Guide

Pubs & Bars

timeout.com/london

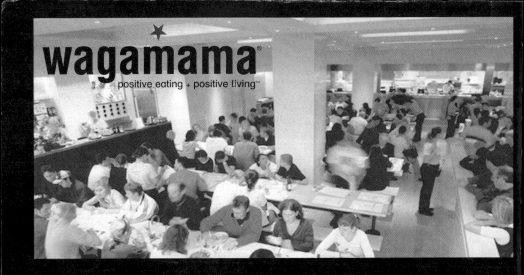

Contents

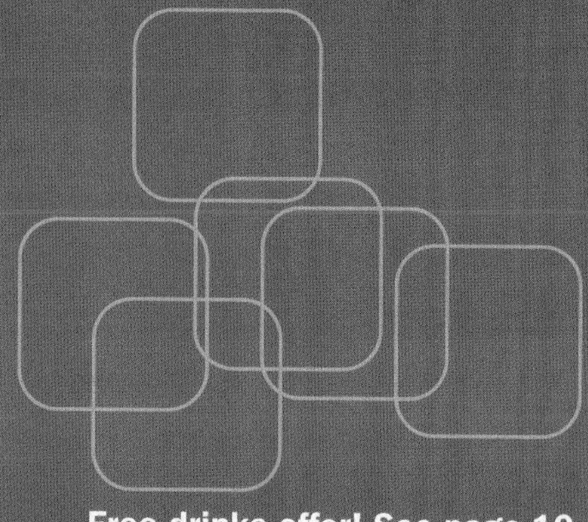

Free drinks offer! See page 10

Central

City

East

North

South

West

Published by
Time Out Guides Ltd
Universal House
251 Tottenham Court Road
London W1T 7AB
Tel + 44(0)20 7813 3000
Fax + 44(0)20 7813 6001
Email guides@timeout.com
www.timeout.com

Editorial
Editor Andrew Humphreys
Assistant Editor Peter Watts
Consultant Editor Jim Driver
Reviewers Abby Aron, Dave Clark, Matthew Colin, Don Connigale, Jonathan Cox, Peterjon Cresswell, Ian Cunningham, Guy Dimond, Jim Driver, Lily Dunn, Steve Fallon, Will Fulford-Jones, Janice Fuscoe, Hugh Graham, Helen Gilchrist, Susie Grimshaw, Oliver Guy, Phil Jones, Arwa Haider, Will Hodgkinson, Andrew Humphreys, Richard Lines, Susan Low, Ted Milton, Chris Moore, Nana Ocran, Laura Paskell-Brown, Lucia Ring-Watkins, William Spencer, Dave Swift, Peter Watts, Tim Wild
Researchers Shane Armstrong, Helen Gilchrist, Cathy Limb, Eleanor Dryden, Holly Furneaux, Rebecca Wootton
Proofreader Tamsin Shelton
Indexer Mike Harrison

Editorial Director Peter Fiennes
Series Editor Sarah Guy
Guides Co-ordinator Anna Norman

Design
Group Art Director John Oakey
Art Director Mandy Martin
Art Editor Scott Moore
Senior Designer Tracey Ridgewell
Junior Designers Astrid Kogler, Sam Lands
Picture Editor Kerri Miles
Acting Picture Editor Kit Burnet
Deputy Picture Editor Martha Houghton
Picture Desk Trainee Bella Wood
Digital Imager Dan Conway
Ad Make-up Charlotte Blythe

Advertising
Group Commercial Director Lesley Gill
Sales Director & Sponsorship Mark Phillips
Sales Manager Alison Gray
Advertisement Sales Terina Rickit, Matthew Salandy, Jason Trotman
Copy Controller Oliver Guy
Advertising Assistant Sabrina Ancilleri

Time Out Group
Chairman Tony Elliott
Managing Director Mike Hardwick
Group Financial Director Rick Waterlow
Group General Manager Nichola Coulthard
Group Circulation Director Jim Heinemann
Accountant Sarah Bostock

Marketing
Group Marketing Director Christine Cort
Marketing Manager Mandy Martinez
Marketing Executives Sandie Tozer, Sammie Squire
Marketing Assistant Claire Hojem
Marketing Designer Stephanie Tebboth

Production
Guides Production Director Mark Lamond
Production Controller Samantha Furniss

All Photography by Tricia de Courcy Ling and Jonathan Perugia except; p11 Frank Bauer, p14 Damian Duncan; p16 Michael Franke; p154, 156. 181 Ulirke Leyens; p217, p233 Thomas Skovsende; p15 Alys Tomlinson; p112, 196, 210, 228, 236 Anthony Webb.
Illustrations Sunil Pawar.

Maps JS Graphics (john@jsgraphics.co.uk)
Street maps based on material supplied by Alan Collinson and Julie Snook through Copyright Exchange.

The editors would like to thank: Guy Dimond, Lesley McCave, Ros Sales.

Repro by Icon, Crown House, 56-58 Southwark Street, London SE1 and Precise Litho, 34-35 Great Sutton Street, London EC1.
Printed and bound by Southernprint, Factory Road, Upton Industrial Estate, Poole, Dorset BH16 5SN.

ISBN 0 903446 839

Distributed by Seymour Ltd (020 7396 8000)

Introduction

Over a thousand pubs and bars visited and a few observations to make.

These are interesting times for London drinkers. While die-hard habitués of grotty locals who believe that the Rovers Return represents the golden pint of pubdom might find current trends unsettling, the rest of us can revel in the capital's ever increasing variety of drinking options. The last 12 months alone have added great new venues in the diverse forms of an American diner-cum-cocktail bar (**Eagle Bar Diner** *see p41*), a South Sea Islands tiki bar (**South London Pacific** *see p216*) and an American Deep South jukejoint (**Boogaloo** *see p168*).

The cocktail revolution continues (although we do have our reservations, *see p113*) with an exciting batch of debutantes devoted to seriously good drinks, notably Chelsea's **Apartment 195** (*see p30*), Notting Hill's **Lonsdale** (*see p71*), the **Townhouse** (*see p55*) in Knightsbridge and the surprisingly good bar attached to the kid wonder's Old Street restaurant **Fifteen** (*see p125*). We still consider DJ bars to be a very good thing – small packages for some very big nights, as we explain on p73 – and although there's been a slowdown in new openings, we welcome Marylebone's **Low Life** (*see p61*), Brixton's **Plan-B** (*see p203*), and **BOD** (*p121*), the improbably-named **dreambagsjaguarshoes** (*see p125*), **Smersh** (*p128*) and **Trafik** (*p130*), all of which are in or about Hoxton.

Hoxton/Shoreditch continues to be the big noise on the scene, but for late nights it's got to be Brixton, which probably has more post-midnight licences per square metre than anywhere else in town. Neighbouring Camberwell has been picking up on some of the overflow and become a decent drinking destination in its own right.

By contrast the prospect of a night out in the West End just gets sadder by the day; Soho, Leicester Square and Covent Garden are all ruined by a glut of lowest common denominator meat markets catering to roaming herds of booze tourists. The brighter bars now settle on the fringes, such as Fitzrovia and Marylebone, both home to tasty burgeoning scenes.

Belsize Park's turning into another bright spot, filling the hole in the band of gastropubs that stretches right across north London from Kensal Rise in the west via Primrose Hill and Tufnell Park over to Islington – providing a vital buffer zone of wadded cash and foie gras ballotine as effective protection against any low-rent attitude creeping down from Luton and beyond.

Opinion is divided on the rapidly spreading gastropub phenomenon. *Time Out London*'s letters column recently blazed against the 'transformation of unpretentious local boozers into bland gastropubs', which our reader reckons are 'overpriced and full of wankers called Sebastian and Ffion'. That's one point of view. Gastropubs come in both good and bad, and they're not always an improvement on the proper boozers they've replaced. Some are, though, and they're the ones that find their way into this guide; note, we review gastropubs primarily as places to drink (if you want to know what the food is like, pick up a copy of *Time Out Eating & Drinking*).

If there is one major trend of the last year, it's the blurring of boundaries. Not so very long ago you knew where (or, rather, in what) you stood. A bar served cocktails and returned change in a small metal dish; a pub was awash with warmish draught beer and dim lighting that meant it was perpetually 10.30pm indoors whatever the time outside; and the term gastropub had never been heard. But take **The Hill** (*see p158*), newly arrived in Belsize Park: Is it a bar? Is it a pub? Is it a gastropub? Who knows and who cares, it's bloody good whatever is it.

Similarly **Dusk** (*p60*) in W1, the **Florist** (*p141*) in E3, and the **Lock Tavern** (*p160*) in NW1, three more new pub-bar hybrids with equal care applied to the kitchens.

It even seems like real beer might be making a comeback, taking pride of place at recent venues the **Microbar** (*see p195*), **Steam** (*see p20*) and the **Greenwich Union** (*see p213*). Equally splendid is the spread of Belgium brews (*see p129*) – oh for a world where the likes of Hoegaarden and Leffe replace old duffers Heineken and Carlsberg.

Is the traditional London boozer, as we hear, under threat and a dying breed? Don't you believe it. It's called a renaissance. *Andrew Humphreys*

The wonder of waxy's...

Waxy O'Connor's has gained world wide acclaim for its spectacular surroundings, traditional, wholesome food and warm hospitality.

Four bars on five different levels, including the amazing Church Bar, offer the ultimate friendly environment in the heart of London's West End.

Open 12 noon - 11 pm Monday - Friday
11 am - 11 pm Saturday
12 noon - 10:30 pm Sunday

14-16 Rupert Street,
London, W1D 6DD
Tel: (020) 7287 0255
Fax: (020) 7287 3962
Email: london@waxyoconnors.co.uk
Web: www.waxyoconnors.co.uk

About **the guide**

Read this first (and it'll all be alright in the morning).

This guide is arranged by area because we reckon that's how most people drink. Area boundaries are often nebulous so we include brief introductions to each section explaining our take on local geography. If you're after something other than just the closest or most convenient good pub or ace bar, then turn to **Where to go for...** (*p247*), a rundown of different types of drinking establishments by theme, from those with great gardens to venues for killer cocktails. Some of the best are highlighted in our **Critics' choice** boxes, scattered throughout the guide and indexed on page 247.

Opening times
We only list the opening times of the bar or pub. We do not list those of any attached restaurant, brasserie or shop (although these may be the same). Note that opening times and food-serving times in particular may change.

Food served
As above, we only list the times that food is served in the bar or pub, not in any attached restaurant or brasserie. 'Food served' can mean anything from cheese rolls to a three-course meal. When the opening times and food-served times are run together (Open/food served), it means that food is served until shortly before closing time. We do not include any establishment that requires you to eat in order to be allowed to drink.

Admission
In some cases, particularly in central London, pubs and bars charge admission after a certain hour. Where there is a regular pattern to this, we list the details. Note that more and more venues are becoming members-only after a fixed time (usually pub closing), although the rules are often blurred. We've chosen not to include in this guide places that are strictly members only, so no reviews here for the likes of Sketch or Soho House.

Credit cards
The following abbreviations are used: **AmEx** American Express; **DC** Diners Club; **MC** MasterCard; **V** Visa.

Babies and children admitted
Under-14s are only allowed into the gardens, separate family rooms and the restaurant areas of pubs and wine bars, unless the premises has a special 'children's certificate'. If the establishment has a certificate, children can go in as long as they're with an adult. Those aged 14-17 can go into a bar, but only for soft drinks. It's an offence for a licensee to serve alcohol in a bar to anyone under 18. Unless drinkers can prove they're at least 18, the licensee can refuse to serve them and can ask them to leave the premises. Look out for *Babies and children admitted* as a guide to whether or not children are welcome.

Disabled: toilet
If a pub claims to have a toilet for the disabled, we have said so; this also implies that it's possible for a disabled person to gain access to the venue. However, we cannot guarantee this, so phone in advance to check feasibility.

Function room
Means the pub or bar has a separate room that can be hired for meetings or parties; some charge for this, some do not.

Late licence
We have listed any pub or bar that is open until midnight or later as having a late licence. Our **Late-night drinking** feature (*see pp28-9*) brings together all those places where it's possible to get a drink *after* midnight.

Music
Unless otherwise stated, bands play in the evening. The same goes for any other form of entertainment listed. For a round-up of our favourite **DJ bars**, *see p73.*

No-smoking room/area
Very few pubs or bars have a no-smoking room or area; we've listed the ones that do. But note that a separate no-smoking area is not necessarily much protection from the usual smoky pub or bar.

TV
Not only do we tell you whether or not the pub has a TV, but also whether it's a subscriber to cable or satellite.

The reviews in this guide are based on the experiences of the Time Out reviewers. Pubs and bars are visited anonymously, and Time Out pays the bill. No payment of any kind has secured or influenced a review.

Sponsors and advertisers
We would like to thank our sponsor Perrier for their involvement in this guide. We would also like to thank the advertisers. However, we would like to stress that advertisers have no control over editorial content. No pub or bar has been included because its owner has advertised in the guide; an advertiser may receive a bad review or no review at all.

Time Out

Free cocktail, glass of wine or bottle of beer for every reader

This year we have linked up with some great bars in the capital to offer every reader the chance to save over £20 off their drinks bills!

Go to any of the bars listed below, cut out the voucher at the bottom of our reply card at the back of this guide and claim your free drink. It's a great chance to try out a new bar or enjoy a drink at your local – absolutely free of charge.

Eclipse 186 Kensington Park Road, W11 (*see p69 for review*)
Living 443 Coldharbour Lane, SW9 (*see p202 for review*)
Lock Tavern 35 Chalk Farm Road, NW1 (*see p162 for review*)
mybar Bloomsbury 11-13 Bayley Street, WC1 (*see p26 for review*)
Plan B 418 Brixton Road, SW9 (*see p203 for review*)
Red Star 319 Camberwell Road, SE5 (*see p205 for review*)

Offer valid until March 31, 2004.
See vouchers for full terms and conditions.

ECLIPSE

LIVING

LOCK TAVERN

MYBAR

PLAN B

RED STAR

plan

myhotel
bloomsbury

The great London **pub game**

Just who owns your local boozer?

Just over a decade ago, most of Britain's pubs changed hands overnight. Traditionally, boozers were owned by brewers, who sold their product direct to a thirsty public. An unencumbered line of supply that worked well for generations. But a 1989 report by the Monopolies and Mergers Commission was the catalyst that changed all that.

By then, three quarters of all Britain's boozers were in the hands of six corporate brewers: 'the Big Six'. In a bid to break their stranglehold it was decreed that pubs owned by brewers with more than 4,000 outlets must be allowed to serve a 'guest beer' from another supplier. Not exactly radical profit-shattering stuff, but enough to send corporate boardrooms into a tizzy. But rather than give up their cosy monopolies, the fat cats found a way around the legislation.

This was to sell off huge parcels of pubs to newly formed pub companies, many of which were run by their former executives and which they financed. Unsurprisingly, these 'new' companies chose to buy their beer from their big brewer pals and not worry about any of this new 'guest beer' malarkey. It was back to square one, except that now two companies had to make a profit out of every pint sold. It was inevitable that prices would rise and standards slip.

There are two basic ways to run a pub: leasing to a tenant (a self-employed publican who pays rent and who has to buy booze only from suppliers you approve); and by installing a manager to run it for you. Either way, it is in the pub-co's best interest to get as high a discount from suppliers as possible – none of which is ever passed on to the customer or even to the tenant. This is why pubs owned by different companies still sell almost identical ranges of beer, usually emanating from the descendants of the Big Six. Big companies can afford big discounts, small companies cannot. It is not uncommon for a tenant to buy a barrel of beer at a higher price than he could if he'd just wandered in off the street, with the missing discount going to the pub company. Any wonder the £3 pint?

Acquiring and disposing of assets has become as much a part of the pub game as pasta of the day, happy hours and 'time, gentlemen, please'. A couple of years ago, the Japanese bank Nomura was the biggest pub landlord in Britain, but now everything's been sold off and huge profits made. Bass Taverns became Six Continents in 2001 and (as of March 2003) are to de-merg, with the pubs group getting the cosy name Mitchells & Butlers. Since Whitbread disposed of its pub division to Laurel – a company set up by Morgan Grenfell/Deutsche Bank – in 2001, the whole lot's been sold to Enterprise Inns and, by the time you read this, might well have been sold again.

Most corporate pubs in central London seem to be owned by Six Continents/Mitchells & Butlers. You can normally spot them by a beer range that will probably include London Pride and Adnams Bitter and by staff who will wander around squirting tables with obnoxious-smelling cleaner at the first sign of an early night.

London's best pubs are independently owned or by regional brewers. Young's and Fuller's houses tend to be concentrated around their south-west and west London bases. Other regionals that have made their mark in London include Yorkshire's Samuel Smith, Dorset's Badger Brewery and Hertford's McMullens.

But it could all change. By this time next year, Young's could be owned by NatWest, Fuller's by Rupert Murdoch and Harveys of Lewes could be an arm of the Anheuser-Busch Budweiser rice-beer conglomerate. It doesn't bear thinking about. *Jim Driver*

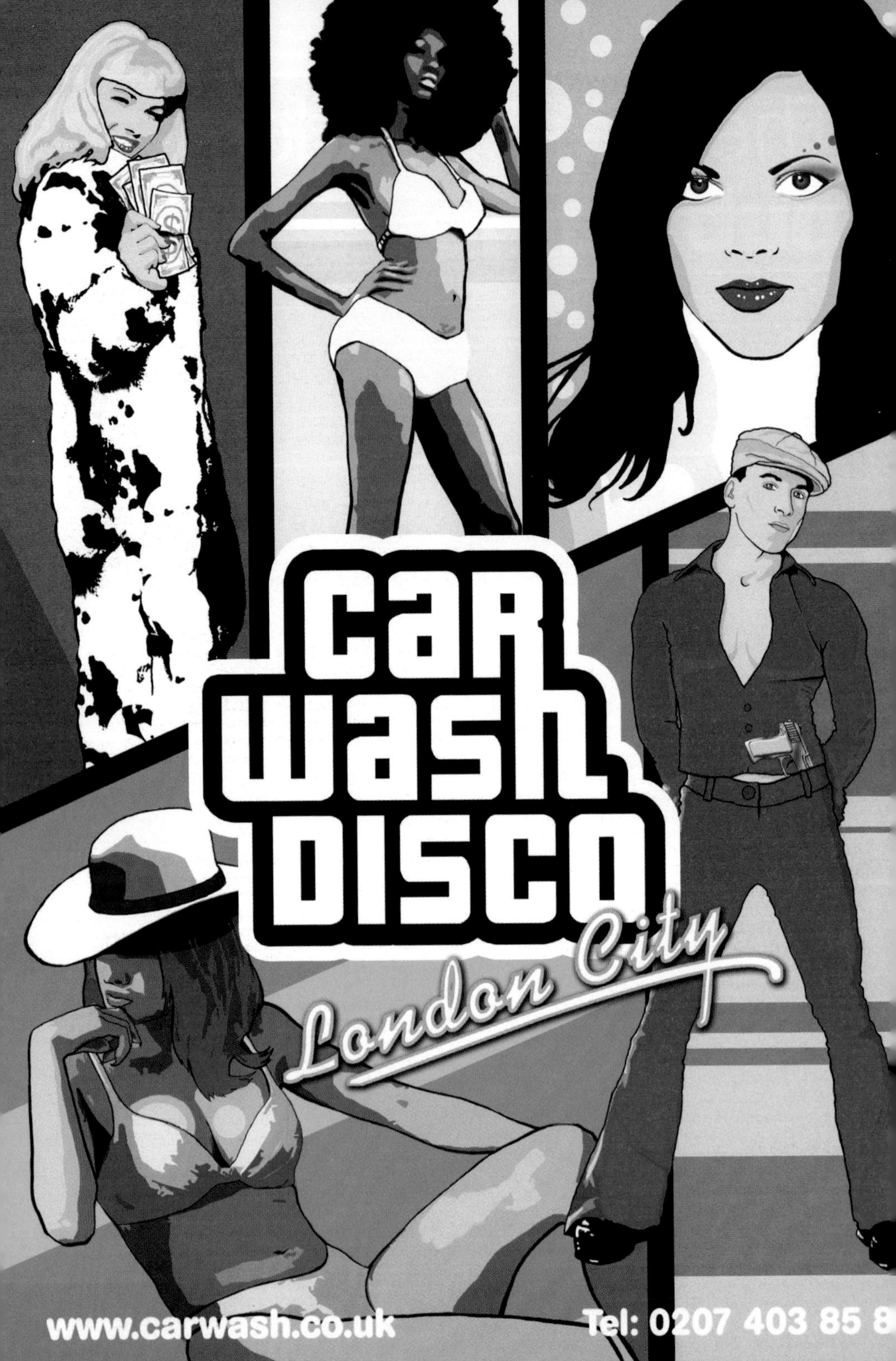
CAR
WASH
DISCO
London City
www.carwash.co.uk
Tel: 0207 403 85 8

The chain gang

The locations may change, but everything else stays the same.

For Dog & Duck and Red Lion read All Bar One and O'Neill's. London pub life has changed in many ways since we started this guide, but the most significant development has been the proliferation of chain bars – identikit pubs dreamed up in boardrooms and dumped on our high streets in place of the banks, cinemas and good old-fashioned spit-and-sawdust boozers that used to live there.

Discerning drinkers have become pretty much immune to these places, so common have they become. Indeed, ask most natives and they couldn't tell you what differentiates one brand from another – All Bar One from Fine Line, Davy's from Jamies. Generally speaking, each attempts to take the same classic formula of meeting, eating and drinking and make it as characterless, undemanding, dependable and comfortable as possible for their core clientele (identified and profiled as a result of focus groups, surveys and sessions with berks from marketing). So while Jamies favours civilised City wine-suppers, Walkabout is aimed at beer-swilling nacho-guzzling party-goers. The ambience may differ slightly, but the ethos remains the same.

You'll find few individual reviews of chain branches in this guide; instead, we give a general write-up here and simply list branches in the **Also in the area...** postscript to each section.

All Bar One

(number of London branches at time of writing, 36)

All Bar One (owned by the massive Six Continents organisation) is about as predictable as drinking can get. Huge wall-to-ceiling windows let plentiful light into pine-saturated Ikea-inspired interiors (rarely have so many trees died for so little), giving passers-by the opportunity to gaze upon dozens of identical young commutobots feverishly texting their identical friends on identical mobile phones. The attractions are as obvious as the deficiencies: plenty of space, lots of seating at big communal tables, and enormous bar counters with a very average selection of not particularly cheap beers (London Pride £2.70; Staropramen £3), plus a slightly better array of wines. They do provide an unintimidating atmosphere for women – but that in turn attracts lots of wolfish males. There's a curious over-21s door policy at most branches, though one wonders why anybody under the age of 30 would want to drink here.

Babushka

(4 in London)

Babushka, along with siblings Bed and Snug, is slowly spreading hip tentacles out from its west London homelands. The Notting Hill original, once the ramshackle boozer in which Richard E Grant was called a 'perfumed ponce' in *Withnail and I*, is still considered the best, but all trade on the same qualities, attracting a young urban crowd to medium-sized darkish, Moorish-influenced and vaguely gothic grottoes that specialise in deafening beat-happy DJ nights and numerous varieties of flavoured vodkas – plus bottled beer, the odd keg of stout or lager and a little wine. Music tends towards the ambient in midweek, but at weekends things can get very noisy indeed, making Babushkas London-wide a favoured venue with those who fancy a night out but really can't be arsed with a club.

Balls Brothers

(18 in London; see p117, p134)

Balls Brothers is the king of fake olde worldeness. It was one of the first in the chain wine bar game and is still firmly holding its own against the younger breed of competitors. Its cellar bars kitted out with wood-panelled walls and drawing room prints originally catered exclusively for noisy gangs of smartly dressed City slickers, but more recently forays have been made west with sites in places like Victoria. Newer venues have a much more contemporary feel aimed at

introducing BB to a younger, more mixed crowd. In keeping with the essentially classical image and clientele, house wine lists tend to be traditional and strong on Old World favourites, particularly Bordeaux and Burgundy.

Bar 38

(5 in London; see p137)

Scottish & Newcastle's brash bar concept, aiming at those who think they're too hip for All Bar One but aren't confident enough for Hoxton-style bars. In fact, the first 38s (in Covent Garden and Hammersmith) started off not too dissimilar in look to the ABOs, but later additions (in Clerkenwell, Canary Wharf and the Minories) have been individually styled and come across as the kind of thing you might find attached to a cinema multiplex – lots of bright colours and cheap finishes. Shooters, long drinks and cocktail pitchers are pushed over beers (are you having fun yet?), plus there's food and a Starbuck's worth of coffees to draw in the lunchtime crowd. About as vital to London drinking culture as Gareth Gates is to the future of British pop music.

Belgo & Bierodrome

(5 in London)

Created in 1992 by a French-Canadian and Anglo-Belgian, Belgo began with a quirky restopub in Camden (Belgo Noord). A more cutting-edge version, Belgo Centraal, opened three years later in Coovent Gaarden, followed by Belgo Zuid in Nootting Hill (which sadly closed in 2002). Three Bierodromes (Clapham, Holborn and Islington) also share the same basic 'Belge est bien' philosophy with house menus of a wide array of Belgian beers – amber, blond, dark or fruity (for more on Belgian brews *see p129*) – backed by huge platters of mussels and chips, or sausage in beer sauces. However, they've never quite got the acoustics right and the venues tend to be loud and shouty, and a touch too corporate and tanked up for the kind of connoisseur who might truly appreciate a choice of several dozen fine ales.

Corney & Barrow

(12 in London; see p131)

Corney & Barrow chooses some prominent sites for its glam City wine bars – Broadgate Circle and Cabot Square being two perfect examples (although it's just let go its prime West End site on the edge of Trafalgar Square). Decor in all the bars is sleek and sexy – as is the clientele, which tends to get younger as the evening goes on. Bar offerings include a substantial mix of designer beers but the real draw is the well-thought out and frequently changing wine list, with more than 60 wines by the glass. Food is a creative take on modern eclectic brasserie fare, with slight variations to suit each bar. Prices aren't the cheapest in town, but then Corney & Barrow customers tend to be aspirational types.

Davy's

(44 in London; see p27)

More of a bar chain with a wine list than a genuine wine specialist, making it less of a destination for oenophiles than, say, branches of Corney & Barrow and Balls Brothers. That said, there is a compact and very approachable wine selection, packed with familiar names like Rioja and Mondavi zinfandel and overflowing with chardonnay options. There are also plenty of Davy's own label options, making choosing even easier as you don't have to negotiate extra hurdles such as names of producers and regions. In addition, the list hasn't changed in the past couple of years, so if you find something you like, chances are it'll still be there next time. Davy's doesn't seem to have a house style and interiors can vary from spit and sawdust to polished, gleaming and spotlit.

Fine Line

(8 in London)

Fuller's take on the style bar follows a familiar formula of big display windows, light wood, light paintwork, and lots of chairs and tables. There's a definite brasserie feel, with a prominence placed on lunch-time food. Menus are sensibly

Shoeless Joe's. See p16.

unambitious and tend toward fish cakes, steak baguettes, fancy sausages and the like, priced around £5-£8. Evenings are more boozy (light snacks are available) but the company's draught beers are largely sidelined in favour of a decent wine list and house cocktails. It's all very female-friendly, welcoming of office crowds and, like the shop-fronts at Gap, perfect for mannequins in suits.

Hog's Head

(22 in London; see p198)

It was only to be expected that the concept of the Hogsheads (note the rebranded title) would fade away once its begetters, Whitbread, sold it on. It was originally conceived as a chain serving a cornucopia of real ales, Belgian beers and other boozy delights, but these days the accent is on lager, alcopops and cheap food. The only cask-conditioned ale available at many branches now is London Pride. A real shame because take away the beers and there's nothing left. Fatuous PR makes claims for 'an entirely new experience which challenges pub orthodoxy', but what this boils down to is table service (the unfortunate waiters are to be officially known as Hoggers). More pig's ear than hog's head.

Jamies

(16 in London; see p132)

Jamies branches vary dramatically in stature and setting from the huge, glam Thameside affair in Docklands at Westferry Circus to the much more intimate and uniquely located bar in the pavilion of an EC2 lawn bowling club. But overall the decor is smart and modish – think high stools and banquettes. The undaunting wine list is split into Old and New World, so you can dive straight in to your preferred section. Each country is represented by a snapshot selection of its best-known wines. Lesser-known producers are also given opportunities to shine, which is great for the more adventurous drinkers. Food is better than average, ranging from nibbles to mains, and served in some bars until 10pm.

JD Wetherspoon

(139 in London; see pp95, 132, 135, 152, 156, 168, 212)

A formula of cheap booze, no smoking, no music and quick-serve canteen cuisine at bargain prices has seen the chain (owned by mullet-haired golden boy of beer Tim Martin) expand to just around 600 pubs nationwide, with 60 more to open in 2003. We like them for their devotion to real ale and for the out-of-the-ordinary premises some of the pubs occupy, including a cinema (Holloway), a ball room (Liverpool Street station) and a chapel (Whitechapel). On the other hand, decor can be cheap and cheesy and the atmosphere more redolent of Batley Labour Club than hip, style-wise London – but where else inside the M25 are you going to get a pint and a curry for £3.95?

O'Neill's

(17 in London; see p180)

This ghastly cod-Irish chain must be doing something right – it's outlasted its marginally more sophisticated rival Scruffy Murphy's for starters, and continues to expand at a relentless pace (worse luck). Every branch is the same, a multi-boothed emporium of manufactured *craic* and falsified blarney, littered with Emerald Isle trinkets, like Donald Duck's idea of Ireland. Guinness, Murphy's and Caffrey's are all on tap, though most drinkers seem to stick to lagers. Food is of the Irish stew variety. Funnily enough, O'Neill's are not usually frequented by the Irish.

Pitcher & Piano

(18 in London)

All Bar One's lairier cousin, P&Ps – again with the pine! – tend to attract lager-swilling young suits on the lash and keen up-for-anything secretaries out splashing the cash on Bacardi Breezers. Add some head-thumping music and a cavernous interior and you've got quite an atmosphere: hectic, smoky, exceptionally noisy and clearly a whole lot of fun for those in the mood. It certainly isn't the place for quiet contemplation,

Jamies. *See p15.*

but fortunately the drinks selection doesn't require much scrutiny: choice is limited to the usual lagers, Pedigree, Scrumpy Jack and the now ubiquitous Hoegaarden, none of which come particularly cheap. Still, if you manage to imbibe enough of what's available you'll probably only count the cost the following morning. The odd sofa is provided for those who can't stand up/it any more.

Shoeless Joe's

(3 in London)

A sports-themed chain originating in Toronto and named after Joe Jackson, the baseball player immortalised in *Field of Dreams* (rather than the short balding pop songsmith from Burton-on-Trent). Last year the Shoeless numbered five but two have recently been sold off leaving just a trio of survivors: on the King's Road (the original and the destination of choice for many Chelsea fans when away games are being televised), on Dover Street in Mayfair and one housed in a snazzy little purpose-built spaceage module just off the north-bank approach to the Millennium Bridge. Expect plenty of bottled beers and testosterone, but little in the way of atmosphere other than during big screenings of major sporting events.

Slug & Lettuce

(17 in London)

The godfather of all chains, Slug & Lettuce was started back in the early 1980s by Hugh Corbett (who subsequently went on to do the Tups and Larricks). Back then it was a breath of fresh air, introducing some revolutionary concepts into the London bar scene such as windows that people could see through, non-sticky carpets and food that someone might actually enjoy eating. But that was some 20 years ago. No one could mistake S&L (now owned by the SFI Group plc) for being revolutionary these days. Suits dominate the current average Slug & Lettuce, with an even split between the sexes, and an age range typically older than that of All Bar One. Food remains central to the operation, with just about every table in the early evening taken up by those soaking up the drink with something decent and edible. Bars for sensible folk.

Tup

(12 in London)

Also founded by Hugh Corbett (*see* **Slug & Lettuce**) but now owned by the Massive Pub Co, the Tups are smart airy pubs that blend a sporting interest with a curious fascination with copulating sheep. Although branches share these common associations, they also retain enough individuality to avoid identikit anodynity. Some can even attain an almost local-like atmosphere. They're customer-friendly too, in a way that doesn't smack of marketing strategy handed down from on high. Many branches allow drinkers to order takeaway food, and even keep menus and cutlery behind the bar for patrons, while the Camden Tup provides plastic glasses so slow drinkers can take unfinished pints with them come closing. Beers are standard, though some branch into adventurous territory (Tonsley has Victoria Bitter from Suffolk's Earl Soham Brewery).

Walkabout Inn

(7 in London)

Antipodean visitors pack these Australian theme bars, despite travelling halfway across the world to escape the very things they celebrate. Rapidly growing in number, they're out-and-out unashamed party joints, where expats, long-term tourists, lost souls and the just plain unadventurous can settle down in a clichéd but familiar environment with like-minded compatriots who don't need every colloquialism or last bit of slang explained to them. Brits who can stand the stench of spilt lager are attracted by the Sheilas and surfer boys and late closing at weekends, but be warned, boasts of sporting supremacy are as legion in conversation as the orange 'Kangaroo Crossing' signs are plentiful on the walls. And no less irritating.

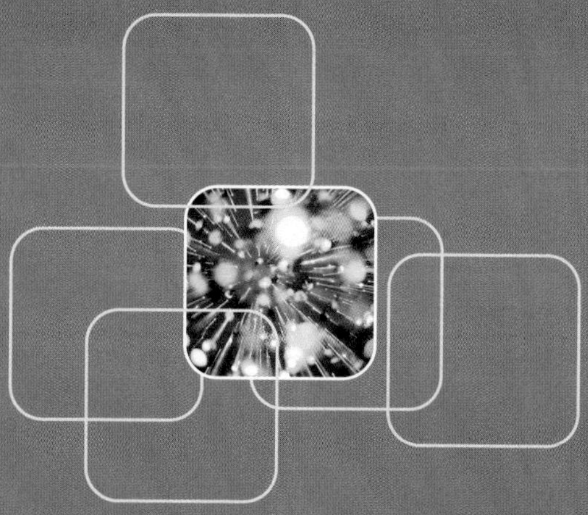

Central

Central

Bayswater & Paddington

For such a vast geographical catchment, pickings are slim. All the way from Edgware Road west to Queensway and the recommendations barely reach double figures. Transient populations of budget and business travellers, Middle Easterners and working girls aren't the types to keep bar culture afloat. 2002 saw the brave arrival of **Cherry Jam** and **Steam**, but will they sink or swim? It's too early to tell.

Archery Tavern

4 Bathurst Street, W2 (7402 4916). Lancaster Gate tube. **Open** 11am-11pm Mon-Sat; noon-10.30pm Sun. **Food served** noon-3pm, 6-9.30pm Mon-Sat; noon-9pm Sun. **Credit** DC, MC, V.

At first glance, the adjacent Village Shop seems rather optimistically named – there are few areas less like a village in central London than Lancaster Gate – but enter the Archery Tavern and you might be persuaded otherwise. It's a fine and sturdy pub, and through the cloud of cigar smoke a cordial welcome will be extended, it seems, to anybody with a nice enough face. The cheery atmosphere is clearly jollied along by the excellent ales on offer – Sussex, Badger and other fine Hall & Woodhouse brews – all given the Cask Marque seal of approval. The main bar is appealingly decked out with potted plants and other horticultural delights and bow and arrow-themed artwork dots the walls. The old tap room at the back is given over to a telly and games. The proximity to Hyde Park stables means horsey types trot in every now and then, barely interrupting the horseplay of the regulars.

Babies and children admitted. Games (board games, darts, fruit machine). Quiz (9pm Sun; £1). Tables outdoors (pavement). TV (satellite).

Cherry Jam

58 Porchester Road, W2 (7727 9950/www.cherryjam.net). Royal Oak tube. **Open/food served** 6pm-2am Mon-Sat; 4pm-midnight Sun. **Happy hour** 6-8pm Mon-Sat; 4-7pm Sun. **Admission** £5 after 8pm, £7 after 11pm Mon-Thur; £6 after 8pm, £8 after 11pm Fri, Sat. **Credit** MC, V.

This DJ bar is one year old, and although the legendary round-the-block queues have thankfully abated since its first appearance, Cherry Jam remains by some distance the hippest venue in the neighbourhood. It's a small place, split into two; a raised area encircling the bar (serving bottled beers and cocktails) and a lower dancefloor, facing a stage on which Rough Trade bands play most Thursday evenings. The place is co-owned by Ben Watt of Everything But The Girl, and its music policy is excellent, making up for the somewhat cheerless boxy interior, occasional cosy snug notwithstanding. Saturday nights are especially popular. Good bar snacks too.

Function area available for hire. Music (DJs 8pm Mon-Sat, 7pm Sun; jazz 8pm Tue; band 8.30pm Thur).

Cubana

36 Southwick Street, W2 (7402 7539/www.cubana.co.uk). Edgware Road tube/Paddington tube/rail. **Open/food served** noon-midnight Mon-Fri; 6pm-midnight Sat; 11am-10pm Sun. **Happy hour** 5-6.30pm, 10pm-midnight Mon-Wed; 5-6.30pm Thur-Sun. **Credit** AmEx, MC, V.

Damn strange, London's ongoing obsession with Cuban-themed bars, but it sure beats having any more of those damned Oirish pubs. Cubana's problem is that it gets rather lost in the spartan backwaters of Paddington, too far from either the station or Edgware Road to attract the numbers it requires for all the themery to seem anything other than a tad sad. When the joint is jumping, though, Cubana's pre-Castro Havana hotel appearance, with palm trees and ceiling fans to provide the Caribbean touch, is just the right side of drop-dead kitsch. The pictures of '50s American cars with gleaming tail fins and portraits of Che Guevera are all to be expected, as are the excellent cocktails that tend to favour rum as their main ingredient. Genuine Cuban food is about as boring as it gets so it's perhaps a good thing that authenticity has been sacrificied to edibility when it comes to snacks. Dead during the week, things get livelier as weekend approaches when bands help to give the place a Latino kick. Cubana might not be revolutionary, but it's still a cause worth supporting.

Babies and children admitted (children's menu). Disabled: toilet. Function room. Music (band 9.30pm Thur-Sat; free). Tables outdoors (pavement).

Leinster

57 Ossington Street, W2 (7243 9541). Bayswater or Queensway tube. **Open** noon-11pm Mon-Sat; noon-10.30pm Sun. **Food served** noon-3pm, 5-10pm Mon-Fri. **Credit** MC, V.

2001's *Time Out* review called the Leinster 'about the best of a decidedly average to awful bunch of locals'. That back-handed compliment has since been translated as 'The best pub in Bayswater – *Time Out*', now emblazoned on the pub's menus and brochures. Cheeky. But actually true enough, depending, of course, on where you consider the borders of Bayswater to be. The decor is simple and airy with wooden floors, white walls and high ceilings. Carrying pints up the steep spiral staircase to the first-floor lounge is a delicate balancing act. Once upstairs there are two diversions: either watch footie on the giant-screen TV, or peer over the balcony at the punters directly below, also watching Premiership action on smaller TVs, or reading from a selection of newspapers. Real ale connoisseurs won't get much satisfaction, but surroundings are convivial enough.

Babies and children admitted (separate area). Function room. Games (board games, chess, fruit machine, golf machine, quiz machine). No-smoking area. Tables outdoors (patio). TV (satellite). **Map 10/B6**

Leinster Arms

17 Leinster Terrace, W2 (7402 4670). Lancaster Gate or Queensway tube. **Open** 11am-11pm Mon-Sat; noon-10.30pm Sun. **Food served** 11am-8pm Mon-Sat; noon-8pm Sun. **Credit** MC, V.

A pair of noisy Kiwis occupied the back room taking part in a very vocal game of carom ('I beatcha again, yoo bastard!'), while the inattentive barman seemed more interested in the Sheila loitering at the other end of the bar. On the neighbouring table a couple of Americans broke off from admiring a collection of US airforce regalia (something of a theme, there's even a pic of air hostesses hanging in the gents') to engage in a passionate debate about Hillary Clinton. There's something about the Leinster Arms, an otherwise inauspiciously traditional place, that seems to attract non-natives in droves. A large front dominated by huge windows lets in plenty of light to the airy interior, though things get rather darker round the back where the TV ominously looms. A raised area by the door is the best place to observe the international comings and goings.

Babies and children admitted (until 8pm). Games (backgammon, darts, fruit machine, quiz machine). Tables outdoors (pavement). TV (satellite).

Mad Bishop & Bear

Upper Concourse, Paddington Station, Praed Street, W2 (7402 2441). Paddington rail/tube. **Open** 7am-11pm Mon-Thur; 8.30am-10.30pm Sun. **Food served** 7.30am-10pm Mon-Sat; 8.30am-10pm Sun. **Credit** MC, V.

Central

Paddington's commuters, boozers and Circle-line cruisers are well catered to at this Fuller's house, up on the first floor of the station concourse. It's large and modern and, although thoroughly ersatz, at least some attempt has been made to recreate the appearance of a grand boozer of the GWNR days (wood panelling, brass fittings, high ceiling). In fact, considering that it's basically a glorified holding pen for passengers on the delayed 5.45 (and cancelled 5.48 and mislaid 5.52...), it's a lot better than we've any right to expect. It does the complete Fuller's range, including seasonal brews, plus a menu of tolerable food. Departure screens are provided for the delayed and expectant, and trainspotting drinkers can spill out on to the upper terrace overlooking the main concourse.
Disabled: lift, toilet. Games (fruit machine, quiz machine). No-smoking area. Tables outdoors (terrace).

Mitre

24 Craven Terrace, W2 (7262 5240). Lancaster Gate tube/Paddington tube/rail. **Open** 11am-11pm Mon-Sat; noon-10.30pm Sun. **Food served** noon-3pm, 6-9.30pm Mon-Sat; noon-9.30pm Sun. **Credit** MC, V.
The venerable Mitre (built 1850-something) is one of those pubs you feel you can get lost in; a series of rambling rooms randomly linked, each offering a different perspective on the drinking experience. There's even a bar in the basement. Enter through a beautifully maintained mosaic and tiled entrance, through the designated no-smoking snug, to the largest room where chatty staff (it was a slow day) serve Greene King IPA and Marston's Pedigree. The food menu proudly proclaims itself to be 'new and exciting' and although it might be the former, it certainly isn't the latter – standard grub down to the last cod and chips. A quiz machine was the only blight on the otherwise charmingly pastoral interior. Comfortable sofas by the marble fireplace in the back space provide the pick of the seating.
Babies and children admitted (separate room). Games (fruit machines, pool table). No-smoking area. Quiz (8pm Sun; free). TV (satellite).

Royal Exchange

26 Sale Place, W2 (7723 3781). Edgware Road tube. **Open/food served** 11am-11pm Mon-Fri; noon-4pm, 7-11pm Sat; noon-4pm, 7-10.30pm Sun. **Credit** MC, V.
Just off the Edgware Road end of Praed Street, the RE's a small Irish-run boozer that's had the same landlord for more than 20 years. In contrast to most of the other pubs in the Paddington area (which cater mostly to a transient crowd), this place is filled most evenings by a dedicated bunch of regulars who either live or work locally. What they lack in youth they make up for in exuberance. It's a little rough around the edges with a fairly devil-may-care attitude to decor (a row of drained traffic cone-sized champagne bottles, an equally dry fish tank, horse pictures, things floral) but it's also comfortably unpretentious. The beers (Boddingtons and Brakspear Bitter on draught) are well kept, and from lunchtime onwards there's a hotshelf of appetising own-made fare (shepherd's pie, roasts and the like) warming behind the bar. Easily the best pub within five minutes' walk of the station.
Babies and children admitted. Tables outdoors (pavement). TV (satellite).

Steam

1 Eastbourne Terrace, W2 (7850 0555/www.steambar.com). Paddington tube/rail. **Open** 11am-1am Mon-Wed; 11am-2am Thur-Sat. **Food served** noon-5pm Mon-Sat. **Credit** AmEx, DC, MC, V.
A strange beast, Steam serves both the five-star patrons of the new Paddington Hilton (of which it's a part) and the commuting community of Paddington station (to which it's also affixed). The result is a pub that thinks it's a style bar. The office set want beer, so Steam serves beer, but not any beer – the bitter is Anchor Steam from San Francisco, the lager is Erdinger and instead of Guinness there's Black Pearl Irish stout. A brave selection, but not one that finds much favour, we bet, with post-office punters gasping for a Carling. The prices are off-putting too. In fact, management would much rather you drink cocktails (£6-£7.50), and the back shelf behind the long, long bar counter is peopled by a Chinese Republic of bottles. Ask for a list to explore the appealing selection, most of which involve the house spirit, gin. There's a daytime menu of British classics; in the evening would-be diners have to make do with a disappointing snack menu.
Babies and children admitted. Disabled: toilet. Music (DJs Wed-Sat). TV (satellite).

Swan

66 Bayswater Road, W2 (7262 5204). Lancaster Gate tube. **Open/food served** 10am-11pm Mon-Sat; 10am-10.30pm Sun. **Credit** AmEx, DC, MC, V.
The one thing the Swan has going for it is its location, just across from serene Hyde Park, and even that ain't great, what with the perennially traffic-choked Bayswater Road coming in between. This is a pub for tourists and the odd businessman staying in one of the local travel-lodges, seduced inside by the perfectly pleasant front patio and exaggerated adverts for London's best breakfast. Once through the door and past the service station food area serving remarkably unappetising nosh (Sicilian, they claim, but as with the breakfast boast, they might not be telling the whole truth), the unwelcoming wooden interior leads to a raised area out back where a piano player from hell serenades assembled wide-eyed tourists with horrendous show tunes and Cockernee classics. 'This isn't our culture,' you want to scream and do so, until forcibly ejected. There used to be some history to this pile – it was opened as the Floral Tea Garden in 1721 – but now better to leave the charmless heap to those that don't know better.
Babies and children admitted (until 9pm). Games (fruit machine). Music (pianist 7.30pm Mon-Sat; free). Tables outdoors (forecourt). TV.

Victoria

10A Strathern Place, W2 (7724 1191). Lancaster Gate or Marble Arch tube. **Open/food served** 11am-11pm Mon-Sat; noon-10.30pm Sun. **Food served** noon-2.30pm, 6-9.30pm Mon-Sat; noon-9pm Sun. **Credit** MC, V.
Sometimes drinkers forget how lucky they are, frequenting as they do some of the most delightful buildings in London. Take the Victoria: an unassuming exterior masks an interior that is utterly gorgeous. Large mirrors, surrounded by gold and exquisitely etched; brass poles topped by spherical glass lampshades along the bar; drapes and curtains; a cute spiral staircase leading to the theatre bar; a beautiful serving hatch through which gammon (£6.25) and jacket potatoes (£3.95) can be delivered. Add a decent pint of one of Fuller's finest and a couple of warming fires and you've got a real gem of a pub, easy on the eye and as comfy as your favourite pair of slippers. But curses on the clod who added the beery promo posters and internet terminal.
Function rooms. Quiz (9pm Tue; £1). Tables outdoors (pavement).

Also in the area...

All Bar One 7-9 Paddington Street, W1 (7487 0071).
Gyngleboy (Davy's) 27 Spring Street, W2 (7723 3351).
Slug & Lettuce 47 Hereford Road, W2 (7229 1503).
Tyburn (JD Wetherspoon) 18-20 Edgware Road, W2 (7723 4731).

Steam

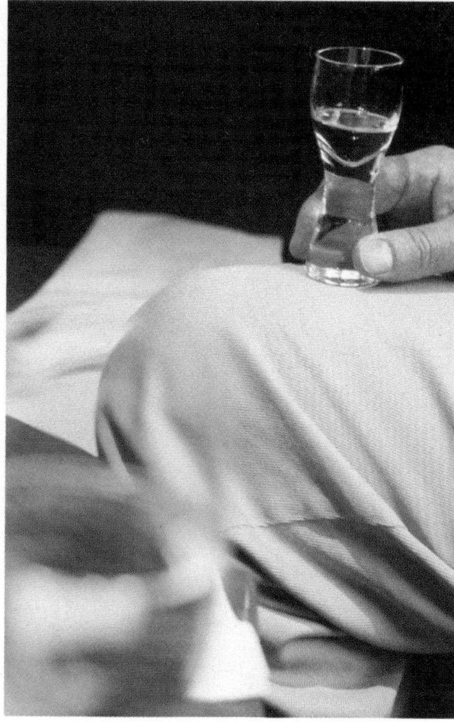

Belgravia

It's been one of the most opulent quarters of London since Thomas Cubitt first laid out its stately streets in the 1820s. Then it was home to the movers and shakers of the British Empire; now its mansions are the ambassadorial offices of foreign powers in England. The pubs were built for the understairs workforce of housekeepers and servants and as such were not great gin palaces but modest little affairs hidden in the mews. They've been remarkably well preserved (the likes of All Bar One have been kept at bay with shotguns) and the side streets around Belgrave Square contain a handful of the city's absolute best model boozers.

Blue Bar

Berkeley Hotel, Wilton Place, SW1 (7235 6000). Hyde Park Corner or Knightsbridge tube. **Open/food served** 4pm-1am Mon-Sat. **Credit** AmEx, DC, MC, V.
Part of the swish Berkeley Hotel, the lovely Blue Bar is a cocktail bar in the classic mould, but stylish hip with it. Artfully, it manages to be both baroque (cherubs, stucco and Wedgwood blue) and boho (leather floor, arty lightshades) at the same time. Champagne buckets line up by the bar counter in readiness for duty – vintage Dom Pérignon (£210-£725) is a speciality. Cocktail classics (around £10 a pop) are worth investigating, or there's a good list of long drinks, Martinis, champagne cocktails, coolers and a range of Highland and Islay malts. To eat, finely chiselled tapas (£5.50) are presented in modern and sweet categories, though bowls of warmed nuts and huge spicy olives will silently arrive with your drink. Service has deteriorated – the girls, clad for a Robert Palmer video, are slow and easily sent into a flap by someone sitting in the wrong place – and on busy nights there's a one in, one out policy, but it's still fabulous all the same.
Disabled: toilet. Function rooms (in hotel).

Grenadier

18 Wilton Row, SW1 (7235 3074). Hyde Park Corner tube. **Open** noon-11pm Mon-Sat; noon-10.30pm Sun. **Food served** noon-1.30pm, 6-9pm Mon-Sat; noon-3pm, 6-9pm Sun. **Credit** AmEx, DC, MC, V.
Some people really shouldn't be working behind a bar. Take the dragon serving at the Grenadier. At a hesitant Frenchman, taking time over his order, she bellows, 'Kelker shows! Kelker shows!' Eh? And before he recovers his wits she turns and, in a whisper loud enough for all assembled to hear, bitches to a minion about 'bloody foreigners' who can't make up their minds. But then it must be something of a comedown when you used to have the likes of Madonna as a regular and now it's just clueless frogs, wops, dagos and krauts. Still, clear-spoken, decisive, native English speakers will find the place appealing for its scuffed board floors, plum-hued walls, 200-year-old pewter bar and general shabby grandeur, for its picturesque military connections (genuine sentry box outside, busby on a shelf inside), and for its legendary Bloody Marys ideally served as an accompaniment to lunch in the rear dining room. You'd just better be bloody quick ordering.
Babies and children admitted.

Horse & Groom

7 Groom Place, SW1 (7235 6980). Hyde Park Corner tube. **Open** 11am-11pm Mon-Fri. **Food served** noon-3pm Mon-Fri. **Credit** AmEx, MC, V.

Blue Bar

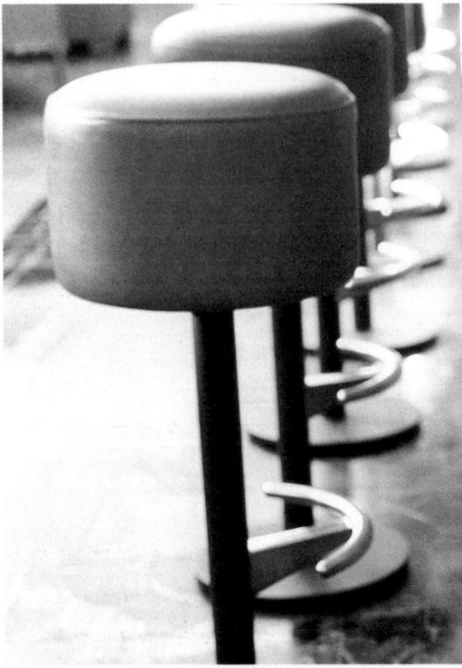

Christopher's. *See p36.*

Anywhere else, the Horse & Groom would be considered a real find, but the presence of the nearby **Grenadier**, **Nag's Head** and **Star** tends to put it in the shade. However, it has perhaps the prettiest location of them all, tucked in the elbow of a small whitewashed and cobbled mews. It also feels like a real local, with a small TV tucked up in one corner, a ciggie machine in the other, Walkers crisps festooning the back wall and a slight smell of disinfectant in the air – none of which spoils the attractiveness of the plain, woody, single-roomed interior. The pub oozes the air of the forgotten and you almost expect to see John Profumo smirking over Christine Keeler beside the bar, one hand on her thigh, the other clutching a pint of Shepherd Neame's finest (Best, Master Brew and Spitfire are on tap). A place for Belgravia boozing without the tourists.
Function room. Games (darts upstairs). TV.

Library

Lanesborough Hotel, Hyde Park Corner, SW1 (7259 5599/www.lanesborough.com). Hyde Park Corner tube. **Open/food served** 11am-1am Mon-Sat; noon-10.30pm Sun. **Credit** AmEx, DC, MC, V.
Monstrously plush though the Lanesborough is, its house bar has a delightfully raffish air. With its two-sizes-too-big white jacketed staff, book-lined walls, roaring open fires and decidedly faux English country-house decor, the Library aims for tradition seekers. But the traditions observed on a recent visit may not be what management had in mind: at the counter an inebriated gent shakily rode his bar stool while tilting comments at passing customers; several of the dimly lit tables were occupied by feline-looking unaccompanied Eastern European ladies with a penchant for tight-fitting trousers and fur. We were offered no menus for drinks but we wouldn't bet on stumping the bar staff with any ad hoc request – the Whiskey Sour and Tom Collins we received were tip-top (although at £10 a time, so they should). Accompany your drinks with a cigar and something from the cheese plate if someone else is paying.
Disabled: toilet. Dress: smart casual. Function rooms. Music (pianist 6.30-11pm Mon-Sat; 6.30-10.30pm Sun).

Nag's Head

53 Kinnerton Street, SW1 (7235 1135). Hyde Park Corner or Knightsbridge tube. **Open** 11am-11pm Mon-Sat; noon-10.30pm Sun. **Food served** noon-9pm daily. **No credit cards.**
From its country-store frontage on a cobbled cul-de-sac (complete with single bench outside and, on our visit, a nostalgic bottle of milk on the doorstep) through the rickety wooden front room and the squeeze of a narrow short stair to the stone-flagged back bar, this is an absolute boozer's dream, with more quirks per square foot than Quentin Crisp's closet. The floor of the serving area, for instance, is sunk a good foot lower than the rest of the room, meaning the bar staff are eye-to-chest with the customers. Bar stools are scaled down to the size of toadstools to fit. Add a glorious old cast-iron fireplace, banking model aircraft, seaside penny-amusements, Adnams Bitter on draught and Bessie Smith on smoky vocals and we reckon that this is arguably the most ridiculously perfect pub in London. Now we've let you in on the secret we ask that you tear this page out and swallow it, and don't say a word to anyone else.

Star Tavern

6 Belgrave Mews West, SW1 (7235 3019). Hyde Park Corner or Knightsbridge tube. **Open** 11.30am-11pm Mon-Fri; 11.30am-3pm, 6.30-11pm Sat; noon-3pm, 7-10.30pm Sun. **Food served** noon-9pm Mon-Fri; 6.30-9pm Sat; noon-9pm Sun. **Credit** AmEx, DC, MC, V.
This is one of only three London pubs to have appeared in all 30 editions of the annual *Good Beer Guide* (the other two are the **Britannia** in Kensington (*see p47*) and the Buckingham Arms in Westminster). But the well-kept Fuller's beers (Chiswick, ESB, London Pride) are possibly only incidental to its popularity, which rests more on several decades of roguish colour involving a glam mix of East End crims and West End celebs. The two elements once dovetailed beautifully in an episode where Liz Taylor was ordered get her 'fat arse' off a bar stool. The full story and others are told in framed clippings hung opposite the bar. These days the main character is the pub itself, particularly the large sitting room warmed by a couple of real fires and adorned with large mirrors and a station concourse-style clock. Drinkers on a recent visit were mainly young Americans slighting the real ales in favour of Coke, although a scuffed British Leyland Range Rover and original Mini Cooper parked outside suggested that there might still have been a bit of true-Brit skulduggery going on in the private room upstairs.
Babies and children admitted. Function room.

Bloomsbury & St Giles

Woolf & co are back c/o *The Hours*, so fancy a bite at the Virginia Woolf Burger Bar & Grill, part of the Bloomsbury Hotel? Thought not. The real period piece is the same establishment's **King's Bar**, or better still, visit the **Museum Tavern** – no known 'Set' connections but it was a haunt of Orwell and Marx. Otherwise, local boozing is becoming ever more focused on New Oxford Street, a spillover for neighbouring Covent Garden and Fitzrovia, with the odd choice venue around the triangle formed with Shaftesbury Avenue and Dyott Street.

AKA

18 West Central Street, WC1 (7836 0110/www.akalondon.com). Holborn tube. **Open** 6pm-3am Tue-Fri; 7pm-7am Sat; 9pm-4am Sun. **Food served** 6pm-midnight Tue-Thur; 6pm-1am Fri; 7pm-1am Sat. **Happy hour** 6-7.30pm Tue-Fri. **Credit** AmEx, DC, MC, V.
Five years on, AKA is still cooler than Christmas, a testament to its brazenly barren layout, to its adherence to a higher class of drinks and snacks and to its fabulous sound system. The ground floor comprises one long zinc bar and floor space barely cluttered by a small helping of curved-back seats in rows; upstairs is clubby with mesh walkways and dining tables. The thin red drinks menu includes a dozen classic cocktails, ten Martinis, ten long shots, five different champagnes by the glass and 22 (!) by the bottle, not to mention a food choice including roasted queen scallops in provençal sauce. Bottled beers include the rarer end of the Belga scale, Brugs Witte, Grimbergen and alike. At the weekend, the place is often used for promo nights, so phone ahead.
Disabled: toilet. Function room. Music (DJs 9pm Tue-Sun; £3 after 11pm Wed; £5 after 11pm Thur; £7 after 10pm Fri; £10 after 9pm Sat). **Map 1/L6**

Angel

61 St Giles High Street, WC2 (7240 2876). Tottenham Court Road tube. **Open** 11.30am-11pm Mon-Fri; noon-11pm Sat; noon-10.30pm Sun. **Food served** noon-9pm Mon-Sat; noon-6pm Sun. **Credit** MC, V.
Set on a gentle incline from the ugly urban hubbub around Centre Point and past the pastoral ambience of St-Giles-in-

the-Fields church (dodging the resident smackheads as you go), here half-a-millennium ago was the Bowl, a pub so named because of the bowl of ale given to condemned Elizabethans before their brief walk to the gallows nearby. The Angel is no less hospitable. A Sam Smith's pub that has lost none of its cosy charm since a refit in 1999, it comprises clusters of twinkling light fittings and an open fire throwing shadows over a small Victorian interior. Music hall-style curtains, flock wallpaper and leatherbound furniture backdrop the huddle of regulars content with the usual stock of Sam Smith's beers, and a reasonable menu of filled Yorkshire puds and six vegetarian options at around a fiver. A side passage in its original tiling hosts summer alfresco supping.
Babies and children admitted (weekend afternoons only). Games (chess, darts, fruit machine). Tables outdoors (courtyard closes 5.30pm). TV. **Map 7/K6**

Grape Street Wine Bar

224A Shaftesbury Avenue, WC2 (7240 0686). Holborn or Tottenham Court Road tube. **Open** 11am-11pm Mon-Fri. **Food served** noon-3.30pm, 5-10pm Mon-Fri. **Credit** AmEx, MC, V.
A wine bar from the old school, where Rigsby might have aspired to corner Miss Jones, Grape Street's basement burrow is still a decent hole to bolt into, away from the frenetic pace of London rumbling above. Decked out in two-tone pastel green and turquoise walls and festooned with viticultural paraphernalia galore, it's a cosy haunt where conversations are conducted in murmurs and a seat is almost always guaranteed (particularly since a recent ground-floor expansion). The 15-strong selection of wines available by the glass isn't hugely inspiring, but Montana's delicious Lindauer at £3.40 is highly satisfactory. The choice is better by the bottle, mixing big names such as Australia's Wolf Blass with a selection of interesting smaller boutique producers on a list that's broad enough to entice but concise enough not to confuse.
Babies and children admitted. Games (board games). Function room. Tables outdoors (pavement). TV.
Map 1/L6

King's Bar

Hotel Russell, Russell Square, WC1 (7837 6470). Russell Square tube. **Open** 7am-11pm Mon-Sat; 7.30am-10.30pm Sun. **Food served** noon-9pm daily. **Credit** AmEx, DC, MC, V.
Now into its second centenary, the resolutely Victorian Russell Hotel, dominating one side of the square of the same name, houses a main bar of similar stately ilk. It features all the trappings of a gentlemen's club: a grand fireplace and bookcases, plenty of sturdy houseplants, dark-wood panelling and formal flunkies' waiting tables. Off to one side is a leather-bound and curtained cocoon of quiet contemplation with vast winged armchairs guarding the windows overlooking the square. In mid-afternoon, tiered stands of high teas are delicately set on white linened tables, later making way for stronger drinks as ladylike chatter gives way to gentlemanly chat after lamplighting time. Then, Glenmorangies of varying era and rarer cousins from the Highlands and Islands make up for a rather limited range of beers and wines.
Babies and children admitted (until 6pm). Dress: no shorts. Function room (call hotel for details). **Map 1/L4**

Museum Tavern

49 Great Russell Street, WC1 (7242 8987). Holborn or Tottenham Court Road tube. **Open** 11am-11pm Mon-Sat; noon-10.30pm Sun. **Food served** 11am-10pm Mon-Sat; noon-10pm Sun. **Credit** AmEx, DC, MC, V.
A classic Victorian creation designed by theatre architect William Finch Hill in the mid-1800s in grand style to complement the British Museum opposite, this ornate tavern is pretty much how an uninitiate from Tokyo or Tallahassee might picture the typical English pub. All that's missing is the pea-souper fog swirling around outside. Within stands a half-moon bar counter embellished by pre-war promotional mirrors (Watney's, Hennessey's et al), old light fittings and, tragically, an eye-level display of alcopops. Perusal of John N Henderson's *History of the Museum Tavern in Bloomsbury*, also on sale, provides further picaresque detail; borrow a copy, order a Theakston's Old Peculiar and shepherds pie from the open kitchen and sit back on one of the handful of patterned wooden chairs, and imagine famous old Museum regulars – Orwell, Marx (both of whom would be pleased to note there's a very popular socialist bookshop just around the corner) – doing likewise.
Children admitted (over-14s only). Tables outdoors (pavement). **Map 1/L5**

mybar

11 Bayley Street, WC1 (7667 6000/www.myhotels.co.uk). Goodge Street or Tottenham Court Road tube.
Open/food served 11am-11pm daily. **Credit** AmEx, DC, MC, V.
As befits a feng-shui'd range of lifestyle hotels designed 'with cutting-edge philosophers, sensitive aromatherapists and seasoned world travellers' in mind, mybar of the myhotel Bloomsbury branch is understatedly branded. It's even got a mysnug at the end for private functions. For the rest of us, mybar provides a fashionable retreat off Tottenham Court Road, comprising a narrow bar space punctured by three open doorways and a fish tank. A bland if rhythmic electronic soundtrack is occasionally fractured by the frantic Latin shake of the cocktail mixer; the Italian staff can't mix music for toffee, but they sure can fix a fine drink. Fruit, herbs and spices are added to ten types of mycocktails, mymartinis, mylongdrinks etc, including a scrumptious mybreeze of berries and Plymouth damson gin for, well, an irksomely uneven amount, courtesy of a 12.5% levy that results in a dish full of small change most punters will be embarrassed to take anyway. That, presumably, is mytip.
Babies and children admitted (until 6pm). Disabled: toilet. Function rooms. Tables outdoors (pavement).
Map 1/K5

Nudge

36-8 New Oxford Street WC1 (7631 0862). Tottenham Court Road tube. **Open** 11am-11pm Mon-Sat. **Food served** 11am-9pm Mon-Sat. **Credit** AmEx, MC, V.
The brashest new kid on the block along an otherwise bland stretch of New Oxford Street, Nudge is trying to be all things to all cosmopolitan bar lovers. Mainly bar with some pub touches – the one main bar is zinc-topped with an imposing carved wooden surround, for example – Nudge has yet to attract a regular lunchtime crowd to complement the post-work horde happy to wash down a day's graft in new surroundings. A shame, because a lot of thought has gone behind the range of food and drinks. Imaginative grilled mains, and smaller dips and stews are concocted in an open kitchen, while drinks include draught Leffe Blonde, Staropramen, Adnams Bitter, obscure cocktails (Brazilian Berry?) and 20-odd wines served in two sizes of glass and by the bottle. Ducts, chandeliers and cabinets are set above a parquet floor upstairs; the cosy DJ bar downstairs deliberately, but not exclusively, attracts private parties. If you like this, there's a near identical sibling venue, the **Interval** (*see p57*) just off Leicester Square.
Babies and children admitted (until 4pm). Disabled: toilet. Function room. Music (DJs 7pm Thur). Tables outdoors (pavement). **Map 1/L5**

Oporto

168 High Holborn, WC1 (7240 1548/www.baroporto.com). Tottenham Court Road tube. **Open** noon-11pm Mon-Sat; noon-9pm Sun. **Food served** noon-10pm Mon-Sat; noon-9pm Sun. **Happy hour** 3-6pm daily. **Credit** AmEx, MC, V.

Also known as the bar with no name; it's the place on the corner of Endell Street, next door to the landmark Oasis sports centre, and although there's no signboard just look out for the big picture windows and welcoming vibe. On a dark night, the place glows, a Hopper-esque scene in studied urbanity with seated coffee and beer drinkers engrossed in newspapers and indulging in chanced conversation. It's suitably American in feel, more cafe-bar than boozer with, at certain times of the day, focaccia and cappuccino as much in evidence as alcohol. There's a pleasing lack of pretension, just mellow music, clean creamy walls, amiable staff and a view of the city lights as they swing round St Giles Circus. If you come with a book, make it Richard Ford.

Function room. Tables outdoors (pavement). TV. **Map 1/L6**

Plough

27 Museum Street, WC1 (7636 7964). Tottenham Court Road tube. **Open** 11am-11pm Mon-Sat; noon-10.30pm Sun. **Food served** noon-7pm, snack menu 7-10pm daily. **Credit** AmEx, MC, V.

'Traditional English Pub' claims the large, brash sign in six languages, each complemented by its own flag. Off-putting to locals, such as they are, but then it's probably the antique-fatigued visitors spilling out of the near-neighbouring British Museum that set the tills ringing here. A shame really, because this Taylor Walker establishment isn't too tacky at all. It comprises two bars, the smaller popular and, indeed, traditional, the larger given over to televised sports and a broad array of wines, fixtures and vintages chalked up by the long bar counter. Beers are a decent bunch and include Bass Ale, Marston's Pedigree, Adnams Bitter and Broadside. Food is of the steak, burger and baguette variety. There's a no-smoking bar upstairs, and a cluster of tables and chairs under baskets of plants outside. A decent alternative when the **Museum Tavern** (*see p26*) is full.

Babies and children admitted (separate room). Function room. Games (fruit machine). No-smoking area. Tables outdoors (pavement). TVs (satellite). **Map 1/L5**

Point 101

101 New Oxford Street, WC1 (7379 3112/www.meanfiddler.com). Tottenham Court Road tube. **Open/food served** 11am-2am Mon-Thur; 11am-2.30am Fri, Sat; 5pm-midnight Sun. **Happy hour** 5-9pm Sun-Thur. **Credit** AmEx, MC, V.

Modern bars based in landmark buildings tend to assume the character of their surroundings and Point 101 is no exception. The trouble is, the building here is Centre Point, the pre-stressed concrete monstrosity famously unoccupied for the first decade of its existence. Although its resident bar rarely suffers from any lack of occupiers, it maintains the family trait of bog-standard wart-on-face ugliness; put simply, Point 101 looks like an open-plan underpass. Heavy concrete surrounds furniture of the shop-floor cafeteria variety, hardly improved by the uncomfortable metal bar stools that only a Play-Doh backside could embrace. The drinks – Staropramen and Grolsch on draught – quench rather than entice. However, there is that late licence and the great appeal it holds. Perhaps its real plus point is the huge glass front that reveals a slow-moving tableau of buses and black taxi cabs crawling down towards Oxford Street. Time for one more before battling the crowds for that last bus back to civilisation?

Babies and children admitted (until 5pm). Function room. Music (DJs 9pm Mon-Sat; 7pm Sun; free). Tables outdoors (pavement). **Map 7/K6**

Queen's Larder

1 Queen Square, WC1 (7837 5627). Holborn or Russell Square tube. **Open** 11am-11pm Mon-Fri; noon-11pm Sat; noon-10.30pm Sun. **Food served** noon-8pm daily. **Credit** MC, V.

'Welcome to this Historic Tavern' beckons the signage above the bar of this cubbyhole on the corner of Queen Square, in the heart of London's traditional medical quarter. During the madness of King George his trusty consort Queen Charlotte used the cellar here as a royal stash (the king was being treated by a Dr Willis in a house opposite). This historical detail inspires decoration of framed beruffed royals in portrait, jug, and tankard form. Custom these days tends toward low-paid ancillaries caning the fruit machine and low-grade Midlands businessmen attracted by a promise of draught Marston's Pedigree while a dumb waiter groans under the weight of pies, puds and potatoes. There's a restaurant upstairs, tables outside in summer.

Babies and children admitted (until 9pm). Games (fruit machine). No-smoking area. Tables outdoors (pavement). TV. **Map 1/L5**

Truckles of Pied Bull Yard

Off Bury Place, WC1 (7404 5338/www.davy.co.uk). Holborn or Tottenham Court Road tube. **Open/food served** 11.30am-10pm Mon-Fri; 11.30am-3pm Sat. **Credit** AmEx, DC, MC, V.

Part of the **Davy's** portfolio (*see p15*), Truckles belongs to a younger generation of wine bars, distinct from the sawdusted Dickensian breed normally associated with the chain. A location on a secluded courtyard (reached via an arch off Bury Place) means that it comes into its own in summer, when there's a little self-contained boozy piazza thing going on. In less clement weather customers are forced inside to be cheered by a vibrant yellow colour scheme. Many of the wines on offer are Davy's own labels, so if you know roughly what sort of a wine you prefer that's as far as the decision-making process has to go. It's not an extensive selection but it does offer enough choice for all but the most choosy, particularly for fans of French plonk. Ale is also served, in pewter tankards unless you request otherwise.

Babies and children admitted. Function rooms. No-smoking area. Tables outdoors (courtyard). **Map 1/L5**

Also in the area...

All Bar One 108 New Oxford Street, WC1 (7307 7980).
Walkabout 136 Shaftesbury Avenue, W1 (7255 8620).

Chelsea

Chelsea's pubs and bars have gained a slightly unfair reputation over the years. True, a good many of the establishments on and around the King's Road do play host to swarms of infuriating, beautiful young people with more money than sense. However, look a little further afield and you'll find plenty of good honest boozers, stylish bars and even an earthy local or two. Note that the boundaries of Chelsea are a bit indefinable, so also see the Fulham and South Kensington sections.

Central

London drinking: late night

Where to keep drinking after the last tube has gone.

We were hoping we wouldn't have to print this section this year, but the much-promised change to the licensing laws allowing all-night drinking has still not come to fruition. So while London may be a thriving cosmopolitan city, it sure ain't a 24-hour kind of place. The truth is, few new bars are being granted late-night licences now that councils such as Westminster (responsible for Soho and Covent Garden), Camden and Kensington & Chelsea are rclamping down on places that might increase night-time activity. The good news, however, is that late licenses – although in too short supply – are still held by around 350 London venues. Door policies vary: some charge admission, while others prefer to keep things free and easy. To help you beat the curfew, we've gathered together a list of bars where you can get a drink even as the clock reaches the witching hour.

Central

Bayswater & Paddington
Cherry Jam *(p18)* until 2am Mon-Sat; midnight Sun.
Cubana *(p18)* until midnight Mon-Sat.
Steam *(p20)* until 1am Mon-Wed; 2am Thur-Sun.

Belgravia
Blue Bar *(p22)* until 1am Mon-Sat.

Bloomsbury & St Giles
AKA *(p25)* until 3am Tue-Fri; 7am Sat; 4am Sun.
Point 101 *(p27)* until 2am Mon-Thur; 2.30am Fri, Sat.

Chelsea
Bluebird *(p30)* until midnight Mon-Thur; 1am Fri, Sat.
Lomo *(p33)* until midnight Mon-Sat.

Covent Garden
Detroit *(p36)* until 12.30am Mon-Sat.
Langley *(p37)* until 1am Mon-Sat.
Retox Bar *(p39)* until 1am Mon-Wed; 3am Thur-Sat.
Roadhouse *(p39)* until 3am Mon-Sat; 1am Sun.
The Spot *(p39)* until 1am daily.

Earl's Court
Troubadour *(p40)* until midnight daily.
Warwick Arms *(p40)* until midnight Mon-Sat.

Fitzrovia
Bar Madrid *(p41)* until 2am Mon; late Tue-Thur; 3am Fri; 3.30am Sat.
Hakkasan *(p42)* until 12.30am Mon-Wed, Sun; 1am Thur-Sat.
Jerusalem *(p43)* Fitrovia.
Open until midnight Tue, Wed; 1am Thur-Sat.
Long Bar *(p43)* until 12.30am Mon-Sat.
Market Place *(p44)* until 1am Mon-Sat; midnight Sun.
Mash *(p44)* until 2am Mon-Sat.
Match *(p44)* until midnight Mon-Sat.
Sevilla Mía *(p45)* until 1am Mon-Sat; midnight Sun.

High Street Kensington
Cuba *(p47)* until 2am Mon-Sat.
Po Na Na *(p48)* until 2am Mon-Sat.

King's Cross & Euston
The Backpacker *(p52)* until 2am Fri, Sat; midnight Sun.
Ruby Lounge *(p53)* until 1am Thur; 2am Fri, Sat.

Knightsbridge
Isola *(p53)* until midnight Mon-Sat.
Mandarin Bar *(p53)* until 2am Mon-Sat.
Townhouse *(p55)* until midnight Mon-Sat.

Leicester Square & Piccadilly Circus
Atlantic Bar & Grill *(p55)* until 3am Mon-Sat.
De Hems *(p56)* until midnight Mon-Sat.
Denim *(p56)* until 1.30am Mon-Sat.
Down Mexico Way *(p57)* until 3am Mon-Sat.
The International *(p57)* until 2am Mon-Sat.
Jewel *(p57)* until 1am Mon-Sat.
On Anon *(p57)* until 3am Mon-Sat.
Saint *(p59)* until 2am Tue-Thur; 3am Fri, Sat.

Mayfair
Claridge's *(p64)* until 1am Mon-Sat; midnight Sun.
The Loop *(p65)* until 3am Mon-Sat.
Mô Tea Rooms *(p65)* until midnight Thur-Sat.
Rosie's *(p66)* until 1am Mon-Sat.
Trader Vic's *(p67)* until 1am Mon-Thur; 3am Fri, Sat.
Windows *(p67)* until 2am Mon-Thur; 3am Fri, Sat.
Zeta Bar *(p67)* until 1am Mon, Tue; 3am Wed-Sat.

Notting Hill, Ladbroke Grove & Westbourne Grove
Eclipse *(p69)* until midnight Mon-Sat.
Lonsdale *(p71)* until midnight Mon-Sat.
Pharmacy *(p72)* until 1am Mon-Thur; 2am Fri, Sat; midnight Sun.
Tiroler Hut *(p74)* until 12.30am Mon-Sat.
Under The Westway *(p74)* until midnight Mon-Sat.

Soho
Akbar *(p75)* until 1am Mon-Sat.
Amber *(p77)* until 1am Mon-Sat.
Bar Code *(p77)* until 1am Mon-Sat.
Bar Soho *(p77)* until 1am Mon-Thur; 3am Fri, Sat; 12.30am Sun.
Bar Sol Ona *(p78)* until 3am Mon-Sat.
Cafe Bohème *(p78)* until 2.30am Mon-Sat.
Candy Bar *(p78)* until 2am Fri, Sat.
Crobar *(p79)* until 3am Mon-Sat.
The Edge *(p81)* until 1am Mon-Sat.
Freedom *(p81)* until midnight Mon-Wed; 2am Thur; 3am Fri, Sat.
Kettner's *(p81)* until midnight daily.
Lab *(p83)* until midnight Mon-Sat.
Opium *(p83)* until 3am Mon-Sat.
Phoenix Arts Club *(p83)* until 12.30am Thur-Sat.
The Player *(p83)* until midnight Mon-Thur; 1am Fri, Sat.
Pop *(p84)* until 3am Mon-Thur; 4am Fri; 5am Sat.
The Soho *(p84)* until 1am Mon-Wed; 3am Thur-Sat.
Thirst *(p85)* until 3am Mon-Sat.
Two Thirty Club *(p85)* until midnight Mon-Sat.
Village Soho *(p85)* until 1am Mon-Sat;midnight Sun.
Waikiki *(p86)* until midnight Thur-Sat.
Zebrano *(p86)* until midnight Mon-Sat.

South Kensington
Cactus Blue *(p88)* until midnight Mon-Sat.
FireHouse *(p90)* until 3am Tue-Sat.
190 Queesgate *(p87)* until 1am Mon-Sat; midnight Sun.

Trafalgar Square & Charing Cross
ICA Bar *(p95)* until 1am Tue-Sat.
Queen Mary *(p96)* until 2am Fri, Sat.
Rockwell *(p97)* until 1am Mon-Sat.
Zander *(p99)* until 1am Wed-Sat.

Waterloo
L'Auberge *(p101)* until midnight Mon-Fri.
Cubana *(p101)* until midnight Mon-Thur, Sun; 1am Fri, Sat.

City

Clarkenwell & Farringdon
Al's Bar Cafe *(p107)* until 2am Mon-Sat.
Cellar Gascon *(p108)* until midnight Mon-Fri.
Charterhouse *(p109)* until 2am Fri, Sat; midnight Sun.
Dust *(p111)* until midnight Mon-Wed; until 2am Thur-Sat.
Easton *(p111)* until 1am Fri, Sat.
Fluid *(p111)* until midnight Mon-Wed; 2am Thur, Fri, Sat.
Match *(p114)* until midnight Mon-Sat.
O'Hanlon's *(p114)* until midnight Mon-Sat.
Pakenham Arms *(p114)* until 1am Mon-Fri; midnight Sun.
Potemkin *(p114)* until midnight Mon-Sat.
Smiths of Smithfield *(p115)* until midnight Fri, Sat.
The Well *(p117)* until midnight Mon-Sat.

Fleet Street, Blackfriars & St Paul's
Nylon *(p118)* until 2am Thur, Fri; 3am Sat.

Hoxton & Shoreditch
Barley Mow *(p121)* until midnight Mon-Sat.
Bluu *(p121)* until midnight Fri, Sat.
BOD *(p121)* until midnight Fri, Sat.
Bridge & Tunnel *(p122)* until 2am Mon-Sat; 12.30am Sun.
Cantaloupe *(p122)* until midnight Mon-Sat.
Cargo *(p122)* until 1am Mon-Thur; 3am Fri, Sat; midnight Sun.
Catch 22 *(p122)* until midnight Tue, Wed; 2am Thur-Sat; 1am Sun.
Charlie Wright's International Bar *(p122)* until 1am Mon-Wed, Sun; 2am Thur; 3am Fri, Sat.
Dragon *(p125)* until midnight Fri, Sat.
dreamsbagsjaguarshoes *(p125)* until midnight Mon-Sat.
Elbow Room *(p125)* until 2am Mon-Sat; until midnight Sun.
Fifteen *(p125)* until midnight Mon-Sat.
Grand Central *(p126)* until midnight daily.
Great Eastern Dining Room *(p126)* until midnight Mon-Wed; 1am Thur-Sat.
Herbal *(p126)* until 2am Wed, Thur, Sun; 3am Fri, Sat.
Home *(p126)* until midnight Mon-Sat.
Hoxton Square Bar & Kitchen until midnight Mon-Sat.
Light Bar & Restaurant *(p127)* until midnight Mon-Wed; 2am Thur-Sat.
Medicine *(p127)* until 2am Wed-Sat; midnight Sun.
Mother Bar *(p127)* until 3am Mon-Wed; 4am Thur, Sun; 5am Fri, Sat.
Pool *(p128)* until 1am Wed, Thur; 2am Fri, Sat; midnight Sun.
Reliance *(p128)* until 2am Fri, Sat.
Shoreditch Electrity Showrooms *(p128)* until midnight Mon-Thur, Sun; 1am Fri, Sat.
Smersh *(p128)* until midnight Tue-Sat.
Sosho *(p130)* until midnight Tue, Wed; until 1am Thur; until 3am Fri, Sat.
Trafik *(p130)* until 2am Mon-Sat; midnight Sun.

Liverpool Street & Moorgate
One of Two *(p132)* until 1am Thur, Fri.

East

Bethnal Green
Pleasure Unit *(p141)* until 2am Fri, Sat.
Sebright Arms *(p141)* until midnight Wed-Sat.

Bow & Mile End
New Globe *(p143)* midnight Mon-Wed; noon-2am Thur-Sat.

Hackney
Aqua Cafe Bar *(p147)* until 2am Fri, Sat.
District *(p148)* until midnight Mon-Wed, Sun; 1am Thur-Sat.
Dove Freehouse *(p148)* until midnight Fri, Sat.
291 *(p149)* until midnight Tue-Thur; 2am Fri, Sat.
Wellington *(p149)* until midnight Mon-Sat.

Limehouse
Booty's Riverside Bar *(p151)* until midnight Fri, Sat.

Whitechapel
Urban Bar (UHT) *(p156)* until 1am Thur-Sat.
Vibe Bar *(p156)* until 1am Fri, Sat.

North

Belsize Park
The Hill *(p158)* until midnight Mon-Sat.

Camden Town & Chalk Form
Bar Solo *(p158)* until 1am daily.
Bartok *(p159)* until 1am Mon-Thur; 2am Fri, Sat; midnight Sun.
Dublin Castle *(p160)* until 1am Mon-Sat; midnight Sun.
Monarch *(p162)* until midnight Mon-Thur; 2am Fri, Sat.
Monkey Chews *(p163)* until midnight Fri, Sat.
Quinn's *(p164)* until midnight Mon-Wed; 2am Thur-Sat.
Singapore Sling *(p164)* until midnight Mon, Tue, Sun; 1am Wed-Sat.

Crouch End
Banners *(p164)* until midnight Fri, Sat.
Bar Rocca *(p165)* until 1am Mon-Thur; 2am Fri, Sat; noon-midnight Sun.
King's Head *(p165)* until midnight Mon-Thur; 1am Fri, Sat.

Finsbury Park & Stroud Green
Triangle *(p166)* until midnight Tue-Sun.
World's End *(p166)* until midnight daily.

Islington
Chapel *(p172)* until midnight Thur, Sun; 1am Fri, Sat.
Elbow Room *(p173)* until 2am Mon-Thur; 3am Fri, Sat; midnight Sun.
Embassy Bar *(p173)* until 1am Fri, Sat.
Filthy McNasty's *(p173)* until midnight Fri, Sat.
Hen & Chickens Theatre Bar *(p174)* until midnight Mon-Wed, Sun; 1am Thur-Sat.
Hope & Anchor *(p174)* until 1am Mon-Sat; midnight Sun.
King's Head *(p174)* until 1am Mon-Thur, Sun; 2am Fri, Sat.
Matt & Matt Bar *(p176)* until 1am Thur; 2am Fri, Sat.
Medicine Bar *(p176)* until midnight Mon-Thur, Sun; 2am Fri, Sat.
Salmon & Compass *(p177)* until 2am Mon-Sat; midnight Sun.

Kilburn
Zd Bar *(p179)* until 1am Mon-Thur; 2am Fri, Sat.

Maida Vale
Otto Dining Lounge *(p179)* until 1am Mon-Sat.

Muswell Hill & Alexandra Palace
Victoria Stakes *(p180)* until midnight Fri, Sat.

Palmers Green
Fox *(p181)* until midnight Tue, Thur; 1am Fri, Sat.

Stoke Newington
Bar Lorca *(p185)* until 1am Mon-Thur; 2am Fri, Sat; midnight Sun.
Londesborough *(p185)* until midnight Fri, Sat.

Swiss Cottage
Zuccato *(p186)* until midnight Mon-Sat.

Tufnell Park & Archway
Progress Bar *(p187)* until midnight Mon-Wed, Sun; 2am Thur-Sat.

West Hampstead
Gallery *(p188)* until midnight Fri, Sat.
No 77 Wine Bar *(p188)* until midnight Wed-Sat.
toast *(p167)* until midnight daily.

South

Balham
Bedford *(p190)* until midnight Thur; 2am Fri, Sat.
Duke Of Devonshire *(p190)* until midnight Mon-Thur, Sun; 2am Fri, Sat.
Exhibit *(p190)* until midnight Fri, Sat.
Lounge *(p190)* until midnight Wed-Sun.

Battersea
Artesian Well *(p191)* until midnight Thur, Sun; 2am Fri, Sat.
Boom *(p192)* until midnight Fri, Sat.
The Common Rooms *(p192)* until 1am Fri, Sat.
Corum *(p192)* until 1am daily.
Drawing Room & Sofa Bar *(p193)* until midnight daily.
Inigo *(p195)* until 2am daily.
S Bar *(p195)* until midnight Sat, Sun.
Tea Room des Artistes *(p195)* until 1am Fri, Sat; 12.30am Sun.

Bermondsey & Rotherhithe
Spice Island *(p197)* until midnight Fri, Sat.

Blackheath
Cave Austin *(p197)* until 1am Fri, Sat.
Zero Degrees *(p198)* until midnight Mon-Sat.

Brixton & Streatham
Bar Lorca *(p201)* until 2am Mon-Thur; 3am Fri, Sat; midnight Sun.
Brixtonian Havana Club *(p201)* until 1am Tue, Wed; 2am Thur-Sat; midnight Sun.
Bug Bar *(p201)* until 1am Wed, Thur; 3am Fri, Sat; 2am Sun.
Dogstar *(p202)* until 2am Mon-Wed, Sun; 2.30am Thur; 4am Fri, Sat.
Fridge Bar *(p202)* until 2am Mon-Thur; 4am Fri, Sat; 3am Sun.
Living *(p202)* until 2am Mon-Thur, Sun; 4am Fri, Sat.
Plan-B *(p203)* until midnight Mon, Tue; 2am Wed, Thur; 4am Fri, Sat; 1am Sun.
SW9 *(p203)* until 1am Fri, Sat.
Telegraph *(p203)* until 2am Mon-Thur; 4am Fri; 6am Sat; midnight Sun.
Tongue & Groove *(p203)* until 2am Wed-Sat; 1am Sun.
White Horse *(p203)* until 1am daily.
Windmill *(p205)* until midnight daily.

Camberwell
Funky Munky *(p205)* until midnight Mon-Wed, Sun; 2am Thur-Sat.
Red Star *(p205)* until 2am Tue-Thur; 4am Fri, Sat; midnight Sun.

Clapham
Arch 635 *(p207)* until midnight Fri, Sat.
Bar Local *(p207)* until midnight daily.
Kazbar *(p208)* until midnight Mon-Sat.
Sand *(p209)* until 2am Mon-Sat; 1am Sun.
SO.UK *(p209)* until midnight Mon-Wed, Sun; 1am Thur; 2am Fri, Sat.
2 Brewers *(p210)* until 2am Mon-Thur; 3am Fri, Sat; 12.30am Sun.
White House *(p210)* until 2am Mon-Sat; midnight Sun.

Dulwich
East Dulwich Tavern *(p211)* until midnight Thur-Sat.
Franklin's *(p211)* until midnight Fri, Sat.

Herne Hill
Escape Bar & Art *(p215)* until midnight daily.

Kennington, Lambeth & Oval
South London Pacific *(p216)* until midnight Tue, Wed, Sun; 1am Thur; 2am Fri, Sat.
White Bear *(p216)* until midnight Mon-Sat.

Putney
Putney Bridge *(p219)* until midnight Mon-Thur; 1am Fri, Sat.

Stockwell
Bar Estrala *(p220)* until midnight Mon-Sat.
Swan *(p222)* until 2am Thur, Sun; 3am Fri, Sat.

Tooting
smoke bar diner *(p223)* until midnight Mon-Sat.
Spirit Cafe Bar *(p223)* until midnight Mon-Sat.

Wimbledon
Bar Sia *(p227)* until midnight Fri, Sat.
Eclipse Wimbledon *(p229)* until midnight Tue, Wed; 1am Thur-Sat.

West

Acton
Grand Junction Arms *(p232)* until 1am Fri; midnight Sat.

Fulham
Fiesta Havana *(p238)* until 2am Mon-Sat; 1am Sun.
Po Na Na Fez *(p239)* until 2am Mon-Sat.

Hammersmith
Autumn House *(p240)* until midnight Fri, Sat.

Kensal Green
William IV *(p242)* until midnight Thur-Sat.

Shepherd's Bush
West 12 *(p246)* until midnight Mon-Sat.

Southall
Glassy Junction *(p246)* until 2am Thur-Sat.

Eagle Bar Diner. *See p41.*

Apartment 195

195 King's Road, SW3 (7351 5195/www.apartment 195.co.uk). Sloane Square tube/11, 22 bus. **Open/food served** 4-11pm Mon-Sat. **Credit** AmEx, MC, V.

Considering all the money around this part of town, the area is notably short on swish, sophisticated bars: so a big welcome, then, to Apartment 195. The name is suggestive of New York, and so is the collection of rooms: urbane, elegant and comfortably understated. The main room is dark and high-ceilinged, the bar staff sleekly professional. Cocktails are the core of the drinks list: manly classics such as the Old Fashioned (Blanton's Bourbon with Bitters: £8), or modern concoctions guaranteed to make you look like a Big Girl's Blouse, such as a Chinese Mule (lightly infused sake muddled with vodka, coriander, ginger and ginger beer: £7). Beer and wine drinkers are more than adequately provided for, and there are some smart bar snacks to pick at. Be warned, though, that a 'swipe card' ID system is being introduced, giving preferential treatment to 'regular customers'.

Function room. TV.

Bluebird

350 King's Road, SW3 (7559 1000/www.conran.com). Sloane Square tube, then 19, 22 bus/49 bus. **Open** 11am-midnight Mon-Thur; 11am-1am Fri, Sat; 11am-10.30pm Sun. **Food served** noon-11pm Mon-Sat; noon-10pm Sun. **Credit** AmEx, DC, MC, V.

Part of Conran's ever expanding Bluebird mall, this stylish, swanky bar nestles in one corner of the equally impressive Bluebird restaurant. It's certainly a pleasant space – comfortable sofas, armchairs, ottomans and large window booths overlooking the King's Road – but it's difficult to escape the feeling that it's been created with a certain brand of customer in mind. The very brand of customer, indeed, that it seems to attract: privileged Chelsea suits with plenty of money to spend on well-made cocktails and upmarket bar snacks (spicy Scotch quail egg, anyone?). As such, at busier times, it's the wrong place to pick for a relaxing drink. Downstairs is the Bluebird supermarket where you can stock up on all manner of international delicacies for a wholesome post-pub snack when you get home.

Babies and children admitted (restaurant only). Disabled: toilet. Function rooms. Music (DJ 9pm-1am Fri, Sat). Tables outdoors (forecourt).

Builder's Arms

13 Britten Street, SW3 (7349 9040). Sloane Square or South Kensington tube. **Open** 11am-11pm Mon-Sat; noon-10.30pm Sun. **Food served** noon-2.30pm, 7-9.30pm Mon-Sat; noon-3pm, 7-9pm Sun. **Credit** MC, V.

Just along Britten Street from the handsome St Luke's Church, the Builder's is a discreet little establishment that the regulars are justified in keeping under wraps. The pastel-toned pub is divided into two rooms by a long narrow bar, but you'll find no public bar/saloon divide here – the ambience is uniformly crisp, comfortable and classy. Low-slung sofas and busy bookshelves abound, while fine art prints offer your eyes something to rest on as they wander lazily over the rest of the clientele. They're mostly young, attractive and wealthy in an understated sort of way. Choice tipple is vino, of which there's an impressive selection here, supplemented by a couple of real ales, as well as around a dozen malt whiskies. Unsurprisingly, food served from a busy kitchen at the rear of the pub is of a higher standard than your average back road boozer. All things considered, it's an inappropriately earthy name for such a well-groomed public house.

Babies and children admitted. Disabled: toilet. Games (chess). Tables outdoors (pavement). TV.

Chelsea Potter

119 King's Road, SW3 (7352 9479). Sloane Square tube. **Open** 11am-11pm Mon-Sat; noon-10.30pm Sun. **Food served** 11am-7pm daily. **Credit** AmEx, DC, MC, V.

Although it maintains a reputation for being a bit 'lively' around kicking-out time, the Chelsea Potter is well past it's premier punk hang out heyday. It's still suitably grotty though. The paintwork has seen better days and the first thing we noticed was a row of noisy fruit machines that runs nearly the whole length of the rear wall. A few tables in a corner of the bar provide the only real seating, otherwise it's down to leaning on the elbow-height pedestal tables that seem so popular with these groups of narky-looking young men. On the beer front, it's the old Foster's, Stella, John Smith's and Guinness combination, and the food is nothing to shout about either. In fact, all that can be said for the Potter is that its prime location allows for a bit of fun people-watching on Saturday afternoons, when the pub itself gets rammed by northern football supporters down for the match and fooled into thinking they are drinking at the epicentre of swinging Chelsea. No wonder they look so disappointed.
Babies and children admitted (until 4pm). Games (fruit machines). Jukebox. Tables outdoors (pavement). TV.

Chelsea Ram

32 Burnaby Street, SW10 (7351 4008). Fulham Broadway tube/Sloane Square tube then 11, 19, 22 bus. **Open** 11am-11pm Mon-Sat; noon-10.30pm Sun. **Food served** 12.30-3pm, 6.30-10pm Mon-Sat; 12.30-6pm Sun. **Credit** MC, V.
Like its near neighbour the **Lots Road Pub & Dining Rooms** (*see p33*), the Ram seems misplaced in the eerily quiet residential area it occupies, sandwiched between the immense Lots Road power station and a large storage depot for Bonham's the auctioneers. You'd never find it unless you already knew it was there. And that seems a shame, given what a convivial place this is. The staff are friendly and on the ball, while the regulars – presumably all locals – are an equally cheerful bunch and, despite the appearance that everyone in the pub knows each other, are more than welcoming of an unfamiliar face. The decor is typical Young's with stripped floorboards and blond wood furniture, although a collection of charcoal drawings that adorns the walls adds a distinctive touch. It's a place well worth seeking out if you find yourself at the nether end of the King's Road.
Babies and children admitted (dining area only). Function room. Tables outdoors (pavement). TV (big screen).

Cooper's Arms

87 Flood Street, SW3 (7376 3120). Sloane Square or South Kensington tube. **Open** 11am-11pm Mon-Sat; noon-10.30pm Sun. **Food served** 12.30-3pm, 6.30-9.30pm Mon-Sat; 12.30-3pm Sun. **Credit** AmEx, MC, V.
The first thing to catch the eye on entering this fine Young's house will almost certainly be the stuffed bear that looms out of one corner of the spacious bar. Second and third glances reveal further examples of the taxidermist's art in the shape of a huge moose head behind the bar and a deer's head over the door to the toilets. And there are plenty more features to admire – a collection of vintage railway company advertisements and a fabulous station clock – in a pub that's big on talking points but, thanks to high ceilings and big windows, never feels overstuffed. Exceptionally friendly bar staff serve a line-up of decent real ales and a great selection of wines with just the right amount of banter to a mixed bag of young trendies and wizened old regulars. Friday and Saturday nights are rammed, as is Sunday lunchtime when the Coop serves up a cracking roast. An all-round winner.
Babies and children admitted (until 6pm). Function room (sit-down meals only). TV.

Cross Keys

1 Lawrence Street, SW3 (7349 9111). Sloane Square tube. **Open** noon-11pm Mon-Sat; noon-10.30pm Sun. **Food served** *Bar* noon-3pm, 6-8pm Mon-Fri. *Restaurant* noon-3pm, 7-11pm Mon-Fri; noon-4pm, 7-11pm Sat; noon-8.30pm Sun. **Credit** AmEx, MC, V.

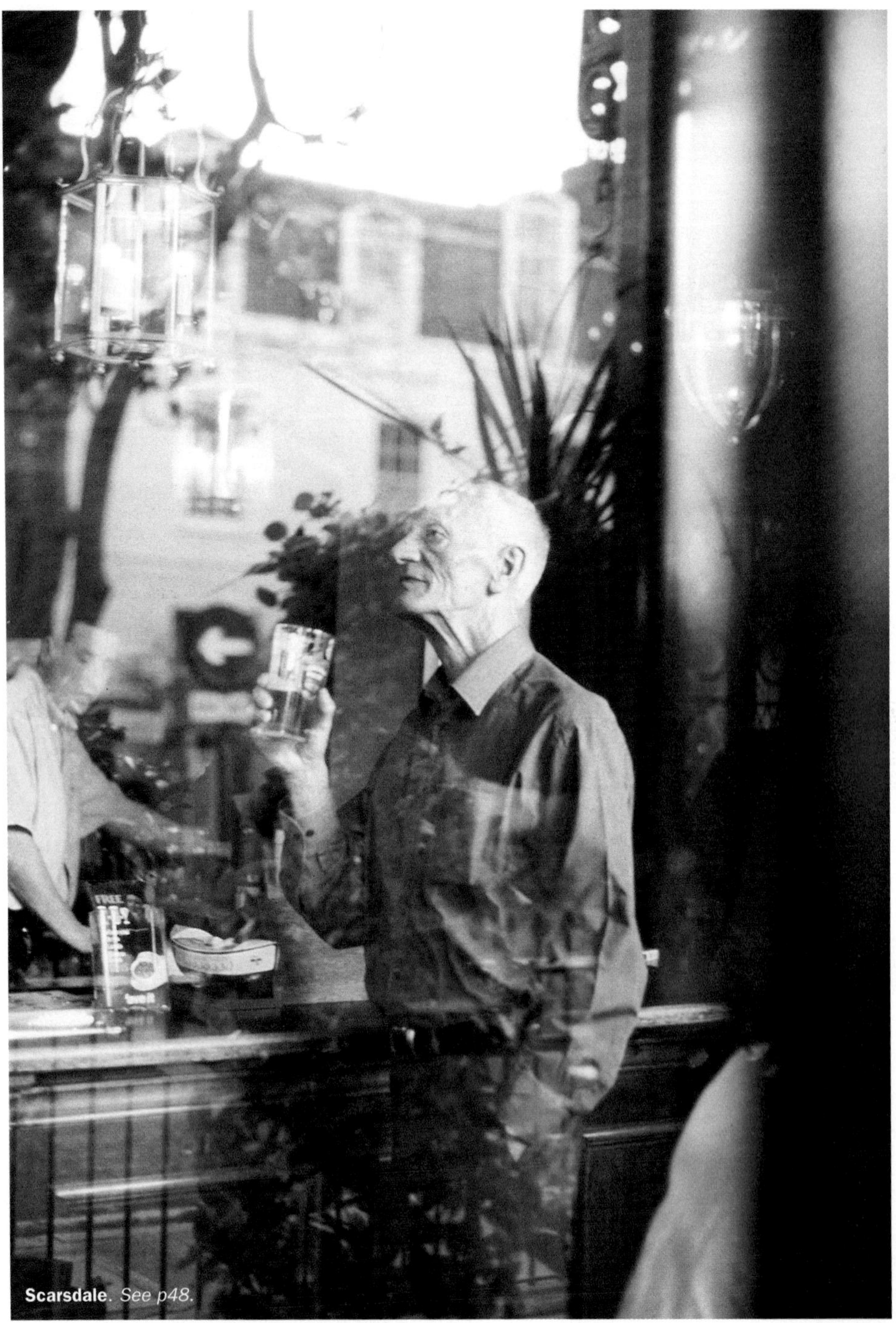
Scarsdale. *See p48.*

A meandering walk from the King's Road through quaint streets that represent some of the most exclusive property in the capital, the Cross Keys is a genuine curiosity. Its modern Gothic interior (created by the same team that designed Notting Hill's **Beach Blanket Babylon**, *see p68*) is punctuated with rococo touches that range from the joyfully tacky – an engraved mirror with a huge embossed lion's head gazing sternly from its centre – to the downright absurd – a plaster monk standing astride one of two roaring fires with his cassock hitched up. It's all charmingly silly and seems to go down well with the self-consciously hip locals who arrive in droves at the weekend and regularly book the upstairs function rooms. To the rear of the bar is a sizeable dining room in which both decor and cuisine lean quite heavily towards the Mediterranean. A fun and funky venue, but the jury's out as to whether it's a genuine treasure or just a passing novelty.
Babies and children admitted (high chairs). Function rooms.

Finch's

190 Fulham Road, SW10 (7351 5043). Earl's Court, Fulham Broadway or South Kensington tube/14 bus. **Open** 11am-11pm Mon-Sat; noon-10.30pm Sun. **Food served** noon-3pm, 6-8pm Mon-Fri; noon-3pm Sat; noon-4pm Sun. **Credit** MC, V.
Squeezed in among the style bars and chain pubs on an energetic stretch of the Fulham Road, this traditional Young's pub has a wilfully forbidding dark wood exterior that shields a gem of a boozer. Many pedestrians scurry past with barely a glance at its shadowy windows, seduced by the bright lights and loud music further down the road. They're missing a genuine treat. Finch's main appeal is in its interior architecture – flamboyant mosaics, private alcoves, an etched mirror on the back wall and, finest of all, a beautiful stained-glass skylight that refracts sunlight into myriad colourful shards. To the rear, a carpeted area complete with low leather sofas and pot plants offers a comfortable spot for leisurely sessions. Equally appealing are the Young's ales on draught, including seasonal specials. Clientele are smiley, nay, even smug in the knowledge they know of the best pub on Fulham Road.
Games (fruit machines). TV (big screen, satellite).

Fox & Hounds

29 Passmore Street, SW1 (7730 6367). Sloane Square tube. **Open** 11am-11pm Mon-Sat; noon-10.30pm Sun. **Food served** noon-2.30pm, 6.30-9.30pm Mon-Fri; noon-3pm Sun. **Credit** AmEx, DC, MC, V.
Until a few years ago, the Fox & Hounds was London's last surviving beer-only pub, serving just pints (plus wine). When it was acquired by Young's in 1999, spirits and a modest food menu were introduced but the Fox retains much quirky charm. The place is small and narrow with low ceilings, cosy corners and open fires. The decor's wonderfully haphazard with hunting prints sharing space with a timeline of the English monarchy and books toppling out of glass-fronted cases. Punters range from sozzled pub philosophers to Chelsea hoorays (we're near Sloane Square) but it's an amiable crowd. Nobody comes to the Fox & Hounds to be seen, or to rate the decor (reviewers excepted), but simply to enjoy a pint and chew the fat. If only there were more places like it.
Babies and children admitted. No piped music or jukebox. No-smoking area.

Lomo

222 Fulham Road, SW10 (7349 8848). Earl's Court, Fulham Broadway or South Kensington tube/14 bus. **Open/food served** 5pm-midnight Mon-Fri; noon-midnight Sat; 5-11.30pm Sun. **Happy hour** 5-7pm daily. **Credit** AmEx, DC, MC, V.

Critics' choice
hip hotel bars

Blue Bar (p22)
Gossipy den of Wedgwood-hued boho chic.

Lobby Bar (p93)
Understated and utterly convivial.

Long Bar (p43)
Top poseurs haunt but worth a look-in for the staring-eye stool backs.

Mandarin (p54)
A performance space for mixological magicians.

Rockwell (p97)
Bourbon specialists and *Time Out* award winners.

A stone's throw from the Chelsea and Westminster Hospital (although throwing stones around a hospital seems a touch uncharitable), Lomo is a modern tapas bar of repute. Darkened windows and occasional doormen are perhaps not the best way to entice in potential customers but those with sufficient front to pass inside are met with an interior that seems nail-bitingly trendy at first – sharp and modern with tall tables, stools and a rusty orange colour scheme – but is surprisingly relaxed on better acquaintance and after the quaffing of some choice tipples. The drinks menu includes bottled Spanish beers, wines and a selection of reasonably priced and reasonably prepared cocktails; the food is surprisingly tasty and inexpensive for a bar in west London. Come for a quick drink and snack, but don't be surprised if you're still here several hours later.
Babies and children admitted. Function room. TV (satellite, available in back room).

Lots Road Pub & Dining Rooms

114 Lots Road, SW10 (7352 6645). Fulham Broadway tube/Sloane Square tube then 11, 19, 22 bus. **Open** 11am-11pm Mon-Sat; 11am-10.30pm Sun. **Food served** noon-3pm, 5.30-10pm Mon-Fri; noon-10pm Sat, Sun. **Credit** AmEx, MC, V.
Lying in the shadow of the imposing Lots Road power station, this former Firkin hostelry has overcome a bleak and unpromising location to become a star venue – recognised as such when it topped the 'Best Gastropub' category in the *Time Out* Eating & Drinking Awards 2002. Its interior is a simple blend of cream walls, dark settles and leather armchairs. Look out over the frosted glass windows for a view of Chelsea Harbour. There's an open kitchen and a blackboard with a daily changing menu; food can be eaten at pub tables or in a separate dining area. Hand-pumped Brakspear Bitter and Courage Directors are backed up by the usual lager standards. An excellent wine list easily trumps the choice of drinks at the bar, with decent choices by the glass and most bottles in the £15-£25 range. When it comes to the food (Modern British), quality is top drawer and includes what the *Time Out* food reviewer reckons is 'the best sticky toffee pudding that we've ever tasted' and trust us, he's tasted plenty. Prices are reasonable too: about £50 for two with drinks. The lack

of a nearby tube station makes the pub a bit of a chore to reach, but that also has benefits – on a Friday or Saturday night you've a good chance of getting a table on spec.
Babies and children admitted. Disabled: toilet.

Orange Brewery

37-9 Pimlico Road, SW1 (7730 5984). Sloane Square tube. **Open** 11am-11pm Mon-Sat; noon-10.30pm Sun. **Food served** 11am-10pm Mon-Sat; noon-6pm Sun. **Credit** AmEx, DC, MC, V.

Since this pub was taken over by Scottish & Newcastle and ceased to brew its own beer, local interest appears to have waned dramatically. Our last end-of-week visit found the formerly bustling establishment bereft of both customers and atmosphere. It's a strange feeling in a pub as large and well known as this one to feel the need to lower the volume of your conversation for fear that the bar staff on the other side of the room might be eavesdropping. It's especially sad because the pub itself still has a lot going for it. The interior may be in need of a little TLC but it's still an attractive place with high ceilings, handsome wooden furniture and some lovely, old-fashioned copper light fittings. Here's hoping that the guys at S&N take notice that the Orange is no longer bearing fruit and hastily off-load the place to someone who knows how to run a decent pub.
Games (fruit machines, Trivial Pursuit machine). No-smoking area in restaurant. Tables outdoors (pavement). TV.

Phene Arms

9 Phene Street, SW3 (7352 3294). Sloane Square or South Kensington tube. **Open** 11am-11pm Mon-Sat; noon-10.30pm Sun. **Food served** noon-3pm, 6-10pm Mon-Fri; noon-4pm, 6-10pm Sat, Sun. **Credit** AmEx, DC, MC, V.

Cynics may suggest that since George Best ditched the bottle (for good this time, again) the Phene might have lost its main selling point – not to mention a major source of income – but there's a lot more to this unusual local than a famous ex-regular. From the outside, it looks every inch the upmarket back street pub: a handsome Victorian building with well-scrubbed brickwork and a pretty little terrace, but inside, it's a different story. The Phene is stuck squarely in the 1960s. It's as though a major refurbishment began at the beginning of that decade and was never quite completed – though new management, installed as we went to press, might decide to ring the changes. From the sleek, square central bar to the starburst clock on the rear wall and the wonderfully kitsch continental-style stemmed beer glasses, the whole place is a picture of retro modernity. But the great thing is, the Phene is no theme pub, this is not a retro re-creation, just a laudable example of some sensible body leaving well alone. Other plus points include Adnams and Fuller's ales, a great garden and convivial clientele.
Babies and children admitted. Function room. Tables outdoors (garden, roof terrace). TV.

Sporting Page

6 Camera Place, SW10 (7349 0455/www.frontpagepubs.com). Bus 11, 14, 19, 22, 328. **Open** 11am-11pm Mon-Sat; noon-10.30pm Sun. **Food served** noon-3pm, 6-10pm Mon-Fri; noon-6pm Sat, Sun. **Credit** AmEx, MC, V.

The rather plain outward appearance of this large local on the corner of quiet Camera Place belies its unusually smart interior. A trim black and white tiled floor and varnished rosewood bar lend an upmarket feel to the surroundings, while a series of sporting heroes depicted in large tiled murals adds a welcome splash of colour to the light airy bar. The punters tend to reflect the upmarket aspirations of the decor, comprising mainly city suits, ex-public school boys and old-school sloanes. Given the calibre of clientele it's perhaps not so surprising that the Sporting Page claims to sell more champagne than any other pub in the country – whether this is a plus or a minus is largely a matter of opinion. As the name suggests, this is very much a sports-orientated pub. Rugby fixtures tend to pull in the biggest crowds but Chelsea FC matches are also understandably popular and even cricket gets the big-screen treatment. Beers on offer include Spitfire and Bombardier and food comes in the shape of classic fish and chips, bangers and mash or roasts.
Babies and children admitted. Tables outdoors (pavement). TV (big screen, digital, satellite).

Surprise in Chelsea

6 Christchurch Terrace, off Flood Street, SW3 (7349 1821). Sloane Square tube. **Open** noon-11pm Mon-Sat; noon-10.30pm Sun. **Food served** noon-2.30pm Mon-Fri; noon-3pm Sat, Sun. **Credit** V.

An enjoyable stroll along Flood Street and through pretty Christchurch Square brings you to the aptly named Surprise. Surprising in that, in an area so flushed with the mega-rich, one should happen across such a down-to-earth local boozer as this. Admittedly, among some of the regulars whose heads turned as we entered we could detect more than a twang of an upper-class accent, but the atmosphere is far more earthy than aristocratic. Half-panelled walls, solid pub furniture and dusty stripped floors offer pleasantly unpretentious surroundings, while Adnams and Fuller's ales make for a decent tipple. The small back room has undergone a mini makeover with the introduction of some mammoth armchairs and a few modern paintings of dubious quality, but otherwise, the Surprise remains quite firmly rooted in the past.
Games (bar billiards, golf machine). Tables outdoors (pavement). TV.

Also in the area...

All Bar One 152 Gloucester Road, SW7 (7244 5861).
Babushka 354 King's Road, SW3 (7352 2828).
Pitcher & Piano 871-3 Fulham Road, SW6 (7736 3910); 316-18 King's Road, SW3 (7352 0025).

Covent Garden

Overrun by tourists and weekenders, this is not the neighbourhood for a quiet pint – far too many venues subscribing to the 'pack 'em in, get 'em pissed' school of hospitality. Yet steer away from the centrepiece Piazza and there are a few places of quality, particularly towards Holborn up and around the top ends of Neal and Endell Streets (**Detroit**, **Freedom Brewing Company**, **Freud**). But if it is a real blast of a lairy, pants-on-head night you're after, this is the place for the perfect stag-and-hen stagger taking in the likes of the **Porterhouse**, **Langley**, **Spot** and **Punch & Judy**, with a final chance to cop off at the **Roadhouse**.

Africa Bar

Africa Centre, 38 King Street, WC2 (7836 1976). Covent Garden tube. **Open** 5.30-11pm Mon-Sat. **Food served** 6-11pm Mon-Sat. **Credit** MC, V.

Tucked down in the basement of the Africa Centre, this is, as the name would suggest, a bar used primarily by Africans. Expats from Kinshasa, Khartoum and Kigali, to be precise, with the odd interloper from Kennington. Like the continent

in question, it's lacking in organisation and funds, but also in pretension, and is best tackled with a sense of adventure and a forgiving nature. Clientele are mainly lone men of, shall we say, character, in semi-somnolent state occasionally rousing themselves to take a sip from a bottle of South African Castle or Kenyan Tusker lager. Most nights nothing more exciting than this goes on. Occasionally, however – typically at weekends, when the upstairs hall hosts live music and party nights – the place is heaving and resembles independence night in Dakar. Either way, it's wholly authentic.
Babies and children admitted (restaurant). Disabled: toilet. Function room. Music (bands Fri; disco 10pm-3am Sat). **Map 2/L7**

Bacchanalia

1A Bedford Street, WC2 (7240 3945). Leicester Square tube/Charing Cross tube/rail. **Open** noon-11pm Mon-Sat. **Food served** noon-10.30pm Mon-Sat. **Credit** AmEx, MC, V.
Just off the Strand, Bacchanalia provides a slice of City cellar wine bar life in the heart of the West End. Dark wood floors with matching furniture and yellow walls hung with belle époque prints mimic the interiors of its EC counterparts, but the WC location and funky soundtrack attract a less suity crowd. A straightforward wine list makes selection a breeze. Prices start at an appealing £9.50 (which gets you a bottle of the house vin de pays de l'Aude) or from £2.50 by the glass, with a choice from 15. Most of the tables tend to get reserved for diners, which means the standing area around the bar can get a little scrum-like at lunchtime and immediately postwork.
Babies and children admitted. No-smoking area. TV (big screen, satellite). **Map 2/L7**

Bar des Amis

11-14 Hanover Place, WC2 (7379 3444). Covent Garden tube. **Open/food served** 11.30am-11pm Mon-Sat. **Credit** AmEx, DC, MC, V.
Close to the Piazza, this buzzy little hangout is tucked down a side street and concealed in the basement of Cafe des Amis – but it's worth the search. Efficient French staff run around behind the large, central bar surrounded by upholstered stools. Clusters of soft banquettes provide further seating by coffee tables. A low ceiling, soft spot lighting and wooden boards create a warm, welcoming feel. A menu of light meals (Malaysian seafood laksa with glass noodles) is served, but a selection of cheeses with fresh baguette and biscuits seems the most popular choice, and there are plenty of gluggable wines to complete the classic French combo. Split 50/50 between France and the rest of the world, the wine list runs to about 50 vins. There are easy drinking vins de pays such as the Wild Trout (a mix of chardonnay and marsanne grapes, perfect for quaffing), as well as heavyweights like the unoaked Glazebrook chardonnay from Gisborne in New Zealand. Eighteen wines come by the glass.
Function room (seats 80). Tables outdoors (terrace). **Map 2/L6**

Box

32-4 Monmouth Street, WC2 (7240 5828/www.boxbar.com). Covent Garden or Leicester Square tube. **Open** 11am-11pm Mon-Sat; noon-10.30pm Sun. **Food served** noon-5pm daily. **Credit** MC, V.
During the day this Seven Dials cafe-bar attracts an appealing mix of local office types, both male and female, plus a smattering of gay sorts. But by night the tightey whitey T-shirt boyz take the ascendancy, lights are dimmed and the

Townhouse. *See p55.*

music gets as pumped up as the displayed pecs. The bar itself has a clean, simple appearance with wooden floor, bright light walls and unfussy small tables – nothing to distract from the main detail, which is, of course, the customers. There are basic lagers (including Hoegaarden and Leffe Blonde) on tap, supplemented by the usual bottled beers, plus slammers and cocktails. There's a pretty good lunch menu, ideally enjoyed at pavement seating, weather permitting. Staff are flirty and easy on the eye.
Babies and children admitted (daytime only). Tables outdoors (pavement). **Map 2/L6**

Brasserie les Sans-Culottes

27-9 Endell Street, WC2 (7379 8500). Covent Garden tube. **Open/food served** 11.45am-11pm Mon-Thur; 11.45am-11.30pm Fri, Sat. **Happy hour** 5-7pm Mon-Sat. **Credit** AmEx, DC, MC, V.
First we had the Czechs, then the Belgians and Dutch, now here come the French to try and teach us a thing or two about beer and how to serve it. Les Sans-Culottes ('without knee breeches', named after the trouser-wearing working class of the French Revolution) is a Froggy brasserie-microbrewery with four own-brewed beers. These are flavourful and heady, and from 5-7pm each night cost only £1.70 a pint (les sans-culottes were a penniless bunch). Food ranges from bar snacks to hearty country fare, and is recommended. Bar staff are Gallic and charming. Decor is nautical but nice, a bit cruise liner-ish, clean and ordered and refreshingly 'foreign'. Best of all Les Sans-Culottes remains undiscovered by the masses, making it top notch for setting a session afloat – and on this boat you can hop off when the room starts to sway.
Babies and children welcome (restaurant). Disabled: toilet. Music (jazz 8pm Sat). TV (satellite). **Map 2/L6**

Brasserie Max

Covent Garden Hotel, 10 Monmouth Street, WC2 (7806 1000/www.coventgardenhotel.co.uk). Covent Garden tube. **Open/food served** 7am-11pm Mon-Sat; 8am-10.30pm Sun. **Credit** AmEx, MC, V.
You'd have to be a very resolute inverted snob with a cast-iron aversion to the smarter-looking bar not to appreciate the charms of Brasserie Max at the Covent Garden Hotel. It's sheer elegance crafted in dark wood and aluminium, with an extensive list of top-shelf brands, a good selection of wines by the glass and alert but friendly staff. Although you may want to dress up to match your Martini, you won't feel out of place if you don't. It makes for the perfect low-lit rendezvous for an intimate pre-dinner drink or somewhere to retire to once the table talk is done and it's locked-eyes-over-cocktails time. There's a further pleasant little kick that comes with the bill, because although the place has an insouciance that whispers 'price gouging' it's actually very reasonable. You get the class without blowing the bank.
Babies and children admitted. Function rooms. **Map 1/L6**

Christopher's

18 Wellington Street, WC2 (7240 4222/www.christophers grill.com). Charing Cross tube/rail. **Open/food served** 11.30am-11pm Mon-Sat. **Credit** AmEx, DC, MC, V.
One of Covent Garden's best restaurants (renowned for its sinful Bloody Mary-led weekend brunches), now comes with a sleek-looking ground-floor bar. Occupying the whole of one long wall, the bar counter itself is a thing of great beauty, a wooden construction of horizontal strips ingeniously lit with strings of pinprick lights to give an all-over copper toning. It's manned by two dextrous wizards who produce the absolute finest of cocktails from a lengthy list of classics (none of your Cocksucking Cowboy nonsense here). Our Whiskey Sour was prepared with egg white, adding a highly unusual, but delightful, viscous fizz – a bargain at £6.50. Sip while gazing heavenward at the floating constellation of globular white lights above. Our only gripe is the VH1 video screen, which is far too intrusive for such a quiet and understated bar. The doorway could also do with screening to avoid that 'waiting room' sensation. But otherwise, sheer class.
Babies and children admitted (daytime only). TV.
Map 2/L7

Coach & Horses

42 Wellington Street, WC2 (7240 0553). Covent Garden tube. **Open** 11am-11pm Mon-Sat; noon-10.30pm Sun. **Food served** noon-2.30pm daily. **Credit** MC, V.
Hiding under a floral display worthy of a Chelsea showing, this is one of the few remaining unspoiled trad pubs in the vicinity of the Piazza. It's a tiny place with scant seating (just a clutch of stools) and unfussy decor: a few theatre posters (this *is* Covent Garden) and a curious bit of a golfing theme. The main attraction is the Guinness; landlord Jim Ryan has been selling Dublin-brewed (non-pasteurised) Guinness here since Covent Garden sold turnips instead of attracting them. And if you fancy a chaser, there's a choice of more than 80 different whiskies. The craic – and the hot Limerick ham baguettes – is mighty enough to draw off-duty barmen from other pubs, as well as Irish expats.
TV. **Map 2/L6**

Cross Keys

31 Endell Street, WC2 (7836 5185). Covent Garden tube. **Open** 11am-11pm Mon-Sat; noon-10.30pm Sun. **Food served** noon-3pm Mon-Sat. **Credit** MC, V.
A traditional, old-school pub fronted by an ivy-woven, flower-bedecked frontage, Cross Keys is utterly out of place in touristy, tat-filled Covent Garden. It's a small and busy single-room boozer, with a bar running down one side, bench seating and tables along the other. The space above the bar is decorated with 1960s pop memorabilia (a signed Elvis napkin, autographed Beatles photos), while brass and copper bits and pieces dangle from the ceiling. No shock to learn, then, that the owner used to be an antiques dealer; he also owns Beak Street's **Old Coffee House** (*see p83*) and Leyton's **William the Fourth** (*see p151*) and Sweet William Brewery. The product of the mini-brewery can be sampled here in the form of Brodies Best. Customers are a complete cross-section of local life, plus the odd tourist showing a bit of initiative and good taste.
Function room. Games (fruit machine). Tables outdoors (pavement). **Map 2/L6**

Detroit

35 Earlham Street, WC2 (7240 2662/www.detroit-bar.com). Covent Garden tube. **Open** 5pm-12.30am Mon-Sat. **Food served** *Bar* 5-10.30pm Mon-Sat. *Restaurant* 6-10.30pm Mon-Sat. **Happy hour** 5-8pm Mon-Sat. **Credit** AmEx, MC, V.
A strange decision to makeover the entrance in such a dismal grey fashion, but thankfully nothing's gone wrong downstairs. It's still the same basement warren of mud-brown, amorphous, cave-like spaces – more Bedrock than Detroit. Likewise, the drinks menu is as comprehensive as it ever was, running to well over 50 classics: Martinis, Collins, shooters and champagne cocktails (£4-£7.50). The iron constitutioned still get to prove their mettle on deadly overproofs such as the lethal sounding Cherry Aid: absinthe, sloe gin, wisnowka cherry vodka, fresh lemon juice, sugar and champagne (£10). There's a small wine selection for the more sensible (three each of red and white by the glass), plus a handful of choice bottled beers for the plain unadventurous. Come between 5pm and 8pm for the 'seven-heaven' ses-

sion: one cocktail and one food platter for seven squids. Otherwise bar snacks of the spring rolls, deep-fried calamari and chicken satay type go from £3.50 to £4.50.
Function rooms. Music (DJs 7.30pm Thur-Sat; free). No-smoking tables. **Map 2/L6**

Freedom Brewing Company

41 Earlham Street, WC2 (7240 0606/www.freedom brew.com). Covent Garden tube. **Open** noon-11pm Mon-Sat; noon-10.30pm Sun. **Food** noon-10pm Mon-Sat; noon-6pm Sun. **Credit** AmEx, MC, V.
A modest makeover has opened out what was the screened dining area and added cartouche-shaped close-quarter counters down the centre of the room and a visual assault of a carpet (also applied vertically – yow!). To the sausage seats and fake leather sofas have been added translucent red plastic chairs that look like cocktail glasses out of which somebody's taken a bite. What hasn't changed is FBC's raison d'être – great drinks and a great atmosphere. Warm tones and mellow lighting make for a relaxed vibe, assisted by attitude-free and friendly bar staff. There are wine and cocktail lists, but given that Freedom is London's most successful microbrewery (although the brewing is no longer done on the premises), choice booze must be one of the own-brand beers: choose between pilsner, wheat, pale ale or fruity Soho Red (£2.95 a pint). Bar snacks run from deep-fried mozzarella (£3.20) to Freedom burgers (£7.50).
Babies and children admitted. Function room. **Map 2/L6**

Freud

198 Shaftesbury Avenue, WC2 (7240 9933). Covent Garden or Tottenham Court Road tube. **Open** 11am-11pm Mon-Sat; noon-10.30pm Sun. **Food served** 11am-4.30pm Mon-Sat; noon-4.30pm Sun. **Credit** MC, V.
There's something a bit self-conscious, over-analytical even, about Freud. Buried in a bunker-like space beneath a home accessories shop of the same name at the Holborn end of Shaftesbury Avenue, it has a divey New York-meets-Murmansk sort of decaying industrial feel. Its canvas-clad record bag-clutching crowd perch less than comfortably on bruised and burst leather cushions that hardly soften concrete bench seating. A board is chalked up with a fair old list of cocktails (good), but there's only a handful of bottled beers (bad) and nothing more than cheap house wine, served in tumblers (ugly). However, for cut-price cred and a great pre-club meet spot, Freud remains hard to beat. Just watch your footing on the staircase going down.
Babies and children admitted. Music (jazz 2.30-5pm Sun). No-smoking tables (until 4.30pm). TV. **Map 1/L6**

Lamb & Flag

33 Rose Street, WC2 (7497 9504). Covent Garden or Leicester Square tube. **Open** 11am-11pm Mon-Thur; 11am-10.45pm Fri, Sat; noon-10.30pm Sun. **Food served** noon-3pm daily. **No credit cards.**
We've always relished the fact that this venerable boozer (17th century or thereabouts) was once known as the Bucket Of Blood. What a name! Perhaps if it still had such a threatening moniker the number of punters would be kept down to the low hundreds and there'd be a chance of getting served at the bar in under an hour. As it is, most nights it's murder here, especially from around 5.30pm onwards when the little cobbled lane out front gets as rammed as an anti-Blair rally. Post-9pm, things quieten down and it becomes possible to appreciate the beam-and-panelled antiquity, and historic quirks like the 'Coutts is in/out' slider. It may even be possible to snag a seat up the creaky stairs, preferably one with a prime position beside the window. Bar staff remain friendly (which seems an almost impossible feat under the crowded circumstances), and serious boozers are kept happy by the generous line-up of real ales (including Courage Directors and various from Young's).
Babies and children admitted (mornings only). Music (jazz 7.30-10.30pm Sun). TV. **Map 2/L7**

Langley

5 Langley Street, WC2 (7836 5005). Covent Garden tube. **Open** 4.30pm-1am Mon-Sat; 4-10.30pm Sun. **Food served** 5pm-midnight Mon-Sat. **Happy hour** 5-7pm daily. **Credit** AmEx, MC, V.
The retro party bar par excellence, themed in test card colours, the Langley hums with post-work chatting up and banter, delivered loud and fast. Past the doormen and down the stairs are two main spaces: the Hudson and the adjoining Geneva. Both are brick-and-pillar jobs with unpretentious air-con interiors and main bar counters buzzing with activity. Happy hour here is a serious business – bottles of wine at £6, a tenner off champagne and reduced bar food (steak or fish finger sandwiches, chicken satay and the like) – but few hightail it out after 7pm. There's enough variety of bottled beer and cocktails to keep the most fickle date interested: Tiger, Corona Extra, Beck's and San Miguel, with the contemporary and classic range of cocktails listed as 'now' and 'then'. Don't be fooled: the Geneva room may look more sedate, but when the cocktails take hold, you'll hear the screams of private parties ringing out from behind the dividing strips of red PVC.
Disabled: toilet. Dress: smart casual. Music (DJs 9pm Thur-Sat; £3 after 10pm Thur; £5 after 10pm Fri, Sat). **Map 2/L6**

Lowlander

36 Drury Lane, WC2 (7379 7446). Covent Garden or Holborn tube. **Open/food served** 11am-11pm Mon-Sat; noon-10.30pm Sun. **Credit** AmEx, MC, V.
Foreign cuisine, bench-type seating around communal tables and speedy service: Lowlander offers an almost Wagamama take on the bar experience. Except here the theming is not Japanese but Benelux. It's a spacious place, made bright by high ceilings and large windows, dominated by a grand bar counter with a handsome display of shiny glasses and trays and an impressive phalanx of tall beer pumps. There are 14 Dutch and Belgian beers on tap at all times, including guests, and up to 30 alternatives by the bottle. Bar snacks are intriguing. Big wheels of waxed cheese can be sampled on a platter that takes in offerings from Bruges as well as old Gouda with sweet mustard and celery salt. You can also get double Dutch fries, vegetable crisps and pitta pizza. Arrive early if you want a seat, as most tables are reserved for parties who are eating.
Babies and children admitted. Function room. No-smoking area. Tables outdoors (pavement). **Map 1/L6**

Opera Tavern

23 Catherine Street, WC2 (7379 9832). Covent Garden tube. **Open** noon-11pm Mon-Sat. **Food served** noon-3pm, 5-8pm Mon-Sat. **Credit** AmEx, MC, V.
One of the nicer old boozers in the area, the Opera Tavern dates from 1879 and the decor remains largely Victorian, with beige painted walls, red upholstery and mellow yellow lighting. It makes for a smooth and relaxed atmosphere, complemented by wise music programming of trad jazz, blues and, of course, opera. There are usually three real ales on tap (typically, Bass, Adnams Bitter and Greene King IPA), as well as a small choice of wines, served in large glasses only. The Theatre Royal is just opposite (at the time we visited it was playing *My Fair Lady*) and the Royal Opera House is down the road, so business fluctuates with performances – which means if you time it right, this is a great spot for a

The Interval. See p57.

quiet drink. Time it wrong and you could be subject to sporadic bursts of 'the rain in Spain' (which falls mainly on the plain, apparently).
Games (fruit machine, quiz machine). Music (8pm last Fri of month). Tables outdoors (pavement). **Map 2/L6**

Porterhouse

21-2 Maiden Lane, WC2 (7836 9931/www.porterhousebrewco.com). Covent Garden tube/Charing Cross tube/rail. **Open** 11am-11pm Mon-Sat; noon-10.30pm Sun. **Food served** noon-3pm, 5-9pm Mon-Fri; noon-9pm Sat; noon-5pm Sun. **Credit** DC, MC, V.
You've been to the superclub, now welcome to the superpub. A labyrinth of interlocking levels, with more piping than the Edinburgh Tattoo, multiple bars, an army of staff and everything swamped nightly by a sea of after-work suits – the Porterhouse is like an Irish pub on steroids. The main attraction, aside from the professional pick-up element, is the beer, brewed by the Porterhouse in Ireland and imported from Dublin. Unpasteurised and outstanding, these brews are fresh and impressively flavourful, not to mention abundant in variety. Trouble is, after the hassle of fording the bodies at the bar and faced with frazzled bar staff and their two-second attention spans, everyone just settles for whichever bog standard lager's displayed most prominently. Food is more restaurant than bar nibbles (steaks, oysters and pasta; to finish, a selection of Irish cheeses), but dodging elbows between fork-fuls isn't our idea of comfortable dining.
Disabled: lift, toilet. Function room. Music (bands 8pm Wed-Fri; DJs 8pm Sat; Irish band 3-7pm Sun; free). Tables outdoors (pavement). TV (big screen, satellite). **Map 2/L7**

Punch & Judy

40 The Market, WC2 (7379 0923). Covent Garden tube. **Open** 11am-11pm Mon-Sat; noon-10.30pm Sun. **Food served** noon-9pm Mon-Thur; noon-7pm Fri, Sat; noon-5pm Sun. **Credit** AmEx, DC, MC, V.
A prime position at the centre of the Piazza makes this place a beacon for tourists (mostly of the impecunious sort), and no matter where in London you are, if you cock your ear to the wind you'll probably be able to discern the beery bellowing emanating from its two floors of bars. Be in no doubt: this is a place to drink and get rowdy. Enter from the market basement into the long stone-flagged cellar bar, or climb the stairs off the Piazza to the square, Regency-style upper bar and the balcony. Conversational babble comes at you in a barrage of languages. Brits are in the minority, but feel free to turn up and share stories of loose bowels in Lagos, the cheapest falafels in Afula and dope smoking in Dahab. Regrettably, the fine view of St Paul's church is spoilt by perpetual overcrowding, but it is a great place to pull. Apparently.
Babies and children admitted (separate area, until 6pm). Games (fruit machines, quiz machines). Music (phone for details). No-smoking area (before 3pm). Tables outdoors (courtyard; terrace). TV. **Map 2/L7**

Retox Bar

The Piazza, Russell Street, WC2 (7240 5330/www.retoxbar.com). Covent Garden tube. **Open/food served** 5pm-1am Mon-Wed; 5pm-3am Thur, Fri; 6pm-3am Sat. **Admission** £5 after 9.30pm Tue-Sat. **Credit** AmEx, MC, V.
Modest from the outside (a sunken entrance on the eastern side of the Piazza) and modest in the early evening (low lighting, gentle mood music for the early drinkers), but drop by

later and the Retox is an absolute hussy of a place. Later is when the party people come calling and all sophistication (such as the minimalist modern furniture) washes out the door on a tide of pernicious cocktails like Nephew's Nipple or one of the many other in-house concoctions designed to do in your liver as fast as possible. The music gets faster, the volume gets louder and the well of good intentions is gatecrashed by crass and wild debauchery. Bottom line: this is a decent, late bar for hard drinking and serious posing among a crowd that considers sleep a thing for wimps.
Dress: smart casual. Music (DJs 9pm Tue-Sat). **Map 2/L6**

Roadhouse

The Piazza, Covent Garden, WC2 (7240 6001/www.roadhouse.co.uk). Covent Garden tube. **Open** 5.30pm-3am Mon-Sat; 5.30pm-1am Sun. **Food served** 5.30pm-1am Mon-Sat; 5.30-10pm Sun. **Happy hour** 5.30-10.30pm Mon-Wed; 5.30-8.30pm Thur, Sat; 5.30-7.30pm Fri. **Credit** AmEx, MC, V.
This basement bar conjures up dirty thoughts. It's big and black and divey and even the bar staff are dressed in tight leather waistcoats and look like they want to have sex with you, whatever your gender. The room is decorated with 1950s Americana: signs and logos, a couple of Harley-Davidsons, and a midget helicopter above the stage. A railroad diner car serves burgers, fajitas and the like, while staff at the three bars dispense bottled beers and cocktails as if they are up against the clock. It's a dedicated party venue where punters take their drinking and flirting seriously – if offering to buy somebody a Bacardi Breezer before sticking a hand down their top can be called flirting. Bands rev up the atmosphere nightly, which is at least preferable to the smooth-talking house DJ. Love it or loathe it, just shut up and dance.
Dress: smart casual. Games (pinball machines). Music (bands nightly; £5 after 9pm Mon-Wed, women free; £7 after 9pm Thur; £10 after 9pm Fri; £7 after 7.30pm, £10 after 9pm Sat). **Map 2/L7**

Round House

1 Garrick Street, WC2 (7836 9838). Covent Garden or Leicester Square tube. **Open/food served** 11am-11pm Mon-Sat; noon-10.30pm Sun. **Credit** AmEx, MC, V.
It's more semicircular than round, but let's not be pedantic. Occupying a corner site where picturesque New Row joins Garrick Street, the Round House has something of the goldfish bowl about it, with customers exposed to the gaze of passers-by, and vice versa, through large windows. Conversely, it's a great place for people-watching. In summer, the large screen doors fold back and punters spill on to the pavement, with drinkers and the public getting in each other's way. A reasonable selection of real ales (Courage Directors and Theakston's Best with occasional guests too), wheat beers, Czech lagers, bottled Belgian specialities and suchlike, is wasted as everybody seems intent on guzzling bog-standard lagers. Food is the usual T&J Bernard pie-based fare. Alternatively, you could nab a bite from the sizeable Tesco Metro just opposite.
Games (fruit machines). TV. **Map 2/L7**

The Spot

29-30 Maiden Lane, WC2 (7379 5900/www.thespot.co.uk). Covent Garden tube/Charing Cross tube/rail. **Open** noon-1am Mon-Sat; 6pm-1am Sun. **Food served** noon-8pm Mon-Sat. **Admission** £3 after 10pm Mon-Thur (incl free drink); £5 after 9pm Fri, Sat; £5 after 8pm Sun. **Happy hour** noon-7pm Mon-Sat. **Credit** AmEx, MC, V.

Divided into four spaces, the Spot is an odd bar-nightclub hybrid that tempts in after-work punters with a generous happy hour (or seven) and aims to keep them there for as long as its late licence allows (currently 1am). Point of entry is a subdued, plain front bar with more seating off in a side room of simple whitewashed stone walls and cream tiled floor. At the back, things get all red and lurid with Amsterdam lighting and lip-shaped sofas broadcasting a message of lurve, reinforced on a recent visit by Luther Vandross on the turntable. Early evening we found several couples ensconced as if they were waiting for something to happen. On past experience, that happening comes around 6pm when loads of off-the-leash officers and officettes pour in and pour down the cut-price bottled lagers. From there, the decline is inevitable as the volume goes up and the Spot becomes a place to sink liquor fast and dance in the same fashion. Enjoy.
Babies and children admitted (restaurant). Function room. Music (DJs 8pm Wed-Sat; open mic 8pm Sun; admission as above). TV (big screen, satellite). **Map 2/L7**

Also in the area...

All Bar One 19 Henrietta Street, WC2 (7557 7941).
Bar 38 1-3 Long Acre, WC2 (7836 7794).
Belgo Centraal 50 Earlham Street, WC2 (7813 2233).
Crusting Pipe (Davy's) 27 The Market, Covent Garden, WC2 (7836 1415).
Henry's 5-6 Henrietta Street, WC2 (7379 1871); 63-6 St Martin's Lane, WC2 (7836 2990).
O'Neill's 40 Great Queen Street, WC2 (7242 5560); 14 New Row, WC2 (7557 9831); 166 Shaftesbury Avenue, WC2 (7379 3735).
Savoy Tup 2 Savoy Street, WC2 (7836 9738).
Tappit Hen (Davy's) 5 William IV Street, WC2 (7836 9839).
Walkabout Inn 11 Henrietta Street/33 Maiden Lane, WC2 (7379 5555).

Earl's Court

Thanks in part to the cliché of drunken Aussies throwing up on pavements outside pubs, drinking in Earl's Court has long been associated with noisy pubs and even noisier punters. And there's some truth in that. However, we may be on the cusp of change. The **Prince of Teck**, bastion of antipodean debauchery – and former home of Stumpy the stuffed kangaroo – has been gutted and steam cleaned and by now should have reopened as a spick and span, shiny boozer under the stewardship of Hugh Corbett, the Terence Conran of the London pub scene. In the past, where Corbett's gone others have followed. Let's hope so, because as it stands (present exceptions given below), boozing round Earl's Court holds about as much joy as the Ashes.

Blackbird

209 Earl's Court Road, SW5 (7835 1855). Earl's Court tube. **Open** 11am-11pm Mon-Sat; noon-10.30pm Sun. **Food served** noon-8.45pm daily. **Credit** MC, V.
A smartly painted black and gold exterior gives way to a less smart interior; nice black and white tiled floor, comfortable booths by the windows for crowds of mates, but shame about the blazing games machines. Nonetheless, the Blackbird does good business with suited-up folk who've wandered over from the Exhibition Centre in search of lunch and a pint of London Pride (usually well kept, this being a Fuller's house). The place is packed through lunch and after knocking-off time with said business types, as well as playing host to a sizeable number of locals. The food is reputed to be among the best pub grub in the area, a fact that's acknowledged in dearer than the norm prices. It's a good solid local in an area that isn't blessed with them.
Games (fruit machines). TV.

King's Head

17 Hogarth Place, SW5 (7244 5931). Earl's Court tube. **Open** noon-11pm Mon-Sat; noon-10.30pm Sun. **Food served** noon-3pm, 6-9.30pm Mon-Thur; noon-9.30pm Fri-Sun. **Credit** AmEx, DC, MC, V.
Tucked away between vibrant Hogarth Road, lined with ethnic supermarkets and restaurants, and sleepy residential Kenway Road, the King's Head is never likely to attract much in the way of passing trade. No matter, it's well known and loved by the locals and is never short of a punter or two, especially on Friday nights when DJs are drafted in, the volume is cranked up and all manner of booze-fuelled mayhem ensues. The splendid bar line up not only offers Fuller's, Greene King and Bass ales on tap but also a good selection of bottled Belgian beers including Duvel, Chimay and De Konnick. There's also a good selection of wine by the glass and a modest array of bar food. The pub itself seems to have been abandoned mid-refurb. The flock wallpaper and fake beams that decorate the rear of the pub are staunchly old fashioned and yet the furniture that fills it is modern and hip. Little foibles such as these only add to the chaotic charm of this fine establishment, however, and only a churl would think to scoff. A real find.
Bar available for hire. Music (DJs Sat, Sun 8pm; free). Games (video game).

Troubadour

265 Old Brompton Road, SW5 (7370 1434/ www.troubadour.co.uk). Earl's Court tube. **Open** 9am-midnight daily. **Admission** free-£5. **Food served** 9am-11pm daily. **Credit** MC, V.
Not to be confused with the large, loud bar next door, the legendary Troubadour – an early London venue for the young pre-electric Bob Dylan – is an almost unspeakably polite and totally charming bar. Its broad double front offers a great view of the cosy interior through huge windows in which hang rows of innumerable coffee pots and grinders, plus further knick-knackery in the shape of stained-glass panels, a giant engraved mirror, attractive prints and all manner of kitchen paraphernalia – all of which combine to create a comfy, cluttered ambience that manages to steer clear of contrivance. The menu seems as catholic as the design, offering as it does everything from bottled beer and wine to coffees and teas, as well as a food selection of pastas, burgers and chips. Refreshingly, you'll generally find the staff seem as happy to be there as the customers, which further adds to the homely, welcoming feel. Downstairs, there's occasional live music, typically folk and jazz.
Babies and children admitted. Comedy (Tue 9pm; £5). Function room (seats 137). Games (board games). Music (singer songwriter evenings Wed; jazz Thur; folk and blues Fri 9pm). No-smoking area (in restaurant). Poetry (Mon 8pm; £5). Restaurant. Tables outdoors (garden, pavement).

Warwick Arms

160 Warwick Road, W14 (7603 3560). Earl's Court or High Street Kensington tube. **Open** noon-midnight Mon-Sat; 10am-10.30pm Sun. **Food served** noon-3pm, 5.30-11.30pm Mon-Sat; 10am-4pm, 5.30-11pm Sun. **Credit** MC, V.

It's a bit of a trek this one, but if you take a right out of Earl's Court tube and walk along the Warwick Road, you'll eventually find a little gem of a pub just over the road. The Warwick's long been a favourite with savvy locals and has benefited recently from a bit of spit and polish sprucing up the fittings without detracting one bit from the pub's lived-in charm. It takes an antique shop approach to decoration with all manner of odds and ends – farming equipment, old prints, advertising signs and the like – filling out what is already quite a small space. Prime spot is a secluded alcove that guarantees privacy, as long as you don't mind being subjected to the stern gaze of WB Yeats who glowers from his gilded frame. The clientele is the traditional mix of suits and scruffs and the atmosphere is welcoming. The recent introduction of some decent Indian food has further added to the pub's plentiful appeal.
Restaurant. Tables outdoors (courtyard, pavement). TV.

Also in the area...

O'Neill's 326 Earl's Court Road, SW5 (7244 5921).

Fitzrovia

The smart alternative to the tired and overexposed drinking dives of Soho. In just the past couple of years the area bounded by Oxford Street, Regent Street, Euston and Tottenham Court Roads (last blooming as a '50s literary bohemia; at its heart, the **Fitzroy Tavern**), has become locale of choice for a string of sharp, sussed operations (**Match, the Social**, **Market Place**) combining cred with commercial know-how. Otherwise, venues on Goodge and Charlotte Streets cater to high street going on high-end tastes; Hanway Street's the place for lowlifers. Just don't call it Noho.

Bar Madrid

4 Winsley Street, W1 (7436 4649/www.barmadrid.co.uk). Oxford Circus tube. **Open/food served** 4.30pm-2am Mon; 4.30pm-late Tue-Thur; 4.30pm-3am Fri; 6.30pm-3.30am Sat. **Happy hour** 4.30-9pm Mon-Sat. **Credit** AmEx, MC, V.
Be warned: this is not a casual beer and feet up sort of joint. An off-Oxford Street walkdown amid sidestreets lined with beckoning happy hours billboards, this is where folks come to shake their tushes. True, the BM does happily dispense San Miguels, sangrias and sundry Spanish tipples, but once imbibed, it's expected that you'll get up off your chair and on to the dancefloor – no bad thing if you've got those happy feet, a little uncomfortable if you'd rather hide them under the tables than dance on them. It's not as if the soundtrack is radical finger-bleeding flamenco – in fact, it's a rather bland Latin mush, the kind of thing you'd barely put up with in Majorca. The place is hugely popular, all the same.
Function room. Music (DJs nightly; musicians Mon; £2 7-8pm, £5 after 8pm). **Map 1/J6**

Bradley's Spanish Bar

42-44 Hanway Street, W1 (7636 0359). Tottenham Court Road tube. **Open** noon-11pm Mon-Sat; 3-10.30pm Sun. **Credit** MC, V.
Bradley's hasn't changed one iota in ten years or more, thank God. Two cramped floors of once plush furniture, decked out in knick-knacks from the pioneering days of package tourism – bullfighting posters and the like – are linked by a busy staircase that allows access to either bar upon entry. Both share the same crackly plonk of a wondrous 45s jukebox – you could be blamed for 'White Horse', 'Waterloo Sunset' or 'Wandrin' Star' – and a pricey selection of draught beers that includes Bitburger, San Miguel and Cruzcampo. Long-term barman, grouchy old Jose, is no longer around to pour them. Instead his photo stares from his old spot downstairs while he sits in enforced exile in Spain. In summer, the dingy alley out front becomes a makeshift patio of bottle-wielding taxi-blocking bonhomie.
TV. **Map 7/K6**

Crown & Sceptre

86 Great Titchfield Street, W1 (7307 9971). Oxford Circus tube. **Open** 11am-11pm Mon-Fri; noon-11pm Sat; noon-10.30pm Sun. **Food served** noon-9.30pm daily. **Credit** AmEx, MC, V.
On a focal corner of Titchfield Village stands this grand tavern, drawing a chapter of motorbike couriers to mill around its exterior, while within media types clink glasses. Thankfully, it's big enough, a pentangle of bar counter allowing a decent expanse of floor space between it and the ornate, glass-framed doorway. For more intimate chat, a rear area features a few half-snugs, with gravitas added by old prints of London history and characters. The patterned ceiling and unusual light fittings hint at previously arty, even pretentious ownerships; these days the C&S does a roaring trade on football nights and rugby afternoons. Choice refreshment includes draught Staropramen, Bass and London Pride; at other times the bar does well on Australian and South African chardonnay by the bottle. Note the extravagant former wrought-iron public toilets immediately outside – recently revived as an art space.
Games (video games). TV (satellite). **Map 1/J5**

CVO Firevault

36 Great Titchfield Street, W1 (7580 5333/www.cvofirevault.co.uk). Oxford Circus tube. **Open** noon-10pm Mon-Fri; noon-6pm Sat. **Food served** 9.30am-9pm Mon-Fri; 10am-5pm Sat. **Credit** AmEx, MC, V.
Many establishments in this guide have constructed their reputations on award-winning bar design, inspired cocktail lists or well-oiled management. This unusual venue is renowned instead for its iconic blue-flame firebowl: the CVO firevault. That's because first and foremost this is a fireplace shop – but it also houses a downstairs lounge bar of the same name. Through accessories and furnishings, warming bowls lead you to price-tagged furniture and comfy alcoves where a menu offers five classic cocktails, five champagnes, hot toddies, Freedom, Budvar and Stella beers, wine and trendy snacks. It's fantastically posh, fantastically pretentious and, in the evenings, fantastically precious (you'll need to book at night). For all that, though, it's unique.
Babies and children admitted. Disabled: toilet. No-smoking tables. Tables outdoors (garden). **Map 1/J5**

Eagle Bar Diner

3-5 Rathbone Place, W1 (7637 1418/www.eaglebardiner.com). Tottenham Court Road tube. **Open** 8am-11pm Mon-Fri; 10am-11pm Sat; 11am-7pm Sun. **Food served** 8am-10.30pm Mon-Fri; 10am-10.30pm Sat; 11am-6.30pm Sun. **Credit** AmEx, DC, MC, V.
This month's flavour is a postmodern diner offering an all-day service – breakfasts, brunch, lunch and louche cocktails – with imaginative touches to decor, drinks and dining. With its small line of signage across the window unfolding like the cellophane wording around a pack of cigarettes, the Eagle gives little away, certainly not the range of its pricey menu. A gutted old Coke machine offering the day's papers and two sides of high-backed green snugs with four brown slatted sofas in front face a long zinc bar. American-themed Eagle

favourite cocktails, eight Martinis (with guava, peanut butter and pumpkin pie), beers including Brooklyn lager (which they're certainly not giving away) and a long list of side orders with the breakfasts, burgers, grills and pancakes, embrace plentiful Americana; the primitive caff letraset on the takeaway menu board of muffins, muesli and salads attracts local shop and office workers from nearby competition. Smart and potentially very successful.
Babies and children welcome. Disabled: toilet. Music (DJs 7pm Thur-Sat). **Map 7/K6**

Fitzroy Tavern

16 Charlotte Street, W1 (7580 3714). Goodge Street tube. **Open** 11am-11pm Mon-Sat; noon-10.30pm Sun. **Food served** noon-2.30pm, 6.30-9.30pm Mon-Thur, Sat, Sun; noon-2.30pm Fri. **Credit** AmEx, MC, V.
'If you haven't visited the Fitzroy, you haven't visited London,' was how dissolute shagaround painter Augustus John put it. For 50-odd years after its conversion from a coffee house in 1897, the Fitz was a playground for the leading lights of pre-pop bohemia. Actors, writers, artists, poets, fops, spies, prostitutes and homosexuals all drank here, most famously under the benign ownership of Charlie and Annie Allchild. John himself – whose portraits line one wall – would pat any children who entered just in case they were his. In 1955, after a police raid, the pub was closed down. Now it's simply a well-stocked Sam Smith's outlet (oatmeal stout, strong Prinz lager, Sovereign Best among many others), with a cosy 'writers' bar' downstairs convivially hosting fireside stand-up each Wednesday. The walls illustrate its legend, no picture perhaps more poignant than the downstairs photo of a Spain-bound Orwell bidding farewell to all and sundry in the heady days of the 1930s.
Function room (seats 35). Games (fruit machine, quiz machine). Tables outdoors (pavement). TV (satellite). **Map 1/K5**

Hakkasan

8 Hanway Place, W1 (7907 1888). Tottenham Court Road tube. **Open** *Bar* 3pm-12.30am Mon-Wed, Sun; 3pm-1am Thur-Sat. **Food served** 6-11.30pm Mon-Wed, Sun; 6pm-12.30am Thur-Sat. **Credit** AmEx, MC, V.
As if it needed it, there's a new buzz about Hakkasan since this superb state-of-the-art Chinese restaurant was bestowed its first Michelin star in January 2003. Star quality has never been short in its adjoining but separate cocktail bar either. Celebs once dined and sipped here in relative privacy; now everyone's taxi driver follows the cobalt blue Hakkasan signs around the corner into secretive Hanway Place. A line of red squares leads down a staircase to an orchid-scented reception area, where diners are assigned seats in the slatted-off restaurant, flanked by a long, slate counter. Delicately illuminated by little lavender lights, staff mix class-A drinks for a narrow corridor of discerning guests. The menu includes ten Martinis, 25 long and short drinks, hot and cold sakes and Yebisu beer, but Hakkas (Cristall vodka, sake and a confusion of lychee and fruit) and Pink Mojitos (made with fresh cranberry) are the flavours of this Michelin-starred month.
Disabled: lift, toilet. Dress: smart casual. Music (DJs 9pm nightly; free). **Map 1/K5**

Hope

15 Tottenham Street, W1 (7637 0896/www.reallondonpubcompany.co.uk). Goodge Street tube. **Open** 11am-11pm Mon-Sat; noon-6pm Sun. **Food served** noon-4pm Mon-Fri; noon-3pm Sat, Sun. **Credit** MC, V.

Windsor Castle. *See p63.*

Not so much a corner pub as a sausage and ale house, with a half-score varieties of bangers to attract a busy lunchtime crowd, equally pleased to find Fuller's London Pride, Everards Tiger, Tetley's and Adnams Bitter served from the pump. Sausages are served, appropriately enough, with mash and beans (although there's the option of gravy), by amiable antipodean bar staff, either in the busy downstairs bar or in the more diner-like space upstairs. A bookcase of standard wine stands behind the downstairs bar should sir be accompanied by a ladyfriend, and social engagement is encouraged with sets of Scrabble and Monopoly piled up by a huge TV that typically dominates proceedings for at least half the week.
Babies and children admitted (until 7pm). Function room. Games (board games, fruit machine). Tables outdoors (pavement). TV (big screen, satellite). **Map 1/J5**

Horse & Groom

128 Great Portland Street, W1 (7580 4726). Great Portland Street or Oxford street tube. **Open** noon-11.30pm Mon-Sat; 11am-3pm, 7-11pm Sun. **Food served** noon-2.30pm, 5.30-8.30pm Mon-Fri; noon-5pm Sat. **Credit** MC, V.
A typically ornate member of the Sam Smith's stable, the Horse & Groom presents a wide-bay front on to this sleek stretch of Great Portland Street, setting out its stall with shining tiles, houseplants and a notice of welcome from 'Chris and Mal'. Apart from the vegetarian slant of the three daily lunch specials, the H&G is as traditional as they come. A pristine interior of a sturdy wooden bar counter, frosted glass windows and leather upholstery leads to a small games room of table football and darts, decorated with old prints including a pre-war football team shot also repeated in the main bar. The sporting theme is presumably attached to the pub's history, although it's the usual range of cheerfully cheap Sam Smith's classics (Extra Stout, Ayingerbräu, D-Pils and alike) that brings the punters in these days.
Function room. Games (darts, fruit machine, quiz machine). Tables outdoors. TV.

Jerusalem

33-4 Rathbone Place, W1 (7255 1120/www.thebreakfast group.co.uk). Tottenham Court Road tube. **Open** noon-11pm Mon; noon-midnight Tue, Wed; noon-1am Thur, Fri; 7pm-1am Sat. **Food served** noon-3pm, 6-10.30pm Mon-Fri; 7-10.30pm Sat. **Credit** AmEx, MC, V.
This cellar bar-restaurant attracts la lively evening crowd with DJs and pitchers of draught Hoegaarden, Leffe Blonde and Beck's. Framed menu boards hanging over rows of heavy wooden refectory benches feature bottled Tiger, Michelob and Pilsner Urquell, wines (ten reds and whites by the bottle, three each by the glass) and a few cocktails. Candlelit nights have been embellished by more generous opening hours, and a strange bar-mounted rotating ball that flashes the almost subliminal message 'Drink More' at the post-workers crowding at the counter. Equally, an almost church-like daytime ambience gives way to an industrial bar feel later on – either way, echoing acoustics challenge even the loudest of conversations.
Music (DJs Wed-Sat; £5 after 10pm Fri, Sat). **Map 1/K5**

Long Bar

Sanderson Hotel, 50 Berners Street, W1 (7300 1400/ www.ianschragerhotels.com). Tottenham Court Road tube. **Open** 11am-12.30am Mon-Sat; noon-10.30pm Sun. **Food served** noon-11.30pm Mon-Sat; noon-10pm Sun. **Credit** AmEx, MC, V.

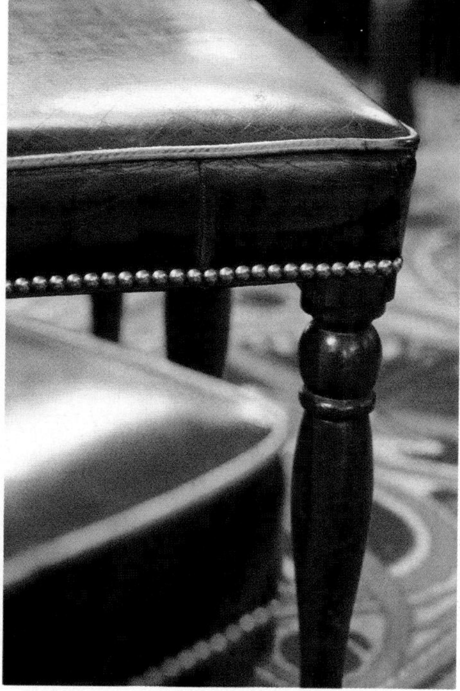

Behind the faceless grey-and-glass facade of the Sanderson and across the dreamily minimalist lobby is this drop-dead glamorous haunt of smugness. A long, chest-high rectangular bar counter is lined with Dali-esque eye-stencilled bar stools, their pupils gazing out from the massaged lower backs of the minor movers and shakers perched there. Their eyes too are big and roving, necks craning to see and be seen – or maybe they're just trying to get the attention of inattentive bar staff. The drinks menu lists a dozen or more Martinis of a natural bent – elderflower, grapefruit and a Sanderson Martini of Wyborowa lemon vodka, Pölstar cucumber, shaken with fresh grapes and brown sugar – plus hi-balls, flutes and rocks, and a whole gamut of champagne. While waiting observe the ripple of delicate curtain fluttering to expose a cheap portrait of a pet dog; outside, a Japanese garden of tiny fountains and tinier shrubbery awaits an almighty power play for the one wicker hammock.
Babies and children admitted (until 6pm). Disabled: toilet. Function rooms (in hotel). Music (DJs 8pm Thur). Tables outdoors (terrace with water garden). **Map 1/J5**

Market Place

11 Market Place, W1 (7079 2020). Oxford Circus tube. **Open/food served** 11am-1am Mon-Sat; noon-midnight Sun. **Credit** AmEx, MC, V.
Branding is the name of the game here. Not only is the Market Place part of the Cantaloupe Group (of **Cantaloupe** and **Cargo** fame; *see p122*), but its slatted wooden two-floor interior has been scorched with slogans: 'Stress relieved here,' it says at the entrance, but that's not bloody likely given the place has been heaving since day one. Luckily, for four months of the year the action takes place outside, a clamour amid the silvery chairs and tables that front the chain of establishments on this little Continental strip north of Oxford Street. The food menu is typical Cantaloupe Group – ie good – and centres on Latin street fare, including rarities such as marinated raw fish (ceviche) from Peru. The drinks are also predominantly Latino (for example, a Batida cocktail of Cachaça, and so on) although bottled beers bafflingly include Old Speckled Hen. Global DJ nights centre on the sauna box basement and have monikers such as Stoned Asia Music.
Babies and children admitted (until 6pm). Disabled: toilet. Music (DJs 8pm daily; £7 after 11pm). Tables outdoors (pavement). **Map 1/J6**

Mash

19-21 Great Portland Street, W1 (7637 5555). Oxford Circus tube. **Open** 7.30am-2am Mon-Fri; noon-2am Sat. **Food served** 7.30am-11pm Mon-Fri; noon-11pm Sat. **Credit** AmEx, DC, MC, V.
Now firmly established as an all-day breakfast-to-bedtime hangout, this former car showroom has attracted a fine mix of swingers and ten-to-fivers thanks to a comfortable, spacious interior with clever retro touches, and a caters-for-all cross-section of menus and drinks. A front-of-house deli sorts out the breakfast crowd, who can also spread out over the main bar area, a roomy, curvy high-ceilinged lounge lined with a long bar counter and bookended by brewing vats. Post-11am, along with original shooters and imaginative cocktails, Mash serves its own microbrewed beers, fruit, wheat, chocolate and house variety, all available on tap. Facing the counter, a chill-out alcove is backdropped by a series of scenes of communal leisure in which one character is grimacing in each. The final touch is an airport departures board announcing wacky messages as you enter the main bar. Supremely multifunctional and fun to boot.
Babies and children admitted (until 8pm). Disabled: toilet. Function room. Music (DJs 10pm Thur-Sat; free). Tables outdoors (pavement). **Map 1/J6**

Match

37-8 Margaret Street, W1 (7499 3443/www.matchbar.com). Oxford Circus tube. **Open** 11am-midnight Mon-Sat. **Food served** 11am-10.30pm Mon-Sat. **Credit** AmEx, MC, V.
Hard to think of this funky little place as one of a chain, but there are four sibling venues in town (plus one in Leicester). This one off Oxford Street was the second (**Match** in Clerkenwell was the first; *see p114*) with the same intelligent cocktail menu (including the legendary Matchnificent Seven), stripy lanterns and iconic design touches as its predecessor. Prime seating is the brown leather stuff at front-of-house, particularly in warm weather when the frontage is folded back (lean back and shake your head sadly at the punters going in and out of the far-less-exceptional chain bar across the road). Otherwise, there's a cosy little back alcove, backdropped by drapes, a raised dining area, and a narrow but sturdy bar counter ideal for bar stool slouching and offering ringside viewing of the whole cocktail-shaking shenanigans.
Babies and children admitted (until 5pm). Disabled: toilet. Function room. Music (DJs 8pm Thur-Sat; free). Tables outdoors (pavement).

Newman Arms

23 Rathbone Street, W1 (7636 1127). Goodge Street tube. **Open** noon-11pm Mon-Fri. **Food served** noon-3pm, 6-9pm Mon-Thur; noon-3pm Fri. **Credit** MC, V.
The petite Newman does a roaring trade of a lunchtime, thanks to the 'Famous Upstairs Pie Room' with its own entrance in an alleyway round the corner from the front door. There, in the same supposed bordello in which Michael Powell's 1960 film *Peeping Tom* is set, steaming beef and ale pies are swiftly followed by jam and treacle sponges of classic yore. Downstairs is a homely, tartan-carpeted ground-floor bar. A small space, when full it can bring on full-blown cabin fever, with its low ceiling, bookcase, englassed model galleon, and military prints over the counter. Although the main board outside boasts 'Premium Brands', Bell's and Archer's are the most prominent spirits at eye level and a huge neon Budweiser ad dominates the front windows – the claim is partially upheld with a modest but cared-for selection of real ales, including Bass and London Pride.
Babies and children admitted (until 3pm). Function room. **Map 1/J5**

Nordic

25 Newman Street, W1 (7631 3174/www.nordicbar.com). Goodge Street or Tottenham Court Road tube. **Open** noon-11pm Mon-Fri; 6-11pm Sat. **Food served** noon-3pm, 5.30-10pm Mon-Fri; 6-10pm Sat. **Happy hour** 5.30-8pm, 9-11pm Mon, 5.30-8pm Tue; 5-11pm Wed, Thur; 6-11pm Sat. **Credit** AmEx, MC, V.
A tidy little operation this, tucked away off Newman Street, and themed right down to its snowshoes. Two areas – the entrance lounge, welcoming you ('Skoal!') with a mural triptych of a pre-*Exorcist* Max von Sydow necking akvavit, and the back restaurant decorated at weekday lunchtimes with a smörgåsbord (crayfish, herring, roast beef) – bookend a narrow bar counter manned by assorted Scando/Baltic staff. Twinkly pine garlands the counter, behind which stretches at eye level bottle after bottle of clear Pölsters, Absolut, Finlandia et al. A cocktail list still in flux currently ranges from the ridiculous (a Horny Viking, an Elke Brooks etc) to the sublime (a Scandapolitan of three vodkas, Cointreau and lingonberry juice). Draught beers include Danish Red Erik, dark and strong, Faxe and Carlsberg, with Lapin Kulta soon slated. A destination of some repute.
Function room. TV (satellite). **Map 1/J5**

Oscar

Charlotte Street Hotel, 15 Charlotte Street, W1 (7806 2000/www.charlottestreethotel.com). Goodge Street or Tottenham Court Road tube. **Open/food served** noon-11pm Mon-Sat. **Credit** AmEx, MC, V.

The Charlotte Street Hotel occupies a prime spot along the spine of media land, its blue-fronted exterior aimed at Fitzrovia's focal local **Fitzroy Tavern** (*see p42*). Through the stylish reception area and past the beady eye of the maître d', residents' bar Oscar operates both as a meeting place for exalted commissioners and broadcasters, and as a holding space for those eating at the trendy restaurant spread out over the rest of the unsurprisingly stylish interior. The kitchen serves both, the bar's thin blue menu featuring snack suggestions of Welsh rarebit, Oscietra caviar and lamb kofta. These complement a page each of vintage, contemporary, classic and champagne cocktails in the £10 range, two pages of Martinis and the signature cocktail, Hush Hush Sweet Charlotte, of Grey Goose vodka, fresh mint and lime juice. Light fittings seemingly converted from old Slinkies, a bust of a forgotten royal and flower-patterned armless chairs add car-boot chic. The name hints at Charlotte Street's vague filmic connections, an image the hotel likes to maintain with its occasional Sunday night meal-and-movie deals in the restaurant and downstairs screening room.

Babies and children admitted. Disabled: toilet. Function rooms. No-smoking area (restaurant, lunch only). Tables outdoors (pavement). **Map 1/K5**

Sevilla Mía

22 Hanway Street, W1 (7637 3756). Tottenham Court Road tube. **Open/food served** 7pm-1am Mon-Sat; 7pm-midnight Sun. **Credit** AmEx, DC, MC, V.

When the licensing hours and familiar patterns of downtown barlife change in a year or two (or maybe less), will we still have any use for the string of Spanish cellar bars that, hand-in-hand with second-hand record shops, set the satisfyingly untrendy tone of pre-Hakkasan Hanway Street? Possibly not. In the meantime, some of us will still find ourselves staggering down these shady steps, too far gone to tell the time let alone to know better, barely even able to walk, into a conspiratorial cavern of flirtatious drinking and standard tapas. It could never be considered classy, not even through sangria-tinted spectacles, but in its time Sevilla Mía has probably allowed an awful lot of people to cop off with entirely improbable bedfellows, and for that, a glass should be raised in its honour whenever the curtain does finally come down.
Map 1/K5

Ship

134 New Cavendish Street, W1 (7636 6301). Oxford Circus tube. **Open** 11am-11pm Mon-Fri. **Food served** 11.30am-5pm Mon-Fri. **Credit** MC, V.

Set on a quiet corner of Fitzrovia between Titchfield Village and assorted university buildings, the Ship takes its name seriously. Its intimate interior is festooned with maritime bric-a-brac, the copper positively gleaming in the array of mirrors promoting unusual British ales or obscure foreign beers. The most prominent is for Wenlock – 'Wenlock's Number One House' – but Dry Blackthorn and Grolsch are also available on draught for the less adventurous. Regimental crests decorate the door of the gents, as well as a notice declaring 'No Soliciting', and talk can be heard of currents and tides. Set breakfasts and burgers can be brought in from the caff next door, regular clients preferring to dine in the cabin than surrounded by moulded plastic furniture.

Function room. Games (fruit machines). Tables outdoors (pavement). **Map 1/J5**

Critics' choice
hotel bars (old school)

American Bar (p91)
Home of the White Lady but welcoming of any suitably attired.

Claridge's Bar (p64)
Attitude in spades, but an absolute classic.

Duke's (p90)
As discreet as it gets and serving possibly the finest Martini in town.

Library (p24)
Great Hyde Park Corner place, but not for bookish types.

Rivoli at the Ritz (p91)
Where to go when you're 'puttin' it on'.

The Social

5 Little Portland Street, W1 (7636 4992/www.thesocial.com). Oxford Circus tube. **Open/food served** noon-11pm Mon-Fri; 1-11pm Sat. **Credit** AmEx, MC, V.

By day, this small cabin bar, well off Oxford Street and almost hidden at street level, cuts through any airs and graces by plonking big bottles of Heinz ketchup and HP sauce on each of its five rounded booth tables, offering student digs fodder of pies and spaghetti hoops on toast (grated cheese is optional), and dispensing top-notch drinks (draught Beck's and Red Stripe, top-end spirits, classic and not-so-classic Martinis, including – ha, ha – the baked bean Martini with said sauce) from a long bar counter. At one end, the excellent Heavenly Jukebox, with Aretha in vintage form, Iggy and his Stooges much in evidence and generally stocked with classics from A to Z. Come evening, the action switches downstairs, its long corridors and alcoves filling with pheromonal fug and loose tongues, while some serious DJing takes place. The quality of music, excellent programming and savvy, not too hip to have fun crowd is guaranteed by the Heavenly Jukebox tag. We still maintain that this is as good a bar as you'll find in all London town.

Babies and children admitted (until 5pm). Music (DJs Mon-Sat, free; occasional bands Mon; £3). **Map 1/J5**

Villandry

170 Great Portland Street, W1 (7631 3131). Great Portland Street tube. **Open** 8am-11.30pm Mon-Fri; 9am-11.30pm Sat. **Food served** 8am-10.30pm Mon-Sat. **Credit** AmEx, MC, V.

The Villandry is nothing if not simplicity done exceedingly well. One third of a sleek operation that also features a plentiful lifestyle deli and abundant florist, this bar-restaurant serves fine produce in spades, but plays its cards very close to its chest. A minimally lit dining area is lined with a side of banquettes divided into three sections, and a smooth stone bar counter embellished by vast stalks of fresh flowers and an understated wooden shelving arrangement behind the bar. Three pumps (Leffe Blonde, Stella, Staropramen) provide shine. The wine list (eight reds and wines, five each by the glass) is classy, as is an imaginative choice of cocktails in the £6.50 range. There are also pitchers for £16, including a

Flightberry Murzenquest of Grey Goose vodka and Galliano, and a Macbeth's Dream of Chivas Regal and white Curaçao. Needless to say, the food is immaculate.
Babies and children (dining only). Disabled: toilet. Tables outdoors.

Also in the area...

Ha! Ha! Bar & Canteen 43-51 Great Titchfield Street, W1 (7580 7252).
Jamies 74 Charlotte Street, W1 (7636 7556).
Lees Bag (Davy's) 4 Great Portland Street, W1 (7636 5287).

High Street Kensington

It might cut a dash with shoppers, but when it comes to drinking the pubs and bars round here are much more reflective of the area's upper-class suburban heritage. Key haunts are places like the historic **Churchill Arms** and **Windsor Castle**, countrified idylls where flat-capped gents take a stout with game pie after walking the setters through Holland Park (except, in reality, fellow customers are more likely to be Bill and Marge from Ohio having halves of lager with their fish and chips).

Abingdon

54 Abingdon Road, W8 (7937 3339). High Street Kensington tube. **Open** 12.30-11pm Mon-Sat; 12.30-10.30pm Sun. **Food served** 12.30-2.30pm, 6.30-11pm Mon-Fri; 12.30-3pm, 6.30-11pm Sat; 12.30-3pm, 7-10pm Sun. **Credit** AmEx, MC, V.
A recent revamp has turned a neighbourhood favourite gathering dust into something akin to a hip hotel bar, and the vaguely recognisable soap stars and other posers and primpers are back – big time. The bright front bar inflicts motion with a dizzy-making faux nouveau ceiling and an amoeba-like mirror that casts even the lesser luminary in a better light. It's a noisy, frenetic space, with the volume (music, voices, egos) up way too high and the sofas too low to truly chill out. The long and narrow restaurant is an attractive annexe, with striped banquettes, slatted wood panelling and an ever-changing menu that ensures a capacity crowd even midweek. But lest patrons forget who and what and where they are, a mirror tilted forward brasserie-style allows diners to catch drinkers spying on diners looking at drinkers.
Babies and children admitted (high chairs). Tables outdoors (pavement).

Britannia

1 Allen Street, W8 (no phone). High Street Kensington tube. **Open** 11am-11pm Mon-Sat; noon-10.30pm Sun. **Food served** noon-2.30pm, 6-9.30pm Mon-Sat. **Credit** AmEx, DC, MC, V.
It's as though they've winched a pub out of deepest Surrey and dropped it into the heart of Kensington. Comfortable, immaculately clean and whisper-quiet, the Britannia is the place to go if you've a wheezing uncle in tow; indeed, few people in the front area dip below 50. In more lively company, head for the ample back lounge or the lush conservatory, replete with rubber and ficus trees. The beer selection (Young's) is legion as is the choice of wine by the glass. The surrounds are warm and cosy, with fires glowing in winter, old china lining the shelves and an altar to the Kensington Cricket Club who frequent the joint. The 18th-century cartoons and caricatures on the walls are didactic; if you've been misbehaving (unlikely in this genteel place), sober up at the print of 'Intolerance & Ridicule'.
Babies and children admitted (conservatory). Function room. Games (darts, fruit machine). No piped music or jukebox. No-smoking conservatory (lunch only). TV.

Catherine Wheel

23 Kensington Church Street, W8 (7937 3259). High Street Kensington tube. **Open** noon-11pm Mon-Sat; noon-10.30pm Sun. **Food served** 12.30-8pm daily. **Happy hour** 7-9pm Mon-Thur, Sun. **Credit** MC, V.
A pub standing shoulder to shoulder with Japanese eateries and rococo antique shops named after Catherine of Alexandria? Huh? She was the fourth-century virgin who lost her head (literally) when the spiked wheel upon which she was to meet her maker broke (hence the catherine wheel). She's the patroness of philosophers and preachers, but both appear to be thin on the ground in this environment. But being within easy sliding distance of the High Street and tube, the place acts as one of those great social levellers, attracting suits, lads and workers in equal numbers. It's a small but jolly place, essentially one main lounge with large windows on two sides, and an upstairs lounge frequently used for private functions. A few original features remain: a large hearth with an impressive etched mirror, an embossed ceiling and antique hanging lamps. Along with the usual Nicholson's offerings, expect Addlestone's Cider and a couple of reds and whites by the glass.
Babies and children admitted (until 7pm). Function room. Games (fruit machines).

Churchill Arms

119 Kensington Church Street, W8 (7727 4242). Notting Hill Gate tube. **Open** 11am-11pm Mon-Sat; noon-10.30pm Sun. **Food served** noon-9.30pm Mon-Sat; noon-4pm Sun. **Credit** MC, V.
At some point in recent history the landlord here determined that the Churchill memorabilia was not enough and began suspending chamber pots, lanterns and golf bags from the ceiling and pinning butterflies under glass. The result is a boozer straight out of central casting, and if Dick Van Dyke isn't doing his Mary Poppins cockney thing somewhere in the corner, he should be. All of which makes the Churchill a big favourite of both locals and tourists, and you'll have to fight your way through scrums of punters at the horseshoe-shaped bar for a pint (Chiswick, ESB, London Pride, plus seasonal ales such as Jack Frost). For more elbow room, head for the rear conservatory bedecked in philodendrons, Swedish ivy and geraniums, where you will find some of the most authentic Thai food to be had in a London pub.
Babies and children admitted (restaurant only). Games (fruit machine). Music (jazz, 7pm every 2nd Sun). TV (satellite). **Map 10/B8**

Cuba

11-13 Kensington High Street, W8 (7938 4137). High Street Kensington tube. **Open/food served** noon-2am Mon-Sat; 2-10.30pm Sun. **Happy hour** noon-7.30pm Mon-Sat; 2-10.30pm Sun. **Credit** AmEx, DC, MC, V.
Has the Cuban revolution fizzled out? You'd never know it from the youthful frenzy of Latin-soundtracked limb-twisters, sloshing drinks and red-blooded pull-on behaviour that goes on in this well-located familiarly styled theme bar. Every night is party night! With special events!! And salsa classes!!! The none-too-salubrious main bar area gives way to a small gallery restaurant beneath a skylight; chico and chica prancing takes place in the downstairs club. The decor is cheesy pseudo-Buena Vista: pre-revolutionary Havana, with the requisite Hemingway additions. Cocktails (mostly rum-based) are plentiful and cheap (£4.95-£5.95; jugs £17.95-£18.95), and the beer is at least Spanish. Food? No

black beans and rice, but lots of south of the border favourites (nachos, fajitas, tortilla wraps). Roll over Papa (and tell Che the news).
Dance classes (salsa daily, times and prices vary). Music (DJ 9.30pm nightly). Restaurant.

Goolies

21 Abingdon Road, W8 (7938 1122/www.goolies-bar.com). High Street Kensington tube. **Open** 5.30-11pm Mon-Sat. **Food served** 6.30-10.30pm Mon-Sat. **Credit** AmEx, MC, V.
If this delightful wine bar-restaurant feels 'foreign' at first – the low-key but inspired decor, the humorous corkscrews on the loo doors (arms up for the gents, demurely down for the ladies), the exceedingly warm welcome – then the answer lies in the antipodean accents of owner and chef. Goolies is essentially an intimate (read cramped) front bar and lounge, with a gallery kitchen a few steps up to the back. Mirrors, an impressive oval-shaped skylight and back-lit niches with light-as-air white alabaster bowls help to lighten things up. The wine list (18 are offered by the glass) is well thought out and very reasonably priced; choose from 'elegant/light', 'aromatic/medium' and 'full-bodied/oaked' whites or 'light/fruity', 'medium-bodied' and 'full-bodied' reds. The menu – essentially Modern British with some Pacific Rim fusions – is inventive but relatively expensive; oenophiles might stick to the wine and order blotter from the Asianesque bar menu.
Babies and children admitted.

Greyhound

1 Kensington Square, W8 (7937 7140/www.theoriginal pubcompany.co.uk). High Street Kensington tube. **Open** 11am-11pm Mon-Sat; noon-10.30pm Sun. **Food served** noon-8pm daily. **Credit** AmEx, MC, V.
The old dog certainly kennels in a pedigree neighbourhood, with a verdant square of blue-plaqued Georgians ('John Stuart Mill lived here') opposite and a turning just south named Thackeray Street in honour of the satirist who (supposedly) imbibed here. With Associated Newspapers just a lurch and stagger away, the Greyhound's inky tradition lives on, and it's not a bad place for stories (both real and imagined). The luridly coloured alcopops and schnapps of lime, orange, raspberry and cranberry attract a younger breed; the beer is the usual Scottish & Newcastle line-up. It's a comfortable place, with a bright front area, a narrow middle space with alcoves facing the bar counter and a large back room, with two pool tables covered in red baize that complement the walls. Be warned, though: the faux Cubist artwork and abstract carpet may have you feeling unsteady on your feet.
Games (fruit machines, quiz machine, pool tables). Music (DJ 8pm 15th and last Fri of mth). TV (big screen, digital, satellite).

Po Na Na

20 Kensington Church Street, W8 (7795 6656/ www.ponana.co.uk). High Street Kensington tube. **Open** 8pm-2am Mon-Thur, Sat; 6pm-2am Fri. **Credit** AmEx, MC, V.
One of a nationwide chain of Maghrebi-themed bars, this downstairs warren goes beyond tassels and hammered brass tables with flamboyant goth sofas in faux leopard skin and an image of Lucifer where he's most comfortable – in the fire. Old Nick lends his name to one of the shooters – the Horny Devil (Red Aftershock and Cointreau alight) – though we searched in vain for the inspiration behind Cocksucking Cowboy (butterscotch schnapps and Baileys). The atmosphere is low-key and candlelit in the early evening, but after the watershed hour (anytime between 9.30pm and 11pm depending on the night) DJs spin hip hop and R&B through to jazz and soulful house and it's party time. Roll up after the DJs hit the decks and you'll have to fork out something between £3 and £7 unless you've downed the required amount of drink at the nearby **Settle Down** (*see below*) to qualify for the reduced cover charge.
Function room. Music (DJs nightly; £3 after 9.30pm Mon-Wed; £5 after 9.30pm Thur-Sat).

Scarsdale

23A Edwardes Square, W8 (7937 1811). High Street Kensington tube. **Open** noon-11pm Mon-Sat; noon-10.30pm Sun. **Food served** noon-9.45pm daily. **Credit** AmEx, MC, V.
The denizens of Edwardes Square, a historic and verdant Georgian space with dubious (both senses) French connections, can lay claim to one of the liveliest locals in Kensington. It's a stylish place in an old-fashioned sort of way with prints and oils in gilt frames, heavy drapes at the windows and stained-glass snob screens. Courage ales are on tap, and there are a half-dozen well-chosen red and white wines by the glass (£3-£5.90); judging from the parade of empty champagne bottles on shelves around the bar the well-heeled and draped locals aren't adverse to a bit of bubbly (£26-£85) either. Lest Americans of a certain vintage think the place has anything to do with the popular high-protein/low-carb Scarsdale Diet of the 1970s, think again. Mains (12oz steaks, sausages) are a carnivore's delight but the chips, rich sauces and calorific puds give the game away.
Babies and children admitted (in restaurant). Games (fruit machines). Tables outdoors (garden). TV.

Settle Down

Barkers Arcade, Kensington High Street, W8 (7376 0008). High Street Kensington tube. **Open** noon-11pm Mon-Fri. **Food served** noon-3pm, 6-10pm Mon-Fri. **Credit** AmEx, MC, V.
The name of this enormous boozer, one of the busiest pubs in Kensington, is something of a misnomer. 'Down', yes – it's in a basement – but 'Settle'? Unlikely. Sitting incongruously below the landmark art deco department store Barkers, it attracts commuters mistaking it for the tube entrance as well as swarms of regulars. It's a feverish and friendly complex of five large rooms, covered in tartan and/or modern art of the cheesy Modigliani print sort. The crowd, in matey groups or on the prowl, is young, multi-ethnic and international. The beer selection is neither here nor there (lagers plus John Smith and Guinness) but priced to please. Many present are drinking their way into **Po Na Na** (*see left*), with which it has a pub-to-club deal.
Babies and children admitted (until 6pm). Function room. TV.

Tenth Bar

Royal Garden Hotel, 2-24 Kensington High Street, W8 (7937 8000/www.royalgardenhotel.co.uk). High Street Kensington tube. **Open** noon-2.30pm, 5-11pm Mon-Fri; 5.30-11pm Sat. **Credit** AmEx, DC, MC, V.
In a quiet corner of the tenth floor of Kensington's only five-star hotel, the Tenth ('X' marks the spot on the lift button) is primarily about views. And should customers be in any doubt, a fold-out photocard tucked inside the drinks list will identify buildings and sites as close as Kensington Palace and as far as St Paul's Cathedral. View duly noted, next peruse the cocktail list: short but sweet (especially the three Tropicals, all of fruits, Kahlúa, Galliano or vodka; £7.95 each), there are aperitifs galore – from Pimms and Pernod to Punt E Mes red vermouth – for those planning to dine next door, and for something post-prandial, a selection of 20 Cuban cigars. The decor's a bit dodgy (burlwood

curlicue-shaped bar counter, barrel armchairs in cabana stripes and a blue and beige herringbone carpet) but then that's not what anybody came to see.
Babies and children welcome. Disabled: toilet. Music (jazz 8pm 1st and last Sat of mth). No-smoking area (restaurant).

Windsor Castle
114 Campden Hill Road, W8 (7243 9551/www.windsor-castle-pub.co.uk). High Street Kensington or Notting Hill Gate tube. **Open** noon-11pm Mon-Sat; noon-10.30pm Sun. **Food served** noon-10pm daily. **Credit** AmEx, MC, V.
The Windsor Castle retains some fine Victorian features – oak-panelled pantry doors separate its three bars – but the bull's-eye windows unnerve. Too much sun through those magnifiers could spark a fire, and no one wants to see yet another Windsor Castle go up in flames. The place is full of high-backed settles and nooks (though the nicotine-coloured walls might do with a lick of paint, or at least more smokers), and there's a delightful courtyard with a shady plane tree. The choice of beer and wine (Adnams Best, London Pride, Grolsch, Staropramen, five reds and three whites by the glass) is unadventurous and expensive; a pint of lager is £3, a 250ml glass of wine £4.60. Food is mostly trad (fish and chips, four types of sausage, Scottish oysters), but with penne and ciabatta added for those with both feet in the 21st century.
No-smoking area (lunchtime). Tables outdoors (garden, pavement). **Map 10/A8**

Holborn

Although it could also furnish the bar crawl from hell – in just 200 metres Kingsway manages to pack in an All Bar One, Pitcher & Piano, Fine Line, Bierodrome, Jamies and a particularly bad Wetherspoon's – Holborn still has a scattering of first choice boozers, none better than the **Lamb** (and Lambs Conduit Street is *so* flavour of the moment), or prettier than the **Princess Louise**. The best food is served at the **Duke (of York)** and **Perseverance**. Our definition of the area runs from the tube station north and east, handing over to Chancery Lane part way along High Holborn and Clerkenwell around Gray's Inn Road.

Calthorpe Arms
252 Gray's Inn Road, WC1 (7278 4732). Russell Square tube. **Open** 11am-11pm Mon-Sat; noon-10.30pm Sun. **Food served** noon-2.30pm daily. **Credit** MC, V.
On a section of the Gray's Inn Road that seems to be fiercely resisting the gentrification that's fermenting all around, this traditional Young's boozer stands resplendent in its old-style green and gold top-coat, looking every inch a throwback to the 1950s. Inside, is a smallish, thin room dominated by the serving area. The carpet's typically psychedelic, the walls are brown painted, and the eight windows and two doors (count 'em) come with extravagant floral drapes. A function room upstairs doubles as a lunchtime dining room, offering the likes of fish and chips, steak pie and lasagne to office workers looking for something that doesn't come with ciabatta. The name comes from the Calthorpe family who at one time owned most of the buildings on this side of Gray's Inn Road – called Gray's Inn Lane until 1862. We hear that the third earl was a keen amateur musician. Maybe that explains the pub's ban on music.
Function room. Games (fruit machine). Tables outdoors (pavement). TV (satellite). **Map 3/M4**

Duke (of York)
7 Roger Street, WC1 (7242 7230). Russell Square tube. **Open** noon-11pm Mon-Fri; 6-11pm Sat. **Food served** noon-3pm, 6-10pm Mon-Fri; 6-10pm Sat. **Credit** MC, V.
A retro gastropub that looks like a backstreet boozer would have looked back in the 1950s, from the Friary Meaux floor tiles to the half-frosted lettered windows, red and white check lino floor and distressed wooden serving area. Now attracting a cross-section of Holborn's arty crowd (yes, they do exist), mixed in with the hipper end of the legal profession and a smattering of actors (we recognised two minor TV names, dahling), the Duke offers a quality drinking and dining experience in an environment that won't give you a headache. Served predominantly in the green-painted back dining room, the food menu is reassuringly brief and will probably include a soup of the day, gourmet sausages, pasta of the day, and specials such as whole roast plaice, lentil salad with roast beetroot and grilled goat's cheese and a steak (maybe with cranberry and roast garlic butter). Keeping up the nostalgia theme, the sole real ale is Ind Coope Burton Ale.
Restaurant. Tables outdoors (pavement). **Map 3/M4**

King's Arms
11 Northington Street, WC1 (7405 9107). Chancery Lane or Russell Square tube. **Open** 11.30am-11pm Mon-Fri. **Food served** noon-2.30pm Mon-Fri. **Credit** AmEx, DC, MC, V.
This is the kind of pub the boss will take his junior employees to after work to encourage them to try 'real beer' (in this case, a choice of Adnams Bitter, Bass or Greene King IPA). There's also a real fire in winter, plus genuine pub mirrors and red velvet curtains and upholstery. It's one of those traditional-looking places you'd expect to be full of grizzled old codgers trying to make their half last all day, but not a bit of it. Instead it's usually packed with twenty- and thirtysomethings talking about torts, football and QuarkXPress. The pavement patio comes into its own in warmer weather; upstairs is a no-smoking area, function room and the narrowest gents' toilet in the world.
Babies and children admitted (separate room). Games (darts). No-smoking area. Tables outdoors (pavement). **Map 3/M4**

Lamb
94 Lamb's Conduit Street, WC1 (7405 0713). Russell Square tube. **Open** 11am-11pm Mon-Sat; noon-4pm, 7-10.30pm Sun. **Food served** noon-2.30pm, 6-9pm Mon-Sat; noon-2.30pm Sun. **Credit** MC, V.
Young's of Wandsworth is extremely proud of the Lamb and with good cause. It's a Grade II-listed structure, built around 1730 and, thanks to a very sympathetic restoration in the 1960s, the ornate Victorian interior is largely intact. The mahogany bar is edged with etched-glass snob screens, complemented by matching windows and mirrors, with dashing racing green upholstery and an angry red gloss ceiling. The 'no-smoking' snug is a nice idea if little more than a partitioned-off area. The sole musical implement is a Victorian polyphon that – in return for a charity donation – will play a 19th-century tune (although one wonders if the charity would be better off if you had to pay the polyphon *not* to play a 19th-century tune). Many contemporary music hall artists appearing in the area used the pub and a selection of their framed portraits lines the walls. The diverse clientele includes a cross-section of local life, from lawyers and thespians to folks who actually work for a living.
Babies and children admitted. Function room. No piped music or jukebox. No-smoking area. Tables outdoors (patio). **Map 3/M4**

Na Zdrowie

11 Little Turnstile, WC1 (7831 9679). Holborn tube. **Open** 12.30-11pm Mon-Fri; 6-11pm Sat. **Food served** 12.30-10pm Mon-Fri; 6-10pm Sat. **Credit** MC, V.

Situated behind Holborn tube in a popular rat-run between an employment exchange and a Thai cafe, this smallish Polish bar is the place to come for 50-odd authentically flavoured vodkas – none of your OTT Smarties and Rollo flavours here – East European beers and real Polish nosh. It's recently gone through a makeover and now boasts greenish-blue walls highlighted by striking lighting. The pleasantly modern-looking nests of tables and chairs fill up first, especially after work, and it doesn't take many in a room this size to make a party. Customers tend to be young Polish expats, local media workers and refugees from the area's rather naff selection of would-be style bars.

Tables outdoors (pavement). **Map 4/M5**

Perseverance

63 Lamb's Conduit Street, WC1 (7405 8278). Holborn tube. **Open** noon-11pm Mon-Fri; 12.30-11pm Sat; 12.30-10.30pm Sun. **Food served** 12.30-3pm, 7-10pm Mon-Fri; 7.30-10pm Sat; 12.30-4.30pm Sun. **Credit** AmEx, MC, V.

Management didn't have to persevere long for this trendy gastropub to pick up a strong and loyal following. Just a couple of years after its opening and you'd be hard pressed to find a seat any night in the ground-floor bar (until about 9pm that is, when the office workers start to drift off home), while booking is almost essential for the swish upstairs restaurant. The decor down in the bar is in the style of a traditional boozer that's been given the Cinderella treatment, with two-tone flock wallpaper hung with grotesquely modern mirrors, stuffed animal heads and cut-price Woollies chandeliers. The sole real ale is Courage Directors, though most drinkers seem content with the usual range of lagers and something from the decent and affordable wine list. The kitchen turns out posh nosh of the confit of duck and foie gras ballotine type.

Babies and children admitted (dining only). Restaurant (available for hire). Tables outdoors (pavement). **Map 3/M4**

Princess Louise

208 High Holborn, WC1 (7405 8816). Holborn tube. **Open** 11am-11pm Mon-Fri; noon-11pm Sat; noon-10.30pm Sun. **Food served** noon-2.30pm, 6-8.30pm Mon-Sat. **Credit** AmEx, DC, MC, V.

Built in 1872 and named after Queen Victoria's fourth daughter, this is very possibly London's finest example of a 19th-century gin palace. The people to thank are WH Lascelles & Co who, in 1891, refurbished the pub in extravagant style. Pride of place goes to the intricately carved, horseshoe-shaped central bar, incorporating a period clock and magnificent etched mirrors. Originally, this would have served several drinking areas, but in the 1960s brewers Watneys knocked the partitions through. Now the pub is under the stewardship of Sam Smith's, so expect the likes of Old Brewery Bitter, Ayingerbräu lager and some tasty bottled brews at very reasonable prices. Seats are hard to come by, especially after work, when hordes of local office types swarm in, searching for decent booze and stunning surroundings.

Function room. Games (fruit machines). No piped music or jukebox. **Map 1/L5**

Vats Wine Bar & Restaurant

51 Lamb's Conduit Street, WC1 (7242 8963). Holborn or Russell Square tube. **Open** noon-11pm Mon-Fri. **Food served** noon-2.30pm, 6-9.30pm Mon-Fri. **Credit** AmEx, DC, MC, V.

Old-school wine bars are getting rarer as chains move in. In these turbulent times, it's reassuring to note that Vats remains resolutely independent and staunchly traditional, with its light wood and dark green paintwork and predominantly French wine list. Customers – a mix of local business people, 'young women who lunch' and Ealing Comedy lookalikes – seem to appreciate the continuity and are a loyal breed. The wine list is traditionally laid out by region; Bordeaux drinkers are well catered for, but fans of the New World might find their options a bit on the sparse side. That said, there's a fine selection of the big names in non-vintage champagne, an excellent selection of half-bottles and 13 wines by the glass. The food menu proffers the likes of risotto, salmon fish cakes and smoked haddock, with main courses around £10-£13.

Babies and children admitted. Function room. Music (jazz 7-10.30pm Tue). Tables outdoors (pavement). **Map 3/M4**

Also in the area...

All Bar One 58 Kingsway, WC2 (7269 5171).
Bierodrome 67 Kingsway, WC2 (7242 7469).
Bung Hole (Davy's) Hand Court, 57 High Holborn, WC1 (7831 8365).
Jamies 50-54 Kingsway, WC2 (7405 9749).
Penderel's Oak (JD Wetherspoon) 283-8 High Holborn, WC1 (7242 5669).
Pitcher & Piano 42 Kingsway, WC2 (7404 8510).
Shakespeare's Head (JD Wetherspoon) 64-8 Kingsway, WC2 (7404 8846).

Holland Park

This is not the greatest part of town in which to be looking for a drink. And it just got a whole lot worse with the closing of the area's only decent old-school boozer, the Prince of Wales, although we're told this is only temporary while the place undergoes a refurb. On the plus side, many of the splendid pubs and bars of Notting Hill Gate and Ladbroke Grove are a brisk ten-minute walk away.

Academy

57 Princedale Road, W11 (7221 0248). Holland Park tube. **Open** noon-11pm Mon-Sat; noon-10.30pm Sun. **Food served** noon-3.30pm, 6-10.30pm Mon-Fri; noon-10.30pm Sat; noon-10pm Sun. **Credit** MC, V.

Once a normal boozer, the Academy is now a laid-back contemporary bar-diner, and so all the better suited to this quiet, whitewashed, residential corner of Holland Park. Unfussily bedecked, it combines spotlights and candles, wooden blinds, a fake fire and modern art on plain white walls to create a relaxed ambience that encourages hardcore lingering. Furniture is an eclectic mix, but one that reflects the clientele, which ranges from well-groomed thirtysomething couples grazing the modish bistro menu to middle-aged guys who've just popped in for a quiet pint before ambling home to their unhumble abodes (there's little that's humble in these parts). The wine list is worth a gander – French-led and affordable, with ten available by the glass.

Babies and children admitted (until 7pm). Function room. Tables outdoors (pavement). **Map 10/Az7**

Castle

100 Holland Park Avenue, W11 (7313 9301). Holland Park tube. **Open** 11am-11pm Mon-Sat; noon-10.30pm Sun. **Food served** noon-3pm, 6.30-10pm Mon-Fri; noon-4pm, 6-10pm Sat, Sun. **Credit** MC, V.

London drinking: jukeboxes

It's not all Wonderwall.

Jukeboxes originally took their name from black slang for disorderly and disreputable behaviour; now they're a byword for somewhere to store unwanted albums by Phil Collins. London's jukeboxes – the ones that haven't been ripped out in favour of decks, so another Hoxton mullethead can play emotionless bleeping white labels picked from his complementary record bag in a soulless DJ bar, that is – are largely an exercise in musical mindlessness. Largely, but not entirely.

Fitzrovia's glorious dive **Bradley's Spanish Bar** boasts London's most renowned jukebox. It plays vinyl, so is gorgeously authentic, providing a crackle, a hiss and a hum as each seven inch whirls around. Dylan, Sam Cooke, Warren Zevon, Love – it's mighty stuff, though some complain of too much swing and an ongoing inability to programme tunes from the downstairs bar. Quirky retreat **Three Kings of Clerkenwell** hides London's other vinyl jukebox. Guvnor Deke chooses from his own collection: Donovan, Led Zep, rare funk and Northern Soul. Hipper than Bradley's and with a higher turnover of tunes, this is the jukey to beat.

Gerry O'Doyle reckons he's got them both licked. Earlier this year he opened the **Boogaloo**, a delightfully louche Highgate local. The only jukebox better than his, he claims, is in NYC. Visually, it's a disappointment, but sonically, it's a real box of delights, with a Deep South bias, be it Willie Nelson, Creedence, Billie Holiday or Muscle Shoals soul. Every month a different musician – Jackson Browne, Robert Plant, Shane MacGowan – programmes their favourite albums. It's value for money, too: use your 50p on the Allman Brothers' extended jamfest 'In Memory Of Elizabeth Reed' or anything from Miles Davis's *Kind Of Blue* and you can take over the mood for an hour.

This approach is at odds with the prevailing climate. Bars simply don't like the customer's ability to drive the atmosphere; hence DJ bars. The **Grand Union** (*see p71*) in Westbourne Grove had a jukebox programmed by Rough Trade. First they took out all the country, then they turned it off altogether, pleading costs and the fact that they'd rather people listened to piped 'lounge music' then make their own selections. Decks won't be far behind. That's already happened at Camden's **Lock Tavern** (*see p162*). Their MP3 jukebox was meant to be revolutionary: customers could download any song they wanted. However, what customers wanted wasn't deemed good enough and the jukebox now operates as a staff-programmed MP3 sound-system. 'We mainly have DJs now anyway,' they told us. If a bar can't trust its customers to provide the right soundtrack, something, somewhere must be horribly wrong.

Top five hit parade

Boogaloo (*see p168*) 312 Archway Road, N6 (8340 2928).
Bradley's Spanish Bar (*see p41*) 42-4 Hanway Street, W1 (7636 0359).
Prince George (*see p148*) 40 Parkholme Road, E8 (7254 6060).
The Social (*see p45*) 5 Little Portland Street, W1 (7636 4992); (*see p177*) Arlington Square, N1 (7354 5809).
Three Kings of Clerkenwell (*see p117*) 7 Clerkenwell Close, EC1 (7253 0583)

It isn't all that way, thank God. Islington's **Social** has a good looking jukey packed with relaxed sounds (Röyksopp, Saint Etienne) while the cosier W1 branch favours louder, more abrasive tunes, from the Stooges to anything off Soul Jazz Records. Soho's the **Endurance** (*see p79*) is good for decent rock, credible indie and a large side order of New Order.

Selections at Hackney's **Prince George** are made by the owner's son and take in Thelonious Monk, T-Rex, Dr John and the White Stripes. If you like guitars turned up to 11, check out the **Crobar** (*see p78*), the metaller's den off Charing Cross Road. With Deep Purple, Iron Maiden, Black Sabbath, this is a jukey with attitude. *Peter Watts*

Situated on busy Holland Park Avenue a short stumble from the tube station, this traditional Victorian pub has been given the modern makeover (what pub hasn't?). High ceilings and bare boards are complemented by low lights and modern artworks by aspiring artists on the walls. Get there early and bag one of the comfortable leather benches by the window to indulge in a spot of people-watching. Drinks lean toward upper-end lagers (Hoegaarden, Staropramen), cocktails and shots like sambuca and tequila (£2.20), and consequently the pub pulls a predominantly youngish crowd who probably enjoy the chilled-out soundtrack played during the week and don't mind shouting their orders at the bar staff when the DJ moves in on Friday night.
Babies and children admitted (restaurant, daytime). Music (DJs 8pm Thur-Sat; free). No-smoking tables. Restaurant. Tables outdoors (pavement). **Map 10/Az7**

Julie's Wine Bar

137 Portland Road, W11 (7727 7985/ www.juliesrestaurant.com). Holland Park tube. **Open** 9am-11.30pm Mon-Sat; 10am-10.30pm Sun. **Food served** 9-11am, 12.30-2.45pm, 7.30-10.30pm Mon-Sat; 12.30-3pm, 7.30-10.30pm Sun. **Credit** AmEx, MC, V.
Julie's Wine Bar sits discreetly behind a sleek, chocolate brown exterior beside a romantic restaurant of the same name. Long-established, the venue remains popular with its effortlessly stylish regulars. Chill out at a pavement table or in the small, intimate bar with its jazzy vibes, bohemian decor and arabesque/Indian-inspired furnishings. Bar staff are flamboyant, friendly and fun, and provide dramatic and leisurely service. In contrast, the concise wine list is classic and slightly conservative, dominated by France, especially Bordeaux and Burgundy. There are also a few New World options such as California's Robert Mondavi, plus a couple of organic wines and even a Tapada Manzanilla sherry available by the glass or half bottle. Ten wines are served by the glass, and about another half dozen by the half bottle. Prices reflect the exceptionally well-heeled location.
Babies and children admitted (crèche 1-4pm Sun, £9.50 including food). Function room. Restaurant. Specialities: wines. Tables outdoors (pavement).

Ladbroke Arms

54 Ladbroke Road, W11 (7727 6648). Holland Park tube. **Open** 11am-11pm Mon-Sat; noon-10.30pm Sun. **Food served** noon-2.30pm, 7-9.45pm Mon-Sat; noon-3pm, 7-9.30pm Sun. **Credit** MC, V.
It's apt that the location of the Ladbroke Arms is so enticingly discreet. The road is quiet (despite the odd police car heading home to Notting Hill cop shop, opposite), adjacent is a cobbled mews, out front a patio with bench seating. Inside, the pub is crammed with tables, numerous framed pictures, and a predominantly public school clientele. There's little space for standing either in the front or the narrow back rooms, both of which are bathed in pleasingly yellow light. Couples aged 25-50, who don't need to dress smartly to exude confidence and wealth, tend to find a home at this cosy spot. In accordance with Al Murray-style stereotypes, males make for the London Pride, Abbot's, Directors or Young's Special, while females drink white wine from a suitably upmarket selection. Dining is the norm, with dishes from sausage and mash to pan-fried sea bass with ink strazzapreti pasta. With its display of fine wines and olive oils, and its rack of well-thumbed and learned journals, this relaxed, convivial place is a little piece of England that is forever Chiantishire.
Babies and children admitted (separate area). Tables outdoors (terrace). **Map 10/Az7**

King's Cross & Euston

The area may be teeming with potential drinkers but most of them are trying to get somewhere, anywhere else. Considering the quality of most of the bars in the neighbourhood, it may be wise to join them. North of the Euston Road, a string of bars gives clubbers drawn to the Cross exactly what they want – loud music and cheap beer. But with the overdue regeneration of the area gathering pace, quality boozers may soon become the norm rather than the exception.

The Backpacker

126 York Way, N1 (7278 8318). King's Cross tube/rail. **Open** 7pm-2am Fri, Sat; 4pm-midnight Sun. **Happy hour** 8-10pm Fri, Sat. **No credit cards**.
Among itinerant antipodeans and members of Her Majesty's forces, Sunday nights at the Backpacker have become legendary. You probably have to be young and on the lash to join the rowdy crowd frantically cruising each other, but as the efforts of at least half the punters tend to be rewarded with a snog, the atmosphere is friendly rather than intimidating. Beer and drinks deals (buy it by the plastic pitcher) accelerate the transformation from someone's wide-eyed sons and daughters to slurring, wild-eyed boozed-up monsters. The large back room literally rocks to the sounds of disco greats, inspiring frenetic dancing, arm waving and massive beer spillage. The Backpacker is so specific in its image of fun, it could almost be a fetish.
Function room. Music (DJs 10pm Fri-Sun, free; band 5pm Sun; £3 after 10pm). Tables outdoors (courtyard). TVs.

Craic House

55-7 Northdown Street, N1 (7837 7758). King's Cross tube/rail. **Open** noon-11pm Mon-Fri; 6pm-11pm Sat. **Credit** AmEx, MC, V.
Believe it or not, there are parts of King's Cross that are already almost gentrified (where the crack addicts use Derwent Crystal syringes), and Northdown Street is one such pocket. At its northern end is this sweet little boozer, unsigned save for a lone illuminated Guinness roundel above a plain deep red frontage. Come evening, and candles in the windows cast a warmly alluring light, beckoning like the gingerbread cottage deep in the forest. Inside is small and woody with a flickering fire and bench seating for no more than a handful, all aligned towards the modest but well-tended bar counter. Guinness is, of course, prominent but there's also San Miguel and Stella on tap, and a real ale called Rebellion IPA, plus a back shelf of choice amber-hued spirits. Despite the cringingly awful name, the place is neither leery nor loud and, on the night we visited, the ethnic quotient was largely Basque, all friends of the charming barmaid.
Bar available for hire. Music (1st Tue of mth jazz 8pm). Tables outdoors (pavement).

Head of Steam

1 Eversholt Street, NW1 (7383 3359). Euston tube/rail. **Open** 11am-11pm Mon-Sat; noon-10.30pm Sun. **Food served** noon-2.30pm, 5-8pm Mon-Fri; noon-3pm Sat. **Credit** MC, V.
Anoraks entering this real ale pub crammed with railway memorabilia must feel they've died and gone to Gortex heaven. It's a boon to commuters too, or at least those of them who are aware that concealed in the unlikely setting of a 1960s office block bordering Euston station concourse is a remarkably good boozer. Stripped floors, dark wooden beams and subdued lighting provide convivial surroundings in which to

sample one of the nine real ales (including lots of obscure brews), two vintage ciders or extensive range of lagers that are always on tap. Many a commuter comes in for a swift one and ends up tired and emotional on the last train home.
Babies and children admitted (separate area, until 9pm). Games (bar billiards, fruit machine). No-smoking tables. TV (satellite).

Ruby Lounge

33 Caledonian Road, N1 (7837 9558/www.ruby-lounge.co.uk). King's Cross tube/rail. **Open** 4-11pm Mon-Wed, Sun; noon-1am Thur; 2pm-2am Fri, Sat. **Credit** MC, V.
With wall projections, leatherette cube seating and an expensive sound system, the Ruby Lounge makes a valiant stab at being a hip DJ bar in grimy King's Cross. But most of the twentysomething crowd that packs the place at the weekend seem to realise it doesn't quite make the grade. They steer clear of the cocktail list, preferring to down pints of Hoegaarden and Staropramen. Perhaps they regard the breast-shaped wall lamps that bathe the walls in a rosy glow as an ironic comment on other economic activities in the area, or perhaps they just think the place resembles a photo processing lab. Either way, everyone seems to have a good time.
Music (DJs 9pm Fri, Sat; free). Tables outdoors (pavement).

Smithy's Wine Bar

Leeke Street, WC1 (7278 5949). King's Cross tube/rail. **Open** 11am-11pm Mon-Fri. **Food served** noon-2.30pm, 6-9pm Mon-Fri. **Credit** AmEx, MC, V.
Difficult to find but well worth the search, Smithy's is a classy bar that makes the most of its former incarnation as a stables. Whitewashed walls and a cobbled floor have been retained and mixed with dark wood tables and monastic candles to produce a dramatic but welcoming atmosphere. Unsurprisingly, it's the venue for a great many office parties, ensuring that toward the end of most weeks Smithy's is surprisingly rowdy. The wine list samples vineyards from Old World and New, running to 40 bottles with 12 priced by the glass. For beer drinkeres, there's London Pride and Greene King IPA on draught and a short menu of high-quality bar snacks to soak up the chardonnay.
Babies and children admitted (until 6pm). Bar available for hire (Sat). Restaurant. Tables outdoors (pavement).

Waterside Inn

82 York Way, N1 (7713 8613). King's Cross tube/rail. **Open** 11am-11pm Mon-Fri; noon-11pm Sat; noon-10.30pm Sun. **Food served** 11am-9pm Mon-Sat; noon-4.30pm Sun. **Credit** MC, V.
With its canal setting and red brick walls, the outside of the Waterside Inn has all the hallmarks of an industrial heritage theme pub, so it's surprising to walk in and find yourself in an Elizabethan barn, complete with leaded windows and wattle and daub walls. Still, the many after-work customers aren't here to ponder architectural conundrums, they're here to watch sport on the big-screen TV and sample a decent pint of Adnams or London Pride. For winter nights there's a pool table and an extensive pizza menu, but it's best to come during the summer when the large terrace overlooking the Regent's Canal really comes into its own.
Bar available for hire. Games (pool table, fruit machines). Jukebox. Music (jazz 7.30pm Wed). No-smoking tables. Tables outdoors (canalside terrace).

Also in the area...

Davy's of Regent's Place Euston Tower Podium, Regent's Place, NW1 (7387 6622).
O'Neill's 73-7 Euston Road, NW1 (7255 9861).

Knightsbridge

Finding somewhere decent to drink in Knightsbridge is hard work. Its two best bars, the **Townhouse** and the **Swag & Tails**, are all but invisible to passing trade: the entrance to the former is slim and subtle, while the latter is hard to find even with an A-Z. Apart from this uncommon pair, the tale is largely one of swanky cocktail bars or slightly down-at-heel boozers, with shamefully little in between.

Australian

29 Milner Street, SW3 (7589 6027). Sloane Square tube. **Open** noon-11pm Mon-Sat; noon-10.30pm Sun. **Food served** noon-9pm daily. **Credit** AmEx, DC, MC, V.
Vast images of Grace et al look down over one room of this handsome local, reminding drinkers of all nationalities that England once offered genuine cricketing competition to its former colony. Other cricketing greats peer down from the walls, and if the rather bright lighting is unsympathetic to those after a little boozy solitude, it at least allows for careful study of the ephemera. The cricketing theme comes from the time when that bastion of willow-based orthodoxy the MCC was based on the green and pleasant fields behind this pub, and the touring Australians stopped in for an evening of good cheer after losing (yes kids, it really used to happen!) to their hosts. And good cheer is what you'll generally find here, from friendly and very capable staff dispensing immaculate Adnams Bitter and less interesting lagers to a well-heeled but approachable group of regulars. Food is of the chicken in a basket variety, the darts scoreboard a clattery, gloriously byzantine contraption.
Babies and children admitted (until 6pm). Games (darts). No jukebox. Tables outdoors (5, pavement). TV (satellite).

Isola

145 Knightsbridge, SW1 (7838 1055). Knightsbridge tube. **Open** 6pm-midnight Mon-Sat. **Food served** 6-10.45pm Mon-Sat. **Credit** AmEx, MC, V.
A classic case of style over content? That may be a little harsh, not least because the style here is something special. The bar occupies the raised ground floor of this operation (the basement below holds the well-regarded Italian restaurant of the same name), and takes the breath clean away. A long counter is lined with bottles, looking out on a room dotted with funky red seating beneath a ceiling high enough to fly a kite under. There's a strong wine list (we can vouch for the £6.20 bottle of chardonnay), but a stronger cocktail menu: our Miss Knightsbridge, taking in amaretto, strawberries and Grand Marnier, was truly gorgeous, and very good value at £6.50. But while staff can certainly mix a drink and hold a conversation, they can't do much else, or at least can't be bothered to. Service was cheerily incompetent, our cheese plate taking 20 minutes to arrive and the bar staff spending five minutes gassing among themselves in Italian as we gestured helplessly for the bill.
Babies and children admitted (high chairs). Disabled: toilet. Dress: smart casual. No-smoking tables. Specialities: Italian wine.

Mandarin Bar

Mandarin Oriental Hyde Park, 66 Knightsbridge, SW1 (7235 2000). Knightsbridge tube. **Open/food served** 11am-2am Mon-Sat; 11am-10.30pm Sun. **Credit** AmEx, DC, MC, V.
During the week this can be quite a calming spot, but the Saturday we swung by this gleaming hotel bar, the bar was two deep with drinkers, grinning, preening and sipping to

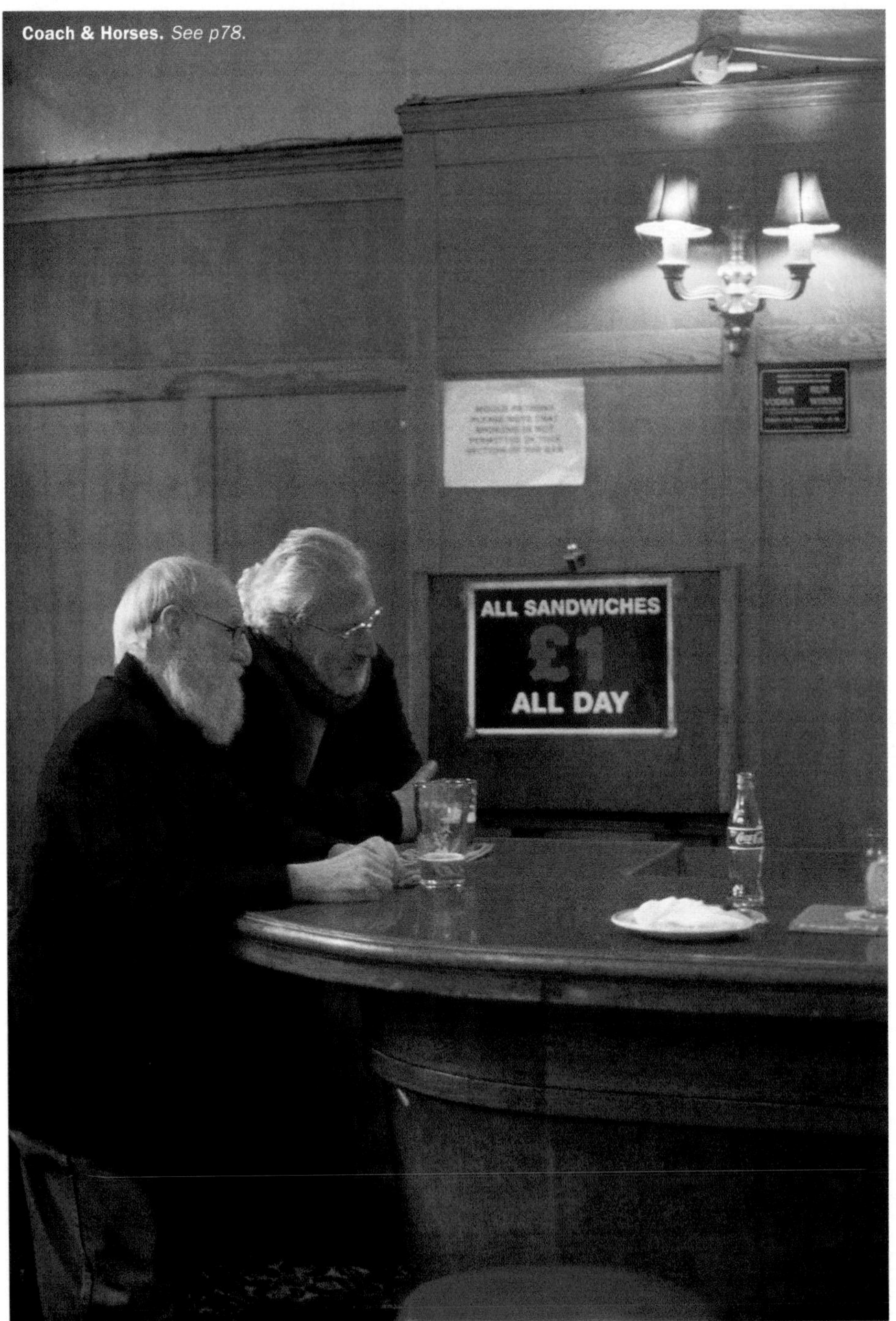

Coach & Horses. *See p78.*

the barely audible accompaniment of a jazz trio. Somewhat fortuitously, we nabbed armchairs and a corner table and looked on at the throng through jaded eyes, but if the drinkers weren't especially stylish, there's no denying the bar itself is quite a looker: daringly colourful yet shiny and sleek, ostentatious in the nicest possible way. The cocktail list is a little less adventurous than the decor, but there's no harm sticking to the classics if you mix them as well as our Godfather (J&B and amaretto). The melon Martini was less perfect, a tad over-sweet, but above-par nonetheless. Added extras: more-ish and colour co-ordinated fancy table snacks, and a vast glass humidor filled with the kind of quality stogies that make emphysema seem a price well worth paying.
Disabled: toilet. Music (jazz 9pm-1am Mon-Sat).

Paxton's Head

153 Knightsbridge, SW1 (7589 6627). Knightsbridge tube. **Open** 11am-11pm Mon-Sat; noon-10.30pm Sun. **Food served** noon-10.30pm Mon-Sat; noon-10pm Sun. **Credit** AmEx, MC, V.

It seems unlikely that the residents of the still-to-be-built Knightsbridge apartments ('The world's most exquisite new residential address') down the street will be using the Paxton's Head as a local. Despite acres of old polished mahogany and etched glass, it's become a dim and rather grubby enterprise. A group of American youths leered and lurched to the numbing thud of dated chart techno, as a fruit machine flickered in some far-off corner and a group of lads looked on pruriently between mulling over that night's Champions' League scores. Only the presence of a few grunting fortysomethings and four real ales on tap (Young's and Pride among them) raised the atmosphere above that of happy hour at a provincial student union, and then not by much.
Babies and children admitted (until 6pm). Function room. Games (fruit machines, games machine, quiz machine). Music (DJ 7pm Fri). TV (big screen, satellite).

Swag & Tails

10-11 Fairholt Street, SW7 (7584 6926/www.swagandtails.com). Knightsbridge tube. **Open** 11am-11pm Mon-Fri. **Food served** noon-3pm, 6-10pm Mon-Fri. **Credit** AmEx, MC, V.

A little intimidating for a pub but not formal enough to be a restaurant, the Swag serves its clientele beautifully. It helps that this is never a pub across which you'd ever stumble: it's hidden away on a teensy street off Brompton Road, in a residential neighbourhood where a couple of million might just net you a garage. The how-the-other-half-live feel extends inside, where Bombardier and wines from an unsurprisingly healthy list are among the drinks served with due decorum on to stripped pine furniture for the benefit of drinkers who earn more in a morning than most do in a year. One look at the lunch menu had both our stomachs and our wallets grumbling; we eventually declined the £12-plus mains and spent a happy lunch hour munching olives, dipping pitta into houmous and trying not to stare at Bernie Ecclestone.
Babies and children admitted (separate area). Bar available for hire. Restaurant. Tables outdoors (conservatory).

Townhouse

31 Beauchamp Place, SW3 (7589 5080/www.labtownhouse.com). Knightsbridge tube. **Open/food served** 4.30pm-midnight Mon; noon-midnight Tue-Sat; noon-11.30pm Sun. **Credit** AmEx, MC, V.

While the skinny three-floor building in which it finds itself is certainly intimate, Townhouse's popularity also means it can get a little uncomfortable. If you haven't booked a table, go during the week, when you can usually bag a seat rather than put up with the discomfiting crush at the bar. Caveat duly outlined, then, we can get on with discussing the good things about Townhouse, of which there are many. The decor, say: clean lines, fingerspot lights and hulking banquettes, surprisingly cool for this part of town. The music is also pitched to perfection through an immaculate sound system: first a mellow, clubby CD, then a DJ who opened his set with Blackstreet's magnificent 'No Diggity'. Staff are happy to help newcomers wade through the modish, approachable 28-page drinks menu, while the drinks themselves, variants on the classics (a rich Townhouse Ice Tea) augmented by newer-fangled concoctions (the tangy, lemony, vanilla vodka-based Bon-Bon) are all mixed immaculately. Recommended.
Babies and children admitted (until 5pm). Dress: smart casual. Games (board games Sun). Music (DJ 8.30pm Wed-Sat; 7.30pm Sun). TV (satellite).

Zuma

5 Raphael Street, SW7 (7584 1010). Knightsbridge tube. **Open/food served** noon-2pm daily; 6-11pm Mon-Sat; 6-10pm Sun. **Credit** AmEx, DC, MC, V.

Its notoriety assured by the beating reputedly taken by a tired and emotional Russell Crowe in the toilets one night, Zuma has settled into its role quite nicely. Exactly what its role is, though, depends entirely on when you go. At lunchtime, it's favoured by power lunchers, talking shop over dishes of excellent Japanese food; the later it gets, the more it fills with SW7's see-and-be-seens. All things considered, its separate bar area is best approached in the early evening, when the ambience is still nicely low-key. Forgoing wine and sake (£3-£5), we hit the cocktails: a Big Appleberry (£8), a mix of cognac and assorted fruits that didn't quite work, and a Sushi Mary (£8.50), a Japanese take on the old bloody classic. Staff were a treat, but on the stroke of eight, a slew of chauffeur-driven Kensingtonians clad in expensive sunglasses and cheap sneers arrived for their dinner appointments, and we made our excuses.
Babies and children admitted (high chairs). Disabled: toilet. Dress: smart casual. Function rooms.

Leicester Square & Piccadilly Circus

Destination of choice for only the most clueless, the pubs and bars here are the nightlife equivalent of a regurgitated Big Mac and fries served up in a bucket. Expect oversized venues peddling piss-poor quality drinks and inedible snacks to hordes of numbskulls prepared to queue all night for the opportunity to ingest this crap then spew it up on the pavement afterwards. With just a couple of shining exceptions, what we list below are the best of the worst that London has to offer. Two words: stay away.

Atlantic Bar & Grill

20 Glasshouse Street, W1 (7734 4888/www.atlanticbarandgrill.com). Piccadilly Circus tube. **Open** noon-3am Mon-Fri; 6pm-3am Sat. **Food served** noon-2.45am Mon-Fri; 6-11.30pm Sat. **Credit** AmEx, DC, MC, V.

With an interior dating back to its original stint as the art deco ballroom of the Regent Palace Hotel, the Atlantic has barely changed course in nearly a century of classy hostelry. Prior to reconversion in the mid-1990s, it had been serving as a disco and it still retains the pillars and mirrors from that era adding a touch of wryly knowing glam. Clientele are expected to make an effort, and have to pass a quick once-over at the roped-off street-level entrance before being allowed

down to casually drape themselves over the furniture. In keeping with the surrounds, the drinks menu leans toward the likes of champagne cocktails, including an Atlantic – a sugar cube soaked in orange bitter with Cointreau, Grand Marnier and Tattinger champers – but there are also choice bottled beers such as Pelforth Brune and Chimay Red. Food takes the form of 'small-bites': smoked haddock, confit duck spring rolls and the like. A restaurant occupies half the downstairs floor space; Dick's bar (after cocktail maestro and original driving force Dick Bradsell) next door is mainly for party hire.
Function room. Music (DJs 10pm-3am Thur-Sat).
Map 2/J7

Blue Posts

28 Rupert Street, W1 (7437 1415). Leicester Square or Piccadilly Circus tube. **Open** 11am-11pm Mon-Sat; noon-10.30pm Sun. **Food served** noon-9pm daily. **Credit** DC, MC, V.
A pilgrim's rest in heaving W1, the Blue Posts modestly occupies a corner of Rupert Street and Court, calmly going about its business while the rest of the known world devours happy hour alcopops. The gimmick-weary are welcomed by an attractive interior, symmetrically constructed from much wood, with barrel tables next to rows of shelving. Books abound, but the brazenly prominent microwave (spag bol, etc) behind the bar quashes any pretension. Best of all, draught beers include Hoegaarden, London Pride and Adnams Bitter, at prices out of step with the over-inflated competition nearby. If ever you're stranded on Leicester Square and a quiet pint calls, you know where to come.
Babies and children admitted (until 6pm). Comedy (8pm Mon, £4-£5). Function room. TVs (big screen).
Map 7/K7

brb

32 Gerrard Street, W1 (7494 1482). Leicester Square or Piccadilly Circus tube. **Open** noon-11pm Mon-Sat; noon-10.30pm Sun. **Food served** noon-10.45pm Mon-Sat; noon-10.15pm Sun. **Happy hour** 5-11pm Mon; 5-7pm Tue-Sun. **Credit** AmEx, MC, V.
Part of the Bar Room Bar chain, the brb sticks out like a sore thumb on the paved Chinatown of Gerrard Street. The 'Carling £1.50 a pint' scrawled in pink lipstick across two of the five mirrors above the bar gives the game away: this is a wolf in chic clothing – chic as in industrial-feel, back chill-out lounge; wolf as in the wolfing down cheap drinks while keeping a look out for an amenable Red Riding Hood to pounce upon. On Thursdays, happy hour is stretched to all night, thus allowing for absurd consumption of very average below-fiver cocktails at a twofer rate. Thankfully, there's reasonable wood-fired pizzas to settle the stomach, although the stern CCTV warning ('You are being watched') written across the length of the urinal should indicate what kind of crowd the management is expecting.
Disabled: toilet. Function rooms. Music (DJs 7.30pm Wed-Sun). **Map 7/K7**

Cork & Bottle

44-6 Cranbourn Street, WC2 (7734 7807). Leicester Square tube. **Open/food served** 11am-11.30pm Mon-Sat; noon-10.30pm Sun. **Credit** AmEx, DC, MC, V.
Scuttle down a scuffed flight of stairs between a sex shop and kebab stall just off Leicester Square, and enter the world of Kiwi Don Hewitson. He's responsible for creating this little subterranean haven, and for the quite fantastic range of wine and champagne it purveys. Ask for 'a glass of wine', and you may as well be at Clapham Junction asking for 'a train, please'. Every inch of this stone-floor cellar for the last three decades has been dedicated to pleasurable intelligent imbibing (the wine complemented by a superb buffet of cheeses and hot mains). Novices can follow the 'Thoughts of Chairman Don', a samizdat wine-zine, which on a recent visit steered us to a glass of Joseph Perrier (with whom Chairman Don 'must confess a long-lasting love affair'). But whatever you choose, it doesn't matter because you can't really go wrong. Just don't plan on doing anything else for the rest of the day.
Babies and children admitted. No-smoking area (daytime).
Map 7/K7

De Hems

11 Macclesfield Street, W1 (7437 2494). Leicester Square tube. **Open/food served** noon-midnight Mon-Sat; noon-10.30pm Sun. **Credit** AmEx, MC, V.
Behind the six big gold letters under the Dutch gables on Macclesfield Street stands more than half a century of tradition, for De Hems has been selling Benelux beers since long before they became fashionable in West End circles (Belgo's, the Lowlander, etc). De Hems – formerly the 'grottoed Macclesfield' – was transformed by a homesick Dutch sailor, whose pub then became a rallying point for the Dutch resistance during the war (cf the **French House** (*see p81*) nearby). Now it's simply a wonderfully friendly wood-interiored pub, decked out in panels and mock Masters, selling draught Oranjeboom, Belgian Belle Vue Kriek and Witte Raaf wheat beer, plus a bunch of interesting Belgians – Palm, Kwak, Trappiste – in bottles. The snacks are the kinds of things – frikandellen, samballetjes – you'd find in street vans all over Holland, and tradition is maintained by the series of framed photos of various Ajax line-ups speckling the walls up to the 'Top Bar', or 't Oude Trefpunt, as it was in the days when you checked your clogs at the door.
Dutch night (6pm 1st, 3rd Thur of mth; free). Function room. Games (fruit machine). No-smoking area. TV (big screen). **Map 7/K6**

Denim

4A Upper St Martin's Lane, WC2 (7497 0376). Leicester Square tube. **Open/food served** 5pm-1.30am Mon-Sat; 5-11.30pm Sun (British summertime only; closed Sun in winter). **Credit** AmEx, DC, MC, V.
Denim's the place for squares. The spirits cabinets behind the bar, the DJ booth, the puffy orange seats, the orange tables (another theme: orange, orange, orange, right down to the goldfish on the long bar counter), the shapes on the glass door-front facing Stringfellow's opposite: all square. Thankfully, the drinks menu is a lot less rigid, with even the odd offbeat beverage, such as Swedish bubblegum shooters. The ground-floor bar's fairly relaxed, and busy with a post-work buzz most week nights, but at weekends when the DJ basement and upstairs restaurant are full to squeezing-point, be prepared for the careful scrutiny of the face police ('Sorry sir, squares only tonight').
Dress: smart casual (Sat). Function rooms. Music (DJs 8.30pm Tue-Sat; £10-£15 after 9pm Fri, Sat). Tables outdoors (pavement). **Map 2/L6**

Dive Bar

48 Gerrard Street, W1 (no phone). Leicester Square tube. **Open** 6.30-11pm Mon; 5.30-11pm Tue-Sat; 7-10.30pm Sun. **No credit cards**.
Down a smoky set of stairs from the King's Head, propping up the end of Gerrard Street, the evergreen Dive Bar is little more than a bare-bones cellar with a long bar serving from a well-below-average selection of drinks, yet it's packed almost every night. Why? Well, it's a mixed, relaxed crowd, happy to mill around two cushioned pillars with a bottle in hand, while a studious DJ delves into bebop and reggae and, well, everything really. Off the main space, two tunnel-like

Bierkellers encourage conspiratorial drunkenness in near darkness. So even though the toilets are as primitive as it gets (bring your own mirror), everyone comes back for more. It's the lack of pretension, the occasional ace tune, the friendly-as-pie bar staff, the overall vibe that everyone is having a fine time, no matter what kind of haircut or shoes they're wearing. Long may it reign.
Music (DJs Fri, Sat). **Map 7/K6**

Down Mexico Way

25 Swallow Street, W1 (7437 9895). Piccadilly Circus tube. **Open** noon-3am Mon-Sat; noon-10.30pm Sun. **Food served** noon-midnight Mon-Sat; noon-10pm Sun. **Happy hour** 5-7pm daily. **Credit** AmEx, DC, MC, V.
Tucked into the elbow of Swallow Street, Down Mexico Way is much better than its rather naff name suggests. A tiled entrance leads to a main reception area; upstairs is the restaurant, to the left, a dark bar occasionally lit with bright sparkles of gold and gleaming decoration. The menu takes itself seriously, with nine brands of tequila in 21 varieties, a similar wealth of rum (including Bajan and Jamaican options), and rarely seen Mexican beers such as Tecate, Bohemia and Rocio. Each of the five house cocktails has a different element – mintini, lemontini, mangotini, etc – after which it is named, and, although we haven't tried it, the south of the border cuisine also looks pretty good. A mainstream disco kicks in at the weekend, while a chill-out lounge overlooking Swallow Street adds a little breathing space.
Babies and children admitted (restaurant only). Dress: smart casual (no trainers). Function room. Music (DJs 9pm Mon-Sat; £7 after 8.30pm Thur-Sat). Salsa lessons (7-8.30pm Mon, Wed; free). Salsa and samba dancers (Mon-Sat evenings; restaurant). **Map 2/J7**

The International

116 St Martin's Lane, WC2 (7655 9810/www.theinternational.co.uk). Leicester Square tube/Charing Cross tube/rail. **Open** noon-2am Mon-Sat; noon-10pm Sun. **Food served** 12.30-3pm, 5-10.30pm daily. **Credit** AmEx, DC, MC, V.
This once classy flagship of City wine merchants **Corney & Barrow** (*see p14*) – facing the National Gallery, don't you know? – has recently undergone a change of ownership, style and, dare we say it, social class. Whereas C&B drew its clientele from the more aspirational end of the market, the International's run by the same people behind Covent Garden party venue the Rock Garden. It's a cut above that though; where the Rock Garden basement hosts rough-arse bands, here it's a champagne bar for hire, and there's a mezzanine restaurant with ambitions beyond dishes of cheesy nachos. The metallic-covered menu offers spirits in three grades (house, premier and deluxe), as well as 20 classic cocktails at £6.95 each, and chilled glasses for the bottled Grolsch, Pilsner Urquell and Bud Anniversary. We're curious to see how this place develops; if nothing else, it's worth a visit for the chance to drink while enjoying Gibb's lovely church opposite.
Disabled: toilet. Function room. **Map 2/K7**

The Interval

14-15 Irving Street, WC2 (7925 1801). Leicester Square tube. **Open** noon-11pm Mon-Sat; noon-10.30pm Sun. **Food served** noon-10pm Mon-Thur, Sun; noon-8pm Fri, Sat. **Credit** AmEx, DC, MC, V.
It may not be the brightest pebble on the beach, but along a neon pizza-and-kebab strewn tentacle of Leicester Square, the pared-down and loungey Interval shines like a lighthouse beacon. Which is why a mixed and far from trendy clientele is here, in a divided dark wood interior, and not meeting in some grotty steakhouse. A simple bar counter dispenses Leffe Blonde, Adnams Bitter and Bass; a kitchen at the end serves customised Brit fare – vegetarian Wellington, venison sausages in chestnut gravy, plus bar snacks of mushy pea fritters and the like. More than 20 of the nearly 30 wines here are available by the glass, and the cocktails combine classic and unconventional. DJs are lined up for Friday and Saturday nights. It's a fair old attempt to cover all bases, from brunch to brazen nights, and sure, it's Boho by numbers, Hoxton, WC2, but surely you wouldn't rather have another smelly soup kitchen, would you?
Babies and children admitted (until 6pm). Disabled: toilet. Function room. Music (DJs 8pm Fri, Sat; free). Tables outdoors. **Map 7/K7**

Jewel

4-6 Glasshouse Street, W1 (7439 4990). Piccadilly Circus tube. **Open/food served** 4pm-1am Mon-Sat; 4-11pm Sun. **Credit** AmEx, DC, MC, V.
An unusual débutante this, which came out at the tail-end of 2002, amid much camera-popping. Just off Piccadilly Circus – you can glimpse a side of it through Jewel's huge curtained windows – this plush four-room operation fits like a long-sleeved glove. The main bar, heavy of chandelier, candle, brick, fireplace and wrought iron, comprises intimate low seating and a main counter dispensing themed cocktails (Ruby, Sapphire, Amber, plus a Jewel in the Crown of Absolut, Midori and Passoa), pâté and cheese platters. Behind an ornate divide, a live rendering of Craig David sets the tone from a small stage in the back room, and is piped into a Moorish-themed room beyond. Upstairs are two further themed rooms, opened for parties and packed at weekends. Jewel treads an awfully thin line between tack and taste, but just about wins out through the sheer enthusiasm of staff and clientele.
Disabled: toilet. Function room. Music (DJs 8pm Wed-Sat; bands 9pm Mon-Sat). **Map 2/J7**

Ku Bar

75 Charing Cross Road, WC2 (7437 4303/www.ku-bar.co.uk). Leicester Square tube. **Open** 1-11pm Mon-Sat; 1-10.30pm Sun. **Happy hour** all day Mon-Thur, Sun; 1-9pm Fri, Sat (cocktails). **No credit cards.**
Shyly hidden under the red-brick arcade opposite the dying second-hand book trade of the Charing Cross Road, the Ku Bar is nothing but bold and brash once you get to know it. Admittedly, 'Fancy a Blow Job for a quid?' is about as indiscreet an icebreaker as it is possible to get, although other choices available but not advertised above the bar include numerous schnapps, sours, tails and shooters. Further investigation of the extensive drinks menu unearths generous until-nine happy hour discounts on two- and four-pint pitchers of many mixes. However, you needn't glug a bucket of Aftershock to appreciate the Ku's sexual orientation. Signed photos of tacky pop and boy bands face a row of cuddly dogs next to the Blow Job proposal, but the space in between is put to friendly interaction between both sexes and several persuasions, beneath a mirror ball spinning out colours from the mosaic by the main door. A mezzanine provides opportunity for more intimate chat.
Jukebox. Tables outdoors (pavement). **Map 7/K6**

On Anon

1 Shaftesbury Avenue, W1 (7287 8008/www.latenightlondon.co.uk). Piccadilly Circus tube. **Open/food served** *Main bar* 5pm-3am Mon-Sat; 5.30-11.30pm Sun. *Study bar* 11am-3am (food: noon-5pm). **Happy hour** 5-7.30pm daily. **Admission** (over-25s only) £3 after 11pm Mon-Wed; £5 after 10pm Thur; £10 after 10pm Fri, Sat. **Credit** AmEx, DC, MC, V.

Salsa!

London's number one Latin venue for live music, dance classes, dance salsa, lambada, merengue, axe and samba.
Our happy hour is daily, come and try the caipririnha.

Opening times
5pm - 2.am, 7 days a week

The best venue in town for private parties.

Phone: 020 7379 3277
Fax: 020 7240 4066
website: http://www.barsalsa.info
email: charingsalsa@sfigroup.co.uk
Nearest ⊖ Tottenham Court Road

Cuba

Cuban bar, restaurant and club. Try our authentic tapas, signature dishes and exotic cocktails, our Mojitos are the best! Fine Cuban cigars & a wide range of tequilas

Opening times
sun 5pm - 10.30pm
mon - thurs 5pm - late
fri/sat 12pm - 2am (free dance classes)

Happy Hour 5pm til 7.30pm daily.
£10 off all Champagne, £5 off wines & half price cocktail jugs

11-13 Kensington High St, London W8 5NP
Phone: 020 7938 4137
Fax: 020 7795 6064
email: cken@sfigroup.co.uk
Nearest ⊖ High Street Kensington

Come to Radius Bar to dance the night away in the club area or smooze in the lounge area!

Radius has it all!

Open Thursday to Saturday, 5pm til 3am. Also available for private hire , Monday - Wednesday.

Stylish and modern bar serving a wide range of cocktails & wines in a luxury environment.
Come along and try our special Cosmopolitan or Mango Daquiri.
Happy hour: 5pm til 7.30pm
£10 off Champagne, £5 off wines.
Restaurant & bar menu available.

5 Goslet Yard • 127-133 Charing Cross Road • London • WC2H 0EH
tel: 020 7437 8595 • fax: 020 7437 0479
email: Radiuscc@sfigroup.co.uk
www.Radiusbar.co.uk
Nearest ⊖ Tottenham Court Road

**Visit our cocktail bar, restaurant and night club to try our famous Multiple Orgasms, fruit daquiris and authentic Latin dishes.
Free dance classes and Latin Dj's**

**490 Fulham Road, SW6 5NH, Tel: 020 7381 5005
email: Fulhamhavana@sfigroup.co.uk
www.fiestahavana.com
Nearest ⊖ Fulham Broadway**

AND

**17 Hanover Square
Mayfair
London W1S 1HU
tel: 020 7629 2552
fax: 020 7491 2821
email: hvhsq@sfigroup.co.uk
website: www.fiestahavana.com
Nearest ⊖ Oxford Circus**

Both bars open Monday to Saturday from 5pm until late. Sunday 5pm til 12.30am

TEX MEX BAR & RESTAURANT

TRY OUR FAMOUS MARGARITAS & WIDE RANGE OF BEERS. A GREAT PLACE TO HANG OUT AFTER WORK, PRE-THEATRE OR LATE INTO THE NIGHT.

COME AND PARTY, WHATEVER THE OCCASION!

FULL RESTAURANT MENU, TRY OUR SIZZLING FAJITAS, GREAT NACHOS, HOMEMADE BURGERS OR RIBS SMOTHERED IN A HICKORY BBQ SAUCE - TO DIE FOR.

DJ'S TIL LATE ON MOST NIGHTS

FAMOUS HAPPY HOUR 2 FOR 1 ON BEERS & OFFERS ON WINES & COCKTAILS

8 ARGYLL STREET (UNDER THE PALLADIUM)
OXFORD CIRCUS
LONDON
TEL: 020 7734 5776 • FAX: 020 7437 5140
EMAIL: OXFORDCIRCUSBFB@SFIGROUP.CO.UK
WWW.BFTB.COM
NEAREST ⊖ OXFORD CIRCUS

Leeds	Peterborough	London
tel: 0113 244 2666	tel: 01733 352412	tel: 020 7734 5776

Somehow prominent and anonymous at the same time – yes, it's that one with the green awning off Piccadilly – On Anon is a huge, bland pleasure palace for undiscerning fun-seekers. Consisting of a street-level cafe, a main bar divided into two main areas – Study and Lounge – and several offshoots it suits all types and all pockets. The Study is a parody of a pub, the Lounge a scuffed-chair parody of a cocktail bar. A tapas menu stretches the genre beyond recognition (chunky chips, baked ciabatta pizza, etc). The place is all about happy hours and after-hours, when you'll have to forget about those trainers and that sports top. And if you like this, see Oxygen on Irving Street, Zoo on Bear Street, or Tiger Tiger on Haymarket, all within gobbing distance of Leicester Square, all part of the Urbium plc 'concept bars in key locations' business plan: 26 of them to date and set to double in number by 2005. Lucky us.
Babies and children admitted (Study bar only, until 5pm) Disabled: toilet. Dress: smart casual. Function rooms. Music (DJs, 9pm Tue-Sat). **Map 7/K7**

Saint

8 Great Newport Street, WC2 (7240 1551). Leicester Square tube. **Open/food served** 6pm-2am Tue-Thur; 5pm-3am Fri; 7.30pm-3am Sat. **Admission** £5 after 9pm Thur; £10 Fri, Sat. **Credit** AmEx, MC, V.
Back in its day, soon after opening in 1996, this unassuming little staircase just off the Charing Cross Road would be graced by gossips and gossipees, slinking down through the bright purple neon haze to a vast apron of diner alcoves and dance space. The throng may have changed, but the space remains the same. And a convivial one it is too: a capacious high-ceilinged room with a main bar counter facing a row of padded green banquettes and a screened-off restaurant area. Bottled beers and other standards are available but far better are the imaginative cocktails, including a Saint Martini of basil-infused Absolut and Saint shots such as raspberry rush with Stoli – plenty of good stuff. Food is similarly excellent. Shamefully wasted on an undiscerning clientele, Saint can still turn a modest evening into a fantastically trashy affair.
Disabled: toilet. Dress: smart casual (Fri, Sat). Music (DJs 9pm Thur-Sat). **Map 7/K6**

Salisbury

90 St Martin's Lane, WC2 (7836 5863). Leicester Square tube. **Open/food served** 11am-11pm Mon-Sat; noon-10.30pm Sun. **Credit** AmEx, DC, MC, V.
Possibly the most perfectly preserved piece of Victorian hostelry in London, the Salisbury is a temple of gorgeously carved mahogany and etched glass, decked out with nouveau statuettes and curved banquettes. Its theatre-friendly location made it an actors' favourite (it pops up in the 1961 Dirk Bogarde movie *Victim*) but in more recent times the thesps have been supplanted by fickle tourists. The pub isn't shy of pandering to passing trade – it sells them branded T-shirts and plies them with alcopops, piled up in neat pyramids on the back bar. To be fair, there is also Young's and Directors on draught, and an attempt to marry traditional sellers (fish and chips, ham and eggs) with modern mores (herb-roasted salmon, roasted red pepper lasagne) on the menu. Avoid the back room and try for a seat in the snug behind the main bar, a cosy little space warmed by a fire in winter.
Games (quiz machine). Tables outdoors (pavement). **Map 2/L7**

Sports Cafe

80 Haymarket, SW1 (7839 8300/www.thesportscafe.com). Piccadilly Circus tube. **Open/food served** noon-3am Mon, Tue, Fri, Sat; noon-10.30pm Sun. **Happy hour** 3-7pm Mon-Fri. **Admission** £3 after 11pm Mon-Thur; £5 after 11pm Fri, Sat. **Credit** AmEx, MC, V.
When will this city of half-a-dozen top football teams, world famous rugby, cricket and tennis arenas and Olympic bids, f'Chrissakes, get itself a proper sports bar? While the well-established Sports Cafe isn't terrible, it is the kind of generic US-style establishment you'll find in the centre of Warsaw or an Abu Dhabi mall, with NFL helmets over the bar, a graffitied streetball court and framed signed shirts over the walls. Oh yes, and TV screens, of course, the biggest being spread across the baying auditorium in the middle, set between a small back bar and the mobbed main bar. Unsurprisingly, this place is most popular for American sporting occasions such as the Super Bowl. Expect high-priced lagers, an atmosphere imbued with the stench of ketchup, and serving girls in short skirts and tight tops. Cocktail nights with free vodka jellos and an 'exclusive' pool lounge try to break the mould, but really, we must be able to do better than this.
Babies and children admitted (until 6pm Mon-Fri; children's menu, play areas). Disabled: toilet. Dress: smart casual. Function room. Games (basketball court, fruit machines, pool tables, table football). Music (DJs 10pm Mon-Sat). TVs (big screens, digital, satellite). **Map 2/K7**

Waxy O'Connors

14-16 Rupert Street, W1 (7287 0255). Leicester Square or Piccadilly Circus tube. **Open** noon-11pm Mon-Fri; 11am-11pm Sat; noon-10.30pm Sun. **Food served** *Bar* noon-5.30pm daily. *Restaurant* 5.30-10.30pm daily. **Credit** AmEx, DC, MC, V.
Somehow, because it is so completely over the top, Waxy's deserves our respect. Many an owner of such a prominent Irish hostelry would have taken the easy route and thrown in a bar counter the size of the *Titanic*, with a kitchen to match. Not here. An innocuous front bar decked out like an old apothecary leads you into a phantasmagorical maze of Irish Gothic and pseudo-religion (even what look like a pulpit and a confessional), divided into many bars, saloons and snugs, on at least three-and-a-half levels (it's very easy to get lost and lose count; it's even easier to mislocate your friends on the way back from the toilet) decorated with any number of sculptures and framed examples of Gaelic literary heritage. The end result, of course, is the same bland meat market as any Rosie O'Grady's or the like, but credit due for architectural effort. Credit also to a superb bar staff. Could you cope with Friday nights here?
Function rooms. Music (band 8.30pm Mon, Tue; free). TV (big screen, satellite). **Map 7/K7**

West Central

29-30 Lisle Street, WC2 (7479 7980). Leicester Square tube. **Open** *Main bar* 2-11pm Mon-Sat; 2-10.30pm Sun. *Theatre bar* 5-11pm Mon-Sat. *Basement bar* 10.30pm-3am Fri, Sat. **Admission** (basement only) from £3. **Credit** MC, V.
One of the brashest gay bars in all the West End, the WC (just a few strides south from homo-central of Old Compton Street) flashes its trade with huge tinted windows, vast fanned rainbow flags, the works. Inside, a video jukebox plays boy band cuts on at least four screens, while a relaxed clientele takes advantage of a handy bar space – long proppable bar, benches, tables, alcoves and still room to dance – over cocktails and Smirnoff Ices. Masses of silly promo nights ensure wild abandon. The upstairs 'Theatre bar' offers less full-on surroundings where you can top up on Dutch courage before descending to the clubby basement space.
Function room (theatre bar). Games (fruit machines, quiz machines). Music (DJs 8pm Mon, Wed-Sun; £1 Mon, free Wed-Sun main bar; £2-£5 in club). TV (satellite).
Map 7/K7

Also in the area...

All Bar One 48 Leicester Square, WC2 (7747 9921); 289-93 Regent Street, W1 (7467 9901).
Hogshead 5 Lisle Street, WC2 (7437 3335).
Moon Under Water (JD Wetherspoon) 28 Leicester Square, WC2 (7839 2837).
O'Neill's 34-7 Wardour Street, WC2 (7479 7941).
Slug & Lettuce 14 Upper St Martin's Lane, WC2 (7379 4880).
Walkabout 136 Shaftesbury Avenue, WC2 (7255 8630).

Marylebone

For the purposes of this guide, our definition of Marylebone stretches from Regent Street all the way west to Edgware Road, and from Oxford Street north to Euston Road. It's a big area and there's lots of good stuff in there. Much of it centres on Marylebone High Street, of late boosted by a Conran shop, classy delis and other eateries drawn by an influx of A-list money. Smart bars **Dusk** and **Low Life** are recent arrivals, and there are surely more to come. Side streets shelter many fine old boozers that have managed to maintain much individuality thanks to loyal local patronage.

Barley Mow

8 Dorset Street, W1 (7935 7318). Baker Street tube. **Open** 11am-11pm Mon-Sat. **Food served** 11.30am-3pm Mon-Sat. **Credit** AmEx, DC, MC, V.

Although it dates back to the days when Marylebone was a village, the Barley Mow (est 1791) retains scant rural appeal – hardly surprising given that what once was a neighbouring lane is now thunderously trafficked Baker Street. At first glance the pub seems barely notable (except for its three real ales) but it possesses some intriguing bits of social history. Set in the bar are ancient inscribed brass price lists and there's an old brass tap that used to dispense gin (bring your own bottle). Best of all are the two small enclosed snob booths, each with a latched door, a pair of facing benches and its own private stretch of bar counter. These were intended to maintain the upstairs/downstairs divide between tippling gentry and ale-swilling servants. Now it's first come first seated. *Vive la égalité*, and a packet of salt and vinegar crisps, please.
Babies and children admitted (until 8pm). Games (fruit machine, quiz machine). Tables outdoors (pavement). TV (satellite).

Beehive

7 Homer Street, W1 (7262 6581). Edgware Road or Marylebone tube. **Open** noon-11pm Mon-Sat; noon-10.30pm Sun. **Food served** noon-2.30pm Mon-Fri. **Credit** MC, V.

Admittedly, our take on this tiny back street bolthole is coloured by the party we walked in on. Everybody obviously knew everybody else and, cast as gatecrashers, we were about to leave until somebody beckoned us to stay. We did, and what a smart decision that was. A boisterous and farcical approximation of the *Weakest Link* provided spectator sport. Someone bought us drinks (London Pride and Young's Bitter are on draught). A well-known soap star (and Beehive regular) collected empties. There was a round on the house. And a raffle. By the time we left at (Mr Plod stop reading here) well gone midnight last orders had still to be called. Not that this goes on every night, but from past editions of this guide (2002: '[regulars] will make you feel more than welcome'; 2001: 'the good-natured regulars seem to relish newcomers') conviviality seems something of a permanent fixture. Could this be the friendliest pub in central London?
Babies and children admitted. Tables outdoors (pavement). TV.

Carpenters Arms

12 Seymour Place, W2 (7723 1050). Marble Arch tube. **Open** 11am-11pm Mon-Sat; noon-10.30pm Sun. **Credit** AmEx, MC, V.

'The Carp', as it abbreviates itself, is one of a trio of tradesmen's pubs established during the building of the Portman estate; the other two being the Bricklayers Arms on New Quebec Street and the **Mason's Arms** (*see p62*). Pleasingly, judging by the overalls and paint-splattered pants on display, the clientele is still largely made up of hands-on grafters. On a Monday night this place was heaving while neighbouring pubs around were looking a little anorexic, a testament to its freehouse status – private landlords tend to be a little more motivated than brewery transplants. So it's cash-prize darts on a Tuesday (there's a dedicated darts alley at the back of the pub), comedy classics on TV on Sunday and top sporting fixtures at other times. Being a freehouse also means there's a constantly changing line-up of real ales with names such as Spittlelicker and Tubby's Foreskin. Note the raised platform under the leather seating by the window: it used to be a stage back in the days when the Carpenters was a gay pub and renowned for trade of a different sort.
Babies and children admitted (until 9pm). Function room. Games (darts, fruit machines). Tables outdoors (pavement). TV (satellite).

Chapel

48 Chapel Street, NW1 (7402 9220). Edgware Road tube. **Open** noon-11pm Mon-Sat; noon-10.30pm Sun. **Food served** noon-2.30pm, 7-10pm daily. **Credit** AmEx, DC, MC, V.

Pubs next to stations are usually ragged old affairs, functional, unpolished stop offs where people await late-arriving acquaintances, sup swiftly and hastily depart. Not so the Chapel, an almost trendy little affair for this part (any part) of the Edgware Road that sits shimmering on its corner location near the District line branch of Edgware Road tube. A table stacked with newspapers greets newcomers: take one, grab a drink (nothing special, though the wines are decent in number) and peel right towards the lounging section of the pub, all spongy sofas, low tables and a general air of taking-care-of-comfort. The remaining space is given over to more austere seating with large wooden tables crowded by large groups of casually dressed, loudly chattering nine-to-fivers, chowing down on adventurous but excellent gastropub offerings from the open kitchen. A shady little garden gives a fine view of a nearby car park.
Babies and children admitted. Function room. Tables outdoors (pavement).

Dover Castle

43 Weymouth Mews, W1 (7580 4412). Oxford Circus or Regent's Park tube. **Open** 11.30am-11pm Mon-Fri; noon-11pm Sat. **Food served** noon-3pm, 6-9pm Mon-Fri. **Credit** MC, V.

The local for the nearby RIBA HQ on Portland Place, the Dover Castle is unobtrusive (slotted into a half-hidden mews), unpretentious, welcoming and deeply traditional – pretty much everything your average contemporary architect seems opposed to, then. It's got one darkly carpeted front-of-house bar with a couple of appealing snugs filling out the back. Mayonnaise and ketchup on the tables attest to busy lunchtimes, but quite what the wilting daffodils signify we've

no idea– other than a lack of water. Boozers were all suited on our visit, men and women both, running up tabs on tomato juices and cigars (men and women both). Being a Sam Smith's house the bar counter options are all Sam Smith's beers – so that'll be another tomato juice, please. OK, unfair: some folk like them, and at under two quid a pint, we could probably get used to them too.
Babies and children admitted (lunchtime only; separate room). Function room. Games (quiz machine). TV.

Duke of Wellington

94A Crawford Street, W1 (7224 9435). Baker Street or Marylebone tube. **Open** 11am-11pm Mon-Sat; noon-10.30pm Sun. **Food served** noon-3pm, 6-9pm Mon-Fri; noon-4pm Sun. **Credit** MC, V.
Windows full of junky antiques, which on closer inspection turn out to have a brass button and plume military theming, make for a beguiling exterior. It's not quite matched by the inside, which is not old enough to be interesting, only plain old-fashioned (rusty red carpet, nicotine ceiling, padded banquettes, polished brasswork). The Napoleonic militaria theme continues with framed badges and medals, cardboard cut-out soldiery, prints, figurines and signposts to Salamanca and Waterloo, although it's too restrained to be truly eccentric. But it's not a bad pub: it is cosy and it has that lived-in-by-the-locals feel. Some of those locals speak Arabic, which may seem odd in such a quaintly English setting, but then Crawford Street has long been a welcoming home to a handful of small Middle Eastern businesses. The beer's also fine, with Adnams Bitter, Bass and London Pride on draught.
Function room. Tables outdoors (pavement). TV.

Dusk

79 Marylebone High Street, W1 (7486 5746). Baker Street tube. **Open** 10am-11pm Mon-Sat; 10am-10.30pm Sun. **Food served** 10am-10.30pm daily. **Credit** AmEx, MC, V.
Last time we passed by this was an old corner boozer called the Rising Sun (with Danny Baker and friends sat in residence). Now it's had a makeover and been reborn as Marylebone High Street's first designer bar, Dusk (Rising Sun to setting sun; clever, eh?). And nice it is too. The pub clutter has been stripped away, along with the lovely ornamental sun that used to hang over the door, drawing attention to attractive structural details like the beautiful arched windows; there's a new polished wood floor, brushed aluminium bar, sleek showpiece furniture and ambient lighting. Drinks are designer too: two pricey white beers (Affligem and the Dutch Wieckse Witte) plus Amstel on draught, plenty of wine (New World and Old) by the glass and bottle, and a select array of cocktails. Food gets prominent billing, with breakfast served from 10am, and a very decent mixed menu (snacks at £5-£6, mains such as confit of duck and a Dusk burger from around £6.50) featured from midday onwards. Other plusses include racked newspapers, table service and super friendly staff.
Disabled: toilet. Music (DJs 7pm Fri). Tables outdoors (pavement).

Golden Eagle

59 Marylebone Lane, W1 (7935 3228). Bond Street tube. **Open** 11am-11pm Mon-Sat, noon-10.30pm Sun. **Food served** noon-2.30pm Mon-Fri. **No credit cards**.
The archetypal London pub, the Golden Eagle, tucked down Marylebone Lane, has a lovely curlicued Victorian frontage wrapped around a single modest bar room with blue velvet banquettes and an almost matching patterned carpet. First thoughts might include the word 'scruffy' but on closer inspection everything's clean and neat, if just a touch eccentric. It's a comfortable haunt, favoured by the local community and occasionally graced by the odd celeb – a photo of John Cleese pint in hand hangs by the fruit machine. The beer's good with a line-up of four real ales, including on our recent visit St Austell's Tribute, a Cornish brew we've never before seen this far east. Prime nights are Thursday and Friday when the dustcovers come off the piano for a right old sing-song. The same pianist's been doing this gig for 12 years so he should know all the notes by now.
Music (pianist 8.30pm Thur, Fri). TV.

Low Life

34A Paddington Street, W1 (7935 1272). Baker Street tube. **Open** noon-11pm Mon-Fri. **Food served** 12-9.30pm Mon-Fri. **Credit** DC, MC, V.
Not the choicest of locations for a DJ bar you'd have thought, but with the offices of Head Candy, Kiss FM and Warner records all local, not to mention the University of Westminster, there's no shortage of party people around. They're met at ground level by two big flat screen TVs, which is misleading given that these are probably the single most expensive parts of the whole operation. The rest is shoestring stuff – student union chic – but it's cheerful and it works. It's also a great little space, partially open to above (so not too smoky) and with three tiny side chambers to fit maybe four, although in one case, not if they all try to stand at once. There is a cocktail list (all £6) but our bar babe seemed so deliriously dance happy we didn't want to trouble her with anything more than flipping the lid on a bottled beer. Food is fish finger sandwiches, pasta and cheese bake and burgers, etc, priced £3.50-£6.
Music (open decks 8.30pm Mon; DJs 8.30pm Tue, Thur, Fri; live acts 8.30pm Wed).

Marylebone Bar & Kitchen

74-6 York Street, W1 (7262 1513). Marylebone tube/rail. **Open** 10am-11pm Mon-Fri; 11am-11pm Sat; 11am-10.30pm Sun. **Food served** noon-10pm daily. **Credit** MC, V.
This rakish, pseudo-scruffy establishment rapidly became the most popular pub in the area when it first flung open its doors a couple of years ago – although competition is not

Critics' choice
pubs on location

Anchor Bankside (p201)
Cruise sups here after successfully performing *Mission Impossible*.

City Barge (p233)
Help! Scenes of madcap Beatlery were shot at this riverside Chiswick pub.

French House (p81)
Setting for Francis Bacon biopic *Love Is The Devil*.

Newman Arms (p44)
Well known to creepy voyeurs for its role in *Peeping Tom*.

Shaw's Booksellers (p120)
Visited by Helena Bonham-Carter in *Wings of A Dove*.

Rosie's. *See p66.*

what you'd call intense in this quiet patch south of the Marylebone Road, just west of Baker Street. It's the wilful eccentricity that attracts, an otherwise straightforward dark-ish square slab of a room given a dab of character by the bric-a-brac furnishings: wicker hanging chairs, bad paintings, a vintage table Space Invader. There's London Pride, Old Speckled Hen and Hoegaarden to be drunk, while the kitchen prides itself on seafood (half-a-dozen rock oysters, £8), although every time we visit the quality seems to have declined in inverse proportion to the price. That hasn't stopped the inoffensively fashionable and besuited clientele from packing it out every evening, though.
Tables outdoors (pavement). TV.

Mason's Arms

51 Upper Berkeley Street, W1 (7723 2131). Marble Arch tube. **Open** 11am-11pm Mon-Sat; noon-10.30pm Sun. **Credit** MC, V.
While the nearby **Carpenters Arms** (*see above*) remains the proles' pub, the Masons has its sights on a more select crowd. All wood-panelled of wall and creaky of floorboard, it's well suited to cosy assignations, particularly the curious little wooden 'roomette', just big enough for man, woman and dog (a floppy-eared red setter roams the pub conveniently for any couple short of a hound). Look out for other fine details too, such as the moulded cornice inset with ventilation grills. The beers are Badger Best, Sussex, Tanglefoot and HB (Hofbräuhaus); ie good. If you ask the amiable antipodean manager nicely, he may guide you down through the private door and show you the storerooms, which used to be dungeons housing condemned prisoners due to be hanged at Tyburn, London's major place of execution (roughly situated where Marble Arch is today).
Babies and children admitted (separate area). Function room. Games (fruit machine). Music (occasional blues musicians). Tables outdoors (pavement). TV.

O'Conor Don

88 Marylebone Lane, W1 (7935 9311/www.oconordon.com). Bond Street tube. **Open** noon-11pm Mon-Fri. **Food served** noon-10pm Mon-Fri. **Credit** AmEx, MC, V.
An Irish pub for folks who can't stand Irish pubs, the O'Conor Don is a handsome place with a minimum of blarney. The beer range is limited to the big black G and sibling products and there's the predictable decor of old tin and enamel ads, but that's about as far as the themeing goes. Otherwise, the interior is all dark scuffed wood (floors and furniture) with chest-high counters to maximise floor space. The absence of soft surfaces or private corners means it's somewhere better suited to post-work camaraderie rather than quiet pints, but no shenanigans – this is a classy place with table service and a lengthy wine list. There's an appealing bar menu of the obvious (filled baguettes, beef and Guinness casserole) supplemented by more wide-ranging fare (fusilli with roasted veg). Down in the basement, 'Moy Mell' is a more intimate space of brick and wood – although its opening hours are limited – while upstairs is the 'Ard Ri' dining room serving 'Modern European food with Irish overtones'. Grand.
Babies and children admitted (until 7pm). Function room. TV.

William Wallace

33 Aybrook Street, W1 (7487 4937/www.ionabar.com). Baker Street or Bond Street tube. **Open** 11am-11pm Mon-Sat; noon-10.30pm Sun. **Food served** noon-3pm, 6-9pm Mon-Fri; noon-8pm Sat, Sun. **Credit** AmEx, DC, MC, V.

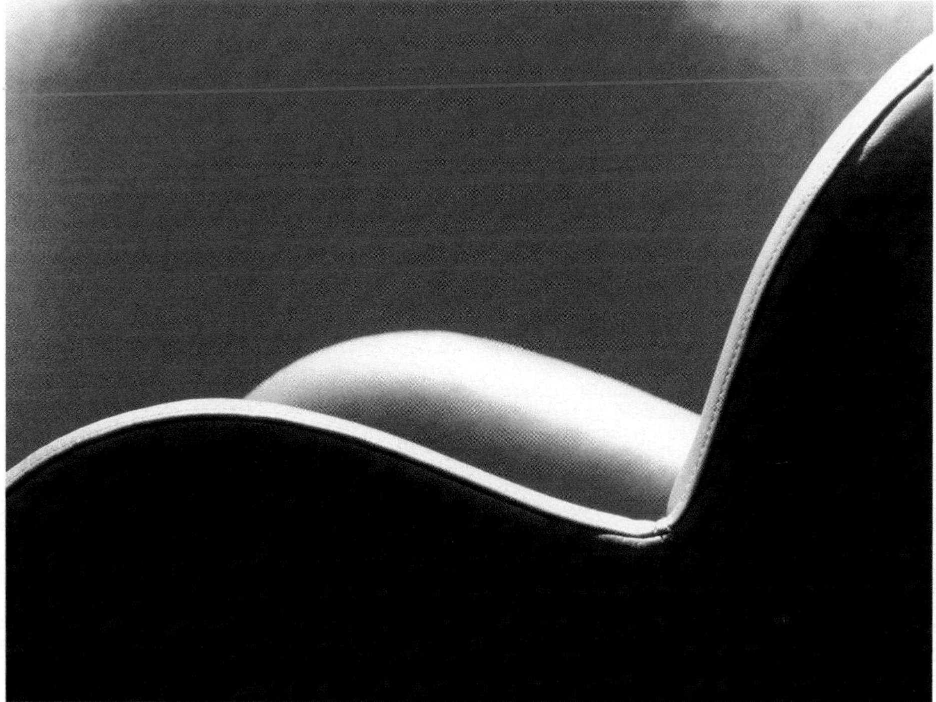

One block back from the High Street overlooking a dour plaza of scrubland – earmarked for a new school building but instead a makeshift car park of long standing – the William Wallace is a gritty boozing bar deep-soaked in raw Scottish spirit. It's got the flags, the signed sports kits, the international footie programmes, the *Braveheart* poster. What it's not got is any tartan or bagpipes or pictures of those wee little Scottie dogs. It's a twee-free zone. What paraphernalia there is hang like trophies in a clubhouse. Hard won. Displayed with pride. It's a pub with a regular crowd who acknowledge each other by name as they come in. There are notices up for pool competitions and darts, and weekly karaoke nights. Also unapologetically Scottish is the poor choice of beer: no fewer than five lagers but just one ale (Calder's). Chase with a shot of fine malt for flavour.
Function room. Games (fruit machine, pinball machines, pool table). Music (DJs 8pm Fri). Tables outdoors (pavement). TV (satellite).

Windsor Castle

29 Crawford Place, W1 (7723 4371). Edgware Road tube. **Open** 11am-11pm Mon-Sat; noon-10.30pm Sun. **Food served** noon-3pm, 6-10pm Mon-Fri. **Credit** MC, V.
This place takes patriotism to extremes. Every inch of available space is dedicated to the royal family and other British institutions: Winston Churchill, Vera Lynn, George Best (?). Photos of Princess Di adorn the mirrors, and famous battles are acted out by toy soldiers. Even the upholstery of the sofas is reminiscent of stately home tapestry. Our table was reserved for the Handlebar Club, whose members meet on the first Friday of every month; their facial foliage is lovingly documented in photographs on the walls. Appropriately enough too, the Small Faces were playing on the sound system on our last visit ('Oh wouldn't it be nice to get on wiv me neighbours'). Perfectly complementing the wilful eccentricity is an extensive menu of finely prepared Thai food (and why not?). Bass and Adnams Bitter are on draught. You don't have to be mad to drink here, but it helps
Babies and children admitted. Tables outdoors (pavement).

Also in the area...

All Bar One 5-6 Picton Place, W1 (7487 0161).
Apollo (Firkin Pub Co) 28 Paddington Street, W1 (7935 0556).
Basement 92 (Davy's) 92 Wigmore Street, W1 (7224 0170).
Dock Blida (Davy's) 50-54 Blandford Street, W1 (7486 3590).
Lees Bag (Davy's) 4 Great Portland Street, W1 (7636 5287).
Marylebone Tup 93 Marylebone High Street, W1 (7935 4373).
Metropolitan (JD Wetherspoon) Baker Street station, Marylebone Road, NW1 (7486 3489).
O'Neill's 4 Conway Street, W1 (7307 9941).

Mayfair

While neighbouring Soho has a bar on every corner, Mayfair's drinking scene is spread a little thinner through its imposingly wealthy streets. But London's poshest neighbourhood isn't as quiet as it may first appear: after all, people live and work here and, regardless of the bulk in their wallets, they still need somewhere to drink. Many of Mayfair's nicest bars, and certainly its most luxurious, are tied to hotels, but wander off the main haunts and you'll find a handful of locals – the **Red Lion** and the **Guinea** chief among them – as lovely as any in central London.

American Bar

Connaught Hotel, 16 Carlos Place, W1 (7499 7070/ www.savoygroup.com). Bond Street or Green Park tube. **Open** 5.30-11pm Mon-Sat. **Credit** AmEx, MC, V.

Gordon Ramsay may have got to its restaurant, but the American Bar at this venerable old hotel is still stuck firmly in the old school: oak panelling, floral sofas, deafening air-conditioning and a young barman of indeterminate accent whose photograph appears in the *Illustrated Oxford English Dictionary* under 'rictus grin'. In fairness, he's a helpful gent, suggesting some suitable cocktails to our party when required to cover for the lack of menu ('being revised,' he offered cheerily). A Bellini was just fine, though a Godfather was somehow a little flimsy, perhaps mixed for too long with ice. Nice olives, though. Grow old, dress up and smoke a cigar the size of a bargepole if you want to fit in.

Disabled: toilet. Dress: smart casual. Function rooms.

The Audley

41-3 Mount Street, W1 (7499 1843). Green Park tube. **Open** 11am-11pm Mon-Sat; noon-10.30pm Sun. **Food served** 11am-9.30pm Mon-Sat; noon-9pm Sun. **Credit** AmEx, DC, MC, V.

What a grand pub this is, a palatial red-brick and terracotta pile constructed in 1889 in high Victorian style, complete with corner turret. And how nice it is to see it being maintained so carefully. You can tell how much attention is being lavished on a building by looking down at the floor and up at the ceiling. The former? Well, the carpet's not great, but at least it's there. And the latter? A glorious shade of deep red, the perfect complement to the vast oval banquettes that line the walls and the dark, heavy furniture scattered around the room. So far so good, yet the Audley should be more appealing than it is. Part of it's the lighting: too bright for a bar with so much gravitas. The mixed signals don't help: pubs this grand should need planning permission to erect large 'Australia Day' party posters of the sort that sat nastily on the bar when we visited. But the real problem with the Audley is that it wants it both ways: to be a local's local and a tourist's souvenir snapshot. Happily, no music; sadly, food is more expensive than it should be.

Babies and children admitted (daytime). Function room. Games (fruit machines). Tables outdoors (pavement). TV.

Cecconi's

5A Burlington Gardens, W1 (7434 1500/ www.cecconis.co.uk). Green Park tube. **Open** 10am-11pm Mon-Sat; 7-10.30pm Sun. **Food served** noon-3pm, 6.30-11pm Mon-Fri; noon-3pm, 7-11pm Sat; 7-10pm Sun. **Credit** AmEx, DC, MC, V.

Quite an achievement, we thought, for someone to look down their nose at you when they're four inches shorter and you're perched on a high stool. But the snotty French barman at this front-of-house designer cocktail bar to the chic, celeb-favoured restaurant managed to make us feel entirely unwelcome while never being anything other than perfectly polite. Very Parisian. Even less welcome was the slapdash fashion in which our cocktails were prepared: when he tasted the Mint Julep before serving and found it, presumably, too weak, another measure of whisky was hurriedly chucked over the top. At these prices (£8.20 a pop), you expect considerably better. Recommended only for thick-skinned rubberneckers (the celebrity quotient is exceptionally high) who are happy to play second-rate voyeur to the pampered and preening diners behind.

Babies and children admitted (high chairs). Disabled: toilet. Restaurant.

Claridge's Bar

Claridge's Hotel, 49 Brook Street, W1 (7629 8860). Bond Street tube. **Open** noon-1am Mon-Sat; 4pm-midnight Sun. **Food served** noon-11pm daily. **Credit** AmEx, DC, MC, V.

Save for the dodgy music, an unlikely mess of Billy Joel and low-key club chic, this is a textbook example of how to update a classic without scaring the horses. The Claridge's revolution continues apace with this fine revamp, sympathetic to the traditions of the bar that once stood here but tilted more towards drinkers who are counting the decades rather than the years until they can collect their free bus pass. Our cocktails were immaculate – a sweet-but-not-sickly forest fruit Mojito, the cognac-and-cream excess of a Pacific Brûlée and a simple, happily tangy Kentucky Highroller – though at £10.50 each, so they should have been. Tips: dress to impress, leave room in your stomach for the fine complimentary table munchies (there's a bigger menu of snacks), and bring a bag of safety flares with which to attract the attention of the easily distracted waiting staff.

Disabled: toilet. Function rooms. Restaurant.

Coach & Horses

5 Bruton Street, W1 (7629 4123). Bond Street or Green Park tube. **Open** 11am-11pm Mon-Fri; 11am-8pm Sat. **Food served** 11am-9.30pm Mon-Fri; 11.30am-6pm Sat. **Credit** AmEx, DC, MC, V.

In fairness, the Coach & Horses isn't the only pub in Mayfair that plays up to its potential tourist market by boosting an olde worlde image and cranking the prices of its (mediocre) food. But it's surely the only one to do so when none of its punters are tourists. This homely (mock?) Tudor boozer draws almost exclusively locals: chiefly workers, and many of those expressing a preference for braces over belts, but with a fair few residents tossed into the mix. Get here at 6pm and you'll be left out in the cold such is its popularity as a post-work boozer in an area short on such options. But later in the evening, when the commuters have commuted and the tables are available, it's a fine spot to while away a pint or two. Beers on our visit included Old Speckled Hen and Bombardier, nicely poured to an unwanted soundtrack of Average White Band.

Babies and children admitted (restaurant). Function room. Games (fruit machines, quiz machines). Restaurant. TV.

Dorchester Bar

Dorchester Hotel, 53 Park Lane, W1 (7629 8888/ www.dorchesterhotel.com). Hyde Park Corner tube. **Open** 11am-11pm Mon-Sat; noon-10.30pm Sun. **Food served** noon-11.45pm Mon-Sat; noon-10.30pm Sun. **Credit** AmEx, DC, MC, V.

On either side of us sit couples, each a wealthy, corpulent foreign gentleman with a younger, slimmer ladyfriend in tow, the former wearing a sour expression as the latter glugs on prohibitively priced wine. Once you've tired of this scene, the bar at this stately yet ostentatious institution doesn't offer much in the way of people-watching, so it's a good job the bar itself merits further examination. The fittings here aren't all original – the hotel, which opened in 1931, had grown shabby prior to an epic two-year refurbishment programme just over a decade ago – but they're every bit as opulent as in the hotel's glory days. The banquettes are plush, the carpet is thick, the piano is covered in tiny mirrors; it's halfway

between sophisticated and kitsch, but only the blue neon underlighting on the steps strikes a truly bum note. The cocktails, while pricey (£10 or so), are among the finest in town. Even better, waiters treat everyone like royalty, a feeling you'll carry with you as you bounce out down the swanky deco lobby, through the revolving door and into the bracing breeze of Park Lane.
Disabled: toilet. Dress: smart casual. Function rooms. Music (pianist Mon, Tue, Sun; jazz 7pm-midnight Wed-Sat). Restaurant.

Ye Grapes

16 Shepherd Market, W1 (no phone). Green Park or Hyde Park Corner tube. **Open** 11am-11pm Mon-Sat; noon-10.30pm Sun. **Credit** (over £15 only) MC, V.
A lovely pub, this. Trouble is, everyone in the area knows it, and given the immediate competition – the garish, touristy King's Arms and, of all things for supposedly select Mayfair, another O'Neill's – it's no surprise this corner boozer does a roaring business. We've rarely found the Grapes anything other than packed; the bitterly chilly Tuesday we popped in, reaching the bar was the height of our ambition, a seat being consigned to the realms of fantasy. Although the original partitions that once divided the interior into numerous intimate spaces are gone, several fireplaces, plenty of polished woodwork and a scuffed bare-board floor remain to imbue the interior with a fine well-seasoned, lived-in feel. Mounted animal heads, fish (stuffed not swimming), huntsmen's rifles, a long-case clock and flying ducks add character of a distinctly masculine sort. Punters are a mix of browsing tourists, diners en route to one of the Market's bargain-basement eateries, and the odd gent grabbing a stiffener before an appointment at one of the shabby flats from which the local hookers conduct their dispiriting business – a Shepherd Market tradition that long predates even the venerable Grapes (1882).
Babies and children admitted (until 2.30pm). Function room. Games (fruit machine).

Guinea

30 Bruton Place, W1 (7409 1728/www.youngs.co.uk). Bond Street or Green Park tube. **Open** 11am-11pm Mon-Fri; 6.30-11pm Sat. **Food served** 12.30-2.30pm Mon-Fri; **Credit** AmEx, DC, MC, V.
Granted, this is London's poshest neighbourhood. But while we weren't expecting the gents' at this centuries-old alehouse to be festooned with typically uncouth pub graffiti, it still came as quite a surprise to find a handwritten notme from Henry Mancini (along with a few scrawled bars of 'Moon River') and the autographs of, among others, Ted Danson and Kelsey Grammer. Sam and Frasier present and correct, we scoured the bar for Norm, but found only Mayfair moneymen, ties and belts loosened to suit the hour (10pm), their braying voices setting our teeth on edge. In fairness, the Guinea's usually quieter than this. Service is a treat, and the beers – it's a Young's pub – top notch. The small bar fronts a restaurant famed chiefly for its award-winning pies, though we couldn't help but wonder, in a whispered football chant, whether the portly, bibulous bugger perched at the bar had already eaten them all.
Function room. No piped music or jukebox. Restaurant. Tables outdoors (pavement).

The Loop

19 Dering Street, W1 (7493 1003/www.theloopbar.co.uk). Oxford Circus tube. **Open/food served** noon-3am Mon-Sat. **Admission** £3 after 10pm Mon-Wed; £5 after 10pm Thur; £10 after 10pm Fri, Sat. **Happy hour** 5-8pm Mon-Wed; 5-7pm Thur-Sat. **Credit** AmEx, MC, V.
The blokes – and they are not gents, or guys, or men, or even chaps, but very definitely blokes – mill around, broad of shoulder and as loud of voice as they are strong of opinion. Those not clad in Top Man sale stock are wearing Burton suits, fat-knotted footballers' ties, loosened with all the hardened insouciance of a third-former waiting for the bus home after double maths. The girls – and they are girls, except to the blokes, to whom they are birds – are secretaries, or temps, or shopgirls, fresh from the changing rooms at Miss Selfridge and travelling in packs of three or more and never venturing to the toilet alone. The girls come here to meet the blokes, the blokes to meet the birds, a ritual carried out nightly in this labyrinthine bar-club to a soundtrack of perfectly dreadful chart music and fuelled by bottled beers (Michelob the most exotic) and hopeless cocktails (we left two thirds of our vile Jackal at the bar). Soon, too soon, their children will be undergoing exactly the same ritual. Still, if it keeps them off the streets and all that.
Dress: smart casual. Music (DJs 9pm-3am Thur-Sat). Restaurant.

Met Bar

Metropolitan Hotel, 18-19 Old Park Lane, W1 (7447 1000/www.metropolitan.co.uk). Hyde Park Corner tube. **Open/food served** 11am-6pm daily (members-only from 6pm). **Credit** AmEx, DC, MC, V.
You won't be able to get in, of course. The entrance rules – hotel guests and members only after 6pm – are enforced by foreboding if thoroughly personable door staff, and only waived for those who can prove they've appeared in the scandal pages of *Heat* at some point during the last two months. Still, its fame and reputation mean we have to include it, although the former is fading (the Met Bar's *so* over, darling) and the latter was never particularly special, unless you find the idea of C-list trolley dollies falling out of their tops and into the arms of some D-list ex-pop star at the first sign of a flashbulb in any way an appealing prospect. Before 6pm? There can't be a bleaker bar in London: at least after dark it has atmosphere, whatever that atmosphere might be. But during the day, there's nothing here. Just a room, a little ragged and hungover from the previous night, counting the hours until it has to grit its teeth and do it all over again.
Disabled: toilet. Music (DJs 10pm Mon-Sat).

Mô Tea Rooms

23 Heddon Street, W1 (7734 3999). Oxford Circus or Piccadilly Circus tube. **Open** 11am-11pm Mon-Wed; noon-midnight Thur-Sat. **Food served** 11am-9.50pm Mon-Sat. **Credit** AmEx, DC, MC, V.
Sister venture to next door's Momo restaurant, this glitzy, over stuffed place has an interior that's more bazaar than bar – appropriate, given that most of what you see (bauble lights, lanterns and chandeliers, kaftans and assorted other clothing, jewellery and graphic art) is for sale at prices bordering on the reasonable. It's a cafe during the day, and a great lunch venue; the Mid East-flavoured sandwiches are excellent, best accompanied with one of six types of mint tea, no less, all showily poured from a great height. It works equally well as an exotic chill-out setting for evening cocktails from a short list (try the Marrakech O' Marrakech of Bacardi, fresh mint, sugar, lemon juice and Apanage champagne, £6.50) and bottled beers (including Casablanca, 'the legendary beer from the legendary city'). A soundtrack of tabla-rattling, oud-strumming raï and an aromatic fug of sheesha smoke (£9 a pop) add further atmosphere. It gets very busy, so come early or be prepared to have to hang around outside while waiting for a table to come free.
Babies and children admitted. Function area available for hire. Restaurant. Tables outdoors (pavement).

Polo Bar

Westbury Hotel, New Bond Street, W1 (7629 7755/ www.westbury-london.co.uk). Green Park or Oxford Circus tube. **Open/food served** 11am-11pm daily. **Credit** AmEx, DC, MC, V.

A corner of Mayfair that is forever England; assuming, that is, you're not English, which most drinkers at the Polo Bar certainly aren't. The 'Polo' of the name refers not to the clothing label, the mint or the car, but to the toffs' sport of choice, and the theme runs throughout: mallet-shaped doorhandles and horsey portraits are among the equine ephemera on display. Yet, hampered by its streetside location and vast glass windows, the Polo Bar never charms: you're always aware you're in a hotel bar, and not in a good way. Meanwhile, the atmosphere-stifling lights put paid to any intimacy that might have been on offer, while also highlighting the hideous chintziness of the soft furnishings. Credit where it's due: our cocktails, a Martini and a Perfect Manhattan, were both terrific, and service struck just the right cocktail-bar balance between deferential and informal.

Babies and children admitted (restaurant). Dress: smart casual. Function rooms. Music (pianist 6-10pm Mon-Fri). Restaurant. TV (satellite).

Punch Bowl

41 Farm Street, W1 (7493 6841). Green Park tube. **Open** 11am-11pm Mon-Fri; noon-6pm Sat. **Food served** 11am-4pm Mon-Fri; noon-5pm Sat. **Credit** DC, MC, V.

The fun is as much in getting to the Punch Bowl as drinking within it. Farm Street is a pleasant enough little road (a five-bed house here was recently on the market for a piffling £2.95 million), but the property opposite this amiable pub is a true peach: Farm House, a marvellously maintained and impossibly desirable ancient wonder gloriously incongruous among its more stately neighbours. The Punch Bowl, sensibly, doesn't try to compete aesthetically: this is just a simple little local, easy on the eye and frequented by a cheery mix of locals and their working-class acquaintances. A recent refurbishment has tarted up the formerly careworn space, sapping it of some of its individuality; we prefer it how it used to be, a little rougher around the edges. These days, it's just another Scottish & Newcastle pub, albeit with a smarter clientele than most. Nice street, though.

Babies and children admitted (until 7pm). Function room. TV (satellite).

Red Lion

1 Waverton Street, W1 (7499 1307). Green Park tube. **Open** 11.30am-11pm Mon-Fri; 6-11pm Sat; noon-3pm, 6-10.30pm Sun. **Food served** noon-2.30pm, 6-9.30pm Mon-Fri, Sun; 6-9.30pm Sat. **Credit** AmEx, MC, V.

No music, no fruit machines, no televisions: just the convivial chink of glasses and the burble of voices as background to an evening – or decadent afternoon – spent downing drinks by the side of the hearth. The surprise, of course, is that this almost bucolic boozer is to be found in the middle of central London, hidden in the crook of an elbow up one of Mayfair's lesser explored streets (not many tourists here), just by a charming baby petrol station. Settle in with a pint – there were four ales on our last visit, including London Pride and Charles Wells Bombardier – and, well, that's about it. There are no distractions: just a handsome, cosy, graciously aged room, a delicious atmosphere, and serviceable pub grub too (sausage and mash is a fiver, not bad for this part of town). Simple but brilliant.

Babies and children admitted. Function room. No piped music or jukebox. Restaurant. Tables outdoors (pavement).

Rosie's

50A Berkeley Street, W1 (7629 0808/www.cafe grandprix.com). Green Park tube. **Open** noon-2.30pm, 5pm-1am Mon-Fri; 7pm-1am Sat. **Food served** noon-2.30pm, 6-10.30pm Mon-Fri; 6-10.30pm Sat. **Credit** AmEx, DC, MC, V.

Deeply strange. On the ground floor is Cafe Grand Prix, a gaudy palace of tack whose trade nonetheless roars about as loudly as the engines of the cars it celebrates. But two floors below – there's a restaurant in between – lies Rosie's, a highly salubrious and approachable cocktail bar. Very handsome it is too, at least below waist level with its gorgeously curvaceous chairs and banquettes. One end of the room is bedecked with a shimmering Klimt-like mural but, sadly, elsewhere the walls are over-crammed with photographs of Formula 1, while the incessant flicker of a TV showing nothing in particular with the sound turned down (piped music was generic dinner-party clubby stuff) hardly aided the atmosphere – of which there was little on our recent visits. The cocktail list is short and, literally, sweet (lots of drinks made with sugar). We noted that the party of women to our left stuck to G&Ts and the dozen burly and besuited blokes three tables away all wielded lagery pints.

Babies and children admitted (dining area). Function room. TV (satellite).

Running Horse

50 Davies Street, W1 (7493 1275). Bond Street tube. **Open** noon-11pm Mon-Sat. **Food served** noon-3pm, 6-9.30pm Mon-Fri; 12.30-4pm Sat. **Credit** MC, V.

Pleasant surprise, this, not to mention easily missed and much needed. Opened in late 2001, the Running Horse is that rare beast: a simple, stylish pub within a shopping bag or two's toss from the business end of Oxford Street, a stretch not exactly over endowed with worthwhile haunts. It makes the most of its corner location, big picture windows drawing the eye into its handsome interior. There's something slightly institutional about the dark-wood panelling that covers the walls, recalling perhaps a library at a minor public school, and the theme continues on the menu, with several varieties of sausage and mash and even sticky toffee pudding. Smaller appetites will be sated by a pleasing array of snacks (pistachios, chips and the like), washed down with a pint of London Pride or a bottle of wine (there are 40 from which to choose, ten of which are available by the glass). Most agreeable.

Babies and children admitted (dining only). Function room. Tables outdoors (pavement).

Scott's Restaurant & Bar

20 Mount Street, W1 (7629 5248). Bond Street or Green Park tube. **Open** noon-11pm Mon-Fri; 5-11pm Sat. **Food served** noon-11pm Mon-Sat. **Credit** AmEx, DC, MC, V.

It was long overdue for a refit, we figured, but we weren't expecting it to be quite so dramatic. After all, to mess with a Mayfair institution like Scott's… it's just not cricket, is it? Regardless, the new Scott's, now operated by Home House, is an improvement on the old version. The central staircase has gone, as – mercifully – has the piano. The decor's homelier now, and more stylish, though if you're lucky or saucy enough to get one of the mysteriously curtained-off booths to one side, you won't notice either the frieze of illustrated flappers lining the back of the bar or the ugly, thoroughly pointless widescreen TV at one end of it. Cocktails were pricey but very good, the pick being a Margarita made with Porfirio tequila. The traditionalists were conspicuous by their absence – as, to be honest, were more or less any other drinkers on this chilly January evening – but we think it's an improvement.

Function room. Restaurant. TV (satellite).

Shepherd's Tavern

50 Hertford Street, W1 (7499 3017). Green Park or Hyde Park Corner tube. **Open** 11am-11pm Mon-Sat; noon-10.30pm Sun. **Food served** 11am-10pm Mon-Sat; noon-9.30pm Sun. **Credit** AmEx, DC, MC, V.

There's a smashing pub here just dying to get out. It's just a pity the management won't let it. Pluses? The location, just near Shepherd Market (when you find **Ye Grapes**, *see p65*, full, as it always is, this is the nearest decent alternative); the food, pricey but perfectly edible pub grub; well-kept ales, the Scottish & Newcastle staples supplemented on our visit by St Austell's Tribute and Pride of the River, a rarely seen Brakspear brew. And yet, and yet, and yet… Every time we swing by here, the music seems to be a half-dozen decibels louder than it was the previous visit, and that much more ill-chosen (gaudy techno on a recent visit), while the incessant, strobing blink from the fruit machine warrants a printed warning to epileptics. The welcome is warm enough, but it's a hard pub to love.

Babies and children admitted (dining area only). Games (fruit machines). Jukebox. Restaurant (available for hire). Tables outdoors (pavement). TV (satellite).

Trader Vic's

Hilton London, 22 Park Lane, W1 (7493 8000). Hyde Park Corner tube. **Open** 5pm-1am Mon-Thur; 5pm-3am Fri, Sat; 5-10.30pm Sun. **Food served** noon-12.30am Mon-Fri; 6pm-12.30am Sat; 6-10.30pm Sun. **Credit** AmEx, DC, MC, V.

Theme bars come and, preferably, go in this never-bored city. That Trader Vic's has held firm through the winds of fashion is testament to the inspired nuttiness of its inventor, Victor Bergeron, who opened his first bar in Oakland 70 years ago and saw his preposterous ethos – essentially, that what the world needs now is a roomful of Polynesian kitsch and cocktails served in fishbowls – take hold around the planet after World War II. This really is a ludicrous place. We ordered a Samoan Fog Cutter, a shamelessly sickly concoction served in *an actual vase*, and a Mai Tai, a Bergeron invention and here mixed very nicely, and watched the frizz-haired house musician run through 'The Girl From Ipanema' and Nino Rota's 'Love Theme' from *Romeo & Juliet*, better known as the background music to Simon Bates' 'Our Tune' slot. Our jaws dropped slowly floorwards – not easy when combined with a big silly grin. Inspired by the South Seas, made in California and a certified London classic.

Babies and children admitted (restaurant). Disabled: toilet. Dress: smart casual. Function room. Music (Latin musicians 10.30pm Mon-Sat). Restaurant.

Windmill

6-8 Mill Street, W1 (7491 8050). Oxford Circus tube. **Open** 11am-11pm Mon-Fri; noon-4pm Sat. **Food served** noon-3pm, 6-9pm Mon-Fri; noon-4pm Sat. **Credit** AmEx, DC, MC, V.

While it's only a stone's throw from the hideous maelstrom of caramelised nut sellers and plastic bag-wielding tourists of Oxford Circus, a hidden location means the Windmill tends to miss out on/escape the heady throngs of daytripping shoppers. Not that they'd like it in here, of course: there's no music, the fruit machine rarely seems to be turned on, and the emphasis is not on Bacardi Breezers but good honest beer. The Windmill is a Young's pub, see, which guarantees at least three ales on tap; the seasonal brew on our most recent visit was the dark and eminently recommendable Winter Warmer. Clientele tends towards knackered staff from local shops. While not unpleasant, the pub's not much to look at and over-lit (a fault common to many Young's houses). But the food's hearty, traditional and a cut above the usual central London pub fare, as you'd expect from a founder member of the Campaign for Real Food. Plain and simple, but then sometimes, ready salted's really just what you fancy.

Function room. Games (fruit machine). No-smoking area (lower bar). No piped music or jukebox. Restaurant.

Windows

Hilton Hotel, Park Lane, W1 (7493 8000). Green Park or Hyde Park Corner tube. **Open/food served** noon-2am, Mon-Thur; noon-3am Fri; 5.30pm-3am Sat; noon-10pm Sun. **Credit** AmEx, DC, MC, V.

Windows reopened in January after a refurbishment programme timed to coincide with the hotel's 40th birthday. Totally needless, of course, for if you're coming here to look at the soft furnishings and check out the tables, the point has been completely lost on you (the clue's in the name). Location, location, location, goes the mantra, though it's not so much Windows' street address – steps from Hyde Park Corner – as its vertical elevation that inspires the alcoholic flâneur to pay it a visit. We're 28 floors above London here, and Windows' windows offer views more panoramic than from any other bar in the capital. It's best at sunset, a hazy wash of pinks and blues and greys if you pick your day carefully, but there's really never a bad time to come up here and fall back in love with the city. Cocktails are fine, music's schlocky, and there's even a £455-a-shot cognac. Like any of that really matters, of course. Bring binoculars.

Disabled: toilet. Dress: smart casual. Music (pianist 6.30pm-2am Mon-Sat). No-smoking tables.

Zeta Bar

35 Hertford Street, W1 (7208 4067/www.zeta-bar.com). Green Park or Hyde Park Corner tube. **Open** 4pm-1am Mon, Tue; 4pm-3am Wed-Fri; 5pm-3am Sat. **Admission** £5 after 11pm Mon-Sat. **Food served** 7pm-1am Mon-Sat. **Credit** AmEx, DC, MC, V.

To say that Zeta Bar is about as modish as this part of town gets is perhaps to damn it with faint praise, but it's also a fair précis. With lighting low and clubbable music pitched at a palatable volume, the decor in the long room is on the approachable side of stylish; it's just a pity the waiting staff are merely on the stylish side of approachable, all preen and little polish. At around £6-£7 each, cocktails are fairly priced (again, with the qualifier 'for this part of town'): our White Russian was over-creamed, but the hazelnut Martini we drained at speed was a success. Drinkers are the usual Hyde Park/Mayfair Eurotrash, slugging back daddy's fortune while pretending they're important. It's a handy alternative when you get turned away from the nearby **Met Bar** (*see p65*), although quite what you were doing trying to get into the Met Bar is another matter entirely.

Bar area available for hire. Dress: smart casual. Music (DJs 9pm Mon-Sat). TV (satellite).

Also in the area...

Balls Brothers 34 Brook Street, W1 (7499 4567).
Chopper Lump (Davy's) 10C Hanover Square, W1 (7409 3201).
Hogshead in St James's 11-16 Dering Street, W1 (7629 0531).
Mulligans of Mayfair (Balls Brothers) 13-14 Cork Street, W1 (7409 1370).
O'Neill's 7 Shepherd Street, W1 (7408 9281).
Pitcher & Piano 1 Dover Street, W1 (7495 8704); 10 Pollen Street, W1 (7629 9581).
Shoeless Joe's 33 Dover Street, W1 (7499 2689).
Slug & Lettuce 19 Hanover Street, W1 (7499 0077).

Electric Brasserie

Notting Hill, Ladbroke Grove & Westbourne Grove

Believe the hype (but not the Hugh Grant movie), Notting Hill is a fantastic place to drink. If you ignore the plethora of slapdash gastro chains and glut of mockney bars, you'll find some real rubies in the dust. There are great old boozers (notably the **Portobello Gold** and **Portobello Star**), a handful of cutting-edge, class-act bars (none better than the recently opened **Lonsdale**), plus more than a fair share of seriously good gastropubs (the **Cow**, **Golborne House**, **Grand Union** and **Westbourne**), where it's not necessary to dine; you can just settle for a pint and salivate.

Beach Blanket Babylon

45 Ledbury Road, W11 (7229 2907). Notting Hill Gate tube. **Open** noon-11pm Mon-Sat; noon-10.30pm Sun. **Food served** noon-3.30pm, 7-10.30pm daily. **Credit** MC, V.

Back in the days when bigger was better, this was the joint to come and show off the size of your mobile phone and stock market portfolio. Tony Weller's ecclesiastical take on Gaudí, the artificial topiary and the theatrical lighting were synonymous with the height of '90s metropolitan élan. Times have changed, but not the BBB. It still draws a crowd of Thatcher's children, empty-headed Eurocrats, bleach-toothed Americans, divorcees and rich tourists who think they've cracked it. It's hard to tell whether the staff are camping it up in response to their showy surroundings or are just plain rude: either way they're tiresome. If you do succeed in snagging some attention, the champagne cocktails are worth a try, but long drinks hover around nightclub prices and the wine list is as ordinary as it is expensive. The Mediterranean food served beyond the labial doorway and over the drawbridge is consistently inconsistent. Best to stick to the bottled beers at the bar and just ogle the restaurant from afar.

Babies and children admitted (daytime). Function rooms. Music (cabaret 9pm Thur). Tables outdoors (garden).
Map 10/A6

Bed

310 Portobello Road, W11 (8969 4500). Ladbroke Grove tube. **Open** 5-11pm Mon-Thur; noon-11pm Fri, Sat; noon-10.30pm Sun. **Food served** noon-9pm Sat, Sun. **Credit** AmEx, MC, V.

Aromatic joss sticks, tea lights and a relaxed trancey vibe make this Moroccan-themed bar in a big old converted pub at the Golborne Road end of Portobello Road a popular hang-out for the scruffily cool crowd. Eyes adjusted to the half light will make out big square tables surrounded by copious amounts of squishy sofas and kilim-covered benches. It's the perfect joint for lounging with mates, something that the management recognises and caters to with drinks by the pitcher. Solo drinkers hang by the bar, checking out each others' purchases from the nearby street markets. The range of drinks is unlikely to impress, but put quantity before quality and you're up for a good lie in. The formula obviously works because it's now been replicated at Bed Smithfield (57-9 Charterhouse, EC1).

Babies and children admitted (until 7pm). Games (board games). Music (DJs 7.30pm Mon-Fri, Sun; 4pm Sat).
Map 10/Az5

Cow

89 Westbourne Park Road, W2 (7221 5400). Royal Oak or Westbourne Park tube. **Open** noon-11pm Mon-Sat; noon-10.30pm Sun. **Food served** noon-4pm, 6-11pm Mon-Sat; noon-4pm, 6.30-10pm Sun. **Credit** MC, V.

According to owner Tom Conran, this is not, repeat *not* an Irish pub – although the shamrocks and Guinness ads sure

suggest otherwise. Actually, we believe him – the food and drink served up here are far too good for a London Irish pub. In fact, this is one of the best foodie pubs in town. Patronised by a late-thirtysomething crowd, in numbers that defy its dimensions (it's tiny), the Cow serves up a quality array of crustaceans and fish with a smile (that would be the service, not the fish), and prices are pretty reasonable for such top notch nosh too. Best of all is the booze: a good set of Irish and other whiskeys, real ales (one of the best pints of Pride in London, plus ESB), Hoegaarden, Guinness, of course, and high-quality house and other wines. There's also a wallet-slimming array of champagnes – this being Notting Hill, people are indeed rich and ostentatious enough to blow money on champagne in a pub.
Babies and children admitted. Function room. Tables outdoors (pavement). TV (satellite). **Map 10/A5**

Elbow Room

103 Westbourne Grove, W2 (7221 5211/www.elbow-room.co.uk). Bayswater or Notting Hill Gate tube. **Open/food served** noon-11pm Mon-Sat; noon-10.30pm Sun. **Happy hour** 5-8pm daily. **Credit** MC, V.
The mothership of the pool-hall chain that's stealthily taking over London with a winning formula of beer and pool and decent DJs, minus the leering, predatory and generally intimidating men that are usually a fixture of the baize. *The Hustler* this most certainly ain't. A bar serving all necessary drinks welcomes you at the front of the space; seven full-size American pool tables lie beyond. While most plump for a pint of lager or spirits, there are also six wines available by the glass and even a choice of champagnes. There's decent fast food (nachos, satays, sandwiches and burgers from £3.95) ferried to the tables along with fresh sets of drinks by friendly and efficient waitresses. Tables cost a reasonable £6 an hour before 6pm Monday to Friday (before 5pm at weekends) and £10 per hour at other times. At night you're restricted to one hour at a time, so everyone can have a good go. Which is fair enough. For the chain's other venues: *See chapters* **Hoxton & Shoreditch**, **Islington** and **Swiss Cottage**.
Games (pool tables). Music (DJs, twice monthly; free). **Map 10/B6**

Eclipse

186 Kensington Park Road, W11 (7792 2063/www.eclipse-ventures.com). Labroke Grove tube. **Open** 5pm-midnight Mon-Fri; 1pm-midnight Sat; 1-10.30pm Sun. **Food served** 5pm-midnight Mon-Sat; 1-10.30pm Sun. **Credit** AmEx, MC, V.
Formerly allied to Cafe Med next door, this is the most recent addition to Kensington Park Road's stellar parade of upmarket bars and restaurants. It also signals another notch on the bedpost for the ever expanding Eclipse family (now five strong in the capital). Despite its diminutive size and new boy status, this plucky bar punches well above its weight with a remorseless sound system orchestrated by a wide-eyed DJ, who, on a recent visit, was accompanied by a bartender beating a bongo to the whooping delight of those crowded by the bar (seating is at a premium). The drinks list is serious and expensive, as are the clientele – men sport perma-tans, slicked back hair and polo shirts, gals opt for hiked-up skirts and flashy jewellery. It's an unashamedly good-time bar for those with the money to enjoy it.
Tables outdoors (pavement). **Map 10/Az5**

Electric Brasserie

191 Portobello Road, W11 (7908 9696/www.the-electric.co.uk). Ladbroke Grove tube. **Open** 11am-11pm Mon-Sat; noon-10.30pm Sun. **Food served** 8am-11pm Mon-Fri; noon-5pm, 6-11pm Sat; noon-5pm, 6-9.45pm Sun. **Credit** AmEx, MC, V.
For too long neglected and empty, the Electric Cinema, England's first purpose-built movie house, was reborn in spring 2002 as a trendy members' club, with a smart bar-

brasserie and restaurant attached for the hoi polloi. Mercifully free of filmic theming, the long, thin brasserie proceeds past a stretch of bar counter that could have been ripped out of an old-style diner, and past a noisy open kitchen to sweep into a den-style 70-cover restaurant, where artfully angled mirrors ensure that everybody gets to gawp at everyone else. The cocktail list contains all the favourites, expertly produced by showy barmen who lap up the praise from giggling singletons. During the day, tables also sprawl out on to the street, where you can dig into a hearty breakfast or lunch or just pour over the papers with a coffee. In the evenings the bar fills with style-conscious, cashmere-clad Hillbillies, who can be overheard telling tales of recent sexual indiscretions in the advertising industry and extolling the expensive virtues of organic milk-fed lamb.
Babies and children admitted. Disabled: toilet. No-smoking tables. Tables outdoors (terrace). **Map 10/Az5**

Golborne House

36 Golborne Road, W10 (8960 6260). Westbourne Park tube. **Open** noon-11pm Mon-Sat; noon-10.30pm Sun. **Food served** 12.30-3.30pm, 6.30-10.15pm Mon-Thur; 12.30-3.30pm, 6.30-10.45pm Fri, Sat; 12.30-3.30pm, 6.30-9.45pm Sun. **Credit** MC, V.
Golborne Road is one of those cusp places, grittily urban but with a tide of new money lapping at its concrete foundations. In the Golborne it has its perfect drinking venue. It's a gastropub for the achingly cool. Plain walls and simple wooden furnishings are a bit All Bar One, but there are plenty of attractive details, like the little Trellick Tower motifs on the windows (through which there are clear views of the real thing beyond). Diners are corralled into one arm of the vast L-shaped open-plan space, divided from the studiedly hip drinking crowd by a barely noticeable partition. The food is excellent, and typically includes dishes like butternut squash risotto (£9.25) or a ham hock with cabbage and mash (£10.50). Bar fare is less inspiring; expect draught London Pride and Hoegaarden, backed by a cosmopolitan wine list and some well-mixed cocktails. For what you get, it doesn't come cheap, but considering that this is the local for folk who've bought into Goldfinger's ex-council block at 250k a pop, value for money isn't always the uppermost consideration.
Babies and children admitted (until 9pm). Function room. Tables outdoors (pavement). TV. **Map 10/Az4**

Grand Union

45 Woodfield Road, W9 (7286 1886). Westbourne Park tube. **Open** noon-11pm Mon-Sat; noon-10.30pm Sun. **Food served** noon-3pm, 7-10pm Mon-Sat; 12.30-4pm, 7-10pm Sun. **Credit** MC, V.
It's been three years since the Grand Union was taken over by neighbouring club Woodys. Despite scaring away the custom from the bus depot opposite, the resulting makeover continues to do good business and the place has bedded down into a much-loved local. It serves great food without the attitude that often comes when sticky carpets are replaced by hard-wood floors and crisps are switched for olives. Unusually for such ventures, the booze is taken as seriously as the food, and handpumps dispensing Adnams Bitter and Broadside complement the lagers and decent house wine. Sadly, the formerly excellent jukebox has been a little temperamental of late and has had its plug pulled; expect something jazzy/loungey on the house sound system instead. If the weather's decent, head downstairs for a table on the terrace beside the canal; by far the best place to wash down a pukka pie and beer for less than a tenner.
Babies and children admitted. Function room. Games (board games). Tables outdoors (canalside terrace). TV. **Map 10/A4**

Harry's Social Club

30 Alexander Street, W2 (7229 4043). Royal Oak tube. **Open** 6-11pm Mon-Sat. **Food served** 7.30-10pm Mon-Sat. **Credit** AmEx, DC, MC, V.
Secreted away down what at first glance appears to be a residential stucco-fronted terrace, this former pub was given a respray and turned into a local members' bar. However, as with so many members' bars, dwindling numbers (hurrah) have forced a rethink on the old exclusivity angle. So Harry's now shares its exotic interior (a cross between a brothel, opium den and a barmy aunt's boudoir) with the masses. Dimly lit tables are filled with locals playing backgammon, fashionable trust funders lolling on cushions, exhausted by the pretence of abject poverty, while drabs of dressy media muppets hover around the zinc. The drinks are fancy, well-crafted cocktails, which are not too badly priced at around the £6 mark, plus a short but sophisticated wine list catering to grown-up tastes. The music is as eclectic as the cramped surroundings – dancing is only for the very brave/drunk. There's also an upstairs restaurant dishing up enticing seasonal fare at a price.
Function room. Music (DJs 9pm Thur-Sat). Tables outdoors (pavement). **Map 10/B5**

Lonsdale

44-8 Lonsdale Road, W11 (7228 1517). Notting Hill Gate or Westbourne Park tube. **Open** noon-midnight Mon-Sat; noon-11.30pm Sun. **Food served** 12.30-3.30pm, 6.30-11.30pm daily. **Credit** MC, V.
The interior is an absolute knockout: walls are studded with rows of aged-bronze hemispheres like some oversized Paracetamol foil packaging; floor and bar are equally hard and sleek, and glossily black. Deeper in, the space flattens out and surfaces soften with lush red carpeting and patterned fake fur upholstery under a luminous sculpted oval skylight. But for such a 'designed' place the mood is improbably relaxed. Menus come in the form of hefty red folders with dividers labelled food, cocktails, wine and spirits. The selections aren't as extensive as at some other places, but what's there is enticing. Cocktails (£7-£8) – masterminded, as at all the best bars, by the ubiquitous Dick Bradsell – are mostly a bit girly but, my god, those we tried were good. The food is also outstanding and far better than we've come to expect from bar snacks. Even from pricey bar snacks. There's also a smaller upstairs bar where walls and ceiling are covered in shiny brushed steel bobbles.
Babies and children admitted (until 6pm). Disabled: toilet. Function room. **Map 10/A6**

Mall Tavern

71-3 Palace Gardens Terrace, W8 (7727 3805). Notting Hill Gate tube. **Open** noon-11pm Mon-Sat; noon-10.30pm Sun. **Food served** noon-3pm, 6-10.30pm. **Credit** AmEx, MC, V.
This grand-looking prominently positioned pub on the Notting Hill-Kensington borders has recently been given a healthy makeover by the team behind the excellent William IV on Harrow Road, and they've done another great job here. Walk straight in and you'll be confronted by a saloon bar, while a slightly quieter dining room (food is taken very seriously in this place) sits further back. The overall look is clean and simple, with white walls, wooden floors and everything bright and as it should be. Beer is from the usual, sadly unimaginative, lager and stout selection but we recommend that drinkers of all persuasions supplement any liquid with a sample of the top-rated sticky toffee pudding.
Babies and children admitted. Function room. No-smoking tables. Tables outdoors (patio). **Map 10/B7**

Market Bar

240A Portobello Road, W11 (7229 6472). Ladbroke Grove or Notting Hill Gate tube. **Open** noon-11pm Mon-Sat; noon-10.30pm Sun. **Food served** *Restaurant* 12.30-3pm, 7-10pm daily. **Credit** MC, V.

It's been more than ten years since this corner plot was refashioned from a cut-throat boozer (the Golden Cross) and styled into a bohemian playpen. Despite alterations over the years that have stripped some of its original atmosphere, this veteran bar remains the master of ceremonies when it comes to market day and carnival weekend. Having shrugged off a nagging reputation as a honey pot for drug dealers and pimps, the Market remains resolutely local in the week; by day it serves the dwindling Guinness-supping Caribbean community and by nightfall the music is cranked up and the giant candles are lit to grotto effect. The bar favours stouts and lagers over bitters and the addition of a wine list and coffee is a nod to the area's changing tastes and the increased tourist trade. Prices are fair and, if you're peckish, bear in mind the Market Thai on the first floor, which serves up competent dishes at competitive prices.

Babies and children admitted (until 9pm). Music (jazz 4-7pm Sun). Restaurant. **Map 10/Az6**

192

192 Kensington Park Road, W11 (7229 0482). Ladbroke Grove or Notting Hill Gate tube. **Open** 12.30-11pm Mon-Sat; 12.30-10.30pm Sun. **Food served** 12.30-3pm, 7-11.30pm Mon-Fri; 12.30-3.30pm, 7-11.30pm Sat, Sun. **Credit** MC, V.

The overstated view that this smart, spartan bar-restaurant acts as the ringmaster in the West London media circus is slightly romantic, but holds some weight. As the Notting Hill outpost of the Groucho Club, Soho's select and grubby den for self-loathing, self-loving celebs, it shares a distinctly clubby atmosphere with personalities to match. On our lunchtime visit we overheard a huddled table of sunglasses indulging in a spot of character assassination and professional bloodletting. But, for those not throwing themselves on the bonfire of the vanities, the global wine list isn't as expensive as you'd expect (the house is £12 and a large glass of the stuff is around the £3 mark). The cocktail list was originally drawn up by legendary barman Dick Bradsell, and remains adventurous and enticing. Beers are limited to bottles. If it's food you're after, the accomplished restaurant knocks out grand global dishes to an established following. Be warned, it could well give your bank balance a good beating.

Babies and children admitted. Tables outdoors (pavement). **Map 10/Az6**

Pharmacy

150 Notting Hill Gate, W11 (7221 2442/www.pharmacy london.com). Notting Hill Gate tube. **Open** noon-3pm, 5.30pm-1am Mon-Thur; noon-3pm, 5.30pm-2am Fri; noon-2am Sat; noon-midnight Sun. **Food served** noon-2.30pm, 6-10.30pm Mon-Sat; noon-2.30pm, 6-10pm Sun. **Credit** AmEx, MC, V.

Damien Hirst's link with this medical theme bar grows ever more tenuous. The management has altered much of the original design and the glass-fronted urinals containing swabs and syringes are more or less the only relics of Hirst's original design. Instead, it's gone for an altogether broader appeal by opening up the clinical white space and warming it with colour and posters. The chemist counter-cum-bar that was tarted up and pushed to one end to make way for dancing is instead used for luggage and stacked chairs. On our recent visit, there was no sign of the dreaded clipboard nazis or the queue that used to snake past Outpatients, the shop next door. The DJ booth remained silent, as did much of the bar, although the group next to us provided a soundtrack with a host of mobile phone ring tones (thanks). Despite all this, the cocktails remain excellent at around the £7 mark – especially the much-vaunted espresso Martini. However, other prices are incredibly steep for a bar stripped of its stardust and core clientele; a real espresso is not much cheaper than the alcoholic version at £3.50 plus service. Pass the formaldehyde, it looks as if Hirst's got another corpse on his hands.

Babies and children admitted (until 10pm; high chairs). Disabled: toilet. Function room. Music (DJs 10pm Wed-Sun; £5 after 11pm Fri, Sat). Restaurant. **Map 10/A7**

Portobello Gold

95-7 Portobello Road, W11 (7460 4900). Notting Hill Gate tube. **Open** 10am-midnight Mon-Sat; 10am-10.30pm Sun. **Food served** noon-11pm Mon-Sat; 1-9pm Sun. **Happy hour** 5.30-7pm daily. **Credit** AmEx, DC, MC, V.

Set among the antiques shops at the south end of Portobello Road, this market mainstay has always nurtured its own individual and charming character. That character is distinctly middle class, not to say public school – a fact that tends to ensure high-quality food and drink. Hence, an impressive wine list, decent real ales (including Courage Directors and Shepherd Neame Spitfire), an array of Belgian and organic beers, and a range of affordable cocktails. Sunday is a particularly popular time for good-value grazing from the all-day bar menu that includes high-grade snacks and a pasta of the day. At other times the food in the conservatory restaurant at the back continues to draw plaudits from lovers of seafood and bistro fare. The Gold also holds the dubious title of the first internet cafe in London – six foldaway computers give access to the net for cyber-idlers.

Babies and children admitted. Function room. Games (backgammon, cards). Internet access. Restaurant. Specialities: organic lager, world beers, wines. Tables outdoors (conservatory, pavement). TV (satellite). **Map 10/A6**

Portobello Star

171 Portobello Road, W11 (7229 8016). Ladbroke Grove or Notting Hill Gate tube. **Open/food served** 11am-11pm Mon-Sat; noon-10.30pm Sun. **No credit cards**.

Regulars held their collective breath when the management updated the signage outside this hell-raising hole in the wall, fearing it was the beginning of the end for the local. They needn't have worried. The smartened exterior hasn't in any way affected the down-at-heel atmosphere in the portakabin interior. The small bar serves a limited range of beers to a hardcore of professional drinkers, made up of hard-worked antiques dealers, ruddy-faced workmen and amateur auteurs who boom and slur, engaging strangers and tourists alike with topics ranging from the dangers of an imperialist America to the death of a pal's budgie. If you want to get involved, put some money in the erratic jukebox, it's a sure-fire way to kick off a conversation. This is as near as you'll get to the Portobello of old and acts as a welcome antidote to some of the more snotty and unfamiliar establishments in the area. The toasted sandwiches are legendary, if a little greasy. We wouldn't have them any other way

Games (fruit machine). Jukebox. Music (duo 8pm Thur; free). Tables outdoors (pavement). TVs (satellite). **Map 10/Az6**

Prince Bonaparte

80 Chepstow Road, W2 (7313 9491). Notting Hill Gate or Royal Oak tube/7, 28, 31, 70 bus. **Open** noon-11pm Mon-Sat; noon-10.30pm Sun. **Food served** 12.30-3pm, 6.30-10pm Mon-Sat; 12.30-9pm Sun. **Credit** MC, V.

London drinking: DJ bars

Big nights in small spaces.

DJ decks have replaced the humble pub jukebox! Or at least it seems that way, as DJ bars continue to mushroom all over London at a giddy rate. Novelty does appear to be a factor, as countless drinking dens undergo clubby revamps – but there's no denying that DJ bars have significantly transformed, from pre-club hangouts in the mid '90s, to buzzy destination venues in their own right.

At their best, DJ bars represent intimate, convivial places to drink and mingle until late, with diverse music programming that appeals to a broader church and age range than just hardcore clubbers. Some do blur the boundary with club venues, such as west London's classy **Cherry Jam**, founded in 2002 as an alternative to brash superclubs.

International name DJs have increasingly been drawn to these relatively bijou settings too: Thursday residency Misdemeanours at **AKA** regularly hosts sets from prominent guests, from Roger Sanchez to Jon Carter. Even at bars that don't have room for a dedicated dancefloor, up-for-it punters won't be deterred from pushing back the seating (or clambering on to the tables) to party.

As DJ bars have multiplied in number, variety and attention to detail have increased. Shoreditch's **Bridge & Tunnel**, founded through record label Nuphonic, takes in swish Cappellini furniture and a state-of-the-art soundsystem for vintage disco to electro nights. 'We've grown up, we're not into being pushed around in big nightclubs,' explains Nuphonic's Sav Remzi. 'It's not a rigid gameplan. In the future, our bar will mutate according to people's responses.' The independent label/bar relationship has also been demonstrated at **The Social**, established by Heavenly Records and a much-loved venue for a midweek boogie.

For DJ culture with an arty twist, try the **ICA Bar**, which has set a standard for brilliant bashes such as Batmacumba (Brazilian music with cocktails to match) and Blacktronica. Now even the **National Theatre** is in on the act; catch DJs on its plush mezzanine level at weekends, with decent house wine and a lovely river view – most civilised.

Because of their widespread popularity, DJ bars generally aren't the place for a low-key drink; the noise and smoke might also put you off eating (some are open for lunch, though). If you're after a table and a more laid-back vibe, get there early, which should ensure free admission as well; many venues charge admission after 9pm.

Whether the decor is swanky or dressed-down, the most striking DJ bars develop their venues through imagination – so it's heartening to witness fun events such as Fair Game (a monthly clubby singles night) at the **Market Place**. Across town, **BOD**, a dashing newcomer in EC1, even features entertainment from an in-house magician! Wherever you are in the capital, having it large at your local has become a reality. *Arwa Haider*

The down 'n' dirty dozen

AKA (*see p25*) 18 West Central Street, WC1 (7836 0110).
BOD (*see p121*) 104-122 City Rd EC1 (7490 7407).
Bridge & Tunnel (*see p122*) 4 Calvert Avenue, E2 (7729 3184).
Bug Bar (*see p201*) St Matthew's Church, Brixton Hill, SW2 (7738 3184).
Cherry Jam (*see p18*) 58 Porchester Road, W2 (7727 9950).
Embassy Bar (*see p173*) 119 Essex Road, N1 (7359 7882).
Fridge Bar (*see p202*) 1 Town Hall Parade, Brixton Hill, SW2 (7326 5100).
ICA Bar (*see p95*) The Mall, SW1 (7930 3647).
Market Place (*see p44*) 11 Market Place, W1 (7079 2020).
Plan-B (*see p203*) 418 Brixton Road, SW9 (7733 0926).
The Social (*see p45*) 5 Little Portland Street, W1 (7636 4992).
Vibe Bar (*see p156*) Old Truman Brewery, 91-95 Brick Lane, E1 (7377 2899).

Johnny Vaughan may have soiled this pub for many people by filming those vacuous Strongbow ads here, but that's now all seemingly forgotten – the barman assured us that nobody has asked where the arrow marks are 'for months'. The look of this roomy, street-corner venue is in keeping with the first wave of gastro-slanted pubs: large windows, a central bar station and open-plan kitchen round the side. The window tables are the province of drinkers – generally, a mix of well-behaved City types and smart students – while the 1940s mess hall at the back takes care of the eaters. Besides a well-travelled line-up of lagers (London Pride's the only ale), there's a wine list that's extensive, global and reasonable. Not as smart, fêted or celeb-haunted as many of its near neighbours, the Bonaparte nevertheless makes for a very good local.
Music (DJ, alternate Sat; free). Quiz (every second Tue). TV. **Map 10/A5**

Tiroler Hut

27 Westbourne Grove, W2 (7727 3981/www.tirolerhut.co.uk). Bayswater or Queensway tube. **Open/food served** 6.30-12.30am Mon-Sat; 6.30-10.30pm Sun. **Credit** AmEx, DC, MC, V.
Lederhosen on for this Westbourne Grove institution, which has been serving up a heady mix of vase-sized steins of Dortmunder Union and high octane Tirol entertainment for more than 30 years. The bar and restaurant remain resolutely Austrian. Buxom Vera is your hostess with the mostess; she acts as the meet and greet on the door, while Joseph, invariably decked out in classic leather shorts, is on crowd control duties, banging out old favourites on his accordion and conducting a surreal cow bell show that will leave you gawping in disbelief. Buy beers at the bar and take them through to the scaled-down artex beer hall where come weekends you're likely to encounter a mix of locals, musos and long-standing cohorts of the Tiroler Hut fraternity. The veteran regulars are engaging enough, happy to tell newcomers their life stories, which may or may not be true.
Music (traditional Austrian 8pm nightly).

Under the Westway

242 Acklam Road, W10 (7575 3123). Westbourne Park tube. **Open** 8am-midnight Mon-Fri; 1pm-midnight Sat. **Credit** MC, V.
The owners could have been slightly more specific when they named this place – like 'Under the Westway at the Little Venice end down a badly lit crack alley off Portobello Road'. As it stands, it's a bitch of a place to find. The bar's lodged in the atrium of the recently refurbished Westbourne Studios, home to a warren of cottage industries, internet upstarts and showrooms churning out homespun design wares and amateurish art products. Having dodged the muggers and slipped through the automatic cargo doors, you'll be confronted by an array of grown-up toys: antique arcade games, beanbags and a pool table. On the far side the bar nods appreciatively to the hand-picked soundtrack. Expect a crowd made up of odds and ends from the record, fashion and fake skate fraternities. Drinks include draught Crest and Kirin, plus an array of rum-based cocktails. This is Notting Hill at its pioneering best, but be warned, Fridays and Saturdays are restricted to members only.
Babies and children admitted (until 7pm). Disabled: toilet. Games (pool table, table football). **Map 10/Az5**

Westbourne

101 Westbourne Park Villas, W2 (7221 1332). Royal Oak or Westbourne Park tube. **Open** 5-11pm Mon; noon-11pm Tue-Fri; 11am-11pm Sat; noon-10.30pm Sun. **Food served** 7-10pm Mon; 12.30-3pm, 7-10pm Tue-Thur; 12.30-3.30pm, 7-9.30pm Fri-Sun. **Credit** MC, V.
The closely packed tables in this open-plan bar guarantee a certain intimacy with strangers, but even those close enough to sniff their neighbour's armpits shouldn't worry – there's no unwashed masses here, just the local media crowd of Notting Hill. Silvery sports car-driving posers sup from a well-chosen wine list, draught Old Speckled Hen, Hoegaarden and Staropramen, jugs of excellent Bloody Mary and – ahem – smoothies. During the colder months, fairy lights and a log fire look incredibly inviting through the glass facade while the front terrace is a favourite with summer brunch-munchers. Food comes from a daily changing menu (dishes such as braised cuttlefish with tomatoes, capers and baby spinach or roasted pheasant with bacon, shallots and mash) and is excellent. A wall of photos and a sideboard full of random bits gives the air of entertaining in your own dining room but without the hassle of the washing up.
Babies and children admitted. Games (board games). Tables outdoors (pavement). **Map 10/A5**

Also in the area...

All Bar One 126-8 Notting Hill Gate, W11 (7313 9362).
Babushka 41 Tavistock Crescent, W11 (7727 9250).

Pimlico

Known for little other than the impressive Tate Britain, Pimlico's unlikely to become a great hub for scintillating nightlife any time soon. The majority of its pubs are archetypal locals that offer little to complain about, but little to send you hurrying back either. There are exceptions, of course, but for the most part, the distances between boozers are too long and the rewards at the end too scant to attract anything other than local workers and residents and the odd passing tourist.

Gallery

1 Lupus Street, SW1 (7821 7573). Pimlico tube. **Open** 11am-11pm Mon-Fri; noon-11pm Sat; noon-10.30pm Sun. **Food served** 11.30am-2.30pm, 5-9pm Mon-Fri; noon-2.30pm, 5.30-9pm Sat; noon-9pm Sun. **Credit** MC, V.
Eighteen months after a major refurbishment and we're assured Pimlico's Gallery is reaping the rewards. An influx of tourists finding their way here from nearby Tate Britain and greatly improved lunchtime trade have seen the work pay off in handsome fashion. The ground-floor bar, once dingy and smoky, is now a light, airy affair that's been modernised by the introduction of pale pastel shades while retaining enough original Victorian features – embossed wallpaper and an imposing wooden bar – to still feel like a pub. Meanwhile, the grandly titled mezzanine level remains something of a mystery. The style is Costa del Sol meets *Crossroads* at Heathrow and the presence of too much stainless steel and laminate wood leaves the whole floor feeling cold and uninviting. A prime example of how not to update a local pub. That misjudgement aside, it's an unremarkable, but perfectly pleasant place to drop in for a pint.
Function room. No-smoking area.

Jugged Hare

172 Vauxhall Bridge Road, SW1 (7828 1543). Victoria tube. **Open** 11am-11pm Mon-Sat; noon-10.30pm Sun. **Food served** noon-10pm Mon-Fri; noon-9pm Sat; noon-8pm Sun. **Credit** AmEx, DC, MC, V.
Looking at the grand neo-classical exterior of this stately building, it doesn't take a genius to work out that the Jugged

Hare used to be a bank. And as useful as that may have been to local residents, there can be no denying that what it is now is a lot more fun. Behind the imposing facade is a gloriously over-the-top re-creation of a posh Victorian drinking house. The walls are coated with rich dark colours and dotted with fading prints, military memorabilia and assorted brewing instruments. A large and suitably chaotic painting of an old London boozer looks down over the main bar area, as do the punters who choose to sit up on the gallery mezzanine level. Furniture is of the heavy, dark wooden variety and you'll go a long way before you'll find a pub that offers such grand surroundings in which to enjoy a simple pint. On the beer front, there are three Fuller's ales to choose from, as tasty as ever, along with the usual selection of draught and bottled lagers. A reasonably priced menu offers a good selection of traditional pub grub, including pies, sarnies and fish and chips.
Bar area available for hire (seats 40). Games (fruit machine). No-smoking area. TV.

Morpeth Arms

58 Millbank, SW1 (7834 6442). Pimlico tube. **Open** 11am-11pm Mon-Sat; noon-10.30pm Sun. **Food served** noon-9pm Mon-Fri; noon-3pm Sat, Sun. **Credit** MC, V.
Built in 1845, the Morpeth retains all the trappings of an authentic Victorian pub, although the spruce state of the carpets and upholstery suggest a welcome refresh may have taken place in the last year. A grand mahogany fireplace and equally imposing bar complete with period clock set the tone for the surroundings, while the liquid refreshment comes in the form of reliable Young's ales from just over the river in Wandsworth. The clientele is a mix of tourists overspilling from Tate Britain and – rather more intriguingly – spooks from the not-so-secret headquarters of MI6, which squats in green and cream on the opposite side of the river. On weekdays in particular there are dozens of stories to be dreamt up about the besuited characters that frequent the secluded corners at the back of the bar. If you're lucky, one of them might even leave their laptop behind. It's a bit livelier as the weekend approaches, but this is never less than a convivial setting for a few cosy drinks.
Function room (seats 30). Games (fruit machine). No piped music or jukebox. Tables outdoors (riverside terrace).

The Page

11 Warwick Way, SW1 (7834 3313/www.frontpagepubs.com). Pimlico tube/Victoria tube/rail. **Open** 11am-11pm Mon-Sat; noon-10.30pm Sun. **Food served** noon-3pm, 6-10pm Mon-Fri; noon-4pm, 6-10pm Sat, Sun. **Credit** AmEx, MC, V.
An outpost of the **Front Page** minichain (*see pXXX*) this friendly boozer offers a pleasant retreat to while away the afternoon. High windows ensure a consistently airy feel while the stripped oak panelling, low sofas and wooden floors provide comfortable surroundings in which to settle. Beers on tap include London Pride and Spitfire, while punters who fancy a feed can order good quality Thai lunches and dinners and can even choose to eat in the slightly more refined surroundings of the first-floor restaurant. Known locally (as many of this chain are) as a bit of a sports pub, the Page is a good bet for rugby, football and cricket matchdays and sports updates are shown consistently – though not obtrusively – throughout the day. Not the most distinctive of Pimlico's boozers, but as with many in this chain, a friendly and relaxed venue nonetheless.
Babies and children admitted. Restaurant (closed Sat, Sun lunch, available for hire). TV (satellite). Tables outdoors (pavement).

White Swan

14 Vauxhall Bridge Road, SW1 (7821 8568). Pimlico tube. **Open** 11am-11pm Mon-Sat; noon-10.30pm Sun. **Food served** noon-10pm Mon-Sat; noon-9pm Sun. **Credit** AmEx, DC, MC, V.
Part of the T&J Bernard brand, the White Swan is somebody's thoroughly misguided attempt at bringing a little bit of country charm to the busy city. It's a totally unexpected barn of a pub full of fake rustic beams, quaint country crockery (bought, no doubt, from a specialist warehouse in Essex) and the odd agricultural implement. On the plus side, you'll find a good selection of ales to accompany the standard lagers including Abbot and Theakston's, plus a couple of regularly changing guests. There's also some reasonably priced (if unspectacular) bar food that can be wolfed down in a seperate eating area if you so desire. The punters tend to be boozy, especially at the weekend, although they never seem intimidating, just dedicated. In fact, if all you're really looking for is a place to go and get leathered with a few like-minded individuals, you could do worse – but with a over-loud, smoky atmosphere and unspeakably naff decor, it will never feature very high up on Pimlico's top pubs list.
Disabled toilet. Games (fruit machine, quiz machine). No-smoking area. Tables outdoors (pavement).

Soho

Despite all the evidence against, Soho remains the prime location for good-time seekers. Weekends can be horrific when the place is packed with leery, amped-up crowds of out-of-towners on the lash, mingling with parading pink priders. Old Compton Street in particular is a nightmare. But at other times, it's worth seeking out some of the old backstreet boozers where it's as if lowlife chronicler Jeffrey Bernard never toppled from his barstool. Truly stylish bars are surprisingly few, although there are a handful of hangouts for the studiedly cool west of Wardour Street (**Alphabet**, the **Player, Sun & Thirteen Cantons**), if you know where to look.

Admiral Duncan

54 Old Compton Street, W1 (7437 5300). Leicester Square or Piccadilly Circus tube. **Open** noon-11pm Mon-Sat; noon-10.30pm Sun. **Credit** MC, V.
The most traditional, least fashion-conscious of Soho's gay bars, the Admiral Duncan became something of a cause célèbre after being the subject of a homophobic bombing attack in 1999. Remarkably, it went pretty much straight back to the way it always was after the necessary rebuilding: the same pink and purple exterior, and the same bare floorboards, low lighting and lack of furniture inside. All that's been added is a doorman and a community consciousness: pamphlets about gay self-help and health groups are now stacked alongside the copies of *Boyz* by the entrance. The clientele are generally thirty- to fiftysomething pint drinkers in bomber jackets and jeans, and beer is at normal pub prices, unlike most other gay bars in Soho.
Games (fruit machines, quiz machine). Jukebox.
Map 7/K6

Akbar

77 Dean Street, W1 (7437 2525/www.redfort.co.uk/akbar). Leicester Square, Piccadilly Circus or Tottenham Court Road tube. **Open/food served** 5.45pm-1am Mon-Sat. **Credit** AmEx, DC, MC, V.

Join us
Monday - Friday 3-7pm
for fantastic drinks deals
and sporty service

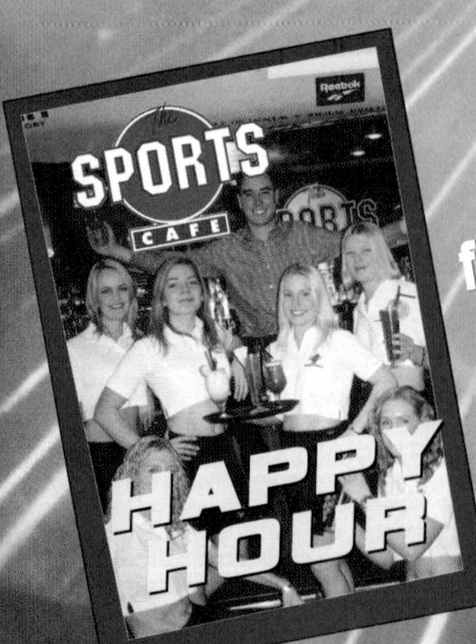

POOL LOUNGE
WITH WAITRESS SERVICE

LIVE
INTERNATIONAL
SPORTS
SCREENED

SERVICE INDUSTRY NIGHT
EVERY MONDAY
DRINKING & DANCING
'TIL 3am

selected bottled beers £1.20
gin/vodka/whiskey/bacardi
and mixer £1.00
along with other great drinks
prices all night

The SPORTS CAFE

www.thesportscafe.com

LONDON	BIRMINGHAM	MANCHESTER
80 Haymarket	240 Broad Street	23 Quay Street
London SW1 4TQ	Birmingham B1 2HG	Manchester M3 4AE
Tel. 020 7839 8300	Tel. 0121 633 4000	Tel. 0161 839 8800
Fax. 020 7839 8303	Fax. 0121 633 4111	Fax. 0161 839 8303

The Red Fort, one of the capital's oldest and best-loved Indian restaurants, went through a revamp a year or so ago, and its new, sleek image demanded a glamorous basement bar. So Akbar was born, complete with girl on the door, floral displays and stone water bowl at its entrance. The style is modern with a touch of Indian: a very long bar, walls in terracotta, sandstone and cream, panels of wood veneer, low-level banquette seating and a plasma video screen. Best of all is the long tunnel-like alcove that occupies an arch underneath Dean Street. Akbar attracts a straighter, more suited crowd than perhaps was aimed for, but it makes a very good venue for a date, with a variety of unusual Indian-themed cocktails and an atmosphere of sophisticated intimacy.
Bar available for hire. Disabled: toilet. Music (DJs 6pm Tue-Sat; free). TV. **Map 7/K6**

Alphabet

61-3 Beak Street, W1 (7439 2190/www.alphabet bar.com). Oxford Circus or Piccadilly Circus tube. **Open/food served** noon-11pm Mon-Fri; 5-11pm Sat. **Credit** AmEx, MC, V.
Media-mobbed bar of the year when it arrived in 1997, Alphabet has since slipped into its comfy jeans and trainers, and is all the better for it. Certainly still popular, but commendably modest, it's a combination of the chic and the shack. Set in a roomy two-floor area with a skylight over the main bar at street level, and a loungeable downstairs featuring a trademark Soho street plan on the floor, the Alph allows for effusive but relaxed chatter. Oiling the gassing are bottles of Pilsner Urquell, Hoegaarden, Asahi and Negra Modelo, as well as two dozen New World reds and whites, and a full set of cocktails. While the main bar does lunch – excellent soups, salads and pastas from the open kitchen beside the bar – downstairs prepares for a night of DJing amid the skip-rescued furniture.
Babies and children admitted (until 5pm). Function room. Music (DJs 7.30pm Thur, Fri, occasional Sat). Specialities: cocktails. **Map 2/J6**

Amber

6 Poland Street, W1 (7734 3094/www.amberbar.com). Oxford Circus tube. **Open** 5pm-1am Mon-Sat. **Food served** 5pm-midnight Mon-Sat. **Credit** AmEx, MC, V.
Sister bar to **Alphabet** (*see above*), Amber is the one that you'd introduce your parents to. Bright, clean and with neither edge nor edges – the curved look built-in furniture of the rather stiff ground-floor bar-diner is punctuated only by cacti – Amber shows her real colours downstairs at night. The basement booms with Latin dance tunes, heavy on the bass and post-work abandonment. Each floor is fed by a similarly Latin-influenced menu of authentic tapas, complemented in style and quality by 12 types each of rum specials and tequilas, the latter essential in the house special of a £12 Margarita Alta of Patron Silver, citronge and fresh lime. Six shooters line up with top-drawer spirits – Patron Anejo tequila, Chivas Regal, sloe gin, Ketel One vodka – plus £3.50 bottled beers including Amber's own, Pacifico Claro, Negra Modelo and Dos Equis.
Function room. Music (DJs 8pm Thur-Sat; free). **Map 2/J6**

Argyll Arms

18 Argyll Street, W1 (7734 6117). Oxford Circus tube. **Open** 11am-11pm Mon-Sat; noon-9pm Sun. **Food served** 11am-5pm Mon-Sat; noon-4pm Sun. **Credit** AmEx, MC, V.
About as close to Oxford Circus tube as you can get without putting a bar in the station itself, the ornate and grand Argyll assumes a weird role as an international platform. The rucksack-bearing clientele are of the email-penpal, 'You-Must-Be-Piotr' type on a nervous first meet. If they recognise each other, and a friendship blooms, how will bespectacled Piotr and buddy remember the first rendezvous venue? A confectioned and confusing Victorian maze of frosted glass, carved dark-wood divisions, covered by a yuk-coloured stucco ceiling and overseen by a large semicircular bar and back bar as elaborate as the Alhambra. Grolsch and Adnams Bitter – isn't London expensive! – were on offer, and the Est 1716 sign above was a major talking point. If any had done extra research, they would have found that Argyll House was demolished in the mid-1800s, and this is an elaborate reconstruction of the original pub. The quieter Palladium bar encourages more like Piotr up the stairs.
Babies and children admitted (restaurant). Function room. Games (fruit machines). No-smoking area (until 4pm in restaurant). Restaurant. TV. **Map 1/J6**

Bar Chocolate

27 D'Arblay Street, W1 (7287 2823). Oxford Circus or Tottenham Court Road. **Open/food served** 10am-11pm Mon-Sat; noon-10.30pm Sun. **Credit** DC, MC, V.
One of Soho's boho bars, the Chocolate (then Tactical) cut its teeth on beatnik nights three or four years ago, with screenings, readings and 'happenings'. The poets' society is now dead, but its Super 8 camera, collection of hip lit and row of bootleg Bukowski tapes stand as some kind of plaque in the central bookcase pillar. Hints at a new identity line the walls, a themed series of – chocolatey? – brown stains, framed as if art. The drinks menu wouldn't be out of place in more self-consciously stylish parts of Soho: rarely found De Vauzelle champagne at £33.50 a bottle, the house cocktail, Chocolate, of Myers rum, crème de cacao, Baileys and chocolate ice cream, plus other alcoholic concotions divided into 'refresher', 'creamie' and 'classic' varieties. For the more penurious: bottled Budvar and Beck's. All are served by willing waitstaff. Lyrical late '50s tunes fill the air, and there's a tangible sense of everything turning black and white – if it wasn't already so brown. Laid-back clientele, though.
Babies and children admitted (until 6pm). Music (DJs 6pm every other Sun; free). Tables outdoors (pavement). **Map 1/J6**

Bar Code

3-4 Archer Street, W1 (7734 3342). Leicester Square or Piccadilly Circus tube. **Open** 4pm-1am Mon-Fri; 3pm-1am Sat; 3-10.30pm Sun. **Admission** £3 after 11pm Fri, Sat. **Happy hour** 5-7pm daily. **Credit** MC, V.
Gay and cruisey Bar Code awakens late, just in time to start the party again as nine-to-fivers close their briefcases and head en masse for the elevators. Early arrivals benefit from generous happy hours, including £1.50 for drinks all night on Mondays. Upstairs, the client base is men of a certain age making the best of neat clipper work to create a favourable immediate impression; downstairs, the entertainment is more communal. Pre-club deep and dirty house at weekends (excellent array of flyers, by the way), comedy nights on Tuesdays, all in a bare blue industrial interior where light is at a premium. Classic Soho stuff, really, re-establishing the concept of the post-work pick-me-up. Bar Code is the tough leather queen to the pretty fashion boys that are **Rupert Street** (*see p84*) and the **Yard** (*see p86*).
Comedy (7pm Mon-Thur, Sat, Sun; free). Games (fruit machine). Music (DJs 9pm Thur-Sat). **Map 7/K7**

Bar Soho

23-5 Old Compton Street, W1 (7439 0439). Leicester Square or Piccadilly Circus tube. **Open/food served** 4pm-1am Mon-Thur; 4pm-3am Fri; 2pm-3am Sat; 4pm-12.30am Sun. **Credit** AmEx, MC, V.

Loud and brash, this large place is the quintessential Soho venue for hedonistic tourism and after-work abandon. It occupies the middle ground between designer bar, modern pub and nightclub, catering to undiscerning needs with plenty of lagers on tap, a late licence, glitter ball and dancefloor. Half the place operates as a restaurant so punters don't need to look elsewhere when the round-midnight munchies strike. At 7.30pm on a Tuesday evening the place was rather calm and refined (oak benches, paving slab floor, heavy wood and cast-iron fittings and candles), with couples on dates and a few friends standing around the bar. Passing by two hours later it was rammed, house music was blasting out and the atmosphere was full-on rowdy party. It may not be sophisticated, but it certainly serves its purpose.
Function room. Music (DJs 9.30pm nightly). Tables outdoors (pavement). TV (satellite). **Map 7/K6**

Bar Sol Ona

13 Old Compton Street, W1 (7287 9932). Leicester Square or Piccadilly Circus tube. **Open/food served** 6pm-3am Mon-Sat; 6-11pm Sun. **Admission** £3 after 8.30pm, £4 after 11pm Fri, Sat. **Credit** AmEx, DC, MC, V.
Essentially, a decent Spanish tapas bar – the six tapas for £13.50 you will get here will be better than the kind found in many of Soho's trendier hangouts – this is a down-to-earth basement dive that, courtesy of a late licence and DJs, performs the function of a club for people who don't like clubbing. On our visit, two large groups dominated each of the couple of basement rooms, all present glugging jugged Margaritas (£12). It has an appealingly clandestine air, enhanced by a blink-and-you'll-miss-it entrance sandwiched between the two branches of **Cafe Bohème** (*see below*), although claustrophobes might get a little panicky on busier nights. Granted that it's somewhat lacking in glamour and panache for a bar named after *la gran encisera*, but a fair few Spanish come here taking a break from Hanway Street.
Music (DJs 10pm Tue-Sat). Tables outdoors (pavement). TV. **Map 7/K6**

Cafe Bohème

13-17 Old Compton Street, W1 (7734 0623). Leicester Square or Piccadilly Circus tube. **Open/food served** 8am-2.30am Mon-Sat; 8am-11pm Sun. **Credit** AmEx, DC, MC, V.
Back in the '80s, when everybody wanted to be Sade or wear a beret, this was such a fashionable hangout. Those days are long gone, but Cafe Bohème has stuck to its guns and remains the closest Soho gets to a proper Parisian brasserie, complete with Guimard-inspired windows, cream walls, shiny bar, long wine list and good-looking, white-smocked waiters and waitresses. It has survived through the years because it's stylish without being pretentious or intimidating, and it attracts an entirely mixed crowd, from young hipsters to old couples. The bar food is what you would find in the real thing – steak frites, moules marinières, etc – and there's Stella on tap and live jazz on Sundays. The more recent Bohème Bar and Kitchen two doors down has more of a modern feel.
Babies and children admitted (eating area). Music (jazz 4pm three days a week including Sun; free). Restaurant. Tables outdoors (pavement). **Map 7/K6**

Candy Bar

4 Carlisle Street, W1 (7494 4041). Tottenham Court Road tube. **Open** 5-11.30pm Mon-Thur, Sun; 5pm-2am Fri, Sat. **Happy hour** 5-7pm Mon-Fri. **Credit** MC, V.
Following a two-year stopover at the other end of Bateman Street, Soho's most celebratory and raucous lesbian bar is back at its original location: a narrow, two-floored former members' club that is perfect for the Candy Bar's mix of exclusivity, fashion-sense and up-for-it action. Upstairs is decked out in a modern style with pastel colours, built-in leather seating, and lots of glass; downstairs is rougher and more barren, with DJs playing hard house and party tunes. Men still won't get in unless they are with a woman, and even then they won't be guaranteed entry – and the door staff can be formidable. The Candy Bar made the break from the traditional lesbian pub, and it has been a huge success as a result.
Function room. Games (pool table). Karaoke (9pm Mon; free). Music (DJs 8pm Thur-Sat; £5 after 9pm Fri, Sat). **Map 7/K6**

Clachan

34 Kingly Street, W1 (7494 0834). Oxford Circus tube. **Open** 11am-11pm Mon-Sat; noon-6pm Sun. **Food served** noon-9pm daily. **Credit** AmEx, MC, V.
Despite a recent revamp, the Clachan remains firmly an old-style boozer (built 1898), complete with original fixtures and fittings (a beautifully etched ceiling, snob screens, chandeliers, oak-panelled bar, deep-cushioned seats). Given its just off Regent Street location, it remains remarkably free of either bag-laden shoppers or satchel-wearing tourists. Instead it attracts more your middle-aged business types, who appreciate a decent drop of real ale. There's also a goodish selection of wines from France, Spain and the New World, including a house wine at only £8.99 a bottle. Fittingly enough for a pub that was for 60 years owned and operated by neighbouring department store Liberty (commemorated in the small upstairs Liberty Bar), the place still attracts plenty of after-work retailers, many of whom often display little regard for the notion of going home.
Function room. Games (fruit machines, quiz machine). TV. **Map 2/J6**

Coach & Horses

29 Greek Street, W1 (7437 5920). Leicester Square or Piccadilly Circus tube. **Open** 11am-11pm Mon-Sat; noon-10.30pm Sun. **Happy hour** 11am-4pm Mon-Fri, Sun. **Credit** MC, V.
This grubby institution, which has always managed to retain an air of genuine old Soho bohemia despite looking like a down-at-heel, knackered old boozer, hardly changes. Prehistoric sandwiches are still only £1, doubles of house spirits are still only £2.80, and all the beers on tap (including London Pride, Pedigree and Burton) are still overpriced. Meanwhile, legendarily rude landlord Norman (who, claims to be 'mellowing with age' – but take it from us, he's not) continues to reign over a clientele typically composed of the same mix of old soaks, pub bores, St Martin's fashion students and the occasional bewildered tourist. It's Soho's last true local, and love it or loathe it, you'll miss it when it's gone.
No piped music or jukebox. TV (cricket only). **Map 7/K6**

Comptons of Soho

51-3 Old Compton Street, W1 (7479 7961/www.comptons-of-soho.com). Leicester Square or Piccadilly Circus tube. **Open** noon-11pm Mon-Sat; noon-10.30pm Sun. **Happy hour** 7-11pm Mon. **Credit** MC, V.
Long before Old Compton Street came out proudly pink there was Comptons, bringing a blush of colour to grey '80s Soho. Venerable enough to be considered a Soho institution, but age certainly hasn't withered her. Pass by the big street-front windows at almost any time of day or night and they'll reveal a tight squeeze of guys of all ages, all looking to make something happen. It's a mix of pick-up joint and party venue: upstairs, where it is pretty much all standing room only, there's usually loud house or disco and groups of friends meeting, while downstairs are plenty of lone sharks who arrive

single but disappear a brief pint later with company. 'Briefcase encounter', as it's known. It's a successful formula and Compton's is rarely anything but busy. It's great when you're not straight, yeah!
Games (fruit machines, pool table, quiz machines). Music (DJs 8-11pm Fri, Sat; free). Tables outdoors (pavement). TV (big screen, satellite). **Map 7/K6**

Couch

97-9 Dean Street, W1 (7287 0150/www.massive pubs.com). Tottenham Court Road tube. **Open** noon-11pm Mon-Sat; noon-10.30pm Sun. **Food served** noon-9pm Mon-Thur; noon-6pm Fri; noon-9pm Sat, Sun. **Credit** AmEx, DC, MC, V.
A gastropub-styled bar aimed at a *Friends*-watching after-work crowd, Couch is an unpretentious place for people who want somewhere more refined than a pub, but nothing too posey. Large wooden tables, little chandeliers, beige walls and scuffed floorboards make for a modern but homely feel, and the regulation brown leather sofas by the windows feel like the perfect addition rather than the 'style' accessory they so often are. It's a place best suited to groups – couples will feel marooned at the big tables – sharing bottles from the long wine list and gossip over dishes from the fusion menu, such as Peking duck (£5.50), pan-fried salmon (£6), or roasts on Sunday. Mainstream but by no means corporate, it's the discerning alternative to All Bar One and a pizza.
Music (DJs Sat; free). TV. **Map 7/K6**

Crobar

17 Manette Street, W1 (7439 0831/www.crobar.co.uk). Tottenham Court Road tube. **Open** 5pm-3am Mon-Sat. **Happy hour** 5pm-9pm Mon-Sat. **Credit** AmEx, MC, V.
When this place went from happy-clappy hippie hangout Acoustic Cafe to the Crobar it became the boozer of choice for London's native metalheads, which is about as extreme a volte-face as Joan Baez jacking in the folk whimsy to join Deicide. A late licence and proximity to the music venues of Charing Cross Road – as well as next door's Borderline – means the long, unfussy but surprisingly tidy bar gets packed post-11pm (when a £3 door charge comes into effect) with a Sabbath-worshipping hair-and-tats-and-leather crowd, necking huge bottles of Budvar and bellowing small talk over Purple, DC and Napalm Death (and that's the easy-listening set). Despite the heavy riffing and the core clientele's somewhat forbidding appearance, this is as friendly a joint as you can imagine, with a happy mix of sexes leaving judgemental cool for Hoxton and instead seeking nothing more in their fellow drinkers than a fondness for liquor and a keenness to rock. And for those about to do so, we salute them.
Tables outdoors (pavement). **Map 7/K6**

Crown & Two Chairmen

31 Dean Street, W1 (7437 8192). Tottenham Court Road tube. **Open** noon-11pm Mon-Sat; noon-10.30pm Sun. **Food served** noon-3pm Mon-Fri. **Credit** AmEx, DC, MC, V.
The Crown was a typical heavy-furnishings London pub until a couple of years back, when it went down the route of blackboards, bare boards and clear (as opposed to frosted) windows. But in spirit, it never changed, and it's still the same laddish, beery place where groups gather to watch football on the big screen, bellow over the anthemic rock and indie hits on the sound system and heckle the comics on Saturday nights. Bavarian wagon wheel chandeliers add an appropriate saloon room touch. The crowd is scruffy, youthful and vibrant, the beer selection surprisingly good (real ales include London Pride, Greene King IPA, Timothy Taylor Landlord and Adnams Best), and food – well, that'll be two packets of salt and vinegar, please.
Comedy (7.30pm Sat upstairs; £8.50). Function room. Games (fruit machines, golf machine). TV (satellite). **Map 7/K6**

Critics' choice theme pubs

Liquid Lab (p127)
Nurse some medicinal alcohol.

Page's Bar (p104)
To boldly go where no bar has gone before.

Sherlock Holmes (p97)
The theme's elementary, my dear Watson.

Smersh (p128)
Cold War cocktails and hammer-and-sickle shots.

South London Pacific (p222)
Waikiki? Wai not? Coconuts, palms and Hawaiian-themed table football.

Dog & Duck

18 Bateman Street, W1 (7494 0697). Tottenham Court Road tube. **Open** noon-11pm Mon-Fri; 4-11pm Sat; 5-10.30pm Sun. **Credit** AmEx, MC, V.
This beautiful little corner place is reputed to be the oldest pub in the Soho area, around since 1734 – although the current premises owe much to a late Victorian makeover. Its tiny proportions mean that evenings can be claustrophobic, so come during the day for the tiled floor mosaic of a quacker copping it (while man's best friend looks on), and handsome high-glaze wall tiles and original etched mirrors. The serving area comes with a fetching curve and occupies half the Lilliputian main bar. The beer range is impressive – Greene King IPA, London Pride, Timothy Taylor Landlord and Adnams Best, plus Addlestone's Cloudy, probably the best cider you'll get in W1. Prime seating (scratch that, the only seating) is in the (you guessed it, tiny) back room, which is warmed by a fire in winter.
Function room. **Map 7/K6**

Dog House

187 Wardour Street, W1 (7434 2116). Oxford Circus or Tottenham Court Road tube. **Open/food served** 5-11pm Mon-Fri; 6-11pm Sat. **Happy hour** 5-7.30pm Mon-Fri; 6-8pm Sat. **Credit** AmEx, DC, MC, V.
A significant bar this, though you'd hardly suspect it from its small, plain, keen-not-to-be-seen office door at the top end of film industry-haven Wardour Street. Look for the signboard of a dog dying of thirst, and a no-entry sign with 'Sorry Guys, No Ties' written on it, and you've come to the right place. Downstairs, a main half-moon bar counter faces a brown leather couch, pedestalled for no apparent reason. A simple bar area of similar brown furniture and smoky chat is accessed through a mosaic-pillared archway, through which some pretty earnest streetwear types, many working in said film industry, pass en route to house cocktails, shooters (Horny Monkey, Cocksucking Cowboy), creamies and fruit Daquiris, none over a fiver. The bottled beer is a solid triumvirate of Budvar, Michelob and San Miguel, and

Grand Union. *See p71.*

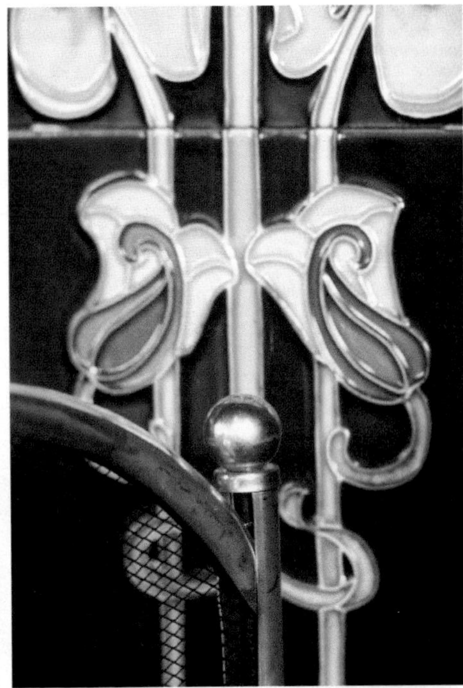

occasionally the kitchen will produce a bowl of potato wedges or calamari. In its own way, it couldn't be more laid-back – or switched on.
Function room (seats 55). Music (DJs Fri). TV (satellite). **Map 1/J6**

The Edge

11 Soho Square, W1 (7439 1313/www.edge.uk.com). Tottenham Court Road tube. **Open/food served** noon-1am Mon-Sat; noon-10.30pm Sun. **Credit** MC, V.
Probably the most accessible of Soho's gay haunts, this is something of a bar multiplex. The ground floor is brasserie style: candles on the little tables, floral displays, a gay/mixed clientele with plenty of women and a fair amount of straight men. But head up the metal stairs and things get increasingly hardcore, until you end up in bare rooms ready-made for partying and cruising at the top of the building. It's a particularly good place for summer drinking, with its Soho Square location, tables on the street, and cheap bar food: brunches for £4.50, burgers for £6. The Edge hasn't been the hippest bar around for a while, but it has settled into being a Soho mainstay and is much loved.
Babies and children (until 6pm). Function room. Music (DJs 9pm Mon, Thur-Sun; jazz and blues 9pm Tue, Wed; free). Tables outdoors (pavement). TV. **Map 7/K6**

The Endurance

90 Berwick Street, W1 (7437 2944). Oxford Circus, Piccadilly Circus or Tottenham Court Road tube. **Open** noon-11pm Mon-Sat; noon-5pm Sun. **Food served** noon-4pm daily. **Credit** MC, V.
Before last June this place was all geezers, being the pub of choice for the Berwick Street market traders. Turn up any night these days, though, and it's wall-to-wall Jarvis Cocker lookalikes. The flock wallpaper and nicotine finish that wer taken for granted by punters of old have been discovered to be ironic. Which is what happens when a boozer gets the gastropub makeover, as happened here to the former King of Corsica. Not that we're complaining. The Corsica was a grim old place. Now there's decent beer (Hoegaarden, Courage Directors), a choice of 20 wines starting at £10.90, and top-drawer food such as bowls of mussels, smoked haddock and salmon fish cakes and slow roast pork belly and sugarsnaps (mains around a tenner). The well-rated jukebox is chock-a-block with cult and indie (after all, choice music shops Sister Ray and Vinyl Junkies are practically neighbours and Selectadisc is just up the road), but be warned, when the 50ps dry-up 'God Save The Queen' and 'Smack My Bitch Up' rotate endlessly and maddeningly.
Babies and children admitted (daytime only). Games (darts). Jukebox. Quiz (7pm Tue). **Map 2/J6**

Freedom

60-66 Wardour Street, W1 (7734 0071). Leicester Square or Piccadilly Circus tube. **Open/food served** noon-midnight Mon-Wed; noon-2am Thur; noon-3am Fri, Sat; 2-10.30pm Sun. **Admission** £3 after 11pm Mon-Thur; £5-£10 after 10pm Fri, Sat. **Credit** AmEx, MC, V.
No longer Soho's trendiest gay bar, perhaps, but pretty groovy all the same. Front of house is a funky mix of dark purples and well-worn giraffe-skin sofas, equally suited to daytime coffee breaks (cappuccinos by Nitzan, who used to have a coffee shop in Haifa) or sultry cool jazz-soundtracked evenings. Push through to the back and this is really a place where boyz and girls just want to have fun. Hi-energy and high spirits reign in slightly shabby surrounds, scuffed and worn to a comfortable fit. Unless you specify to the contrary, spirits are automatically served as a double. Drink prices are over the odds but by the time Freedom really gets going most punters are well past caring, especially at weekends when packed polysexuality throbs to funky and uplifting grooves down in the basement bar until three in the morning.
Disabled: toilet. Function room. Music (DJs 10pm Wed-Sat). **Map 7/K6**

French House

49 Dean Street, W1 (7437 2799). Leicester Square or Piccadilly Circus tube. **Open** noon-11pm Mon-Sat; noon-10.30pm Sun. **Food served** *Bar* noon-3pm Mon-Sat. *Restaurant* noon-3pm, 6pm-midnight Mon-Sat. **Credit** AmEx, DC, MC, V.
One of the most historically and artistically important of Soho dives, this beautiful old bar – it can't really be called a pub as it doesn't serve pints – was a centre for the French Resistance in Britain during World War II, and the louche dive par excellence in the years that followed: Brendan Behan, Francis Bacon, Samuel Beckett and Dylan Thomas all went to seed here in the company of original owner Gaston. The boho spirit continues to be nurtured by the predominantly wine-guzzling and dishevelled set of local eccentrics that frequent the place. They aren't the most welcoming of bunches but polish your bon mots and persevere and maybe you'll eventually be accepted. Otherwise, fuck 'em, just come anyway (afternoons especially when the place isn't so crowded) to clock the drawings of actors and actresses and theatrical memorabilia on the walls, and to revel in a slightly decadent charm that has all but disappeared from Soho.
No piped music or jukebox. Restaurant. **Map 7/K6**

Intrepid Fox

99 Wardour Street, W1 (7494 0827). Leicester Square or Piccadilly Circus tube. **Open** noon-11pm Mon-Sat; 3-10.30pm Sun. **No credit cards.**
'Yeah, got a gig at the Sow & Sprocket and we're after a roadie. There's a cut of the door for ya. Innarested?' Somewhere in the dark recesses of Goth Central on Wardour Street, plastic glasses will squidge together in honour of another speaker set to be shifted in the name of rock 'n' roll. Here, amid the gig posters, skeletons and skulls, pony-tailed leathered longhairs in tour T-shirts do that awful hippie handshake thing around a permanently crowded four-square bar counter totally geared to serving pints of Strongbow or snakebite and black (still £2.60). In actual fact, all these 'geezers' are called Jeremy and they scrub up beautifully for the next evening's job artfully lounging for a Pimms ad being shot in W11. You see, the Intrepid Fox is really a concoction of some pin-sharp intern at the UK tourist office, designed to keep the wide eyes agog of American and Japanese tourists. It's far cheaper than keeping the royal family, apparently.
Function room. Games (fruit machine, pool table). Music (DJs Tue-Sun; free). **Map 7/K6**

Kettner's

29 Romilly Street, W1 (7734 6112). Leicester Square or Piccadilly Circus tube. **Open/food served** noon-midnight daily. **Credit** AmEx, DC, MC, V.
Founded in the 1860s by Napoleon III's chef, Kettner's is famous for serving pizzas (it's now owned by the Pizza Express people) in opulent surroundings. It's almost equally well known for its champagne bar, which, following a recent redesign, looks smarter than ever: large oil portraits of proud, haughty lords, leather armchairs, brown leather pouffes, a cream colour scheme and little spotlights, combining to create a sort of gentlemen's club feel. The wallful of champagne bottles behind the bar looks pretty impressive too. Prices start at under £30 a bottle. Unsurprisingly, there are a lot of businessmen impressing clients here, but this is a great place to take a date – you'll be bound to impress 'em too.

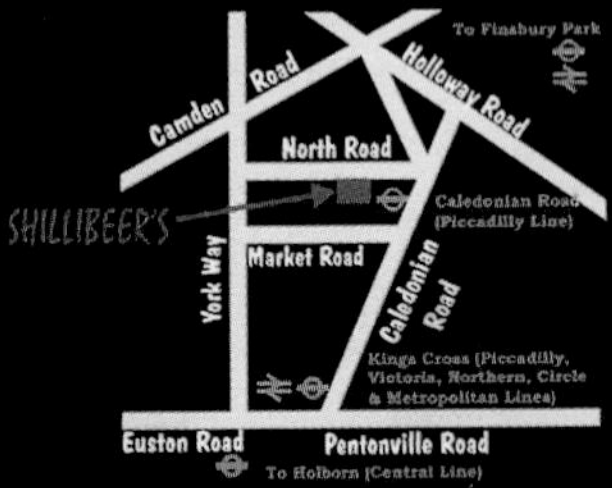

Babies and children admitted. Function room. Music (pianist 1-3pm, 6.15pm nightly). Restaurant. Specialities: champagnes. **Map 7/K6**

Lab

12 Old Compton Street, W1 (7437 7820/www.lab-bar.com). Leicester Square or Tottenham Court Road tube. **Open** 4pm-midnight Mon-Sat; 4-10.30pm Sun. **Food served** 6pm-midnight Mon-Sat. **Credit** AmEx, MC, V.

The cocktail list at tiny two-level Lab comes in the form of a booklet that's as weighty as your average computer manual. Fortunately, it's entirely more comprehensible and makes for lip-smacking reading with lengthy entries for classics, shooters, shorts and longs, Collins, Martinis, juleps, breezes, Daiquiris and fruit Caipirinhas – every spirit going mixed, dashed, shaken, muddled, splashed, strained and flambéed (all around £6-£7). For best effect pull up a seat at the bar to closely observe the mixological magicians at work. Add to this funky retro space age decor, all curves and brown and orange, pumping music (courtesy of regular DJs in the basement) and a lively snack menu and you've also got all the ingredients for an excellent bar. Combine with a stylish, good-natured, up-for-it crowd, mix well and enjoy.

Music (DJs Mon-Sat). **Map 7/K6.**

Old Coffee House

49 Beak Street, W1 (7437 2197). Oxford Circus or Piccadilly Circus tube. **Open** 11am-11pm Mon-Sat; noon-3pm, 7-10.30pm Sun. **Food served** noon-3pm Mon-Sat. **Credit** MC, V.

This place stands in defiance of west Soho's gradual shift toward sushi, Starbucks and shitty pubs. Although you'll probably find the odd media type sucking on a Bud, this isn't prime Bud-sucking turf. Expect instead a diverse mix of old and new Soho as well as Polish barmaids and mercifully low beat of sub-club something. Although most punters seem intent on dicing with Kronenbourg, gourmets can check out three real ales: Courage Directors, Marston's Pedigree and Brodie's Best, the latter from Leyton's Sweet William Brewery. Every spare cubit of wall and ceiling space is crammed with odd artefacts, from stuffed fish to phoney gold discs. Despite the proximity to Carnaby Street few tourists ever make it here, perhaps put off by the effortlessly ugly brown exterior. Don't take fright at the signed photo of Phil Collins, he's never been here. But Frank Bruno has.

Function room. Games (fruit machine). Restaurant. TV. **Map 2/J6**

Opium

1A Dean Street, W1 (7287 9608/www.opium-bar-restaurant.co.uk). Tottenham Court Road tube. **Open/food served** noon-3am Mon-Fri; 7pm-3am Sat. **Admission** £15 after 10pm. **Credit** AmEx, MC, V.

There is an insurmountable problem in opening a place like Opium. In aiming to create a flashy, exclusive and glamorous bar/club/restaurant, the owners inevitably want to attract the hippest of the hip. But hipness and wealth rarely meet, which means that those artistic types who set the scene haven't got a spare pound coin to tip the toilet attendant. The result is that the core clientele are always going to be made up of businessmen and footballers' wives. The Orient theme is vague but effective – low lighting, carved wood and gilded chinoiserie create an exotic mood – while prices are unsurprisingly high. There is something a little calculated and soulless about the place, with the oriental mishmash cuisine (honey-glazed chicken and Asian mushroom risotto, £16.50) coming off as a bit pretentious. It certainly looks impressive, though.

Bar available for hire. Dress: smart casual. Music (cabaret Wed, Tue; DJs Thur-Sat). Restaurant. **Map 7/K6**

Phoenix Artist Club

1 Phoenix Street, Charing Cross Road, WC2 (7836 1077/www.thephoenixartistclub.co.uk). Leicester Square or Tottenham Court Road tube. **Open/food served** 5-11.30pm Mon-Wed; 5pm-12.30am Thur, Fri; 1pm-12.30am Sat. **Happy hour** 5-8pm Mon-Thur; 1-8pm Sat. **Credit** AmEx, MC, V.

About ten years ago, this peculiar, previously ignored basement bar became a place to be seen, and it's managed to retain its cool status through no effort of its own whatsoever. For that alone it deserves to be commended. The Phoenix looks like a cross between a Bavarian bierkeller, a Cajun speakeasy and the theatre bar it actually is, with stuffed crocodiles and nauticalia hanging from the Gothic rafters, theatre posters on the walls, plus some fantastic cubby holes at the back – we once succeeded in occupying the curtained circular stone room reserved for special guests, until the red-faced manager threw us out. For some reason, the beer never seems to taste very good here, but the atmosphere is always great and the late licence is a bonus, although this is only achieved through a members policy, so arrive early, especially on weekends, to be guaranteed entry.

Dress: smart casual. Games (fruit machine, quiz machine). Restaurant. **Map 7/K6**

Pillars of Hercules

7 Greek Street, W1 (7437 1179). Tottenham Court Road tube. **Open** 11am-11pm Mon-Sat; noon-10.30pm Sun. **Food served** 11am-10pm Mon-Sat; noon-10pm Sun. **Credit** AmEx, DC, MC, V.

One of Soho's old faithfuls, the Pillars, found just south of Soho Square, is a traditional and earthy pub of scuffed floorboards, heavy wood panelling and snob screens, enjoyed by a particularly catholic crowd that could include anyone from earnest lookers from St Martin's art school to brash but honest media movers to the old duffers who drop by for the real ales in which the pub specialises (expect Marston's Pedigree, Theakston's Best, plus regularly changing guest ales). Being Soho, there are also the requisite oddballs that drop in of an evening: look out on Sunday nights for the guy with a shopping trolley-mounted sound system, who goes by the name of DJ Wheeliebag. Staff are young and the atmosphere is typically vibrant going on raucous.

Games (fruit machine, quiz machines). TV. **Map 7/K6**

The Player

8 Broadwick Street, W1 (7494 9125/www.thplyr.com). Tottenham Court Road tube. **Open** 5.30pm-midnight Mon-Thur; 5.30pm-1am Fri; 7pm-1am Sat. **Food served** 5.30-11pm Mon-Fri; 7-11.30pm Sun. **Credit** AmEx, MC, V.

Now part of the Match chain, the Player started life as a sought-after members' bar run by cocktail guru Dick Bradsell. Although closed for a while before Match took it on, the cachet still stuck. Since opened to the hoi polloi – many in trainers, jeez! – the Player hasn't lowered its standards, although it has chucked up some catch-all touches, such as Elia Kazan film posters in the hall, and esoteric triptychs of still life photos in the main alcoved seating area. The menu is now the neat size of a bus pass, and the charming staff, perhaps the most polite in all of Soho – 'And how are you this evening, Sir?' – wear pin-striped shirts. The rest is more Match than mix, the stripy lanterns, the degree logo on the back-bar fridge doors, the Match-themed selection of drinks. Food is of the snack variety and doesn't lend itself to vegetarians. Occasional camera flashes testify its popularity as a post-work party destination.

Music (DJs 8pm Fri, Sat; £3 after 10pm). **Map 7/K6**

Pop

14 Soho Street, W1 (7734 4004/www.thebreakfast group.co.uk). Tottenham Court Road tube. **Open** 5pm-3am Mon-Thur; 5pm-4am Fri; 8pm-5am Sat; 6-11.30pm Sun. **Admission** £3-£5 after 9pm Mon-Thur; £7 guest list, £10 door after 9pm Fri; £10 guest list only Sat; £5 Sun. **Credit** AmEx, DC, MC, V.

Pop looks great, a space age '60s/'70s *Barbarella* fantasy in primary colours, complete with a forest scene on one wall, plastic banquette seating and backlit neon plastic panels. The entrance is opulent, with velvet drapes and strange futuristic chandeliers making it look like the gateway to some Bond villain's underground lair. The problem comes with its size – London doesn't have enough women with flicks and polyester trouser suits or moustachioed men with wing collars to fill a place this big so it's all too often embarrassingly devoid of the kind of custom it's looking for. Which is a shame, because the capital needs a glorious piece of retro-escapism like this. It's also far too pricey for truly uninhibited fun – cocktails are £6-£9, doubles are £6-£8. That said, the '60s-themed club nights are recommended.

Function room. Music (DJs nightly). TV (satellite). **Map 7/K6**

Revolution

2 St Anne's Court, W1 (7434 0330/www.revolution-bars.co.uk). Tottenham Court Road tube. **Open/food served** noon-11pm Mon-Sat; noon-10.30pm Sun. **Happy hour** 5-7pm Mon-Wed, Sun. **Credit** AmEx, MC, V.

London came late to the Revolution, a chain already some 20-odd strong and stretching from Dundee to Swansea before the addition of this Soho link (since joined by another in Clapham). It fills all the requisite needs of the style-conscious urbanite (cool loungey interior of minimalist fittings and dim lighting), but the size of the place, the clear glass facade and the resolutely upbeat atmosphere make it unintimidating and pose-free. Its large, loud and leery nature ensures popularity with boisterous parties intent on getting bevied as odourlessly as possible on the house special of vodka in all its forms (95 varieties), traded in shots (six for £9!), cocktails (try a Barbarella: zubrowka, bison grass, raspberries and chambord, £6) and – my God – pitchers. Unsophisticated? Yes. Dangerous? Possibly. Fun? You bet.

Disabled: toilet. Music (DJs 7pm daily; free). Specialities: vodkas. **Map 7/K6**

Rupert Street

50 Rupert Street, W1 (7292 7141). Leicester Square or Piccadilly Circus tube. **Open** noon-11pm Mon-Sat; noon-10.30pm Sun. **Food served** noon-5pm Mon-Thur; noon-6pm Fri-Sun. **Credit** AmEx, DC, MC, V.

The cries of Rupert Street costermongers on one side of the epic plate-glass picture windows – Oh to be seen! – vie on the other with a domineering sound system set to funk. Pompidou pipes traverse the ceiling, nautical metal decks the floor. The seating's unforgivably hard. It's civilised and cafe-like during the day serving cappuccinos and snacks (including chips and fish in a Caffrey's-based batter – 'Nothing without alcohol,' quips the manager) to a mixed crowd of boyz, men and women. All change when the evening shift comes in and the volume's hoisted to a level that precludes conversation – but that's OK because the elderly suits and Colt Studio poster boys are there primarily to check each other out. There's Guinness, Grolsch, Caffrey's and Strongbow on tap, plus bottled beers and bubbles, and Tom of Finland to look at while you make a play for the bartender's eye.

Disabled: toilet. No-smoking area. Tables outdoors. **Map 7/K6**

Shampers

4 Kingly Street, W1 (7437 1692). Oxford Circus or Piccadilly Circus tube. **Open/food served** 11.30am-11pm Mon-Sat. **Credit** AmEx, DC, MC, V.

The place was heaving when we paid it an early-evening visit one recent Monday; if the wine bar is an endangered breed (*see p89* **London Drinking: Wine bars**), nobody told Shampers. It has the traditional wine bar look, with dark green walls largely hidden by mirrors, paintings, wine racks, chalk boards and bottles, bottles and more bottles. The stand-up bar to the rear jostles with drinkers, in contrast to the more orderly (but also packed) dining area at the front. Food is bistro and choice is vast, but quality varies and specials aren't always good value. The seasonally changing wine list, however, is exceptional, offering stacks of choice from the big names like Mondavi from California to small boutique producers, with an extensive Spanish section to boot.

Babies and children admitted (restaurant). Function room. Restaurant. TV (satellite). **Map 2/J6**

The Soho

12-13 Greek Street, W1 (7025 7844/www.thesoho bar.co.uk). Leicester Square or Tottenham Court Road tube. **Open/food served** 4pm-1am Mon-Wed; 4pm-3am Thur-Sat. **Happy hour** 5-7pm daily. **Credit** AmEx, DC, MC, V.

Taking over from Mondo, which had the dubious distinction of being the hottest, most pretentious bar in London for a few minutes in the mid-'90s, the Soho opened last July with minimal fuss. It launched as an out-and-out wine bar, but has already undergone a transformation into a cocktail bar with a reasonable wine list. Although the selection has gone from extensive to succinct, the list still incorporates a good spread of geographical locations and features eight wines by the glass. Prices are the norm for the locale (ie rather too expensive), but 5-7pm is happy hour when all wines are half price, and cocktails are £2.50. The switch from wine to cocktails has also been accompanied by a welcome refit getting rid of the old dark panelling and giving the place a lighter, brighter feel. Already an improvement on the stuffy, snobby place it has thankfully replaced.

Map 7/K6

Spice of Life

37-9 Romilly Street, W1 (7437 7013/www.thespiceof lifesoho.com). Leicester Square or Tottenham Court Road tube. **Open** 11am-11pm Mon-Sat; noon-10.30pm Sun. **Food served** noon-9pm daily. **Credit** AmEx, MC, V.

Thanks to a prime location on Cambridge Circus – next to the Palace Theatre, long-standing home of *Les Miserables* – it's largely passing trade that rings the tills at the Spice Of Life. A recent tart-up has added large chandeliers, swanky thick-pile carpet and plush red upholstery, and the stained-glass window tops and bar surround have been spruced up and mirrors now circle columns giving the effect of a comfortable saloon. But it remains very impersonal. No faulting the beers, though, which come from Hertford brewery McMullen & Sons (the distinctively dry Original AK and fruity Country Best Bitter). Nosh includes the likes of bangers and mash, fish and chips and other similar tourist-pleasing fare, with the odd dish like curried black-eye beans (£6.95) as a sop to the locals. There's regular live music and comedy in the basement bar.

Disabled toilet. Function room. Games (fruit machines). Music (open mic 7pm Mon; jazz 8pm Wed, Thur; blues 7.30pm Tue; acoustic guitar and live bands 7.30pm Fri). Tables outdoors. TV. **Map 7/K6**

Sun & Thirteen Cantons

21 Great Pulteney Street, W1 (7734 0934). Oxford Circus or Piccadilly Circus tube. **Open** noon-11pm Mon-Fri; 6-11pm Sat. **Food served** noon-9pm Mon-Fri. **Credit** AmEx, DC, MC, V.

Apparently, the sun was the sun on a clock face when once upon a time this corner of London was home to a small community of Swiss clockmakers, and as there are 12 cantons in Switzerland, this was the 13th. There's been a pub on the site for 500 years, and the present building's been here for 125. It's got the feel of a Parisian brasserie – polished brass foot rail, varnished wood panelling, bentwood chairs and scrubbed wooden tables – especially the back room, set out for the renowned and extremely reasonably priced lunches prepared by Dominique, the French-Portuguese chef. Downstairs in the low-ceilinged, multi-mirrored function room occasional techno and hip hop events take place (heralded only by word of mouth); Carl Cox, Mr E and DJ Sneak have all played here. It's also where the Chemical Brothers are said to have made their debut (and where Underworld penned the sublime 'Born Slippy').

Function room (seats 50). Music (DJs Thur, Fri; free). **Map 2/J6**

Thirst

53 Greek Street, W1 (74371977/www.thirstbar.co.uk). Tottenham Court Road tube. **Open/food served** 5pm-3am Mon-Sat. **Happy hour** 5-10pm Mon-Sat. **Credit** DC, MC, V.

This is the latest bar to make a go of it at the cursed Bateman/Frith Street corner. First came Riki-Tik's, which had its moment of glory but tripped up over its ridiculous 'no suits' policy. Then there was Ego, whose rapid demise was hastened by that bloody awful name (what were the thinking?). The **Candy Bar** (*see p78*) dallied awhile here before returning to its original premises. Now there's Thirst, heading full throttle down the designer route. The ground floor looks like a mini unused gallery space (just a solid plastic Thirst sign in the window); downstairs is where the action is, decorated by underlit plastic squares on the walls, accessorised with super-fashionable staff, DJs, an intimate dancefloor and practically nowhere to sit. The owners stress a policy of good music and unshocking bar tabs (bottled beer under £3, cocktails £5-£6.50). Will it work where so many have failed? So far so good, but watch this space.

Music (9pm-3am daily). **Map 7/K6**

Toucan

19 Carlisle Street, W1 (7437 4123/www.thetoucan.co.uk). Tottenham Court Road tube. **Open/food served** 11am-11pm Mon-Fri; 1-11pm Sat. **Credit** MC, V.

Central London's finest Irish pub is a modest little operation. The tiny ground-floor bar looks like Paddy McGinty's parlour. The basement bar we can't comment on because we've never been able to ford the massed bodies to get there (12's a crowd at the Toucan). Adornment is provided by a smattering of Guinness-related ephemera: the walls are covered in posters, cartoons, murals, adverts and signs; the bar is weighed down by wooden big-billed birds. Staff pull a fine pint of the black stuff (well, they'd have to really, wouldn't they), there's a huge range of Irish whiskeys, and food is cheap and hearty (Guinness pie and champ, £6). Finding room to eat, however, could be a problem given that most nights the massed Toucaneers swell out of the pub on to Carlisle Street and neighbouring Soho Square, hassling passing motorists and sloshing Guinness all over the cluttered pavement. For more space, more suits but considerably less atmosphere there's the **Toucan Two** on the other side of Oxford Circus on Wimpole Street – same formula but with the added attraction of doors that open up to the street and a pool table in the quiet basement.

TV (satellite). **Map 7/K6**

Two Floors

3 Kingly Street, W1 (7439 1007). Oxford Circus or Piccadilly Circus tube. **Open** 11am-11pm Mon-Sat. **Food served** 11.30am-5pm Mon-Sat. **Credit** MC, V.

Two Floors, one of the first West End joints to abandon shopfront signage and still attract enough of the right crowds, has always been a home to the hip, so it came as little surprise that on our visit a soundtrack of AC/DC, Pixies and Chilli Peppers was entertaining the too-cool-for-school clientele who've read *Dazed And Confused* and so are well versed on the fact that it's now OK to like rock. Two Floors is as comfy as it is trendy. The coffee's excellent, candles burn on the bar, the furniture's a bit scruffy, Ola the barman's friendly and tells you he plays sax – but for the lack of that certain scent you'd believe you were in Amsterdam. There's no beer on draught, only bottles, but cocktails are popular – they all cost six quid and contain a double measure. Sandwiches and ciabattas are available in the daytime when the vibe's well laid-back and you can bump into musicians, lazy people, out-of-work actors, or trendies working in fashion accessories. Thirsty office workers swell the ranks after six, but generally the crowd's hip, knows it and is in its 20s. The second floor (hey, the clue's in the name) is a maroon-walled bunker with enough room for half-a-dozen extremely worn sofas.

Babies and children admitted (daytime only). Function room. **Map 2/J6**

Two Thirty Club

23 Romilly Street, W1 (7734 2323). Leicester Square or Piccadilly Circus tube. **Open** 5.30pm-midnight Mon-Sat. **Food served** 5.30-11.30pm Mon-Sat. **Credit** AmEx, MC.

This is one of our favourite Soho hangouts, a stylish basement bar that still feels like a bit of a secret, five years after it first opened as the public part of a private members' club. Entrance is by way of an understated and unannounced (save for the smallest sign) dark brown door. It gives into a small rectangular room with wood veneers and black leather seats, polite, good-looking bar staff and a dressed-up crowd. It feels right to drink cocktails in here, and the central location on a quiet side street, makes for a great place to take a date. Watch out for the private parties that get booked in here regularly, however, which undoubtedly fill the little room to bursting.

Music (DJs 8pm Tue-Sat; free). **Map 7/K6**

Village Soho

81 Wardour Street, W1 (7434 2124). Piccadilly Circus tube. **Open/food served** noon-1am Mon-Sat; noon-midnight Sun. **Happy hour** noon-8pm daily. **Admission** £2 after 11pm Fri, Sat. **Credit** AmEx, MC, V.

Two gay bars in one, this, each with its own entrance, one in Wardour Street, the other in Brewer Street. The latter is more shambolic, a shack slapped together with candlesticks and fireplaces, surrounding a crush of fairly cruisey people at an old wooden bar counter. Karaoke provides regular entertainment. Enter from Wardour Street for the public face of the operation, with a far more mixed crowd enjoying bursts of loud, tacky pop and house drinks with silly names. At happy hour, you can't move in either bar, tourists seem to join in with the fun, and Soho's mandate of a mixed melting pot where marginal and mainstream can get off their faces communally is well and truly served. The strictly mainstream O Bar sits nicely in between the two.

Function rooms. Music (DJs 8pm nightly). Tables outdoors (patio). TV (music videos). **Map 7/K6**

Waikiki

28 Frith Street, W1 (7434 3881). Leicester Square tube. **Open** noon-11pm Mon-Wed; noon-midnight Thur-Sat; 5-11pm Sun. **Food served** noon-3pm, 5-10.30pm Mon-Sat; 5-10.30pm Sun. **Credit** AmEx, DC, MC, V.

The strange phenomenon that is tiki – Polynesian pop culture imported into the States by returning GIs and mixed in with '50s Americana – never really took off on these shores, perhaps having too little to do with European sensibilities. But three tiki bars sprang up in London in 2002 – one on Essex Road, **South London Pacific** in Kennington (*see p222*) and this one in Soho. But this is a curious tiki in that its influences are more South-east Asian: bamboo surfaces, a wallpapering of Asian pop magazine covers from the '50s and '60s, a big red porcelain Buddha on the bar. Not Waikiki then, but Thai-tiki. Whatever – it makes for a kitschy atmosphere that's fun without being tacky. Drinks of choice are well-made cocktails (£4.50 for shorts such as Brambles, Mojitos and Caipirinhas; £6 for long drinks such as Mai Tais and Moscow Mules). And the bar food is, surprise, surprise, not bad at all – green papaya salad, pad Thai and green curry and the like at around £6.50. The best new bar in Soho for some time.

Function room. Music (DJs 7pm nightly). Tables outdoors (pavement). **Map 7/K6**

Yard

57 Rupert Street, W1 (7437 2652/www.yardbar.co.uk). Piccadilly Circus tube. **Open** noon-11pm Mon-Sat. **Happy hour** 5-8pm Mon, Tue, Sun. **Credit** AmEx, DC, MC, V.

Set back from the hurly-burly of the stallholders and dodgy chemical characters of Rupert Street, the Yard (a courtyard with bar attached) provides a rare opportunity for alfresco drinking in W1. Punters stand in the small flagged square open to the sky above (covered with an awning in winter), stepping inside for top-ups of lager, wine or shampers. On screens above the bar counter Muscular Marys combat chromium machines. Upstairs is a more subdued second bar space with Chesterfield seating and colonial-style ceiling fans twirling indolently from a beamed barn roof.

Function room. Music (DJs 8pm Fri, Sat). Tables outdoors (covered/heated and open courtyard). **Map 7/K6**

Zebrano

14-16 Ganton Street, W1 (7287 5267). Oxford Circus tube. **Open** 5pm-midnight Mon-Sat. **Food served** 5-10.30pm Mon-Sat. **Credit** AmEx, MC, V.

A slick, seductive and sexy operation this, part of the **Freedom Brewing Company** stable (*see p37*). Few are here for the co's own-brewed beer, however. They've slinked down the staircase – passing up the street-level cafe-diner – to plunge into a red-tinged world of zebra striping and zingy drinks. The drinks menu shows admirable panache, with unusual finds in the Martini list (one with strawberry, berry and basil, for example), and house shooters of Kahlúa, Baileys and Blavod. Barmen with improbable handles such as Bartek B and Pete O contribute specials such as Caribbean Stud and Sweet Cheeks. Spirits can be sold by the bottle, and it's a young, moneyed clientele, many looking to pick up, show her off, or just have a flashy, funky time. The vats that used to be such a big feature of this place – hey, what's sexy about vats? – are now hidden behind red perspex. Alcoves divided by rows of house plants provide much-needed smooch zones.

Bar available for hire. Restaurant. Tables outdoors (pavement). **Map 2/J6**

Also in the area...

All Bar One 84 Cambridge Circus, WC2 (7379 8311); 36-8 Dean Street, W1 (7479 7921).
Jamies 58-9 Poland Street, W1 (7287 6666).
Moon & Sixpence (JD Wetherspoon) 185 Wardour Street, W1 (7734 0037).
Moon Underwater (JD Wetherspoon) 105-7 Charing Cross Road/20 Greek Street, WC2 (7287 6039).
O'Neill's 38 Great Marlborough Street, W1 (7437 0039).
Pitcher & Piano 69-70 Dean Street, W1 (7434 3585).
Slug & Lettuce 80-82 Wardour Street, W1 (7437 1400).

South Kensington

Strange, given the fabulous gin palaces built elsewhere in London during Queen Vic's reign, that the ambitious scheme that was once known as 'Albertopolis' (the grouping of grand museums, royal concert hall and Hyde Park memorial named in honour of the Prince Consort) didn't incorporate any notable boozers. Instead, visitors to the area have to wander widely, down the Brompton Road, or even as far as Fulham Road (connoisseurs zero in on the **Anglesea Arms**). Equally strange, given the big money in SW3 and SW7, that neither has the area ever been known for stylish bars, although the recent arrival of **FireHouse** may go some way to changing that.

190 Queensgate

190 Queensgate, SW7 (7581 5666). Gloucester Road or South Kensington tube. **Open** 11am-1am Mon-Sat; 11am-midnight Sun. **Food served** *Bistro* 7am-midnight Mon-Fri; 7.30am-midnight Sat; 7.30am-11.30pm Sun. *Restaurant* 5.30-11pm Tue-Sat. **Credit** AmEx, DC, MC, V.
This annexe of the Gore Hotel is everybody's secret find for a nightcap after a concert at the Royal Albert Hall. But don't expect quite the Victorian splendour of the anchor tenant, with its Turkish carpets, stained glass, aspidistras and 4,500-plus paintings and prints. Instead, settle for (or rather into) button-upholstered leather chairs, oak-panelled walls, portraits and a long bar counter with shelves of backlit bottles. The drinks list is extensive; bouquets for the wonderful choice of wines, cocktails and single malts, brickbats for the single beer (Tiger) on offer. Demure by day, the atmosphere at night is louche, attracting both a spirited younger crowd and the expense account brigade, with a few natashas livening up the mix. Music is well selected – Nitin Sawhney, Thievery Corporation – but a titch too loud for a place that has better acoustics than the concert hall across the way.
Babies and children admitted (high chairs; restaurant and bistro only). Bistro. Function room. Restaurant.

Admiral Codrington

17 Mossop Street, SW3 (7581 0005/www.estreet.com). South Kensington tube. **Open** 11.30am-11pm Mon-Sat; noon-10.30pm Sun. **Food served** noon-2.30pm, 7-11pm Mon-Fri; noon-3.30pm, 7-11pm Sat; noon-3.30pm, 7-10.30pm Sun. **Credit** AmEx, MC, V.
Resting more on labels than laurels, this erstwhile Sloane Ranger fave once hosted the likes of Lady Di and the then-happy couple Fergie and Andy. It's been a tough act to follow;

nowadays you're more likely to encounter Irish lads laying into the Guinness or a trio of PAs in M&S cashmere necking the Chilean chardonnay (£17 a bottle). The surrounds – a bit of distressed furniture in muddy tones, dark wood panelling, photos and prints of cricketer Ian Botham, motorcycle jumper Chris Bromham, fox-hunters – are comfortable in a rough-edged sort of way. A real plus is the Codrington's conservatory restaurant, Cod (geddit?), with a fine selection of fish dishes (£9.95-£13.25) and an ichthyo-theme throughout. The pub's name honours the hero of the Battle of Navarino (1827); interesting to speculate what would have appeared on the menu had it been named after Horatio Hornblower.
Babies and children admitted. Games (backgammon). Restaurant (available for hire). Tables outdoors (garden).

Anglesea Arms

15 Selwood Terrace, SW7 (7373 7960 /www.capitolpubcompany.co.uk). Gloucester Road or South Kensington tube. **Open** 11am-11pm Mon-Sat; noon-10.30pm Sun. **Food served** noon-3pm, 6-10pm Mon-Fri; noon-10pm Sat; noon-9.30pm Sun. **Credit** MC, V.
It could well be that this museum-quality Victorian pub experiences the odd quiet, uncrowded moment, but just when, pray tell, might those be? Like Venice, the Taj Mahal and the Riviera, it's just too pretty for its own good. With original etched-glass snobscreens, chairs upholstered in green leather, ornate lampshades of varying styles and eras and William Morris-style wallpaper, it's an embodiment of drawing room elegance lifted from the pages of Dickens. (We knowingly drop in that reference as a link to the fact that as a young man of 22 Dickens lodged just a couple of doors away at No 11.) In addition to Old England splendour, the long bar provides Adnams and Brakspear on draught (supplemented by regularly changing guest ales) and a good selection of wine by the glass. The restaurant – a proper dining room rather than a gastropub-style back room – serves affordable traditional English fare, as well as contemporary faves such as mussels provençal and pumpkin risotto (mains £6.95-£12.95). Add a flowery front terrace for summer drinking and a cosy cast-iron and tilework fireplace in winter and you have near pub perfection.
Babies and children admitted (restaurant; before 6pm in bar). No piped music or jukebox. Tables outdoors (terrace). TV (satellite).

Blenheim

27 Cale Street, SW3 (7349 0056). South Kensington tube. **Open** noon-11pm Mon-Sat; noon-10.30pm Sun. **Food served** noon-2pm daily. **Credit** AmEx, DC, MC, V.
This extremely comfortable Georgian pub bordering the grassy spaces of St Luke's church is a major beneficiary of a doting brewery – in this case, Dorset-based Hall & Woodhouse, trading under the name Badger, which owns and manages a good number of London's better boozers. Its pubs tend to be immaculately kept with an emphasis on conservation of character, with the Blenheim being a fine case in hand. The framed pictures of the King's Road at the turn of the 20th century, the wall of Chelsea FC team line-ups dating from the 1907-8 season, one of their first after formation, the gorgeous stained-glass cupola – all whisper the gentle notion of time slowly passing. And then there are the beers: three Badger Brewery ales (including Tanglefoot by the four-pint jug) and a rare drinkable lager in Hoffbräu. Two-hour tranches of lunchtime pub grub, a burbling CD player, TV and a pinball machine are concessions to those on a stricter, nine-to-five schedule.
Function room. Games (fruit machines, pool table). TV (big screen, satellite).

Cactus Blue

86 Fulham Road, SW3 (7823 7858). South Kensington tube. **Open/food served** 5.30pm-midnight Mon-Fri; noon-midnight Sat; noon-11pm Sun. **Happy hour** 5.30-7.30pm daily. **Credit** AmEx, DC, MC, V.
The space occupied by this theme bar is decidedly more Shinjuku than South Ken. From the ground-floor bar (gun metal counter, Navajo blanket patterns and portraits of Sitting Bull in all guises but generally seated) rises an astonishingly high atrium; reach the mezzanine via the glass-enclosed staircase, complete with brass handrail in the shape of a rattler (as in snake). Behind lies the restaurant serving the usual Tex-Mex dishes (£9.95-£18.95) and such 'errant' (their word not ours) entrées as jambalaya and salmon sabayon. Up at the bar, most of the Cactus classic cocktails (£5.95 to £6.25) are tequila-based, which is hardly surprising given that the back shelving displays more than 40 types. There are seven additional mescals, and, for the sensible, a decent selection of wines from the New World. Good music too – completely native to the UK.
Babies and children admitted (restaurant only). Function room. Music (DJs Thur; jazz 7pm Sun; free). Restaurant. Tables outdoors (pavement).

The Collection

264 Brompton Road, SW3 (7225 1212/www.the-collection.co.uk). South Kensington tube. **Open/food served** *Bar* 5-11pm Mon-Sat; noon-10.30pm Sun; *Restaurant* 6.30-11.30pm Mon-Fri; noon-4pm, 6.30-11.30pm Sat; noon-4pm, 6.30-10.30pm Sun. **Credit** AmEx, DC, MC, V.
It's an impressive entry, to be sure: an illuminated footbridge leading to an impossibly long bar and one of the largest arrays of spirits in town. But there ends the razzle-dazzle. The space is huge and completely overpowers a bizarre mix of Polynesia (split bamboo walls, beaded curtains, trunk-like posts) and SoHo (NYC) warehouse conversion. Approach the bar with caution: it's on a slip-sliding gradient that may provoke giddiness well before any encounter with alcohol. The list of cocktails (£7.50-£8.50) spans the globe, from north and south of the border (Chivas Manhattan to Mojito) to Eastern Block (*sic*) and the Orient (but ignoring Asia's greatest contribution to mixology, the Singapore Sling). The peckish head for the loft restaurant or choose one of the 'sharing plates' (£22/£36 for two/four people): oriental, Arabic meze, antipasti or mixed sushi. Map not included.
Babies and children admitted (restaurant only; high chairs). Bar available for hire. Disabled: toilet. Dress: smart casual. Music (DJs 7.30pm nightly; free). Restaurant.

Drayton Arms

153 Old Brompton Road, SW5 (7835 2301). Earl's Court or Gloucester Road tube. **Open** noon-11pm Mon-Sat; noon-10.30pm Sun. **Food served** noon-10pm Mon-Fri; noon-9pm Sun. **Credit** MC, V.
Lavish use of terracotta, marble and mahogany, plus oxblood walls and potted plants hark back to fusty Victorian origins; sinuous tendrils and curlicues above the windows and the doors add bijou art nouveau, while table football and pinball machines bring the whole shebang crashing and blinging into the 21st-century world of pubdom. It's grand and solid with a reassuring air of permanence. For such a well-aged institution the crowd is surprisingly young, but aat the same time pleasingly laid-back. The line-up of beers is fairly unexciting (Bass, London Pride and Staropramen) but the service is friendly. Various filled paninis (£5.25) are served throughout the day, more substantial main courses (£6.95-£7.95) in the

London drinking: wine bars

What ever happened to the wine bar?

Back in the '70s and early '80s, wine bars were the posh alternative to the pub. They were the sort of places where punters could go and get a seat, a bite to eat and admire the chintz curtains over a bottle or two of Blue Nun, far away from the smoky, downmarket environs of the local boozer.

And now? Many of London's drinkers would rather poke their eyes out with knitting needles than be caught dead in a wine bar. And, really, who could blame them? Many of those shedlike old boozers, the sort that used to smell of fags and tramp's trousers, have been smartened up and transformed into gastropubs or DJ bars. And there's an ever growing list of style bars serving up the right mix of music, decor, beautiful people and decent cocktails for more serious boozing and schmoozing. Wine bars, in comparison, are about as hip as a shellsuit.

So, what went wrong with the wine bar? Its decline and fall isn't down to just one factor, but to several – most attributable to the wine bars themselves. To start with, too many London wine bars are just plain boring. They are monuments to mediocrity, from the staid food offerings, to the uninspiring interiors, to the naff muzak. Few wine bar owners seem to have taken notice of what successful style bars do to attract customers and they remain stuck in a swag-curtained '80s time warp as a result. Two notable exceptions here are the **Corney & Barrow** (*see p14*) and **Jamies** (*see p15*) chains, two slick predominantly City-based operators determined to drag corporate wine drinking into the 21st century.

Then there's the wine itself. Strange as it may seem, the list served at many London wine bars is likely to be boringly unadventurous, even downright bad. The first duty of a wine bar ought to be to serve excellent wine, but even with this humble goal, many fail. Quite why this should be is very difficult to say, as London is a world capital for the wine trade. Finding interesting, well-made wines here is far easier than it is in most other cities. Serving crap wine in a wine bar is inexcusable. Wine bars with dull wine lists deserve to go under.

These days, more people are likely to know the difference between bad wine and good. Back in the 1970s, drinking wine had an appealing mystique about it. People didn't really know that much about the subject and wine was still an aspirational drink. Now, wine has become demystified to such an extent that it's just another commodity. About 90 per cent of the adult population who drink alcohol drink wine. The majority of that wine is being drunk at home. Supermarkets are the biggest wine retailers and they make no bones about selling wine as a beverage for everyday consumption.

A top five for vino

Bleeding Heart Tavern (*see p108)* Bleeding Heart Yard, 19 Greville Street, EC1 (7404 0333).
Cork & Bottle (*see p56*) 44-6 Cranbourn Street, WC2 (7734 7807).
Cellar Gascon (*see p108*) 59 West Smithfield, EC1 (7796 0600).
Gordon's (*see p95*) 47 Villiers Street, WC2 (7930 1408).
Wine Wharf (*see p201*) Vinopolis, Stoney Street, SE1 (7940 8335).

From the consumer's point of view, when you can buy better wine at Sainsbury's or Oddbins than you can in a wine bar, why go to a wine bar? One could argue, with some success, that the role of the wine bar has simply been superseded by gastropubs and cocktail bars. Both make a point of selling a few decent wines by the bottle and glass. Even so, wine bars are thriving in cities such as San Francisco, New York, even Buenos Aires – cities with no shortage of good watering holes. So, could the wine bar become trendy in London again? With so many of our drink trends being imported from the US, the revivification of the wine bar can't be ruled out. But don't hold your breath. *Susan Low*

evening, and there's a popular Sunday lunch. It may be a modest, workaday, ordinary boozer, but of the pure pub with no-frills genre, the Drayton is up in the premier league.
Disabled toilet. Music (DJs 8pm Fri). Tables outdoors (pavement).

FireHouse

3 Cromwell Road, SW7 (7584 7258 /www.firehouse sw7.com). South Kensington tube. **Open** 6pm-3am Tue-Sat. **Food served** 7pm-1am Tue-Sat. **Credit** AmEx, DC, MC, V.
FireHouse began as yet another private members' club, but now ordinary mortals (ie those who haven't shelled out £300 for yearly membership) are permitted – although not at weekends – to pass through the grand entrance, set within a mid-Victorian terrace built by Sir Charles James Freake in 1862, and enter this shrine to beautiful and well-heeled gentility. Those cursed with the ugly gene might feel awkward among the Pierces and Sophies lounging artfully on modish red and black sofas beneath provocative wall-hung photo art ('Shooting Sex: the Definitive Guide to Undressing Strangers') but service is surprisingly warm. Order drinks from a list as long as the Book of Job. From the back bar, french doors give way to a small dining room hung with black and whites of '60s icons, a discreet nod to past lives played out on the premises: Jimi Hendrix performed in a club on this site in 1966 and this was where (allegedly) Lord Lucan was last seen before his famed disappearance.
Dress: smart casual. TV (satellite).

Latitude

163-5 Draycott Avenue, SW3 (7589 8464). South Kensington tube. **Open** 5-11.30pm Mon-Sat. **Food served** 5-11pm Mon-Sat. **Credit** AmEx, MC, V.
Despite all the style-bar hype and hullabaloo, London remains a pub city. The number of bars is on the increase but they're still something of a novelty, largely reserved for a night up West or a Hoxton trawl. Truly local bars are a rarity. This little venue is one. Rustic white tiles on the floor, tawny textured walls and comfy leather armchairs and sofas are well suited to trad pub-type pursuits of catching up with mates and having a good old natter over a few jars of something loosening. The list of classic cocktails (£7.50) is brief but packed with good stuff, although almost everyone seems to stick with the chardonnay or rioja. So endearing is Latitude that we even forgive the conceptual nonsense of the drinks menu (lower case typography festooned with mixed fonts and irrelevant punctuation marks); 'Available on [rikwest'] – n,' it says. 'Who's Rick West?' asked one understandably confused punter. See what we mean?
Function room. Games (backgammon). Music (occasional DJs).

Also in the area...

Abbaye 102 Old Brompton Road, SW7 (7373 2403). **All Bar One** 152 Gloucester Road, SW7 (7244 5861).

St James's

There is occasional activity around St James's Street – a new restaurant here and there, though rarely anything earth shattering – but otherwise the stately byways of this part of town are impervious to change. Waterstone's **Studio Lounge** appeared a year or so ago, but as far as St James's is concerned the line-up for this guide was set in the first edition. Expect a handful of classic old pubs plus the odd hotel bar of distinguished pedigree. Note: we define St James's as the area wholly north of the park of the same name; for pubs in the vicinity of St James's tube station *See chapters* **Westminster** (p104) and **Victoria** (p98).

Che

23 St James Street, SW1 (7747 9380/www.cherestaurant. co.uk). Green Park tube. **Open** 11am-11pm Mon-Fri; 5-11pm Sat. **Food served** 11am-2.45pm, 6-11pm Mon-Fri; 6-11pm Sat. **Credit** AmEx, MC, V.
A peculiar mix of ancient and modern, Che is not your usual cigar bar. The ageing St James's fat cats, who stock their humidors with visits to Davidoff and James J Fox nearby, are put off by the clubby music that booms out in the main bar, but barely permeates the smoking room in the back. Guevara-admiring radicals pour scorn on the concept and return immediately to Stoke Newington. This leaves Che's main clientele as the young and the flashy, who we suspect – and Sigmund would surely have pointed out – regard a fat cigar more as an ostentatious penis extension than as a tasty and relaxing treat to be savoured. If you can hack the smoke (or if you fancy a puff; the cigar menu is lengthy and impressive), the dimly lit back room is a far more comfortable place in which to enjoy a glass of wine or a cocktail.
Babies and children admitted (restaurant). Disabled: lift, toilet. Dress: smart casual. Function room. **Map 2/J8**

Duke's Hotel Bar

Duke's Hotel, 35 St James's Place, SW1 (7491 4840/ www.dukeshotel.co.uk). Green Park tube. **Open** noon-11pm Mon-Sat; noon-10.30pm Sun. **Credit** AmEx, DC, MC, V.
Venue of choice for the last of the country gentry, Duke's is secluded (in fact, devilishly hard to find unless you know exactly where to look), discreet and ultimately classy, without being at all show-offy. Its two lordly drawing room spaces are soberly coloured in Wedgwood blue, and comfortably furnished with red leather bucket chairs. House special is a Martini, prepared with Grey Goose vodka and hypnotic grace at your table. Ours was immaculate – but then for 13 squids you'd expect it to be, wouldn't you? Crunchy table snacks are of superior quality. This is the perfect bar in which to meet your paramour; credit Di and Dodi with some taste, then, for this is where they reputedly used to hook up. But it's a delight whatever the company.
Dress: jacket and tie. Function room. **Map 2/J8**

Golden Lion

25 King Street, SW1 (7925 0007). Green Park or Piccadilly Circus tube. **Open** noon-11pm Mon-Fri. **Food served** noon-2.30pm Mon-Fri. **Credit** AmEx, MC, V.
It's a pity the Nicholson's staff responsible for refitting the **Red Lion** (*see below*) on Duke of York Street weren't called in to work on this, its near-neighbour. For while that pub has been looked after beautifully, this one – vintage c1732 – hasn't been treated nearly as well. Sure, the Jacobean-style frontage with protruding windows is handsome (it's been awarded a London Heritage Inn plaque), but inside, it's the usual Nicholson's story of severe lighting, ugly upholstery, bland muzak and an especially luminescent fruit machine (housed in its own snuggly fitting dark wood booth – do you think it's original 18th century?). On the plus side, it is considerably larger than most other pubs in the area – and floor space is boosted at lunchtimes by the upstairs 'Theatre bar' – with less of a crush. Sadly, since our last visit the selection of beers has declined to the sad but common pairing of Adnams Bitter and Tetley's.
Function room. Tables outdoors (pavement). **Map 2/J8**

Red Lion

23 Crown Passage, off Pall Mall, SW1 (7930 4141). Green Park or St James's Park tube. **Open/food served** 11am-11pm Mon-Sat. **Credit** MC, V.

If a deficiency of heritage disqualifies you from the stately clubrooms of Pall Mall, then the Red Lion might make a more than acceptable substitute. It's not just the proximity: there's also a certain air of gentility about the place, conferred through a combination of the half-hidden passage approach and an interior of dark wood panelling, leaded windows and red velvety banquettes. It claims to be the second-oldest continuously licensed pub in the West End (what the oldest is the landlord can't say) but there are no obvious signs of great age. The well-bred punters tend to be possessed of fruity public-school tones, employed in ordering pints (just Adnams Bitter and Bass on draught), wines from a small but well-chosen list or a splash from a rich choice of two dozen or more amber-hued bottles of Glen-this and Glen-that.

Babies and children admitted (daytime). Function room. TV. **Map 2/J8**

Red Lion

2 Duke of York Street, SW1 (7321 0782). Piccadilly Circus tube. **Open** 11.30am-11pm Mon-Sat. **Food served** noon-3pm Mon-Fri; noon-5pm Sat. **Credit** MC, V.

A come-hither frontage of flowers and frills to catch the eye of passers-by on busy Jermyn Street means that this dinky Victorian place is almost permanently blockaded by pavement drinkers, forced out into the open by the massed bodies within. On the rare occasions on which the pub is quiet, patronsadmire walls so covered in etched glasswork that the impression is of a fairground hall of mirrors. The framing and the central island bar are all lustrous mahogany and things of great beauty. Games machines, music and TVs are banished so that entertainment is unwittingly provided by the cross-purpose attempts of Japanese tourists to communicate with the Eastern European bar staff. A Cask Marque attests to the well-kept state of the Burton, Bass and London Pride.

Map 2/J7

Rivoli at the Ritz

Ritz Hotel, 150 Piccadilly, SW1 (7493 8181). Green Park tube. **Open** 11.30am-11pm Mon-Sat; noon-10.30pm Sun. **Food served** noon-10pm daily. **Credit** AmEx, DC, MC, V.

In 1972, after 65 years of stylishly boozy history, the Ritz Hotel closed its legendary Rivoli Bar. In 2001 it reopened as a fantastical creation fashioned in early art deco style. Walls are panelled in polished camphor wood inset with Lalique glass panels, the bar is in pale polished onyx and everything is reflected in verre églomisé mirrors painted with prancing deer. It's all very florid and OTT (leopard-print chairs!) and, given the cabin-sized dimensions of the place, slightly cloying. But gorgeous all the same. Bottled beers start at an absurd £5.50, cocktails at £10. We sipped an Old-Fashioned (£12) and a Black Almond (black vodka, amaretto, Frangelico; £11); the latter came in a glass with a rim stuck with crushed almonds and pistachios. We felt like a million dollars – until the bill came. Jacket and tie is requested for gents, and a healthy bank balance required by all.

Children admitted. Disabled: toilet. Dress: jacket (no jeans or trainers). No-smoking tables. TV. **Map 2/J8**

Studio Lounge

5th floor, Waterstone's, 203-6 Piccadilly, W1 (7851 2400). Piccadilly Circus tube. **Open** 11am-11pm Mon-Sat; noon-6pm Sun. **Food served** noon-4pm, 6-9pm Mon-Sat; noon-5pm Sun. **Credit** AmEx, MC, V.

Up on the fifth floor of Waterstone's flagship Piccadilly store the reverent silence gives way to one hell of an un-bookish racket. The atmosphere in the Studio Lounge is arts theatre bar – chatty, smoky, photo exhibits on the walls, cool jazz soundtrack – fuelled by a well-travelled range of bottled beers, wines by the glass and cocktails. Prices, like the elevation, are a little higher than the norm. Tables by the picture windows offer views of the rooftops of St James's (spoiled at night by the reflected glare of the lighting) or there are a handful of prized couches. It makes for a great place to meet someone: the bar is beside the Arts section with the most browsable titles helpfully displayed on a table beside the entrance.

Babies and children admitted (until 5pm). Disabled: toilet. Function rooms. **Map 2/J7**

Also in the area...

Balls Brothers 20 Ryder Street, SW1 (7321 0882).
Crown Passage Vaults (Davy's) 20 King Street, SW1 (7839 8831).
Davy's at St James's Crown Passage, Pall Mall, SW1 (7839 8831).

Strand & Aldwych

This south-eastern extremity of 'theatreland' borders the touristy glitz of Covent Garden to the north and the legal and financial edge of the City to the east. It could be the influence of students and staff from the LSE and King's College plus media types from the BBC World Service at Bush House that injects the area with added sparkle, but there's plenty of choice and enough going on to keep everyone happy. This diversity encompasses slick modern bars like **Bank** and **Columbia**, as well as neighbourhood boozers such as the **Nell Gwynne**, **Seven Stars** and **White Horse**. And possibly the best cocktails in town can be had at the Savoy's **American Bar**.

American Bar

Savoy Hotel, Strand, WC2 (7836 4343/www.the-savoy.co.uk). Charing Cross tube/rail. **Open** 11am-11pm Mon-Sat. **Food served** 11am-1.30pm Mon-Sat. **Credit** AmEx, DC, MC, V.

The old-school art deco bar at the Savoy attracts the great and good, particularly American tourists and those with generous expense accounts. Expect to be scrutinised by a uniformed flunky before being offered a seat – the official dress code is jacket and tie, but a black polo neck passed muster. As you'd expect from the place where Britain's first Martini was mixed, cocktails are king, with vodka Martinis (served in frosted glasses) and absinthe concoctions reputedly the finest in town. Be warned, prices can top a tenner. The 69 malt whiskies range from the bog standard to the rare, and bottled beers are (just) under a fiver. Service is of the highest order, and a query on the definition of a 'cocktail' earned us a concise history of said beverage from our supremely well-informed waiter.

Disabled: toilet. Dress: smart; jacket and tie. Function rooms. Music (pianist 7-11pm Mon-Sat). No-smoking area. **Map 2/L7**

Bank

1 Kingsway, Aldwych, WC2 (7379 9797/www.bankrestaurants.com). Covent Garden or Holborn tube. **Open** 11am-11pm Mon-Sat; 11.30am-10pm Sun. **Food served** noon-3pm, 5-11pm Mon-Fri; 11.30am-3pm, 5.30-11pm Sat; 11.30am-3pm, 5.30-9.30pm Sun. **Credit** AmEx, DC, MC, V.

Let's get it straight from the off: this successful and imposing bar-restaurant luxuriating behind huge picture windows caters exclusively to winners . Only those who have succeeded in their chosen fields will ever feel truly comfortable eating, drinking and being themselves among the comfortable modern seating, surrealist American seaside scenes and self-realised patrons of Bank. Only they can identify whatever that shards-of-glass installation thingy is that occupies most of the ceiling. Winners. The cool and efficient door and bar staff are never less than charming – so long as you look as if you can afford a dozen quid for a bottle of house plonk. We winners enjoy spending time at Bank. We even guessed (correctly) that it was so-called because the building used to be a financial institution. The food in the large, clattering restaurant at the rear is an acclaimed mix of Modern European and British staples at a price considerably more than losers would be prepared to pay.
Babies and children admitted (children's menu, high chairs, restaurant only). Disabled: toilet. Dress: smart casual. Function room. Music (jazz 11.30am-3pm Sat, Sun). Restaurant. **Map 4/M6**

Coal Hole

91 Strand, WC2 (7379 9883). Embankment tube/ Charing Cross tube/rail. **Open** 11am-11pm Mon-Sat; noon-6pm Sun. **Food served** noon-5pm daily. **Credit** MC, V.
This is the pub the late, great, hell-raising Ireland-born actor Richard Harris used to slip into whenever he was staying at the adjacent Savoy Hotel and, although it has faded somewhat since its glory days at the early part of the 20th century (haven't we all?), the Romantic Period decor is still worth a long look. Built in 1904 and named after a succession of pubs in the area used by riverside coal-haulers – then the lowest of the low – the Hole was deliberately designed fancy. So expect period-style wood beams on nicotine-painted high ceilings, some very fancy stained glasswork and fine Greco-Roman marble nymph friezes. Upstairs is the Wolfe Room, contemptuously named after Victorian actor Edmund Kean's club for henpecked husbands. The chunky L-shaped serving area occupies most of the long, dark ground-floor room and dispenses real ales that have shrunk in recent years to just the standard, although not unpleasant, trio of Tetley's, Adnams and London Pride.
Games (fruit machine). Tables outdoors (pavement). **Map 2/L7**

Columbia Bar

69 Aldwych, WC2 (7831 8043). Covent Garden or Holborn tube. **Open** 11am-11pm Mon-Thur; 11am-1am Fri. **Food served** noon-10pm Mon-Fri. **Credit** AmEx, DC, MC, V.
Young's foray into the style-bar market has been remarkably successful, managing to combine the wine and cocktail-quaffing crowd with lovers of real ale. The lines are clean and modern, with the ground floor almost exploding in angles, a psychedelic pattern carpet and striking orange pillars. The basement is less frenetic with more in the way of brickwork. Overall, imagine All Bar One designed by a Goldsmith's acid casualty. More clued-in students from the nearby London School of Economics mix freely with hipper office workers and representatives of the designer-arty-crafty world. And was that Alan Alda we saw dining quietly in the corner? Although most of the drinkers are on bottled beers and wines, the real ale gets more of a look-in than you'd think. Quality will out?
Disabled: toilet. Games (fruit machines). Music (DJ 9pm-1am Fri; free). No-smoking area (restaurant). Restaurant. TV. **Map 4/M6**

Edgar Wallace

40 Essex Street, WC2 (7353 3120). Temple tube. **Open** 11am-11pm Mon-Fri. **Food served** noon-3pm Mon-Fri. **Credit** MC, V.
This friendly corporate boozer just off the Strand is named after one of Britain's most influential (and forgotten) thriller writers. Between 1905 and his death in 1932 (he'd gone to Hollywood to script the first film of *King Kong*), Wallace wrote a staggering 957 short stories, 15 plays and 175 novels. Prolific ain't the word. 1975 was the centenary of his birth and it gave the pub company the excuse to rename the Essex Head in his honour. It's a late-Victorian pub built on the site of a much older tavern frequented by the likes of Dr Johnson. The internal walls have been knocked through to make one square-shaped bar, with a serving counter at one end knocking out some decent beers, including the fine Timothy Taylor Landlord bitter. The walls are covered in Wallace memorabilia as well as a more recent addition: a menu signed by what looks like 'Lucy Sprigget'. Tireless research revealed that it is, in fact, the signature of one Jerry Springer, a man obviously not as gifted with the pen as he is with the gob. Most customers are lawyers (Temple's just a stagger away), with the odd smattering of academics from King's College and Wallace devotees.
Babies and children admitted (lunchtimes). Function room. Games (darts, quiz nights). No-smoking tables. TV. **Map 4/M6**

George IV

28 Portugal Street, WC2 (7831 3221). Holborn or Temple tube. **Open** 11am-11pm Mon-Fri. **Food served** 11am-3pm, 5-9pm Mon-Fri. **Credit** MC, V.
Operating unashamedly as a fun pub in order to attract students from the nearby LSE, and the younger end of local office and legal workers, this high-ceilinged Edwardian boozer is loud, brash and invariably busy. The big screen is used for 'major' sporting events (aren't they all, these days?) and the Capital FM-style soundtrack is usually a few notches louder than most over-30s would like. The original architecture – engraved mirrors, carved woodwork and exposed floorboards – fits in surprisingly well with the posters advertising cheap drink and food deals (predominantly involving burgers, chicken tikka masala and chilli). Upstairs is used as a games and function room with a pool table and assorted board games. Confirming that real ale is on a climb-back to favour with younger drinkers, regular London Pride is joined by occasional guests from time to time.
Function room. Games (fruit machines, pool table). TV (big screen, satellite). **Map 4/M6**

Lobby Bar

One Aldwych, 1 Aldwych, WC2 (7300 1000/ www.onealdwych.com). Covent Garden tube/Charing Cross tube/rail. **Open** 9am-11pm Mon-Sat; 10am-10.30pm Sun. **Credit** AmEx, DC, MC, V.
The lobby in question is that of One Aldwych, a hotel so exclusive it thinks the very word 'hotel' is vulgar. The bar is a vast, airy space, more like a banking hall, with light spilling in from tall arched windows on both long sides. A statue of an oversized rower in a small boat uses his considerable oar to direct visitors towards the bar counter. This is where efficient uniformed bar staff mix a variety of superior Martinis, cocktails, long drinks, Bellinis and Collins for under a tenner. You can get a beer but the choice includes nothing too fancy. The seating comprises oversized chairs and low sofas, the decor incorporates flowers (both fresh and dried), simple colours and understated lines. Although the adjacent Axis restaurant offers superior meals, bar snacks

of the satay, sushi and caviar with blini variety are available from 5.30pm, but at prices that reflect the surroundings. You see how high that ceiling is?
Babies and children admitted. Disabled: toilet. Function rooms. Restaurants. **Map 4/M7**

Lyceum Tavern

354 Strand, WC2 (7836 7155). Covent Garden, Embankment or Temple tube/Charing Cross tube/rail. **Open** 11.30am-11pm Mon-Sat; noon-10.30pm Sun. **Food served** noon-3.30pm, 5-8.30pm Mon-Thur, Sat; noon-5pm Fri; noon-4pm Sun. **Credit** MC, V.
The ground-floor bar of this popular Sam Smith's boozer is where the real drinkers hang out. A melange of office workers, blue-collar types and more adventurous tourists occupy the useful row of wood and glass cubicles that run down one long wall, prop up the opposite long bar, or cram themselves into the small seated 'sports' area at the rear. Upstairs is where the bosses and more squeamish tourists hang out, plus those looking for the traditional pub grub that's a speciality up here. This is a world of leather armchairs, low glass tables and faux wall-tapestries. Even the music is different: upstairs we encountered John Lee Hooker, while down below vintage Kylie was bemoaning her lack of luck. Being a Sam Smith's pub everything – including the stout, Old Brewery Bitter and fancy-sounding lagers – is cheaper than you'd usually find in the West End.
Babies and children admitted (before 9pm). Games (darts, quiz machines). No-smoking tables (when food is served). TV. **Map 2/L7**

Nell Gwynne

1-2 Bull Inn Court, WC2 (7240 5579). Embankment tube/Charing Cross tube/rail. **Open** 11am-11pm Mon-Sat. **Food served** (sandwiches) noon-3pm Mon-Sat. **No credit cards.**
It's long been a semi-secret drinking destination for theatrical and media types but now that a proper sign has finally arrived in the Strand, this small, intimate boozer has become known to a wider public. The tiny raised seating area at the back makes it look bigger than it is, but the whole pub is no larger than the average sandwich bar. Bathed in a scarlet glow, thanks to the ubiquitous dark red ceiling and upturned glass nipple lampshades, a blackboard behind the bar reads 'Jerry and Trish welcome you to the friendliest freehouse in the West End', a proposition certainly worth discussing. We found the Pixies on the sound system, and the Korean judo team thrashing Britain on twin TVs. The pick of three cask-conditioned bitters are Courage Directors and Greene King Old Speckled Hen. Bitter seemed the beverage of choice on the Wednesday night we called by, with Baileys-ice nudging lager into third place.
Babies and children admitted. Comedy (8pm every 2nd Mon of mth; free). Jukebox. Games (fruit machines). Tables outdoors (pavement). TVs (satellite). **Map 2/L7**

Seven Stars

53-54 Carey Street, WC2 (7242 8521). Chancery Lane, Holborn or Temple tube. **Open** 11am-11pm Mon-Fri; noon-11pm Sat. **Food served** noon-3pm Mon-Fri; noon-9pm Sat. **Credit** AmEx, MC, V.
The arrival of Ms Roxy Beaujolais – cookery writer, socialite and late of the Three Greyhounds, Soho – a couple of years ago, added a touch of pizzazz to this dry old boozer. Situated at the back of the Royal Courts of Justice and within easy strolling distance of the old bankruptcy court, it's not surprising that the majority of customers are lawyers. Add a few visiting Soho eccentrics and those attracted by the historic associations, and this small, narrow pub can get mighty crowded. Built in 1602 and originally called the Leg & Seven Stars (after the naval flag of Holland) in a bid to attract visiting Dutch sailors, it retains low-beamed ceilings, narrow wood settles and rough plasterwork. There's been a dab hand at work, adding joyous reds and yellows, framed British legal film posters (*Brothers in Law*, *Action for Slander* with Ann Todd, *Trial and Error*) and a shot of Tom Paine (the cat not the essayist). The three real ales we found were Broadside and Bitter from Adnams and Harveys fine Sussex Best. Superior lunchtime food ('Marvellous Milly is cooking for you today') might include bistro classics, gourmet sandwiches, kedgeree, ribeye and what-have-you.
Babies and children admitted. Function room. **Map 4/M6**

Ye Old White Horse

2 St Clement's Lane, WC2 (7242 5518). Holborn or Temple tube. **Open** 11am-10.30pm Mon-Fri. **Food served** noon-2pm Mon-Fri. **Credit** MC, V.
Now that the Brakspear brewery has gone, this smallish trad boozer has widened its repertoire to include the likes of Timothy Taylor Landlord, Greene King Abbot and Flowers IPA. It's a cosy, red-painted pub, with a tiny raised seating area at the back and a landlord and landlady in smart braces and perm. The 'No Students' sign that used to hang on the door was absent when we last called by – maybe it was being cleaned – but the sentiment remains and this is the only pub within pissing distance of the LSE not to encourage the educational elite with karaoke, jugs of tequila and melted-cheese-on-chips style promotions.
Games (fruit machine). **Map 4/M6**

Also in the area...

Savoy Tup 2 Savoy Street, WC2 (7836 9738).
Walkabout Temple Place, The Embankment, WC2 (7395 3690).

Trafalgar Square & Charing Cross

Most of the pubs and bars around Charing Cross rail station exist to winkle out the tourist and commuter dollar, but if you know where to look, diamonds can be found. **Gordon's** wine bar bucks the trend as do neighbouring back street boozers such as the **Ship & Shovell** and **Sherlock Holmes**. Smarter alecs rate **Rockwell** as one of the capital's best (and most expensive) style bars, worth the dosh if only for views of the Square and the opportunity to sample 2,000,000 different bourbons.

Clarence

53 Whitehall, SW1 (7930 4808). Embankment tube/Charing Cross tube/rail. **Open** 8am-11pm Mon-Sat; 10am-10.30pm Sun. **Food served** 8am-9pm Mon-Sat; 10am-9pm Sun. **Credit** AmEx, DC, MC, V.
The sign on the door says 'famous since 1862' and the decor of bare brick walls, ancient beams and wooden floorboards (said to have been snatched from a demolished pier) points in that direction. Named after King William IV (an early Duke of Clarence) and known as 'the copper's nark' in the days when nearby old Scotland Yard was the Met's HQ, it has become a place that's popular with tourists and civil servants from the government buildings that surround Whitehall. The two or three real ales that are always on offer are invariably well kept and will probably include Adnams Bitter and Broadside. Food is strictly 'traditional' pub grub of the fish and chips to ploughman's type and the brief but enterprising wine list doesn't allow for many either/ors.

Babies and children admitted. Function room. Games (fruit machine, golf machine). Tables outdoors (pavement). TV. **Map 2/L8**

Gordon's

47 Villiers Street, WC2 (7930 1408). Embankment tube/ Charing Cross tube/rail. **Open** 11am-11pm Mon-Sat; noon-10pm Sun. **Food served** noon-10pm Mon-Sat; noon-9pm Sun. **Credit** MC, V.

A long-cherished institution, Gordon's is to wine bars what Rules is to steak restaurants. Consequently, there are usually more bottoms than there are seats for them to sit on, even if the air is occasionally reminiscent of a Whitby smokery. When everything's right, the atmosphere in the subtly lit subterranean bar with its candles in bottles and dusty nooks can be intense. And when a hundred conversations start reverberating off the low, grime-encrusted brick alcoves, you know you're in business. Although the casual wine drinker is well looked after, so is the connoisseur. Specialities stretch across the spectrum, with the sherry, madeira and port part of the menu particularly worth plundering. Wines come from all corners of the globe, start at around a tenner a bottle and you can get something very decent for double that. Food is of the cold salad and cheeseboard type and served from the counter at the foot of the stairs. In warmer weather the tables in the outside court are highly sought after.

Babies and children admitted (lunchtime). Tables outdoors (terrace). **Map 2/L7**

Harp

47 Chandos Place, WC2 (7836 0291). Charing Cross tube/rail. **Open/food served** 11am-11pm Mon-Sat; noon-10.30pm Sun. **Credit** AmEx, DC, MC, V.

A friendly community boozer that's narrow enough to ensure you meet people – even if you're only squeezing past them. It's decorated in the avant-garde way of an eccentric rural freehouse: extravagant brass chandeliers drop from a deep red ceiling, with a wall of painted '60s celebrities (James Mason, Elizabeth Taylor) opposite a row of mirrors. It's too thin for traditional tables and chairs, so once you squeeze past the geezers at the bar, you find rows of raised bench-like tables with tall stools. Clientele ranges from off-duty coppers from Charing Cross nick over the road to off-duty charity workers and their past clients. It's a mildly bohemian little oasis that serves good beer (Harveys Sussex, and a guest or two) and great lunchtime sausages (O'Hagan's) in wonderfully unhealthy crusty bread.

Dress: smart casual. **Map 2/L7**

ICA Bar

The Mall, SW1 (7930 3647/www.ica.org.uk). Charing Cross tube/rail. **Open** noon-11pm Mon; noon-1am Tue-Sat; noon-10.30pm Sun. **Food served** noon-3pm, 5-10.30pm Mon; noon-3pm, 5-11pm Tue-Sat; noon-10pm Sun. **Admission** £1.50 (free to ICA members). **Credit** AmEx, DC, MC, V.

Be prepared to pay £1.50 temporary membership just to get to the ICA cafe and bar. Enough people feel the charge is worth it to find a healthy smattering enjoying their after-work tipple, with numbers increasing as the night meanders on and the adjacent cinema and art gallery start to empty out. At weekends this turns into a flood when black-clad crop-headed chain-smokers (death is good for the image) turn up for ear-shattering club nights, hosted by celebrity DJs. But the charge does keep out the riff-raff, keeping faces like us safe from grizzled old locals trying to tap us for the price of a pint. Your companions are much more likely to be vaguely familiar, either because they are or because they look like someone who is. Whoever they are, they won't talk to you so don't try for any small talk. Real ale is a real no, the nearest options being Hoegaarden or Leffe. There's also Guinness. Cocktails are OK, if run-of-the-mill, but happily the wine list is better.

Babies and children admitted (nappy-changing facilities). Disabled: lift, toilet. Function rooms. Games (chess). Internet access. Music (DJs 9pm nights vary). No-smoking area. **Map 1/K8**

Lord Moon of the Mall

16-18 Whitehall, SW1 (7839 7701). Embankment tube/ Charing Cross tube/rail. **Open** 10am-11pm Mon-Sat; noon-10.30pm Sun. **Food served** 10am-10pm Mon-Sat; noon-10.30pm Sun. **Credit** AmEx, MC, V.

This was one of the JD Wetherspoon chain's early flagship boozers and the portrait of the grand Regency nobleman over the fireplace is none other than the company's founder, Tim Martin. Built in 1872 as the headquarters of Cocks Biddulph & Co (Bankers) and sold by Barclays in 1992, the property is a typical high-ceilinged Victorian banking hall that's been cleverly adapted for drinking purposes. The toilets occupy the old vault and the no-smoking area is roughly where defaulters used to be strung up as a warning to the poor. Although the rows of comfy armchairs and sofas, decent range of real ales and opulent surroundings lure in local white-collar workers and tourists by the cartload, it has to be said that the place lacks any real atmosphere and looks something like a Butlins version of Boodles.

Babies and children admitted (until 5pm). Disabled: toilet. Dress: no football colours on match days. Games (fruit machine, quiz machine). No piped music or jukebox. No-smoking area. **Map 2/K8**

Marquis of Granby

51 Chandos Place, WC2 (7836 7657). Covent Garden tube/Charing Cross tube/rail. **Open** noon-11pm Mon-Sat; noon-10.30pm Sun. **Food served** noon-5pm daily. **Credit** MC, V.

This wedge-shaped pub is ideally situated midway between the orchestra pit of the Coliseum and Charing Cross police station. That it's also beside the major commuter rat-run between Covent Garden, London's main post office and one

Critics' choice
rock history

Camden Head (p171)
An early rehearsal venue for the Kinks.

Intrepid Fox (p81)
Where Rod Stewart and Ronnie Lane formed the Faces.

Slug & Lettuce (p60)
The Upper St Martin's Lane premises in which Keith Moon spent the evening the night he died.

Telegraph (p207)
Where the late, great Joe Strummer played his first ever gig with the 101ers.

Troubadour (p40)
Venue for one of Dylan's first UK gigs.

Freedom. See p81.

of London's busiest railway stations doesn't hurt any either, nor does the reasonable range of cask-conditioned bitters that usually features the divine Timothy Taylor Landlord. The decor comes from the Victorian age (though not all was originally installed in this pub) and includes carved wooden screens, glorious etched glass and two of the biggest and brashest Victorian gas heaters this side of David Dickinson's loft. In winter the cast-iron fireplace belts out a fierce heat, and in summer all windows are cranked open to allow the London air in. The kitchen comes into its own with its bargain Sunday lunches served in the Tesco tradition: 'Pile 'em high, sell 'em cheap'.

Babies and children admitted (upstairs, until 5pm). Dress: smart casual. Function room. Games (fruit machines). **Map 2/L7**

Old Shades

37 Whitehall, SW1 (7321 2801). Embankment tube/ Charing Cross tube/rail. **Open** 11am-11pm Mon-Sat; noon-10.30pm Sun. **Food served** noon-8pm Mon-Thur; noon-5pm Fri, Sun; noon-8pm Sat. **Credit** AmEx, DC, MC, V.

Although the neo-gothic facade of this popular top-end-of-Whitehall boozer points to ancient beginnings – and, in fact, there has been a pub of some description on this site since before the Reformation – this particularly striking building is only around a century young (built 1898). Still the carved spandrels, cross-mullioned casements and other Flemish-Gothic features (ask your dad to explain the terminology) make it a Grade II-listed building. Inside it's comfortably furnished with wood-panelled walls, prints of old London and several worthy attempts at faux stained glass. The cupola over the serving area has been known to attract gasps of admiration from the knowledgeable, as have the couple of real ales offered in addition to the usual bog-standard selection of lagers, stouts and cider.

Function room. Games (fruit machines, quiz machine). No-smoking tables. TV (big screen, satellite). **Map 2/L8**

Queen Mary

Waterloo Pier, Victoria Embankment, WC2 (7240 9404/ www.queenmary.co.uk). Embankment or Temple tube. **Open** *Summer* noon-11.30pm Mon-Thur; noon-2am Fri, Sat; noon-10.30pm Sun. *Winter* noon-11.30pm Mon-Thur; noon-2am Fri, Sat; noon-6pm Sun. **Food served** *Summer* noon-9pm daily. *Winter* noon-9pm Mon-Sat; noon-6pm Sun. **Admission** £7 after 9pm Fri, Sat. **Credit** AmEx, MC, V.

There is a certain type of individual – could be a young backpacking tourist; could be a similar-aged office worker – who enjoys nothing better than lounging on boat-decks during the less inclement months of the British summer. This moored hulk, in teh shadow of Waterloo Bridge, and the nearby **Tattershall Castle** (King's Reach, Victoria Embankment, SW1; 7839 6548) both fit the bill admirably. OK, so the range of beers never rises above the usual nitro-keg offerings and prices are hardly in the 'duty free' bracket, but the experience is the thing. These vessels are so popular, you'd be hard pressed to find any deck-space during hot weather, and the myriad of bars and function rooms each possesses offer popular pubby food during the day with fun clubby experiences to follow into the early hours.

Babies and children admitted (until 6pm). Dress: smart casual. Function rooms (seat 100-170). Games (fruit machine). Music (DJs 9pm Fri, Sat). Tables outdoors (deck). **Map 2/L8**

Rockwell

Trafalgar Hotel, 2 Spring Gardens, SW1 (7870 2959/ www.thetrafalgar.hilton.com). Embankment tube/Charing Cross tube/rail. **Open** 7am-1am Mon-Sat; 7am-10.30pm Sun. **Food served** 11am-11pm Mon-Sat; 10.30am-10pm Sun. **Credit** AmEx, DC, MC, V.

Although this spacious and very classy bar primarily serves the residents of the Trafalgar Hotel, it also attracts a cosmopolitan cocktail crowd in its own right (after all, it was the *Time Out* Eating & Drinking awards Best Bar winner in 2002). Keywords are 'vast', 'chic' and 'exclusive'. Add 'pricey' if £8 for a cocktail seems a lot. The house speciality is bourbon, and the room-long bar displays just about every variety known to man; more than 100, they say, though who has time to count? The decor is subdued but chic, with huge picture windows (partially overlooking Trafalgar Square), ranked chaise longues, lots of marble, and uniformed staff who know exactly what they're about and think you should too. The Trafalgar Hilton is pitched as the Hilton Group's first 'lifestyle hotel'. If that description sounds like bollocks to you, you're probably not the Rockwell type.

Disabled: toilet. Tables outdoors (roof garden). **Map 2/K7**

Sherlock Holmes

10 Northumberland Street, WC2 (7930 2644/ www.sherlockholmespub.homestead.com). Embankment tube/Charing Cross tube/rail. **Open** 11am-11pm Mon-Sat; noon-10.30pm Sun. **Food served** noon-10pm daily. **Credit** MC, V.

One of London's first theme pubs (created in 1957, capitalising on an exhibit left over from the '51 Festival of Britain), the Holmes may be a little cheesy (paw prints of the Hound of the Baskervilles, etc), nevertheless, it's a pleasing Victorian-style pub on the site of what used to be the swanky Northumberland Hotel (famous as the accommodation of Dr Mortimer in *The Hound of the Baskervilles*). The speciality of the house is real ale, and up to five are available on tap, including an own-label that turned out to be Adnams Bitter last time we checked. Upstairs is a restaurant where fanciful names disguise standard pub fare: Sherlock's Own Favourite (8oz sirloin), the Six Napoleons (mussels), the Illustrious Client (melon), the Sign of Four (soup of the day). You'll also find a mock-up of Holmes's study reputedly provided by the Conan Doyle family.

Babies and children admitted. Games (fruit machine). Restaurant (no smoking; available for hire). Tables outdoors (pavement). **Map 2/L7**

Ship & Shovell

1-3 Craven Passage, WC2 (7839 1311). Charing Cross tube/rail. **Open** 11am-11pm Mon-Fri; noon-11pm Sat. **Food served** noon-3pm Mon-Fri; noon-4pm Sat. **Credit** AmEx, MC, V.

The name of this idiosyncratic Hall & Woodhouse boozer comes from the English admiral Sir Cloudisley Shovell, who had the misfortune to lose his fleet off the aptly named Scilly Isles in 1707. The gimmick is that the pub is actually two pubs, standing opposite each other on either side of narrow Craven Passage. Not just a marketing ruse, but it makes sound business sense too, as one staff can run what effectively are two boozers. Although the pub has no history to speak of – one side was until quite recently a model soldier shop – the decor throughout is traditionally styled wood panelling, bare board floors and etched glass. The beers come from Dorset's

Badger Brewery and include IPA, Tanglefoot and Best Bitter. Customers tend to be commuters passing through nearby Charing Cross station mingling with various groups of local office workers.
Babies and children admitted (Sat only). Function room. Games (fruit machines). TV (satellite). **Map 2/L7**

Also in the area...

Champagne Charlie's (Davy's) 17 The Arches, Villiers Street, WC1 (7930 7523).
Ha! Ha! Bar & Grill 6 Villiers Street, WC2 (7930 1263).
Pitcher & Piano 40-42 William IV Street, WC2 (7240 6180).

Victoria

Commuters can't be choosy – a swifty before the 5.50pm to Uckfield is all dependent on ease of access, hence the plethora of grotty, undistinguished, yet heavily patronised boozers around the periphery of the station. The search for something superior means putting distance between yourself and the concourse (although the Wetherspoon's up above WH Smith combines decent beer with views of the departure boards, and the Thistle Victoria Hotel offers the gentlemen's club-like ambience of the Harvard Bar). Happiest hunting grounds are east along Victoria Street (for the **Albert Tavern**) and the narrow lanes to the north where there are a few small local pubs of character, notably the **Cask & Glass**.

Albert Tavern

52 Victoria Street, SW1 (7222 5577). St James's Park tube/Victoria tube/rail. **Open/food served** 11am-11pm Mon-Sat; noon-10.30pm Sun. **Credit** AmEx, DC, MC, V.
A wonderfully ornate wedding cake of Victoriana, built in the mid-1800s and in dutiful service as the Albert since the 1860s. Its most famous connection is parliamentary; in the upstairs carvery is a division bell to usher honourable members back to lobby, while the staircase is lined with a gallery of portraits of PMs. Thatcher unveiled hers personally, Blair offered a full-colour signed version. The nobs can feast on prime succulent beef and roast Norfolk turkey – the plebs downstairs make do with scampi and Scotch eggs. Scampi and Scotch eggs in superb surroundings, mind, downstairs being a huge bar space in three areas, dominated by an imposing counter offering Abbot Ale, Charles Wells Bombardier and Courage Directors. PCs might join off-duty MPs, as New Scotland Yard's just round the corner.
Babies and children admitted (restaurant, weekends only). Function room. Games (fruit machines).

Bbar

43 Buckingham Palace Road, SW1 (7958 7000/ www.bbarlondon.com). Victoria tube/rail. **Open** 11.30am-11pm Mon-Fri (available for hire at weekends).
Food served noon-10.30pm Mon-Fri. **Credit** AmEx, DC, MC, V.
A new addition this, and a slick operation – if a bit of a laboured gimmick. The theme is 'hunting lodge' (why? God knows) and the place is done up like a set from *Daktari*. A classy façade under a black awning hides a fairly small bar area filled with the trappings of the savannah: a model of a cheetah at pace, pictures of fellow Attenborough-favoured mammals, a zebra stripe here and there. The cocktails follow the theme, for example, 'Shark Infested Island Tea', which is Absolut, Gordon's gin, Bacardi, Cointreau, blackcurrant and toy shark. The menu also features an impressive array of Highland malts, ports and fortified wines, and some quite pricey cognacs. Still, it's hugely popular with (black-hearted) white City hunters, and any new venture around Victoria is one to be welcomed.
Babies and children admitted. Function room. No-smoking area. Tables outdoors (pavement).

Boisdale

13 Eccleston Street, SW1 (7730 6922/www.boisdale.co.uk). Victoria tube/rail. **Open** noon-1am Mon-Fri; 7pm-1am Sat. **Food served** noon-2.30pm, 7-11pm Mon-Fri; 7-11pm Sat. **Admission** £10 (£3.95 if already on premises) after 10pm Mon-Sat. **Credit** AmEx, DC, MC, V.
Inaugurated in 1988, Boisdale – 'of Belgravia' if you please – peddles a classy dining and drinking experience. First off, the whole joint is done out in the dark green and red of the Macdonald clan, mounted claymores, four rows of whiskies behind the main bar counter, the whole bit. In addition to stocking every single malt under the sun, the Boisdale boasts every Cuban cigar brand known to man, because above all else this canny two-room (Mac and back bars) establishment is a jazz-and-cigar club. Live music happens six nights of the week, the best examples are released on the Boisdale label. Dining involves fine Scottish cuisine, often sourced from across the border: Orkney salmon, pure-bred Highland steaks and alike. Wines, bought directly from continental vineyards, are remarkably cheap for the surroundings – 20 types of quality French and Spanish brands at under a tenner a bottle. A pretty courtyard with a retractable roof completes the picture. There is now a second Boisdale in the vicinity of Liverpool Street station.
Babies and children admitted. Function rooms. Music (jazz 10pm-midnight Mon-Sat). Tables outdoors (conservatory).

Cardinal

23 Francis Street, SW1 (7834 7260). Victoria tube/rail. **Open** 11.30am-11pm Mon-Sat; noon-10.30pm Sun. **Food served** noon-3pm, 5.30-9pm Mon-Fri; noon-3pm Sat. **Credit** AmEx, DC, MC, V.
Tucked in along a dark tributary of the Vauxhall Bridge Road behind Westminster Cathedral, the imposing Cardinal looks every inch the traditional (posh) boozer. Yorkshire brewery Sam Smith's was responsible for the complete refurb; the place is all decked out in regal greens, deep reds and browns with lots of carved wood and engraved mirrors. Ever present are the prying eyes of any number of historic cardinals, captured in portrait. Around the main three-square bar counter, the whole Sam Smith's range is available from the keg; on the far side is a separate dining area with an open kitchen. Attached to another side, what was once a sherry bar – and still ornately inscribed as such on the door to the street – is now a place to escape the laddish beery conversation drowning out the beep of the fruit machine.
Babies and children welcome. Function room. Games (darts, fruit machine, quiz machine). No-smoking area (lunchtime). TV (big screen).

Cask & Glass

39-41 Palace Street, SW1 (7834 7630). Victoria tube/rail. **Open** 11am-11pm Mon-Fri; noon-8pm Sat. **Food served** 11am-2.30pm Mon-Fri; noon-2.30pm Sat. **Credit** AmEx, DC, MC, V.
One of the more maverick of Shepherd Neame's roster of pubs in central London, the C&G occupies a tiny corner of an otherwise faceless grid of streets between Victoria station and Westminster. And we mean tiny. Post-work, you have to cut

a square through the cigar smoke to get to the bar, and the limited table space is at a premium. Why here and not any number of anodyne hostelries delaying the commuter journey home? Well, pedigree, really. Along with the idiosyncratic touch of lining shelf space and skirting rail with toy aeroplanes modelled on every conceivable international carrier, it offers quality ales from Faversham's Shepherd Neame brewery, including Spitfire and Master Brew, plus fine wines chalked on a board by the fireplace. The house plants outside could have been landscaped.
Tables outdoors (pavement). TV (satellite).

Christopher's Victoria

Thistle Victoria Hotel, 101 Buckingham Palace Road, SW1 (7976 5522). Victoria tube/rail. **Open** noon-11pm Mon-Sat; noon-10.30 Sun. **Food served** noon-10.30pm Mon-Sat; noon-10pm Sun. **Credit** AmEx, DC, MC, V.
Based on the grand steak and lobster houses on America's Eastern seaboard (and younger sibling to the Covent Garden branch; *see p36*), Christopher's bar-restaurant in Victoria's Thistle Hotel takes full advantage of a large room dating back to the mid-19th century. The restaurant has its own entrance facing the bus terminal; the bar, accessible through the station, ushers in its guests with understated class. A destination in its own right, the bar comprises a long granite counter and comfy divided seating areas, with a casual scattering of pillars and large cushions, almost Arab by design. The menu is nothing if not stylish, with cocktails based on fruit purées and classic mixes, including a house Bellini-tini of vodka, peach schnapps and peach purée. 'Tiny snacks' start at £1, and run up to sizzling mains of grilled sirloin steaks.
Babies and children admitted (restaurant).

Goring Hotel Bar

Goring Hotel, Beeston Place, Grosvenor Gardens, SW1 (7396 9000). Victoria tube/rail. **Open/food served** 7am-11pm Mon-Sat. **Credit** AmEx, DC, MC, V.
A very neat operation this, a quality hotel bar whose clientele, staff and surroundings conspire in a high but not stifling sense of decorum. Lunchtimes are relaxed, but come evening and your coat is taken by a smiling flunky on the main door, and a jacket and tie, though not obligatory, are the passport to erudite conversation and extra olives. The bar leads to a series of three lounge areas, porticoed or alcoved, where efficient waiters serve classic cocktails, a long selection of aperitifs (all £5, including akvavit and Punt E Mes), sherries and ports, digestifs, armagnacs and the whole geography of Scotland in a whisky-shaped bottle: Speyside Highland vintages, Island malts, even Lowland varieties. Liqueurs are given equal prominence, and ales include Ram Rod and Sam Smith's.
Babies and children welcome (lounge area). Disabled: toilet. No-smoking tables.

Plumbers Arms

14 Lower Belgrave Street, SW1 (7730 4067). Victoria tube/rail. **Open** 11am-11pm Mon-Fri. **Food served** 11am-9.30pm Mon-Fri. **Credit** AmEx, DC, MC, V.
The food's average, the beer selection is so-so, the decor's drab, the lights are too bright and the staff are surly. However, none of these things mattered much to the clearly distressed lady who burst into the Plumbers Arms one November night in 1974 and informed the assembled company that her husband had just killed their nanny at their Chester Square home. Lord Lucan hasn't been seen since, of course, but it's unlikely he misses this undistinguished boozer too much. There's nothing especially unpleasant about it (a traditional single-bar boozer), but there are several far nicer places for a pint on the other side of Eaton Square (see the Belgravia section).
Function room. Games (darts, fruit machine). Quiz (mini bar quiz daily). Tables outdoors (pavement). TV (satellite).

Tiles

36 Buckingham Palace Road, SW1 (7834 7761). Victoria tube/rail. **Open** noon-11pm Mon-Fri. **Food served** noon-2.30pm, 5.30-10pm Mon-Fri. **Credit** AmEx, DC, MC, V.
A continental-style wine bar that carries off the laid-back brasserie feel with aplomb despite the constant roar of taxis and tourist coaches en route to nearby Victoria termini. Behind a pretty red facade, a scattering of white tableclothed wooden tables are invariably full, particularly at early evening. The choice of wines is diplomatically divided between Old and New Worlds, with some 20 reds and whites, six each by the glass; prices are similarly well spread. The names are chalked over the bar and the staff are happy to offer recommendations. Bar snacks are served at lunch and dinner, the speciality being potato skins with various complements – bacon, smoked cheddar, and so on. Downstairs is a less staid lounge area, decked out with comfy sofas and coffee tables.
Babies and children admitted. Function room. Tables outdoors (pavement).

Zander

45 Buckingham Gate, SW1 (7379 9797/ www.bankrestaurants.com). Victoria tube/rail. **Open** *Bar* noon-11pm Mon, Tue; noon-1am Wed-Fri; 5pm-1am Sat. **Food served** noon-2.45pm, 5.30-11pm Mon-Fri; 5.30-11pm Sat. **Credit** AmEx, DC, MC, V.
Being the biggest in Europe doesn't necessarily mean being the best, but the labyrinthine Zander at least gives it a good shot. Blessed with Europe's longest bar counter – and a cocktail menu of equal dimension – the Zander is also able to hide scores of casual/trendy customers in its mirror-free warren of alcoves. The complex links with its sister Bank restaurant, but could come in handy should London ever suffer another Blitz. If it does, then it won't be stout and Ovaltine underground; 20 Zander cocktails (including a house iced tea of Absolut Blue, absinthe, citronge, Havana Club rum, lemon and cranberry juices), 15 Martinis, ten scrummy fresh fruit Martinis, champagne and classic cocktails, plus fruit breezes and caipirinhas, complement Zander bar food (from 5.30pm only) of Indian, Spanish or vegetarian plates in the £10 range. Not cheap, and a confusing place to meet on a first date, but worth the walk through St James's Park.
Babies and children admitted (restaurant only; children's menus, high chairs). Function rooms. Music (DJs 8.30pm Fri, Sat; free). Tables outdoors (conservatory).

Also in the area...

Balls Brothers 50 Buckingham Palace Road, SW1 (7828 4111).
Tapster (Davy's) 3 Brewers Green, Buckingham Gate, SW1 (7222 0561).
Wetherspoon's Unit 5, Victoria Station, SW1 (7931 0445).
Willow Walk (JD Wetherspoon) 25 Wilton Road, SW1 (7828 2953).

Waterloo

'Terry meets Julie at Waterloo station, every Friday night,' – but where on earth did they go for a drink? Like many parts of London that are dominated by a mainline railway station, spruced-up Waterloo lacks a

quality boozing or bar scene. There are some able venues on Lower Marsh (**Cubana**, **Elusive Camel** and a branch of the Ruby Lounge: *see p53*) and commuters do OK by the **Fire Station** and **Hole in the Wall** (both just outside station exits). But visitors to the sprawling South Bank arts complex have few options other than the so-so **Film Cafe** and various faceless theatre bars. There is a shining light further east, though, where the stylish **Baltic** might point at treats to come.

Archduke

Concert Hall Approach, South Bank, SE1 (7928 9370). Waterloo tube/rail. **Open** 8.30am-11pm Mon-Fri; 11am-11pm Sat. **Food served** 11am-11pm Mon-Sat. **Credit** AmEx, DC, MC, V.

As rush hour trains thunder overhead, no one bats an eyelid in this unfalteringly popular watering hole, tucked under the arches of Waterloo Bridge. An interior like a giant conservatory is divided into several areas: a formal restaurant on top, a casual mezzanine and ground-floor bar, an alfresco gravel patio, and an enclosed terrace that doubles as a function room. Ceilings are high and arched, walls are exposed brick. Large amounts of glass, mammoth terracotta pots and hanging flora create a light, tropical feel. The place attracts a mixed and casual crowd who on the night we dropped by were being treated to some mellow and unobtrusive live jazz. The wine choice is ample, but not overwhelming, with plenty of familiar names from classic Euro regions, plus some tasty New World numbers. Easy drinking wines that don't demand food predominate; almost all are under £20. The weekly promos of wines by the glass are also worth a look.

Babies and children admitted. Conservatory (available for hire). Disabled: toilet. Music (jazz 8.30-11pm Mon-Fri; 9-11pm Sat). No-smoking areas. Tables outdoors (conservatory, garden, pavement).

L'Auberge

1 Sandell Street, SE1 (7633 0610). Waterloo tube/rail. **Open/food served** noon-midnight Mon-Fri; noon-11pm Sat. **Credit** AmEx, DC, MC, V.

Anyone seeking respite from the commuter chaos at Waterloo and unable to afford a Eurostar escape to Brussels will find some sanctuary at least in L'Auberge, nestling 100ft below the station. It's Belgian-themed but Tintin-free, and a choice of five different mussels dishes can be washed down with a variety of interesting beers, ranging in potency from a 4.5% raspberry-flavoured number (£3.45) to a sobriety-clattering 9.2% Rochefort (£4.75). One, the daffy-named Kwak, is served in a surrealist version of an hourglass so anorexic as to merit its own peculiar wooden holder, apparently designed by somebody's talentless dad in a shed in Ghent. It works well enough, though, as does the muted decor and unobtrusive lighting, which is perfectly complemented by the unshowy efficiency of the staff. All in all, a place where, once you've got your head round some of the prices, offers cosy relaxation with gourmet possibilities.

Babies and children admitted. Function room (Sat only). Tables outdoors (roof terrace).

Baltic

74 Blackfriars Road, SE1 (7928 1111/www.baltic restaurant.co.uk). Southwark tube/Waterloo tube/rail. **Open** noon-11pm daily Mon-Fri, Sun; 6-11pm Sat. **Food served** noon-3pm, 6-11pm daily. **Credit** AmEx, DC, MC, V.

Baltic is a treat. A place to gawp – and not merely because of the place's growing reputation as London's latest luvvy-drome. The owner, a half-Polish prince called Jan Woroniecki, is a man on a mission to both educate and pamper the palate and the eyes. Architect Seth Stein was called in to realise the proprietor's vision of a tastebud-tantalising experience in relaxed and understated surroundings, and this former coach-builder's factory was converted into its angular and spacious and very contemporary self. The 'is-it-an-Indian-restaurant?' door wrong-foots you towards the long bar, which further opens out into a high-vaulted restaurant area, where a wide range of moderately priced and damn tasty Eastern European cuisine is on offer. The attractions of the bar are even greater with 100-strong spirits, champagnes and Polish beers, followed by 32 different flavours of vodka at £2.50/£2.75 a shot (prices overall are a lot less than the seriously classy ambience would lead you to expect). The inspired use of amber, both as part of the bar structure and combined with optic fibre to create the most beautiful chandelier, confirms this as what it is: a rare gem on the south side of the river.

Babies and children admitted. Disabled: toilet. Function room. Music (jazz 7-11pm Sun; free). Tables outdoors (patio). TV (big screen, satellite).

Cubana

48 Lower Marsh, SE1 (7928 8778). Waterloo tube/rail. **Open/food served** noon-midnight Mon-Thur, Sun; noon-1am Fri, Sat. **Happy hour** 5-6.30pm daily; 10pm-midnight Mon, Tue. **Credit** AmEx, DC, MC, V.

This nation's Cuba obsession shows no signs of abating, as this joint shows with its now familiar celebration of Caribbean/Communist culture (no matter that the Cubans themselves are more interested in Coca-Cola and CNN). A heavy-lidded, cigar-chomping Fidel Castro grins down amid the weaponry, parrots and revolutionary-themed posters that jostle for space on walls painted to evoke sun-faded hues. Vertigo-indifferent couples whisper sweet nadas at the tables-for-two, individually perched in their own little tower overlooking the compact lower bar. While rum-based cocktails are the order of the day, an appetising array of Creole food is also available in tapas or main dish form. You can find plantain rosti with black bean houmous or marinated free-range chicken breast with fresh papaya salsa at both under £4. Laid-back in the week, it gets more lively at weekends, when waitresses move gingerly through a mayhem of dancers buzzing on booze and live tropical music. The theme might be tiring, but Cubana still manages to chill and rock with much aplomb.

Babies and children admitted. Disabled: toilet. Music (salsa 10.30-1pm Fri, Sat). Tables outdoors (terrace).

Elusive Camel

121 Lower Marsh, SE1 (7633 0270). Waterloo tube/rail. **Open** noon-11pm Mon-Sat; noon-10.30pm Sun. **Food served** noon-9pm daily. **Credit** MC, V.

David Byrne welcomes us into the Elusive Camel with the mantra 'same as it ever was'. Not entirely, David, not entirely. Nowadays, the lights are blue outside this reputed former whorehouse that is now an Aussie-run venture that still pulls quite a crowd. Local office bods pop in at lunchtime to sample the all-continents-covered bar food: cajun chicken, carbonara and Thai platter, each made with ingredients taken from the street's vibrant market right outside the front door. Grub can be accompanied by a glug or two of the imported Australian beers on offer, such as VB (£2) or Crown Lager (£2.80). A fine original staircase leads to the comfortable upstairs area, where the evening clientele can enjoy the angular blue shadows cleverly cast on to the ceiling from light sources outside and the view through the banister rails to where the sports screen-ogling punters are gathered in the bar below. From cathouse to frathouse, they might find themselves pondering.

Baltic. *See p101.*

Games (fruit machine). Music (rock/pop 8.30-11pm Thur). Tables outdoors (beer garden). TV (big screen, satellite).

Film Cafe

National Film Theatre, South Bank, SE1 (7928 3535). Waterloo tube/rail. **Open** *Bar* 11am-11pm Mon-Sat; noon-10.30pm Sun. *Cafe* 9.30am-9pm daily. **Food served** *Cafe only* 9.30am-9pm daily. **Credit** MC, V.

The warm and vibrant hues of the NFT foyer provide a welcome contrast to the grimy starkness of the South Bank. Turquoise pillars complement purple and pink carpeting, while reviews of the latest productions adorn the walls and a gauntlet of stills from the current season lines the corridor that leads off to the box office. The bar has a brief but promising wine list of New World varieties and if the selection of bottled beers is limited it does at least include Beck's and Budvar. Apparently, the two Young's ales (Special and Ordinary) are dispensed by a state-of-the-art electric pump, the only such beast in London. Scoffable-looking sandwiches hover in the background. On sunny days, the outdoor tables get packed with drinkers, not all of them there to discuss the merits of the latest Buñuel season, while a fiercely bearded ageing fiddler rasps the catgut with gusto. Institutional and concrete-swathed it may be, but in a city not blessed with accessible central riverside drinking areas, you takes what you can get.

Babies and children admitted. No-smoking tables. Tables outdoors.

Fire Station

150 Waterloo Road, SE1 (7620 2226). Waterloo tube/rail. **Open** 11am-11pm Mon-Sat; noon-10.30pm Sun. **Food served** *Bar* 11am-9pm Mon-Sat; noon-9.30pm Sun. *Restaurant* noon-3pm, 5.30-11pm Mon-Fri; noon-11pm Sat; noon-9.30pm Sun. **Credit** AmEx, DC, MC, V.

Though cavernous, the Fire Station – which proudly proclaims its emergency service origins in red girders, cream-tiled decor and fire engine-sized doors – still strains to contain all who nightly crowd within. It's popular with local suits killing time before the beckon of suburbia, as well as with the pre- and post-theatre crowds from the nearby Old Vic and National. The range of beers is excellent, with real ales to the fore (expect Brakspear, Young's, Adnams and a house brew) backed by upper-end lagers (Affligem and a Belgian abbey beer), plus a well-balanced (if pricey) wine list. Prominently displayed throughout is the establishment's award-winning menu, offering the likes of braised pheasant with risolette potatoes, sugar snaps and red wine reduction. If they served that in the average fire station canteen, the firemen would never fit down the pole.

Babies and children admitted (children's menu at weekends, high chairs). Function room. Games (fruit machine). Tables outdoors (pavement). TV (big screen, satellite).

Hole in the Wall

5 Mepham Street, SE1 (7928 6196). Waterloo tube/rail. **Open** 11am-11pm Mon-Sat; noon-10.30pm Sun. **Food served** noon-8pm Mon-Sat; noon-4pm Sun. **Credit** MC, V.

Gone are the days when a carelessly discarded cigarette butt would carbonise one of the highly flammable dossers that once congregated in the railway arch here. That apart, the unpretentious and welcoming Hole in the Wall is essentially unchanged. The lovely range of beers available reflects the passionate knowledge of the landlord: the common Old Speckled Hen, Young's Winter Warmer, Fuller's London Pride and Adnams Broadside sharing cellar space with the more elusive but admirably characteristic and organically brewed Battersea Bitter (£2.35 a pint). The food is basic hearty pub fare, grilled ribeye steak the dearest thing on the menu at £6.85. A word of advice: non-lovers of rugby looking for a quiet pint should steer well clear on international days, when the collective quaffing from the wall-to-wall scar-tissue brigade provokes a value surge for Guinness plc and a rapid exodus for everybody else.

Babies and children admitted (until 6pm). Games (fruit machines, golf machine, pinball). TV (big screen, satellite).

King's Arms

25 Roupell Street, SE1 (7207 0784). Waterloo tube/rail. **Open** 11am-11pm Mon-Sat; noon-10.30pm Sun. **Food served** noon-3pm, 6-10.30pm Mon-Fri; 6-10.30pm Sat; noon-5pm Sun. **Credit** AmEx, DC, MC, V.

The 'coal' fire might not be the real thing, but the warm welcome most certainly is. It emits from the period film-looking Victorian terraced location, from the genuine decor and from the conversation of the locals nattering and nodding at the bar counter. Equally warming is the range of alcohol: nine choices of white wine, seven of red, plus an awesome array of single malts at £2.25 a snifter, including some truly distinctive examples of the genre – a Bunnhabhain Single Islay Malt or a 15-year-old Glenfiddich Solera Reserve. Two guest ales accompany the three always on tap (Adnams Bitter, Marston's Pedigree and Tetley's). The chosen beverage can then be taken out to the conservatory, where the atmosphere of the former funeral parlour is anything but funereal, and press-rated English and Thai food can be sampled at long, solid wooden tables. Retro isn't always right, but at the King's Arms we wouldn't have it any other way.

Babies and children admitted (until 6pm Mon-Fri, all day weekends). Disabled: toilet. Function room. TV.

Laughing Gravy

154 Blackfriars Road, SE1 (7721 7055). Southwark tube/Waterloo tube/rail. **Open** 11am-11pm Mon-Fri; 7pm-midnight Sat. **Food served** noon-10.30pm Mon-Fri; 7-11pm Sat. **Credit** MC, V.

It's stuck out on a limb on a grim bit of bar-bereft Blackfriars Road, but the Laughing Gravy (named after Laurel & Hardy's dog) is definitely worth a detour. It's a bar-restaurant majoring in aspirational international cuisine (very good food, but pricey) and wine. There's a main dining area with a small quiet bar area that's invitingly unpretentious and atmospheric with a few homely touches such as Tiffany lamps, a piano and a dresser, and art for sale on the walls. The wine list is ample and straightforward and includes some easy drinking quaffers like a Montepulciano from Italy, as well as more sophisticated food wines like Chablis and Pouilly Fumé.

Babies and children admitted (high chairs). Games (board games). Tables outdoors (pavement).

The Ring

72 Blackfriars Road, SE1 (7928 2589). Southwark tube. **Open** 11am-11pm Mon-Sat; noon-10.30pm Sun. **Food served** 11am-2.30pm Mon-Fri; noon-2.30pm Sat, Sun. **No credit cards.**

The Ring is a rare example of sensitive refurbishment. The new manager – replacing long-term publican Neville Axford, counted out by the great referee in the sky last year – has retained respect for a boxing heritage that has long characterised this traditional and really rather lovely boozer. The walls are absolutely covered with framed photographs of the pugilists who once frequented the upstairs gym and would then visit the bar itself, for the requisite post-exercise refreshment. The gym's long gone, but new windows have effectively opened out the small space downstairs and muted

lighting adds to the welcoming air. Wooden tables and floor are spotless. The Ring provides a good range of single malts while Marston's Pedigree and Brakspear are the real ales on offer. A two-course lunchtime set menu combines Thai or English fare, and continental-quality coffee is available. Nice to see that trend and tradition needn't always be knocked out for the count.
Tables outdoors (pavement). TV (satellite).

Also in the area...

All Bar One 1 Chicheley Street, SE1 (7921 9471).
The Hop Cellars (Balls Brothers) 24 Southwark Street, SE1 (7403 6851).

Westminster

Parliament and Parliamentarians dominate this small area of governmental London. Our version of Westminster runs from the Palace of Westminster, north up Whitehall and west to just shy of the great Romanesque cathedral (called Westminster, but we reckon you're in Victoria by then). This year's terrible loss will be the art deco heaven of the **Paviours Arms**. As we go to press, it's destined for the wrecker's ball. That this fate should befall what is (was) London's most elegant, original and remarkably preserved late-1920s pub is little short of scandalous. Hopefully next year we will be able to report that landlords, Land Securities, have had a change of heart. But don't hold your breath.

Page's Bar

75 Page Street, SW1 (7834 6791/www.pagesbar.com). Pimlico or St James's Park tube. **Open** 11.30am-11pm Mon-Fri; 5-11pm Sat. **Food served** noon-2pm Mon-Fri; 6-10pm Sat. **Credit** AmEx, MC, V.
From the outside, this tarted-up former pub looks quite ordinary, but step inside and you're suddenly part of your favourite science fiction/fantasy fantasy. Most Saturdays there's a theme night based around the likes of *Nosferatu*, *Star Trek*, *Dr Who* and others ordinary mortals shouldn't have heard of. Similarly, many familiar faces have guest-starred – Dave Prowse (Darth Vader's body, althouth his strong Cornish accent meant he was never allowed to become his voice), Jon Pertwee, Craig Charles and the bloke who plays Mr Sulu – as well as loads of B-listers only the truly devoted would ever recognise without their make-up. The decor follows the theme with plenty of hidden lighting, a giant *Star Trek* model that flies over the pool table and glass cases full of stuff such as 3-D chess, models of Kirk, Picard and the rest, and signed photos of the great and the gory. Staff are also very proud of their *Star Trek* logo carpet. London Pride stands in for Klingon Ale as the beer of choice, and football and karaoke cater to the more down-to-earth locals who drink here during the week.
Games (fruit machine, pool table). Karaoke (1st and last Fri of mth). TV (satellite).

Paviours Arms

75 Page Street, SW1 (7834 2150). Pimlico or St James's Park tube. **Open** 11am-11pm Mon-Fri. **Food served** noon-2.30pm, 6-9.30pm Mon-Fri. **Credit** AmEx, DC, MC, V.
Admirers of art deco will already know about Page Street, with its Lutyens checkerboard flats and this deliciously unspoilt boozer. Though the chevron-design upholstery seems to have been replaced by a more standard pattern, the bulk of the decor remains authentic. The black surround bar with its leg-mirrors is particularly fine, as are the lashings of mahogany and chrome, but the best is to be found in the dining room (also good for reasonable quality Thai food), with its small, square, black and silver lacquered dining tables, curved glass lighting feature above the bar and upright deco lamp standards. The beers come from Fuller's, so no complaints there either, and the regulars are a mix of unimpressed locals, visiting office workers and the odd refugee from nearby Parliament. We once encountered a well-known TV B-lister canoodling with someone clearly not his wife (or daughter), but that's another story.
Babies and children admitted (until 7pm, restaurant only). Function room. Games (darts, fruit machine, pool table). Restaurant. TV (big screen, satellite).

Red Lion

48 Parliament Street, SW1 (7930 5826). Westminster tube. **Open** 11am-11pm Mon-Sat; noon-7pm Sun. **Food served** noon-3pm Mon-Sat; noon-2.30pm Sun. **Credit** MC, V.
Anyone who prefers *not* to mix with politicians, wannabe MPs gaining extensive photocopier experience, civil servants and political journalists should steer well clear of this, the Palace of Westminster's nearest boozer. On the other hand, if the BBC Parliamentary Channel is a source of thrills and if the idea of a division bell going off at odd moments fills you with knee-trembling excitement, then step right on in. The present Gothic pile was erected in 1900 over the pub where David Copperfield called for a glass of 'genuine stunning ale' and was served it with a kiss. These days, it's more likely to be Adnams or London Pride, and no kiss. The original hand-carved mahogany and etched glasswork in the ground-floor bar are worth a gander, as is the subterranean cellar, where NUM banner postcards commemorate the pub's role as the union's unofficial HQ during the miners' strikes of the 1980s. Two flights up is the soberly panelled dining room,where MPs and minor Treasury officials lunch unimportant VIPs.
Babies and children admitted (dining area). Function room. No-smoking area. Tables outdoors (pavement). TV (satellite).

Westminster Arms

9 Storey's Gate, SW1 (7222 8520). St James's Park or Westminster tube. **Open** 11am-11pm Mon-Fri; 11am-8pm Sat; noon-6pm Sun. **Food served** 11am-8pm Mon-Fri; noon-4pm Sat, Sun. **Credit** AmEx, DC, MC, V.
Attracting politicians like losers to a betting shop, this solid old warhorse lays claim to the title of best real ale boozer in SW1. A beast of many parts, it also comprises a downstairs wine bar (Storey's) and a traditional first-floor grill restaurant (Queen Anne's English Dining Room). Back at the bar, the serving area takes up most of one wall and is stacked with beer pump handles. There were eight real ales available when we last visited, ranging from Adnams Bitter to a superb Gale's GB from Horndean in Hampshire and the pub's own-label Westminster Bitter. Usually, staff are happy to reveal the real identity of the own ale, but here the barman kept commendably schtum. A good selection of cigars is available for those with shares in Sketchleys, and the wine list is impressive and caters to paupers and politicians alike. Expect to find aforementioned political types, civil servants and journalists, together with visiting tourists in search of photo opportunities.
Babies and children admitted. Function room. Games (fruit machine). No-smoking tables. Tables outdoors (pavement).

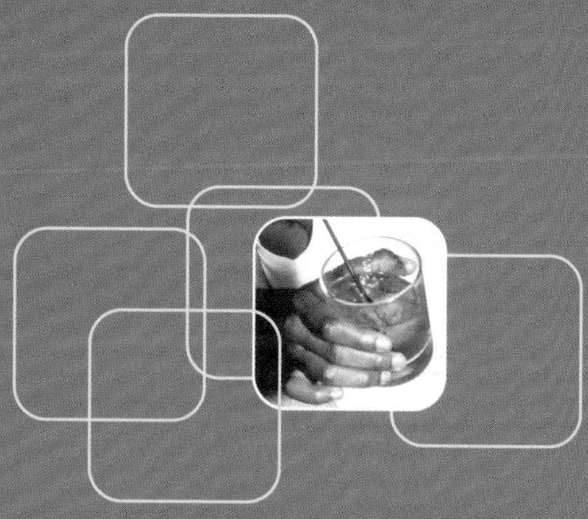

City

City

Chancery Lane

Occupying the City edge south and east of High Holborn, this is one of those nameless areas where legal and financial offices flourish, and a smattering of printworks remain after the mass exodus of the late 20th century. Early on a Friday night the best bars and boozers are packed with post-work revellers, but once the last tube has left, it's a ghost town until the office cleaners return early on Monday morning. Architectural tourists would do well to check out **Ye Old Mitre** and the showy **Cittie of Yorke**, which – like Paris – has to be experienced at least once.

Castle

26 Furnival Street, EC4 (7404 1310). Chancery Lane tube. **Open** 11am-11pm Mon-Fri. **Food served** 11am-2.30pm Mon-Fri. **Credit** MC, V.

This tiny corporate boozer, tucked away in the print and industrial enclave between Holborn and Fleet Street, doesn't have much going for it, on paper, at least. The views are grim – a brick wall in one direction, a *Third Man*-style desolate street scene in the other – but the welcome's usually friendly and the decor is of a type (comfortable inner city) that's fast disappearing. There's not much in the way of furniture, just bar stools and shelves, but hey, there's not a lot of room for luxuries. Silent Sky Sports, robust rock music and the flashing of the fruit machines offer entertainment to the solo drinker. Lunchtime food is popular, if much reliant on the frying pan. Tetley's and Adnams are the usual real ales.

Function room. Games (darts, pool, quiz machines). TV (satellite). **Map 4/N6**

Cittie of Yorke

22 High Holborn, WC1 (7242 7670). Chancery Lane or Holborn tube. **Open** 11.30am-11pm Mon-Sat. **Food served** noon-9pm Mon-Sat. **Credit** AmEx, DC, MC, V.

Dating from 1430, but substantially rebuilt in 1923, this Gothic pile owes much of its eccentric look to the time it spent (1890-1979) as flagship of the Henekey's wine bar chain. In the vast back room is the legendary Henekey's long bar – once the longest in the empire – and tall butts that used to hold spirits, wines and sherries, but which were emptied as a safety precaution during World War II. The wooden cubicles are Victorian and were intended for lawyers to consult with their clients, while the triangular metal stove that appears to have no chimney dates back to 1815 and was half-inched from the hall at nearby Gray's Inn. Now run by Samuel Smith's of Tadcaster, its Old Brewery cask-conditioned bitter and improbably named lagers are sold at good old Yorkshire prices. When Sam Smith's took over it opened up part of the 17th-century cellar as a wine bar and made the relatively modern front bar look ancient.

Babies and children admitted (downstairs). Function rooms. Games (darts, fruit machine). **Map 3/M5**

Mucky Duck

108 Fetter Lane, EC4 (7242 9518). Chancery Lane tube. **Open** 11am-11pm Mon-Fri. **Food served** noon-2.30pm Mon-Fri. **Credit** MC, V.

When Fleet Street (the industry rather than the thoroughfare) was thriving in the locale, this was where you'd find a goodly selection of boozed-up journos and overpaid printworkers. And, by the look of the decor – all dark woods, patterned carpet, framed naughty seaside postcards and metal advertising signs – not a lot has changed since. This traditional boozer survives by nurturing a loyal following among local office workers and, on a cold Monday night when most of the area's other pubs and bars were empty, the Duck had a healthy roomful. The barman seems to know everybody's name and also their tipples of choice. The real ales – London Pride, Greene King IPA – are toothsome enough and the jukebox full of singalong classics helps make this one of the area's best, if least assuming, boozers.

Dress: smart casual. Function room. Games (darts). Quiz. TV. **Map 4/N6**

Ye Old Mitre

1 Ely Court, Ely Place, EC1 (7405 4751). Chancery Lane tube/Farringdon tube/rail. **Open** 11am-11pm Mon-Fri. **Food served** 11am-9.30pm Mon-Fri. **No credit cards**.

We've heard it called 'the explorer's pub', for the simple reason that you've got to be a good map-reader or extremely dogged to find this tucked-away gem. Originally built in 1546, it was restructured in the 18th century using the original plans and materials and comes with an appealing warren of wood-panelled rooms, plenty of low beams, exposed stonework and a ghost. The name comes from its original purpose as the servants' quarters for the Bishops of Ely, whose London palace stood nearby. Previous landlords have included Sir Christopher Hatton and Oliver Cromwell, who made it a prison and then a hospital during the Civil War. Our favourite room, the largest, is to the right of the main entrance. Here you'll encounter a variety of local legal types, jewellers and some of London's more adventurous tourists. Look out for three or four real ales, as well as comfort snacks such as Scotch egg and farmhouse cheddar sarnies.

Dress: smart casual. Function room. **Map 3/N5**

Tooks Bar & Restaurant

17-18 Tooks Court, Cursitor Street, EC4 (7404 1818). Chancery Lane tube. **Open** 11am-11pm Mon-Fri. **Food served** noon-3.30pm, 5-8.30pm Mon-Fri. **Credit** AmEx, DC, MC, V.

Tooks is secluded, set up a narrow alley off a little-trafficked sidestreet at the back of Chancery Lane, which is all the better for languorous afternoons spent sharing briefings over the Môet (core clientele are affluent legal types). The look of the place is modern, with plenty of light wood, beige paintwork and greenery. During the day, the light spills in through large picture windows and gives the place a Mediterranean feel. Food falls into one of two types: bar snacks (soup, fish cakes, rice salad, etc) and more substantial Modern European entrées in the attached restaurant. Neither offers much in the way of budget eating. The sole draught lager is Bitburger, bottled beers come from Adnams of Suffolk, and wine via a substantial and well-thought-out list.

Babies and children admitted. Disabled: toilet. Function room. **Map 4/N6**

Also in the area...

Bottlescrue (Davy's) 53-60 Holborn Viaduct, EC1 (7248 2157).

Clerkenwell & Farringdon

Second only to Hoxton in the new bar stakes, the Clerkenwell/Farringdon area (stretching in our definition from Gray's Inn Road east to Goswell Road) has been transformed in just a handful of years from suits to ravers, from nine to fivers to people up for drinking and socialising into the early hours. And still the venues keep coming. The last 12 months have seen the arrival of Bed, Lifthouse and the Living

Room (all on Charterhouse Street, Smithfield), all welcome additions, and worth a look once you've worked your way through the following.

Abbaye

55 Charterhouse Street, EC1 (7253 1612). Chancery Lane tube/Farringdon tube/rail. **Open** noon-11pm Mon-Fri; 5.30-11pm Sat. **Food served** noon-10.30pm Mon-Fri; 5.30-10.30pm Sat. **Credit** AmEx, MC, V.

Exuding continental elegance in both decor (wooden floorboards, delicate cream walls decorated with porcelain plates) and staff training (they carefully steam glasses before pouring), Abbaye is a sophisticated moules restaurant that also happens to have a mean selection of Belgian beers and world wines that are definitely worth exploring. After all, it's not that often you get to try plum, banana and pineapple beer or such a wide variety of Leffe's quality ale, Pils and Trappist monastery beers. We recommend accompanying any booze with the moules Ostendaise (mussels steamed with Leffe Blonde, bacon and savoy cabbage, £8.50 a kilo). Visit Tuesday for Musselmania (as much as you can eat for £8.50) with Leffe's 12% Bush (Belgium's strongest lager, £3.65) to help turn the continental sophistication and suave dignity of the diners a little woozy.

Babies and children admitted. Disabled: toilet. Function room. No-smoking area. Restaurant. **Map 3/O5**

Al's Bar Cafe

11-13 Exmouth Market, EC1 (7837 4821). Angel tube/ Farringdon or King's Cross tube/rail/19, 38 bus.
Open 8am-2am Mon-Fri; 10am-2am Sat; 10am-11pm Sun.
Food served 8am-10pm Mon-Sat; 10am-9.30pm Sun.
Credit AmEx, DC, MC, V.

The short and pleasingly pedestrianised stretch of bookshops and trendy bars that is Exmouth Market is anchored firmly at its lower end by Al's, a large, bustling bar that makes up in popularity what it lacks in character. A vibrant blue on the outside, the decor of its main room (a concrete slab of a bar, bare walls, laminate tables) would surely harbour an echoey lack of warmth were it not so consistently lively. Al's manages to grab the crowds with an array of attractions. All-day breakfasts, burgers, and other affordably priced quality pub grub pulls in the hungry. The thirsty, meanwhile, can find a decent array of European beers (Warsteiner, Amstel and Pilsner Urquell, for example), while those seeking loud, late-night mingling, lubricated with cocktails and accompanied by DJs, head for the kitschy downstairs bar. Al's really comes to life in the summer, when the big windows fold back and its pavement tables and late licence make it a guaranteed draw for the weekend crowds.

Babies and children admitted (until 7pm). Function room. Music (DJs 9pm Fri, Sat). Tables outdoors (pavement). **Map 3/N4**

Al's Bar Cafe

City

Bear

2 St John's Square, EC1 (7608 2117). Farringdon tube/rail. **Open** noon-11pm Mon-Fri. **Food served** noon-2.30pm, 6-9.30pm Mon-Fri. **Credit** AmEx, MC, V.

The Bear's been taken over by the owners of **19:20** (*see p114*), which is why the dining room upstairs has now become a very hip bar christened Hibernate with low-slung leather sofas as far as the eye can see, square pouffes and a '50s vibe evoking a murky world of Arthur Daley spivs and Jack Hawkins gangsters. It's immensely popular with the EC1 boys and girls in their voluminous jeans and heavy oblong glasses – they all work in galleries, style journalism or photographic studios. Down on the ground floor it's business as usual: a safe and comfortable environment of nothing too challenging. Drinks are kept simple (Stella, Guinness and Hoegaarden on tap, with a limited selection of wine and cocktails for a fiver), as is the food, which is beloved of City gents, some of whom visit so regularly that they're on first-name terms with the chef. Lunchtime specials are popular, and we would particularly recommend the rocket, spinach and warm chicken liver salad.

Function room. Disabled: toilet. Tables outdoors (pavement). TV (satellite). **Map 3/O4**

Bishops Finger

9-10 West Smithfield, EC1 (7248 2341). Farringdon tube/rail. **Open** 11am-11pm Mon-Fri. **Food served** noon-3pm, 6-9pm Mon-Thur; noon-3pm Fri. **Credit** AmEx, MC, V.

Thatched Kentish country pubs may be brewer Shepherd Neame's traditional style, but it's also done a pretty fine job with this very tasteful City pub. In contrast to some of Farringdon's dingier historical taverns, this place is bright and warm with crisp yellow walls, candles and fresh flowers on the tables, and plants and vines adorning the huge window that looks out on to West Smithfield. Although the decor and mellow jazz may seem more bistro than boozer, the Kentish countryside lives on here in the great selection of English cask ales (Master Brew, Spitfire and, naturally, Bishops Finger). Winner of Shepherd Neame's Pub Food of the Year 2003 award, the Bishop is also justly proud of its grub, serving up fresh-from-the-market sausages (including lamb, lime and chilli; venison and red wine; tomato and mozzarella) and innovative creations such as stuffed chicken with mozzarella and spinach burgers.

Babies and children admitted. Disabled: toilet. Function room. Tables outdoors (pavement). **Map 3/O5**

Bleeding Heart Tavern & Bistro

Bleeding Heart Yard, 19 Greville Street, EC1 (7404 0333). Farringdon tube/rail. **Open** 11am-11pm Mon-Fri. **Food served** 11.30am-10.30pm Mon-Fri. **Credit** AmEx, DC, MC, V.

Oozing with a rich history of bloody murders and royal weddings (all celebrated in its publicity literature, so we needn't repeat it all here), the Bleeding Heart Tavern is a great place for rich wines and spit-roasts in lavish if sombre surroundings of red ceilings, fireplace, crimson flowers and a fine mahogany mirrored bar. Inspired by its history, the menu is traditional (whole roast suckling pig with crackling and apple sauce, £9.95) but luxurious (steamed steak, kidneys and stout puddings with fresh Irish oysters, £8.75) and tremendous value all at the same time. Although most people packed around the Tavern's tables were enjoying its culinary delights, the extensive wine list and quality Adnams ales (including Bitter and Fisherman) make it an enticing stop for a drink or two, if you can find any room at the bar. Further into the yard, the **Bleeding Heart Bistro** keeps up the good work, with an outstanding wine list that reads like a who's who of the viticultural world, and quality dining in more sedate surroundings.

Function room. **Map 3/N5**

Cafe Kick

43 Exmouth Market, EC1 (7837 8077). Angel tube/ Farringdon tube/rail/ 19, 38 bus. **Open** noon-11pm Mon-Sat; 5-10.30pm Sun. **Food served** noon-3pm Mon-Fri. **Happy hour** 4-7pm Mon-Sat; 5-8pm Sun. **Credit** MC, V.

Très continental and très chic, Cafe Kick goes from strength to strength; after the fabulous Moro restaurant opposite, this must be Exmouth Market's primo crowd-puller. The theme is simple: table football; but with that comes all manner of European sophistications from the quality bottled lagers (drink your way around the world) to the large front windows that open out on to the street to let air and light into the intense and smoky interior. The gloriously shambolic bar is long and thin, dotted with classy football memorabilia – pennants, programmes and portraits – and with a service area at the back, where boothed seating areas are planted in concession to those not taking part in the beautiful game. And the game's the thing. While the posing patrons of its sister establishment, **Bar Kick** (*see p121*), seem to think the René Pierre tables are clever-clever retro art installations rather than a form of entertainment, players at Cafe Kick take their game very seriously indeed, so remember: no spinning.

Games (table football). TVs. Tables outdoors (pavement). **Map 3/N4**

Cellar Gascon

59 West Smithfield, EC1 (7796 0600). Farringdon tube/rail. **Open** noon-midnight Mon-Fri. **Food served** noon-11.30pm Mon-Fri. **Credit** AmEx, MC, V.

'We're like the embassy for Gascon wines in London,' says the enthusiastic French barman explaining Cellar Gascon's impressive and intriguing list of 120 wines exclusively from Alsace. Just joking. Gascony. Indeed, Cellar Gascon is where suave embassy-style leather scoop bar stools, banquettes and elegant copper hanging lamps mix effortlessly with rustic brick, wood and candles of the rural France this place represents. Knowledgeable bar staff are happy, nay eager, to guide novices through lesser-known areas of winery such as Irougleguy and Pacherenc. A selection of 35 degustations (French-style tapas) includes more familiar regional classics like foie gras, while traditional aperitifs and digestifs such as Floc de Gascoigne and a huge selection of cognac and armagnac complete the Gasconomic experience.

Babies and children admitted (3-6pm). **Map 3/O5**

Cicada

132-6 St John Street, EC1 (7608 1550). Farringdon tube/rail. **Open** noon-11pm Mon-Fri; 6-11pm Sat. **Food served** noon-3pm, 6-11pm Mon-Fri; 6-11pm Sat. **Credit** AmEx, DC, MC, V.

There is affluence and a certain amount of sophistication in Clerkenwell, and those seeking it – or wishing to display it – may well head for Cicada. Large windows reveal comfortable sofas on stone flooring, with rectangular wall panels on serene, sand-coloured walls completing the understated decor. Neatly dressed barmen await behind the square, central bar, mixing up an enjoyable range of classic, champagne and Martini cocktails (£5.50-£6.50). Side of the bar is a sectioned-off dining area, serving a limited but interesting pan-Asian menu, including the likes of dim sum, chilli-salt squid and spicy pork ribs. Draught beers include Hoegaarden and Leffe, and there's a reasonably comprehensive wine list. The background chatter of the urbane crowd sums up the atmosphere,

which is noisy without being obtrusive, lively without being boisterous. Tasteful modernity – for those who like that kind of thing (and plenty do).
Babies and children admitted. Function room. No-smoking area (restaurant). Tables outdoors (piazza). **Map 3/O4**

Charterhouse

38 Charterhouse Street, EC1 (7608 0858). Farringdon tube/rail. **Open** noon-11pm Mon-Thur; noon-2am Fri; 10am-2am Sat; 10am-midnight Sun. **Food served** noon-10pm Mon-Fri; 10am-10pm Sat, Sun. **Happy hour** 5-7pm Mon-Wed. **Credit** MC, V.
Wedged into the narrow fork of Charterhouse Street, this bar occupies one of those buildings that look so narrow and slice-of-pie like from the outside that you can't help but be curious about what it's like within. The answer is thin at one end and fatter at the other. Architectural curiosities aside, it's an upbeat and stylish place that buzzes with a post-work/pre-club crowd who don't mind a bit of a squeeze round the bar area. Draught Beck's and Guinness, but particularly bottled St Peter's ales, complement a menu that, while it's not going to sweep any prizes for originality (grilled goat's cheese with marinated vegetables, £6.50; steak with shallot and brandy sauce, £10.95), offers food that's fresh, flavoursome and reasonably priced. Expect lashings of shooters, cocktails and house spirits in the lively company of vaguely hip but universally employable clientele.
Games (board games at weekends). Music (DJs 8pm Thur-Sun; free). TV (big screen, satellite). **Map 3/O5**

Clerkenwell House

23-7 Hatton Wall, EC1 (7404 1113). Chancery Lane tube/Farringdon tube/rail. **Open** noon-11pm Mon-Fri; 6-11pm Sat; noon-10.30pm Sun. **Food served** noon-3pm, 6-10pm Mon-Fri; 6-10pm Sat; 1-7pm Sun. **Credit** AmEx, MC, V.
Sandwiched between the diamonds of Hatton Garden and diamond geezers of Leather Lane market, Clerkenwell House is just oh so loungerooney. So laid-back! So spacious and hip! Ground floor is a favourite jumper of a room – slouching and ageing leather sofas and furniture chosen at random from several house clearances, arty exhibits – with bar and kitchen at the end. A half-naked gilded lady watches over a winding wrought-iron stair down to a pool room that boasts four tables and its own bar. Draught beers are mostly duffers (Hoegaarden the worthwhile exception) but cocktails are affordable at £7, and there are six wines by the glass. Remo the Italian chef works his Mediterranean cuisine all day long. A DJ plays house and funk on Friday evening but few people dance. Locals turn up at the weekends, especially on Sunday for the roasts and free pool.
Games (4 pool tables; £6 per hour, free Sun). Music (DJs Fri; free). **Map 3/N5**

Cock Tavern

East Poultry Avenue, Central Markets, EC1 (7248 2918). Farringdon tube/rail. **Open** 6am-3pm Mon-Fri. **Food served** 6am-2.30pm Mon-Fri. **Credit** AmEx, MC, V.
The place in London that you're least likely to encounter Moby or any other vegetarians of your acquaintance, the Cock is the haunt of butchers, bloody and true. Buried beneath the market building, this is the real deal Smithfield pub, the social centre for the market traders once their hard day's morning's at an end. It's not pretty: a three-room bunker of fluorescent strip lights, formica tops and lino floors, a loud TV and radio, and the smell of hot fat. In fact, it's more greasy spoon than tavern, from 6am five mornings a week it does a huge trade in dishing up heart attacks on a plate (sausage, egg, bacon, baked beans, kidneys, black pudding, liver and tomato, £6.65) and cheap pints (Foster's £2.30) to tables of blood-spattered white-coated meatpackers. It's an intimidating scene and interlopers may be eyed with suspicion, but if you do happen to be up, around and gagging for a pint at dawn, well, you know where to come.
Babies and children admitted. Function room. Games (fruit machine). TV (satellite). **Map 3/O5**

Crown Tavern

43 Clerkenwell Green, EC1 (7253 4973). Farringdon tube/rail. **Open** noon-11pm Mon-Sat. **Food served** noon-10pm Mon-Thur; noon-6pm Fri, Sat. **Credit** AmEx, MC, V.
Intensely popular during the week with the people from *Bizarre* magazine, gallery owners and loft dwellers, quieter at the weekend when Clerkenwell Green goes dark, the Crown was formerly a Victorian music hall called the Apollo. What's left of the concert hall is upstairs, with its high, lovingly maintained tobacco-tinted ceiling, candelabra and imitation flock wallpaper. Downstairs is a recently overhauled cavernous wood-panelled and windowless oversize snug, with ceiling fans and prints on the walls. The infinitely more luminous bar area has mirrors and cut-glass windows inscribed 'Gin', 'Vodka', 'Rum'. Tipples of choice today are more likely to be something from the line-up of Staropramen, Hoegaarden, Grolsch or London Pride, or a glass of one of the proffered 20 wines. It's particularly fine in summer courtesy of plenty of outside seating in highly attractive surrounds.
Function room. Tables outdoors (pavement). **Map 3/N4**

Dovetail

9 Jerusalem Passage, EC1 (7490 7321). Farringdon tube/rail. **Open** noon-11pm Mon-Sat. **Food served** noon-3pm, 6-10pm Mon-Sat. **Credit** MC, V.
Its 14-page menu includes an accessible wine list and eclectic food selection (from grilled goat's cheese to duck sausages, provençal mussels to Thai fish cakes) but pride of house are the 101 Belgian beers. Trappist, fruit, Abbey, Gueze, Pilsner and wheat (most served in their own specific-shaped and labelled glass), the choice is daunting; however, knowledgeable and approachable bar staff are on hand to advise.

Critics' choice
irish pubs

Auld Shillelagh (p184)
A boozy old Stokey fave with a great entertainment programme.

Coach & Horses (p36)
The finest Guinness in the West End.

O'Hanlon's (p114)
Pastoral Irishness and a fine line up of independently brewed beers.

Power's Bar (p178)
A younger, hipper take on Irish pubbery with regular live music.

Toucan (p85)
Best little Irish house in Soho.

City

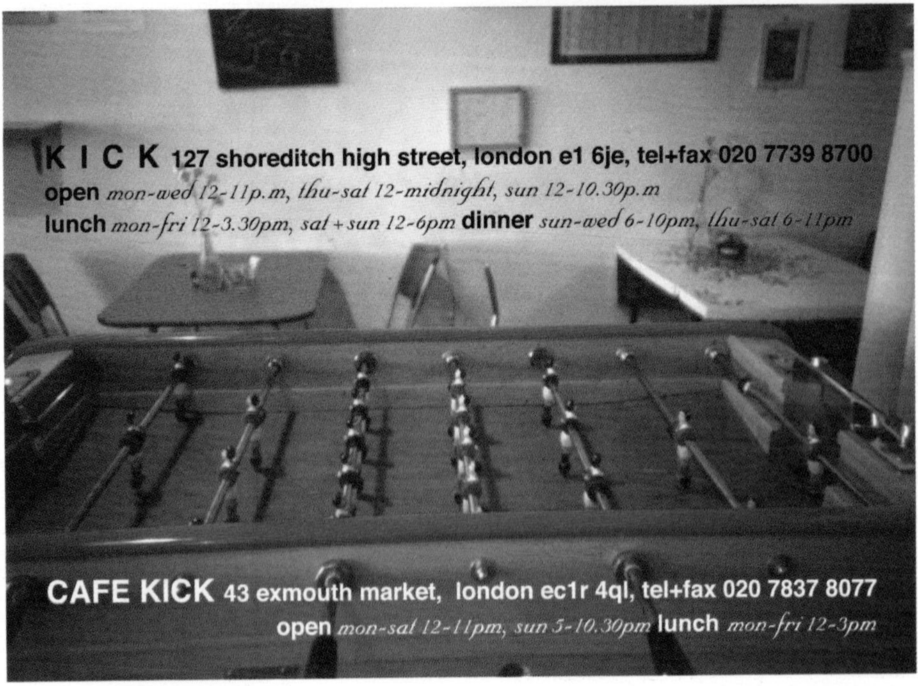

They're even happy to draw off samples. In terms of decor it's a small bare-brick and stone-floor bar, softly lit and sparsely decorated aside from the fun if somewhat incongruous Asterix prints (he was a Gaul). The barman's Latvian but, in such pleasant surrounds, who's keeping score?
Bar for hire (Sun). Disabled: toilet. No-smoking area. **Map 3/O4**

Duke of York

156 Clerkenwell Road, EC1 (7837 8548). Farringdon tube/rail. **Open** 11am-11pm Mon-Sat; noon-10.30pm Sun. **Food served** noon-3pm, 6-10pm Mon-Fri; 6-10pm Sat. **Credit** MC, V.
But for the vast acreage of picture window (gorgeously illuminated at night by forests of candles), the DoY has a very traditional feel. It also prides itself on a democratic clientele, 'from cycle couriers to suits'; salsa dancing has been known to spontaneously erupt on occasion (a Latin American dance class meets somewhere in the neighbourhood). Co-licensee Doey, who's worked here for ten years, reckons it's a 'lovely crowd'. They're kept fuelled from a bar line-up of Bombardier, Stella and Guinness, with added nourishment courtesy of a cooked-to-order menu by the resident Thai chef (individual dishes rarely cost more than £5). There are monthly changing art exhibitions (Snapshots of California on our last visit) and pool and table football at the back. It's the perfect antidote to all that tiresome designerdom going on a few blocks down the Clerkenwell Road.
Babies and children admitted (until 7pm). Games (fruit machine, pool, table football). Tables outdoors (pavement). TVs (digital). **Map 3/N4**

Dust

27 Clerkenwell Road, EC1 (7490 5120). Farringdon tube/rail. **Open** 11am-midnight Mon-Wed; 11am-2am Thur, Fri; 7.30pm-2am Sat. **Food served** noon-3pm, 6-10pm Mon-Thur; noon-3pm, 6-8.30pm Fri. **Credit** AmEx, DC, MC, V.
'A haven for trendsetters,' says the blurb outside. Beware the self-publicising, say we. Mind you, there can be few who haven't heard of Dust, which first settled on this bit of Clerkenwell Road quite some years ago now. Its 'earthy urban' look has been much copied – exposed brick, stripped floorboards, vintage leather sofas – but is holding up well, complemented at present by an exhibition of huge acrylic paintings. Upstairs has recently been done up as a dining room, with exotic orchids on the bar and tables for 30 covers – the cuisine's Modern British though the chef tells us he's looking forward to introducing kangaroo and ostrich. Busiest times are end of the week/weekend when a DJ plays hip hop and house for the pre-Turnmills/Fabric crowd. That's when they shift a lot of cocktails, although there's also an interesting wine list including curiosities such as a Lazy Lizard Syrah and Starved Dog Lane Cabernet. Why 'Dust' you may wonder? 'Dust thou shall eat all the days of thy life'? No, the answer's that a watchmaker used to work on these premises: ergo, after time comes dust. Most sagacious.
Disabled: toilet. Music (DJs Thur-Sat; £2-£5 after 10pm Fri, Sat). **Map 3/O4**

Eagle

159 Farringdon Road, EC1 (7837 1353). Farringdon tube/rail. **Open** noon-11pm Mon-Sat; noon-5pm Sun. **Food served** noon-2.30pm, 6.30-10.30pm Mon-Fri; 12.30-3.30pm, 6.30-10.30pm Sat; 12.30-3.30pm Sun. **Credit** MC, V.
The Eagle has a ramshackle allure. No two plates match, the beaten-up tables and chairs aren't related and music is turned up full blast. This was one of the first gastropubs in the UK, and it still makes a feature of its open kitchen, letting diners observe the bustle of aproned sous chefs dissecting onions and delivering some full-on performance cuisine. The menu's chalked up, nothing printed, so that with each day comes fresh inspiration. You're spoilt for choice for beer and real ales: Eagle Lager, Kirin, Red Stripe, Leffe, Hoegaarden, Lowenbrau, even a Banana Bread Beer. And that's just the pumps. On Saturdays large boisterous parties of youths congregate, while weekdays feature a faithful clientele from the adjoining offices of the *Guardian* newspaper.
Babies and children admitted. Tables outdoors (pavement). **Map 3/N4**

Easton

22 Easton Street, WC1 (7278 7608). Bus 19, 38. **Open** noon-11pm Mon-Thur; noon-1am Fri, Sat; noon-10.30pm Sun. **Food served** noon-3pm, 6-10pm Mon-Sat; 1-4pm, 6-10pm Sun. **Credit** MC, V.
In recent years this hard-to-find Clerkenwell boozer (look out for a handpainted sign that points the way) languished as an unlovely strip joint (the Queen's Head). Now, the new owners have cleaned it up, let the light back in through its big Edwardian windows and turned it into yet another bare-boards gastropub. As a result, it now attracts more regulars from the Amnesty International offices at the end of the road than from the Mount Pleasant mail sorting office that used to form the core of its clientele. Unfortunately, beers are limited to the usual nitrokegs and Hoegaarden but the wine list is better, with a short selection of inexpensive, good-value bottles. The main trade here is food, though. A blackboard menu is brief, with just a handful of well-priced dishes chalked up (grilled mackerel with grapefruit salsa, gratin dauphinois with Italian sausage). On a weekday lunchtime visit the Easton was empty, but the service exemplary. But on a return evening visit, the service fell apart and it took nearly an hour for our food to arrive. Our advice: go for a leisurely Sunday roast and keep your fingers crossed.
Babies and children admitted (daytime only). Music (DJs 9pm Sat). Tables outdoors (pavement). **Map 3/N4**

Fluid

40 Charterhouse Street, EC1 (7253 3444/www.fluidbar.com). Barbican tube/Farringdon tube/rail. **Open** noon-midnight Mon-Wed; noon-2am Thur, Fri; 7pm-2am Sat. **Happy hour** 5-7pm Mon-Fri. **Admission** £4 after 10pm Fri, Sat. **Food served** noon-10pm Mon-Fri. **Credit** AmEx, MC, V.
The kitschy manga comic strips of yesteryear may have been replaced by sultry black and white screen prints, but this 'bar music sushi' hang out still harbours enclaves of Japanese tack. Sprinkled between two floors of burnt orange ambient lighting, leather sofas and industrial metal vents and flues, are a Japanese photo-sticker booth, bright orange Sapporo beer machine and huge comic-style Fluid logos. But who cares? Certainly not the hip young crowd lounged around the low tables, drinking their crisp Kirin lagers and nibbling on sushi to the smooth jazz, electronica, trip hop and downbeat house sounds around them. Like its neighbour at No 38 (**Charterhouse**, *see p109*), Fluid provides a good setting for hard-earned after-work unwinding or pre-club vibing, but, with its late licence and own fine selection of weekend DJs, ordering a few more sakes and digging in your heels isn't such a bad option either.
Babies and children admitted (until 9pm). Function room. Games (retro video games). Music (DJs Wed-Sat). Tables outdoors (pavement). **Map 3/O5**

Fox & Anchor

115 Charterhouse Street, EC1 (7253 5075). Barbican tube/Farringdon tube/rail. **Open** 7am-7pm Mon-Fri. **Food served** 7am-3pm Mon-Fri. **Credit** AmEx, MC, V.
Above the listed cut-glass windows of this inn's magnificent art nouveau facade, the stuffing's beginning to leak out of the fox who's inexplicably taken refuge with a ship's anchor. The place is famous for its breakfasts, opening at 7am to serve the traditional full English and steaks of all sizes and weights. Lucky diners – or those who reserved – are seated in wood-panelled and windowless cubicles at the rear – on a cold winter's morning what could be cosier? The clientele are mostly office workers from nearby architects' offices and sundry design studios – market workers drink in the nearby **Cock Tavern** (*see p109*) – who down Stella, Carlsberg Export, Adnams Bitter, Guinness and Blackthorne cider, but only until seven in the evening, and not at all at the weekends, when the area roundabout is largely moribund.
Babies and children admitted (lunchtime). Function room. Tables outdoors (pavement). **Map 3/O5**

Hand & Shears

1 Middle Street, EC1 (7600 0257). Barbican tube. **Open** 11am-11pm Mon-Fri. **Food served** noon-3pm Mon-Fri. **Credit** AmEx, MC, V.
History lingers on in the Hand & Shears; from its faded pictures of bygone London to the pages recounting this boozer's own slice of history proudly mounted on the cluttered walls. Built in 1849 on the site of an alehouse dating back to 1123, the pub used to serve condemned prisoners their last drink before going to the scaffold at Newgate, and has also welcomed historical diners such as Baldwin and Churchill. Seeping from the wood-panelled walls and bare floorboards surrounding the small central bar, the air of the past ensures there is no jukebox or fruit machine – friendly chatter between barman and regulars and subdued conversations of a suited post-work crowd are as loud as it gets. Courage handles the real ales supplemented by monthly guest beers, while the traditional no-frills pub grub menu comes at good old-fashioned prices (ham, egg and chips, £3.80; fish and chips, £3.90).
Babies and children admitted. Games (darts). Function room. **Map 3/O5**

Hope

94 Cowcross Street, EC1 (7250 1442). Farringdon tube/rail. **Open** 6-10.30am, 11.30am-9pm Mon-Fri. **Food served** 7-10am Mon-Fri (restaurant only); noon-2pm Mon-Fri. **Credit** MC, V.
If the early bird catches the worm, then Hope could be a plump little sparrow. Opening its doors at 6am, this pub gives busy workers from the market opposite a good hearty breakfast accompanied by an early morning pint or two – or even a champagne breakfast (full English with half a bottle of bubbly, £19.50). Bright and cheery as the morning may or may not be, Hope's fresh peppermint green walls, high ceilings, large mirrors and big glass frontage make it a pleasant and airy place to start the day. The chandeliers and antique tiling may give the place a faded grandeur, but the service is down-to-earth and friendly, and the Young's 'ordinary', John Smith's, Guinness and Kronenbourg good value. Upstairs, the cunningly named Sir Loin restaurant is perfect for tucking into a meaty treat while overlooking the market from whence it was so recently delivered.
Tables outdoors (patio). **Map 3/O5**

Jerusalem Tavern

55 Britton Street, EC1 (7490 4281). Farringdon tube/rail. **Open** 11am-11pm Mon-Fri. **Food served** noon-3pm Mon-Fri. **Credit** MC, V.
Charming and so tiny it would only take 20 or so punters to pack it out – maybe the customers were a lot smaller in 1720 when this place opened as a coffee house – you could be below decks on the *Mayflower*. Six small barrels protrude behind the bar, pewters are hanging at the ready overhead. This is the solitary London representative of the St Peter's Brewery, based near Bungay in North Suffolk, making it a mecca for CAMRA types. The brewery does a roaring trade exporting its classic fruit beers made with elderberry and ales brewed with juniper, dried fruits and nettles to all over the world – it's even sold at Helsinki railway station. But the Jerusalem's here so you don't have to travel that far. At lunchtime there are baguettes, bangers and mash or beef and Yorkshire pudding. But the beers are a feast in themselves.
Babies and children admitted. Tables outdoors (pavement). **Map 3/O4**

Fox & Anchor

London drinking: cocktails

We talkin' bout a revolution?

To us, 'cocktail revolution' conjures up images of flaming Molotovs, police barricades and running street battles, not a fancy drink served in a Martini glass and topped with a Cape gooseberry.

But it seems that most other Londoners have a different take on things. And who'd blame them? Thousands of column inches have been dedicated to singing the praises of London's cocktail revolution. If you believe the spin, we've become a nation of connoisseurs. Whereas once we were happy to make do with a weak G&T, we now spend our time leaning against the polished surfaces of style bars, requesting bar tenders to conjure up exotic concoctions made with our specified brands of bourbon, gin or flavoured vodka.

But how true is any of this? Next time you slink into your favourite posh bar, take a good butcher's at what the people around you are drinking. Lots will be necking bottles of imported lager. Nothing revolutionary there. Next, check what's in the fridges behind the bar. In many places you'll see rows of pre-mixed drinks. Ask the barman to mix you, say, a Sidecar and you're likely to receive a blank stare instead.

The fact is, the skills of many bar staff don't go much beyond pulling a swift pint of lager or flicking the cap off a bottle – and lots of drinkers wouldn't know the difference between a good drink and a bad one anyway.

The cocktail ain't new to London. During Prohibition, when the self-proclaimed 'freest country in the world' banned booze (but not guns), sensible Yanks – particularly the barmen – left the country in droves. Some of them set up bars in Europe (including London), where they could continue to dabble in the demon drink without some mad Temperance Nazi shaming them out of town. The **American Bars** at the Savoy and Connaught are still very much alive – and both still serve extremely good cocktails.

Yet even an old cynic has to concede that it's far easier to get a properly made, innovative cocktail in London than it ever has been. Barmen, led by the likes of Dick Bradsell (who has consulted to more bars than most of us have had hot toddies) and Douglas Ankrah (the creative barman behind **Lab** in Old Compton Street and **Townhouse**), take their craft seriously.

Another thing that's changed is that modern bars, like travel agents or sex trade workers (well, so we're told), are specialists. Vodka fans can visit **Baltic** (*see p101*) in Southwark or the **Revolution** (*see p84*) minichain. For bourbon, there's **Grand Central** (*see p126*) in Shoreditch and **Rockwell** (*see p97*) just off Trafalgar Square. If rum's your thing, there's **Anda de Bridge** (*see p120*) in Hoxton. So, yes, there are a lot more cocktail bars in London serving great drinks made with good alcohol as well as with creativity and care. But there's a lot of bandwagon-jumping too. Somebody once said that a revolution was a process rather than a single event. If that's so, London's bar scene adds weight to that theory. *Susan Low*

Ten magic mixers

American Bar (*see p64*) Connaught Hotel, 16 Carlos Place, W1 (7499 7070).
American Bar (*see p91*) Savoy Hotel, Strand, WC2 (7836 4343).
Apartment 195 (*see p30*) 195 King's Road, SW3 (7351 5195).
Christopher's (*see p36*) 18 Wellington Street, WC2 (7240 4222).
Lab (*see p83*) 12 Old Compton Street, W1 (7437 7820).
Lonsdale (*see p71*) 44-8 Lonsdale Road, W11 (7228 1517).
The Player (*see p83*) 8 Broadwick Street, W1 (7494 9125).
Sosho (*see p130*) 2A Tabernacle Street, EC2 (7920 0701).
Townhouse (*see p55*) 31 Beauchamp Place, SW3 (7589 5080).
Trader Vic's (*see p67*) Hilton London, 22 Park Lane, W1 (7493 8000).

City

Match

45-7 Clerkenwell Road, EC1 (7250 4002). Farringdon tube/rail. **Open** 11am-midnight Mon-Fri; 5pm-midnight Sat. **Food served** noon-11pm Mon-Fri; 6-11pm Sat. **Credit** AmEx, DC, MC, V.

In San Francisco in '34 an event of earth-shattering proportions took place: a barman added lime juice, apricot brandy and orgeat to a double shot of dark rum, sampled it, and screamed, 'Mai Tai!' (Tahitian for 'just out of this world'). Pete's telling this story and he knows at least 200 cocktail recipes by heart. Come to Match midweek when it's a bit quieter and Pete will invent a cocktail on the spot specifically for you. The staff are all equally inspirational and their love of Bees Knees, the Blood and Sand, Beneath the Sheets, Mojito, Stolipolitan and, above all, the Wibble, knows no bounds. The Match Hangover Sandwich (Suffolk bacon, black pudding, free-range egg and brown sauce) is served at tables ranged around the walls, with the bar a sunken six steps down. This is still an unbeatable venture, the quality not dissipated since it branched out with further siblings in the West End (*see p44*) and Shoreditch (*see p130*).

Bar area for hire. Disabled: toilet. Tables outdoors (pavement). **Map 3/O4**

19:20

19-20 Great Sutton Street, EC1 (7253 1920). Farringdon tube/rail. **Open** noon-11pm Mon-Fri; 6pm-1am Sat. **Food served** noon-3pm, 6-10pm Mon-Fri. **Credit** AmEx, MC, V.

Pool bars can suffer from being overly male environments, and often tend toward a lack of atmosphere. 19:20 manages to address this by having clearly defined games (above) and bar (below) areas. If the four large, orange baize rectangles aren't a giveaway to the presence of pool-playing facilities, a numbered guide displayed in the moon-landing mural on the ground floor makes it all clear. Between entrance and ornamental water feature, a staircase sweeps down to the large, warmly lit bar, where City-types gather amid red-padded furnishings, listening to MTV and enjoying the 'Clerkenwell Collection' of cocktails. The food menu, based around meat and fish platters, burgers and nachos, is decent if unadventurous, as is the beer selection (Beck's, John Smith and Beamish on tap). Still, it is undeniably popular, with regulars who consider it a fun and lively post-work getaway.

Babies and children admitted (lunchtimes only). Function room. Games (4 pool tables). Music (DJs 7pm Thur-Sat; free). Tables outdoors (pavement). TV (satellite). **Map 3/O4**

O'Hanlon's

8 Tysoe Street, EC1 (7278 7630). Angel tube/19, 38 bus. **Open** 11am-midnight Mon-Sat; 11am-8pm Sun. **Food served** noon-2.30pm Mon-Fri; 6-9pm Tue-Thur; noon-3.15pm Sun. **Credit** MC, V.

The last decade witnessed the opening of a virtual deluge of faux-Irish pubs amid which this, the genuine article, represents pleasantly high ground. Its founder, originally from Kerry, has departed, but his legacy remains – not least in the form of O'Hanlon's beers, which are now brewed in the West Country and are offered here alongside a number of other ales, including several guest beers and some fine Belgian ales. These are served by friendly bar staff in the narrow front room (painted a lurid egg-yolk yellow), as are generous lunches and reasonably priced Irish dinners. The pub opens out into an uncluttered back room that, although small, feels light and airy due to a large skylight and pale wooden floor. Memorabilia such as posters from forgotten Irish musicals adorns the walls, but the traditional charm feels mercifully unforced. The character comes to the fore for rugby games involving Leinster, Munster or London Irish when crowds gather under the pull-down screen.

Music (bands Thur). No-smoking tables (12.30-2.30pm Mon-Fri). Tables outdoors (pavement). TV (satellite). **Map 3/N3**

Pakenham Arms

1 Pakenham Street, WC1 (7837 69339). King's Cross tube/rail/Russell Square tube. **Open** 9am-1am Mon-Fri; 9am-midnight Sat; 9am-10.30pm Sun. **Food served** 9am-3pm, 6-10pm Mon-Fri; 9am-10pm Sat; 9am-6pm Sun. **Credit** MC, V.

To succeed in today's climate, independently run pubs can't just be good, they have to diversify. During the day this large, single bar, backstreet local serves postmen from the nearby sorting office and neighbourhood office workers. In the evening, darts players and sports fans – served by one big screen and two even bigger screens – join real ale freaks and daytime stragglers. Serious drinkers will be relieved to know that spillover is minimal and football phobics are allowed to slink into quiet corners. As the night wears on, late-night drinkers join post-shift posties in the mix. No post modern 'beer is the new black' crap here, just a down-to-earth boozer serving a decent selection of six or so real ales, mostly under two quid a pint. In the centre of town too. Is the guvnor mad? Maybe not. The Pakenham opens for breakfast at nine – kippers and muffins plus the usual coronary-inducers – then it's simple but upmarket lunches (chicken satay, minted lamb and veg pie, all around £4), and similar in the evenings. Students of pub decor will appreciate the internal placing of pawnbroker's balls and illuminated beer signs, and the cheery red, primrose and lemon paintwork.

Babies and children admitted (daytime). Games (cards, cribbage, darts, fruit machines). Outdoor tables (pavement). **Map 3/M4**

Peasant

240 St John Street, EC1 (7336 7726). Angel tube/Farringdon tube/rail. **Open** noon-11pm Mon-Fri; 6.30-11pm Sat; noon-5pm Sun **Food served** 12.30-3pm, 6.30-11pm Mon-Fri; 6.30-11pm Sat; noon-3.30pm Sun. **Credit** AmEx, DC, MC, V.

A common criticism of gastropubs is that they try just too hard to be 'classy', but this place fairly oozes quality and demonstrates that it is possible to be modern and sophisticated, without losing that essential pub warmth. It's a large corner building and its spacious layout and high ceiling could drain it of atmosphere, but dark wooden fittings and deep red walls keep it fairly intimate. The restaurant upstairs receives fine reviews, but those simply seeking a relaxed drink will find plenty to occupy them below. A modest range of draught beers includes WT, Bombardier and Hoegaarden; more impressive is the array of bottles, including Budvar, Bishops Finger, San Miguel and Leffe, and balanced selection of wines. A blackboard proclaims splendid bar snacks of Mediterranean origin, while the merely peckish can nibble from bowls of roasted almonds or mixed olives. A pub successfully blending English cosiness with continental style: who says European integration can't work?

Babies and children admitted. Games (board games). Tables outdoors (conservatory, garden). **Map 3/O4**

Potemkin

144 Clerkenwell Road, EC1 (7278 6661/www.potemkin.com). Farringdon tube/rail. **Open** 6pm-midnight Mon-Wed, Sat; noon-3pm, 6pm-midnight Thur, Fri. **Food served** noon-3pm, 6-10.30pm Mon-Fri; 6-10.30pm Sat. **Credit** AmEx, DC, MC, V.

Totally unique, sleek, suave, small and Russian-themed – Potemkin is named after the mutineering Russian battleship as filmed by Eisentstein and/or Gregory Alexandrovich, Catherine the Great's lover. A classy minimalist design: full length windows curve gracefully above light brown leather banquettes, and at the bar – the business! A choice of some 130 vodkas: cannabis flavoured! Sweet dark chocolate! Luksowa potato! Polster cucumber! Zubrowka bison grass! Or Stolnaya Jewel of Russia at £288 the bottle! Chase them down with Baltika beer. Journalists from the nearby *Guardian* and members of the local business community ease their way downstairs to the award-winning restaurant for caviar, borscht, and pelmeni dumplings galore. When leaving it's worth noting that the door opens outwards.
No-smoking area (restaurant). **Map 3/N4**

Rising Sun

38 Cloth Fair, EC1 (7726 6671). Barbican tube/ Farringdon tube/rail. **Open** 11.30am-11pm Mon-Fri; noon-11pm Sat; noon-10.30pm Sun. **Food served** noon-2.30pm, 6-8pm Mon-Fri; noon-2.30pm Sun. **Credit** AmEx, MC, V.
A refreshing change from the trendier and more expensive watering holes on the other side of Smithfield Market, the Rising Sun sits comfortably on this narrow backstreet as a healthy bastion of the good old-fashioned British pub. Laughter echoes on to the quiet street outside, while inside tracksuits and trainers mix happily with suits and overcoats; game machines and television screens blend in with old mahogany bookcases and antique glass panels. The atmosphere is friendly and laid-back; solitary drinkers sit happily supping the Rising Sun's selection of Sam Smith's standards while groups play darts in a smaller room blessed with an attractive fireplace. Food here is traditional pub fare (steak pie cooked in stout, fish and chips) but with a twinge of Modern British (salmon and dill fish cakes) gradually creeping on to the reasonably priced menu.
Function room. Games (chess, darts, dominoes, fruit machine, golf machine). Quiz (8.30pm Tue; free). TV. **Map 3/O5**

St John

26 St John Street, EC1 (7251 0848). Farringdon tube/rail. **Open** 11am-11pm Mon-Fri; 6-11pm Sat. **Food served** 11am-11pm Mon-Fri; 6-11pm Sat. **Credit** AmEx, MC, V.
How high the ceilings and how white the exposed brick walls of this Victorian industrial building originally used for smoking meat – look up above the bar, that's where they once hung the carcasses. It's now home to the St John bar and restaurant with its renowned philosophy of nose-to-tail eating – braised squirrel and fennel, rabbit saddle and dandelion; not for the squeamish. The adjoining bar, with its shoulder-high zinc and bakery where Justin slaves all night long to feed his crusty whites and browns to the famished queue that's already formed at 7am, opens at 11am. Perhaps at that time it's a bit early to choose from the exclusively French list of more than 80 wines and champagnes, but why not, especially if you're one of the not-so-YBAs that are regulars, along with their dealers and legal minds from Lincoln's Inn Fields. You can order oysters, langoustines, rabbit offal and mash at the bar where Guinness, 6X and Black Sheep are ready to be pulled. Very soon another St John will open in Spitalfields.
Babies and children admitted (11am-5pm). Disabled: toilet. Function room. **Map 3/O5**

Sekforde Arms

34 Sekforde Street, EC1 (7253 3251). Farringdon tube/rail. **Open** 11am-11pm Mon-Fri; 11am-6pm Sat; noon-4pm Sun. **Food served** noon-9.30pm Mon-Fri; noon-3pm Sat; noon-3pm Sun. **Credit** MC, V.
This friendly hostelry was named in honour of Thomas Sekforde, a public benefactor of Tudor England, and his good work continues, if only in lending his name to this fine example of an old-fashioned local. Cosy and welcoming (a sign above the bar introduces you to the proprietors, Bill and Wendy), it's a corner pub where it's easy to quickly feel at home. It's also as unaffectedly and traditionally British as they come, from the pictures of former Young's regular the Queen Mum on the wall to the dartboard in the corner, and from the unglamorous furnishings to the weekly football quiz. There are quality beers, with the mostly regular crowd enjoying Young's Bitter and seasonal ales (the aptly named Winter Warmer featured on our last visit). A blackboard menu offers mountainous roast dinners (almost large enough to share), followed by rib-sticking and appropriately nostalgic puddings such as spotted dick and custard.
Babies and children admitted (restaurant only). Function room. Games (bridge club, darts, fruit machine). Quiz (sports, 2-3 per week). Tables outdoors (pavement). TV (satellite). **Map 3/O4**

Smiths of Smithfield

67-77 Charterhouse Street, EC1 (7251 7950/ www.smithsofsmithfield.com). Farringdon tube/rail. **Open** *Ground floor* 7.30am-11pm Mon-Thur; 7.30am-midnight Fri; 10.30am-midnight Sat; 9.30am-10.30pm Sun. *Cocktail bar* 5.30-11pm Mon-Thur; 5.30pm-midnight Fri, Sat. **Food served** *Ground floor* 7.30am-5pm Mon-Fri; 10.30am-5pm Sat; 9.30am-5pm Sun. **Credit** AmEx, DC, MC, V.
Located bang opposite the market, this impressive warehouse dating back to 1886 used to service meat traders with butchers' supplies – these days it does a fantastic job servicing the glugging and gastronomic needs of local office workers and hip urbanites. Renovated by Smiths to retain many of the building's original features, walking through the huge front doors of SOS is like walking straight on to the factory floor – but with a whole lot more panache. Long tables and benches take centre stage in front of the vast stainless steel bar, while the sofa area in the corner is perfect for chilling out (literally, it can get quite parky) with a Kozel beer after a hard day – or preparing to face it with a coffee and paper, as the doors and cafe kitchen open at 7.30am. Upstairs, through transparent red plastic abattoir-style curtains and into cosy velvet booths, the darker, bustling cocktail bar deals in a menu of quality cocktails and champagnes, while up and up again are a further two floors of fine dining.
Babies and children admitted (daytime; high chairs). Disabled: toilet. Function room. Music (DJs Thur-Sat; free). Outdoor tables (pavement). TV (big screen, sporting events only). **Map 3/O5**

Sutton Arms

16 Great Sutton Street, EC1 (7253 2462). Barbican tube/ Farringdon tube/rail. **Open** 11am-11pm Mon-Fri. **Food served** noon-3pm Mon-Fri. **Credit** DC, MC, V.
Clerkenwell is awash with places catering to suited City workers and affluent twenty- and thirtysomethings; wannabe sophisticated bars drawing punters with putative hip tunes and international cuisine. It is somewhat refreshing, then, to find a pub without gimmicks, airs or graces. This is a comfortable, street corner place with a friendly landlord who doesn't pretend to offer much besides a bar, seating, welcoming staff, a pleasing selection of draught beers (including Flowers IPA, London Pride and Hoegaarden), and a lunchtime menu comprising unpretentious pub grub. It is a place to chat, rather than a place to be seen, and while the slightly drab decor may drive away the bright young things, who needs 'em? The Sutton provides a more than acceptable backdrop

Three Kings of Clerkenwell

for its regulars – largely a mix of locals and those seeking a quiet after-work pint – to meet and relax. They come to enjoy the Sutton for what it is – a traditional, no-frills public house. Raise a glass to it.
Function room. Tables outdoors (pavement). TV (digital). **Map 3/O4**

Three Kings of Clerkenwell

7 Clerkenwell Close, EC1 (7253 0483). Farringdon tube/rail. **Open** noon-11pm Mon-Fri; 7.30-11pm Sat. **Food served** noon-3pm Mon-Fri. **No credit cards.**
A rhino has only just managed to thrust its vast head through the wall above the blazing log fire. Jason has worked behind the bar on and off for 15 years. He tells us the bat-eared fox dines exclusively on insects quite near the Sahara. His boss chooses the music for the upstairs vinyl jukebox, definitely nothing mainstream, favouring the Ethiopians, the Cramps and the Staple Singers. This idiosyncratic bar is small and intimate, the customers more boho than besuited. On tap you have Hoegaarden, Grolsch and Young's Bitter. Sue cooks the lunchtime specials, at between £4 and £5 just try and find a better deal in any white-collared neck of the woods. Enjoy your meal upstairs while James Dean looks down from a poster and Tommy Tucker's 'Hi-Heel Sneakers' plays on the jukey. Gaze out on the secluded, almost rural, churchyard of St James, Clerkenwell, and its London lime trees. All the while, the Three Kings – Elvis, King Kong and Henry VIII – swing on the inn sign.
Function room. Games (board games). No-smoking area (lunchtime upstairs). TV (satellite). **Map 3/N4**

The Well

180 St John Street, EC1 (7251 9363). Farringdon tube/rail. **Open** 11am-midnight Mon-Sat; 11am-10.30pm Sun. **Food served** noon-3pm, 6-10pm Mon-Wed; noon-3pm, 6-10.30pm Thur, Fri; noon-10.30pm Sat; noon-10pm Sun. **Credit** AmEx, DC, MC, V.
Local pub, cocktail bar, quality restaurant and wine bar: places trying to be jack of all trades often end up being master of none – but the Well is a reasonable success. The large windows of the main bar reveal comfortably robust furnishings: chunky wooden tables sit atop bare floorboards, surrounded by simple, bare brickwork. The food may be pricier than standard pub grub, but it's interesting, well prepared, pleasantly presented and consumed in a warm and intimate atmosphere, so no complaints there. Despite a background of clinking glasses and conversation, socialising is not obligatory: newspapers and fresh coffee are provided for those seeking a quieter escape. A wide selection of draught (Leffe, San Miguel, Budvar) and bottled (Kirin, Corona, Tiger) beers are available above, while downstairs, fish gliding through the aquarium gaze out at the fine wines and cocktails that are served to a lively crowd. Self-consciously trendy, perhaps – but an air of contentment permeates throughout.
Aquarium Bar available for hire. Babies and children admitted. Games (board games). Music (DJs Sun; free). Tables outdoors (pavement). **Map 3/O4**

Also in the area...

All Bar One 91-3 Charterhouse Street, EC1 (7553 9391).
Bar 38 89-97 St John Street, EC1 (7253 5896).
Betjeman's (Jamies) 43-4 Cloth Fair, EC1 (7600 7778).
Burgundy Ben's (Davy's) 102-8 Clerkenwell Road, EC1 (7251 3783).
Jamies 64-6 West Smithfield, EC1 (7600 0700).
The Printworks (JD Wetherspoon) 113-17 Farringdon Road, EC1 (7713 2000).
Sir John Oldcastle (JD Wetherspoon) 29-35 Farringdon Road, EC1 (7242 1013).
Slug & Lettuce 36-42 Clerkenwell Road, EC1 (7608 1929).

Fleet Street, Blackfriars & St Paul's

When the last of the newspapers – the *Daily Telegraph*, as ever the last to catch on – moved away in 1990, Fleet Street lost much of its character. Deprived of core custom some pubs (like Ye Olde Cock) have tarted up and now appeal to nobody. But a trawl on and off Fleet Street still remains one of the best pub crawls in London, beginning on St Andrew's Hill, progressing via the gorgeous **Black Friar** and down the former street of shame via choice boozers, the delicious **Tipperary** and the modern Fuller's conversion at the **Old Bank of England**. Winos will enjoy the boozy charms of **El Vino**.

Balls Brothers

6-8 Cheapside, EC2 (7248 2708). Bank or St Paul's tube. **Open** 11am-10pm Mon-Fri. **Food served** 11am-9pm Mon-Fri. **Credit** AmEx, DC, MC, V.
One of the oldest links in the **Balls Brothers** chain *(see p13)*, this particular wine bar has become a City institution thanks to a prime site at the western end of Cheapside bang opposite St Paul's. Think wood, think wine, think suits. In addition to the signature Balls cellar-style space, there's also a high-ceilinged, airy bar on the ground floor, plus a big summer bonus of a sunken outdoor terrace with cracking views of Wren's great edifice. The choice of wine is, in keeping with the establishment, traditional, and largely French, led by Bordeaux and Burgundian classics. New World product has just a token representation. A modest selection of five whites and five reds are available by the glass.
Games (competitions). Function room. Tables outdoors (garden). **Map 4/O6**

Black Friar

174 Queen Victoria Street, EC4 (7236 5474). Blackfriars tube/rail. **Open** 11.30am-11pm Mon-Fri; noon-4pm Sat. **Food served** noon-2.30pm Mon-Fri. **Credit** AmEx, MC, V.
When this mid-Victorian boozer was refurbished in 1903, the owners asked Henry Poole to give its wedge-shaped exterior an art nouveau facade. Because a nearby Dominican monastery had dominated the area for 317 years until Henry VIII's Dissolution in 1538, the theme was obvious. A couple of years later, H Fuller Clarke – a leading light in William Morris's Arts & Crafts Movement – turned up and went to work on the inside, adding marbled walls, pillared fireplaces and bas-reliefs of monks working and relaxing in gilt and silvered scenes. Immediately after World War I a snack bar was added at the rear and that's where those elaborately mirrored alcoves come from. All this survived remarkably well through the last century – although the last few years have given some cause for concern – and this landmark pub is regarded as one of London's most beautiful and eccentric. Unfortunately, the present custodian is a major pub company so expect fruit machines and loud 'background' music, uninspired real ales (London Pride, Adnams), typically bland pub food and that annoying habit of cleaning up around drinkers when staff decide it's time for bed (usually around 9.30pm).
Games (fruit machine). Tables outdoors (garden). TV. **Map 4/O6**

City

City

Cockpit

7 St Andrew's Hill, EC4 (7248 7315). Blackfriars tube/ rail. **Open** 11am-11pm Mon-Sat; noon-2.30pm, 7-10.30pm Sun. **Food served** 11.30am-2.30pm, 5-8pm Mon-Fri. **Credit** MC, V.

A pub has stood on this site since the time William Shakespeare lived nearby. The area was then a centre of fowl bloodsports in this part of town, hence the name. From 1849, when cockfighting was finally banned, the name was altered to the Three Castles, but a revisionist renovation in the 1970s restored it and added a rough approximation of what the place would have looked like in its gory and feather-strewn heyday. The small single ground-floor bar is decked out in red velvet with a running motif of poultry: framed prints and as many examples of the Courage brewery cock logo as could be squeezed in. A mock viewing gallery looking down from the first floor isn't high enough for anyone much over a metre tall, but it's a good example of late 20th-century pub company folly. Patrons of standard height gather round the serving area, swap stories and guzzle decent Courage Best and Directors or Marston's Pedigree.

Games (fruit machine). TV (satellite). **Map 4/O6**

El Vino

47 Fleet Street, EC4 (7353 6786). Chancery Lane or Temple tube/Blackfriars tube/rail. **Open** 8.30am-9pm Mon; 8.30am-10pm Tue-Fri. **Food served** 8.30am-9pm Mon-Fri. **Credit** AmEx, MC, V.

It was 1879 when El Vino first opened its doors, and little appears to have changed since. The bar has an appropriately dingy wooden interior furnished with well-worn leather chairs and sturdy tables, dusty bottles and ageing barrels. Pin-striped City males come and settle for a hearty lunch in the old-school basement restaurant, followed by a drop of vino. Smartly clad staff help customers navigate their way around the substantial, Euro-centric wine list. Claret and champagne sections contain a thoughtful cross-section of vintages and prices, including a good number of half bottles. Fans of fortified and dessert wines have plenty to ponder, including luscious Alsatian Vendange Tardive 1997, made from gewurztraminer. The New World isn't overlooked either. Bar food is sturdy pub fare: ox tongue and tomato sandwich; ploughman's lunch. City hours are adhered to, so come lunchtime or early evenings weekdays only.

Dress code: smart casual. Function room. **Map 4/N6**

Evangelist

33 Blackfriars Lane, EC4 (7213 0740). Blackfriars tube/rail. **Open** noon-11pm Mon-Fri. **Food served** noon-9pm Mon-Wed; noon-8pm Thur, Fri. **Credit** AmEx, MC, V.

Is it a pub, is it a bar, is it a restaurant? (The first time we walked past we thought it was the headquarters of a global Christian Right newspaper.) In fact, the Evangelist is all these things (except a newspaper). Housed in a modern office building, the large right-angled interior is decked out with comfy sofas, dining tables and wilfully mismatched furniture. As the name suggests, there's a vaguely ecclesiastical theme going on with the tiles and a mosaic of a medieval saint. Draught lagers (of course) rub shoulders with decent real ales (including Bombardier and the ubiquitous London Pride) along with a wine and champagne list that would tempt an archbishop. The open kitchen shuttles out gastropub-style dishes such as honey roast ham, seared salmon and new wave pasta stuff. The clientele tend toward more upmarket office types with a high proportion of women.

Disabled: toilet. Function room. TV (big screen). **Map 4/O6**

La Grande Marque

47 Ludgate Hill, EC4 (7329 6709). Blackfriars tube/rail. **Open** 11.30am-9.30pm Mon-Fri. **Food served** 11.30am-3pm Mon-Fri. **Credit** AmEx, DC, MC, V.

The former City Bank (1891-1990, RIP) is now a grandly appointed wine bar that leaves absolutely no doubt as to its speciality: champagne. Bottles of the stuff line the windows and just about every nook and cranny inside. Otherwise, elegant wood-panelled walls reach to an ornate and lofty ceiling under which is the very grand central marble-countered bar. Well-respected wine merchant Lay & Wheeler supplies the bottles on the considerable, French-led list, which includes impressive selections of vintage and non-vintage champagne and fine wines. More affordable are several interesting New World options, such as the chardonnay Los Vilos from Chile's Concha y Toro, and Madfish shiraz from Australia (both under £20). A good cross-section of the list is available by the glass. A small concession is made to beer drinkers, with Bitburger on draft and bottles of Peroni.

Function room. **Map 4/O6**

Nylon

1 Addle Street, EC2 (7600 7771). St Paul's tube/ Moorgate tube/rail. **Open** 4.30-11pm Mon-Wed; 4.30pm-2am Thur, Fri; 4.30pm-3am Sat. **Food served** 5-10.30pm daily. **Credit** MC, V.

One of a scant handful of City-style bars, this is an expansive two-floor, three-bar operation thriving behind a faceless office. The bright, curvy, chandeliered lounge bar (dotted with occasional plants and illuminated frosted-glass tables) is slightly kitschy, slightly sexy, and open to all comers; the first-floor lounge (cream and brown leather sofas, cylindrical floor to ceiling fish tanks) has recently become a members only construct. The whole package is from the same team that brought you the chain **Babushka** (*see p13*) and **Bed** (*see p71*) and just like its siblings, Nylon's trade ebbs and flows around a range of quality, chilled and occasionally infused Icelandic, Polish and Russian vodkas. Look out for 'home-styled' flavours that include delights such as Mars Bar, Milky Way and Skittles. Just remember to leave your satchel and homework in the cloakroom by the main entrance.

Dress: smart casual. Music (DJs 6pm Thur, Fri). Function room. **Map 6/P6**

Old Bank of England

194 Fleet Street, EC4 (7430 2255). Temple tube. **Open** 11am-11pm Mon-Fri. **Food served** noon-9pm Mon-Thur; noon-8pm Fri. **Credit** AmEx, MC, V.

Probably London's grandest example of what can be done with a converted bank, this was once the Law Courts branch of the Old Lady of Threadneedle Street. High ceilings don't come much more ornate or higher – 30 metres above the tiled floor – and the five huge arched and draped windows go all the way up to the top. Add intricate giant chandeliers, art nouveau lamps, a balcony that runs the length of the place and a central carved-wood serving area and you've got to be pretty blasé not to be impressed by where you're drinking. But the gaggle of lawyers and their minions who flock here for the full range of Fuller's beers, wines and near-pies (it's now a Fuller's Ale & Pie House) don't seem to take much notice of their surroundings. The bank/pub stands on the site of two historic old boozers: the Cock (commemorated in a grotesquely modernised namesake across the road) and the Haunch of Venison, supposed local of pie-loving barber Sweeney Todd. Grandeur *and* irony.

Babies and children admitted. Games (fruit machines). Function room. **Map 4/N6**

Old Bell Tavern

95 Fleet Street, EC4 (7583 0216). Blackfriars tube/rail. **Open** 11.30am-11pm Mon-Fri. **Food served** noon-3pm, 4-9pm Mon-Fri. **Credit** AmEx, MC, V.

When Sir Christopher Wren was rebuilding St Bride's following the destruction wrought by the Great Fire, he erected this tavern to house his craftsmen – cheaper than the Strand Palace, we presume. Before that the premises housed the printshop where Wynkyn de Worde operated the press he inherited from William Caxton. These days the pub is owned and run by the ubiquitous Six Continents, and for a chain boozer it's pretty well run, in addition to being amazingly well preserved. The floors are mixed stone flagging and bare wood, the walls are stone and the facing fireplaces are the originals. The small front room used to be an off-licence, but now it comes crammed with tables and curious triangular stools. The real ales will probably include Timothy Taylor Landlord, London Pride and Brakspear. For lunchtime food, read 'pie of the day', fancy sandwiches and chilli and rice.

TV. **Map 4/N6**

Ye Olde Cheshire Cheese

145 Fleet Street, EC4 (7353 6170). Blackfriars tube/rail. **Open** 11.30am-11pm Mon-Fri; noon-3pm, 6-11pm Sat; noon-2.30pm Sun. **Food served** noon-9.30pm Mon-Fri; noon-2.30pm, 6-9.30pm Sat; noon-2.30pm Sun. **Credit** AmEx, DC, MC, V.

Built over medieval cellars that survived the Great Fire, the present incarnation of the great Cheese has been a major feature of London life ever since the flames were doused. Looking something like Hollywood's idea of a London pub, it's all rambling wooden staircases, small rooms edged with black oak panelling and backside-numbing settles. Old regulars – Dr Johnson, Dickens, Thackeray, GK Chesterton, Conan Doyle and Stanley Baldwin – would still recognise the place today, even if the number of rooms has crept up over recent years. Now there are six separate areas for drinking and four for dining. Say what you like about owning-brewery Sam Smith's, it does do a good job on restoration, even if the vaulted cellar bar is likely to reverberate to overloud Kylie. Not all of the pretence is modern: 'Boswell's chair' was half-inched from the Mitre way back in 1819: it looks like they've got away with it.

Babies and children admitted (restaurant). No smoking tables. Function rooms (seat 15-50). TV. **Map 4/N6**

Punch Tavern

99 Fleet Street, EC4 (7353 6658). Blackfriars tube/rail. **Open** 11.45am-11pm Mon-Fri. **Food served** 11.45am-3pm Mon-Fri. **Credit** AmEx, MC, V.

Not too long ago there were two pubs, both called the Punch Tavern, both on the same site, a result of a lease disagreement. Now, what was once the Sam Smith's Punch Tavern is boarded up leaving the last laugh to this elegantly decorated boozer, with its red and gold paintwork, framed magazines (the eponymous humour title was conceived here in 1841) and Mr Punch motif. The walls are crammed with marionettes and representations of the unhappily wooded couple, as well as posters for chocolate and soap powder sharing the name. We always take time to inspect the original Victorian tiling around the front entrance and try at least one of the decent real ales on offer. No marks for imagination, but the London Pride and IPA usually do it for us. Customers tend to be local office workers – many known by name – and the few tourists brave enough to venture this far east along Fleet Street.

Babies and children admitted (until 3pm). Games (quiz machine). Music (live bands 7pm Fri). Function room (seats 50). TV (satellite). **Map 4/N6**

Red Herring

49 Gresham Street, EC2 (7606 0399). St Paul's tube. **Open** 11am-11pm Mon-Fri. **Food served** noon-9pm Mon-Fri. **Credit** AmEx, MC, V.

Although boozers in modern office buildings are invariably naff, this modern corner bar's not at all bad. Young(ish) office workers appear to be the core clientele and the combination of Fuller's fine ales, a decent wine list and good bistro-style food seems to be a winning formula. We've always found both drinking areas – on the ground floor and down in the basement – busy at times that other venues in the area were closing early for lack of trade. Comfortable sofas, easy chairs and potted plants constitute decor, while acres of glass allow views toward the building site opposite – a view that can only get better. You may prefer to focus on the simple but spectacular backlit bottle display behind the main serving area. Nice. We nattered about it all night.

Disabled: toilet. Games (fruit machine). Tables outdoors (pavement). TV (big screen, satellite). **Map 6/P6**

Rising Sun

61 Carter Lane, EC4 (7248 4544). St Paul's tube/ Blackfriars tube/rail. **Open** 11am-11pm Mon-Fri. **Food served** noon-3pm, 5.30-10.30pm Mon-Fri. **Credit** AmEx, DC, MC, V.

Traditional in style, but cheerier in spirit than most – with external orange and green paintwork and beige and primrose inside – this friendly corner pub manages to appeal to practically all strands of local drinker. Guinness appears unduly popular, so too the duo of real ales (usually Spitfire and Bombardier), with lager, wine and Breezer-type popsicles bringing up the rear. Food is proper Thai and the sound system offers an intelligent mix of ancient and modern pop and classic rock (is there any other type?). The pub lies at the heart of a historic area of narrow sloping thoroughfares: Guy Fawkes met his fellow conspirators at the Hart's Horn Tavern, roughly where we stand now, and Carter Lane used to be one of the City's main thoroughfares before the Dean finally allowed a route through St Paul's Churchyard.

Babies and children admitted. Function room. TV (satellite). **Map 4/O6**

Samuel Pepys

Stew Lane, High Timber Street, EC4 (7634 9841). Mansion House or St Paul's tube. **Open** noon-11pm Mon-Fri. **Food served** noon-3pm, 5-9pm Mon-Fri. **Credit** AmEx, MC, V.

Stew Lane was where ferries left for the 'stews', or brothels, of the fleshpot parade that was Tudor Southwark, hence the name. There's little that is historic (or racy) about the Pepys, however, which is a pleasingly modern brick and bare-wood conversion near the northside of the wobbly Millennium Bridge. Subsequently, the views across the Thames towards the South Bank are superb. Inside, expect a combination of comfortable leather sofas, high bar tables and solid dining furniture spread over a first-floor loft conversion. The long serving area running almost down one side offers two real ales (Cask Marque certificate, London Pride and Adnams Bitter) as well as bottled continental delights such as Chimay, Liefman's Kriek, Duvel, Orval, plus Anchor Steam and Freedom lagers. The wine list is no slouch either, with a suggested 'wine of the month' (usually between £15-£18) and a house wine at £13.50 a bottle. Food is simple but well-cooked trad British fare; expect the likes of peppered lamb fillet, beer-battered cod and steak and kidney pie, all at gastropub prices. Not bad, but did we mention the view?

Disabled: toilet. Games (fruit machine, quiz machine). No-smoking tables. Function room. **Map 6/P7**

Shaw's Booksellers

31-4 St Andrew's Hill, EC4 (7489 7999). St Paul's tube/Blackfriars tube/rail. **Open** noon-11pm Mon-Fri. **Food served** noon-3pm, 6-9pm Mon-Fri. **Credit** AmEx, DC, MC, V.

There never was a Shaw, nor was there ever any bookselling business at 31-4 St Andrew's Hill, just an imagining of such mocked up on these premises for a couple of scenes in the 1997 Helena Bonham Carter flick, *Wings Of A Dove*. Still, this sizeable two-room Fuller's pub proves popular with the area's younger business types, who slouch over the mismatched rustic dining tables and loll in leather sofas, discussing Blake, Heaney and Tinky Winky. Perhaps. The lurid red and magnolia colour scheme suggests dotty individualism but, in fact, food and wine menus offer the sort of thing you'd expect to find in a Fine Line. Among our specials were pan-fried scallops, gruyere, artichoke and spinach risotto and skate wing. Beers will include a couple of Fuller's cask-conditioned bitters (London Pride and Chiswick, most likely) as well as Hoegaarden and the usual suspects in the lager department. Slick and contrived but likeable all the same.

Babies and children welcome (until 6pm). Disabled: toilet. Function room. TV. **Map 4/O6**

City

Tipperary

66 Fleet Street, EC4 (7583 6470) Blackfriars tube/rail. **Open** 11am-11pm Mon-Fri; noon-6pm Sat, Sun. **Food served** 11am-10.30pm Mon-Fri; noon-5pm Sat, Sun. **Credit** MC, V.

Despite the sentiments of the song, it's not that far to the Tipperary: in easy ten minutes' walk from Blackfriars station, tops. This became London's first Irish pub in 1700, when Dublin brewer SG Mooney took over the lease of this tall narrow boozer, then called the Boar's Head. Legend has it that it had been constructed in 1605 from the ruins of the Whitefriars monastery (demolished at the Dissolution), and that its stone construction helped it survive the Great Fire of 1666. It was certainly London's first pub to sell both bottled and draught Guinness, and was renamed in 1919 in honour of the famous marching song, thanks to the efforts of returning Fleet Street print workers from the hellish trenches of World War I. Suffolk's Greene King brewery bought the place in the 1960s and restored it to its 18th-century glory, using mostly original fittings. The ground floor comes with shamrock mosaic floor and panelled walls slung with giant mirrors, maps and prints. Drinkers are a diverse bunch, ranging from local blue-collar workers to what appear to be junior members of the aristocracy, drawn here by the friendly antipodean couple who run the place, the atmosphere and a brace of well-kept real ales: Abbot and IPA.

Babies and children admitted. Games (fruit machine). TV. **Map 4/N6**

Viaduct Tavern

126 Newgate Street, EC1 (7600 1863). St Paul's tube. **Open** *Oct-Apr* noon-11pm Mon-Fri. *May-Sept* noon-11pm Mon-Fri; noon-5pm Sat. **Food served** *Oct-Apr* noon-3pm Mon-Fri. *May-Sept* noon-3pm Mon-Sat. **Credit** AmEx, MC, V.

Although the pub company (good old Six Continents again) painted over the beaten copper ceiling in a 2001 refurbishment, this grand old corner gin palace has been remarkably well preserved. Opened in 1869 and named in honour of William Heywood's impressive new Holborn Viaduct, the architects took further inspiration from the Old Bailey across the road and added busts of the 16 hanging judges of the time to the murals of the four viaduct statues (Commerce, Agriculture, Science and Fine Arts), a carved mahogany bar and giant gilt and silvered mirrors. Almost half-moon in shape, tall windows look out on to Newgate Street and it's said that the cellars are remnants of Newgate Prison cells. Beers are usually in tiptop condition and the last time we visited included Timothy Taylor Landlord and Badger Tanglefoot. It has long been traditional for lawyers, their clients (assuming they've got something to celebrate) and distraught relatives to flock here after long trials, so if you encounter a corner of Littlewood suits, peroxide blondes and steely glares just be careful whose pint you knock over.

Map 4/O6

Also in the area...

All Bar One 44-6 Ludgate Hill, EC4 (7653 9901).
Balls Brothers 5-6 Carey Lane, off Gutter Lane, EC2 (7600 2720).
Centre Page 29 Knightrider Street, EC4 (7236 3614).
City Pipe (Davy's) 33 Foster Lane, EC2 (7606 2110).
Corney & Barrow 3 Fleet Place, EC4 (7329 3141).
Davy's 10 Creed Lane, EC4 (7236 5317).
Heeltap & Bumper (Davy's) 2 Paul Street, EC2 (7247 3319).
Jamies 34 Ludgate Hill, EC4 (7489 1938).
Knights Templar (JD Wetherspoon) 95 Chancery Lane, WC2 (7831 2660).
O'Neill's 2-3 New Bridge Street, EC4 (7583 0227).
Shoeless Joe's 2 Old Change Court, EC4 (7248 2720).
Walkabout Hill House, Shoe Lane, EC4 (7353 7360).

Hoxton & Shoreditch

The style journos may crow that Hoxton's done and dusted and that the scene has moved on elsewhere, but the Shoreditch Triangle (formed by Old Street, Shoreditch High Street and Great Eastern Street) still has the largest concentration of cool bars attracting beautiful people in London. This remains the place for top cocktails, great bar snacks, the best international DJs and other assorted nightlife diversions, from art events to strippers. But be warned, unless your idea of a good night out is standing in a queue for a couple of hours, the most popular venues are best appreciated during the week. Oh, and the 'Shoreditch Twat' is either a publication, a DJ or that guy with the mullet behind you in the queue – or all three.

Anda de Bridge

42-4 Kingsland Road, E2 (7739 3863). Old Street tube/rail/55 bus. **Open** 11am-11pm Mon-Fri; 5-11pm Sat. **Food served** 11am-3pm, 6-10pm daily. **Credit** AmEx, MC, V.

A great understated bar, which is quiet and cosy early, when the music ranges from Air to mellow reggae, and entertains a genuine mixed bag of locals and office workers who sit at candlelit tables or settle back on hessian couches for a quick drink (all spirits are double measures). Perhaps they'll also grab something from the decent, reasonably priced Spanish/Caribbean menu (chorizo £3.50, jerk pork £5, rice 'n' peas £2).Things get busier and livelier later when pre-clubbers are served by friendly staff apparently unfazed by the enormous drinks menu – a short, well-chosen wine list, cocktails, overproofs, shooters, 29 liqueurs, 15 rums, 16 vodkas down to a more pedestrian pint of Stella, or Leffe Blonde.

Disabled: toilet. Function room (seats 25-30). Music (DJs 8pm Thur-Sat; free). Games (theme nights, call for details). **Map 5/R3**

Artillery Arms

102 Bunhill Row, EC1 (7253 4683). Old Street tube/ rail. **Open** 11am-11pm Mon-Fri; noon-11pm Sat; noon-10.30pm Sun. **Food served** noon-3pm Mon-Fri. **Credit** AmEx, MC, V.

This cosy little Fuller's pub sits opposite Bunhill Fields cemetery, the last resting place of William Blake. A bit blokey and smoky, it's nonetheless very likeable, fitted out with wooden tables and chairs, and bright green walls bedecked with cigarette card collections and period photographs. Friendly bar staff serve a mixed bag of City workers and locals with good cheer and quality beer at reasonable prices (Chiswick Ale at £1.85). If you can play anything more complex than 'Chopsticks', you have the landlord's permission to entertain the punters on the pub piano, otherwise leave it to the CD player behind the bar. The upstairs function room is opened when the bar gets too busy; it can also be hired out for meetings or quiz nights.

Function room. Games (darts, fruit machine). Tables outdoors (pavement). TV (satellite). **Map 5/P4**

Bar Kick

127 Shoreditch High Street, E1 (7739 8700/www.cafe kick.co.uk). Old Street tube/rail/55 bus. **Open** 11am-11pm Mon-Sat; noon-10.30pm Sun. **Food served** noon-4pm Mon, Tue; noon-4pm, 6-11pm Wed-Sat; noon-10pm Sun. **Happy hour** 4-7pm daily. **Credit** MC, V.

Bigger and less cluttered than its original sister bar (**Cafe Kick**, *see p108*) in Exmouth Market, this place is just sooooo continental – from the no-smoking area (two small tables in the corner of the room), to its huge range of international bottled beers (14 of them: beware the French Jenlain, 6.5% at £3.50), litres of Cruzcampo (£6) and overhanging flags and pennants boasting the crests of exotic European football teams. Even the food menu of tapas, boquerones and manchego cheese with membrillo (quince) adds to the flavour. Then, of course, there's the table football (four upstairs, three down); tables cost 50p a game. Spirits are anything from £2 to £7 for absinthe (liable to affect your game). Bar staff are young and friendly, much like the punters, and even the music has an eclectic feel – check out jazz from Brazil on Wednesdays. When you've played the game and tasted the food, you can even buy the Kick T-shirt (as well as the olive oil!). Branding aside, this remains a terrific hang out, well in control of its image and still a long goal kick away from the danger of franchise hell.

Disabled: toilet. Function room. Games (backgammon, table football). Music (musicians 7pm Tue, Wed; 6.30-10.30pm Sun; free). TVs (big screen, satellite). **Map 5/R4**

Barley Mow

127 Curtain Road, EC2 (7729 0347). Old Street tube/ rail/55 bus. **Open** 11am-midnight Mon-Sat; 1-10.30pm Sun. **Credit** MC, V.

No longer the overflow pub for the neighbouring **Bricklayer's Arms** (*see p122*), the Barley Mow has come into its own in the last couple of years and is often even busier than the Brickies itself. This may have something to do with the warm atmosphere, ambient lighting (candles, muted wall lights and fairy lights), friendly bar staff, intimate seating areas and live events, including comedy and magicians, as well as regular live music. Drinks are impressive too – real ales include BOB (from Gloucestershire's Wickwar Brewing Company) and Ridleys IPA at £2.50 a pint, then there's double-brewed Wieckse Witte and Affligem at £2.20 a half (you'll only want a half at 6% abv). Unbelievably, for Shoreditch at least, children and babies are welcome until 9pm. There are also DJs from Thursday to Sunday.

Babies and children admitted (until 7pm). Function room. Music (DJs 9pm Thur-Sat; 7pm Sun). Tables outdoors (pavement). **Map 5/R4**

Bluu

1 Hoxton Square, N1 (7613 2793). Old Street tube/rail/55 bus. **Open** 11am-11.30pm Mon-Thur, 11am-10.30pm Sun; 10am-midnight Fri, Sat. **Food served** noon-10pm daily. **Credit** AmEx, DC, MC, V.

On the bottom corner of Hoxton Square, this is a good-looking, stylish bar with retro furnishings – from '60s lamps to '70s leather chairs – cowed into submission by a long (and we mean long) concrete and steel bar. Great cocktails (from a Passion at £5 to a French 75 at £9.50) are served with some confidence; shooters cost from £4.50 to £7. There's also a smaller, cosy (nay, cramped) bar below for a more intimate experience. It's just a shame about the clientele. On Friday night expect to be jostled by lager-swilling louts talking in decibels and brandishing their nipples at each other. The burly security geezers on the door don't exactly embrace the notion of cool either. In fact, better avoid the weekends altogether, except for brunch. Try midweek, when it's strictly locals and much more laid-back.

Disabled: toilet. Function room. Music (DJs 9pm Fri, Sat; free). **Map 5/R3**

BOD

104-22 City Road, EC1 (7490 7407). Old Street tube/ rail. **Open** 11am-11pm Mon-Thur; 11am-midnight Fri, Sat. **Food served** 11am-10pm Mon-Fri. **Credit** AmEx, MC, V.

Stumble out of Old Street (exit eight for those confused by the subterranean labyrinth) and fall straight into BOD – latest in the area's ever-increasing line-up of DJ bar/restaurant/clubs. This one's USP is a resident magician called Magic (what else?), who roams around the two-floor 200-capacity joint entertaining punters with his tricks. The L-shaped basement boasts a bar made from the reflective material used in Formula 1 cars, and is host to a number of free-entry parties ranging from Music For Grown Ups, which offers varied tempo music, food, drink and board games, to Bad Bad Simba

Critics' choice historic boozers

Black Friar (p117)
It's not that old, but boy is it beautiful.

Lamb & Flag (p37)
Formerly the 'Bucket of Blood' – we can't think why they changed the name.

Ye Olde Cheshire Cheese (p119)
London's archetypal ye olde worlde pub.

Prospect of Whitby (p155)
The former Devil's Tavern, built in 1520.

Spaniards Inn (p167)
Turpin, Keats, Dickens, Byron, Lamb et al.

with Groove Armada's Tom Findlay playing funk rarities. The food is strictly organic and generally excellent (£5 mains), and the booze includes great cocktails and an innovative and well-chosen wine list, with bargain house available at £10. Magic, indeed.
Babies and children admitted. Disabled: toilet. Games (chess, Jenga, Monopoly). Music (DJs 9pm-midnight Fri, Sat; free). **Map 5/Q4**

City

Bricklayer's Arms

63 Charlotte Road, EC2 (7739 5245). Old Street tube/ rail/55 bus. **Open** 11am-11pm Mon-Fri; noon-11pm Sat; noon-10.30pm Sun. **Food served** noon-3pm, 6pm-midnight Mon-Fri; 2.30pm-11pm Sat; 1.30-9pm Sun. **Credit** MC, V.

Something of a Shoreditch institution, but this old boozer is in need of a little TLC. The battered sofas and wooden floors remain, and its regular core of studenty/grungy/groovy clientele is still packing it out, but a big-screen TV and dangling wires where the lighting once was don't bode well. On our last visit even the ubiquitous fire was off – replaced by an electric heater – when the snow lay deep and crisp outside. On the upside, there are six bitters offered (including Old Speckled Hen), draught cider and Stella Artois. And if a pickled egg (65p) won't sate your appetite, there's fine Thai food served in the slightly cooler, less busy restaurant-bar area upstairs. Sunday roasts are a reasonable £7.95. DJs wreck decks from Thursday to Sunday.
Games (quiz machine). Jukebox. Music (DJs 8.30pm Thur-Sun; free). Restaurant available for hire. Tables outdoors (pavement). TV (satellite). **Map 5/R4**

Bridge & Tunnel

4 Calvert Avenue, E2 (7729 6533). Old Street tube/rail/ 55 bus. **Open** 5pm-2am Mon-Sat; 12.30pm-12.30am Sun. **Food served** 5-11pm Mon-Sat; 12.30-2.30pm Sun. **Credit** MC, V.

It was inevitable that the hype would prove too much for this place to deliver. Set up by the people behind Nuphonic Records and the fabulous but sadly defunct Blue Note club, it promised to be the coolest new DJ bar around. And, even if it looks something like a tarted-up wine bar, it definitely does plenty of things well. Upstairs the high ceilings are accentuated by long red drapes at the windows, while soft lighting gives the place an intimate feel. A discerning but friendly crowd is drawn in by an unrivalled wow of a sound system and some great club nights with DJ luminaries such as Andrew Weatherall and J Swinscoe (Cinematic Orchestra). The well-stocked bar serves a good selection of spirits and cocktails (around the £6 mark), as well as draught beers at £2.90; a small open kitchen offers simple cheap pastas and tasty sandwich/bruschetta options.
Disabled: toilet. Function room. **Map 5/R4**

Cantaloupe

35 Charlotte Road, EC2 (7613 4411). Old Street tube/ rail/55 bus. **Open** 11am-midnight Mon-Fri; noon-midnight Sat; noon-11.30pm Sun. **Food served** noon-close daily. **Credit** AmEx, DC, MC, V.

In spite of its age – this is considered the first of the groovy bars in Hoxton – Cantaloupe still does everything better than most of its johnny-come-lately competitors. The vast NYC-style front bar, filled with chunky tables and benches, is always packed with office workers early evening, gently nudged out by a trendier contingent later on. Despite its size and varied custom, the place always manages to feel like your own local. There's a vast array of cocktails (all £5), exemplary wines (from £9.90), and strange-sounding beers (aromatic Dutch wheat beer Korenwolf, £1.80 a half). You'll also find a great street-food menu with tapas-sized plates and prices, and a fine Spanish-based restaurant out the back. With its sound music policy (not too loud, at least until the place is heaving) and friendly bar staff (take heed, rivals), this one is undeniably set to run and run.
Babies and children admitted (restaurant only). Disabled: toilet. Music (DJs 8pm Wed, Fri-Sun; free). **Map 5/R4**

Cargo

83 Rivington Street, EC2 (7749 7844/www.cargo-london.com). Old Street tube/rail/55 bus. **Open** 6pm-1am Mon-Thur; noon-3am Fri; 6pm-3am Sat; noon-midnight Sun. **Food served** 6-11pm Mon-Thur; noon-3pm, 6pm-midnight Fri; 6pm-midnight Sat; 1-5pm, 6pm-midnight Sun. **Admission** £4-£9 (depending on DJ/band). **Credit** MC, V.

Cargo is a multipurpose, multimedia, multi-play venue within a bunker-sized space of stripped-down wood and brick, all housed in three converted railway. arches. There's a huge back-of-house dance area where musicians and DJs play, a decent-sized bar area and a food bit where Latin-influenced dishes are served. Drinks include cocktails (£6), litres of Cruzcampo (£5.90) and a choice of bottled beers (£2.90). Punters queue around the block for regular club nights such as Barrio (Afro, Latin and vocal-infused house) and specials such as the Remix with Asian Dub Foundation playing live. In spite of its popularity, Cargo remains friendly and unpretentious. If the great programming continues, it will always be rammed. One of London's finest.
Disabled: toilet. Film projections. Music (bands and DJs nightly). **Map 5/R4**

Catch 22

22 Kingsland Road, E2 (7729 6097). Old Street tube/ rail/55 bus. **Open** 5.30pm-midnight Tue, Wed; 5.30pm-2am Thur, Fri; 6pm-2am Sat; 5.30pm-1am Sun. **No credit cards.**

Catch isn't following any Hoxton rules on the music front – there are no 'names' playing here and you're often listening to loud 1980s hits. But pick your night and you can have a rollicking good time (we recommend Sunday's reggae night). Alternatively, it's just a comfortable place to hang out – woody booths on a raised platform overlooked by huge copper lamps, a mishmash of sofas and chairs in a small window area (making you the window display), a makeshift DJ booth in the corner and a spiral staircase leading to the space upstairs, which is often hired out for party nights. Midweek draws an inoffensive, trend-free crowd, while weekends attract a more dressed-up bunch ready to party. Drinks are the standard fare of draught and bottled beers. There's no food but staff are happy for you to bring in your own kebab, so long as you don't make a mess.
Function room (club upstairs). Games (pool). Music (DJs Wed-Sun; free). **Map 5/R3**

Charlie Wright's International Bar

45 Pitfield Street, N1 (7490 8345). Old Street tube/rail/ 55 bus. **Open** noon-1am Mon-Wed, Sun; noon-2am Thur; noon-3am Fri, Sat. **Admission** £3 after 10pm Fri, Sat. **Food served** noon-3pm, 5-11pm daily. **Credit** DC, MC, V.

Can this really be Hoxton? We sweated on a slithering dance floor, saved the last dance for half the bar, supped a score of quality beers, rubbed shoulders with backpackers and bruisers alike and laughed it all off the next day over a game of pool at the very same venue. Welcome to the domain of Mr Wright, a Ghanaian power-lifter with a yen for delicate statuettes of jazz musicians and the provider of welcome proof that Hoxton is not just the playground of shark-finned Nathan

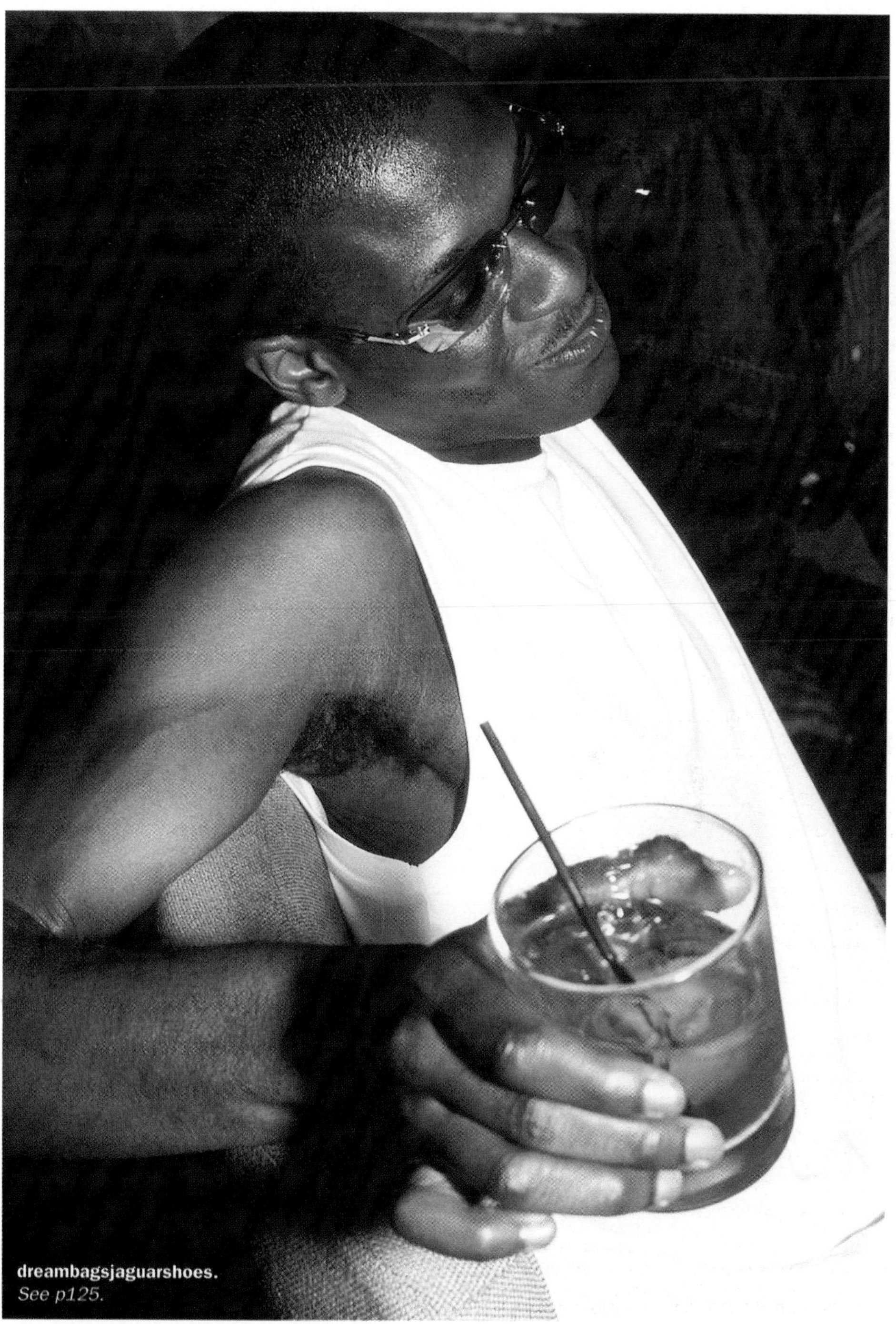

dreambagsjaguarshoes.
See p125.

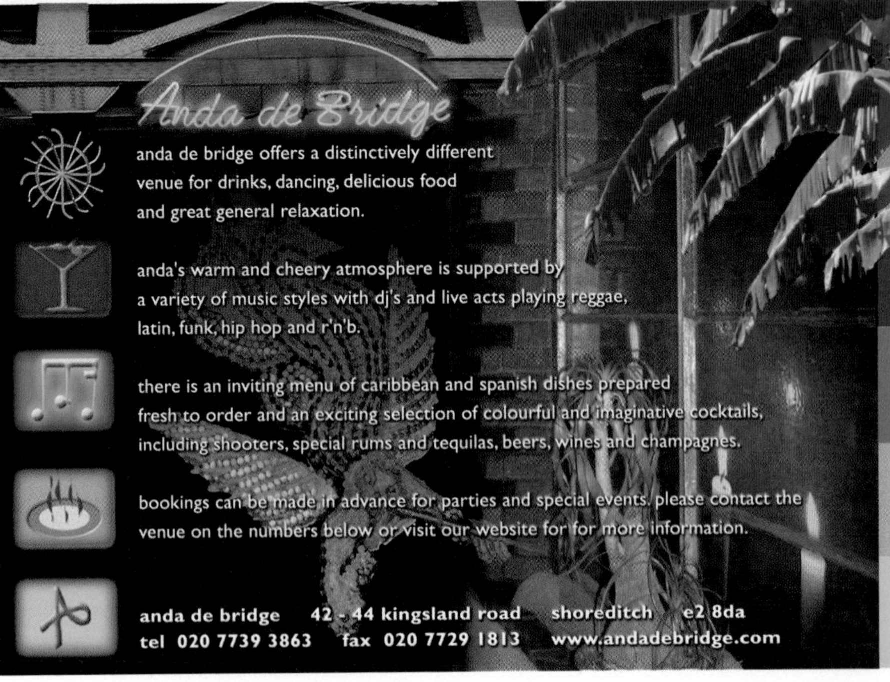

Anda de Bridge
anda de bridge offers a distinctively different venue for drinks, dancing, delicious food and great general relaxation.
anda's warm and cheery atmosphere is supported by a variety of music styles with dj's and live acts playing reggae, latin, funk, hip hop and r'n'b.
there is an inviting menu of caribbean and spanish dishes prepared fresh to order and an exciting selection of colourful and imaginative cocktails, including shooters, special rums and tequilas, beers, wines and champagnes.
bookings can be made in advance for parties and special events. please contact the venue on the numbers below or visit our website for for more information.
anda de bridge 42 - 44 kingsland road shoreditch e2 8da
tel 020 7739 3863 fax 020 7729 1813 www.andadebridge.com

Barleys and micro-scooting posers. Instead, you'll find an outstanding choice of draught (Affligem, Warsteiner, Wieckse Witte) and bottled beers (Lapin Kulta, Jinzu and Zywiec), Thai food, and some fine DJing after dark. It all takes place in a simple bar space, so simple it almost beggars description, with the counter in one corner, a kitchen at the end and a pool table down one side.
Babies and children admitted (until 7pm). Games (fruit machine, pinball, pool). Music (DJs Thur-Sun). TV (big screen, satellite). **Map 5/Q3**

Cocomo

323 Old Street, EC1 (7613 0315). Old Street tube/rail/ 55 bus. **Open/food served** 11am-11pm Mon-Fri; 5-11pm Sat, Sun. **No credit cards**.
Hookahs (with an 'ah', not 'er') might be a familiar sight around the Edgware Road, but not so in this part of the city, especially at the bargain rate of £2.50. If you're intrigued, then head for Cocomo, an intimate space reminiscent of a Moroccan coffee house where a flavoured puff on an ancient water pipe is one of the treats. Less exotic – and without that intoxicating whiff of decadence – are smoothies at £2.80 and decent cocktails from £5. A slightly roomier (but not much) downstairs area usually has bodies filling every inch of limited floor space, slumped on rugs, leather stools and couches, chilling to the sounds of the funky DJ. The mixed crowd might include some Romford lads who've headed into town looking for 333... If they linger here, they might not care to make it.
Babies and children admitted (daytime). Function room. Music (DJs 7pm Wed-Sun; free). **Map 5/R4**

Dragon

5 Leonard Street, EC2 (7490 7110). Old Street tube/rail/ 55 bus. **Open** 11am-11pm Mon-Thur; 11am-midnight Fri, Sat; noon-10.30pm Sun. **Credit** MC, V.
Tucked in its own little lair in Leonard Street, the Dragon rarely sleeps. Packed to the gills most nights, it's a trend-proof den of trash and tack, home to a refreshingly enthusiastic crowd, getting off on the music as much as each other, crammed into a narrow, radiantly unpretentious bar (bare brick, old leather sofas and dimmed lights). If this bunch (not least the vivacious DJ at the far end of the bar counter) turned up en masse at your birthday party, you'd be delighted (though you might hide the breakables). Provided the bar staff aren't too pushed, they can rustle up a decent cocktail (around £6), but most settle for pints of Scrumpy Jack, Staropramen or Guinness, with occasional chasers of absinthe (£3.50-£4.50). In fine weather, the atmosphere, bottled up behind the curtains at the front and the blocked-off exhibition space above, escapes into the backyard, to drift over the basketball court beyond. The underused room downstairs (a comfy sofa space lit by little red lights and candles) serves as a spillover area as well, but in reality you don't mind a bit if someone sloshes a little Staropramen over your sneakers.
Art gallery. Babies and children admitted (until 6pm). Music (DJs 8pm nightly). **Map 5/Q4**

dreambagsjaguarshoes

34-36 Kingsland Road, E2 (7739 9550). Old Street tube/rail/55 bus. **Open** 5pm-midnight Mon-Sat; 5-11.30pm Sun. **Credit** MC, V.
With its half-finished look and quirky work-in-progress wall art, DBJS has become a Shoreditch success story. The goldfish (once swimming under your glass-topped table) have gone, but the regularly changing displays by local artists, as well as the battered sofas and plastic bucket chairs, all remain. Club nights like 'All Records 99p' where eight DJs spend £10 on charity shop records and spin away, are pulling them in – expect to be surrounded by photographers, musos, pseuds and crowds of office girls. A smaller, more intimate space downstairs can get smoky. Drinks include Korenwolf wheat beer at £2 a half, and there's a short wine list (£10-£22), plus Japanese nibbles for dins.
Music (DJs 8pm Tue-Sun; free). **Map 5/R3**

Elbow Room

97-113 Curtain Road, EC2 (7613 1316). Old Street tube/rail/55 bus. **Open/food served** noon-2am Mon-Sat; noon-midnight Sun. **Happy hour** 5-8pm Mon-Fri. **Credit** MC, V.
The nearest thing Shoreditch has to a chain, this bar/restaurant/club is the latest addition to Arthur Baker's empire (*see also* Westbourne Grove, Islington and Swiss Cottage). Anyone from groups of pink-shirted estate agents to baggy-trousered funksters comes here to shoot pool on one of the eight signature purple-baize tables, while listening to top tunes provided by the likes of Tummy Touch or Heavy Rotation. The space is enormous, but well designed; there are booths that seat up to 30 people, and you can watch soundless videos of the likes of *Reservoir Dogs* (or at least a loop of the most violent bits). The drinks menu includes draught and bottled beers, plus basic cocktails – some of which are included in the two-for-one deal. A char-grilled buffet menu is available as well as light bites from £3.95. Quibbles? No ashtrays when we were there.
Disabled: toilet. Games (8 pool tables). Music (DJs 8pm Thur-Sat; 4pm Sun; free). TV (plasma screens).
Map 5/R4

Fifteen

15 Westland Place, N1 (7251 1515). Old Street tube/rail. **Open** 11am-midnight Mon-Sat. **Food served** *Deli* 7.30am-midnight Mon-Sat. **Credit** AmEx, DC, MC, V.
Runaway reality TV success means that dinner at Fifteen tops half the country's 'to do before I die' list, so unless you booked at birth, forget it. However, the restaurant comes with a swish bar attached, and you can usually get into it without too much trouble. It's certainly pretty: all backlit pink, violet neon tables and opal leather banquettes. Wine is expensive (£20-£30 a bottle), so we recommend choosing from the impressive cocktail list or the huge range of whiskies, rums, tequilas, gin and vodkas. Bottled beers cost more than £3. Service is poor and the loos are uninspiring, while your fellow Fifteeners will be more highlights and high heels than Hoxton hip. But order one of the well-made snacks served with freshly baked bread (bacon sarnie £3.50, big breakfast £7) and you can at least truthfully boast, hand on heart, that you've eaten at Jamie's gaff. Next, sex with the cast of *Friends*.
Babies and children welcome (high chairs, nappy-changing area). Disabled: toilet. No-smoking area (restaurant). TV (satellite). **Map 5/Q3**

Fox Dining Room

28 Paul Street, EC2 (7729 5708). Old Street tube/rail. **Open** noon-11pm Mon-Fri. **Food served** 12.30-3pm, 6.30-10pm **Credit** MC, V.
Brought to you by one of the former partners in Farringdon's famous **Eagle** (*see p111*), the Fox is a lovingly restored old boozer, warmly lit with table lamps and chandeliers, and embellished with a centrepiece rich, dark-wood, island bar. Catering predominantly to a post-work City crowd (and so closed at weekends), the bar dispenses just the one real ale (Charles Wells Bombardier) but it has a short, good wine list. Upstairs, the 'Gentleman's club' area is a plush leather sofa'd dining room for top-drawer gastropub grub (the Fox was a runner-up in the Best Gastropub category of *Time Out*'s 2002 Eating & Drinking awards). Good simple lunches of the likes

of ploughman's and own-made sausage rolls can also be had in the non-gentleman's downstairs bar.
Babies and children admitted. Pub available for hire at weekends. Tables outdoors (terrace). **Map 5/Q4**

George & Dragon

2 Hackney Road, E2 (7012 1100). Old Street tube/rail/ 55 bus. **Open** noon-11pm Mon-Sat; noon-10.30pm Sun. **Credit** MC, V.

Since their move from Hoxton's **Red Lion** (*see p128*), Richard and Julie have opened the George & Dragon at the top of Hackney Road and brought new life to this dismal bit of Shoreditch. The makeover retains plenty of that old pub feel – tasselled table lamps, leather armchairs, pub stools, heavy curtains, jukebox of choice 'classics' (a concession maybe to the high 'codger factor' found here most early evenings). Regular DJs play quirky delights, while local designers and artists give the place a friendly vibe that is less evident in the trendified bars close by. A full bar includes novel items such as draught Double Diamond (!) served in a jug or straight glass, as well as a Fluffy Nutnot (advocaat, lemonade, Frangelico, £3).
Disabled: toilet. Music (DJs 8pm nightly). **Map 5/R3**

Grand Central

93 Great Eastern Street, EC1 (7613 4228/www.grand central.org.uk). Old Street tube/rail/55 bus. **Open/ food served** 8am-midnight Mon-Fri; 6pm-midnight Sat; 11am-5pm Sun. **Happy hour** 5-7pm Mon-Fri. **Credit** AmEx, MC, V.

With 2,000sq ft of smooth lines, wood and glass with a post-industrial feel and raised seating areas enclosed by neon-lit borders (grand indeed), the Grand Central is all things to all people. Early morning it dishes out great breakfasts (£5.50) accompanied by 16 different coffees, and it's also surprisingly good as a lunch venue with a varied menu of large salads and plates of pasta alongside sandwiches and burgers. Come evening, punters are more interested in the wonderful multi-coloured neon bar and the liquids it dispenses: specifically myriad cocktails and spirits (including a great range of bourbons), and draught and bottled beers (including the excellent Anchor Steam). Early birds can take advantage of the 6x6 Special (5-7pm Mon-Sat) when six cocktails cost £3 each, a bottle of house wine with nachos is £9, and two pints and two flavoured bourbon shots go for £6. Kicking DJs provide new wave disco, electro pop and everything in between as soundtracks to a frequently great late-night sesh.
Babies and children admitted (until 5pm). Music (DJs 8pm Thur-Sun; free). **Map 5/Q4**

Great Eastern Dining Room

54-6 Great Eastern Street, EC2 (7613 4545). Old Street tube/rail/55 bus. **Open/food served** noon-midnight Mon-Wed; noon-1am Thur-Sat. **Credit** AmEx, DC, MC, V.

Some come here for food (the dining crew at *Time Out* reckon it's fab), but we less sophisticated types at the *Pubs & Bars Guide* just come to booze. Head upstairs to a chic and sophisticated space of high ceilings, dark wood, stylish chandeliers and leather bucket chairs. There, at the chrome bar, join assorted groovy muckers selecting from a huge range of decent cocktails (from £5), whiskies (from £2) and cognacs (from £2.50), or more pedestrian draught and bottled beers (under £3). The Great Eastern is a superb post-work venue (though avoid Friday nights when it's positively rammed and fairly unpleasant) and attracts a mixture of office workers, young creatives and up-for-it clubbers who will later head downstairs to Below 54 where they'll expect, and likely get, a night of sweat, dim lighting, projectors screening very arty visuals and leather sofas.
Babies and children admitted (restaurant). Dress: no ties (downstairs Thur-Sat). Function room (Mon-Wed only). Music (DJs 7.30pm Thur-Sat). **Map 5/R4**

Herbal

10-14 Kingsland Road, E2 (7613 4462/www.herbal uk.com). Old Street tube/rail/55 bus. **Open** 9pm-2am Wed, Thur, Sun; 9pm-3am Fri, Sat. **Admission** £3-£6 (depending on DJs) after 10.30pm Wed, after 10pm Fri, Sat. **No credit cards.**

It's bleak at the southern end of the Kingsland Road, but enter through the green astroturf doors into a beautifully converted oak-veneer warehouse – all exposed brick and reclaimed timber – turned supreme late-night venue. On the first floor is an intimate, ambiently lit space good for chilling, while the ground floor is presided over by a roster of resident and guest DJs. The programming is generally excellent, but the big nights are Bitches Brew (Afro-Latin soulful deep house) and Care in the Community. Drinks are nothing too exciting (although prices are at 'pub' level) but the crowd's comfortably mixed in age, friendly and up-for-it, making this one of the coolest bars around. Small wonder that clubbers continue to beat a path to the green door.
Disabled: toilet. Music (DJs Tue-Sun). **Map 5/R3**

Home

100-106 Leonard Street, EC2 (7684 8618/www.home bar.co.uk). Old Street tube/rail/55 bus. **Open** 5pm-midnight Mon-Fri; 6pm-midnight Sat. **Food served** 12.30-3pm, 7-10.30pm Mon-Fri; 7-10.30pm Sat. **Credit** AmEx, MC, V.

How do they do it? Trailblazer Home, the laid-back, lived-in basement bar that helped Hoxton earn its Hip Square Mile title, is now practically an emporium. Still central to the operation, though, is the three-roomed basement bar filled with low-level tables, Chesterfields and sofas, ambient '70s-style lights, and ever busy, but helpful and efficient staff manning the (too) small bar. Drinks include decent wine (250ml, £4.20-£4.60), cocktails (from £5.50) and shooters (£3.50), but a woefully pedestrian selection of draught and bottled beers. The demographics of the sleek 80-seat (Modern British) restaurant upstairs might be felt down in the bar but it's still basically a fun-loving crowd. DJs liven up proceedings in the latter part of the week. Click the heels of your ruby red slippers and repeat, 'There's no place like...'
Babies and children admitted. Function room. Music (DJs 8pm Thur-Sat; free). No-smoking area (lunchtime, restaurant). TV (big screen, satellite). **Map 5/R4**

Hoxton Square Bar & Kitchen

2-4 Hoxton Square, N1 (7613 0709). Old Street tube/rail/ 55 bus. **Open/food served** 11am-midnight Mon-Sat; noon-10.30pm Sun. **Credit** AmEx, MC, V.

Still known to locals as the Lux Bar, despite the demise of the landmark cinema of that name next door, this stark concrete bunker bar looks something like an airstrip with its now famous plate-glass window that seems to be playing chicken with oncoming traffic, delivering a frisson to punters as the car headlights appear to be aiming straight for them. It's like something from JG Ballard's wet dream. Otherwise, it's a comfortable, popular venue filled with spinning bucket chairs, leather sofas and good-looking folk noshing on good-looking, fairly priced food (winter veggie soup with ciabatta, £3.50). Highlights of the huge drinks list include draught Affligem and Erdinger (£2.20 a half/£4 a pint), bottled Kirin and a short but decent selection of wine by the glass. There's usually a photographic or art exhibition to look at too. All these years on, if you walk past this bar, particularly when it's in full

swing, you feel that you're missing out on something, and few other Hoxton venues can say that.
Babies and children admitted (until 6pm). Disabled: toilet. Tables outdoors (pavement). **Map 5/R3**

Light Bar & Restaurant

233 Shoreditch High Street, E1 (7247 8989). Liverpool Street tube/rail. **Open/food served** *Bar* noon-midnight Mon-Wed; noon-2am Thur, Fri; 6.30pm-2am Sat; noon-10.30pm Sun. *Restaurant* noon-3pm, 6-10.45pm Mon-Fri; 6.30-10.45pm Sat. **Admission** £2 Thur-Sat (upstairs bar). **Credit** AmEx, DC, MC, V.
'More Light, More Power' is the motto of Shoreditch. Really. And here they take it more seriously than most. Two airy warehouse-sized floors of bare brick and wooden beams are home to a stylish bar, swish restaurant and an upstairs cocktail lounge with views right over the City (foregrounded, unfortunately, by Liverpool Street station's sidings). Unusually, since it is on the edge of the Square Mile, there's a 'no suits' policy in the lounge, hence the crowd tends to be fairly casual and under-30. Bar staff are better-looking than is good for service (don't expect eye contact). That aside, this is a fine place to hang after work. Cocktails cost a reasonable £5 to £6, shots are £3, and half a pint of Bellevue cherry beer (yum!) is £2.60. More power to it!
Disabled: toilet. Dress: no suits in upstairs bar. Function room (Sun-Thur only). Music (DJs Thur-Sat). Tables outdoors (courtyard, lawn, roof terrace). **Map 5/R5**

Liquid Lab

20 City Road, EC1 (7920 0372/www.liquidlab.co.uk). Moorgate/Old Street tube/rail. **Open** 11am-11pm Mon-Fri. **Food served** 11am-10pm Mon-Fri. **Credit** AmEx, DC, MC, V.
The theme is medical, with sterile white walls 'decorated' with backlit X-rays. Patients – predominantly City folk – sit at wooden tables and chairs, and are served from a cool 'ice' bar where friendly waitresses administer cocktails with names like Sperm Bank (honey liqueur, crème de cacao, vanilla, schnapps, £5.50). If you find that amusing, you might need an 'Appointment with the house doctor' (£20), which starts with a shot of Viagra (absinthe, midori and Baileys) and ends with a sugar cube soaked with brandy. Actually, we needed no professional help to diagnose our problem: migraine, brought on by Robbie Williams on the sound system at great volume (though any volume is bad enough). Sustenance for the stomach comes in the form of tapas (from £3.50) and mains, which are thankfully theme free (except for the Liquid Lab burgers – we shudder to think what goes in those).
Disabled: toilet. Games (board games). Function room. Tables outdoors (pavement). **Map 5/Q4**

Medicine

89 Great Eastern Street, EC2 (7739 5173/www.medicine bar.net). Old Street tube/rail/55 bus. **Open** 5-11pm Mon, Tue; 5pm-2am Wed-Sat; 5pm-midnight Sun. **Food served** 5-10pm daily. **Happy hour** 5-9pm Sat. **Admission** £6 after 9pm Fri, Sat. **Credit** MC, V.
Such is the success of Islington's **Medicine Bar** (*see p176*), that its younger Shoreditch sibling is reaping big rewards, packed to the max most weekends. On two levels, the huge ambiently lit, leather sofa-filled space offers plenty of good music, with the main bar area playing funky classics, while the club downstairs (with excellent sound system) hosts regular big nights attracting names such as Andy Weatherall, Jon Carter and Norman Cook. Fame costs, however, and on Friday and Saturday after 10pm you'll have to cough up a not unreasonable six squids. Cocktails are keenly priced and good (an ace Mojito at £5.90). Between 5pm and 9pm on Saturday all bottled beers or vodka and splash are £1.95. We do have our gripes, though, with the surly door staff and the atrocious, verging on non-existent, bar service.
Disabled: toilet. Function room. Music (DJs 9pm Thur-Sun). Tables outdoors (pavement). **Map 5/Q4**

Mother Bar

333 Old Street, EC1 (7739 5949/www.333mother.com). Old Street tube/rail/55 bus. **Open** 5pm-3am Mon-Wed; 5pm-4am Thur, Sun; 5pm-5am Fri, Sat. **Food served** 5-11pm daily. **Credit** MC, V.
Above the scruffy-looking 333 (covered in billposters loudly advertising its own nights), the bar that was once pleasingly intimate and inviting is starting to look a little dark and dingy – the loos were always grim. The mirror balls, chandeliers, flock wallpaper and DJs (playing anything from the Beach Boys to the Beastie Boys) remain, but sadly the predominantly male clientele is often as rough as a badger's backside, comprising a lairy mix of locals, out-of-towners and bemused foreign tourists in varying stages of drunkenness, slavering over the sofas and each other. It is still possible to meet some quirky folk, like the Chinese guy who felt he was a little bit too 'tree' (who knows?), but he was in a minority of one. Oh, and expect major queues.
Music (DJs 10pm Mon-Thur; 8pm Fri, Sat; 5pm Sun; free). **Map 5/R4**

New Foundry

84-6 Great Eastern Street, EC2 (7739 6900). Old Street tube/rail/55 bus. **Open** 4-11pm Tue-Fri; 2-11pm Sat; 4-10.30pm Sun. **No credit cards.**
As chaotic and squat-like as the day it first opened, the Foundry remains one of the most chilled-out places in Shoreditch. Housed in what was a big old corner bank, it's two floors of scruffy tables, odd chairs, strange wall hangings and a host of defunct computer screens. The basement (former bank vaults) is a gallery space hosting exhibitions of local artists, while the ground floor holds irregular DJ sessions and one-offs such as Micro-band night, hosted by Masse and including live performances and midi-bouzouki players (!?). There's also the regular Welcome to Wormworld, a poetry and performance event. Drinks include draught Pitfield Organic and bottled Pitfield Eco Warrior as well as absinthe (£3). The loos are shambolic.
Art gallery. Babies and children admitted (separate area). Music (DJs 6pm Thur-Sun; free). Poetry readings (9pm Sun; free). **Map 5/Q4**

New Inn

1 New Inn Broadway, EC2 (7739 7775/www.new inn.co.uk). Old Street tube/rail/55 bus. **Open** 5-11pm Mon-Fri; 6-11pm Sat; 6-10.30pm Sun. **Credit** DC, MC, V.
Enjoy a different kind of night on the tiles at this Scrabble-happy little bar, tucked down a side street where the lifestyle tourists won't find it. With no door policy, and no trend-pleasing, this intimate space – packed with mismatched tables, chairs and benches – caters to a mixed-age clientele with friendly bar service, an indifferent range of draught beers strengthened by bottled Belgian stuff, and a load of board games. There's a quieter area downstairs and, to top it off, a mellow jukebox. For quirkiness sake there hangs upon the wall a framed pair of pants that have apparently travelled the world; ask the barman about them if you dare.
Function room. Games (board games). Music (jamming session 9pm Mon). Quiz (8pm Tue; free). Tables outdoors (pavement). **Map 5/R4**

City

City

Owl & the Pussycat

34 Redchurch Street, E2 (7613 3628). Liverpool Street or Old Street tube/rail. **Open** noon-11pm Mon-Fri; 5-11pm Sat; noon-10.30pm Sun. **Food served** noon-3pm, 7.30-9pm Mon-Fri; 7.30-9pm Sat; 1-5pm Sun. **Credit** MC, V.

Relatively unscathed by the brown-leather-sofa-and-DJ-decks madness surrounding it, the Pussycat is one of the scarce few quality boozers left in Shoreditch. It's got a log fire burning in winter and a walled garden to loaf in during the summer, a bar billiards table and a piano. The food is highly recommended: daily lunches cost £6.50 to £8.50, while one of the best Sunday roasts in town comes in three courses for £13 (it's recommended that you book in advance). There's London Pride and Bass on tap, and children are welcome. On Wednesday the landlord stands drinks on the house at half-hour intervals and gives a piggyback home to any customer without a car. OK, that last sentence is a lie, but don't you wish you had a local as good as this one?

Babies and children welcome. Games (bar billiards, fruit machine). Quiz (8.30pm Tue; £1). Restaurant (available for hire). Tables outdoors (garden). **Map 5/R4**

Pool

104-8 Curtain Road, EC2 (7739 9608). Old Street tube/rail/55 bus. **Open** noon-11pm Mon, Tue; noon-1am Wed, Thur; noon-2am Fri; 5.30pm-2am Sat; noon-midnight Sun. **Food served** noon-3.30pm, 6-10.30pm Mon-Fri, Sun; 5.30-10.30pm Sat. **Credit** MC, V.

This spacious two-floor bar has plenty to recommend it, apart from just the pool tables. It's free every night, open until 2am on Fridays and Saturdays, has decent programming five nights a week, and even hosts a film club. But the pool's the main thing – there are two American-sized (huge pockets) tables upstairs, and a standard table downstairs for those prefer to keep things British. All are available to hire by the hour (with a free hour thrown in if you get your pool card stamped four times on four separate days), but on Sundays, when brunch is also offered, table's are free to all. There's also a good, reasonably priced menu, varied seating (including arthritis-inducing bean bags), and a relaxed crowd – and no door attitude, so far. We like.

Babies and children admitted (until 5pm). Games (pool; £5 per hour before 6pm, £7 after 6pm; Sun free). Music (DJs 8pm Wed-Sat; 6pm Sun). Outdoor tables (pavement). **Map 5/R4**

Red Lion

41 Hoxton Street, N1 (7739 3736). Old Street tube/rail/55 bus. **Open** 6-11pm Mon, Sat; noon-11pm Tue-Fri; 6-10.30pm Sun. **Credit** MC, V.

Its future looked uncertain when Richard and Julie left to open the **George & Dragon** (*see p126*) but since Laura, the ex-manager of the **Bricklayer's Arms** (*see p122*), took over, the place has hardly changed. That may not last because we hear a major refit is due in March, but for now, the place is wonderfully cosy, with a clientele of friendly locals (couriers, designers and smoochers) who perch on faux-leopard/tiger skin bar stools, or lounge in front of one of the only real log fires in Shoreditch, surrounded by potted palms and beneath starry, twinkly ceiling lights. The famous jukebox has gone, but in the small side room, with a huge backlit photograph of what looks like a wildebeest, DJs play a mess of reggae and old faves. The range of drinks is disappointing, but it's nothing we can't live with.

Music (DJs 8pm nightly; free). Tables outdoors (yard). **Map 5/R3**

Reliance

336 Old Street, EC1 (7729 6888). Old Street tube/rail/55 bus. **Open** noon-11pm Mon-Thur; noon-2am Fri; 6pm-2am Sat. **Food served** 12.30-3pm, 6-10pm Mon-Fri; 6.30-10pm Sat. **Admission** £2 after 11pm Fri, Sat. **Credit** AmEx, DC, MC, V.

Look for an incongruous sail flapping around on the frontage and you've found the Reliance. We haven't managed to discover the provenance of the name but with plenty of boating and sailing photos upstairs, as well as what looks like part of a boat's hull, you can draw your own conclusions. That aside, it's a comfortable, exposed brick and wood (chairs, tables, floors, bar) sort of pub serving far better than average food and drink. Lager lovers have a knock-out trio of Affligem, Wieckse Witte and Litovel to choose from, while real beer drinkers should have no complaints with Ridleys Old Bob. Sparkling wine costs £2.50 a glass or £10.50 a bottle. There are bar snacks of olives and bread, or for more substantial fare head to the restaurant upstairs. Toward the end of the week and at weekends, guest DJs crank it up for a pre-club crowd. The place is always busy.

Babies and children admitted (restaurant). Function room. Music (DJs 8pm Thur; 10.30pm Fri, Sat). **Map 5/R4**

Shoreditch Electricity Showrooms

39A Hoxton Square, N1 (7739 6934). Old Street tube/rail/55 bus. **Open** noon-midnight Mon-Thur; noon-1am Fri, Sat; noon-midnight Sun. **Food served** 12.30-3.45pm, 6.30-10.30pm Tue-Fri; 12.30-4.45pm, 6.30-10.30pm Sat, Sun. **Credit** AmEx, MC, V.

Old-guard Hoxton but still holding its impressive own despite the rate of new bars opening in the area standing at roughly one every 17 minutes. The SES thrives because it's stylish, spacious (loads of seating), and slickly professional. Beyond that, the formula is no secret and is spelled out on the facade: 'Eat till 11, drink till 12, dance till 1'. Eating is dealt with in the small but decent restaurant area out back, dancing downstairs, but it's the main bar where most of the action takes place, overlooked (currently – but the scene is always changing) by an enormous photo of a zebra. Beneath said mammal, staff dole out mainly bottled beers – though there are good draught options – and cocktails. (One suggestion: the bar boys and girls could do with getting over themselves and attempting the occasional smile; they give the impression that they'd rather be almost anywhere else in Shoreditch than serving you.) SES is also very handy for watching the (non)progress of the queue for 333 opposite.

Babies and children admitted (until 7pm). Disabled: toilet. Film projections (Mon). Function room (weeknights only). Music (DJs 9pm Fri-Sun; free). **Map 5/R3**

Smersh

5 Ravey Street, EC2 (7739 0092). Old Street tube/rail/55 bus. **Open** 5pm-midnight Tue-Fri; 8pm-midnight Sat. **Happy hour** 5-7pm. **No credit cards.**

Inspired by events behind the Iron Curtain and located just behind Curtain Road, Smersh apparently derives its name from the Russian 'smert shpionam' or 'Death to Spies!' Apparently. So, with collar turned up, step into this cosy little hard-to-find and red (of course) venue and be prepared to be charmed into submission. There are two little rooms off the bar area, each furnished with just a few well-rationed chairs and tables (the hammer and sickle jigsaw table was missing on our last visit) – creature comforts are limited. Beer comes in bottles and is from Poland: Brok (£2.60). There's also absinthe (from £4.10), spirits and lots of shots. Service is friendly, and punters even more so; one sweet soul offered

London drinking: Belgian beer

In beer terms, this year's black is Belgian.

These days, no bar worth its salt would dare open to the public without at least one mainstream and a couple of lesser-known Belgian beers. As soon as a new venue opens – **Nudge** (*see p26*) on New Oxford Street or **Lowlander** on Drury Lane, for example – it looks to the Low Countries for alcoholic inspiration.

The trend began with **Belgo**, the brainchild of restaurateurs Denis Blais and André Plisnier, who opened **Belgo Noord** in north London in 1992. With £5 mussels-and-chips lunch specials, a range of strange beers and staff in monk's habits (a hint at Belgian ale's Trappist heritage), the gimmick stuck. Three years later, **Belgo Centraal** opened near Covent Garden, keeping with the Belgian theme, but three times the size. Alongside the Belgos came the more bar-oriented **Bierodromes**, with flagship venues in Upper Street and Kingsway.

Sleeker, hipper but equally specialised spots cropped up, the domino effect seeing a Belgian hegemony at many mainstream outlets.

Where will it end? Under the table, no doubt, as part of the attraction of Belgian beer, along with its variety (Raspberry! Strawberry! Honey! Banana!) is its strength. In the meantime, many of the rarer types previously left on the shelf are now enjoying star status with their own beer tap on bar counters across the city (the increasingly common Leffe Blonde being a case in point).

Belgian-beer lovers wishing to sample the tip of a 600-variety iceberg now have a wealth of choice around town. At the Clerkenwell **Dovetail**, 101 Belgian beers are described and explained in painstaking detail, the drinks menu divided into sections for lagers, pilsners, wheat beers and less familiar lambics and gueuze, spontaneously fermented varieties known for their strength and unusual flavours. As befits Belgian tradition, each beer is served in its own logoed glass, plonked on to its own logoed beermat. Glasses may be goblet-shaped (De Koninck), thin-stemmed (Kriek) or a complicated test-tube-and-wooden-holder arrangement (Kwak). The ritual is almost as attractive as the raison d'être.

Abbaye is a more upmarket chain of Belgian bar-brasseries, where office workers can dive into the darkened recesses of obscure Trappist ale genres. The initiated now know that Belgium has five authentic monastic varieties: Chimay; Orval; Rochefort; Westmalle; and Westvleteren. Wheat beers needn't stop at Hoegaarden: there's Brugs and Limburgse too. Ever more present are Duvel (a golden ale), Kriek (a fruit lambic) and De Koninck (a pale from Antwerp).

Want more? The **Lowlander**, enjoying much success since its opening in 2001, offers 12 Benelux varieties on tap; **L'Auberge** by Waterloo station provides a range of bottled types in half-pint glasses or sociable two-pint pitchers. The **Microbar** in Battersea and the **Porterhouse** (*see p38*) in Covent Garden, boast a dizzying array of varieties. Out west, **Portobello Gold** on the Portobello Road features Leffe on tap, and **Quinn's** of Camden even has cherry-flavoured Bellevue Kriek on draught. A fad's fine, but here's hoping this lasts. *Peterjon Cresswell*

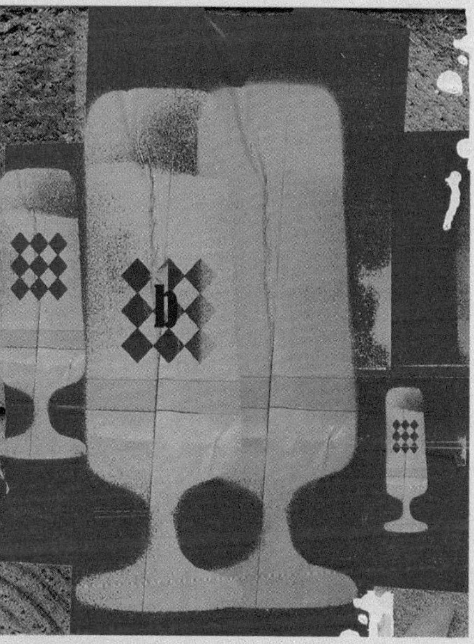

Les huit premières Belges

Abbaye (*see p107*) 55 Charterhouse Street, EC1 (7253 1612).
L'Auberge (*see p101*) 1 Sandell Street, SE1 (7633 0610).
Belgo Centraal (*see p15*) 50 Earlham Street, WC2 (7813 2233).
Dovetail (*see p109*) 9 Jerusalem Passage, EC1 (7490 7321).
Lowlander (*see p37*) 36 Drury Lane, WC2 (7379 7446).
Microbar (*see p195*) 14 Lavender Hill, SW11 (7228 5300).
Portobello Gold (*see p72*) 97 Portobello Road, W11 (7460 4900).
Quinn's (*see p164*) 65 Kentish Town Road, NW5 (7267 8240).

to make up our beer money as we rummaged for change. Events include 'Brastuff presents Great Western' – country music brought to you by the best honky tonkin' Norwegian DJ in town – and 'Cutting Tongues', an open mic session for performers and readers.
Music (DJ 8pm nightly; free). Poetry readings (Tue mid-month). **Map 5/Q4**

Sosho

2 Tabernacle Street, EC2 (7920 0701). Moorgate or Old Street tube/rail. **Open** 11.30am-11pm Mon; 11am-midnight Tue, Wed; 11.30am-1am Thur; 11.30am-3am Fri, Sat. **Food served** 11am-11pm Mon-Sat. **Admission** £3 after 10pm Thur; £3 after 9pm Fri, Sat. **Credit** AmEx, DC, JCB, MC, V.
Still in a class of its own, the City branch of the Match family (now just known as Sosho) hasn't had to change tack, decor or cocktail choice since winning the *Time Out* Best Bar award in 2001. It's a beautiful and stylishly designed venue that continues to do everything well. Along one side a smoothly run bar, offering five champagne, 12 original and nine classic cocktails complementing eight 50ml premium house spirits and four beers (Kölsch, Union, Anchor Steam and Proof Pilsen). Facing the bar is the American Midwest of legend, in giant blow-up photographic form, offset by the occasional chandelier and glitterball. The tables trail off from the main bar area towards the door, allowing conversational space before quality DJing; watch out for Mindfluid until 3am on a Saturday night. Food ranges from freshly made organic soup (£3.50) to seasonal dishes like roast haunch of venison (£8.50), and lunchtime specials.
Disabled: toilet. Function room. **Map 5/Q4**

Trafik

331 Old Street, EC1 (7613 0234). Old Street tube/rail/bus 55. **Open/food served** 6pm-2am Mon; noon-2am Tue-Sat; noon-midnight Sun. **Happy hour** Wed (student night). **Credit** AmEx, MC, V.
Open for a year now, Trafik seems to have found its feet – though how is anybody's guess since it's pretty dark inside. The long corridor bar, opening on to both Old Street and Hoxton Square, boasts a simple bar, small DJ area and a few leather seats around formica tables. So what's the draw? Friendly bar staff for a start, and decent, inexpensive food. Then there are the deckmeisters (including Fabric's Terry Francis) who don't mind you having a conversation early on, but when the clock strikes 10pm… House cocktails are particularly good (all £6), although draught beers (from £2.50) are limited to Red Stripe, Guinness and Erdinger, or choose from seven bottled varieties (£2.60). The wines aren't bad

Trafik

either (but avoid the house, which isn't great) and Modern European food is also available. Add to that a pretty relaxed lot of punters, and getting stuck in Trafik for the night suddenly doesn't seem such a tragic option.
Babies and children admitted (restaurant, until 9pm). Games (carom). Music (DJs 8.30pm Wed-Sun, free; 9pm Thur-Sat, £3). Tables outdoors (pavement). TV (big screen, satellite). **Map 5/R4**

Wenlock Arms

26 Wenlock Road, N1 (7608 3406). Old Street tube/rail. **Open** noon-11pm Mon-Sat; noon-10.30pm Sun. **Food served** noon-9pm daily. **No credit cards.**
Regarded as one of London's very best real ale pubs, this old-fashioned boozer serves eight regularly-changing real ales, including on our most recent visit Pitfield's Organic, East Kent Goldings (light bitter, 4.2%), a real cider and a mild, all at around £2 a pint. You'll also find a wide selection of bottled beers and ciders. Jazz sessions are held several times a week and the locals also take part in darts tournaments and quiz nights. Food includes delights such as blood pudding, salt beef sandwiches and Cornish pasties that actually come from Cornwall. It's a little gem.
Babies and children admitted. Function room. Games (board games, cards, darts). Music (jazz 9pm Fri, 3pm Sun; jazz/blues 9pm Sat; free). Quiz (9pm Thur; free). TV (satellite).

Also in the area...

Colonel Jaspers (Davy's) 190 City Road, EC1 (7608 0926).
Heeltap & Bumper (Davy's) 2-4 Paul Street, EC2 (7247 3319).
Masque Haunt (JD Wetherspoon) 168-72 Old Street, EC1 (7251 4195).
Pulpit (Davy's) 63 Worship Street, EC2 (7377 1574).

Liverpool Street & Moorgate

With hundreds of thousands of Essex boys and girls passing through the area on the way to and from Liverpool Street station every working day, it's little wonder that this is the City's liveliest party zone. All the chains are here, with their offerings of pre-packaged drinks and chicken tikka parcels to pre-packaged consumers. But there are other, worthier choices. Conran's **George** offers style, if not real ale; **Twentyfour** and **Vertigo 42** appeal to well-heeled high-fliers; and **City Limits** is a wine bar with a soul. For head-down, no-nonsense boozing there's **Hamilton Hall**, where at session's end you can topple out of the door and roll down the stairs straight on to your tube/train.

City Limits

16-18 Brushfield Street, E1 (7377 9877). Liverpool Street tube/rail. **Open/food served** 11.30am-3pm, 5-11pm Mon-Fri. **Credit** AmEx, DC, MC, V.
The days when this good-looking bar-restaurant on the fringes of the Square Mile was a banana wholesaling business are long gone and, although it's been here for coming up to 20 years, there's maybe more of the new Shoreditch about it than the old. On a midweek evening, we found a healthy crowd of mostly twentysomethings sipping on bottled beers and glasses of wine chosen from an impressive list of over 50. The emphasis is on the French vineyards and more affluent drinkers can splash out on some classic vintages. The atmosphere is relaxed, and although there was no music, satellite TV comes into play when great sporting moments present themselves. There's a downstairs restaurant offering bistro food of the steak and veal escalope variety.
Babies and children admitted (restaurant). Function room (seats 60). Restaurant. Tables outdoors (pavement). TV. **Map 5/R5**

Corney & Barrow

19 Broadgate Circle, EC2 (7628 1251/www.corney-barrow.co.uk). Liverpool Street tube/rail. **Open** 7.30am-11pm Mon-Fri. **Food served** 7.30-11.30am; noon-10pm Mon-Fri. **Credit** AmEx, DC, MC, V.
If you think of Broadgate Circle as a clock face laid flat, then this glamorous megabar occupies one through 11. Choose from the slick glass-fronted interior or the large outside terraces at either end and enjoy a bird's-eye view of the seasonally changing entertainment in the circle below, which transforms from an ice rink in winter to a stage for concerts and events in the summer. Expect the usual **Corney & Barrow** bar offerings (*see p14*) including a fabulous world-encompassing selection of easy drinking wines, laid out by grape variety with succinct tasting notes for extra help. As a bonus, the choice by the glass more or less runs to the length of the list. Food is modern brasserie style and each dish has its own wine recommendation.
Disabled toilet. Tables outdoors (terrace). TV. **Map 5/Q5**

Dirty Dick's

202 Bishopsgate, EC2 (7283 5888). Liverpool Street tube/rail. **Open** 11am-10.30pm Mon-Fri; 11am-3pm Sun. **Food served** noon-2.30pm Mon-Fri; 11.30am-2.30pm Sun. **Credit** AmEx, MC, V.
Although the basement bar, with its cobwebs and petrified animal remains, has long been cleaned up by order of environmental health officers, traces of the original idea remain. 'Dirty Dick' was a wealthy ironmonger called Nathaniel Bentley, whose wife died on the night before their wedding day. A precursor of and maybe the inspiration for Dickens' Miss Haversham, he locked up his house – complete with wedding breakfast – and retreated into a life of filth and squalor. When he died in 1809, a budding Bransonesque entrepreneur of the day bought up all his possessions and displayed them in his house, recently converted to a tavern. The building was rebuilt in 1870 and all that remain of the old house are the cellars. Young's of Wandsworth now have the place and have made sure that every level is used to the full, from the downstairs wine bar to the ground-floor bar and first-floor dining room. Expect bare bricks, bare wood floor and plenty of olde worlde charm, with synthetic cobwebs restricted to the basement.
Bar for hire. Games (fruit machines). No-smoking area. Restaurant. TV. **Map 6/R5**

Fleetwood Bar

36 Wilson Street, EC2 (7247 2242). Liverpool Street or Moorgate tube/rail. **Open** 11am-11pm Mon-Fri. **Food served** 11.30am-9pm Mon-Fri. **Credit** AmEx, DC, MC, V.
It has the most unappealing of locations, on a corner of the ghastly Broadgate Centre, but there's something about this stylish Fuller's-operated bar that makes it so much more user-friendly to the less thrusting drinker than the same brewery's **One of Two** (*see p132*). Maybe it's the staff who always seem to radiate friendliness, maybe it's the customers who appear to come from the more mellow end of the area's young office workers; or perhaps it's just the clean lines and uncluttered decor of the two-level modern bar. Peering in through

City

smoked-glass picture windows at the orange-sand coloured walls, light wood floor and IKEA furniture, you could be forgiven for thinking it is the rest area of an advertising agency or design company. Peering out through those same windows, the world beyond looks rather mean and distinctly drabber. After finishing our two pints of excellent ESB, we discovered this was indeed the case.
Games (fruit machines, quiz machine). Tables outdoors (pavement). TV. **Map 5/Q5**

City

The George

Great Eastern Hotel, 40 Liverpool Street, EC2 (7618 7400). Liverpool Street tube/rail. **Open** 11am-11pm Mon-Fri; noon-11pm Sat; noon-10.30pm Sun. **Food served** 11am-4pm, 5-10.30pm Mon-Sat; noon-4pm, 5-10pm Sun. **Credit** AmEx, DC, MC, V.
Oh Sir Terence! Despite making it appear that there are real ales on offer, even down to a blackboard boasting 'guest ales' and prominent use of cask-beer names such as Marston's Pedigree and London Pride, all four bitters here are dispensed through gas pressure and therefore about as real as unicorn shit. Odd for a bar that claims to offer 'the best of British food and drink'. But even if he can't be bothered with quality beer, this oak-panelled adjunct of the £70 million Great Eastern Hotel is a gorgeous space in which to watch City slickers get out of their skulls, with its tall baronial ceiling, big windows and refectory-style benches and high tables. Food – which, after all, is what Conran does best – is served in an attached smaller marigold and beige dining room and offers variations on traditional British fare at top-end bar prices. The somewhat clubby atmosphere is reinforced by a no-signpost rule, making trips to the toilets more of an adventure that is perhaps necessary.
Babies and children admitted (high chairs). Disabled: toilet. Function room. Restaurant. **Map 6/R6**

Golden Heart

110 Commercial Street, E1 (7247 2158). Liverpool Street tube/rail. **Open** 11am-11pm Mon-Sat; 11am-10.30pm Sun. **No credit cards.**
This small corner Victorian pub received serious coverage when its landlady, Sandra Esquilant, took 80th place in a recent list of the 100 most powerful figures on the contemporary art scene. The inclusion was partly ironic and partly because several influential artists – including the dreaded Tracey – drink here. Once a haunt of Shoreditch Market workers (opposite), these days the clientele is more likely to be young, studiedly-scruffy and carrying a portfolio of supermarket bean logos. They'll also be a smoker – take a herring in here for a drink and it'll leave a kipper. Don't expect fancy service or any major amenities – we arrived at peak hours to find a two-deep queue at the bar, ashtrays overflowing, and one server trying to cope. Still it was fun, the beer (a couple of Adnams ales are available) was good and the atmosphere crackling. Decor-wise, it's a good-looking, two-bar boozer with stripy wallpaper, original dark-wood panelling and a mishmash of furniture. One side has been transformed into the 'Shoreditch Wine Bar' with twinkly lights and lager the vintage of choice; the other, a tarted-up version of how the pub has looked for 100 years. Ghoulish tourists might be interested in the vague Jack The Ripper connection.
Babies and children admitted. Function room (wine bar). Tables outdoors. TV (satellite).

Hamilton Hall

Unit 32, Liverpool Street Station, EC2 (7247 3579). Liverpool Street tube/rail. **Open** 10am-11pm Mon-Sat; noon-10.30pm Sun. **Food served** 10am-10.30pm Mon-Sat; noon-9.30pm Sun. **Credit** AmEx, MC, V.
Whatever you think of the ubiquitous **JD Wetherspoon** (*see p15*) chain, it certainly does things on a grand scale. This used to be the ballroom of the Great Eastern Hotel – still adjacent and now under Conran control – and it's been restored to a publican's idea of the glory it might have enjoyed a century or more ago. Pale blue and lemon paintwork comes decorated with gilt and opulent chandeliers, with a mezzanine offering a seated no-smoking area. To say that this place gets busy is an understatement, and the high ceiling means that the reverberating racket of conversation completely drowns out the roar of the trains from Liverpool Street station below. You know what to expect by now: around six real ales, including the usual suspects plus (hopefully) one East Anglian guest; and bargain food that's tasty, edible and plentiful.
Disabled: toilet. Games (fruit machine, quiz machine). No piped music or jukebox. No-smoking area. Tables outdoors (pavement). **Map 6/R5**

Jamies at the Pavilion

Finsbury Circus Gardens, EC2 (7628 8224). Liverpool Street or Moorgate tube/rail. **Open** 11.30am-11pm Mon-Fri. **Food served** noon-3pm, 6-9pm Mon-Fri. **Credit** AmEx, MC, V.
This branch of the **Jamies** chain (*see p15*) must surely win the prize for the most original wine bar location in London – cohabiting with the City of London Bowling Club in a slick clubhouse conversion, amid the slightly surreal green oasis of Finsbury Circus Gardens. It's a particularly good place to head for in the summer, and a few laps of the bowling green works wonders to sober you up before hitting the tube for the long ride home. Lunchtimes and early evenings, the place heaves with a youngish crowd of stressed-out City suits unwinding on champagne, vino and copious bottles of beer, and it provides a lively and unintimidating environment in which to enjoy a few experimental forays into the world of wine. The manageable list offers a broad global selection accompanied by helpful tasting notes, and almost every wine is also sold by the glass.
Babies and children admitted (restaurant). No piped music or jukebox. Restaurant (available for hire). **Map 6/Q5**

One of Two

45 Old Broad Street, EC2 (7588 4845). Liverpool Street tube/rail. **Open** 11am-11pm Mon-Wed; 11am-1am Thur, Fri. **Food served** 11.30am-10pm Mon-Wed; 11.30am-midnight Thur, Fri. **Credit** AmEx, DC, MC, V.
London's two regional breweries have both dabbled with modern bars, but Fuller's seems far more committed to keeping abreast of the drinking times. Situated on a busy corner with London Wall, this is a thoroughly modern first-floor bar, reached via stone stairs and a mini conservatory. Larger than you'd expect, the space is subtly lit and usually pulsating with rapid bpms. In a reversal of the traditional, lager taps loom large over the long bar, overshadowing tiny handpumps for London Pride and a seasonal bitter. The youngish office types who pack the place seem split between spirits, lager and bitters. Out on the terrace you'll probably find couples sharing wine or sucking longer drinks through straws. There's also an attached restaurant space.
Function rooms. No-smoking tables. Restaurant. Tables outdoors (terrace). **Map 6/Q6**

Public Life

82A Commercial Street, E1 (7375 2425). Aldgate East tube. **Open/food served** noon-midnight Tue-Fri. **Credit** MC, V.
Here's an idea: a subterranean 'events-led artists' bar' (in the words of one of the artists who run it) in a former public toilet beside Nicholas Hawksmoor's grand and spooky Christ

Church. The lavatory itself is of a more recent vintage: Victorian, tiny and oval-shaped. We adore the original black and white tiles, although it's hard not to imagine cubicles where the serving area now squats. These days, Public Life is not so much a bar as a place in which to experience loud DJ-driven music while gulping down bottled beer and Breezer-type things. It only opens at weekends or when there's a special event on and that will only happen if anyone can 'get it together'. These people are artists, after all. Don't come down looking for a three-course meal, as food is more snacky than substantial. Jokes about 'piss artists' are unhelpful and very juvenile.
Music (DJs 8pm most nights; £2-£3 Fri, Sat).

St Paul's Tavern

56 Chiswell Street, EC1 (7606 3828). Moorgate tube/rail. **Open** noon-11pm Mon-Fri. **Food served** noon-8pm Mon-Thur; noon-6pm Fri. **Credit** AmEx, MC, V.
One of the few corporate boozers in the area to offer dignified drinking without the hard-sell and 'two-for-the-price-of-one' Breezer and Carling posters. This used to be the house pub for the Whitbread Brewery, which stood next door from 1750 until a couple of years ago, when Sam's descendants decided that the future was pizzas and burgers. The building's still there, but now it's been converted to offices and function suites. At the St Paul's, around six real ales are usually available; we found Abbot, Boddingtons, Old Hooky (that's better!), London Pride, Brakspear Bitter and Caledonian Deuchars. The ongoing popularity of the pub is self-evident and extra rooms have been added to make one long, thin brick and bare wood boozer. Staff are friendly, the atmosphere is good-natured and you tend to get a better class of pissed-up office worker than in the All Bar One up the road.
Games (fruit machines). No-smoking tables (lunchtime only). **Map 5/Q5**

Twentyfour/Vertigo 42

Level 24, Tower 42, 25 Old Broad Street, EC2 (7877 2424). Bank tube/DLR/Liverpool Street tube/rail. **Open** 11.45am-11pm Mon-Fri. **Food served** 6-9pm Mon-Fri. **Credit** AmEx, DC, MC, V.
The former NatWest Tower may no longer be the tallest building in London, but it can boast the bar with the most altitude. Due to security arrangements you've got to book first (avoiding names such as Saddam and Bin Laden). The 24th floor houses a bar of the same name, usually filled with suits lounging in grey armchairs, chomping on cigars and downing cocktails. And the men are even worse. From here, the view of St Paul's and Tower Bridge is great, but there's even better to be found 18 floors higher. Up on the 42nd floor, Vertigo is the apt name of the game, with comfortable electric blue furniture and spectacular views over most of metropolitan London and three counties beyond. Champagne and oysters are the preferred fare (well, that's what management would prefer you consumed – don't even think about requesting something as plebeian and cheap as a beer) and anybody dressed in anything that cost less than a hack's annual expenses will feel out of place. Every student in London should be made to come here: they'll either end up a confirmed socialist or work all the harder to achieve the thrusting, grasping life for themselves.
Disabled: toilet. Function rooms. Restaurant. **Map 6/Q6**

Also in the area...

All Bar One 18-20 Appold Street, EC2 (7377 9671); 127 Finsbury Pavement, EC2 (7448 9921); 106-7 Houndsditch, EC2 (7283 0047).
Balls Brothers 158 Bishopsgate, EC2 (7426 0567); 11 Blomfield Street, EC2 (7588 4643).
Bangers (Davy's) 2-12 Wilson Street, EC2 (7377 6326).
Bishop of Norwich/Bishop's Parlour (Davy's) 91-3 Moorgate, EC2 (7588 2581).
City Boot (Davy's) 7 Moorfields Highwalk, EC2 (7588 4766).
Corney & Barrow 19 Broadgate Circle, EC2 (7628 1251); 5 Exchange Square, Broadgate, EC2 (7628 4367); 114 Old Broad Street, EC2 (7638 9308); 1 Ropemaker Street, EC2 (7382 0606).
Davy's 2 Exchange Square, EC2 (7638 6341).
Jamies 155 Bishopsgate, EC2 (7256 7279).
O'Neill's 31-36 Houndsditch, EC3 (7397 9841); 64 London Wall, EC2 (7786 9231).
Orangery (Jamies) Cutlers Gardens, 10 Devonshire Square, EC2 (7623 1377).
Pitcher & Piano 200 Bishopsgate, EC2 (7929 5914).

Mansion House, Monument & Bank

A drinker's paradise – though there's still plenty of crap to wade through to find the gems – this central part of the Square Mile is stuffed with traditional old pubs of character (plus the rare stylish bar). Expect to be rubbing shoulders with eager young financiers and shrewd operators who wouldn't think twice about gypping a desperate *Big Issue* seller out of a quid. Typical behaviour involves drinking fast and furiously for a couple of hours, then wending off home. Places often close surprisingly early (8pm-ish) as takings begin to drop, and anyone hoping for a drink at the weekend will either have to cross the river for the fine pickings of Borough & Southwark or head back into the ever-buzzing West End.

Critics' choice
views

Barley Mow (p151)
For vistas of Limehouse and the Thames.

Phoenix (p180)
Capital views from north London's highest point (Ally Pally).

Tenth Bar (p49)
Lord it over west London from this swanky Kensington hotel bar.

Vertigo 42 (p133)
Killer cocktails and a bird's-eye panorama of the city from 42 floors up.

Windows (p67)
Mayfair from on high at the 28th floor of the Park Lane Hilton.

City

Bar Bourse

67 Queen Street, EC4 (7248 2200). Mansion House tube/Cannon Street tube/rail. **Open** 11.30am-11pm Mon-Fri. **Food served** 11.30am-3pm Mon-Fri. **Credit** AmEx, MC, V.

As basements go, this stylishly realised space, with its alternating light/dark wooden floor, oversized red and gold striped seats and giant tilted mirrors, is not so much dungeon as palace. We love the dinky blue and chrome stools arranged along the front of the elegant curved bar. Customers tend to be from the more affluent end of City life (so, not short of a bob), with the beautiful and the sharply dressed prevailing over the usual grey banking types. It can get pretty crowded here and the party atmosphere – fuelled by a soundtrack you'd expect to find when Jazz FM is in a good mood – although invariably genteel, can occasionally teeter into mild debauchery. Black and white publicity shots in the entrance hall upstairs attest to that. Champagne is the choice drink, with wine (two score of each to choose from), spirits and upmarket continental lagers rolling in behind. Food choices include steak sandwich, 'pizzetta' and chilli burgers; don't expect much change out of a tenner.

Babies and children admitted. Bar area available for hire. Disabled: toilet. Restaurant. TV. **Map 6/P7**

Bar Under the Clock

74 Queen Victoria Street (entrance on Bow Lane), EC4 (7489 9895). Mansion House tube. **Open** 11am-11pm Mon-Fri. **Food served** 11am-3pm, 5.30-9pm Mon-Fri. **Credit** AmEx, DC, MC, V.

There's something very bright and pleasing about this modern basement bar. Part of the **Balls Brothers** chain (*see p13*) – though you'd never have guessed it – you enter by means of a yellow painted staircase to find a brightly painted room with modern furniture and stone flagging. The serving area occupies most of one wall and is invariably awash with bright young City types, reclining on minimalist light wood and silver bar stools or standing, shooting the breeze. Belgian ales and other fine continental beers are on offer, as well as vodka and tequila shots, but most drinkers seem intent on sampling the wine. Choose from five types of champers/sparklers, and another ten each of red and white. Food offers a modern twist on typical wine bar fare, with the likes of teriyaki (veggie or ribeye), baked salmon steak and liver and bacon all well priced at under a tenner.

Bar area available for hire. **Map 6/P6**

Bell

29 Bush Lane, EC4 (7626 7560). Cannon Street tube/rail. **Open/food served** 11am-10pm Mon-Fri. **No credit cards.**

Anyone whose idea of heaven is the All Bar One drinking experience will detest this quiet little boozer. The rest of us quite enjoy the lack of jukebox and fruit machines and the fact that it looks like it's not been decorated since the Coronation. When the Thames was wider, this was a riverside inn that largely survived the Great Fire. The two small rooms come with timbered beams, tiled floors and tinted walls packed with framed prints and newspaper clippings, mostly relevant to the pub but some (the Quorn Hunt, for example) seemingly apropos of nothing. Otherwise, the main decor is brass, copper and pewter mugs, brasses and measures. Showing just how important a good cellarman is, the Courage Best and Directors are among the tastiest we've ever sampled. Food is limited to individually produced sandwiches and seating is restricted to a few settles and bar stools. Visit before the developers get their hands on it.

Map 6/P7

Bonds Bar & Restaurant

Threadneedle Hotel, 5 Threadneedle Street, EC4 (7657 8088). Monument tube/Bank tube/DLR. **Open** 11am-11pm daily. **Food served** 6-11pm daily. **Credit** AmEx, DC, MC, V.

If ever a hotel bar was well located, it's Bonds, centrally placed in the financial district, within easy staggering distance of the Bank of England and the Stock Exchange. Depending on your viewpoint, the name might conjure up images of the suave super spy and/or debentures and/or tea-drinking chimps, and this diversity comes over in the clientele. We were surprised to find almost as many smart polo necks as pinstripes, and an average age nearer 25 than 50. A cross between former banking hall opulence and up-to-date bar chic, the decor incorporates tall windows, hidden lighting and large beige lampshades overhanging the metal serving area. Drinkers tended to favour wines (especially champers), cocktails and long spirit drinks, with pale, golden lagers served in elegant tall schooners. Food is a definite feature, with a Modern European meets trad Brit menu offering – when we called by, at least – free champagne. Encouraging, but don't go expecting a bargain.

Disabled: toilet. Function room. **Map 6/Q6**

Bow Wine Vaults

10 Bow Churchyard, EC4 (7248 1121). Mansion House tube/Monument tube/Bank tube/DLR. **Open** 11am-11pm Mon-Fri. **Food served** noon-3pm Mon-Fri. **Credit** AmEx, DC, MC, V.

Not so much a vault as a wood-panelled ground-floor wine bar-restaurant with a U-shaped extruding serving area and modern art that might have come from South America, the Left Bank or Fenn Street Juniors. Head chef Giuseppe Stantomauro offers such delicacies as risotto, butterfly sardines and steak and kidney pie, served at white-clothed tables in the left-hand dining area. The wine list is French-dominated and contains a broad selection of styles and types, though most are only available by the bottle. We thoroughly enjoyed our Beaujolais Villages (£16.50), the classical music soundtrack and silent boxing on the small television screen. Unfortunately, the majority of our fellow diners/winos were the type of boorish middle-aged banking types we normally do our best to avoid, but maybe we were just very unlucky.

Function room. Restaurant. Specialities: European and New World wines. Tables outdoors (pavement). TV (satellite). **Map 6/P6**

Counting House

50 Cornhill, EC3 (7283 7123). Monument tube/Bank tube/DLR. **Open** 11am-11pm Mon-Fri. **Food served** noon-10pm Mon-Fri. **Credit** AmEx, DC, MC, V.

In the days when high street banks cared enough about their customers to offer displays of their wealth, this was the headquarters of the NatWest. When Fuller's converted it into a branch of its Ale & Pie chain, it won a City Heritage award – the first pub ever to receive one. It's big, the floors are bare board, the walls marble and studded with huge gilt-framed mirrors and portraits. A wrought-iron balcony runs around three edges and above the large island bar a spectacular domed skylight allows in summer sunshine and winter half-light. You'll find the complete range of Fuller's beers, bottled Budvar and draught Hoegaarden. The food's hearty if predictable, and the staff know their stuff. Customers are the usual financial types, augmented by blue-collar workers and commuters stopping off before laughing all the way to Bank.

Disabled: toilet. Function room. Games (fruit machine). No-smoking area (dining area). **Map 6/Q6**

Crosse Keys

9 Gracechurch Street, EC3 (7623 4824. Monument tube/Bank tube/DLR. **Open** 10am-11pm Mon-Fri; 10am-7pm Sat. **Food served** 10am-10pm Mon-Fri; 10am-6pm Sat. **Credit** AmEx, MC, V.

The Wetherspoon chain's answer to the **Counting House** (*see p134*), this is the former Hong Kong and Shanghai Bullion Bank, a Grade II-listed building. It's big, it's brash and it's pretty impressive, with massive green marble pillars and high, ornately draped picture windows that reach high up to the rococo ceiling. Nests of tall stools and clusters of conventional pub furniture provide support for the bums of corporate wheeler-dealers and their underlings who flock here, seemingly in their thousands. Just as traffic flow seems to expand to clog up wide new arteries, so Wetherspoon's have proved that if you build 'em big enough, enough drinkers will come to squeeze the walls. We've been here on a busy Friday evening when the place was absolutely packed; the noise level (even taking into account the chain's ban on music) was bordering on unbearable and the atmosphere was electric. The central island bar is topped off with four satin tents in a style Sir Richard Burton would have approved of, and dispenses a handful of the usual real ales as well as JDW's expected bargain-priced bottles.

Babies and children admitted (in family area until 9pm). Disabled: toilet. Function room. Games (fruit machines, quiz machines). No piped music or jukebox. No-smoking area. **Map 6/Q7**

Hatchet

28 Garlick Hill, EC4 (7236 0720). Mansion House tube. **Open** 11am-10pm Mon, Tue; 11am-11pm Wed-Fri. **Food served** noon-2.30pm Mon-Fri. **Credit** AmEx, DC, MC, V.

The combination of Suffolk's Greene King ales (Abbot and IPA) and traditional decor attracts a loyal band of lunchtime and after-work non-executive drinkers and you'll seldom find the Hatchet empty. There are two drinking areas on the ground floor: a tiny back room with comfortable banquettes and a moderately larger front bar where the ability to fight over a bar stool or stand are seemingly essential. An attractive leaded front window and a picaresque row of jugs form the main decorative points. It's a friendly, no-frills boozer, with no theme to speak of, that'll probably never win an award or be mentioned in any kind of dispatch. Still, the atmosphere is hard to beat and it remains one of our very favourite City pubs.

Function room. Games (fruit machine). Quiz (every other Wed 7.30pm). TV. **Map 6/P7**

Jamaica Wine House

12 St Michael's Alley, EC3 (7626 9496). Bank tube/DLR. **Open** 11am-11pm Mon-Fri. **Food served** noon-3pm Mon-Fri. **Credit** AmEx, DC, MC, V.

This misleadingly named old pub has certainly seen some history. Said to be the site of the first London coffee house and haunt of Jamaican slave and sugar plantation owners – which explains the moniker – it opened in 1652, was destroyed by the Great Fire and then finally reconstructed again in 1862 in the style of a grand Victorian public house. Around a year ago it went through another renovation. We think that maybe the new owners have spruced it up a little too much, taking away the black lino, tobacco-stained mahogany and Victorian character, replacing it with new wooden partitions, bench seating, concealed lighting and overloud club music. The former incarnation's lip-smackin' line up of real ales has been replaced by the less inspiring triumvirate of Courage Best, Adnams Broadside and Flowers IPA. Still, the place is usually busy, though a younger crowd has replaced the more traditional and media mix that used to frequent what was once the area's most atmospheric boozer. Still, tempus fugit, innit?

Babies and children admitted. Function room. Games (fruit machine). **Map 6/Q6**

Lamb Tavern

10-12 Leadenhall Market, EC3 (7626 2454). Monument tube/Bank tube/DLR. **Open** 11am-9pm Mon-Fri. **Food served** noon-2.30pm Mon-Fri. **Credit** AmEx, DC, MC, V.

Lamb Tavern

Built in 1880 and run by the same family for half a century, this four-storey-high boozer has been the pub of choice around Leadenhall Market for yonks. The tiled basement used to be a Victorian toilet and a spiral staircase leads up to the 'mezzanine' and a carpeted second-floor no-smoking area – the first in the City – where lunchtime food is served to those with sufficient puff. French breadsticks well filled with roast rib of beef, loin of lamb and suchlike are the cornerstone of the limited but popular menu. The exterior is, like all the other Market buildings, painted dark red, and the ground-floor bar has been stripped down to the Victorian bare boozing minimum. Check out the impressive Victorian tile painting by the side door and the ambrosial Young's beers. You'll not find them better kept anywhere. And that's a promise.
Function room. Games (darts, fruit machine). No-smoking room. **Map 6/Q6**

Leadenhall Wine Bar

27 Leadenhall Market, EC3 (7623 1818). Monument tube/Bank tube/DLR. **Open** 11.30am-11pm Mon-Fri. **Food served** 11.30am-10pm Mon-Fri. **Credit** AmEx, MC, V.
Olé! With decent tapas on the menu – £2.95-£4.75 a pop – and a distinctly Spanish feel, a new dimension has been added to what last year was just another traditional City wine bar. Ignore the tacky art and Iberian knick-knacks on the way upstairs, allow yourself to be propelled instead by the flamenco and Latin dance music that wafts out of not so hidden speakers beside the front door. In the first-floor bar-dining area, you'll probably be greeted by an over-cheery Spaniard with a ponytail; let him lead you to a red-clothed table to inspect the largely Spanish wine list and tapas menu. When we last popped along, 80% of the clientele were women, aged between 18 and 45 and seemingly loving every raucous second of their EC3 Spanish experience. Remember: every Wednesday is Paella Day.
Function room. Restaurant. **Map 6/Q7**

Ye Olde Watling

29 Watling Street, EC4 (7653 9971). Mansion House tube. **Open** 11am-11pm Mon-Fri. **Food served** 11am-3.30pm Mon-Fri. **Credit** AmEx, MC, V.
When Sir Christopher Wren was working on St Paul's Cathedral in 1668, he rebuilt this pub to use an an office. There's probably been some sort of tavern here since Roman times, when the thoroughfare linked to the old Roman road of Watling Street. But thanks to a huge makeover in 1901, it doesn't look that old, even after taking into account the distressed wood flooring and half-panelled walls constructed from timbers that reputedly came from sailing ships. Historians are grateful for this insight into how Victorians thought old inns should look. The upstairs restaurant knocks out fish and chips and steak and kidney pie to local office workers and the occasional tourist. Downstairs you've got the choice of a small games room at the rear or the virtually standing-only front bar. Real ales are a feature and will likely include London Pride, Adnams Bitter, Bass and – if you're lucky – Harvey's Sussex.
Babies and children admitted (restaurant). Function room. Games (darts, fruit machines, pool table). Restaurant. Tables outdoors (courtyard). **Map 6/P6**

1 Lombard Street

1 Lombard Street, EC3 (7929 6611). Monument tube/Bank tube/DLR. **Open** 7.30am-11pm Mon-Fri. **Food served** 7.30-11am, noon-3pm, 6-10pm Mon-Fri. **Credit** AmEx, DC, MC, V.
A haunt of upper crust financiers and their aspiring underlings – but despite that, still worth trying to front your way past the greeters at the door just to gaze at the domed skylight and inner sanctum below it. By day rows and rows of crisply linened tables are filled with power lunchers, but after work the place takes on more of the air of a bar. Drink prices aren't that much more than elsewhere in the area, and there's the plus of being looked after by some of the most on-the-ball serving staff in the entire Square Mile. Expect fellow customers to be wearing made-to-measure suits, designer dresses and boasting well-manicured nails. Food is 'European-style cuisine' and *is* very pricey, with starters such as salad of crab and lobster with tarragon and acidulated lobster veloute (whatever that is!) for almost £20 a head, and mains at least a tenner more.
Babies and children admitted (restaurant). Disabled: toilet. Function room. Restaurant. **Map 6/Q6**

Pacific Oriental

1 Bishopsgate, EC2 (7621 9988). Monument tube/Bank tube/DLR/Liverpool Street tube/rail. **Open** 11.30am-11pm Mon-Fri. **Food served** 11.45am-3pm, 6-9pm Mon-Fri. **Credit** AmEx, DC, MC, V.
Although the six copper microbrewing vessels are the focal point of this vast but stylishly realised blue and cream-painted basement space, the beer end of the operation seems little more than a gimmick. Pils and some form of bitter are usually available, with occasional guests thrown in from time to time, but when the ultra-helpful barman allowed us an unbidden taste, we were less than impressed, especially by the over-chilled bitter. Practically all the bright young City things we encountered were drinking wine (22 to choose from, including a rosé and four champers) and fancy cocktails. We were tempted by the Bombay Sling, repelled by the French Martini (vodka, Chambord and pineapple) and surprised to see that the only vaguely malt whisky available was Johnny Walker Black Label (not).
Babies and children admitted (restaurant). Disabled: toilet. Function room. Restaurant. TV (digital). **Map 6/Q6**

Prism

147 Leadenhall Street, EC3 (7256 3888). Monument tube/Bank tube/DLR. **Open** 11.30am-11pm Mon-Fri. **Food served** 11.30am-3pm, 6-10pm Mon-Fri. **Credit** AmEx, DC, MC, V.
Owners Harvey Nichols have transformed this former Bank of New York building into a slick modern lounge bar and restaurant. Although the marble hallway hints at grandeur, the light and airy, cream-dominated basement bar, with its wood parquet flooring and suede sofa-cubes, still comes as a surprise. Clever hidden lighting all but convinces you that there's a view available, but in reality drinkers have only themselves – usually an elegant mix of well-to-do local bankers and their paramours – to gaze upon. It doesn't take a genius to work out that these were once the bank vaults. Drinks of choice are cocktails and wine, chosen from a 200-strong list. The spacious upstairs restaurant continues the cream and white theme with high pillars, a modern backlit bar, neat rows of modern art and masses of white linen covered tables. Prices are pretty high but not outrageously so.
Babies and children admitted (restaurant). Disabled: toilet. Function room. Music (jazz weekly). Restaurant. **Map 6/Q6**

Swan Tavern

Ship Tavern Passage, 77-80 Gracechurch Street, EC3 (7283 7712). Monument tube/Bank tube/DLR. **Open** 11am-11pm Mon-Fri. **Food served** noon-3pm Mon-Fri. **Credit** AmEx, MC, V.
Fatties tend to avoid the Swan, as the tiny ground-floor bar is among London's thinnest. It's not much better upstairs in the red painted, rectangular and grandly named Swan Room,

which is about the size of your average council-flat kitchen. Downstairs, the ornately curved Edwardian serving area takes up most of the room, and when a row of tall stools in front of the bar is added into the equation, what's left is best suited to besuited businessmen who don't mind claustrophobia. Maybe serving time at a good school prepares one for such proximity to one's fellow man. Still, this is a good traditional-style pub, serving the full range of Fuller's beers and a choice selection of wines. Lunchtime food is basic but good and the lack of fruit machines (there's no room!) and no jukebox attracts the less hedonistic of local drinkers.
No piped music or jukebox. TV. **Map 6/Q7**

Williamson's Tavern

1 Groveland Court, off Bow Lane, EC4 (7248 5750). Mansion House tube. **Open** 11am-11pm Mon-Fri. **Food served** noon-3pm Mon-Fri. **Credit** AmEx, MC, V.
The site of the Lord Mayor's official house after the Great Fire, what we see now came from a major rebuild in 1932. Before that it had been Williamson's Hotel and long before that, the site of Sir John Fastolf's house, later immortalised by the dyslexic Will Shakespeare. Although the pub is an unimaginatively corporate-run boozer ('this week's guest ales are London Pride and Brakspear'), the atmosphere is lively and students of pub architecture will be overjoyed by what they find within. The wrought-iron gates at the entrance to the court were donated by William and Mary and the fireplace in the smaller front bar incorporates Roman tiles found during the rebuilding. Most drinkers, who tend to be office workers celebrating their post-work freedom, simply prefer the larger back room with its open kitchen, Sky Sports and minimalist furniture.
Function room. Games (fruit machine). TV (big screen, satellite). **Map 6/P6**

Also in the area...

All Bar One 103 Cannon Street, EC1 (7220 9031); 34 Threadneedle Street, EC2 (7614 9931).
Balls Brothers Budge Row, Cannon Street, EC4 (7248 7557); 3 Kings Arms Yard, EC2 (7796 3049); 52 Lime Street, EC3 (7283 0841); Minster Court, Mark Lane, EC3 (7623 2923); Mincing Lane, EC3 (7283 2838); 2 St Mary-at-Hill, EC3 (7626 0321).
Bangers Too (Davy's) 1 St Mary-at-Hill, EC3 (7283 4443).
City Flogger (Davy's) Fenn Court, 120 Fenchurch Street, EC3 (7623 3214).
City FOB (Davy's) Lower Thames Street, EC3 (7621 0619).
City Tup 66 Gresham Street, EC2 (7606 8176).
Corney & Barrow 2B Eastcheap, EC3 (7929 3220); 1 Leadenhall Place, EC3 (7621 9201); 12-14 Mason's Avenue, EC2 (7726 6030); 16 Royal Exchange, EC3 (7929 3131).
Fine Line 1 Bow Churchyard, EC4 (7248 3262); 1 Monument Street, EC3 (7623 5446).
Green Man (JD Wetherspoon) 1 Poultry, EC2 (7248 3529).
Heeltap & Bumper (Davy's) 2-6 Cannon Street, EC1 (7248 3371).
Jamies 5 Groveland Court, EC4 (7248 5551); 54 Gresham Street, EC2 (7606 1755); 107-112 Leadenhall Street, EC3 (7626 7226); 13 Philpot Lane, EC3 (7621 9577).
Liberty Bounds (JD Wetherspoon) 15 Trinity Square, EC3 (7481 0513).
Number 25 (Jamies) 25 Birchin Lane, EC3 (7623 2505).
O'Neill's 65 Cannon Street, EC4 (7653 9951).
Pitcher & Piano 67-9 Watling Street, EC4 (7248 0883); 28-31 Cornhill, EC3 (7929 3989).
Slug & Lettuce 25 Bucklersbury, EC4 (7329 6222); 100 Fenchurch Street, EC3 (7488 1890).

Tower Hill & Aldgate

Just starting to see the development its City neighbours to the north and west have become used to, the area between the river, Bishopsgate and Whitechapel is currently at the halfway point between the old East End and its new role as southern extremity of the financial district. Bangladeshi restaurateurs and slick corporate pub companies are falling over themselves for their share of the area's leisure cash, while to the south, the false community around St Katharine's Dock shows how far you can go in chasing the tourist dollar. A casualty since our last guide is Tsunami, a stylish stand-alone bar turned into (yet another) branch of the Davy's wine bar chain. A sign of the times?

Bar 38 Minories

St Clare House, 30-33 The Minories, EC3 (7702 0470). Aldgate or Tower Hill tube/Tower Gateway DLR. **Open** 11am-11pm Mon-Fri. **Food served** 11am-10pm Mon-Fri. **Happy hour** 5-7pm Mon-Sat. **Credit** AmEx, DC, MC, V.
This flagship branch of Scottish & Newcastle's style bar chain (*see p14*) has become a major attraction in the Minories. On the Friday night we happened along, the place was thoroughly jammed with wall-to-wall suit-, jean- and micro-clad junior execs and PAs. The glass-fronted exterior allows those on the outside to watch and envy revellers on two floors (not forgetting the mezzanine) enjoying themselves among the garish purple, blue and chrome decor. As if it were a showroom for a modern bar design and shopfitting service, every trick in the book is brought into play, from the backlit bar and corrugated walls to pinhole illuminated tables and space age furniture. Only the kicked-in glass at the bottom of one door suggested that this is not to everyone's taste. Uniformed waiting staff – seemingly chosen more for their looks than their efficiency – fetch keg and bottled beers, wines, shooters, cocktail pitchers and what-have-you. Food-wise expect the usual low-res, easy-to-prepare favourites: principally, variations on the theme of sandwich (ciabatta melts, burgers, pockets, etc).
Babies and children admitted (3-5pm). Disabled: lift, toilet. Venue available for hire (Sat only). **Map 6/R7**

Crutched Friar

39-41 Crutched Friars, EC3 (7264 0041). Tower Hill tube/Tower Gateway DLR. **Open** 11am-11pm Mon-Fri. **Food served** 11am-4pm (bar snacks), 4-8pm Mon-Fri. **Credit** AmEx, MC, V.
Imagine a City pub decorated by the people who make El Paso tacos? Well, this is it – almost. The three large rooms that make up the Crutched Friar may be painted in happy shades of yellow, green and aubergine-cream but thankfully the effect is not so much garish as summery and subsequently rather pleasant, which is easy to achieve in July, but no mean feat in February. When the sun does shine, the nifty rear patio comes into its own and the predominantly youngish office workers who flock here take up every centimetre of space. It can and does get noisy, but that's the way it is in EC3. Poets have long since learned to head for open countryside. The food continues the vaguely Mediterranean theme with lots of

pasta, fish and any excuse to chuck in an olive or sun-dried tomato. Our favourite room is to the left of the main entrance, a forest of fanciful icons and nifty metal lamps.
Disabled: toilet. No-smoking area (lunchtime). Tables outdoors (pavement, patio, garden). **Map 6/R7**

Dickens Inn

St Katharine's Way, E1 (7488 2208). Tower Hill tube/ Tower Gateway DLR. **Open** 11am-11pm Mon-Sat; noon-10.30pm Sun. **Food served** noon-4pm Mon-Fri; noon-6pm Sat, Sun. **Credit** AmEx, DC, MC, V.
This three-storey wooden boozer was originally built as a warehouse sometime around 1795 on some riverside site, but not here. In the late 1960s demolition contractors put the framework on wheels and rolled it along St Katharine's Dock to where it sits now, surrounded by expensive but characterless flats and in full view of some gorgeous yachts. The weatherboard exterior and semi-enclosed wooden balconies strewn with hanging baskets and window boxes arrived in 1974. There are sunken outside drinking areas to accommodate sunken outside drinkers, and the large ground-floor bar – with its wooden floor, lengths of rope and other kitsch maritime devices – caters for the rest of us. Beers include Adnams Broadside and 1744, but don't come cheap, even for the area. The top floor houses Grill on the Dock, a steak and fish restaurant (starters well over a fiver, mains three or four times that), while at Pizza on the Dock (first floor) cheese and stuff on dough will cost anything up to £36.90 (it's called a 'Beast' and is supposed to serve six).
Babies and children admitted (high chairs, nappy-changing facilities). Disabled: toilet. Function room. Games (fruit machine, quiz machine). No-smoking area (restaurant). Tables outdoors (garden). TV.

Market Bar & Restaurant

1-2 Crutched Friars, EC3 (7480 7550). Aldgate or Tower Hill tube/Tower Gateway DLR. **Open** 11am-11pm Mon-Fri. **Food served** 11am-3pm (bar snacks), 3-8pm Mon-Fri. **Credit** AmEx, MC, V.
The name comes from the stock market and not only do drink prices rise and fall depending on in-house demand – but don't get too excited, it's only a few pence either way – screens also keep drinkers informed of the real market prices. A gimmick? Almost certainly, but it's one that works because it isn't taken too seriously. Enter through a shared entrance hall, up some stairs and then down into the basement. Surfaces are a mixture of beige and red semi-panelled walls, with soft lighting, big leather sofas and screened Kiss TV to augment the market theme. There's also plenty of intimate corners and alcoves in which to negotiate important deals. Drinks are standard and on the night we last called in the most popular were Guinness, Hoegaarden, Stella, Stella, Stella and white wine. The restaurant space is tucked away behind a glass screen and boasts not only a Mediterranean menu but also a section of genuine Roman wall.
Babies and children admitted. Disabled: lift, toilet. TV (satellite). **Map 6/R7**

Old Dispensary

19A Leman Street, E1 (7702 1406). Aldgate East tube. **Open** 11am-11pm Mon-Fri. **Food served** 11am-3pm Mon; 11am-3pm, 5.30-9pm Tue-Fri. **Credit** AmEx, DC, MC, V.
We've always found this vast, high-ceilinged Victorian conversion to be one of the better watering holes on this side of London. Staff are welcoming, the food is decent – ranging from deep-fried camembert and pasta to stone-baked pizzas – and the drinks list is comprehensive. Half-a-dozen wines come by the glass, more by the bottle and the cask-conditioned beers include Adnams Bitter and Broadside plus guests for under £2 a pint. The place used to be a charitable dispensary for the poor children of the area; it's since been painted cream, a wooden balcony added as well as a couple of smaller rooms for those more intimate moments. The happy mix of customers includes a good proportion of office types blending in with blue-collar workers and locals.
Babies and children admitted. Function room (seats 40). Games (golf machine). No-smoking area. TV (digital).

Poet

82 Middlesex Street, E1 (7422 0000). Liverpool Street tube/rail. **Open** 11am-11pm Mon-Fri. **Food served** noon-3pm, 5-9pm Mon-Fri. **Credit** AmEx, DC, MC, V.
Petticoat Lane's not the obvious location for a classy pub like this; with its glass, brick and steel exterior, it's pretty hard to miss. And that's the end of the rhyming. This is a lively ground-floor pub painted beige and deep red, subtly lit and decorated with silhouettes of city skylines, with a gentle backing of sub-club beats. Being just off the edge of the financial district, clientele tend to be a mix of young City whizz-kids and neighbourhood artists. The beer choice seems to have settled down to a choice of Adnams Bitter and Broadside, with the usual nitrokeg stuff for the packaged beer lover. Wine seems popular, with a small but decent list. The name is commemorated by a bust of Shakespeare and intellectuals are promised participation in 'the biggest pub quiz ever seen'.
Babies and children admitted (11am-5pm). Bar area available for hire. Disabled: toilet. Karaoke (once a month). TV (satellite). **Map 6/R6**

White Swan

21 Alie Street, E1 (7702 0448). Aldgate tube/Tower Gateway DLR. **Open** 11am-11pm Mon-Fri. **Food served** noon-3pm Mon-Fri. **Credit** AmEx, MC, V.
Seemingly a haunt of bankers, local geezers and other assorted Jack the Lads, the White Swan nevertheless feels like a neighbourhood local. Divided into two small bars – more for structural reasons than anything to do with class, we feel – with decor that's somewhere between traditional and modern in style. The paintwork is white, dark cream and red and there's a mixture of big armchairs and bar stools scattered around the bare wood floor. Being a Shepherd Neame pub, you'll find the full range of bitters (Master Brew and Spitfire being the perpetuals) plus Orangeboom lager. There's a function room upstairs that we've found in use every time we've been in, although we've yet to decide whether the occupants were sales people celebrating hitting targets or merely junior management out on the piss.
Function room (seats 25). Games (fruit machine). TV (satellite).

Also in the area...

All Bar One 16 Byward Street, EC3 (7553 0301).
Corney & Barrow 37A Jewry Street, EC3 (7680 8550).
Fine Line 124-7 The Minories, EC3 (7481 8195).
Grapeshots (Davy's) 2-3 Artillery Passage, E1 (7247 8215).
The Habit (Davy's) 65 Crutched Friars, EC3 (7481 1137).
Hogshead 1 America Square, EC3 (7702 2381).
Jamies 119 The Minories, EC3 (7709 9900).
Liberty Bounds (JD Wetherspoon) 15 Trinity Square, EC3 (7481 0513).
Pitcher & Piano 9 Crutched Friars, EC3 (7480 6818).
Slug & Lettuce 9 Stoney Lane, E1 (7626 4994).
Vineyard (Davy's) 1 St Katharine's Way, E1 (7480 6680).

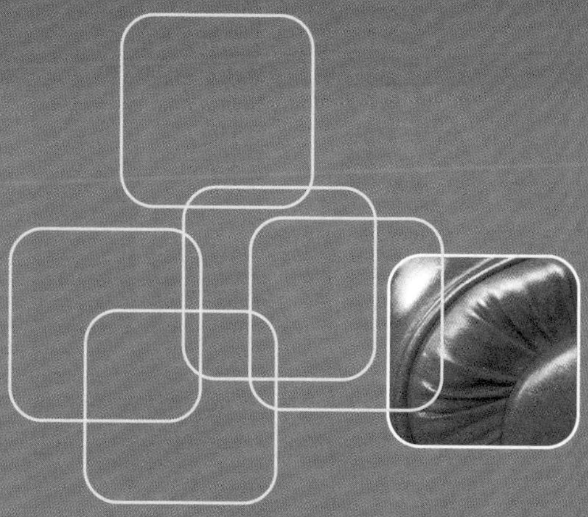

East

The Florist

Bethnal Green

Although gentrification is creeping over from the Hackney and Shoreditch boundaries, most drinking options here are unreconstructed old boozers, and pretty basic boozers at that. Step off the main thoroughfares and you'll likely find a locals-only, real ale-free zone where women are treated like objects from Mars (or the *Sun*). But there are exceptions that prove the rule. Columbia Road's **Royal Oak** prospers as a gay pub and the **Pleasure Unit** and newly arrived **The Florist** cater successfully to the young and hip. And when a boozer in Approach Road is lauded in the mainstream press (twice in one week!) as the new 'in' celebrity hangout, you know the times they are a-changing...

Approach Tavern

47 Approach Road, E2 (8980 2321). Bethnal Green tube/rail. **Open** noon-11pm Mon-Sat; noon-10.30pm Sun. **Food served** noon-2.30pm, 6-9.30pm Mon-Fri; noon-3.30pm, 6-9.30pm Sat; noon-4pm Sun. **Credit** MC, V.

We were amazed to find – on a Monday night at that – Catherine Zeta Jones and Michael Douglas in one corner of this gently restored Victorian pub, quietly sipping Ridleys IPA and Prospect respectively. Beside the open kitchen (variations on the theme of the gastropub staples), Nigella and Charles were caning the chardonnay and talking profiteroles; while over at the bar, Michael Caine was railing against the British tax laws. Well, maybe not, but if you believe what you read in the press then this place is an absolute celeb-fest, with staff beating back the A-list with sticks. Now part of the small but worthy Remarkable Restaurants chain, there's been the inevitable loss of service that occurs when manager replaces landlord, but overall things are tickety-boo. Good food, decent beer (real ales from Chelmsford's Ridleys brewery), heated outside terrace and even a small upstairs art gallery.

Art gallery (noon-6pm Thur-Sun). Babies and children admitted. Jukebox. Quiz (8.30pm Tue; £1). Tables outdoors (pavement, yard). TV (satellite).

The Florist

255 Globe Road, E2 (8981 1100). Bethnal Green tube/rail/8 bus. **Open/food served** 4-11pm Mon-Fri; 3-11pm Sat; 1-10.30pm Sun. **No credit cards**.

Just off the north side of Roman Road, the Florist is an old East End corner boozer barely converted into a bar aimed squarely at E2's trendies. It's been given a minimum specs makeover: dark varnishing on the bare wooden flooring, a deep maroon paint job and velvet drapes instead of doors on the toilets. Little candles in saucers, one big leather sofa and three tables with chairs constitute clear-out sale furnishings. (Money obviously was an object.) Which is not to denigrate anybody's efforts – it's a nice laid-back space. Shame about the drinks range, then, which runs to just three beers on tap (a lager, Guinness and London Pride). Then again, the kind of punters that the Florist is hoping to attract are likely to favour their booze in chuggable bottles, and there's plenty of that along with slammers, shorts and wines by the glass. Food comes in the form of Spanish tapas.

Games (backgammon, chess). Music (DJs Wed-Sun). Tables outdoors (summer).

Pleasure Unit

359 Bethnal Green Road, E2 (7729 0167). Bethnal Green tube/rail/8 bus. **Open** 5-11pm Mon-Thur; 5pm-2am Fri; 4pm-2am Sat; 3-10.30pm Sun. **Food served** Fri, Sat evening (bar snacks). **Credit** MC, V.

'Bar, lounge, art' says the sign outside, which sums up the way this enterprising DJ bar sees itself. While most of its neighbours – with the exception of the nearby Camdens Head, JD Wetherspoon boozer – growl at strangers, the Pleasure Unit greets them with open arms and till. Despite the blocked-up windows, it's a friendly, would-be hip joint with decor not much changed from when it was the Cock & Comfort gay hangout (hence the wooden windows). On Bethnal Green Road? Yep, these premises seem destined for a trailblazing role. Furniture is the kind you'd find in a posh church hall (mismatched stacking chairs, utilitarian tables, battered sofas) and the paintwork is pastel with the merest hint of glitter. With a late licence, regular live bands and a roster of DJs (including the long-running, Led Zep-worshipping monthly Heavy Load '70s rock night), and free admission (at the time of writing, at least), it looks as if the new name is every bit as appropriate as the old.

Art gallery. Music (8pm Thur-Sun; occasional charge Fri, Sat). TV (satellite).

Royal Oak

73 Columbia Road, E2 (7739 8204). Bethnal Green tube/ Old Street tube/rail/26, 48, 55 bus. **Open** 1pm-11pm Mon-Sat; 8am-10.30pm Sun. **Food served** 8am-2pm Sun. **No credit cards**.

You may recognise the Oak from its frequent media appearances. Starring roles in *Goodnight Sweetheart*, the scene of Victor Meldrew's last drink and even a *Blue Peter* Christmas decoration project have made this well-preserved 1940s-looking, single-bar boozer a face to remember. During the week it's a gentle mixed gay pub, attracting a good proportion of local artisans, who sit around the bar drinking lager and other more colourful concoctions, talking iMacs, eye-scans and the big 'I am'. It almost goes without saying that there's no real ale. On Sunday market mornings the mood changes dramatically. At 8am a post-club crowd of booted, shaven-headed clones stomps in, intent on continuing the party. Add a smattering of sightseers, market traders and general flower lovers as the morning wears on, and the mixture is akin to adding saltpetre to charcoal and sulphur. It's an East End institution.

Babies and children admitted (until 6pm). Function room. Games (fruit machine, pool table). Jukebox. Quiz (9.30pm Thur; £1). Tables outdoors (pavement; yard). TV (big screen, satellite).

Sebright Arms

34 Coate Street, E2 (7729 0937). Bethnal Green tube/ rail/Cambridge Heath rail. **Open** 11.30am-11pm Mon, Tue; 11.30am-midnight Wed-Sat; noon-10.30pm Sun. **Food served** noon-4pm Sun only. **Happy hour** 1-7pm Mon-Fri. **No credit cards**.

Real ales may have been inexplicably plucked from the equation since our last visit, but this esoteric gay-friendly boozer off Hackney Road has retained its enterprising entertainment policy. The traditional pub decor is as dreamt by Laurence Llewelyn-Bowen after one opium pipe too many, and although the long thin serving area takes up the whole of one wall, the focus of attention is the glittery backed, red velour-framed corner stage. Look out for a mixture of bands, drag and karaoke. On Thursdays, 'Docklands Famous Music Hall Continues': a weekly event that carries on from where the late and lamented Dockyard Doris left off. Expect a mixture of old-fashioned music hall and camp comedy designed to appeal to the fashion-conscious, largely gay crowd who don't shy away from audience participation. The Sebright is also renowned for its mammoth Sunday lunches (for which booking is advisable), with a seated courtyard that's one of the choicest alfresco drinking spots this side of the gasworks.

Babies and children admitted (restaurant). Function room. Games (darts, fruit machine, pool table). Music (music hall 9pm Thur; entertainment 9pm Fri; jazz 9pm Sat). Quiz (9pm occasional Tue). Restaurant. Tables outdoors (courtyard).

Also in the area...

Camdens Head (JD Wetherspoon) 456 Bethnal Green Road, E2 (7613 4263).

Bow & Mile End

Respectively named after the bow-shaped bridge built by Henry I and because of the distance from the City boundary (d'oh!), in the 19th century this was an area of semi-industry intermingled with back-to-back workers' housing. Now it's an up-and-coming slice of the East End dominated by Queen Mary College, with Mile End and Bow Roads peppered with noisy bars and pubs designed to appeal to students. The arrival of the **Crown**, a branch of the small and organic singhboulton chain – a skip away from Bow Dock – was a brave move that seems to have paid off.

Bow Bells

116 Bow Road, E3 (8981 7317). Bow Road tube. **Open** 11am-11pm Mon-Sat; noon-10.30pm Sun. **Food served** 11.30am-2.45pm Mon-Fri. **No credit cards.**

Although the Bow Bells of legend are actually a good few miles away at St Mary-Le-Bow, Cheapside, you can't let a minor detail stand in the way of a good name. This is a modernised Victorian pub near enough to Bow Church DLR to make it a handy waiting room. It's the type of east London boozer that attracts all types of locals, plus students and beer drinkers gasping for London Pride, Adnams or the guest ale in an area otherwise bereft of cask-conditioned goodness. The single ground-floor bar forms an L-shape around the central serving bit, with a small stage area to one end. Friday night is parteeee night, with karaoke or – if God is smiling – a diminutive Elvis impersonator of Indian or Bangladeshi origin. Top stuff, and very popular with the Bow belles. It was someone's birthday and we encountered a group of 12 women who could have been the same woman in different stages of life. It turned out to be three generations of the same family, plus sisters, nieces, etc. Oddly enough, they all smoked the same brand of cut-price cigs and nearly all wore glasses. Buzzing around were a load of 30-plus guys discreetly wearing Elvis belt-buckles. It's wild out east.

Babies and children admitted (until 7pm). Function room. Games (darts, fruit machines, pool table). Jukebox. Karaoke. Music (DJs 8.30pm Fri, Sat). Quiz (8.30pm Wed). Tables outdoors (pavement). TV (big screen, satellite).

Coborn Arms

8 Coborn Road, E3 (8980 3793). Bow Road or Mile End tube. **Open** 11am-11pm Mon-Sat; noon-10.30pm Sun. **Food served** noon-2pm, 6.30-9.30pm Mon-Fri; 1-9pm Sat, Sun. **Credit** MC, V.

It was someone's birthday and the champagne was flowing like Cava the Friday night we last called here, though celebrations were kept politely low-key so as not to disturb other drinkers. This large Young's boozer centres around a comfortably decorated main room that's a cut above most of Bow's other boozers. The paintwork's cream, the upholstery's green and gold, and it's all heaped on top of a red patterned carpet: an agreeable combination, even if it doesn't sound like it. If there's a fault, it's the over-chintzy lampshades, but we're growing to like even those. The Coborn is a great place to come to play darts, with two boards in a pair of small and separate side rooms. Drinkers are a mix of local couples, academics and students from the college and groups of geezers out for a quiet pint. Young's 'ordinary' and Special are dispensed by pleasant staff and food (fish and chips, steak and kidney pie, etc) is simple but good and – a must for genuine darts players – agreeably plentiful.

Disabled: toilet. Games (darts, fruit machine, golf machine). Tables outdoors (patio). TV (big screen, satellite).

Crown

223 Grove Road, E3 (8981 9998). Mile End tube, then 277 bus. **Open** 5-10.30pm Mon; noon-11pm Tue-Fri; 10.30am-11pm Sat; 10.30am-10.30pm Sun. **Food served** 6.30-10pm Mon; noon-3pm, 6.30-10.30pm Tue-Fri; 10.30am-4pm, 6.30-10.30pm Sat; 10.30am-4pm, 6.30-10pm Sun. **Credit** AmEx, DC, MC, V.

The only place to get organic booze and grub in E3 – and we do mean the only place – this good-looking eastern outpost of the small but significant singhboulton chain (**Duke of Cambridge**, *see p172*) is an oasis in a sea of pub mediocrity. Although Bow Lock is less than a dribble away, the principal views from the light and airy ground-floor bar are of a mini-roundabout and the visage of Victoria Park's Crown Gate. You get a much better view of the greenery from the two upstairs no-smoking rooms, which can be reserved for dining. Everything on the menu is organic and, wherever possible, fair trade. This means that prices tend to be at the higher end of the gastropub range, though the old adage 'you get what you pay for' is never more applicable. Expect rustic European-style home-cooking that will probably include a risotto, a tart and something pan fried. Drink-wise the beers (all of which come from the rather fine Pitfield Brewery) are entirely organic and will probably include Eco Warrior, own-label singhboulton bitter and Shoreditch Stout. But expect to pay up to £3 a pint. Wines are better value and even come marked as vegan and vegetarian, as applicable. Watch out for some of the ever-so-low-slung sofas – in some cases it's like sitting in a marsh.

Babies and children admitted. Disabled: toilet. Function rooms. No-smoking area (restaurant). Restaurant. Tables outdoors (pavement, courtyard.)

New Globe

359 Mile End Road, E3 (no phone). Mile End tube. **Open** noon-midnight Mon-Wed; noon-2am Thur-Sat; noon-10.30pm Sun. **Food served** noon-3pm Mon-Fri. **Admission** £2 after 11pm Thur-Sat. **Credit** MC, V.

Not to be confused with the Old Globe, and especially not Ye Olde Globe, this is a pub desperate to be a bar and attract lots of lovely young students. However, on our visit the ground-floor booths were filled with mean-looking types sporting rugged tattoos – and the men weren't much better. Plenty of promotions, late opening at weekends and loud clubby music. Photocopied A4 posters advertise regular drink promotions: wannabe rockers' tipple Jack Daniels was going cheap on our visit and windows were plastered with notices offering bottles of a lager we'd not heard of for just £1.50. Not exactly looking as if the management leads from the front, we noted a lack of real ale but a notice asking for suggestions for the future. Pool is played on two tables upstairs, while outside tables of the baize-less kind offer romantic interludes beside the picturesque Grand Union Canal (with an equally grand view of the Canary Wharf tower twinkling by night).

Disabled: toilet. Games (fruit machine, pool table, quiz machine). Jukebox. Music (DJs Thur-Sat). Tables outdoors (canalside).

Also in the area...

Match Maker (JD Wetherspoon) 580-586 Roman Road, E3 (8709 9760).

Clapton

Pub and bar-wise, there's not much to shout about in E5, aside from these two boozers, both perched on the towpath of the River Lea. Both are outposts of breweries from the other side of London (Fuller's and Young's) and both cater largely to a transient water-appreciating clientele. Most of the other drinking places we tried had the friendliness and charm of Wild West saloons.

Anchor & Hope

15 High Hill Ferry, E5 (8806 1730). Clapton rail. **Open** 11am-3pm, 5.30-11pm Mon-Fri; 11am-11pm Sat; noon-10.30pm Sun. **No credit cards.**

Unless you arrive by boat (or the riverside towpath) you'd never find this odd little boozer nestling between the banks of the Lea and the High Hill housing estate. The view's not brilliant – a water filtration plant and the electrified railway – but the swans gliding by add grace to what is essentially an urban waterway. The pub's not changed a lot since the Coronation, which is around the time the current landlord moved in. The flooring's red lino, and the two-tone paintwork is dotted with reminders of the recent past and of local events. If you think the 'main bar' is tiny, wait until you see the 'sports room': barely enough room to chuck a dart. Beers come from Fuller's and include well-kept London Pride and ESB, something the mixed-sex regulars who pack the pub most nights seem to appreciate. That and a good singalong.

Babies and children admitted. Games (dominoes, cribbage). TV.

Princess of Wales

146 Lea Bridge Road, E5 (8533 3463). Clapton rail/48, 55, 56 bus. **Open** 11am-11pm Mon-Sat; noon-10.30pm Sun. **Food served** noon-2.30pm, 6-8.30pm Mon-Sat; noon-3.15pm Sun. **Credit** MC, V.

It's an impressive, cottage-style riverside pub, even if the H_2O that brings boats to the riverside terrace is not the mighty Thames but the lithesome Lee. For 137 years the pub was happy as the Prince of Wales until, in 1997, Lady Diana Spencer was murdered by the security services (afraid she was going to reveal that the Queen Mum had been the second JFK gunman) and the name was changed. This gross sentimentality extended to screwing a framed copy of a poem 'A Nation Mourns Diana' on to the panelled saloon bar wall and to the English rose pub sign. But do not be deterred. The Wales's two bars offer contrasting aspects of the convivial Clapton riverside experience: the long, thin public bar is devoted to Young's bitters, darts and big-screen sport; while the saloon offers more genteel vibes, allowing you to sit and nosh while the swans drift by. In summer, the mini conservatory is perpetually busy, and if you want a weekend picnic table, arrive at dawn.

Games (darts). Tables outdoors. TV (satellite).

Docklands

Creating Docklands from scratch meant that developers got to choose most of the area's bars, restaurants and pubs. It also meant that a traditionally working-class area such as the Isle of Dogs was turned upside down in a generation. The south and east of the peninsula are least affected, with old-school boozers like the **Ferry House** and **Lord Nelson** still catering to descendants of dockers and their families. But around Canary Wharf the corporate operations rule the roost: this is the (un)natural home of the chain bar. As if to drive the point home, in the last year alone three independent places – Harry's Bar, the Gun and Tollesbury Barge, all formerly featured in this guide – have closed. Woe to the Docklands drinker.

Cat & Canary

1-24 Fisherman's Walk, Canary Wharf, E14 (7512 9187). Canary Wharf tube/DLR. **Open** 11am-11pm Mon-Sat. **Food served** 11am-11pm Mon-Fri; 11am-4pm Sat. **Credit** AmEx, MC, V.

Built in 1992 but looking (inside at least) like it has been around for a century or more, this large dockside Fuller's pub attracts a complete cross-section of local life. Taxi and delivery drivers and blue-collar workers slurp down pints of ESB, London Pride and lager, while media types and financial managers raid the wine list. Fuller's has done a good job here, installing woodwork that's said to have come from an Essex church and a phone kiosk modelled from the former pulpit. Dark-wood panelling and terracing give the impression of age, while bright paintwork (a cross between orange and parchment) stops the place looking dowdy. The drinkers slump in cosy armchairs, noshing good pub grub.

Disabled: toilet. Function room. Games (darts, fruit machines, quiz machine, golf machine). No-smoking area. Tables outdoors (terrace). TV (big screen, satellite).

City Pride

15 Westferry Road, E14 (7987 3516). Canary Wharf tube/DLR/South Quays DLR. **Open** noon-11pm Mon-Sat; noon-10.30pm Sun. **Food served** noon-9.30pm daily. **Happy hour** 6-9pm Mon-Fri. **Credit** AmEx, MC, V.

Don't be fooled by the obviously fake wooden beams, yo-ho barrels and exposed stonework, this is a genuinely old boozer, built just before World War I as a beer saloon for dockers. Now that dockers are a little thin on the ground – unless you include people who move dollars across computer screens – the emphasis has changed. City Pride is probably trying to appeal to the junior end of the local office worker market, and that's who were in the majority the last time we visited. There's a single real ale (Tetley), contemporary clatter that'd be considered too tame for Capital Radio and a food menu based around the concept of 'large plates' and 'small plates'. Odd combinations like chicken arrabiatta with mushrooms, Hungarian stroganoff and fish and chips (too traditional to mess with) are offered on various-sized crockery for between a fiver and a tenner.

Babies and children admitted (until 5pm Fri). Function room. Games (fruit machines, pool tables, quiz machines). Music (vocal 6pm Fri). Tables outdoors (garden).

Ferry House

26 Ferry Street, E14 (7537 9587). Island Gardens DLR. **Open** 2-11pm Mon-Fri; 11am-11pm Sat; noon-10.30pm Sun. **No credit cards.**

This traditional pub used to be the official residence of the ferry master who, until the foot tunnel arrived a century ago, presided over the only route to the south bank of the river. Although there's been a hostelry here since Henry VIII was a lad, the current building went up in 1823. With the area's residents now a dichotomy of loftlivers and blue-collar flat dwellers, it's the latter who largely frequent this unspoilt family boozer. It boasts an original metal fireplace that would

London drinking: real ale

What's so funny about beer with flavour?

In Britain, real ale has acquired a stigma. The image of the average drinker, carefully fostered by years of extra-smooth bitter and lager advertising, is of a bearded bore with a big belly. But let's not drag Anne Widdecombe into it.

Real ale is the name given to cask-conditioned beer, a living, breathing entity that's the beer drinker's equivalent of a decent farmhouse cheese. Most of the beers and practically every lager offered in the average bar are lifeless, processed product that's been pasteurised for a longer, trouble-free shelf-life. In other words, they are the Kraft cheese slices of beer. Cask-conditioned ale is naturally effervescent, whereas 'keg' beer requires bottled carbon dioxide or even nitrogen to inject that artificial sparkle.

Other northern European countries revere their beers, treating them with the same regard Mediterraneans afford to wine. Belgium, Holland and Germany are proud of their brewing traditions, whereas we seem embarrassed by ours. The snob factor plays a part and may explain why the previous generation, desperate to appear middle class, shied away from proper beer. But thanks to a new generation of bitter drinkers, real ale is coming back into favour, seen now again as a quality product that deserves attention.

London is both a good place and a bad place for decent beer. It's good in that we have two exemplary regional breweries – Young's and Fuller's – whose pubs sell cask-conditioned beer that's invariably in top condition, and because there's a huge choice of real ale pubs to choose from. Bad, because most pubs that sell real ale don't give a damn.

As a general rule, educated drinkers prefer to only drink real ale in pubs of the brewery that produced it. There's no doubt that a pint of London Pride tastes far more toothsome in a Fuller's pub than it does in a corporate West End boozer where the staff have maybe had an hour's tutelage between them in the art of keeping cask-conditioned beers.

The **Royal Oak** in Southwark serves the best Harveys bitter in London. There's the added advantage of having the entire range to choose from (including seasonal beers and mild) and an environment that doesn't include overloud Kylie, a pool table or fruit machine pollution. Similarly, Badger beers taste pretty good at the **Ship & Shovell** at Charing Cross and the peak place for St Peter's ales is the brewery's own **Jerusalem Tavern** in Farringdon.

There are exceptions to this brewery-beer rule. In south-east London, for example, the **Dog & Bell** and **Rutland Arms**, neither of which is a Fuller's house, both sell perfect Fuller's pints and offer a choice of ambrosial guest ales.

If it's choice you're after, then London has three destination pubs of distinction. The **White Horse** at Parsons Green offers up to half-a-dozen real ales and a huge selection of Belgian delicacies; Old Street's **Wenlock Arms** is the CAMRA supporter and jazz-lover's paradise; and Borough's **Market Porter** has a frequently changing range of eight bitters. *Jim Driver*

A real ale eight

Dog & Bell (*see p211*) 116 Prince Street, SE8 (8692 5664).
Jerusalem Tavern (*see p112*) 55 Britton Street, EC1 (7490 4281).
Market Porter (*see p199*) 9 Stoney Street, SE1 (7407 2495).
Royal Oak (*see p200*) 44 Tabard Street, SE1 (7357 7173).
Rutland Arms (*see p206*) 55 Perry Hill, SE6 (8291 9426).
Ship & Shovell (*see p97*) 1-3 Craven Passage, WC2 (7839 1311) .
Wenlock Arms (*see p121*) 26 Wenlock Road, N1 (7608 3406).
White Horse (*see p240*) 1-3 Parsons Green, SW6 (7736 2115).

The Lane. *See p156.*

warm an antique dealer's heart, wood-slatted walls and ceiling, and old-fashioned globe lights. The dartboard remains the original London Fives – none of this modern 1-20 stuff – and there's good Courage Best at well under £2 a pint. You'll find every age and type in here from 18 year olds – though their natural haunt would seem to be the nearby Nelson – to pensioners and all ages between. Staff can be abrupt.
Children admitted (over 14). Games (darts, fruit machine). Jukebox. Tables outdoors (pavement). TV (satellite).

Rogue Traders

25 Westferry Road, E14 (7987 3439). Canary Wharf tube/South Quay DLR/D3, D7 bus. **Open** 11am-11pm Mon-Sat; noon-10.30pm Sun. **Food served** noon-3pm, 5-10pm Mon-Fri; noon-10.30pm Sun. *English & Indian takeaway service.* **Credit** AmEx, DC, MC, V.
First it was a dockworkers' boozer called the Blacksmith's Arms, then it underwent a makeover and name change to become a sort of style bar, with an in-house Indian takeaway now added. Change indeed in E14. 'Enjoy a great selection of eclectic fusion dishes along with classic Indian dishes put together by our seasoned chef,' says the blurb (watch that salt and pepper) and now it's possible to nosh on pepper bahar, murgi masala or cheatal (fish) jalfrezi while supping Greene King IPA or an Indian lager. The decor is modern in style, with mauve and cream walls, a small serving area crowned with a dining area enlivened by orange paint. Service is friendly and customers are a cross-section of Docklanders from young locals to besuited salesmen out on the razzle.
Babies and children admitted. Games (fruit machine). Tables outdoors.

Spinnaker

19 Harbour Exchange Square, E14 (7538 9329). South Quay DLR. **Open** 11am-11pm Mon-Fri. **Food served** 11am-3pm Mon-Fri. **Credit** AmEx, DC, MC, V.
From the outside there's nothing very special about this large single-room Greene King pub, purpose-built as part of a modern dockside office and shop complex. The nautical window display hardly inspires and the entrance hall is more Woolworth's than modern pub. But once inside you can see the value of this large, bright and airy boozer. For a start, big picture windows and an enclosed balcony offer an unhindered view of the water, and the yellow and beige colour scheme keeps everything cheerful. Worth noting is a psychedelic carpet, reminiscent of Tony Hancock's work in *The Rebel.* A pleasantly curved serving area dispenses lager and bottled beer, plus a decent selection of wine and Abbot and IPA. Food is of the 'fun food now' snacky type and includes pasta, chilli and rice and popadoms with dips for a bargain £2.25.
Disabled: toilet. Games (fruit machine, golf machine, pool table, quiz machine). TV.

Via Fossa

West India Quay, Canary Wharf, E14 (7515 8549). West India Quay DLR. **Open** 11am-11pm Mon-Sat; noon-10.30pm Sun. **Food served** *Bar* 11am-10.30pm Mon-Sat; noon-10pm Sun. *Restaurant* noon-2pm, 6-9pm Tue-Fri; 6-9pm Sat, Sun. **Credit** AmEx, DC, MC, V.
The old stone warehouse of which Via Fossa occupies three floors was built by Napoleonic prisoners and remained in gainful employee up until the 1970s as a sugar warehouse.

Inside, the decor is 'baroque meets modern art' (imagine El Cid on GHB), with orange-ragged stone walls, masses of wrought ironwork and doors that look as if the mad brother's tucked away behind them. There's a maze of drinking dens, alcoves and eating areas in which you'll find a high proportion of the area's younger drinkers, competing to be heard over the commercial club music. Those intent on finding the restaurant can follow the complicated instructions provided by the main entrance. Food is typically grill- and microwave-friendly pub grub, tarted up to look posh: duck with jalapeno jelly, chicken satay, beef and Theakston pie. This place seems to have given up pretending that real ale is an option as the last couple of times we've visited, the pump's been empty.
Disabled: lift, toilet. Function room. Karaoke (3rd Wed of mth). No-smoking area (restaurant). Restaurant. Tables outdoors (pavement).

Also in the area...

All Bar One 42 Mackenzie Walk, South Colonnade, Canary Wharf, E14 (7513 0911).
Bar 38 16 Hertsmere Road, West India Quay, E14 (7515 8361).
Corney & Barrow 9 Cabot Square, Canary Wharf, E14 (7512 0397).
Davy's at Canary Wharf 31-5 Fisherman's Walk (7363 6633).
Fine Line 10 Cabot Square, 29-30 Fisherman's Walk, Canary Wharf, E14 (7513 0255).
Jamies Unit 1, 28 West Ferry Circus, Canary Wharf, E14 (7536 2861).
Ledger Building (JD Wetherspoon) 4 Hertsmere Road, West India Quay, E14 (7536 7770).
Slug & Lettuce 30 South Colonnade, Canary Wharf, E14 (7519 1612).

Hackney

If you can tell a neighbourhood's character from its drinking, which of course you can, then while Hackney is definitely improving, it's still got a long way to go. The smattering of DJ bar openings and pub redecorations of the last few years are still wildly outnumbered by rank, dank boozers straight from the old school, and not in a good way. Scattered throughout the borough, from Dalston's welcoming **Prince George** to the decidedly modish **District** a mile or more away, are some fine spots, but you'll need to look hard to find them. 'Up and coming', anyone?

Aqua Cafe Bar

270 Mare Street, E9 (8533 0111/www.ocean.org.uk). Hackney Central or Hackney Downs rail. **Open** 10am-11pm Mon-Thur; 10am-2am Fri, Sat; 6-10.30pm Sun. **Food served** noon-3pm, 6-10pm Mon-Sat; 6-10pm Sun. **Credit** MC, V.
The house bar of the Ocean music complex aims for a community feel and, we think, succeeds. A brasserie-style hangout during the day, it segues into a bar in the evening. How busy it is depends on who's playing the hall that night.

There's nothing too fancy about the place: decor is formula modern with vivid blue walls, cafe-style furniture and picture windows, which bring the Hackney streets into the bar (although after-dark bouncers keep out the grittier elements). The bar is canteen-like with the usual beers on draught supplemented by cocktails, plus tea and coffee. Food is serviceable if uninspiring, and it is at least served late. Regular DJs enliven the proceedings. One other plus: it's one of the few bars in E8 that draws a genuinely racially mixed crowd and a range of ages too.
Children admitted (until 6pm). Function rooms. Disabled: lift, toilet. Games (fruit machine, quiz machine). Music (DJs 7pm Wed-Sat; bands nightly in main venue; prices vary, call box office for info).

brb at the Alex

162 Victoria Park Road, E9 (8985 5404). Bethnal Green or Mile End tube/277 bus. **Open** noon-11pm Mon-Sat; noon-10.30pm Sun. **Food served** noon-10.30pm Mon-Sat; noon-10pm Sun. **Credit** MC, V.
The pub used to be called the Alexandra until it was taken over by the brb people. The name switch from Alexandra to Alex is quite fitting, as the place has taken on something of a masculine air. On our Sunday afternoon visit, the place was rammed with a post-club, post-football crowd (big matches play on the big screen) shouting over hardcore music. Not a place for a quiet pint and read of the papers then. But the pub itself is an attractive number, with a circular sweep of a bar counter, big bursting comfy sofas, leather beanbags and artworks on the walls. Food and drink conform to the usual brb formula of lager, lager, lager plus cheap shooters and cocktails, and pizzas, whose appeal is heightened by two-fer deals. A good venue if you're in a loud and lively mood, but a little wearing otherwise.
Babies and children admitted. Music (DJ 8pm Thur-Sat). Tables outdoors (pavement). TV (big screen, satellite).

District

19 Amhurst Road, E8 (8985 8986). Hackney Central rail. **Open/food served** 5pm-midnight Mon-Wed; 5pm-1am Thur; 4pm-1am Fri; 2pm-1am Sat; noon-midnight Sun. **Happy hour** 5-8pm Mon-Fri; 4-8pm Sat, Sun. **Credit** MC, V.
District is a funky, dark and ever-so-slightly edgy late-night bar at the Hackney Central end of Amhurst Road. It's got that Hoxton thing going of bare brick walls, low leather sofas and a pool table. Five nights a week it operates as a DJ bar, with deck jocks spinning everything from deep house through tech-edged funk to roots reggae. The late licence attracts a strong presence of laddish gangs looking for continuance after the pubs have closed, and things can get a little lairy – unaccompanied females beware. But staff are friendly enough. Drinks are standard spirits, cocktails, shooters, bottled beers and draught lagers. Definitely at the trendy edge of Hackney drinking, but the neighbourhood needs to catch up and chill-out a little before this becomes the truly laid-back and sweet little venue it could be.
Films. Games (board games, chess, pool table). Music (DJs 9pm Wed-Sun; after 10pm Fri, Sat £3). Tables outdoors (pavement).

Dove Freehouse

24-28 Broadway Market, E8 (7275 7617). Bus 55. **Open** noon-11pm Mon-Thur; noon-midnight Fri, Sat; noon-10.30pm Sun. **Food served** noon-3pm, 6-10pm Mon-Thur; noon-3pm, 6-10.30pm Fri; noon-10.30pm Sat; noon-10pm Sun. **Credit** MC, V.
Though it's shaggy around the edges (a multi-layered and multi-roomed rambling place, with rickety old furniture, benches covered in cushions and ethnic knick-knacks on the walls), the Dove remains an outstanding pub. We love it first and foremost for its Belgian beers, both draught – including De Koninck and delicious cherry-flavoured Kriek – plus a great range by the bottle. These are complemented by a wholesome range of food of the order of sausages and flavoured mash, and excellent prime beef burgers in focaccia. Evenings here are typically warm, cosy and lit by candles. Staff are professional and charming. Our only grouch is that the place might benefit from a bit of DIY – tables are precarious, particularly when covered with slidey silk saris, and banisters look ready to topple. Then again, we'd hate for it to lose any of its skewed, slightly off-kilter charm.
Babies and children admitted (restaurant; children's menu). Games (board games). No-smoking area. Restaurant. Specialities: Belgian beers. Tables outdoors (pavement).

Prince George

40 Parkholme Road, E8 (7254 6060). Bus 38, 242, 277. **Open** noon-2.30pm, 5-11pm Mon-Fri; noon-11pm Sat; noon-10.30pm Sun. **Food served** noon-3pm Sun. **Credit** MC, V.
This is the kind of pub for which people travel. The Monday night quiz is famous and a very serious business that has the place bursting at the seams with furrowed-browed trivialists. The jukebox is also a cracker, with Thelonious Monk sharing space with the White Stripes. Drinking is another thing the George's patrons do well, furnished by a great selection of real ales (Abbot Bitter, London Pride, Marston's Pedigree, Adnams Bitter and Flowers IPA), and a reasonable range of good wines and bottled beers. The pub's held out against the vogue for modernisation and has remained true to its traditional vibe: little bar stools and tables too heavy to move, frosted windows over which velvet curtains are drawn as it nears closing time and a pool table that should have a waiting list. Punters range from artists and academics to the local soaks who smoke over the bar staff. In the summer the feel-good factor spills out on to the street benches and tables.
Babies and children admitted (until 8.30pm). Games (pool table). Jukebox. Quiz (9pm Mon; £2 per team). Tables outdoors (heated forecourt). TV (satellite).

Royal Inn on the Park

111 Lauriston Road, E9 (8985 3321). Mile End tube, then 277 bus. **Open** noon-11pm Mon-Sat; noon-10.30pm Sun. **Food served** noon-2.30pm, 6-9.30pm Mon-Fri; noon-9.30pm Sat; noon-4pm Sun. **Credit** MC, V.
Handsome, high-ceilinged and bang next to Victoria Park, the Royal Inn is a fine venue with a grand wooden bar, drapes and wooden settees furnishing alcoves, and big windows overlooking the greenery. The crowd is mostly gossipy – even occasionally rowdy – trendies who enjoy the pub's proximity to their posh Vic Park homes. Their custom dictates a long chalk-boarded list of wines, appended with recommendations of the week. There's also real ales that might include Ridleys IPA, Old Bob and Pedigree, plus London Pride. Food's a feature and Sunday lunches are especially popular when the hordes descend with dogs and kids in tow (there's a dedicated dining room, plus a heated tent area out the back, but food can be eaten anywhere). Another bonus is the phenomenal jukebox, with choice cuts drawn from early Stevie Wonder, James Brown, Al Green and Billie Holiday.
Babies and children admitted (high chairs, nappy-changing facilities). Disabled: toilet. Function rooms. Jukebox. Life-drawing classes (7.30pm Mon; book in advance). No-smoking area (restaurant). Quiz (8.30pm Tue; £1). Restaurant. Specialities: Belgian and Czech beers, real ales. Tables outdoors (garden). TV.

Critics' choice
pub games

BOD (p121)
Land on Old Street at Old Street with Monopoly at BOD, plus chess and Jenga.

Cafe Kick (p108)
The only place for serious table footie fans, beside Bar Kick (p121), of course.

Elbow Room (p69)
The Westbourne Grove branch was the first in this pool bar chain and it's still the best.

Queen's Head (p152)
Keeper of one of the few remaining London Fives dartboards.

Surprise (p229)
A lovely Stockwell local brings boules to south London.

291

291 Hackney Road, E2 (7613 5676). Bus 26, 48, 55. **Open** 6pm-midnight Tue-Thur; 6pm-2am Fri, Sat. **Admission** £3 after 10pm Fri, Sat. **Credit** MC, V.

One of the city's more unusual drinking venues, 291 is a church conversion. A stunning space then, but also difficult to fill. Whenever we've visited it's been uncomfortably empty and echoey. In large part, that's down to its out-of-the-way location. To compensate, it has a lively programme of screenings, live bands, DJs and all manner of other events intended to pull the punters in. A screening of *The Exorcist*, complete with incense and upturned crucifix, apparently drew a packed house. At other times, surroundings are striking if stark, with a bar on one side and tables across on the other, and a line up of sofas in front of a huge screen. Drinks are a bit dull: house wines and bottled Kronenbourg and San Miguel. Bar staff are kinda arty, but that comes with the territory.

Art gallery. Babies and children admitted (high chairs). Cinema-sized screen. Disabled: toilet. Function rooms. Music (DJs 9pm Fri, Sat). Tables outdoors (garden).

Wellington

119 Balls Pond Road, N1 (7275 7640). Dalston Kingsland rail/Highbury & Islington tube/30, 38, 56, 277 bus. **Open** 4pm-midnight Mon-Fri; noon-midnight Sat; noon-11.30pm Sun. **Food served** 5-9.30pm Mon-Fri; noon-midnight Sat; 1-5pm Sun. **Credit** MC, V.

The Wellington is so female friendly that on our recent visit, it was mostly populated by lesbians. A makeover of a year back reconceived the place as a bright, warm and very welcoming haunt. To the existing large central circular bar, glass partition and flock wallpaper were added care worn leather sofas, fresh flowers and house quirks such as the ceramic leopard leashed to the bar with a bicycle chain. Other pleasing features include fresh juices and better-than-average pub grub (Sunday lunch is popular). Drinks are standard for a London pub, but most bases are covered. The Wellington's aim seems a modest one: to be a good local. It succeeds, and we wish there were more places around like it.

Babies and children admitted (separate room). Disabled: toilet. Function room. Games (backgammon, cards, chess). Music (Dj s and occasional live music; free). Tables outdoors (pavement). TV.

Leyton & Leytonstone

Leyton and its eastern neighbour Leytonstone both lack a well-defined centre, which is probably why their best pubs are scattered haphazardly around the area. If it's just a quick pint you're after, then you won't go thirsty for long – there are plenty of standard boozers on main arteries Leyton High Road and Leytonstone High Road. If you're choosy, however, you may have a longish walk on your hands, though the excellent **William the Fourth** is – to borrow one pub chain's former slogan – worth passing a few pubs for.

Birkbeck Tavern

45 Langthorne Road, E11 (8539 2584). Leyton tube. **Open** 11am-11pm Mon-Sat; noon-10.30pm Sun. **Food served** noon-6pm Mon, Wed-Sat. **Credit** MC, V.

Entering the Birkbeck is a bit like arriving late at a party in someone's palatial sitting room – it's such a long walk from the door to the bar that everyone gets a good long look at you. It's a generously proportioned Victorian boozer boasting a huge island bar and a fine selection of ales, notably including Rita's Special, named after the landlady and a bargain at £1.70 a pint. Neat, tidy and freshly decorated, the place is happily lacking in the acres of bought-by-the-yard pub drek that disfigures so many of its rivals. Food's perhaps not a strong point, but fresh sandwiches are served from noon to 6pm (although, peculiarly, not on Tuesdays).

Function room. Games (darts, fruit machine, pool table). Jukebox. Quiz (8.15pm Sun). Tables outdoors (garden). TV (satellite).

North Star

24 Browning Road, E11 (8532 2421). Leytonstone tube. **Open** noon-11.30pm Mon-Sat; noon-10.30pm Sun. **Food served** noon-3pm, 6-9pm Mon-Fri; noon-5pm Sat, Sun. **Credit** MC, V.

Tucked away in a side street off the High Road, the North Star is an unpretentious but friendly local, taking its name from the Great Western Railway's first successful locomotive. The railway theme, such as it is, pretty much ends there: decor consists of a few brewery posters and paintwork the colour of red leicester. The long, double-sided bar serves both the saloon and public lounges, and features include a Monday to Friday happy hour with Carling and Guinness at £1.90, John Smith's £1.60 and a selection of house doubles for £2.30. It's hard to imagine the North Star ever becoming fashionable, but it's a cheerful little oasis in this otherwise faintly depressing area near the Green Man roundabout.

Games (fruit machine). Tables outdoors (garden, pavement). TV (digital, satellite).

Sir Alfred Hitchcock Hotel

147 Whipps Cross Road, E11 (8530 3724). Leytonstone tube/Walthamstow Central tube/rail. **Open** 11am-11pm Mon-Sat; noon-10.30pm Sun. **Food served** noon-3pm, 7-10.30pm Mon-Sat; 1-5pm Sun. **Credit** MC, V.

The Hitch is very much a pub in search of a theme: photographs of the 'Master of Suspense' (brought up in nearby Leytonstone) jostle with Irish beer signs, miscellaneous football memorabilia and, perplexingly, lobster pots. Still, the large, rambling building (incorporating a restaurant and

East

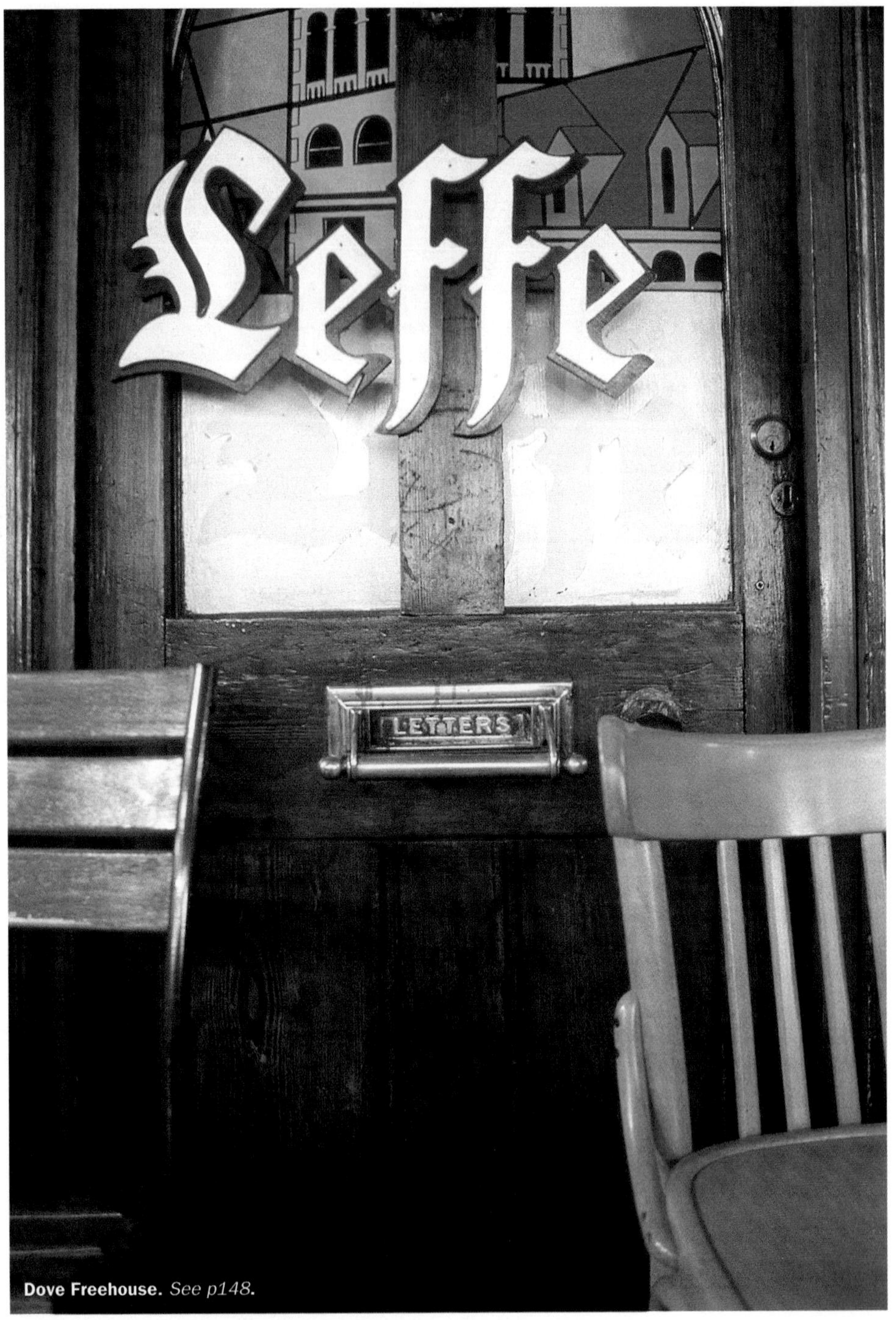

Dove Freehouse. *See p148.*

hotel, and strangely reminiscent of Hitch's own Jamaica Inn) is a welcome sight at the end of an invigorating walk around Epping Forest. The bar area, however, is seriously in need of refurbishment, with carpet worn to the felt and upholstery that has your bottom plunging dangerously close to floor-level. There's a good selection of beers (Brakspear Bitter, London Pride and Hoegaarden on tap) and – thanks to South African owners – biltong and droewors take pride of place among the bar snacks.
Babies and children admitted (restaurant). Games (fruit machine). Quiz (8pm Tue; £1). Restaurant (available for hire). Tables outdoors (garden). TV.

William the Fourth

816 Leyton High Road, E10 (8556 2460). Leyton tube/ Walthamstow Central tube/rail. **Open** 11am-11pm Mon-Sat; noon-10.30pm Sun. **Food served** noon-10pm Mon-Sat; 12.30-10pm Sun. **Credit** MC, V.
It's a bit of a trek if you're not local, but don't be put off – the William IV is probably the best thing on Leyton High Road. The long, serpentine bar offers a dazzling variety of beers, not only from the pub's own Sweet William microbrewery but from other sources too: on our visit, there were no fewer than six guest ales, including King & Barnes Festive and the surprisingly palatable Wychwood Dog's Bollocks. The large front windows are practically hidden behind giant tropical plants, apparently half-inched from the set of *Bridge on the River Kwai* and chosen to complement the lengthy and very edible Thai menu. A quieter, more anonymous, back room is used mainly for eating said Thai but also has its own bar for boozehounds.
Babies and children admitted (until 7pm). Games (fruit machines, quiz machine). Music (bands 8.30pm Sat) Quiz (8.30pm Sun; £1). Tables outdoors (paved area). TV (big screen, satellite).

Also in the area...

Drum (JD Wetherspoon) 557-9 Lea Bridge Road, E10 (8539 9845).
George (JD Wetherspoon) 159 Wanstead High Street, E11 (8989 2921).
O'Neill's 762 Leytonstone High Road, E11 (8532 2411).
Walnut Tree (JD Wetherspoon) 857-61 Leytonstone High Road, E11 (8539 2526).

Limehouse

This mean-looking patch by the side of the river was London's original Chinatown, peppered with opium dens and illegal gambling joints. From early Victorian times up until the decline of the dockyards, Limehouse was a place into which respectable people thought twice before stepping out. No change there, then. Except the revamping of Docklands, the arrival of the DLR and the general gentrification of the area mean that there is a gradual change. It's very slow, it started in Narrow Street, and it's definitely coming.

Barley Mow

44 Narrow Street, E14 (7265 8931). Limehouse or Westferry DLR. **Open** noon-11pm Mon-Sat; noon-10.30pm Sun. **Food served** noon-2pm, 6.30-9.30pm Mon-Thur; noon-2pm, 6.30-10pm Fri; noon-3pm, 6.30-10pm Sat; noon-9.30pm Sun. **Credit** AmEx, MC, V.
The graceful Edwardian red-brick building became a pub in 1989; before that it was the Limehouse Basin's dockmaster's house. Named after a long-defunct nearby brewery, you enter down stone stairs that rise over the dock wall, past the flagged riverside terrace (bring your Uzi if you want a good spot) and into an olde worlde pub that looks like it's been doing the job for decades. There's plenty of exposed brick, chunky wood furniture, panelling and spectacular views across the water. Customers tend to be local business types, tourists festooned with guide books and cameras and couples out for a romantic riverside stroll, bless 'em. Two or three regular real ales keep the connoisseurs happy and there's above-average pub food (plenty of pasta and fish dishes) in the enclosed restaurant area. Staff always seem unusually pleasant and, despite the corporate feel and West End prices, it remains one of our favourite new riverside pubs.
Babies and children admitted. Disabled: toilet. Games (fruit machine, quiz machine). Music (jazz last Tue of mth; free). Restaurant. Tables outdoors (riverside terrace). TV.

Booty's Riverside Bar

92A Narrow Street, E14 (7987 8343). Westferry DLR. **Open** 11am-11pm Mon-Thur; 11am-midnight Fri, Sat; noon-10.30pm Sun. **Food served** 11am-9.30pm Mon-Fri; 11am-7.30pm Sat; noon-9.30pm Sun. **Credit** AmEx, DC, MC, V.
Not a Caribbean bottom-fanciers club as you might expect, but a converted 17th-century barge builder's store that was turned into a pub, the Waterman's Arms, taking on its present moniker in 1979. It's a comfortable and hospitable place that aspires to be a wine bar – featuring as it does a decent, predominantly French list – but the atmosphere is that of a venerable and aged pub. The single split-level ground floor falls to a drinking/dining area, scattered with gingham-clothed tables overlooking the Thames. Food is simple and comes from a serving area beside the traditional heavy wood bar. Expect a couple of decent real ales (probably Bass and Tetley's), a strong local following with thirtysomethings in the majority and a scatter of tourists drawn by the location. When the river floods, Booty's is less of a riverside bar and more of an in-the-river bar.
Babies and children admitted. Games (fruit machine, quiz machine). Specialities: wines. Tables outdoors (pavement). TVs (digital, satellite).

Grapes

76 Narrow Street, E14 (7987 4396). Westferry DLR. **Open** noon-3pm, 5.30-11pm Mon-Fri; noon-11pm Sat; noon-10.30pm Sun. **Food served** noon-2pm, 7-9pm Mon-Sat; noon-3.30pm Sun. **Credit** AmEx, DC, MC, V.
Although a couple of other pubs claim the honour, we're convinced that Charles Dickens wrote about the Grapes in *Our Mutual Friend*, disguising it as the Six Jolly Fellowship Porters. A pub's been on this site since 1583, though the present upstart only dates from 1720. Although you'd hardly credit it, looking at the upmarket locals, tourists and financial whizz-kids who these days form the core clientele, up until the 1970s this was a serious working-class boozer. There's been a major refit since, with the wooden platform on the river strengthened and the odd creak and loose board straightened. Happily, the chunky wood floor remains deliciously off-kilter and the antique panelling still looks awry. An ancient, noisy wooden staircase leads up to the very good first-floor fish restaurant and looks out on to a scene little changed since Charlie's day. Real ales will probably include London Pride and Adnams Bitter and the wine list is brief but very much to the point. And food? 'Best seafood pub in England 2002' say the notices. But don't believe everything you read.
Games (board games). Restaurant (available for hire). Tables outdoors (riverside balcony).

Queen's Head

8 Flamborough Street, E14 (7791 2504). Limehouse DLR. **Open** 11am-11pm Mon-Sat; noon-10.30pm Sun. **Food served** 11.30am-3pm Mon-Fri. **No credit cards.**
This two-bar local is one of the handful of Young's pubs in east London. In days gone by the beer used to come up the Thames on a barge, but now it's delivered from Wandsworth by lorry. The front saloon bar is where most of the action takes place, with easy chairs and bar stools occupied by the local cabbies, couples and tradesmen who make up the pub's main clientele. A gang of off-duty traffic wardens have made themselves regulars and we've found the sex-split most evenings not far off 50-50. Both bars and the connecting games room (London Fives dartboard, naturally) are decorated in similar style with check curtains, carpets and comfortable banquettes. Friday nights tend to be lively affairs and Wednesday night quizzes are fun.
Babies and children admitted. Games (darts). Quiz (8.30pm Wed; £1). TV.

East

Plaistow

The name derives, apparently, from the Old English for 'a place to play', but 21st-century Plaistow isn't exactly awash with desirable drinking places, playful or not. The **Black Lion**, a few minutes' walk from the tube station, is the only half-decent place (and it's a pub that would be a winner whatever part of town it was in). Students at local East London Uni head up the road to the pubs in nearby Stratford.

Black Lion

59-61 High Street, E13 (8472 2351). Plaistow tube. **Open** 11am-3.30pm, 5-11pm Mon-Wed; 11am-11pm Thur-Sat; noon-10.30pm Sun. **Food served** noon-2.30pm, 5-7.30pm Mon-Fri. **Credit** MC, V.
The courtyard at the side betrays the pub's origins as a coaching inn, dating from the time when Plaistow was a hamlet. The pub is deservedly popular – our first impression was of a wall of noise, as locals tucked into dishes of chips and chicken legs thoughtfully distributed along the long, half-moon bar. It has a long-standing reputation for its guest ales, which on our visit included Adnams Fisherman and Tally Ho. The boisterous crowds and in-your-face music may not be to everybody's taste, especially if you're in search of a quiet pint, but the drinkers are of satisfyingly mixed stock and the staff friendly and efficient. An excellent local.
Babies and children admitted (until 7pm). Function room. Games (fruit machine). Tables outdoors (garden). TV.

Stratford

Despite being several miles from the centre of London, Stratford is built around the capital's most comprehensive transport nexus – passenger and goods trains, the tube, DLR and numerous buses all converge here. Given this, you would expect a myriad hostelries offering sustenance to the weary traveller; sadly, few of them (noted exceptions reviewed below) merit more than a passing visit.

Goldengrove

146-8 The Grove, E15 (8519 0750). Stratford tube/DLR/rail. **Open** 11am-11pm Mon-Sat; noon-10.30pm Sun. **Food served** 10am-10pm Mon-Sat; noon-9.30pm Sun. **Credit** AmEx, MC, V.
Taking its name from a poem by Stratford lad Gerard Manley Hopkins ('Margaret, are you grieving/Over Goldengrove unleaving?'), the Goldengrove is part of the not-all-bad **JD Wetherspoon** chain (*see p15*), so while there's little real individuality there is a concerted attempt to cater for all-comers in relatively civilised surroundings. The place was packed out on our visit, at around half-three on a Friday afternoon, by a mainly working, blue-collar (as Bruce Springsteen might put it) clientele of all ages. The seating area boasts numerous booths if you're looking for a wee dab of privacy, and includes a huge no-smoking area. A garden increases the capacity even further. Food is the usual cheap and cheery Wetherspoon's fare, but the well-stocked bar offers one or two pleasant surprises, such as, on our visit at least, Addlestone's Cloudy Cider and Rebellion ale.
Babies and children admitted (until 6pm). Disabled: toilet. Games (fruit machines). No piped music or jukebox. No-smoking area. Specialities: guest ales. Tables outdoors (garden).

King Edward VII

47 Broadway, E15 (8534 2313/www.kingeddie.co.uk). Stratford tube/DLR/rail. **Open** noon-11pm Mon-Sat; noon-10.30pm Sun. **Food served** noon-7pm Mon-Fri; noon-6pm Sat, Sun. **Credit** MC, V.
If you're organising an East End pub crawl, don't keep the Eddie for last – the step just inside the door can be unforgiving if you're a little unsteady on your feet. It has two distinct drinking areas: the exceptionally wide public bar at the front is pleasingly dark, despite big windows looking on to busy Broadway. The larger saloon is reached via an unmarked door next to the counter and is characterised by dark wood and, on winter days, a fire in the grate (though, disappointingly, only of the gas variety). It takes a while to realise that the whole pub is on several levels, rather like one of those MC Escher prints showing impossible perspectives and endless staircases. The landlord, Jim, takes his real ales seriously – our visit found four on display, including London Pride and Old Speckled Hen – though the droning and over-amplified jukebox may put off those who like to enjoy their bitter in reverent silence. A student favourite.
Function room. Games (arcade game, fruit machines, quiz machine). Quiz (8.45pm Sun). Tables outdoors (yard). TVs (big screen, digital, satellite).

Also in the area...

Hudson Bay (JD Wetherspoon) 1-5 Upton Lane, Forest Gate, E7 (8471 7702).

Walthamstow

Walthamstow has two main thoroughfares: Hoe Street, which bears most of the through traffic, and High Street, home to mile-long Walthamstow Market. Both have their fair share of pubs, but the best of them are to be found in the 'Village' area at the eastern end of Orford Road, where the **Nag's Head** is an especially welcome new arrival. Beer lovers might want to make a note of the Flower Pot, on the eastern flank of Walthamstow at 128 Wood Street, which has been praised by CAMRA for its well-kept Bass.

Goose

264 Hoe Street, E17 (8223 9951). Walthamstow Central tube/rail. **Open** 11am-11pm Mon-Sat; noon-10.30pm Sun. **Food served** 11am-9pm daily. **Credit** AmEx, MC, V.

London drinking: absinthe

The little green drink that can cause a whole lot of damage.

'Oh my God! What have I done?!?' The head of a French family awoke from an alcoholic stupour to find his wife and kids at his feet, slain by his own hand. The case achieved notoriety because it led to the banning of the drink that pushed a generation over the edge: absinthe.

Banned, it became the heroin of its day – Manet, Toulouse Lautrec and Degas all indulged, although only Van Gogh sliced off his own ear afterwards. Almost as soon as a wormwood-free pastiche of Swiss Dr Ordinaire's 18th-century concoction had been invented in 1920 – Pastis, as it came to be known – the French public were happy to sip quiet glasses of aniseed flavouring and yellowing water over a game of boules. In Czechoslovakia, much to Green Bohemia's delight, absinth (no 'e' in these parts) was also a semi-secret indulgence, carried out by burning the demon juice with sugar.

Prohibition remains in France to this day, but in the UK it was never banned, and the skull-and-crossbones reputation has ensured that it's the most cachet-laden drink in town.

Discerning travellers to Prague, Portugal and beyond have long returned with tales of a strange green drink that summoned the demons when lit with sugar; their bragging would be embellished by a clandestine bottle unveiled from wrappings of newspaper. La Fée, 'the fairy', as it was known, loved and abused in 19th-century France, was well-known amid certain elite circles. It took a quartet from the brotherhood calling themselves Green Bohemia Ltd – two magazine editors, an alcohol importer with Czech know-how and a pop star – to share their naughty little habit with the rest of London. On the same night in 1998, at 15 key central bars, barmen had matches, spoons, sugar and glasses at the ready for the 9pm lift-off. Such a limited, exclusive and sought after promotion relit the absinthe legend overnight. And nobody had to die, get rushed to A&E or taken in for questioning for it to happen.

Positive media coverage fanned the flames and the torch was passed from W1 to the upmarket hotel bars (the **American Bar** at the Savoy, the **Zeta Bar** at the Park Lane Hilton and the **Met Bar** at the Metropolitan), to hip Hoxton (**Cantaloupe** and the **Dragon**) and on to Brixton, where the **Fridge Bar** wanted a rite of its own, jealously guarding little green monsters of all makes and mixes, and attracting a regular clientele delighted with the shady legality, quasi-narcotic ritual and, most of all, the effect.

The two most popular brands – available at £35-£45 a bottle at stores such as **Soho Wine Supply** or **Gerry's** – are Hill's Absinth (distilled in Bohemia since the 1920s) and La Fée Absinthe, remade and remodelled solely for the UK market. The Czech version is taken *au feu*, the French with water. The latter is endorsed by Marie-Claude Delahaye, founder and curator of the Absinthe Museum, outside Paris at 44 rue Calle, Auvers-sur-Oise, the same village where Vincent and his brother Theo are buried. Any attempt to join them in spirit at the museum bar will have to be done without the aid of absinthe: the bottles there are authentic but empty. *Peterjon Cresswell*

A deadly octet

American Bar (*see p91*) Savoy Hotel, Strand, WC2 (7836 4343).
Cantaloupe (*see p122*) 35 Charlotte Road, EC2 (7613 4411).
Dragon (*see p125*) 5 Leonard Street, EC2 (7490 7110).
Fridge Bar (*see p202*) 1 Town Hall Parade, SW2 (7326 5100).
Gerry's 76 Old Compton Street, W1 (7734 2053).
Met Bar (*see p65*) Metropolitan Hotel, 18-9 Park Lane, W1 (7447 1000).
Soho Wine Supply 18 Percy Street, W1 (7636 8490).
Zeta Bar (*see p67*) 35 Hertford Street, W1 (7208 4067).

East

Grapes. See p151.

Thronged most weeknights with after-work drinkers (it's directly opposite Walthamstow Central station and just down the road from the bus hanger), the spacious, dark-wooded Goose works better as an unwinding zone once the punters have gone home for dinner. For much of the '90s, it was resolutely seedy and permanently two thirds empty; it was a relief, then, when new owners, recognising the potential, gave it the refit it had been crying out for. It's a huge place, with two enormous bars built at right-angles to each other, but varying levels and strategically placed pillars prevent it seeming too barn-like, and there are plenty of nooks and crannies if you're looking for peace and quiet. Draught beers include Tetley's, Bass and Calders.
Disabled: toilet. Games (fruit machines, golf machine). No-smoking area.

Nag's Head

9 Orford Road, E17 (8520 9709). Walthamstow Central tube/rail. **Open** noon-11pm Mon-Fri; noon-11pm Sat; noon-10.30pm Sun. **Food served** noon-4pm Mon-Sat; noon-2pm Sun. **Credit** MC, V.
The name may be bog-standard but so, until recently, was the pub. Recently, though, the Nag's Head has been transformed into an exemplary little neighbourhood bar, full of pleasing details: candles on tables, printed cards inviting you to bring your favourite CDs on DJ nights (Mondays) and seasonal drinks such as mulled wine. Decor is fashionably plain and the place attracts a clean-cut, middle-class Walthamstow Village clientele. The small, well-stocked bar has a good selection of wines, plus Kronenbourg, Shepherd Neame Spitfire and Hoegaarden on draught. Other pluses include a garden and a no-smoking area at the rear of the pub, with obligatory leather couch – though, as one regular warned us, it's not as soft as it looks. Recommended.
Music (DJs 7pm Mon; jazz 3pm Sun). No-smoking tables. Tables outdoors (courtyard).

Village

31 Orford Road, E17 (8521 9982). Walthamstow Central tube/rail. **Open** 11am-11pm Mon-Sat; 11am-10.30pm Sun. **Food served** noon-2.30pm daily. **Credit** AmEx, MC, V.
'The only pub in Walthamstow where you don't have to leave your brain at home,' according to one local website. It is the pub of choice for the more discerning E17 crowd (there is such a thing), with an atmosphere reminiscent of a student haunt in a small university town. It's got a rough-hewn wood bar and tables typically filled with garrulous young punters knocking back pints of Broadside and Tiger. The music is surprisingly current, much to the bemusement of the handful of old regulars who grumble into their Guinness. It's a friendly place that comes dangerously close to being cool.
Babies and children admitted (garden only). Games (fruit machines). Quiz (8.30pm Wed; £1). Tables outdoors (garden). TV.

Wapping

Until Dirty Digger Rupert Murdoch moved his News International plant here during the reign of Maggie the Impaler, Wapping was a tired old riverside area, quietly rotting into the Thames. There's still not much happening and despite bars and clubs coming and going (these journalists and printworkers are a fickle lot), the best bets for a Thameside drink remain these two ancient boozers.

Prospect of Whitby

57 Wapping Wall, E1 (7481 1095). Wapping tube. **Open** 11.30am-11pm Mon-Sat; noon-10.30pm Sun. **Food served** *Pub* 11.30am-10pm Mon-Sat. *Restaurant* noon-3pm, 7-10pm Mon-Fri; 7-10pm Sat; noon-3pm Sun. **Credit** AmEx, DC, MC, V.

Built in 1520 but extensively remodelled in 1777, this historic boozer has seen some action over the years. The first fuchsia ever to enter the country was exchanged for a scoop of rum here in 1780, and in 1953 an armed robbery on a party being held upstairs resulted in a villain called Scarface (Robert Harrington-Saunders at prep school) being hanged after shooting one of his pursuers. Charles Dickens, Samuel Pepys and the 'Hanging Judge' Jeffreys have all drunk here. Perhaps the most photogenic of London's historic pubs, it comes with a pewter-topped bar supported on old beer barrels, exposed beams and white-painted plaster. The small riverside terrace offers a good waterside drinking spot on days without rain, hail or snow (the best of luck finding one). Upmarket modern-meets-trad food is served in the restaurant. The three or four real ales regularly on offer might include Old Speckled Hen, Courage Directors and Theakston Black Bull.

Babies and children admitted (dining area). Function room. Games (fruit machine). No-smoking area. Restaurant. Tables outdoors (riverside terrace). TV.

Town of Ramsgate

62 Wapping High Street, E1 (7481 8000). Wapping tube/100 bus. **Open** noon-11pm Mon-Sat; noon-10.30pm Sun. **Food served** noon-3pm Tue-Sat; noon-4pm Sun. **Credit** MC, V.

The name came about because fishermen from Ramsgate unloaded their catches via the Wapping Old Stairs, which run beside the pub. Prior to that, it was called the Red Cow. Being old and by the water, it's a pub with a chequered history. Criminals and labour organisers were chained up in its cellars before being transported to Australia and our old friend, 'Hanging Judge' Jeffreys, was all but lynched as he looked for passage to Hamburg following a regime change in 1688. Captain Bligh and Fletcher Christian had a farewell noggin here before setting off on the *Bounty* and Captain Kidd shivered his timbers nearby. It's a long, narrow pub, with plenty of old dark-wood panelling and ancient-looking windows. Expect up to three real ales, including Adnams Bitter, Young's and London Pride. Drinkers tend to be local loft dwellers, disgruntled sport hacks, gangs of office-workers on after-work binges and tourists.

Tables outdoors (riverside).

Whitechapel

A rich melting pot of cultures and styles makes Whitechapel one of London's most interesting areas. This is a major centre of Islam in Britain – good for restaurants, not so for bars – with immigrants from Bangladesh and Pakistan having followed the Jews and Huguenots into E1. Meanwhile, the old Whitechapel of Jack the Ripper tours, bagel shops and backstreet boozers is squaring up to the gentrification caused by an influx of artists, media types, City workers and the style bars that have sprung up to serve them.

Black Bull

199 Whitechapel Road, E1 (7247 6707). Whitechapel tube. **Open** 11am-11pm Mon-Sat; noon-10.30pm Sun. **Food served** (sandwiches only) noon-3pm Mon-Fri. **No credit cards**.

Of all the least likely places to find beers from Suffolk's small but worthy Nethergate Brewery, this vaguely scruffy one-bar local in the heart of Whitechapel Market is it. Here, among the bull motifs, big-screen sport/VH1 and cor blimey cockneys, you'll find one, maybe even two Nethergate real ales. It's a basic pub with comfortable bench seating, solid wood furniture and a clientele that stretches from students to market workers and the odd City gent. The view as you pee in the gents' urinal is worth the price of a pint in itself: a linguine junction of tracks and points leading out of nearby Whitechapel tube station. After dark, the fireworks caused by a train shooting over the points can be quite spectacular, especially after a half-dozen pints of Old Growler.

Games (fruit machine). TV (big screen, satellite).

Blind Beggar

337 Whitechapel Road, E1 (7247 6195). Whitechapel tube. **Open** 11am-11pm Mon-Sat; noon-10.30pm Sun. **Food served** noon-2.30pm Mon-Sat; noon-3pm Sun. **Credit** MC, V.

For years the Blind Beggar underplayed its notoriety as the pub in which Ronnie Kray shot George Cornell, but now that the brothers have all gone to that great nightclub in the sky, it's obviously been deemed safe to add a few pictures of the criminally insane siblings. Just in the interests of 'istory, y'understand. In those days (9 March 1966) the pub consisted of several bars and Cornell was shot in the public one. Now it's just one giant L-shape around the serving area. Possibly as a tribute to the deceased, the overriding colour is blood-red, with matching carpets, lampshades and upholstery. We've always thought the twinkling white fairy lights in the lean-to conservatory tasteful, and the bench-tabled garden is one of the East End's best. The beer range varies, but expect Courage Best, Brakspear and the usual line-up of stouts and lagers. The clientele is a mixture of students, local couples and large men in overcoats sipping bottled beer.

Babies and children admitted (conservatory and garden only). Function room. Games (fruit machines, pool table). Music (cabaret last Fri of month). Restaurant. Tables outdoors (garden). TV (big screen, satellite).

East

Half Moon

213-23 Mile End Road, E1 (7790 6810). Stepney Green tube. **Open** 11am-11pm Mon-Sat; noon-10.30pm Sun. **Food served** 11am-10pm Mon-Sat; 11am-9.30pm Sun. **Credit** MC, V.

Formerly a fringe theatre and before that a Welsh Calvinist chapel, this expansive JD Wetherspoon conversion has won awards from organisations as diverse as CAMRA and the Design Council. The main part of the pub features a small wooden gallery and occupies what was the old chapel/auditorium. Much of the original woodwork is still intact, offering a temperate reminder to the diverse groups of drinkers who congregate here. Being a Wetherspoon's (*see p15*), you can expect grizzled old geezers grateful for the cut-price booze (including five or six real ales), students on the razzle, and gangs of office workers noshing pub grub. The modern, chrome and glass side of the pub is accessed through a short gallery. Looking not unlike the entrance hall to a go-ahead 1960s cheese company, this is the no-smoking/dining area.

Babies and children admitted (until 6pm). Disabled: toilet. No piped music or jukebox. No-smoking area. Tables outdoors (garden).

The Lane

12 Osborn Street, E1 (7377 1797). Aldgate East tube. **Open** 11.30am-11pm Mon-Sat. **Food served** noon-3pm, 6pm-10pm Mon-Sat. **Credit** AmEx, DC, MC, V.

In nearby Hoxton, the Lane's open plan and video fractals would be as unremarkable as an androgynous student dating a Japanese moppet with an art folder. But here it feels impossibly smart. It's a gamble, but the reasoning is to market the Lane's proximity to London's 'square mile'. Judging from the customers we saw planted on charcoal cubic pouffes and backless couches, the ploy is working; three were clustered around a laptop, others were in suits. Drinks are adequate but unexciting, with classic cocktails and a reliance on bottled beers. A single, functional menu stretching from lunch through to dinner has welcome, unfussy mains (around £7) such as Cumberland sausages and onion mash, crispy fried cod and tagliatelle carbonara.

Disabled: toilet. Function room. Music (DJs 7pm Thur-Sat).

Pride of Spitalfields

3 Heneage Street, E1 (7247 8933). Aldgate East tube. **Open** 11am-11pm Mon-Sat; noon-10.30pm Sun. **Food served** noon-2.30pm Mon-Fri. **No credit cards.**

This traditional two-bar boozer is like a perfect village local. Customers are a diverse bunch and vary with the time of day and day of the week. Lunchtime trade is largely local businessmen and workers, augmented by local pensioners. As afternoon turns into evening they're replaced by the first wave of curry-holics arriving for their pre-Brick Lane pints. Then come locals plus students and visiting twentysomething arty/media types – rolling cigarettes, drinking Crouch Vale IPA and talking *essente da bollo* – plus real ale aficionados after a decent pint. The decor is comfortable, with red upholstered banquettes and framed prints of old Spitalfields. Seating is at a premium and anyone who is anyone will head into the small antechamber and try for a table there.

Babies and children admitted (annexe area). Tables outdoors (pavement). TV (big screen, satellite).

Urban Bar (LHT)

176 Whitechapel Road, E1 (7247 8978). Whitechapel or Aldgate East tube/25 bus. **Open/food served** 11am-11pm Mon-Wed; noon-1am Thur-Sat; noon-11.30pm Sun. **Credit** MC, V.

There's something about a 'Live Snake Bar' that makes our flesh creep and it's not just the reptiles in glass cages nobody seems to look twice at. Billed as 'hot music, cool drinks, great food', it's the corporate way to create a student-friendly party venue. As we went to press, London had three, and this was the first. The concept involves painting the exterior of this large Victorian boozer (formerly the London Hospital Tavern) in gaudy orange and black zebra stripes and adding flashing coloured lights and orange paint to the original wood panelling, cubicles and flooring. Drop in loud clubby music, a late licence and enough lager to sink a battleship and you're in business. Real ale is usually an item and we found Spitfire and London Pride on tap.

Function room. Internet access. Jukebox. Music (band Tue, Sun; free).

Vibe Bar

Old Truman Brewery, 91-5 Brick Lane, E1 (7377 2899/www.vibe-bar.co.uk). Aldgate or Aldgate East tube. **Open** 11am-11.30pm Mon-Thur; 11am-1am Fri, Sat; 11am-11.30pm Sun. **Food served** noon-5pm daily. **Credit** AmEx, MC, V.

A pioneer of the Shoreditch bar phenomenon, Vibe still manages to keep ahead of the competition. The latest idea was to have its own Indian restaurant, Red Chilli, housed in a tent in the large, seated and heated courtyard. Groovy, baby. The Vibe's share of this former brewery includes an enclosed terrace, a large strikingly painted central bar area with giant Cuban and Afro-influenced wall designs and a perpetually throbbing beat. A long metallic serving area at one end dispenses standard beers such as Grolsch, Staropramen and Guinness, though the young arty crowd who flock here would rather be seen with a cocktail or something long and thin. Evening DJs and internet access help keep the buzz going.

Function room. Internet access (free). Music (DJs 7pm daily; £3 after 8pm Fri, Sat. Band Sun eve; £1 after 5pm). Tables outdoors (heated courtyard, marquee). TV (big screen, satellite).

Also in the area...

Goodmans Field (JD Wetherspoon) 87-91 Mansell Street, E1 (7680 2850).

Slug and Lettuce The Courtyard, E1 (7626 4994).

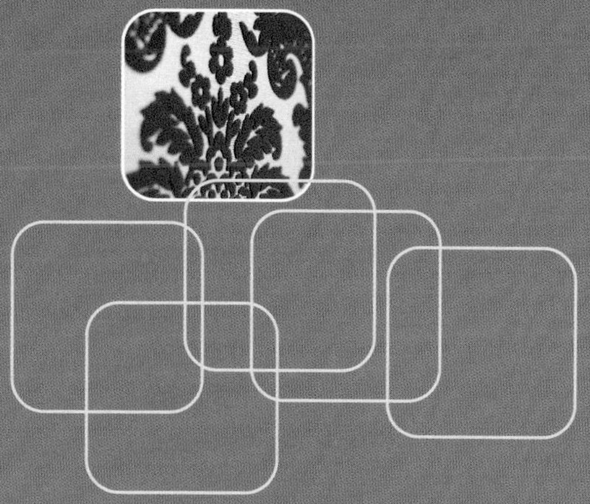

North

Belsize Park

At last, competition for the **Sir Richard Steele**. This used to be a strictly one-pub part of town, but the past 18 months have seen three great new refurbs (the three listed below that aren't the Richard Steele) of bedraggled old boozers. The results are fantastic, and where Belsize Park was once the black hole between the twinkling nightlife of Camden and Hampstead, it's now turned into a bright spot that eclipses both of its neighbours.

The Belsize

29 Belsize Lane, NW3 (7794 4910). Belsize Park tube. **Open/food served** 5-11pm Mon-Thur; noon-11pm Fri, Sat; noon-10.30pm Sun. **Credit** AmEx, MC, V.

Belsize Lane is pure Mary Poppins territory: fancy houses with gables, fancy houses with turrets, fancy houses so big they've got wings. What, you wonder, must the local boozer be like? Fancy. It's a gorgeous, high-ceilinged place recently done up with no expense spared; a painted floral frieze, tailored Roman blinds, dangly chandeliers – even the flickering candles are set in golden candelabras. Ranked above the acres of polished bar counter are phalanxes of gleaming underslung wine glasses to be filled on request from an extensive list. By contrast, beer drinkers must choose between a pair of lonely pumps (Adnams Bitter or London Pride), or settle for bog-standard lagers. Two ritzy back rooms serve gastropub standards, but drinkers settle into velvet benches, perch atop leather cube pouffes or cosy up on a tan sofa. It's seductive and dreamy. Tipple downed, you reach into your pocket for the keys to your fuck-off 4x4 only to pull out the monthly travelcard that's your ticket back to reality. Rats.

Babies and children admitted. Function room.

North

The Hill

94 Haverstock Hill, NW3 (7267 0033). Belsize Park or Chalk Farm tube. **Open** noon-midnight Mon-Sat; noon-11pm Sun. **Food served** 6.30-10.30pm Mon-Fri; noon-3.30pm, 6.30-10.30pm Sat; noon-10pm Sun. **Credit** MC, V.

Pub, gastropub or bar? It's getting harder to distinguish these days. But however you classify the Hill, it's an absolute winner. Makeovers of formerly grotty old boozers are ten-a-penny, but this one is executed with real panache. Enter into a room where winking fairy lights and candlelit illumination casts a beguiling glow over massed high-winged leather armchairs and sofas, overlooked by a giant black and white photo of a pair of laughing girlie heads. The modestly sized bar counter was charmingly staffed on our visit by a whispering Italian waif, who apologised that the one beer of interest (something called Gulpener with a hamster for a logo – really) was off. We settled for Staropramen and watched flashes of flames dancing behind the shelved bottles, which is where the semi-visible kitchen space lies. We didn't eat but the smart fodder ferried out by cheerfully knackered waiting staff looked excellent (without a menu we'd call it lamb shanks, chicken steaks, grilled fish, but there's doubtless a more florid description to be had). Tuesday night and the place was full and buzzing, no mean feat given the quality competition of nearby **Sir Richard Steele** (*see below*).

Babies and children welcome. Function room. Tables outdoors (garden). **Map 8/G25**

Sir Richard Steele

97 Haverstock Hill, NW3 (7483 1261). Belsize Park or Chalk Farm tube. **Open** 11am-11pm Mon-Sat; noon-10.30pm Sun. **Food served** noon-8pm Mon-Sat; noon-5pm Sun. **Credit** MC, V.

Theatrically, not to say ridiculously, over the top – this is a mansion of a boozer up on the hill, with an interior that has the aesthetics of a Portobello junk stall. It inspires utter devotion in its regulars, a raffish bunch of blaggers, chancers, wide boys, party girls, musos and minor Haverstock Hill celebs. Some of the crowd have been included in the Renaissance-style fresco on the ceiling. Pull up at the massive set piece of a bar (choice draught options include Flowers IPA, London Pride, Hoegaarden), bunk up on a bench, or lurk hopefully for a chance of snagging one of the little snug rooms round the back: one with a TV, the other with the open fire. Regular live music helps the descent into good-natured bacchanalia.

Babies and children admitted (until 6pm). Function room. Music (rock Sun afternoon; Irish Sun night; trad jazz Mon; jazz or blues Wed). Tables outdoors (patio). TV (satellite).

Washington Hotel & Bar

50 England's Lane, NW3 (7722 8842). Belsize Park or Chalk Farm tube. **Open/food served** noon-11pm Mon-Sat; noon-10.30pm Sun. **Credit** MC, V.

Just far enough into the quiet wealth of England's Lane to be truly a local, but at the same time smart enough to pull 'em in from far afield, the Washington has its cake and scoffs it. A recent refit lovingly buffed up original etched mirrors and polished woods, and counterpointed these old riches with a nicely chafed mishmash of retro furniture. Customers can now choose from butcher-block tables and scruffy sofas or drawing room chairs set on oriental rugs. Or, just pull up a stool at the bar, rest forearms on silky mahogany and indicate your preference from a line-up of white beer (Leffe, Hoegaarden), decent cider (Addlestone's) or one real ale (London Pride). There's also a lengthy list of wines by the glass. Best enjoyed on lazy Sundays with papers, a replenishing Bloody Mary and a substantial lunch of modern bistro mains.

Babies and children admitted (until 5pm). Comedy (8pm Sat; £6/£5 concessions). Function room. Tables outdoors (pavement).

Camden Town & Chalk Farm

Briefly trendy a decade or so ago, Camden has ever since traded on memories and a market-led tourist crowd too young to know better. A hellish High Street of fast food and chain bars stretches from Mornington Crescent to the Lock, while – the **Dublin Castle** and **Spread Eagle** aside – Parkway is just another indentikit slice of Anywheresville, UK. There are some bright one-offs (all described below), and the patch north of the Lock up toward Chalk Farm (**Lock Tavern** to **Monkey Chews**) is worth a gander.

Bar Solo

22 Inverness Street, NW1 (7482 4611). Camden Town tube. **Open** 8am-1am daily. **Food served** 8.30am-midnight daily. **Happy hour** 5-7pm daily. **Credit** MC,V.

Halfway down one of Camden's busiest drinking strips, Bar Solo is a popular haunt with local workers. During the day, patrons sip lattes or tuck into the excellent breakfasts and burgers but as the evening draws on, the regular weeknight happy hour ensures a steady flow of half-price cocktails and bottled beers are served from the ornate faux deco bar at the back. Weekends are crammed with a younger crowd preparing for clubbing in town or downstairs in the basement. The decor won't win any awards for originality, but the prices and quality of drinks and food more than make up for it.

Babies and children admitted, Music (jazz 7.30pm Sun). Function room. Tables outdoors (pavement). **Map 8/H1**

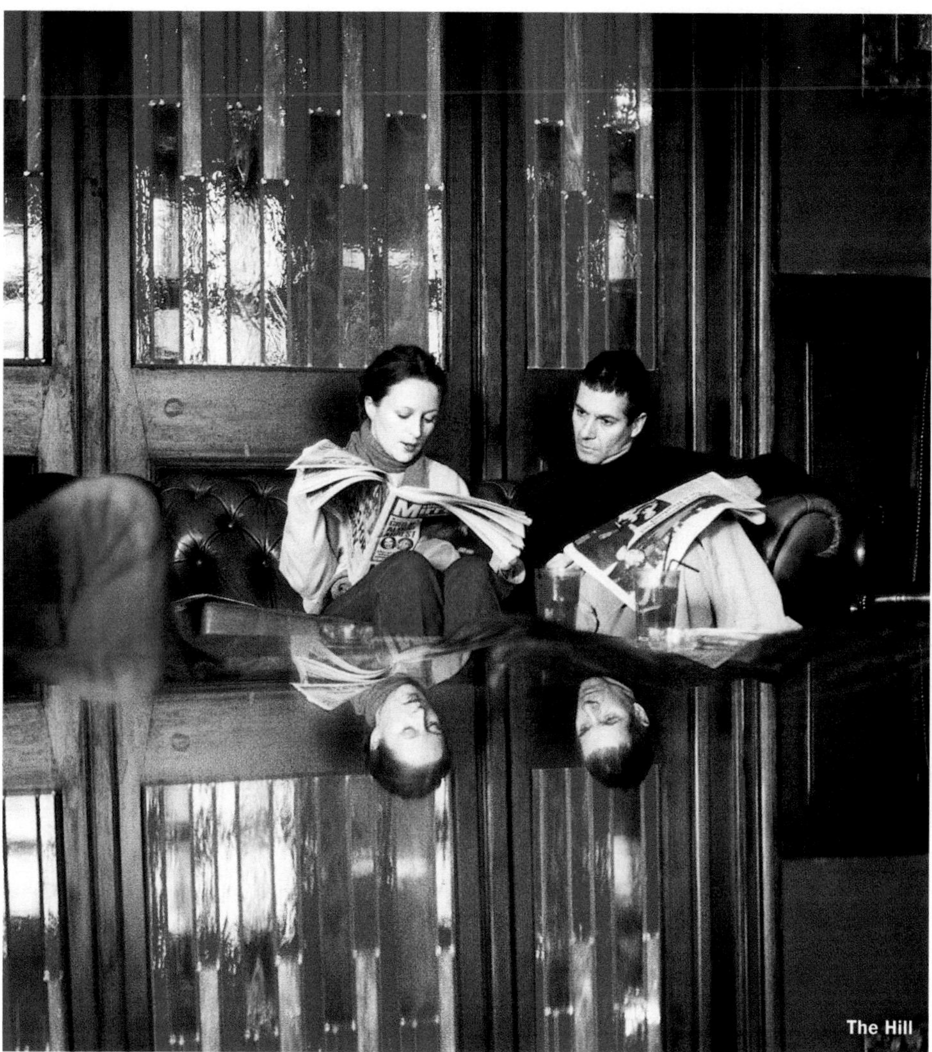

The Hill

Bartok

78-9 Chalk Farm Road, NW1 (7916 0595). Chalk Farm tube. **Open/food served** 5pm-1am Mon-Thur; 5pm-2am Fri; noon-2am Sat; noon-midnight Sun. **Happy hour** 5pm-1am Mon, Thur; 5-8pm Fri. **Credit** MC, V.

At first, it seems like nothing you haven't seen before in London's smarter bars, with its darkened hotel lobby vibe. Small chandeliers? Check. Low sofas? Check. Huge drapes? Check. Chi-chi cocktails and bottled beers? Check. The difference is that Bartok is the capital's only classical music bar, dedicated to strutting its refined stuff every night of the week with different DJs and themes. When we visited, it was Debussy, but they dance it up at weekends when some astute mixing takes you from Bach to beats without breaking stride. Whether you think that atonal violins are a suitable accompaniment to drinking and merriment is entirely up to you, but it's plenty popular (amazing what an extra hour or two on your licence can do).

Games (chess, Pictionary). Music (DJs Tue, Fri, Sat; live music Wed, Thur; string quartet Sun). **Map 8/G26**

Bar Vinyl

6 Inverness Street, NW1 (7681 7898). Camden Town tube. **Open/food served** 11am-11pm Mon-Sat; noon-10.30pm Sun. **Credit** MC, V.

Open a dictionary, look under DJ bar and you'll probably come across a picture of Bar Vinyl. This is the original, the real deal, the epitome of effortless cool. There's a permanent set of decks at the back, DJs most nights and a record shop down the backstairs. A curving concrete bar dominates front of house (Budvar and Hoegaarden are on tap) with celeb

portraits and record sleeves adding a splash of colour to the walls. Happily, the urban vibe doesn't extend as far as the kitchen, whose menu is tasty and adventurous (roast pumpkin salad with feta and chilli, for example), all served up canteen style on the big plastic tables. At weekends this is the beating heart of buzzing Inverness Street.
Babies and children admitted. Music (DJs 8pm Wed-Sun; daytime Sat, Sun; free). Tables outdoors (patio). **Map 8/H1**

Blakes

31 Jamestown Road, NW1 (7482 2959). Camden Town tube. **Open** 11am-11pm Mon-Sat; noon-10.30pm Sun. **Food served** noon-10.30pm daily. **Credit** AmEx, MC, V.
A class act, Blakes. Its imposing dungeon doors (with blood red drapes behind) are a little out of place opposite the new Holiday Inn and corporate offices of Jamestown Road. But with a new Wetherspoon's over the road, it must look ever more appealing for those who don't find bingo carpets or cheap hamburgers all that exciting. It's of the wooden floor and big candles school of pub decor, and punters share chunky tables, ordering cocktails, with only lager on draught (no real beer, for shame). Upstairs is an intimate restaurant with modern bistro menu. Bar snacks are served downstairs, where large modern paintings, high prices and well-dressed punters all help Blakes keep its nose firmly in the air.
Babies and children admitted (until 6pm). Function room. Tables outdoors (patio). **Map 8/H1**

Camden Brewing Co

1 Randolph Street, NW1 (7267 9829). Camden Town tube/Camden Road rail. **Open** noon-11pm Mon-Thur, Sun; noon-midnight Fri, Sat. **Food served** noon-3pm Mon-Fri; 1-6pm Sat, Sun. **Credit** MC, V.
Despite living in the shadows of Camden's tower blocks, this is no battle-scarred boozer with safety-glass windows and big-screen football. Far from it, it's a bright and welcoming cheery bar liberally scattered with comfortable chairs and sofas, striking a balance between living-room comfort and sleek design. There's the odd naff touch, such as the faux literary drinking quotes on the tables, and the bright colour scheme has a slightly stapled-on feel, but the original fireplace and wrought-iron staircase are pleasing and the beer garden out back is a real winner in warmer months. A compact horseshoe, polished tugboat of a bar serves a decent choice of drinks including three cask ales (Wadworth's 6X and Flowers IPA, plus a regularly changing guest).
Disabled: toilet. Games (table games). Tables outdoors (garden, pavement). TV (satellite). **Map 8/J26**

Crown & Goose

100 Arlington Road, NW1 (7485 8008). Camden Town tube. **Open** 11am-11pm Mon-Sat; noon-10.30pm Sun. **Food served** noon-3pm, 6-10pm Mon-Sat; noon-9pm Sun. **Credit** MC, V.
In comparison to the coloured-alcohol tourist traps that litter the nearby High Street, this cosy, friendly pub, once a gastropub pioneer and still blessed in the kitchen department, is a treat. No sofas, cocktails, blond wood or similarly modern touches lurk to scare off local workers and Camden residents who dodge the mêlée here. Instead there are soothingly green walls, gilt-framed portraits and scuffed wooden furniture offering unfussy surrounds in which to wind down for a mixed crowd, heavy in the couples department. The small open kitchen is kept busy dishing out ambitious pub food as well as more prosaic fare such as cheeseburgers. There's Leffe and London Pride on tap, plus a reasonable wine list. It's nice to find a pub in Camden catering to grown-ups.
Babies and children admitted. Disabled: toilet. Function room. Restaurant. Tables outdoors (pavement). **Map 8/J1**

Dublin Castle

94 Parkway, NW1 (7485 1773/www.dublincastle.co.uk). Camden Town tube. **Open** 11am-1am Mon-Sat; noon-midnight Sun. **No credit cards**.
The Dub was built as one of a British Isles quartet of Castles, each catering to a different nation of navvies working on the railroads and canals. Nearby is the Edinboro (57 Mornington Crescent; good beer garden, not much else) and up in Primrose Hill there's the **Pembroke Castle** (*see p183*). The Windsor Castle has been transformed into style-bar-by-numbers NW1. Happily, the shabby old Dub hasn't changed in years, and there's no reason it should as it's still one of the best live music pubs in London, putting on three bands almost every night. The few tables out front are crammed with band members, their mates and punters, while the glitter-topped bar dishes out basic beers in plastic glasses, as well as individual bottles of Mateus Rosé. Testaments from bands that have played here – Madness and Travis – are proudly displayed, but everyone's here to try and spot who'll replace them and boast about it in years to come. And here's a nice touch – all the local bus timetables are pinned up by the door.
Babies and children admitted (daytime). Games (fruit machine). Jukebox. Music (indie/rock bands nightly; admission varies). TV. **Map 8/H1**

Enterprise

2 Haverstock Hill, NW3 (7485 2659). Chalk Farm tube. **Open** 11am-11pm Mon-Sat; noon-10.30pm Sun. **Happy hour** 11am-7.30pm Mon-Sat; noon-7.30pm Sun. **No credit cards**.
This is the place opposite the Roundhouse, the pub that most punters scurry past, put off by the garish rainbow colour scheme. Shame, because they're missing out on a fine boozer. The carnival paint masks a lovely sepia-toned inside, scuffed and worn like a pair of old brogues, and just as comfortable. It attracts the Camden indie crowds in jovial numbers for its extended happy hour, frequent drinks promos and scruffy-go-lucky atmosphere. Although nominally Irish (portraits of Joyce and Flann O'Brien, quotes from Behan), it's also the local for those using the Roundhouse – artists and punters – and so has a certain appealing theatrical loucheness. With a big range of regularly changing guest ales and music and poetry nights upstairs, those with a hankering for a sticky carpet and a touch of the raucous will love it.
Function room. Music (acoustic band 8pm Tue, Thur; £3). Spoken word (8pm Wed; £3). Tables outdoors (pavement). **Map 8/G26**

Hawley Arms

2 Castlehaven Road, NW1 (7428 5979). Camden Town tube. **Open** noon-11pm Mon-Sat; noon-10.30pm Sun. **Food served** noon-4pm, 6-9pm daily. **Credit** DC, MC, V.
Considering the mayhem of the market is just a stone's throw away, the Hawley Arms is surprisingly refined (though Saturday afternoons can get a bit manic). With big arched windows, high ceilings, walls covered with light-oak panelling and sporting a huge, brickwork open fireplace in the centre, it makes for a fine place to park a shopped-out body and reward it with a drink (Greene King IPA and Hoegaarden being the pick of the draught). Church pews and stout chairs surround the tables and there's also a tiny but useful beer garden at the back. The food's decent as well, turned out of a kitchen that's partially open to the bar area so nostrils are set twitching by the smells. A pub that does simple things well – and if that doesn't sound like praise, we should point out that it's an achievement well beyond most London boozers.
Babies and children admitted (daytime). Function room. Tables outdoors (garden patio). **Map 8/H26**

JD Young Sports Bar

2 Lidlington Place, NW1 (7387 1495). Mornington Crescent tube. **Open** 11am-11pm Mon-Sat; noon-10.30pm Sun. **Food served** noon-3pm, 5-8pm Mon-Fri; noon-4pm Sat. **Credit** MC, V.

It does what it says on the tin all right. Football flags, shirts, hats, an imitation World Cup trophy and a raised section made to look like a boxing ring are just some of the heavy-handed hints as to what this place is about. Add two giant screens at either end of the pub, a couple of pool tables, plus weekly darts competitions and this could be either heaven or hell depending on the amount of testosterone you're packing. So it's a great place for watching the footie or for a session round the baize with mates, but on the evening we last dropped by (admittedly, a rare date free of major fixtures of any kind) it also worked equally well as a venue for a quiet pint and a read of the paper – sports pages, of course.

Babies and children admitted (until 7pm). Function room. Games (darts, fruit machines, pool tables). Tables outdoors (garden). TVs (big screen, satellite). **Map 8/J2**

Lock Tavern

35 Chalk Farm Road (7482 7163). Camden Town or Chalk Farm tube. **Open** noon-11pm Mon-Sat; noon-10.30pm Sun. **Food served** noon-3pm, 5-10pm Mon-Fri; noon-5pm, 6-9pm Sat. **Credit** MC, V.

Formerly a right old dive but one with a prime spot opposite Camden market, smart money (some of it belonging to DJ Jon Carter) has reinvented the Lock into the very essence of the modern public house. They've done an excellent job of it too. It's roomy and laid-back, with polished leather banquettes, swivel armchairs and big tables facing off against a long main bar (London Pride and IPA on tap, plus the usual lagers). An open kitchen at the back serves pies, excellent roasts and assorted snacks. Upstairs is a separate and slightly more intimate bar that gives access to the lovely roof terrace, from where you can survey the fluorescent madness of the market down below. Atmosphere is stoked along by the occasional name DJ, though the much-heralded 1,000-song jukebox is no more. Expect big crowds on weekends looking for the faint whiff of celebrity, but it's well worth joining them.

Music (DJs Thur-Sun; free). Function room. Tables outdoors (roof terrace, garden). **Map 8/H26**

Lord Stanley

51 Camden Park Road, NW1 (7428 9488). Camden Town tube/Camden Road rail, then 29, 253 bus. **Open** 6-11pm Mon; noon-11pm Tue-Sat; noon-10.30pm Sun. **Food served** 7-10pm Mon; noon-3pm, 7-10pm Tue-Sun. **Credit** AmEx, DC, MC, V.

Although they live in a bit of a no man's land, residents of Camden Square must feel blessed all the same – at the top of the road they've not only got a comfortable, no-bullshit boozer, but the open kitchen at the back of the bar serves superb dishes worthy of any metropolitan restaurant – the fish and seafood are particularly outstanding. Drinkers hang around the U-shaped bar, or slump in large couches and armchairs – if the pub pets haven't bagged them first (dogs and cats are the best-treated regulars). Choice beers include Abbot Ale, Adnams Bitter and Young's Special, and there's also a generous wine selection. Diners take their cue from a blackboard menu offering a small but well-chosen selection of traditional British and global dishes. The one perplexing matter is how this truly excellent operation comes packaged in such an off-puttingly seedy exterior of stained green tiles – could it be a deliberate ploy to keep a good thing secret?

Babies and children admitted. Music (jazz 8pm Mon; free). Tables outdoors (garden, pavement).

Mac Bar

102 Camden Road, NW1 (7485 4530/www.macbar.co.uk). Camden Town tube/Camden Road rail. **Open** noon-11pm Mon-Sat; noon-10.30pm Sun. **Food served** noon-3.30pm, 6-9.30pm Mon-Fri; noon-9.30pm Sat, Sun. **Credit** MC, V.

This is a different beast from the rest of Camden's (mostly) scruffy pubs – and a far cry from the raucous Irish bar Rosie O'Grady's that used to inhabit the same spot. Staffed by some of the best cocktail makers in north London, the Mac serves up exotic combinations of booze to a loud, hip crowd artfully draped over low maroon furniture beneath high-concept photographic displays. Name your drink and the mixologists will magic it. There's also a good range of lagers (though no real ales – it's not that sort of place) and fine, if pricey, food. Given the generally dire state of the bar scene in Camden, this is a class venture well worth supporting.

Music (jazz 8.30pm Wed; DJs 8.30pm Fri, Sat; free). Games (board). Tables outdoors (pavement). **Map 8/J26**

Monarch

49 Chalk Farm Road, NW1 (7916 1049). Camden Town or Chalk Farm tube. **Open** 8pm-midnight Mon-Thur; 8pm-2am Fri, Sat. **Admission** club/gig nights £5. **No credit cards**.

Lock Tavern

North

Fading black paint, UV lighting and cider on tap – it can only be a live music pub. The Monarch has been entertaining the indie/rock crowds of Camden for years, and since the Barfly organisation started doing the gigs the quality of the acts has greatly improved. Downstairs is a functional bar that hasn't seen a paintbrush in a while, but has plenty of seats and a suitably anticipatory atmosphere as gossipy crowds get stuck into the standard range of beers and spirits before heading upstairs to the stage. It can get mighty crowded up there, so this is not a place for the timid. A cashpoint by the loos helps ensure that punters spend more than intended.
Music (DJs, bands nightly). **Map 8/H26**

Monkey Chews

2 Queen's Crescent, NW5 (7267 6406). Chalk Farm tube. **Open** 3-11pm Mon-Thur; 3pm-midnight Fri; noon-midnight Sat; noon-10.30pm Sun. **Food served** 5-11pm Mon-Fri; noon-11pm Sat; noon-10.30pm Sun. **Credit** MC, V.
Odd name, odd place. Monkey Chews' dark and sinister exterior conceals an alluringly low-lit and seedy bar. It's a wonderfully rumpled dive with hundreds of empty spirit bottles covering walls and the shelves behind the horseshoe bar, and a chromatic array of movie posters and paper lanterns adding to the DIY decor feel. It's the perfect shady setting for a Herbert Lom or Sidney Greenstreet or any fat man in a sweat-stained white suit, although in reality the crowd tends to be youngish and black clad. They tuck themselves away in screened cubbyholes or in giant red armchairs, poison of choice to hand (all cocktails are £3.50). Meanwhile, a DJ booth hints at lively weekends. Should hunger strike, there's a restaurant at the back, specialising in seafood.
Function room (seats 50). Music (DJs 9pm Thur-Sun; free). Tables outdoors (5, pavement). **Map 8/G25**

113 Bar

113 Bayham Street, NW1 (no telephone). Camden Town tube. **Open** 11am-11pm Mon-Sat; noon-10.30pm Sun. **Food served** noon-3pm, 5-10pm Mon-Fri; 5-10pm Sat, Sun. **Credit** MC, V.
Brand spanking new. Formerly the Laurel Tree, 113 still sports the old sign, but the split-level interior is now defined by cream walls, sofas, chunky tables and a bar stocked with exotic beers, displayed in one of those chiller cabinets station newsagents keep dodgy pasties in. The present owners have made the most of the huge arching windows, even if the view is only of the Bayham Street bus stands. Although this is nothing you haven't seen before, there's plenty to recommend,

North

including the comfortable atmosphere, a downstairs space that plays host to regular comedy nights and a Thai snack menu. A damn sight more convivial than anything you'll find one block over on the High Street.
Comedy (8.30pm; £10 inc food). Function room. TV (plasma screen). **Map 8/J1**

Quinn's

65 Kentish Town Road, NW1 (7267 8240). Camden Town tube. **Open/food served** 11am-midnight Mon-Wed; 11am-2am Thur-Sat; noon-10.30pm Sun. **Credit** DC, MC, V.
Now to us, Quinn's doesn't look anything like an Irish pub, but according to landlord Kevin Quinn that's because we're not Irish. Can't argue with that. We're particularly misled by the beer selection – Irish pubs traditionally serve Guinness and little else besides, but Quinn's has a 22 draught beers plus 40-odd Belgian brews by the bottle (including the marvellously named Delirium Tremens, 9% abv). The place is lovingly tended by at least two generations of Quinns (ma and pa plus sons), who indeed are Irish. It also has that very desirable late licence, offering three hours extra boozing time come the week's end. For all of these reasons, not to mention an appealing mix of punters, we make Quinn's one of the best pubs in NW1. The combination of a green carpet and orange walls is a bit of a strain on the vision, but feast your eyes on that long polished bar instead and all the wonders it holds.
Tables outdoors (garden). TV (satellite). **Map 8/J26**

North

Singapore Sling

16 Inverness Street, NW1 (7424 9527). Camden Town tube. **Open** 11am-midnight Mon, Tue-Sun; 11am-1am Wed-Sat. **Food served** noon-3pm, 5-11pm Mon-Thur; noon-3pm; 5-11.30pm Fri, noon-11pm Sat, Sun. **Happy hour** 5-7pm daily. **Credit** DC, MC, V.
Ostensibly a pan-Asian restaurant, Singapore Sling has a little secret up its sleeve – a small but perfectly formed cocktail bar up the back steps. With its dark wooden decor, exotic plants and two tables, it's a great place to sneak into for a clandestine late drink as it serves until midnight or later. You can order some of the restaurant dishes at the bar, look out at the water feature through the back window, or sample some of the cocktails on offer with the bottled beers and wines (nothing on draught). The staff are nice too – when we winced at the taste of our Chartreuse concoction, they refused to let us pay for it and replaced it with something nicer.
Babies and children admitted (restaurant). Function room (seats 40). Music (jazz 7pm Mon, Sun). Tables outdoors (2, patio; 4, pavement).

Spread Eagle

141 Albert Street, NW1 (7267 1410). Camden Town tube. **Open** 11am-11pm Mon-Sat; noon-10.30pm Sun. **Food served** noon-7.30pm Mon-Sat; noon-5pm Sun. **Credit** MC, V.
Like a tobacco-stained middle finger raised to the chain-pub domination of Camden Town, the Spread Eagle sits defiant on its handsome perch halfway down Parkway. The ornate woodwork gives it a cosiness and familiarity that can't be manufactured, and regulars sit contentedly at the public bar picking the day's winners. There's the full range of Young's ales and a surprisingly long wine list too, but this is a pints and whisky pub at heart. Striped wallpaper and sporting prints adorn the walls and, if it weren't for the traffic outside, you could be forgiven for thinking you were in a small country village. An excellent place for a pre-dinner drink – many of Camden's best restaurants are just a few doors away.
Games (board games). Tables outdoors (pavement). TV (satellite). **Map 8/H1**

World's End

174 Camden High Street, NW1 (7482 1932). Camden Town tube. **Open** 11am-11pm Mon-Sat; noon-10.30pm Sun. **Food served** 11am-3pm, 6.30-10.30pm Mon-Fri; 6.30-10.30pm Sat, Sun. **No credit cards**.
Tip, if new to Camden: never arrange to meet anybody in 'the pub by the station', 'cos this is it and it's one busy boozer, supposedly shifting more pints – more than a million a year – than any other in the country. There's a head-down-and-booze section at the front, which leads to the cavernous tramshed of the main bar, followed by another separate section above the bar, while yet more tables are crammed into a step-down annexe off to one side. Lost yet? You soon will be. Around the edges, high tables and stools hide the imitation Camden shopfronts painted on the walls and offer good views of the tide of humanity that sweeps in and out, all looking for their mates, their date, their wallet, your wallet, their dealer, their mother… Things get even more crowded when there's a gig on at the Underworld downstairs. It's not everyone's pint of snakebite by any means, but there's more energy in here than a thousand chain pubs could ever hope for.
Games (fruit machines). Music (in club: bands most nights 7-11pm; admission varies). TV (big screen, satellite). **Map 8/J1**

Also in the area...

Bar Risa 11 East Yard, Camden Lock, NW1 (7428 5929).
Belgo Noord 72 Chalk Farm Road, NW1 (7267 0718).
Camden Tup 2-3 Greenland Place, NW1 (7482 0399).
Edward's 1 Camden High Street, NW1 (7387 2749).
Hog's Head 55 Parkway, NW1 (72841675).
Man in the Moon (JD Wetherspoon) 40-2 Chalk Farm Road, NW1 (7482 2054).

Crouch End

There are two things you can't move for in Crouch End: cafe-bars and cxelebs. With both, the quality is variable. People have been known to move to Crouch End just to be near **Banners**. Relative newcomers **Bar Rocca** and the eyesore that is **Ice** draw their younger clientele from further afield, while for a good solid local try the **Harringay Arms**.

Banners

21 Park Road, N8 (8348 2930). Finsbury Park tube/rail/ Crouch Hill rail. **Open/food served** 9am-11.30pm Mon-Thur; 9am-midnight Fri; 10am-midnight Sat; 10am-11pm Sun. **Credit** MC, V.
This lively, friendly bar and restaurant is one of Crouch End's best loved. Stripped floorboards and a large, dark wood bar give a distinctly pub-like feel, while colourful paintwork, a Cuban flag and global music add a bit of boho chic. The clientele is an equally mixed bunch. Rarely short of packed – even on a weekday afternoon – Banners is as likely to play host to a sprawling family group as a gang of local trendies and can, especially in the afternoon, resemble a parenting club. A tempting menu roams widely, from Jamaican jerk chicken to a cracking English breakfast. Likewise, the drink selection is refreshingly international. Bottled beers include Mexican, Caribbean, Cuban and Belgian, and there's also a reasonable wine list and a fine selection of rum. A jack of all trades perhaps, but Banners also comes close to mastering most. A new branch in Archway points to the beginnings of a minichain.
Babies and children admitted (crayons, high chairs, toys). Music (world music). TV (satellite).

Bar Rocca

159A Tottenham Lane, N8 (8340 0101). Hornsey rail. **Open** 5pm-1am Mon-Thur; 5pm-2am Fri; noon-2am Sat; noon-midnight Sun. **Food served** 5-10pm Mon-Fri; noon-10pm Sat, Sun. **Credit** MC, V.

The attractive Victorian chapel that was once home to Hornsey Snooker Club now houses a spacious tapas and salsa joint. Its single, high-ceilinged hall easily accommodates a long bar to the right, a narrow raised seating area to the left and a broad expanse of polished laminate flooring in between. The decor is anodyne – lots of blond wood accessorised with chrome and arty prints – but the atmosphere's generally friendly and relaxed. Come Friday or Saturday night and it all gets a bit raucous with loud dance music and R&B whipping up a crowd to the point of being intimidating. A sign at the door reads 'no trainers, no baseball caps, no sportswear' but also the oddly ambiguous 'mixed couples only'. Eh?

Babies and children admitted (daytime). Disabled: toilet. Music (acoustic 9pm Thur. DJ 9pm Fri, Sat; free. Salsa 7.30pm Wed; £6).

Harringay Arms

153 Crouch Hill, N8 (8340 4243). Finsbury Park tube/rail, then W3, W7 bus/Crouch Hill rail. **Open** noon-11pm Mon-Sat; noon-10.30pm Sun. **Food served** noon-3.30pm daily. **No credit cards.**

The Harringay first entered the rates book in October 1851, and was described there as a 'beer shop'. Its present look dates from around a century after that – the smooth laminate wood panelling is straight out of a 1950s working men's club. The character of decor is matched by the character displayed at its tables, roosts for a bunch of grizzled locals who look as though they've been in place since the panelling was fitted. These days there's also an increasing number of trendy media types finding their way here. Despite this odd mix, the atmosphere is consistently convivial and very conducive to transforming a quiet pint into the launch of a good session.

Games (fruit machine). No piped music or jukebox. Quiz (9pm Tue; £1). Tables outdoors (garden). TV.

Ice

18-20 Park Road, N8 (8341 3280). Crouch Hill or Hornsey rail. **Open/food served** 5-11pm Mon-Sat; 5-10.30pm Sun. **Happy hour** 5-8pm daily. **Credit** AmEx, MC, V.

Heading down from the clock tower you'll hear Ice before you see it, as loud house wafts out of the open doors. Inside, the decor's minimal with an industrial edge – the floors are bare concrete while uniform grey walls are punctuated by odd lengths of exposed pipe and hazy neon light. Stylish, yes, but also very predictable. The sleek, modern furniture is attractive but not particularly comfortable. But that doesn't really matter because Ice is not a venue made for slouching and chat. The music is prohibitively loud for conversation and the contact here is all of the eye variety as punters nonchalantly check each other out. Hit and miss during the week, Ice hums come the weekends, pulling in crowds with DJs spinning rare groove and funky soul classics. It makes for a reasonable pre-club bar – but Crouch End's got no clubs.

Bar available for hire (Mon-Thur). Music (DJs 8pm Fri-Sat; free).

King's Head

2 Crouch End Hill, N8 (8340 1028). Finsbury Park tube/rail/Crouch Hill rail. **Open** *Ground-floor bar* noon-midnight Mon-Thur; noon-1am Fri, Sat; noon-10.30pm Sun. *Cellar bar/comedy club* 8pm-midnight Mon-Thur; 8pm-1am Fri, Sat; 7.45-10.30pm Sun. **Food served** noon-8pm Mon-Sat; noon-4pm Sun. **Credit** MC, V.

The bar looks very much the same as a hundred other town centre pubs: an interior of faux Victoriana, deep pile carpets and a brightly lit bar with an unremarkable beer selection. What draws most people here, however, is the basement. It's small (too small) and it's smoky, but it's also home to the hugely popular King's Head Comedy Club every Saturday night, which features anything from established acts such as Ed Byrne to up-and-coming talent and open-mic stand-up. Other nights see more comedy acts, plus jazz, soul and salsa, dance classes, record fairs, poetry sessions and other community bonding enterprises.

Comedy (8pm Thur, Sat, Sun; £5-£7). Function room (daytime only). Games (fruit machines, pool). Music (bands 8pm Tue, Fri; £3-£6. Jazz noon-5pm Sun; £3). Salsa club (7.30pm-midnight Mon; £5). TV (satellite).

Also in the area...

All Bar One 2-4 The Broadway, N8 (8342 7871).
Tollgate (JD Wetherspoon) 26-30 Turnpike Lane, N8 (8889 9085).

Finsbury Park & Stroud Green

Most of the pubs in the area have been revamped in the last few years, but as they've invariably all followed fashion by stripping down to hard seats and bare floorboards, they're pleasant but nothing special. For a more unusual and certainly more lively drinking experience, there's a clutch of rough and ready Irish boozers that still manage to cling on in the area around Finsbury Park station.

Old Dairy

1-3 Crouch Hill, N4 (7263 3337). Finsbury Park tube/rail/ Crouch Hill rail. **Open** noon-11pm Mon-Sat; noon-10.30pm Sun. **Food served** noon-9.30pm Mon-Sat; noon-5pm Sun. **Credit** AmEx, MC, V.

This cafe-bar north of Finsbury Park certainly makes the most of the building's prior history – the decoration contains more references to dairy products than you'd find in the Delia Smith Bumper Book of Cheesy Milky Goodies. The preservation of

Critics' choice
beer gardens

Black Lion (p152)
A courtyard beside a converted Plaistow coaching inn.

Canonbury Tavern (p171)
A grassy Islington paddock fit for a gymkhana.

Drayton Court (p233)
Arguably the best pub garden in west London.

Duke of Edinburgh (p205)
Hugely popular beer garden beloved by Brixton's young trendies.

Freemasons Arms (p166)
A fine location by Hampstead Heath with a massive garden.

original architectural features such as the exterior murals depicting heroic scenes from the milk industry (squeeze that teat!) and the glazed wall tiles of the former shop certainly provide for a unique atmosphere. And with a gallery/restaurant serving food that bit classier than the usual pub grub, this is more than just a straight boozer. On the other hand, if it's a straight boozer you want, head for the central room where you'll find a big screen and Young's, Adnams and HSB on tap.
Babies and children admitted (until 6pm). Disabled: toilet. Function rooms. Games (golf machines). Music (DJ 9pm Fri; free). No-smoking areas. Quiz (9pm Tue, Thur; £1). Restaurant. TVs (big screen, satellite).

Triangle

1 Ferme Park Road, N4 (8292 0516). Finsbury Park tube/rail then W3 bus/Crouch Hill rail. **Open/food served** 6pm-midnight Tue-Fri; 11am-midnight Sat, Sun. **Credit** MC, V.

North Africa's long been a destination du jour with the design crowd, but it's debatable whether style fascists on a budget would settle for a visit to Triangle's hippie drop-out warren of pot plants, screens and multicoloured lamps. With its bright walls and Middle Eastern soundtrack it's a fun place to perch at the small bar and swig a bottle of lager or sip a cocktail from a list of standard recipes. That said, Triangle really operates as more of a restaurant than a bar and most punters are sufficiently encouraged by their surroundings to scoff something from the short but good value menu. Outside is a conservatory garden, for those summer days when this corner of N4 seems not that far from Marrakech at all.
Babies and children admitted (high chairs, nappy-changing facilities). Disabled: toilet. No-smoking area. Music (jazz 7pm Sun). Tables outdoors (garden, pavement).

North

World's End

21-3 Stroud Green Road, N4 (7281 8679). Finsbury Park tube/rail. **Open** noon-midnight daily. **Food served** noon-9pm daily. **Credit** MC, V.

The World's End may have recently been tarted up by the Barracuda pub chain, but this old favourite, slapped next to a bus station, still attracts an eclectic mix of suits, pensioners and musos. The refit has the standard features of stripped floorboards and leather sofas, but the designers must have been bored by the time they got to lighting – every type of illumination is here from art nouveau extravaganzas to IKEA spots. Music fans come to hear bands in the back room, which resembles a small, but well-equipped village hall. When no one's on stage, the lights are dimmed, the big screen is lowered and the World's End worships at the altar of Arsenal FC.
Games (board games, fruit machine, pinball, pool table, quiz machine, video games). Music (DJ 8pm Fri; bands 9.30pm Sat; free). Tables outdoors (pavement). TVs (big screen, digital, satellite).

Also in the area...

White Lion of Mortimer (JD Wetherspoon)
125 Stroud Green Road, N4 (7561 8880).

Hampstead

Grand old Hampstead, pretty as a picture with its rural, rambling heath, leafy lanes and tall, expensive houses. It's an ale drinker's dream. The bar culture that is so prevalant in the rest of London has not yet infiltrated this old-moneyed manor, so instead come and enjoy the most marvellous selection of beautiful, historic and genuinely welcoming taverns.

Bar Room Bar

48 Rosslyn Hill, NW3 (7435 0808). Hampstead tube/Hampstead Heath rail. **Open** 11am-11pm Mon-Sat; noon-10.30pm Sun. **Food served** noon-10.30pm Mon-Sat; noon-10pm Sun. **Credit** MC, V.

At the foot of Hampstead's main drag is one of the few chain bars in the village, and the funny thing is, it provides a real breath of fresh air. Walk by on any given night and the scene behind the big picture window is like one of those cool bars in the Southern Comfort ads – a crush of fuckable people, limbs waving, heads snuggling, teeth shining, hips swaying, eyes gleaming. Come in, come in, come in, it all says. Wow. And we do. This is bright and airy enough to make for a decent cafe during the day, before shifting up a few gears for the evening. That's when the crowd assembles, foregoing the edging of tables and chairs for a prime spot up among the chitchat at the central island bar. Drinks are lifestyle accessories like designer beers and cocktails. Successful pairings can transfer to the attractive little covered courtyard out back.
Babies and children admitted (until 7pm). Music (DJs Fri, Sat; free). Tables outdoors (garden).

Flask

14 Flask Walk, NW3 (7435 4580). Hampstead tube. **Open** 11am-11pm Mon-Sat; noon-10.30pm Sun. **Food served** noon-3pm Mon; noon-3pm, 6-8.30pm Tue-Sat; noon-4pm Sun. **Credit** MC, V.

In contrast to the restyled upmarket establishment of the same name in nearby Highgate (*see p168*), this Flask is a largely unreconstructed village boozer. Of its two rooms, the public bar has been least tampered with; the saloon boasts some horrible wallpaper and a tasteless oak screen, but it's still an attractive place, and is unsurprisingly popular with the local over-50s. The bar line-up includes a choice of Young's cask ales as well as around 17 wines. Standard pub grub is served in a conservatory at the rear, while the atmosphere created by the well-worn furnishings admirably suits the main event: steady drinking.
Babies and children admitted (until 7pm). Disabled: toilet. Function room (conservatory). Games (fruit machine, quiz machine). No piped music or jukebox. Restaurant. Tables outdoors (pavement, terrace). TV (big screen, satellite).

Freemasons Arms

32 Downshire Hill, NW3 (7433 6811). Belsize Park or Hampstead tube/Hampstead Heath rail. **Open** noon-11pm Mon-Sat; noon-10.30pm Sun. **Food served** noon-10pm Mon-Sat; noon-9.30pm Sun. **Credit** MC, V.

A huge 1930s mock-Victorian pub, situated on one of the loveliest residential streets in London. It's also ideally placed for the heath. The interior strikes a bit of a bum note – tiled floor, curtained windows, dressers laden with crockery: all very happy Harvester – but that's more than made up for by a very large garden. It's a popular lunch/dinner place with an extensive and eclectic menu. At the bar are 17 wines available by the glass, Tetley's and Bass bitter, and Hoegaarden. Unfortunately, the pub's famous skittle alley was out of action when we visited due to an unexpected spot of flooding; the owners hope to get it back in action before the end of the year.
Babies and children admitted (dining area and garden). Disabled: toilet. Games (fruit machine). No-smoking area. Tables outdoors (garden, patio).

Holly Bush

22 Holly Mount, NW3 (7435 2892). Hampstead tube/Hampstead Heath rail. **Open** noon-11pm Mon-Sat; noon-10.30pm Sun. **Food served** 6.30-10pm Mon; 12.30-4pm, 6.30-10pm Tue-Sun. **Credit** MC, V.

Before it became a pub, the Holly Bush building was a stable block belonging to painter George Romney, who fled to the wilds of Hampstead in 1796 to escape from his obsession with Lady Hamilton (of Nelson fame). It's been a boozer since the mid-19th century, as much loved for its secluded position on top of the hill as for its antique interior. Surprisingly spacious, its four wood-panelled rooms are cosy in winter (there's a real coal fire in one and snug alcove in another) although seats at tables can often be at a premium. As befits such a destination, the beers are notably well drawn (including Adnams Broadside and Old Speckled Hen on our visit) and there's an excellent wine list. Food is hearty and a cut above the norm with a decent selection of pies and four different sausages to accompany cheddar mash, onions and gravy. Yum.
Babies and children admitted. Benches outdoors (pavement). Function room. No piped music or jukebox.

Magdala

2A South Hill Park, NW3 (7435 2503). Hampstead Heath rail/24, 168 bus. **Open** 11am-11pm Mon-Sat; noon-10.30pm Sun. **Food served** noon-2.30pm, 6-10pm Mon-Fri; noon-10pm Sat; noon-9.30pm Sun. **Credit** MC, V.
Like Whitechapel's **Blind Beggar** (*see p156*) and the **Plumbers Arms** (*see p104*) in Westminsterthe Magdala is more famed for its ghoulish past than its healthy present. Ruth Ellis shot her lover here back in 1955, earning her the notoriety of becoming the last woman to be hanged in Britain. The pub frontage still displays the bullet holes. Inside is split into two strikingly different rooms; the larger is bright and cheerful, and kitted out for diners with plenty of pine tables and chairs, potted plants, candles and framed prints. The kitchen has quite a good rep. The back bar has been allowed to retain more of its original character and has been preserved as a quieter, darker, more traditional, drinking hole. A framed newspaper clipping maintains a link to the murder.
Babies and children admitted. Function room. Restaurant. Tables outdoors (patio).

Ye Olde White Bear

New End, NW3 (7435 3758). Hampstead tube. **Open** 11am-11pm Mon-Sat; noon-10.30pm Sun. **Food served** noon-9.30pm daily. **Credit** MC, V.
Like many of Hampstead's drinking establishments, this one is also set back off the main thoroughfare, in a picturesque spot at the bottom of New End. A pretty, white-shuttered house, festooned with flowers in the summer, it has a cosy appeal inside on chilly winter days. There's a homely feel to the place with its wooden surround fireplace and dark green walls strewn with prints, plates and even a fine pair of antelope antlers. The overriding impression is friendly, and it is obviously a favourite with locals from across the age ranges including families at weekends. Food is straightforward, served in the bar and has a good reputation.
Quiz (9pm Thur; £1). Tables outdoors (courtyard, pavement). TV (satellite).

Spaniards Inn

Spaniards Road, NW3 (8731 6571). Hampstead tube/ 210 bus. **Open** 11am-11pm Mon-Sat; noon-10.30pm Sun. **Food served** noon-9pm daily. **Credit** MC, V.
In an area in which every pub lays claim to some historical significance, it takes an extraordinary pedigree to secure the crown of NW3's most famous inn. Step forward the Spaniards. In its time home to the Spanish ambassador to the court of James I, rumoured birthplace of Dick Turpin and certainly one of his later hangouts (Black Bess was stabled in the tollhouse opposite), a stopover for Byron, Lamb and Joshua Reynolds and an inspiration to Bram Stoker, Dickens and Keats (a pint in the pretty, light-festooned beer garden started the latter on his 'Ode to a Nightingale'). The pub's been cashing in on its history for some time. Beer prices match those of the West End. Even so, with its unpretentious low-ceilinged woodiness and resistance to the obvious temptations to theme, the place remains a refreshing spot close to Kenwood. In summer its garden draws substantial crowds.
Babies and children admitted. Function room. Games (board games, fruit machine). No piped music or jukebox. Tables outdoors (garden).

toast

First floor, 50 Hampstead High Street, NW3 (7431 2244). Hampstead tube. **Open/food served** 6pm-midnight Mon-Fri; 11am-midnight Sat, Sun. **Credit** AmEx, MC, V.
Blink and you'll miss it, as you walk past the discreet doorway that leads to this glamorous and unlikely find directly above Hampstead tube. Popular with a young well-off local set, attracted by an imaginative cocktail list (including a Sake-Tine made with chilled citroen sake) and a tempting eclectic brasserie style menu, toast (far too cool for capitals) feels more like a venue from the West End that has just popped up the Northern line for the evening. It's sleek and sophisticated, with subdued, ambient lighting, mirrors, creamy walls and high-backed, upholstered seating. Tables are attended by glam waiting staff, although they seem to be more for show than service. Sit at the bar and save yourself the 12.5%.
Babies and children admitted (high chairs). Music (DJs 10pm Mon, Fri; free).

Wells Tavern

30 Well Walk, NW3 (no phone). Hampstead tube/ Hampstead Heath rail. **Open** 11am-11pm Mon-Sat; noon-10.30pm Sun. **Food served** noon-3pm daily. **Credit** MC, V.
Sitting on an imposing corner site halfway down the hill, the Wells was built in 1837 – on a site at which John Keats once lodged but countless refits later it has lost all of its original features and become a straightforward, no-nonsense local, with a fittingly loud carpet and ceiling. These days, entertainment is provided by the fruit machine, dartboard and there's even an old joanna for that impromptu singalong, making NW3's East End diaspora very happy indeed. Footie fans are also well catered to, particularly Arsenal supporters as the Wells shows all their matches. A great summer destination due to its location near the heath and outdoor seats that are quickly bagged when the sun's got his hat on.
Babies and children admitted (daytime). Games (darts, fruit machine, quiz machine). Music (acoustic band 8pm Thur; free). Quiz (9pm Mon). Tables outdoors (garden, terrace). TV (big screen, satellite).

White Horse

153-4 Fleet Road, NW3 (7485 2112). Belsize Park tube. **Open** 11am-11pm Mon-Sat; noon-10.30pm Sun. **Food served** noon-9pm daily. **Credit** AmEx, MC, V.
An old Victorian pub-cum-lively-bar, set on a busy triangular site just down the road from the Royal Free, and therefore a popular hangout for its doctors and nurses. A big TV screen, loud piped music, flashing fruit and game machines, daily 2-4-1 promos and a dazzling array of multicoloured drinks and shots appeal to a youthful crowd. A choice of three ales and a smaller, screened area with an original fireplace, a bookshelf, comfy seats and daily papers act as a concession to oldies. The only way to look when quaffing at the bar is up, as the pub boasts a remarkable painted tile coffered ceiling and some intriguing giant red bell lampshades.
Comedy (8pm Sat; £7). Function room. Games (fruit machines, golf machine, quiz machine). No-smoking area (noon-5pm only). Tables outdoors (yard). TV (big screen, digital, satellite).

Also in the area...

Babushka 58-62 Heath Street, NW3 (7431 0399).
Three Horseshoes (JD Wetherspoon) 28 Heath Street, NW3 (7431 7206).

Highgate

Distant Highgate is one of the few places in London that fully deserves its 'village' title. There's a real community feel here, and subsequently dozy old boozers of gossipy locals are the predominant strain of pub life (cf the **Flask**). Which makes new arrival the **Boogaloo**, a rock 'n' roll jukejoint of Deep South persuasion, an all the more surprising and welcome addition to the area. As the man said, there's gonna be a whole lotta shakin' goin' on. Can Highgate cope?

Boogaloo

312 Archway Road, N6 (8340 2928). Highgate tube. **Open** noon-11pm Mon-Sat; noon-10.30pm Sun. **Food served** noon-3pm, 5-9pm Mon-Fri; noon-7pm Sat, Sun. **Credit** MC, V.

Run by the same people that used to have **Filthy McNasty's** (*see p173*), Boogaloo is an ace new bar on the Archway Road just down from Highgate tube. The star attraction is one that it is refreshing to see brought out of near retirement – the jukebox. It contains only classic tracks that are at least ten years old, and each month a celeb muso gets to do some reprogramming. As for the bar itself, it's decked out something like a Deep South jukejoint. Music is the dominant theme, from the old piano in the corner (more than just decoration) to the oil painting of Elvis draped in a Confederate flag with the motto 'the South will rise again'. The one drawback is an unspectacular range of beer and wine but the tapas-munching clientele is very laid-back and, judging by the amount of people that were in the place on the Monday evening we visited, it's already a welcome addition to the area. Visit on Tuesday for the 'Who Shot Bambi?' pop quiz.

Jukebox. Music (band 5.30-8.30pm Sun; free). Quiz (music only, 8.30pm Tue; £1). Tables outdoors (garden).

Flask

77 Highgate West Hill, N6 (8348 7346). Archway or Highgate tube/143, 210, 214, 271 bus. **Open** *Apr-Oct* 11am-11pm Mon-Sat; noon-10.30pm Sun. *Nov-Mar* noon-11pm Mon-Fri; 11am-11pm Sat; noon-10.30pm Sun. **Food served** noon-3pm, 6-10pm Mon-Fri; noon-10pm Sat; noon-4pm, 6-9.30pm Sun. **Credit** MC, V.

The Flask certainly packs them in, particularly since its latest refurbishment, which has added some comfy leather sofas and relaxing banquettes to the furniture inventory. Dating back to 1663, it's set in a fine brick building opposite a small green in the heart of Highgate. A seat in the spacious front yard – heated in winter – transports you to the depths of rural England, while inside, the warren of convivial low-ceilinged rooms and timbered corners retains plenty of charm. Beer lovers are spoilt for choice by a range of bottled Belgian and US brews, and a wide choice of continental lagers and British ales on tap. Wine lovers don't do too badly either. Nineteen wines are on the blackboard including ten by the glass. The recently expanded kitchen serves modern eclectic food.

Babies and children admitted. Function room. Tables outdoors (garden).

Also in the area...

Gatehouse (JD Wetherspoon) 1 North Road, N6 (8340 8054).

Holloway

In the past drinking on the Holloway Road was all right, if you wanted a fight. But with half the watering holes taken over by chains (even the Nag's Head is now an O'Neills) and the other half gentrified, they've calmed down considerably. Away from the main thoroughfare, rising house prices ensure that the chardonnay flows as freely as the Guinness. For those who prefer their pints with added excitement, a few of the old-school boozers remain, mainly clustered just south of the Archway roundabout.

Coronet

338-46 Holloway Road, N7 (7609 5014). Holloway Road tube. **Open** 10am-11pm Mon-Sat; noon-10.30pm Sun. **Food served** 10am-10pm Mon-Sat; noon-9.30pm Sun. **Credit** AmEx, DC, MC, V.

Just as in its heyday as a cinema in the 1930s, the whole of Holloway seems to have walked through the Coronet's handsome art deco doors. From the gaggles of students, to the lone white-haired drunk, they're all here, and despite the fine range of real ales on offer, they're all drinking Guinness. Bravely, Wetherspoon (*see p15*) has kept the cavernous space of the main auditorium, but what it loses in intimacy, it gains in convenience: there's space for literally hundreds of seats, so it's not hard to find an empty one. One inevitable decision was to decorate the interior with silver screen memorabilia, but in the end it's the eclectic mix of customers, rather than Hollywood glamour shots that engenders nostalgia for the golden age of cinema-going.

Disabled: lift, toilet. Games (fruit machines). No piped music or jukebox. No-smoking area. Specialities: guest real ales. Tables outdoors (patio).

Landseer

37 Landseer Road, N19 (7263 4658). Archway tube/43, 217 bus. **Open** 5-11pm Mon-Fri; noon-11pm Sat; noon-10.30pm Sun. **Food served** 6-10pm Mon-Thur; 6-10.30pm Fri; 12.30-4.30pm, 6-10.30pm Sat; 1-5pm, 6-9.30pm Sun. **Credit** MC, V.

The Landseer may stick to a tried and tested gastropub recipe – a light stripped-out room filled with church furniture, olives and pistachios on the tables and Coldplay on the stereo – but it follows the formula so expertly it's hard to quibble. The short menu with dishes such as French shepherd's pie has a Gallic rustic slant and the plates arrive stacked, steaming and smelling delicious. The hand pumped Pedigree retained a pleasingly hoppy bite and there are more than 15 wines to choose from, most of them sold by the glass. So it's no wonder there are more than a few dressed-down professionals flicking through the Landseer's extensive collection of Q magazines while waiting for their mobile phones to vibrate. Excellent, but it still seems rather odd for Holloway.

Babies and children admitted. Function room. Games (board games, quiz machine). Tables outdoors (pavement). TV (big screen, digital).

Swimmer at the Grafton Arms

13 Eburne Road, N7 (7281 4632). Holloway Road tube/ Finsbury Park tube/rail. **Open** 5-11pm Mon-Thur; noon-11pm Fri, Sat; noon-10.30pm Sun. **Food served** 6-9.20pm Mon-Sat; noon-2.20pm Fri, Sat; noon-4pm Sun. **Credit** MC, V.

Residents of the elegant enclave surrounding the Grafton Arms may well object to another good review, for not only is their local a top boozer, it's also a pretty thin, already packed, top boozer. It's not difficult to understand its popularity – the

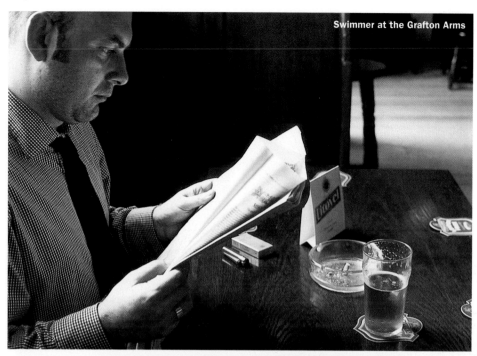

Swimmer at the Grafton Arms

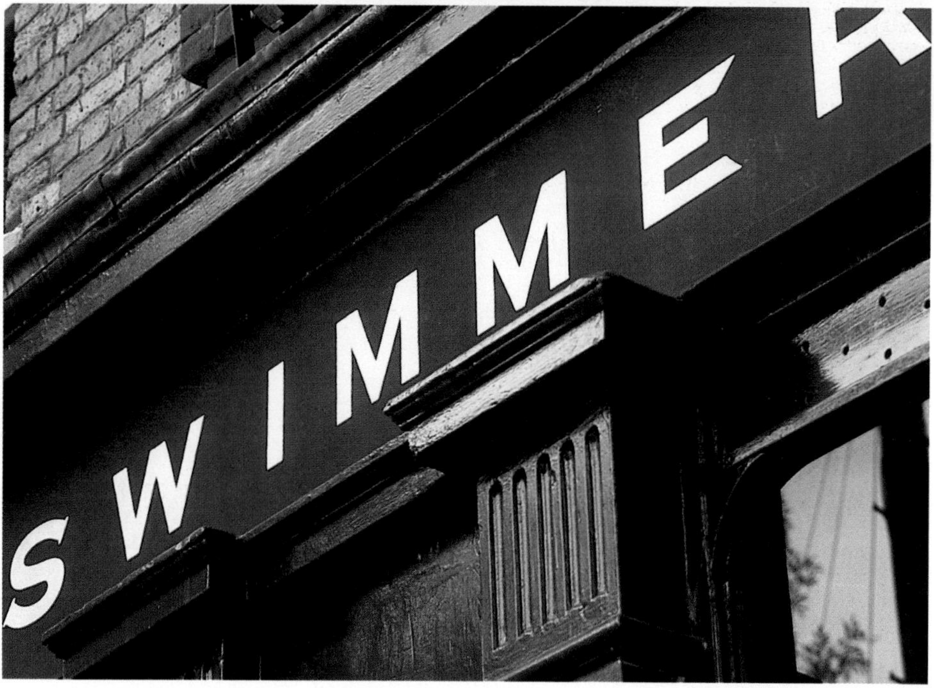

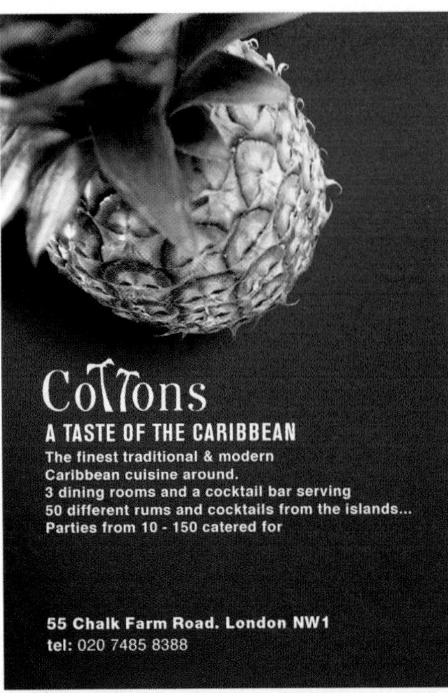
Cottons
A TASTE OF THE CARIBBEAN
The finest traditional & modern
Caribbean cuisine around.
3 dining rooms and a cocktail bar serving
50 different rums and cocktails from the islands...
Parties from 10 - 150 catered for
55 Chalk Farm Road. London NW1
tel: 020 7485 8388

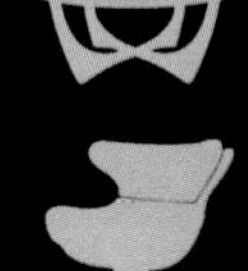

THE HARRINGAY ARMS
A good old fashioned pub where
conversation is the key to entertainment!
Opening times
Mon - Sat: 12.noon to 11pm
Sunday: 12 noon to 10.30pm
THE HARRINGAY ARMS
153 Crouch Hill, Crouch End, N8 9QH
Tel: 020 8340 4243

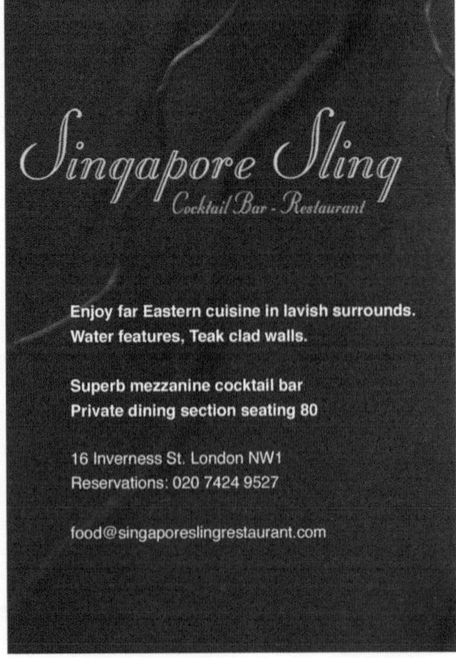
Singapore Sling
Cocktail Bar - Restaurant
Enjoy far Eastern cuisine in lavish surrounds.
Water features, Teak clad walls.
Superb mezzanine cocktail bar
Private dining section seating 80
16 Inverness St. London NW1
Reservations: 020 7424 9527
food@singaporeslingrestaurant.com

open kitchen serving warm salads and superior grills visually complements the well-preserved Victorian interior, there's a beer garden out the front, and the pub quiz isn't exactly *University Challenge* (although we still fared miserably). Couple all this with a wine list running to 20 bottles, most of which are sold by the glass, plus a bar serving a selection of Litovel quality Czech lagers and Ridleys excellent hand-pumped ales and there's only one conclusion to be drawn: the Swimmer's a winner.
Disabled: toilet. Quiz (9pm Mon; £2). Music (9pm, 1st Sat of mth). No-smoking tables (during meals). Tables outdoors (7, patio). TV.

Also in the area...

O'Neill's 456 Holloway Road, N7 (7700 8941).

Islington

There's more to the Islington bar scene than focaccia and Beaujolais. True, gastropubs are spreading through N1 like a particularly virulent rash. And admittedly, the relentlessly middlebrow chain pubs that line Upper Street are rather dispiriting. But venture away from that well-trodden thoroughfare and Islington has tons going for it. This is probably the late licence capital of London, while clubby types have a thoroughly credible selection of DJ bars to choose from. Add to this a smattering of good old-fashioned working men's boozers, four theatre pubs, a few terrific beer gardens, and – of course – all that posh nosh, and you can appreciate that Islingtonians have good cause to be so bloody smug.

Albion

10 Thornhill Road, N1 (7607 7450/www.thealbion.co.uk). Angel tube/Highbury & Islington tube/rail. **Open/food served** 11am-11pm Mon-Sat; noon-10.30pm Sun. **Credit** AmEx, DC, MC, V.
Although just a few minutes' walk from the madding crowd of Upper Street, the Albion belongs to another world altogether. It's an ivy-covered former Georgian coaching inn and a throwback to the country pub of yore, with busy floral carpets, hunting prints and cosy nooks and crannies. A true neighbourhood local, the pub is filled with all walks of life, from well-heeled new Islingtonians to craggy old-timers waxing nostalgic for the area's pre-ciabatta glory days. Not that there's much yuppie food on the menu here: it's stodgy fare, with a few Mediterranean specials to please more sophisticated types, who also can choose New World and European wines by the glass or bottle. There's London Pride for the rest of us. The pub's biggest asset is a gloriously quaint beer garden, which is one of the prettiest in north London.
Babies and children admitted (weekends). Disabled: toilet. Games (fruit machine, table games). No-smoking area. Tables outdoors (patio, garden). TV. **Map 9/N1**

The Angelic

57 Liverpool Road, N1 (7278 8433). Angel tube. **Open** noon-11pm Mon-Sat; noon-10.30pm Sun. **Food served** noon-10pm Mon-Sat; noon-9.30pm Sun. **Credit** MC, V.
The Angelic is one of Islington's more cultured gastropubs. The dining experience is raised by decor loaded with neoclassical references – marble busts, mosaics and Corinthian pillars – as well as lavish floral displays. Food, from roast guinea fowl to portobello mushroom burgers, is top notch and arrives in generous portions. Healthy types have a full selection of freshly squeezed fruit juices and smoothies to choose from. During the week, the place is positively romantic, with its candlelight, crimson walls and brown leather couches (make a note in your diary for 14 Feb). The tranquillity is shattered at the weekend, when half of young Islington descends to drink swish cocktails and pints of Guinness, and then relieve themselves in toilets prettified with Greek god statues, ornamental wishing well and a talking book reading of James Joyce.
Babies and children admitted (until 6pm). Disabled: toilet. Function room. TV (satellite). **Map 9/N2**

The Bull

100 Upper Street, N1 (7354 9174). Angel tube. **Open** noon-11pm Mon-Sat; noon-10.30pm Sun. **Food served** 6-10pm Mon; noon-3pm, 6-10pm Tue-Thur; noon-7pm Fri-Sun. **Credit** AmEx, MC, V.
The Bull's another in a seemingly endless string of tasteful gastropubs to open in Islington. The decor is familiar: crimson and taupe walls, wooden floors and those preposterous steel air ducts meant to lend yuppie bars a hint of industrial chic. Draught beers include Witches Brew, London Pride, Leffe and Hoegaarden. Should you order a glass of wine, attentive bar staff will quiz you on exactly what vintage and vineyard you require. A wrought-iron staircase leads to a first-floor lounge, where couples whisper sweet nothings on squidgy beige sofas. All very nice, but there's nothing at all original or distinguished about it; the avant-garde chandelier and B&Ws of skinheads are lame attempts to add a bit of edge. Still, the pub does what it's supposed to, and is particularly pleasant in summer, when the full-length windows are opened to the street lending the place a breezy, cheery feel.
Disabled: toilet. Games (arcade machine). **Map 9/O1**

Camden Head

2 Camden Walk, N1 (7359 0851). Angel tube. **Open** 11am-11pm Mon-Sat; noon-10.30pm Sun. **Food served** 11am-9pm Mon-Sat; noon-9pm Sun. **Credit** AmEx, DC, MC, V.
Period pubbery doesn't get much better than this. Looming grandly over the Camden Passage antiques market (held Wednesdays and Saturdays), this opulent Victorian pile has been around since 1899 and, thanks to a painstaking restoration in the 1960s, retains many original features, including a ridiculously ornate island bar, lots of gorgeous acid-etched glass and wonderful Edwardian lamps. The red velvet drapes, floral carpets and patterned wallpaper are deliciously gaudy. By contrast, the punters are 'north London bloke' writ large: market traders, builders and errant hubbies knocking back real ales – Charles Wells Bombardier and Courage Directors – to a 'Now That's What I Call Sixties' soundtrack. In the evenings, a more studenty crowd takes over.
Comedy club (8.30pm Thur-Sat and every other Mon; £3-£5). Function room. Games (fruit machines, quiz machines). Jukebox. Tables outdoors (terrace). **Map 9/O2**

Canonbury Tavern

21 Canonbury Place, N1 (7288 9881). Highbury & Islington tube/rail. **Open** noon-11pm Mon-Sat; noon-10.30pm Sun. **Food served** noon-3pm, 6-9pm Mon-Fri; noon-4pm, 6-9pm Sat; noon-6pm Sun. **Credit** MC, V.
On some levels, the Canonbury Tavern is the meat and potatoes of Islington pubs: a back-to-basics local, with no gimmicky themes or style mag delusions, where you can slob out with a pint and a fag with nary a poseur in sight. It has simple, stripped-down decor: wooden floors, red and green walls, and a pool table in the corner. There's a studenty atmosphere and a soundtrack to match: the Strokes, Radiohead, New Order. The draught selection is small but well chosen, including Adnams Bitter and Timothy Taylor's Landlord. But the Canonbury stands out from the crowd by dint of its staggering selection of bottled beer, which hails from Belgium

(Duvel, Liefmans, Chimay red), America (Anchor Steam, Anchor Liberty) and Germany (Beck's, Schneider Weisse). Should all the beer sampling stimulate your stomach, a blackboard menu offers an impressive array of grub, from basic BLT sarnies to more upmarket nosh like fried camembert. Best of all is the grassy paddock of a beer garden at the back – watch that the squirrels don't grab your nuts.
Babies and children admitted (in summer, garden only until 7.30pm). Games (fruit machine, pool table, quiz machine, table football). No-smoking tables. Tables outdoors (garden). **Map 9/P26**

Centuria

100 St Paul's Road, N1 (7704 2345). Highbury & Islington tube/rail/30, 277 bus. **Open** 5-11pm Mon-Fri; noon-11pm Sat; noon-10.30pm Sun. **Food served** 6-10.45pm Mon-Fri; 12.30-4pm, 6-10.30pm Sat; 12.30-10.30pm Sun. **Credit** MC, V.
A gastropub that's a little bit of rough. Sure, the Centuria's got the obligatory high falutin' menu – mussel and saffron soup anyone? – the textbook country-kitchen-by-candlelight aesthetic, and young media types wolfing down (gorgeous) bruschetta. But look a little closer and there's character too: the flowers on the bar come in a tin bucket; the paint's chipping a bit, and the candles are shoved in wine bottles, student-style. Even the fabulous people seem less smug and self-satisfied than in your standard Islington eaterie. To that end, the Centuria could be considered a gastropub for those who hate gastropubs: terrific food, homely setting, few posers. On the night we visited, there were even a few solo drinkers quaffing pints at the bar, a couple of builders, the odd baseball cap, and, heaven forbid, a fat man! The staff are lovely. When they had to cut off a drunk – another gastropub rarity – they handled him beautifully and a scene was averted. Later, surveying the mixed room of punters, one of the barmen commented to himself, 'Nice crowd tonight.' He was right.
Babies and children admitted. Dining room. Disabled: toilet. Tables outdoors (pavement). TV. **Map 9/P25**

Chapel

29A Penton Street, N1 (7833 4090). Angel tube.
Open/food served 5-11pm Mon-Wed; 5pm-midnight Thur; noon-1am Fri, Sat; noon-midnight Sun. **Happy hour** 5-9pm Mon-Wed; 5-7pm Thur-Sat. **Credit** MC, V.
For a trendy Islington DJ bar, the Chapel is highly original. Taking their cue from the name, the decorators have adhered strictly to an ecclesiastical theme: the stained-glass front doors are funeral parlour chic, the ornate stone bar resembles a little chunk of Notre Dame, and Gothic arches separate the front bar from the sunken 'vestry' lounge. In keeping with the 'God is in the details' theme, the light fixtures are adorned with crosses, the bog doors are straight from a medieval abbey and the elegant frosted urinals would do Norman Foster proud. During the week, a reverent hush fills the place – all chill-out music, squashy sofas and quiet conversations. Come the weekend, soothing trip hop gives way to a ballsier mix of funk and house. A clubbier, gay-friendly crowd fills two floors (and a terrace) until 1am. Zest, a funky Sunday club night, welcomes people of all sexual persuasions. Staff are friendly and slightly goth in keeping with the surroundings.
Function room. Music (band 6pm Thur; DJs 9pm Fri). Tables outdoors (terrace). **Map 9/N2**

Compton Arms

4 Compton Avenue, N1 (7359 6883). Highbury & Islington tube/rail. **Open** 11am-11pm Mon-Sat; noon-10.30pm Sun. **Food served** noon-2.30pm Mon-Fri; noon-4pm Sat, Sun. **Credit** MC, V.
With its low, beamed ceilings, wood benches and minuscule tables, the cosy Compton Arms calls to mind the Seven Dwarfs' half-timbered cottage. On the night we visited, a delightful barmaid engaged in banter with a group of balding men at the bar (really!), adding to the Snow White feel of it all. During the week, it's a quiet little haven, with vintage photos of old Islington covering the walls and no music to spoil conversation; an ivy-covered beer garden out back gives further respite from the 21st century. As you'd expect from a pub that feels more Ambridge than Angel, there's a good selection of real ales – Abbot and IPA from Greene King, 6X from Wadworth – and plenty of sausage-and-mash type fare. The only concession to modernity is the giant TV screen at one end of the room, with a televised fixture list posted by the door. Even quiet types need their fix of Sky Sports.
Babies and children admitted (separate area). Games (quiz machine). Quiz (8.30pm Sun). Tables outdoors (garden). TV (big screen, satellite). **Map 9/O26**

Crown

116 Cloudesley Road, N1 (7837 7107). Angel tube.
Open noon-11pm Mon-Sat; noon-10.30pm Sun.
Food served noon-3pm, 6-10pm Mon-Sat; noon-3pm, 6-9pm Sun. **Credit** AmEx, MC, V.
You know a pub has gone posh when you ask for a packet of crisps and are offered cashews in a cocktail glass instead. Or when fish and chips is substituted by shark steak with sautéed potatoes. Welcome to the Crown, another trad local turned destination gastropub. Credit to the designers who've done a good job of preserving the pub's best features – gorgeous etched glass windows, elaborate cornices and magnificent oak bar – while keeping the rest of the decor pleasingly simple. As with other pubs of this ilk, there are rustic wooden tables, rough-hewn wood floors, and, in the back room, squishy leather sofas on which to sip expensive cocktails or cabernet sauvignon while gazing into the open kitchen. Punters seem to be a mixture of trust fund kids, serious diners and locals who are still pinching themselves that a pub so lovely has opened up on their quiet little street.
Babies and children admitted. Function room (seats 14). Tables outdoors (patio). **Map 9/N1**

Drapers Arms

44 Barnsbury Street, N1 (7619 0348). Angel tube/ Highbury & Islington tube/rail. **Open** noon-11pm Mon-Sat; noon-10.30pm Sun. **Food served** noon-4pm, 7-10pm Mon-Sat; noon-4pm Sun. **Credit** MC, V.
Gastropubs are ten a penny in these parts, but the Drapers is clearly aiming to run clear of the pack. In Georgian house surrounds and more gastro than pub, the place resembles an elegant restaurant. It has a delicate, feminine decor: the dusky rose walls are adorned with antique mirrors and modern art; there's a scent of fresh lilies on the air; and the soft candlelight is flattering to the older, moneyed crowd. The food has received good reviews in the past, but on our visit, the traditional pub grub was disappointing. You don't have to eat; when we visited, there were several well-groomed punters sitting at the bar drinking pints of Courage Best and Old Speckled Hen, and 'ladies who lunch' types sipping wine on leather sofas by the fire. In summer, a pretty garden offers alternative sanctuary. It's all very posh – but why not? Posh people need watering holes too.
Babies and children admitted. Function room. Tables outdoors (garden).

Duke of Cambridge

30 St Peter's Street, N1 (7359 3066/www.singhboulton.co.uk). Angel tube. **Open** noon-11pm Mon-Sat; noon-10.30pm Sun. **Food served** 12.30-3pm, 6.30-10.30pm Mon-Fri; 12.30-3.30pm, 6.30-10.30pm Sat; 12.30-3.30pm, 6.30-10pm Sun. **Credit** AmEx, MC, V.

Fancy a beer? That'll be a pint of Eco Warrior then. The DoC is an organic pub, and all its drinks are Soil Association-approved: Luscombe Devon cider, Freedom and St Peter's ales, and a range of organic soft drinks (ginger beer, pear juice) of which Prince Charles would heartily approve. There's a plethora of signs outlining, in minute detail, the worthy pedigree of the various foods and beverages. It gets a bit much and the urge to order a pint of Bacardi and Coke and a large bucket of pork scratchings may become overwhelming. Still, this is a good-looking rusticated place, with bare-board floors, chunky wooden tables and a neutral colour scheme. The food is excellent. There's no music either, which makes conversation possible. And, when it comes down to it, any business supporting independent British farmers and breweries deserves your patronage.
Babies and children admitted (children's portions, high chairs). No jukebox or piped music. No-smoking areas. Restaurant. Specialities: organic beers and food. Tables outdoors (conservatory, courtyard). **Map 9/O2**

Elbow Room

89-91 Chapel Market, N1 (7278 3244/www.elbow-room.co.uk). Angel tube. **Open/food served** 6pm-2am Mon; noon-2am Tue-Thur; noon-3am Fri, Sat; noon-midnight Sun. **Happy hour** 5-8pm daily. **Admission** £2 9-10pm, £5 after 10pm Fri, Sat. **Credit** MC, V.
There are two equally weighted reasons to come to this cavernous, aircraft hangar of a bar: pool and pulling. Part of an American-style chain of pool parlours, this place boasts ten signature purple baize tables in a slick, middle-of-the-road setting. During the week, a mixture of suits, boy-next-door types and girlfriends dally to a soundtrack of dance and indie. However, at the weekend the late licence and club choons result in a meat market extraordinaire drawing good-time boys and gals from far and wide. In keeping with the knocking-shop ethos, the women's toilets have a two-way mirror with a view of the men's urinals (from behind). The drinks line-up is nothing special, but it all gets you pissed, and the bar does food of the snacky, burger and potato-skin genre.
Disabled: toilet. Games (pool; noon-6pm £6 per hour, after 7pm £9 per hour). Music (DJs nightly). TVs (big screen, plasma screen, satellite). **Map 9/N2**

Embassy Bar

119 Essex Road, N1 (7359 7882). Angel tube/Highbury & Islington tube/rail. **Open** 5-11pm Mon-Thur; 5pm-1am Fri, Sat; 5-10.30pm Sun. **Credit** AmEx, DC, MC, V.
The Embassy has been Islington's hippest DJ bar for a few years now, and yet, curiously, it still feels like a secret. Housed in an anonymous building, the bar has stayed successful by pretending not to be. The sign is barely visible, the interior is understated and the drinks are cheap. In fact, the place is downright cosy. The room is small and dimly lit, dominated by a horseshoe bar, and decorated with red and gold Chinesey wallpaper, twinkly Christmas lights and lived-in furniture. During the week, candles add a touch of romance, and Tetley's sooths purists. Come the weekend, the place becomes a madhouse, with a ton of drunken bodies rammed in for edgy club nights. Success has necessitated the opening of a basement bar (all cherry wood and padded vinyl panels) that does little to ease the biggest problem: congestion.
Function room (seats 40). Music (DJs 8pm Thur-Sun; Fri, Sat £3 after 10pm). **Map 9/O1**

Filthy McNasty's

68 Amwell Street, EC1 (7837 6067). Angel tube. **Open** noon-11pm Mon-Thur; noon-midnight Fri, Sat; noon-10.30pm Sun. **Food served** noon-3pm, 6-10pm Mon-Fri; noon-6pm Sat; noon-8pm Sun. **Credit** MC, V.
It's an Irish pub, but there's not a trace of theme parkery about it. The decor is stubbornly plain, but for a few framed photos of iconoclasts: Sid Vicious, Kurt Cobain, The Stranglers. A huge traffic light in the corner, permanently on red, casts a gritty urban light on the place. The soundtrack on a Friday night was loud, edgy rap and R&B, and with all the guys in hooded tops and baseball caps, one couldn't help but think of House of Pain rather than U2. During the week, things are a bit quieter. Certainly, the folk acts are more conducive to savouring the Guinness. The pub's Vox 'n' Roll nights may have come to an end since the departure of Filthy founder Gerry O'Doyle (although they are set to continue at his new Highgate gaff, **Boogaloo**, *see p168*) but there's still enough other good stuff going on to lift it above the average boozer.
Babies and children admitted (daytime). Disabled: toilet. Function room. Literary readings (8.30pm Wed, Thur). Music (band 8pm Sat, 4pm Sun; DJs 8pm Fri, 3pm Sun). Quiz (8pm Mon). Tables outdoors (pavement). TV (digital). **Map 9/N3**

Hemingford Arms

158 Hemingford Road, N1 (7607 3303). Caledonian Road tube. **Open** 11am-11pm Mon-Sat; noon-10.30pm Sun. **Food served** 12.30-2.30pm, 6.30-10.30pm Mon-Fri; 6.30-10.30pm Sat; 12.30-4pm, 6.30-10.30pm Sun. **Credit** MC, V.
The *Old Curiosity Shop* of pubs, the Hem deserves a Michelin star for atmosphere. The ivy-covered exterior is positively luxuriant, while the smoky interior is crammed with bric-a-brac and memorabilia. Forget about people-watching, you'll spend most of your time gaping at the ceiling and its treasure trove of hanging copper pots and pans, deer antlers, stuffed badgers, old instruments, tennis rackets, antique bird cages... Walls are plastered in classic film and theatre posters – from *Vertigo* to *Kiss Me Kate* – and the lower parts half hidden behind dusty old bookcases. The crowd's boisterous and manly, the beer selection good (Adnams Bitter, Courage Best and Directors), and the Thai food cheap and filling. A piano in the corner is sometimes dusted off for a rowdy singsong.
Babies and children (until 6pm). Games (fruit machine). Music (bands 9pm Mon-Wed, Fri-Sun). Quiz (9pm Thur; £2 per team). Tables outdoors (pavement). TV (satellite). **Map 9/M26**

Critics' choice
pub quizzes

Boogaloo (p168)
North London jukejoint with a good specialist music quiz.

Half Moon (p220)
A Tuesday night draw for (Herne) Hillbillies.

Mistress P's (p212)
Brilliant and quirky quiz for which punters will even cross the river.

Prince George (p148)
A great jukebox and also a legendary quiz at this cracking Hackney local.

Shakespeare (p186)
A Stokey standby that draws the odd celeb.

Hen & Chickens Theatre Bar

109 St Paul's Road, N1 (7704 7621/ www.henand chickens.com). Highbury & Islington tube/rail. **Open** noon-midnight Mon-Wed, Sun; noon-1am Thur-Sat. **Admission** £3 after 11pm Fri, Sat. **Credit** MC, V.

Islington has no shortage of theatre pubs (see also the **King's Head, Old Red Lion** and **Rosemary Branch**), but of them all, the Hen & Chickens feels the least theatrical, both in terms of decor and punters. It's a simple, slightly scruffy, single-room boozer with wood floors and cheery green and yellow walls. A couple of ornamental roosters and a plastic bull's head lamp are about as arty as it gets. And unlike its counterparts, there are very few Quentin Crisp types floating about the place, just a down-to-earth north London crowd – jeans and T-shirts, shaggy haircuts – knocking back pints like there's no tomorrow. Come 8pm, half of them disappear to watch the goings-on upstairs (fringe plays, comedy and bands) seated on hardback rows rescued from the old music hall on Brighton Pier. Afterwards, it's back downstairs for more beery oblivion courtesy of a thoughtful late licence. Draught beers include London Pride and Staropramen.

Comedy (Mon, Sun). Games (fruit machine, quiz machine). Music (bands 10pm Thur, Sun; 11pm Fri, Sat). Theatre (eves Tue-Sat, matinées Sun; box office 7704 2001; £6-£10). TV. **Map 9/O25**

Hope & Anchor

207 Upper Street, N1 (7354 1312). Highbury & Islington tube/rail. **Open** *Ground floor* noon-11pm Mon-Sat; noon-10.30pm Sun. *Basement* 8.30pm-1am Mon-Sat; 8pm-midnight Sun. **Food served** noon-4pm Mon-Fri; noon-7pm Sat, Sun. **Credit** MC, V.

At the Hope & Anchor, a beer-stained, smoky, blokey, London legend, they don't just rock – they rrrrrrrawk. The Clash and the Sex Pistols got their start in its sweaty basement bar, still home to nightly gigs that range from folk to heavy metal. Pictures of rock icons line the walls of the ground-floor pub, which comes complete with tacky carpet, long-haired guys in black T-shirts, and a rocktastic jukebox booming thunderous tunes by the likes of Metallica and The Cult. Staff are dead friendly – rockers are so much sweeter than club kids. Draught beers include Greene King IPA, John Smith's and Abbot Ale. Not the best place to come if you're a Chilled Ibiza kind of a gal, but if you like your beer cheap and your Motörhead loud, welcome home.

Disabled: toilet. Games (fruit machines, pool tables, table football, video games). Jukebox. Music (bands 8.30pm nightly; £5, £4 concessions; DJs 11pm Thur-Sat). **Map 9/O26**

The House

63-9 Canonbury Road, N1 (7704 7410/www.inthe house.biz). Highbury Corner tube **Open** 5-11pm Mon; 11am-11pm Tue-Sat; noon-10.30pm Sun. **Food served** 6-10.30pm Mon; noon-3.30pm, 6-10.30pm Tue-Fri; 6-10.30pm Sat; 6-9.30pm Sun. **Credit** MC, V.

One for the grown-ups, this. The House has taken the tried-and-true gastropub formula and upped the ante a couple of notches. The decor is exquisitely yuppie: taupe walls, smoked mirrors and polished wood everywhere, set off by candlelight, fresh flowers and B&Ws of the Manhattan skyline. Add a famous chef (Jez Hollingsworth, formerly of Quo Vadis) and the chattering classes come running. And so they should. The food is delicious – short on the flowery descriptions, long on hearty ingredients – and the wine list is helpfully divided into categories such as 'warm and cheerful', 'fruity and easy-going' 'crisp and lively'. Not that the smartly dressed customers look like they need any help sorting out their Beaujolais from their pinot grigio. There's also Tetley's and San Miguel on tap, but you somehow feel it would be more appropriate to order a champagne cocktail. Even if the whole gastropub epidemic is getting a bit old, you have to admit the House is a class act.

Babies and children admitted. Disabled: toilet. Music (DJs 1-7pm Sun). No-smoking tables. Tables outdoors (terrace, pavement). **Map 9/O26**

Island Queen

87 Noel Road, N1 (7704 7631). Angel tube. **Open** noon-11pm Mon-Sat; noon-10.30pm Sun. **Food served** noon-3pm, 6-8pm Mon-Fri; noon-5pm Sun. **Credit** AmEx, MC, V.

Tucked away on a quiet residential avenue, the gorgeous Island Queen is one of Islington's best-kept secrets – and one of the most beautiful historic boozers in London. Fronted by a great curve of wood and etched glass, is a wondrously high-ceilinged single room dominated by a massive, dark wood central island bar. Pink Christmas lights twinkle on rose walls, which are adorned with exotic palm-fringed mirrors and nautical prints; the pub was named after a ship, and a wave-battered wooden figurehead flanks the ladies' toilets. A screened snug holds a pool table. Beers include London Pride and Bass on tap. So why, on the Saturday night we visited, was the place so empty? Not trendy enough for Islingtonians we suppose. More fool them.

Function room (seats 45). Games (fruit machine, pool table). No-smoking tables. Tables outdoors (pavement). **Map 9/O2**

King's Head

115 Upper Street, N1 (7226 0364/www.kingshead theatre.org). Angel tube/Highbury & Islington tube/rail. **Open** 11am-1am Mon-Thur; 11am-2am Fri, Sat; noon-1am Sun. **Food served** noon-3.30pm Tue-Sat; noon-9pm Sun. Pre-booked theatre dinner available Tue-Sat.
No credit cards.

Islington's best-loved theatre pub, the King's Head is one of the most eclectic watering holes in London. The building dates from the mid-19th century and, although not quite that old, the fringe theatre at the back has been around yonks. Old playbills and production photos on the walls remind drinkers that the likes of Kenneth Branagh and Victoria Wood all began by treading the boards here. After the show, an odd-ball crowd – students, drama queens, old queens, rockers and rastas – spill into the fabulously scruffy pub for a serious assault on decent beers at decent prices. At weekends, the place gets boisterous with wall-to-wall bodies bellowing along to indie covers until God knows what time. Fans of *Withnail & I* will feel right at home. Long may the show go on.

Babies and children admitted (until 7pm). Disabled: toilet. Music (bands 10pm nightly). Theatre. Tables outdoors (pavement). **Map 9/O1**

Marquess Tavern

32 Canonbury Street, N1 (7354 2975). Highbury & Islington tube/rail. **Open** 11am-11pm Mon-Sat; noon-10.30pm Sun. **Food served** noon-3pm, 6-9pm Mon-Sat; noon-6pm Sun. **Credit** MC, V.

The Grand Old Dame of Islington pubs, the Marquess makes a majestic first impression, its neoclassical exterior lit dramatically by spotlights. The interior used to be just as show-stopping – so kitsch we called it the Bet Lynch of pubs. Tragically, the management felt it was time for an image re-haul, and stripped away the glitzy flock wallpaper and gaudy carpets. It's still handsome – oak panelling, red walls, Victorian chandeliers – just not as glamorous: Bet Lynch without her slap. Despoiling aside, this is a great local. The beers are Young's so they're good too. Further renovations are planned; let's hope it's nothing too tasteful.

North

The House

Babies and children admitted (until 6pm). Games (fruit machine). Tables outdoors (patio). TVs (satellite). **Map 9/P26**

Matt & Matt Bar

112 Upper Street, N1 (7226 6035). Angel tube. **Open** 6pm-1am Thur; 6pm-2am Fri; 8pm-2am Sat. **Happy hour** 6-8pm Thur, Fri. **Credit** MC, V.

If there can be such a thing as a homely neighbourhood DJ bar, then Matt & Matt is it. It's a long narrow room with plain walls, exposed brick, and a couple of sofas with white sheets thrown over them – all mercifully simple. This leaves the staff, punters and DJs to create the atmosphere – which is chilled, ultra-casual and far less snooty than nearby rivals. During the week, this is a loungey kind of place for catching up with the neighbours. Weekends hot up when the DJs spin a spiky mix of house, trance and techno. But even then it feels more like a local than a posy club. Drinks include flavoured vodkas and cocktails, with lagers and Guinness on draught.

Music (DJs 9pm Thur-Sat; £4 after 10pm Fri, Sat). **Map 9/O1**

Medicine Bar

181 Upper Street, N1 (7704 9536/www.medicinebar.net). Angel tube/Highbury & Islington tube/rail. **Open** 5pm-midnight Mon-Thur; 5pm-2am Fri; noon-2am Sat; noon-midnight Sun. **Admission** £4 (non-members) after 10pm Fri, Sat. **Credit** MC, V.

The Medicine Bar is that rare creature: a fashionable bar with soul. There's a whiff of bohemian chic about the place, with its palm trees, worn leather sofas and patio-style lanterns. The panelled walls and cosy first-floor drinking dens add to the louche, loungey-ness of it all. Shagadelic bars require good cocktails, and the Medicine comes through: house favourites the Italian Job (Bombay Sapphire, Martini, and orange juice) and Medicine Lemonade (Jack Daniels, Cointreau, lemon juice and lemonade) are spot on. There's no dancefloor, but DJs spinning a mix of funk, house and soul ensure that standing still is just not an option. And any bar that plays Dionne Warwick's 'Do You Know the Way to San Jose' is good by us.

Function room. Music (DJs 9pm Thur-Sun). Tables outdoors (pavement). **Map 9/O1**

Narrow Boat

119 St Peter Street, N1 (7288 9821). Angel tube. **Open** noon-11pm Mon-Sat; noon-10.30pm Sun. **Food served** noon-3pm Mon-Fri, Sun. **Credit** MC, V.

Sandwiched between the organic ab fabness of the **Duke of Cambridge** (*see p172*) and smart canalside offices, the Narrow Boat is a last gasp of the Islington of yore. It's housed in a couple of old workers' cottages and has a distinctly nautical feel. There's a cosy narrowboat-style snug, and a view of the water; in summer, snag a table on the balcony. The rest of the year, grab a couch by the fire, watch some footie and savour a real ale from the rotating line-up that includes London Pride and Badger IPA. Bar staff are friendly, and there's an endearing naffness to the handbag house soundtrack. Punters are more East End than Essex Road, but, given the area's rapid gentrification, one wonders for how long.

Babies and children admitted (until 6pm). Music (DJs 7pm Thur, Fri). No-smoking tables. Tables outdoors (balcony, towpath). TV. **Map 9/P2**

Northgate

113 Southgate Road, N1 (7359 7392). Essex Road rail/ 38, 73 bus. **Open** 5-11pm Mon-Fri; noon-11pm Sat; noon-10.30pm Sun. **Food served** 6.30-10.15pm Mon-Fri; noon-4pm, 6.30-10.15pm Sat; noon-4pm, 6.30-9.15pm Sun. **Credit** MC, V.

The chic, pea-green restaurant at the rear of the Northgate buzzes nightly with gastro connoisseurs, and there's lots to buzz about because the food is wonderful. But the best thing about this place is that despite the big gastro-makeover, the oldies haven't been squeezed out. Sure, the airy front pub area has gone all smart – and at one of the next tables, a group of interior designers pored over plans for, you guessed it, a new gastropub – but, on the night we visited, an old man and his dog sat at one corner of the bar nursing his pint and, as we were leaving, two fishermen entered, rods in one hand, towing their dogs behind them. The staff are amiable and attentive (and tattooed – there's a gastropub rarity) and there's a good selection of real ales on tap: London Pride, Adnams Bitter, Old Speckled Hen. N1 may have got itself yet another gastropub, but more importantly, the residents of Southgate Road have got themselves an excellent local.

Babies and children admitted (restaurant). Restaurant. Tables outdoors (yard).

Old Queen's Head

44 Essex Road, N1 (7354 9273). Angel tube. **Open** noon-11pm Mon-Sat; noon-10.30pm Sun. **Credit** MC, V.

Like many a pub along this increasingly worthwhile stretch of Essex Road, the OQH is a hip refurbishment of a formerly shabby old boozer. A carved fireplace too fantastic to remove remains, but that's the only concession to tradition. Set in one cavernous room done out in deep red and dark blue, there's a bar, a large B&W of a stylus on a record, and that's about it. Apart from the punters, that is, who seem to be equally vocal (and drunk) whenever there's a football game on the big screen, a club night on later, or a mate's birthday to celebrate: in other words, most of the time. This certainly isn't a quiet venue, but with a 'pick your own' CD collection behind the bar and friendly staff, it's exuberant rather than aggressive. Our only quibble (although it's quite a big quibble) is the booze: a lame selection of nitrokegs and alcopops.

Babies and children admitted (until 9pm). Function room. Games (board games, table football). Tables outdoors (pavement). TV (satellite). **Map 9/O1**

Old Red Lion

418 St John Street, EC1 (7837 7816). Angel tube. **Open** noon-11pm Mon-Sat; noon-10.30pm Sun. **Food served** noon-3pm Mon-Fri. **Credit** MC, V.

Cheap glamour is hard to find these days in polished, perfect Islington. So the Old Red Lion, a smoky old theatre bar, is a treasure. Situated down the road from Sadler's Wells and down the stairs from its own auditorium, the Lion is full of theatrical history (photos of past productions line the walls). Although you may chance to eavesdrop on audition gossip, and luvvie types do pop down to the bar for drinkies during intermission, the Old Red Lion hasn't a pretentious bone in its body. The drama crowd is outnumbered by hardened brickies, tattooed punks and a smattering of oldies savouring a decent pint of Adnams Bitter, Greene King's Abbot Ale, Fuller's London Pride or Tetley's. As with the **King's Head** (*see p174*), the combination of heavy drinking, rowdy blokes and theatrical personalities results in one very merry throng.

Babies and children admitted (until 6pm). Games (fruit machines, quiz machine). Music (DJs 3pm 2 Sun per month). Tables outdoors (patio). Theatre (Tue-Sun 8pm; £8-£10). TVs (satellite). **Map 9/N3**

Rosemary Branch

2 Shepperton Road, N13 (7704 2730/ www.rosemary branch.co.uk). Angel tube/Old Street tube/rail. **Open** noon-11.30pm Mon-Thur; noon-midnight Fri, Sat; noon-10.30pm Sun. **Food served** noon-2.30pm, 6.30-9.30pm Mon-Sat; noon-4pm Sun. **Credit** MC, V.

In bland Blairite Britain, unusual pubs are increasingly hard to find. But a few genuinely eccentric places still exist and this is most definitely one of them. Check the weird metallic sculptures and model aeroplanes hanging from the ceilings, the plaster ear protruding from the wall, the raunchy tabloid headlines are taped to the bar. Pink twinkly Christmas lights and black velvet drapes add to the theatrical effect (offbeat productions are, in fact, staged in the small auditorium upstairs). There's an impressive selection of beers (Affligem Blonde, Lituvel, Ridleys Old Bob on our visit) and the place does good, fun food (steak sarnies, nachos with salsa, guacamole and sour cream). Turn up for the pub quizzes: Monday for music, Thursday for general knowledge.
Babies and children admitted (until 8pm). Function room. Jukebox. No-smoking area. Quiz (8.30pm Mon, Thur; £1). Theatre (Tue-Sat). TV (satellite). **Map 9/P1**

Salmon & Compass

58 Penton Street, N1 (7837 3891). Angel tube. **Open** 5pm-2am Mon-Sat; 5pm-midnight Sun. **Admission** £3 after 9pm Thur-Sat. **Credit** MC, V.
The name suggests a nautical pub, perhaps full of old seafaring types with weather-beaten faces and peg legs. Not a bit of it. This is party central, where a friendly, unpretentious crowd congregates to shoot vodka and shout over urban beats, trancey whooshes and old skool dance. The decor is purple walled with ridiculous exposed air ducts and leather cubes for chairs – redeemed by dim lighting, weird cinematic projections on the walls and a glittering disco ball. Drinks are restricted to bottled lagers and cocktails, though nothing too grown up: think Sex on the Beach served by the pitcher (£15). Staff are as sweet as pie, and the late licence is a winner. However, all or none of the above may soon change as the place is about to come under new management.
Games (pool table). Music (DJs 8pm daily). **Map 9/N2**

The Social

Arlington Square, N1 (7354 5809/www.thesocial.com). Angel tube. **Open** 6-11pm Mon-Fri; noon-11pm Sat; noon-10.30pm Sun. **Food served** 7-10.30pm Mon-Fri; noon-5.30pm, 6.30-10.30pm Sat; 12.30-5pm, 6-9.30pm Sun. **Credit** AmEx, DC, MC, V.
Eventually, even clubbing types grow old, buy Gap, take up mortgages, have babies and seek out more leisurely forms of hedonism. Which explains the thinking behind the latest venue to call itself the **Social** (*see p45*), yet another fine Heavenly Records' venture and currently the liveliest gastropub in N1. It's a bar with the red velour, oak-panelled ambience of a local (it was formally the Hanbury) but with an open kitchen that justifies gastropub prices; and, crucially, an excellent big old jukebox you actually want to play (the Strokes! the Avalanches! Johnny Cash!). Chatty bar staff pull pints of Eagle IPA, Kirin and Duff, while fashionably sloppy types (lots of hooded parkas, combat trousers and general overdressed casualness) lounge on the leather sofas. Eating is optional but recommended. There's also a cosy upstairs lounge and, come the weekend, top DJs provide feel-good sets (although we felt just fine without them).
Babies and children admitted. Function room. Games (board games, pool). Music (DJs 6pm Wed-Sun). Quiz (8pm every other Tue; £2 per person). **Map 9/P2**

Stone

201 Liverpool Road, N1 (7607 7710). Angel tube/ Highbury & Islington tube/rail. **Open** noon-11pm Mon-Fri; 11am-11pm Sat; 11am-10.30pm Sun. **Food served** noon-3pm, 6-10pm Mon-Fri; 11am-3pm, 6-10pm Sat; 11am-3pm, 6-9.30pm Sun. **Happy hour** 6-8pm Fri, Sat. **Credit** MC, V.
Sitting forlornly on a wild stretch of Liverpool Road, the Stone is all dressed up with no place to go. It's one of Islington's more stunning bars: the slate grey interior, minimalist white couches and diaphanous curtains bring to mind the Sanderson Hotel. It has the compulsory cocktail menu with the tongue-in-chic concoctions (Italian Valium, Painkiller and the like) and a good range of bottled beers. Plus there's the up-to-date menu – sea bass with pak choi – and pan-Asian bar snacks. In short, it's got it all, except for one thing: people. Perhaps scared off by the no man's land location, the trendy young things are staying away. As are the neighbours – it's too spiffy for locals. Right bar, wrong location.
Function room. Music (DJs 8pm Fri, Sat). Tables outdoors (pavement). TV (satellite). **Map 9/N1**

25 Canonbury Lane

25 Canonbury Lane, N1 (7226 0955). Highbury & Islington tube/rail. **Open** 5-11pm Mon-Fri; noon-11pm Sat, Sun. **Food served** 6-10pm Mon-Thur; 6-8pm Fri; 12.30-3.30pm, 6-8pm Sat; 12.30-3.30pm Sun. **Credit** MC, V.
Islington has a plethora of beautiful little bars for beautiful people, but 25 Canonbury Lane remains the benchmark. The look is tasteful modern classical: chandeliers, rococo mirrors, faux Renaissance art, mixed with sunken leather couches, slick backlit bar and stripped wood floors. By candlelight, the place almost seems romantic; softly played house leaving room for hushed conversation. A blackboard is filled with immaculate cocktails – Martinis range from vanilla to kiwi; £5-£8 – and there's a sophisticated wine list, complemented by a de rigueur tapas menu: Thai fish cakes, grilled goat's cheese, char-grilled squid and the like. There are four draught beers and numerous bottled varieties, but no real ales. No matter, this is a cocktail crowd, for which the phrase 'upwardly mobile' was coined. Oh, to be young and loaded in Islington.
Babies and children admitted (until 6pm). **Map 9/O26**

Also in the area...

All Bar One 1 Liverpool Road, N1 (7843 0021); 131-2 Upper Street, N1 (7354 9535).
Angel (JD Wetherspoon) 3-5 Islington High Street, N1 (7837 2218).
Babushka 125 Caledonian Road, N1 (7837 1924).
Bierodrome 173-4 Upper Street, N1 (7226 5835).
Islington Tup 80 Liverpool Road, N1 (7354 4440).
O'Neill's 59 Upper Street, N1 (7704 7691).
Pitcher & Piano 68 Upper Street, N1 (7704 9974).
Slug & Lettuce 1A Islington Green, N1 (7226 3864).
Walkabout Inn 56 Upper Street, N1 (7359 2097).
White Swan (JD Wetherspoon) 251-5 Upper Street, N1 (7288 9050).

Kentish Town & Gospel Oak

A poor relation to nearby Camden, Kentish Town has a collection of particularly perilous boozers that you'd only frequent if drunk or otherwise mentally addled (and there's no shortage of that kind of punter round here). Unlike most areas of London where the number of venues we cover grows with each edition, Kentish Town shrinks; a shooting incident further winnowed our list this year.

Bull & Last

168 Highgate Road, NW5 (7267 3641). Kentish Town tube/rail, then C2, 214 bus. **Open** 11am-11pm Mon-Sat; noon-10.30pm Sun. **Food served** noon-3pm, 6.30-10pm Mon-Fri; noon-10pm Sat, Sun. **Credit** MC, V.

Ideally located opposite the tennis courts at the bottom of the heath on Parliament Hill, this quiet and unpretentious gastropub does the basics, but does them well. No flashy refit or expensive lighting here, just excellent food and drink in comfortingly weather-beaten surroundings (the decor's a study in brown). London Pride, Greene King IPA, Hoegaarden and Pilsner Urquell cater for the tastes of the gently bohemian locals and there's also a lengthy wine list to complement the European-leaning menu and tasty bar snacks. Weekends (Sundays especially) can be busy with families fresh off the heath, but that's no reason to stay away.
Babies and children admitted (until 8.30pm). Function room. Restaurant. Tables outdoors (pavement).

Jorene Celeste

256 Kentish Town Road, NW5 (7485 3521). Kentish Town tube/rail. **Open** 11am-11pm Mon-Sat; noon-10.30pm Sun. **Food served** noon-3pm, 5-10pm Mon-Fri; 5.30-10pm Sat; noon-5pm Sun. **Credit** MC, V.
What was once the ailing Vulture's Perch has been revived as probably the most characterful pub in central Kentish Town. Named, apparently, after the landlord's actress mum, it's easy to miss, hidden behind fruit and veg stalls on a corner just south of the tube station. Inside, an imposing great bar dominates front of house, but ease by the locals propping up the counter to the large and high-ceilinged back room, with framed portraits, mirrors, elegant wall lamps and upholstered chairs. There's Greene King IPA and London Pride on tap, a well-stocked wine rack and inexpensive Thai food to eat.
Babies and children admitted (until 8.30pm). Function room. Games (fruit machines). Restaurant. **Map 8/J25**

North

Pineapple

51 Leverton Street, NW5 (7284 4631). Kentish Town tube. **Open** noon-11pm Mon-Sat; noon-10.30pm Sun. **Food served** noon-2.30pm, 7-10pm Tue-Sat; 1-4pm Sun. **Credit** MC, V.
This pub has a heart-warming tale to tell. Faced with the impending sale of the place to a property developer (boo! hiss!), the loyal Kentish Town locals simply clubbed together, bought the place back for themselves (hurrah!) and redecorated, adding a restaurant to the upper floor. The result is a triumph – a cosier, more relaxed atmosphere would be hard to find. Behind the thick curtain at the door is the tiny but lovingly restored bar typically crammed with genial locals patting themselves on the back (and why not?) and sampling the extensive wines and draught beers (Pedigree, Bass, London Pride). The restaurant's also very popular – book in advance, you've been warned – but if you turned up unannounced, the wait downstairs wouldn't be a hardship. A beautifully lit garden extends the limited space.
Babies and children admitted (until 7.30pm). Games (chess, cards, darts). Music (folk/jazz/soul 8.30pm Wed). Quiz (8.30pm Mon; £1). Tables outdoors (garden, pavement). TV. **Map 8/J24**

Vine

86 Highgate Road, NW5 (7209 0038). Tufnell Park tube/ Kentish Town tube/rail. **Open** 11am-11pm Mon-Sat; noon-10.30pm Sun. **Food served** 12.30-3.30pm, 6.30-10.30pm Mon-Sat; 12.30-9pm Sun. **Credit** AmEx, DC, MC, V.
A long-standing gastropub with a good track record among the plummy residents of the Highgate Road, the Vine is strikingly Edwardian on the outside, elegantly lazy on the inside (leather sofas and around an open fireplace). If there's a fault, it's that the focus on food (a stout range of British and European bistro dishes) is at the expense of the drinkers. There's also a huge, Mediterranean-style covered patio out the back for summer barbecues and the like. Baby-phobes be warned, it can sometimes resemble a crèche on Sundays.
Babies and children admitted (high chairs). Function rooms. Restaurant. Tables outdoors (conservatory, paved garden).

Also in the area...

Ruby in the Dust 86 Highgate Road, NW5 (7482 7037).

Kilburn

Wedged between well-to-do locales is scruffy Kilburn High Road, heart of Irish London. Advantages? A living homage to the Emerald Isle and all attendant dipsomaniac pleasures: pop in anywhere and you'll find cheap stout, folky music and garrulous punters. (Is there a cliché we've missed here?) Disadvantages? A living homage to the Emerald Isle and all attendant dipsomaniac pleasures: pop in anywhere and you'll find cheap Guinness, folky music and garrulous punters.

Black Lion

274 Kilburn High Road, NW6 (7624 1520). Kilburn tube/Brondesbury rail. **Open** 11am-11pm Mon-Sat; noon-10.30pm Sun. **No credit cards**.
Dublin meets London in the gloriously faded Victoriana of this Kilburn favourite. Grandeur comes in the form of wall-mounted copper reliefs of Georgian gentility and a mind-boggling chocolate box ceiling embossed in deep red, green and gold. Yet nicotine-laced curtains and adhesive carpets paint a truer picture of a joint that's had one too many nights on the black stuff (they serve little else, and certainly not without a frown). In the snug, ladies take their darts seriously, while in the larger front bar gents squint over their pints at the *Racing Post*. TVs throughout are permanently tuned to anything sporty and a jukebox blurts out a mixture of unabashed trash and chirpy singalongs. Out the back there's a dingy dancefloor tickled by the occasional band.
Babies and children admitted (until 7pm). Function room. Games (darts, fruit machines). Music (band 9pm Fri, Sat; free). TV (big screen, satellite).

Power's Bar

332 Kilburn High Road, NW6 (7624 6026). Kilburn tube/ Brondesbury rail. **Open** noon-11pm Mon-Sat; noon-10.30pm Sun. **No credit cards**.
Power's might well be compared to your slightly embarrassing best mate. Like them, the place has appalling dress sense, borne out in the bohemian figures adorning the deep blue walls. Musically, your pal's never really got over student union days either – with a worrying penchant for timeless jukebox anthems (Marley, Elvis, Dire Straits) and indie classics played at full pelt. And you can forget any interest in suave new drinks – tonight you're on the cheap Guinness (£1.90) and cheaper cocktails (have a go at the aptly named Brain Haemorrhage). But God love 'em all the same, for a warm welcoming nature and good conversation. And in Power's case add the glow of open fires, a comfort food menu and regular live bands in the back room to ensure a boisterous good time being had by all. Like the **Zd Bar** (*see p179*), this is owned by the Mean Fiddler group run by Irishman Vince Power (hence the name).
Babies and children admitted (Sun afternoons only). Jukebox. Music (acoustic 9pm Tue, Wed; DJs 8.30pm Thur-Sat; Irish band 4-7pm Sun; free). Tables outdoors (pavement). TV.

Salusbury

50-52 Salusbury Road, NW6 (7328 3286). Queen's Park tube. **Open** noon-11pm Mon-Sat; noon-10.30pm Sun. **Food served** 12.30-3.30pm, 7-10.15pm Mon-Sat; 12.30-3.30pm, 7-10pm Sun. **Credit** MC, V.

The Salusbury pulls off the key elements of the gastropub with relative aplomb. Its hazy candlelit bar with deep red paint job and B&Ws of Afro-Caribbean communities is a successful, if generic, rendition of the contemporary British pub. Perched on rickety wooden furniture decoratively coiffeured young folk reminisce over gap-year shenanigans and check out club flyers on the walls, while young mothers peruse the ads for post-natal yoga classes. Drink options cover a similarly broad church, with imported lagers (Staropramen) lining up alongside real ales (Adnams Bitter, London Pride) and an estimable wine list. Past the open kitchen and round the back is the bright, rustic-looking dining area, with an expansive Mediterranean-ish menu, but you can also eat the same food in the main bar.

Babies and children admitted (restaurant). Restaurant. Tables outdoors (pavement).

Zd Bar

289 Kilburn High Road, NW6 (7372 2544). Kilburn tube/ Brondesbury rail. **Open/food served** 5pm-1am Mon-Thur; 5pm-2am Fri, Sat; private bookings only Sun. **Admission** £3 10-11pm, £4 after 11pm Fri, Sat. **Credit** MC, V.

Kilburn High Road's most popular late-night drink and dance venue appears to operate on the principle that 'if it ain't broke…' Behind its big copper door is a well-worn formula of polished wooden floor, deep leather chairs and raw industrial vents hanging from the ceiling. DJs spin tunes most nights of the week offering everything from salsa to '70s funk. But potential strutters beware, the sunken dancefloor is tiny and can swiftly morph from Travolta's paradise into a sweaty pit. Despite its longevity, however, you can't help feeling this place is unhappy on the Kilburn High Road – shuttered windows are clearly designed to allow patrons to forget the scuzz outside and dream of Hoxton. Early-evening drinking, meanwhile, can be a soulless experience – a lack of custom is not helped by the uninspiring range of alcopops and bottled lagers.

Disabled: toilet. Function room.. Music (DJs 9pm Mon, Wed, Fri, Sat; band 9pm Thur). TVs (satellite).

Maida Vale

Maida Vale or Little Venice? There's always been an indistinctness about the Vale but one redeemed by its dominant feature, the meandering Regent's Canal. True to form, locals are a mixed bag of über-wealthy St John's Wood overspill and those drawn from the rough-round-the-edges borders with Kilburn and Paddington. They seem happy enough mingling in the neighbourhood's choice boozers, although on balance the toffs are stealthily easing out the proles.

Bridge House

13 Westbourne Terrace Road, W2 (7432 1361). Warwick Avenue tube. **Open** noon-11pm Mon-Sat; noon-10.30pm Sun. **Food served** noon-3pm, 6-9.30pm Mon-Sat; noon-3pm, 6-9pm Sun. **Credit** MC, V.

Occupying a plum site overlooking the canal (a pub's been here since 1731), the Bridge House has miraculously managed to avoid visits from pine-wielding interior designers and remains resolutely down-to-earth, dumpy, dishevelled and decidedly ordinary looking. While it's just a short trip in the Jag from millionaires' row, most punters are drawn from the local estates with a mildew-scented smattering ashore from the live-aboard barges that line Blomfield Road. The dark L-shaped room boasts a large telly in one corner and plenty of drinkers enjoying standard London Pride and Bass, and bravely noshing warmed pies or fish and chips. Upstairs hosts the Comedy Cafe Theatre, whose myriad fringe offerings have for years gone unnoticed by the gossiping locals below.

Comedy (7.30pm & 9.30pm nightly; £7). Games (fruit machine, golf machines). Tables outdoors (terrace). Theatre. TV (big screen, satellite).

Otto Dining Lounge

215 Sutherland Avenue, W9 (7266 3131). Maida Vale tube. **Open** 6pm-1am Mon-Sat. **Food served** 7pm-1am Mon-Sat. **Credit** AmEx, MC, V.

Otto's occupies a spot once taken by a Mongolian barbecue and the new owners have worked a miracle with the space they inherited. Enter through confusing glass doors (mind your head!) to a small lobby from where a staircase leads up to a long, sleek and stylish dark-wood lounge bar. The bar counter stretches along the whole of one side of the large room, with the remaining space given over to smart tables and banquettes. The room has a distinct odour of young money, given out by the thirtysomething sophisticated cocktail-drinking set who pack out the place at weekends talking consultancy fees and second homes. The drinks list boasts classic longs and shorts, with a score each of wines red and white. Regularly changing bottled beer is available to the riff-raff. The adjacent restaurant serves well-regarded international cuisine. Everything is done in exceedingly good taste, bar the name, which can't help but remind you of the greasy bus driver from *The Simpsons*.

Babies and children admitted. Dress: smart casual.

Prince Alfred & Formosa Dining Rooms

5A Formosa Street, W9 (7286 3287). Warwick Avenue tube. **Open** 11am-11pm Mon-Sat; noon-10.30pm Sun. **Food served** noon-3pm, 5.30-10.30pm Mon-Sat; noon-4pm, 6-10pm Sun. **Credit** AmEx, MC, V.

Grade I-listed and gorgeous, the Victorian marvel that is the Prince Alfred is divided into five distinct but interconnected areas – Public, Ladies', Gentlemen's, Private and Snug. The quintet is separated by the most elaborate of glass and mahogany partitions and entry into each is facilitated by tiny doorways designed for slim-line dwarfs. Beer bellies thus discouraged, the owners have decided to focus on the wine list and offer a commendable range of Old and New World bottles (though, there's not much wrong with the choice of beers either). A recent refit did nothing to harm the huge sculpted ceilings, etched glass and preponderance of mahogany, but it did turn the games room into an excellent restaurant.

Babies and children admitted (dining area, high chairs). Disabled: toilet. Tables outdoors (pavement).

Warrington Hotel

93 Warrington Crescent, W9 (7286 2929). Maida Vale tube. **Open** 11am-11pm Mon-Sat; noon-10.30pm Sun. **Food served** noon-2.30pm, 6-10pm daily. **Credit** MC, V.

A huge and extravagant Edwardian gem, and – so they say – a former brothel. The area once had a reputation for sexual dalliances, and it's the claim of some etymologists that the term 'randy' derives from the collection of nearby Randolphs (Road, Crescent and Avenue), favoured addresses for well-kept mistresses. The Warrington is big, stunningly beautiful and unsurprisingly popular. In summer most forego its interior charms of ornate ceilings, marble bar counter, art nouveau etchings and saucy wallpaper, and venture down the mosaic steps to drink on the spacious outdoor pavement. Fuller's and Young's

North

are both on draught, though wine and bottled lagers are a more popular tipple with the young posh types that linger here. Up the staircase (another arresting feature) is Ben's Thai, one of the first such restaurants to associate itself with a pub.
Babies and children admitted (restaurant). Games (darts, fruit machine, quiz machine). No piped music or jukebox (main bar). No-smoking areas. Restaurant. Tables outdoors (courtyard, pavement). TV (satellite).

Warwick Castle

6 Warwick Place, W9 (7432 1331). Warwick Avenue tube. **Open** noon-11pm Mon-Sat; noon-10.30pm Sun. **Food served** noon-2pm Mon-Fri; noon-6pm Sat, Sun. **Credit** AmEx, MC, V.
There's a quaint normalcy about the Warwick that makes you wish it were your local. It's not so special it is filled with tourists, but it is lovely enough to justify frequent revisits. Close to the canal and based on a street that is quiet enough to allow the pub to throw open its doors on warm evenings without disturbing either local residents or the studious drinkers inside, the Warwick is based around four simple square rooms, with a marble fireplace making the back room the pick of the bunch. With a good but standard range of drinks and unremarkable but filling menu, it's a thoroughly pleasant place to while away a few hours.
Games (fruit machine, quiz machine). No piped music (after 5pm). Tables outdoors (pavement). TV.

The Waterway

54-6 Formosa Street, W9 (7266 3557/ www.thewaterway.co.uk). Warwick Avenue tube. **Open** noon-11pm Mon-Sat; noon-10.30pm Sun. **Food served** 12.30-3.15pm, 6.30-10.15pm daily. **Credit** MC, V.
This striking, very modern canalside gastropub was once a candidate for grottiest boozer in London. A friend recalls being here some years ago when in walked a chap with a baseball bat, which he took to the cubicles of the gents bellowing for 'George' to come out. Those days are long gone. The same utilitarian '70s building now houses a retro-modern wood-based chic chalet-style bar that serves nitrokeg lagers and interesting wines to a clientele drifted east from Notting Hill. The food's received mixed reviews, but our pan-fried chicken livers and lamb burgers were fine. Chief selling point is the slatted outside decking that allows the Vale's schmoozers to drink in the urban charms of the adjoining waterway.
Babies and children admitted (daytime only). Tables outdoors (pavement).

Also in the area...

Slug & Lettuce 47 Hereford Road, W2 (7229 1503).

Muswell Hill & Alexandra Palace

There's not much to Muswell Hill. We do like the **Phoenix**, but it's a hell of a trek for a pint (although there's reward in the views). The neighbourhood also boasts one of the few **O'Neill's** worth talking about, but that's a bit like saying genital warts is the best form of VD. Last year's arrival of the **Victoria Stakes** was promising, but nothing's happened since. There's always the bus down to Crouch End.

O'Neill's

87 Muswell Hill Broadway, N10 (8883 7382). East Finchley or Highgate tube/43, 134 bus. **Open** noon-11pm Mon-Sat; noon-10.30pm Sun. **Food served** noon-7pm daily. **Credit** MC, V.
Better known locally as 'the church pub', this branch of the most ubiquitous of chains announces its Irish theme in no uncertain terms. A giant Guinness Toucan hangs from the high beamed ceiling while several similar birds peer out from the walls and perch behind the bar. Despite the gargantuan size of the pub, its atmosphere remains pleasantly homely – even on a quiet weekday afternoon – thanks to the various levels that break up the space and the wide variety of battered leather sofas and low tables that fill it. The pub's popularity is confirmed as the weekend approaches and the locals turn out in force. At such busy times, a large galleried first-floor seating area opens up to accommodate the extra customers, although it still gets uncomfortably crowded.
Disabled: toilet. Games (board games, fruit machine). Music (occasional bands). No-smoking area. TVs (big screen, digital).

Phoenix

Alexandra Palace Way, N22 (8365 2121). Turnpike Lane or Wood Green tube/Alexandra Palace rail/W3 bus. **Open** *Winter* noon-8pm Mon-Thur; noon-11pm Fri, Sat; noon-10.30pm Sun. *Summer* 11am-11pm Mon-Sat; noon-10.30pm Sun. **Food served** 11.30am-7pm daily. **Credit** MC, V.
If you've never had a good reason to make the trek all the way up the hill to Alexandra Palace, this weird and wonderful pub-cum-cafe could provide enough on its own. Located on the end of the fabulous Victorian building, the Phoenix is an outpost of bygone seaside chic. The large, square lounge, with its high ceilings, mahogany fittings and tall, elegant pot plants, has the feel of an old-fashioned seafront hotel – right down to the worn fittings. Meanwhile, the teas and coffees, fish and chips, and ice creams (advertised enthusiastically even on a dismal February afternoon) available at the bar only serve to strengthen the holiday atmosphere. To cap it all, the clientele consists of just the right combination of prim old ladies, confused tourists and loafing locals to complete the picture. For sheer surreal ambience it's hard to beat.
Babies and children admitted (indoor beer garden; nappy-changing facilities). Disabled: toilet. Function rooms. Tables outdoors (patio, terrace). TV (satellite).

Victoria Stakes

1 Muswell Hill, N10 (8815 1793/www.victoria stakes.co.uk). Bus 144, W7. **Open** 5-11pm Mon-Wed; noon-11pm Thur; noon-midnight Fri, Sat; noon-10.30pm Sun. **Food served** 6-10.30pm Mon-Wed; noon-4pm, 6-10.30pm Thur-Sat; 1-5pm, 5-10pm Sun. **Credit** MC, V.
Once a grimy local pub, the Victoria Stakes is now a gem of a gastropub that serves up good cheer, good beer and great food in roughly equal measure. The downstairs bar is a typical but well-executed update of the traditional pub with lots of solid wooden tables, leather armchairs and reclaimed Victorian banisters. The bar menu offers superb Modern British food including venison steak and chunky chips to be tucked in to along with one of three guest real ales. Upstairs, there's a dining room characterised by voluptuous dark wooden furniture. A fuller menu is available in the restaurant where the food is gaining such a reputation that booking at the weekend is essential and even the minor celebrities that tried to grab a table on our last visit were turned away.
Babies and children admitted (high chairs). Restaurant.

Also in the area...

Ha! Ha! Bar & Canteen 390 Muswell Hill Broadway, N10 (8444 4722).
JD Wetherspoon 5 Spouters Corner, High Road, Wood Green, N22 (8881 3891).
Ruby in the Dust 256 Muswell Hill Broadway, N10 (8444 4041).

Palmers Green

Such charms as the area has are concentrated on Green Lanes: ace for all devotees of lifeless locals and dreary chain pubs. Giggle hunters and tree lovers should make the trip for the two pubs below.

Fox

413 Green Lanes, N13 (8886 9674). Palmers Green rail/ 329, W2 bus. **Open** noon-11pm Mon, Wed; noon-midnight Tue, Thur; noon-1am Fri, Sat; noon-10.30pm Sun. **Food served** noon-9pm Mon-Sat; noon-7pm Sun. **Credit** MC, V.
This huge Edwardian alehouse is widely known for its Bound & Gagged comedy nights. Weekly jape seekers have tittered here to a roll call of the best in British stand-up. As a pub, there's something of a hole where the character should be. This was not improved by a recent makeover in pastels, with insipid sports collages. Hair-gelled lads and mini-skirted lasses supply plenty of oomph, tanked up on jugs of cocktails and alcopops, fired by loud sounds and live football. Some of them crawl back the next day for recovery breakfasts at £3.95.
Comedy (8pm-1am Fri; £5-£8). Disabled: toilet. Disco (8.30pm Sat; free). Function room. Games (pool). Karaoke (8.30pm Tue, Thur; free). Tables outdoors (garden). TVs (big screen, satellite). Video jukebox.

Woodman

128 Bourne Hill, N13 (8882 0294). Southgate tube. **Open** 11am-11pm Mon-Sat; noon-10.30pm Sun. **Food served** noon-2.30pm, 6.30-9.30pm Mon-Fri; noon-3pm, 6.30-9.30pm Sat; noon-4pm Sun. **Credit** AmEx, MC, V.
Tucked away in affluent suburban streets on the edge of Grovelands Park, the Woodman's a bit of a rustic oasis. The low-beamed ceilings of the tiny front bar bow over a bevy of locals emitting the earthy odour of wellies and cigar smoke. Images of cricket, horse racing and the great outdoors clutter the walls, while at the back, there's a more modern dining room leading to an attractive beer garden and children's playground to ensure the little ones aren't left out. In accord with the general homely ambience, the cuisine casts a nod to Sundays with the folks: ample roasts, bangers and mash and similar comfort fare tucked into beside an open fire. There's a standard selection of beers and an extensive but unambitious wine list.
Babies and children admitted (high chairs). Games (fruit machine). Music (singer, occasional Sun). Restaurant. Tables outdoors (garden, patio). TV.

Also in the area...

Whole Hog (JD Wetherspoon) 430-34 Green Lanes, N13 (8882 3597).

The Waterway

North

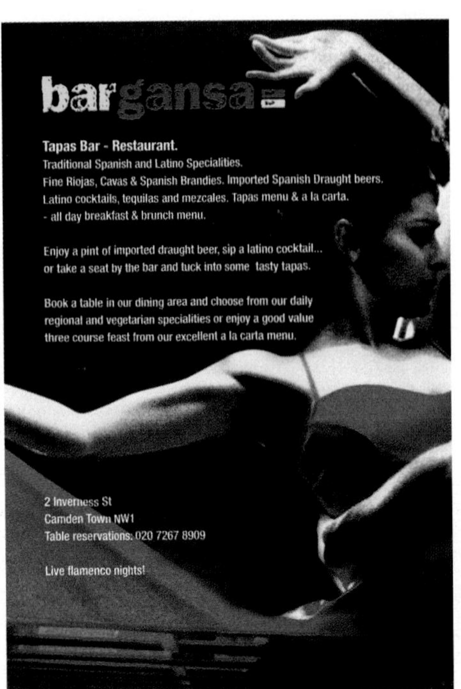
bargansa
Tapas Bar - Restaurant.
Traditional Spanish and Latino Specialities.
Fine Riojas, Cavas & Spanish Brandies. Imported Spanish Draught beers.
Latino cocktails, tequilas and mezcales. Tapas menu & a la carta.
- all day breakfast & brunch menu.
Enjoy a pint of imported draught beer, sip a latino cocktail...
or take a seat by the bar and tuck into some tasty tapas.
Book a table in our dining area and choose from our daily
regional and vegetarian specialities or enjoy a good value
three course feast from our excellent a la carta menu.
2 Inverness St
Camden Town NW1
Table reservations: 020 7267 8909
Live flamenco nights!

salon
at the house hotel

The Gallery
Bar and Restaurant
190 Broadhurst Gardens, West Hampstead, London NW6
tel: 020 7625 9184
Lunch for a fiver
Tuesday – Friday 12.30pm - 3.30pm
(closed for lunch week days during winter)
Lunch: 12.30pm - 4.30pm
Traditional Sunday Lunch
Dinner 7pm - 10pm everyday
Bar hours:
Sunday & Monday: 12pm - 11pm
Tuesday, Wednesday, Thursday: 12pm - 11.30pm
Friday & Saturday: 12pm - midnight
Bar snacks everyday 5pm - 8pm (except Sunday)

londons' only combined bar,
restaurant and record store
bar vinyl café
6 inverness street, camden nw1
www.vinyladdiction.co.uk
020 7681 7898

Primrose Hill

It's just across the tracks from Camden and Chalk Farm but Primrose Hill offers a very different take on the drinking experience. Forever bathed in sunshine, the few scant clouds in the sky lined with silver both inside and out, every day a Sunday afternoon... It's a pub lover's paradise. The venues are lovely, the beers are 'real' and the food's out of this world. And isn't that Jude over there with Nicole? And Jamie at the bar? And that bloke out of...

Engineer

65 Gloucester Avenue, NW1 (7722 0950). Camden Town or Chalk Farm tube. **Open** 9am-11pm Mon-Sat; 9am-10.30pm Sun. **Food served** 9-11.30am, noon-3pm, 7-10.30pm Mon-Fri; 9am-noon, 12.30-3.30pm, 7-10pm Sat, Sun. **Credit** MC, V.

It's as much restaurant as pub, with half the downstairs space and the entire second floor devoted to the seating of diners (plus the garden out back in good weather). Most nights there's not a single one of those seats spare, such is the good rep of the food served here. Although the bar often functions as little more than a holding area for those waiting to eat, it still caters to the pint-and-packet-of-crisps crowd. It has an understated, countrified look, with a monotony of stripped wood relieved by edgings of bright tiling, scattered candles and gorgeous flower arrangements. Big mirrors make the small space look bigger. Accomplished bar staff dispense an excellent range of wines by the glass and there's Old Speckled Hen and London Pride on tap.

Babies and hildren admitted (children's menu, high chairs). Disabled: toilet. Function room. Tables outdoors (garden). TV. **Map 8/G1**

Lansdowne

90 Gloucester Avenue, NW1 (7483 0409). Camden Town or Chalk Farm tube. **Open** *Bar* 6-11pm Mon; noon-11pm Tue-Sat; noon-10.30pm Sun. **Food served** noon-2.30pm, 7-10pm Mon-Sat; 1-9.30pm Sun. **Credit** MC, V.

The epitome of the scruffily chic gastropub, from the outside the Lansdowne looks like the kind of gaunt and hardened estate pub you'd cross the street to avoid if it was in Streatham. But this is Primrose Hill, and behind the cold tiled frontage is a big welcoming square of a room over filled with artfully distressed low-slung furniture. The blackboards covered with scrawled listings of choice vintages red, white and rosé, plus fussy Mediterranean fare and fancy bar snacks, really give the game away. The only threat here is matching the wrong plonk to your Connemara oysters. (Real foodies should head for the dining room upstairs for superb Modern British cuisine.) It's noisy and cheerful and an altogether classy experience, but don't make the mistake of saying so – here it's all about pretending not to notice.

Babies and children admitted (high chairs, nappy-changing facilities). Disabled: toilet. No piped music or jukebox. Restaurant. Tables outdoors (pavement). **Map 8/G26**

Pembroke Castle

150 Gloucester Avenue, NW1 (7483 2927). Chalk Farm tube. **Open** noon-11pm Mon-Sat; noon-10.30pm Sun. **Food served** noon-3pm, 6-9pm Mon-Fri; noon-8pm Sat; noon-6pm Sun. **Credit** AmEx, MC, V.

The down-to-earth Primrose Hill pub that looks like a Victorian railway station waiting room. There's even a clock built in as part of the dark wooden porch, iron columns support a magnolia ceiling edged with moulded cornices, and the intercity services rattle the leaded-glass windows as they brake into Euston. Beer includes Abbot and IPA from Greene King, plus there's a decent choice of wine. Upstairs is a lounge with big-screen sports and pool; outside is a paved terrace for summer drinking. A place for those who prefer a pint and the beautiful game to a glass of wine and the beautiful people.

Babies and children admitted (until 7pm). Function room. Games (fruit machine, pool tables). Tables outdoors (terrace). TVs (big screen, satellite). **Map 8/G26**

Queen's

49 Regent's Park Road, NW1 (7586 0408). Camden Town or Chalk Farm tube. **Open** 11am-11pm Mon-Sat; noon-10.30pm Sun. **Food served** noon-2.30pm, 7-9.45pm Mon-Thur; noon-2.30pm, 7-10.15pm Fri; noon-3pm, 7-10.15pm Sat; 12.30-4pm, 7-9pm Sun. **Credit** MC, V.

Primrose Hill's best and friendliest pub is this neo-Georgian Young's house, which pulls off the seldom achieved double of good beer (Young's own plus offerings from West Country brewery Smiles) and praiseworthy food. It's shaped like a Christmas cracker, with a central bottleneck corridor around the bar, flaring out into seated areas at either end – choose between chunky farmhouse tables or the slightly raised area with the (highly prized) sofa. Upstairs is a dining room (a solid, unpretentious menu supplemented by daily specials); downstairs is the cellar purportedly haunted by the ghost of Lillie Langtry, who once lived next door. Across the road is the hill, with one of the finest of London views.

Babies and children admitted. Restaurant. Tables outdoors (balcony, pavement). TV (satellite). **Map 8/G1**

St John's Wood

Tourists frequently shatter the leafy opulence of St John's Wood, joining overjewelled lunching housewives and their overworked au pairs as they descend on the area's two cultural landmarks: Lord's cricket ground and Abbey Road's pedestrian crossing. Accordingly, there are few down-to-earth boozers in this scattered selection, but the **Clifton**, the once great **Crocker's Folly** and the **Salt House** all offer a disparate but moneyed charm.

Clifton

96 Clifton Hill, NW8 (7372 3427). Maida Vale or St John's Wood tube. **Open** noon-11pm Mon-Sat; noon-10.30pm Sun. **Food served** noon-3pm, 6-10pm Mon-Sat; noon-9pm Sun. **Credit** AmEx, MC, V.

Hard-to-find but worth the trek, the Clifton is one of those cute-looking pastoral boozers that looks as if it belongs in Esher – or at the very least Hampstead – than in the qunmistakably urban streets of NW8. Essentially a converted stuccoed terrace, a small front garden leads into a much-wooded low-ceilinged interior where, period gossip would have it, Edward VII would meet his mistress Lillie Langtry. These days it's more likely to be frequented by cricket fans and the odd sub-Primrose Hill minor actor, skulking behind well-pulled pints. Those seeking more air with their London Pride should head for the conservatory and garden out back, where noshable food can be had. A snug place for a drink.

Babies and children admitted (until 7pm). Tables outdoors (garden, patio).

Crocker's Folly

24 Aberdeen Place, NW8 (7286 6608). Edgware Road or Warwick Avenue tube. **Open** noon-11pm Mon-Sat; noon-10.30pm Sun. **Food served** noon-3pm, 6-9pm Mon-Fri; noon-3pm, 6-8pm Sat; noon-8pm Sun. **Credit** AmEx, MC, V.

North

This, perhaps the most spectacular pub in London, was almost lost to us last year when, unable to find a buyer, the owner-brewery threatened to close it down to concentrate on other interests (Jongleurs, Walkabout – classy stuff). For a while there were rumours that this magnificent late-Victorian pile would be converted into an Indian restaurant. It hasn't happened. The pub now trades under new ownership, although apparently it's on borrowed time. The decline and neglect isn't obvious at first. Crocker's still looks extraordinary: three rooms, all marvels of the palatial and extravagant, with intricate Jacobean-style coffered ceilings, gleaming woodwork, beautiful mirrors and, in the aptly named marble bar, an immense fireplace. But service is desultory, the food is poor, and what kind of a crowd does a pub attract that it is sometimes forced to exercise an over-25s only policy? We'd say give it a miss until things improve, but without sustained custom we might just lose the place altogether and that would be an even greater disaster.
Babies and children admitted (restaurant only). Disabled: toilet. Games (darts, fruit machines, table football). Music (jazz 8pm occasional Sun; free). Quiz (9pm Thur; free). Restaurant. Tables outdoors (pavement). TV (big screen, satellite).

Duke of York

2A St Anne's Terrace, NW8 (7722 1933). St John's Wood tube. **Open** 11am-11pm Mon-Sat; 11am-10.30pm Sun. **Food served** noon-11pm Mon-Sat; noon-10pm Sun. **Credit** MC, V.
A curio this, formerly a standard-issue corner boozer now done up to look like an Irishman's idea of a Persian brothel with polished brass lamps, mosaic tables, beaded rugs, cushions and curtains, and plentiful adverts for Guinness. Eccentric maybe, but endearing. For a while there was North Africa-influenced food to match the visuals, but on recent visits we've noticed a retreat to pub basics with just the odd concession to the original theme. Shame. It's still a perfectly enjoyable place to have a drink (from a limited selection), especially if you can bag one of the outside tables to sit and watch the supremely self-satisfied locals go about their no-accounting-for-cost, less-accounting-for-taste business.
Babies and children admitted (daytime). Restaurant. Tables outdoors (pavement). TV.

Lord's Tavern

Grace Gates, St John's Wood Road, NW8 (7266 5980). St John's Wood tube. **Open/food served** 11am-11pm Mon-Sat; noon-10.30pm Sun. **Credit** AmEx, MC, V.
Tucked smack-bang beneath HQ (fan terminology for Lord's cricket ground), the ugly boxlike Tavern oozes masculinity as only a darkish hued pine-and-brick based sports bar can. A nightmare on matchdays when the Barmy Army come to roost, the place is half empty the rest of the time, despite its decent range of ales (Charles Wells' Bombardier, Brakspear Bitter) and reasonable food (served in a side-room dining area). The leather-and-willow theme is kept to a minimum and the cosy Chesterfields in the corner would be quite enticing if there was more of an atmosphere.
Babies and children admitted. Restaurant. Tables outdoors (terrace). TV (big screen, satellite).

Salt House

63 Abbey Road, NW8 (7328 6626). St John's Wood tube. **Open** noon-11pm Mon-Sat; noon-10.30pm Sun. **Food served** 12.30-3pm, 6.30-10.30pm Mon-Fri; 12.30-4pm, 7-10.30pm Sat, Sun. **Credit** AmEx, MC, V.
It took a while for a gastropub to appear in St John's Wood, but when it did, it was this corker, located 100 yards or so up the road from The Beatles' iconic crossing. It's a big place that makes full use of its corner setting with a pleasant roadside front garden leading to an airy but slightly cramped main bar space, all bare boards and blackboard menus – you know the look by now. Down wooden steps is a larger dining area, but the menu – variable, but a dream when on form – can be enjoyed anywhere. Home to the Wood's younger set (yes, there is such a thing), the prices still favour the affluent, but if you want to settle in a corner sofas with a free newspaper and half an ale, the attractive bar staff don't look the type to object.
Babies and children admitted (children's room, high chairs). Function room. Restaurant. TV.

Star

38 St John's Wood Terrace, NW8 (7722 1051). St John's Wood tube. **Open** 11am-11pm Mon-Sat; noon-10.30pm Sun. **Credit** MC, V.
A local's local, the Star is blissfully out of step with the rest of a high street given over to chains-u-like, children's clothes shops and ludicrously expensive minimarkets. The fact it's slightly off the beaten track might help, but chances are this kind of big-beamed boozer will never go totally out of fashion. A large Victorian fireplace dominates, complemented by multicoloured stained-glass windows and lovely lillies lining the shelves. The back room's big screen marks it down as the place to come and watch our brave boys in ball-busting action. The beer selection is nothing special but the convivial and easy going atmosphere more than makes up for it.
Games (fruit machine). Tables outdoors (garden). TV (big screen).

Also in the area...

All Bar One 60 St John's Wood High Street, NW8 (7483 9931).

Stoke Newington

Granted, there are a couple of decent watering holes on the High Street, and a couple more tucked away in the heart of residential neighbourhoods (seek out the **Shakespeare** if you can), but it's still all about Church Street, a skinny stretch of road lined with bookshops, pubs, restaurants and London's loveliest cemetery. Remember Islington a decade or so ago, before property prices surged skywards and the chains moved in and killed Upper Street? Well, that's what Stokey's like today: modest, approachable and, put plainly, nice. Bring a copy of the *Guardian* to blend in.

Auld Shillelagh

105 Stoke Newington Church Street, N16 (7249 5951/ www.theauldshillelagh.com). Bus 73, 105. **Open** 11am-11pm Mon-Sat; noon-10.30pm Sun. **Credit** AmEx, DC, MC, V.
The place has changed but the names have stayed the same. A refurb inside and out has done wonders, but this remains at heart an age-old (130 years) Irish pub, with same age-old Irish crew propping up the bar morning, noon and night. The once grubby, still skinny room has been extended at the back and opened up into a beer garden beyond. More of a surprise is the entertainment here: the Sinatra-themed Frank's Happy Hours nights have bitten the dust, but Peel Me a Grape on Sundays has plugged the gap with a mix of music and film. This is still an Irish pub, though, and pint-proud bartenders ensure that the Guinness is nothing short of exceptional.
Babies and children admitted. Film screenings (1st and 3rd Sun mth). Games (fruit machine). Music (band occasional Fri; 1st and 3rd Sun mth). No-smoking area. TV (satellite).

Bar Lorca

175 Stoke Newington High Street, N16 (7275 8659/ www.barlorca.com). Bus 73, 476. **Open** noon-1am Mon-Thur; noon-2am Fri, Sat; noon-midnight Sun. **Food served** noon-11pm Mon-Thur; noon-midnight Fri, Sat; noon-11pm Sun. **Admission** £4 after 10pm Fri, Sat. **Happy hour** 6-9pm Mon-Sat. **Credit** AmEx, MC, V.

On a large corner site at the High Street end of Church Street, the 'lucky Lorca' has long been pulling a wide variety of hard-drinking and dancing punters. It's a huge place, decorated in a colourful Iberian theme and split into three areas: bar, restaurant, dancefloor. It's big enough that you can still find quiet(ish) corners even on party nights – particularly among the palms and pretty Mediterranean pottery of the (fairly expensive) dining section. At the high mosaic bar, where the lively, often Spanish, crowd slugs bottles of Estrela, Latin cocktails are a speciality (by the jug, £15). During the day the continental tradition of welcoming children holds, with occasional clowns to distract the bambinos.

Babies and children admitted (until 8pm; clowns, high chairs, toys). Dance classes (7.30-9.30pm Mon, Fri; £5). Disabled: toilet. Games (fruit machine, pinball machine). Music (jam session 9pm Sun; free). Restaurant. TV (big screen, satellite).

Coach & Horses

178 Stoke Newington High Street, N16 (7254 6697). Stoke Newington rail/67, 73, 106 bus. **Open** 11am-11pm Mon-Sat; noon-10.30pm Sun. **Food served** noon-10pm Tue-Sat; 1-9pm Sun. **No credit cards.**

A one-time Irish boozer and former punk hangout, the Coach has been transformed into a kind of Thai theme bar. Buddhas, shadow puppets and Eastern prints adorn tan-coloured walls, while large ceiling fans rotate indolently (not to say superfluously) above. Although a fair proportion of the clientele is here to enjoy the very fine and competitively priced South-east Asian food, the place remains very much a bar rather than a restaurant, with dumpy Guinness-pint bar stools and a laserdisc jukebox. The choice of beers is a slight let-down (Stella, Tetley's, Blackthorn), but the genial good humour of the staff and the majority of the punters, is a winner.

Babies and children admitted (until 7pm). Disabled: toilet. Games (fruit machine). Tables outdoors (pavement). TVs (satellite).

Daniel Defoe

102 Stoke Newington Church Street, N16 (7254 2906). 73, 393, 476 bus. **Open** 1-11pm Mon-Fri; noon-11pm Sat; noon-10.30pm Sun. **Food served** 1-10pm Mon-Fri; noon-6pm Sat-Sun. **Credit** MC, V.

Totally trad, the Defoe attracts an older crowd than most Stokey pubs. It's got a large front room and a smaller back room with pool table. The big draw, however, for those who care about such things, is the range of real ales, which will quite possibly include Adnams Broadside, Charles Wells' Bombardier, Old Speckled Hen and something called Defoe Ale – all badged with a Cask Marque testifying to what a good job the landlord does of keeping his pipes clean. Real ale drinkers should also check out the Rochester Castle on the High Street, a JD Wetherspoon pub with a good selection of beers.

Games (fruit machine, golf machine, pool table). Tables outdoors (garden).

Fox Reformed

176 Stoke Newington Church Street, N16 (7254 5975). Bus 73, 393, 476. **Open** 5-11pm Mon-Fri; noon-11pm Sat, Sun. **Food served** 6.30-10.30pm Mon-Fri; noon-3pm, 6.30-10.30pm Sat, Sun. **Credit** AmEx, MC, V.

One of the pack leaders in the rush to gentrify the area in the 1980s, the Fox is more adult in tone than many a Stokey establishment. Brightly decked out in hunting pink, it has a style much appreciated by a loyal bunch of regulars. The bar is always busy: even early on a Monday evening we were only just in time to grab the last two seats (although Monday does play host to the regular backgammon fixture). The wine list is compact, yet still manages to encompass a good range of drinker-friendly grape varieties and styles. Choice of wine by the glass is limited but the bottles are superb value for money.

Babies and children admitted (high chairs). Games (board games). No-smoking tables. Tables outdoors (heated garden). Theme nights (backgammon 7.30pm Mon; book club last Tue mth; investment club 1st Sun mth; wine-tasting club every other Thur; all £30 per year).

Londesborough

36 Barbauld Road, N16 (7254 5865). Bus 73.
Open. 4.30-11pm Mon-Thur; 4.30pm-midnight Fri; noon-midnight Sat; noon-10.30pm Sun. **Food served** 6-10pm Mon-Thur; 6-11pm Fri; noon-4.30pm. 5-9pm Sat, Sun. **Credit** MC, V.

It used to be a gay bar but since reopening after a refurb the Londesborough seems to have no particular sexual orientations and is welcoming to all comers. It sports a modish dark-wood interior filled with a liberal scattering of low tables and sofas, with a modest DJ booth in the corner screened by perspex. The selection of drinks is excellent and includes 55, 60 and 70% absinthe (they're all artists in Stokey, you know), 20-year-old bourbon and a good cocktail list. For the less adventurous there's London Pride and Hoegaarden on tap. The food looks good too, and in wamer months the existing menu will be supplemented by BBQs in the beer garden out back. The place is slightly off the beaten track, which cuts down on casual High Street riff raff.

Babies and children (until 6pm). Music (DJs 7pm Tue-Sun). No-smoking tables. Tables outdoors (garden).

The Prince

59 Kynaston Road, N16 (7923 4766). Bus 73. **Open** 4-11pm Mon-Fri; 11.30am-11pm Sat; noon-10.30pm Sun. **Food served** 5.30am-9.45pm Mon-Fri; 11am-4pm, 5.30-9.45pm Sat; 12.30-4pm, 5.30-9.30pm Sun. **Credit** MC, V.

Bought and done up a couple of years back by the owner of the highly successful Cooler deli on nearby Church Street, the scruffy old pub that was once the Prince of Wales has come of age. The interior has also been sharpened with a few fancy design features – a stainless-steel bar and cranky lights – and a lick of battleship grey and maroon paint. As a result, the place has become the current Stoke Newington hangout of choice. A large part of its popularity is due to the reliably delicious food (a comfort-oriented global pick 'n' mix, at very fair prices), sourced from the deli and served in a separate restaurant area at the back. This gives on to a outside yard that looks like the *Big Brother* house garden but makes a refreshing alternative to the regular crush at the bar. In addition to the interesting wine list, beers on draught include Flowers IPA, Staropramen and Hoegaarden, plus bottled organics such as Golden Promise and Freedom.

Babies and children admitted (children's games and menu, high chairs). Disabled: toilet. Function room. Games (board games). Tables outdoors (garden, pavement). TV (satellite).

Rose & Crown

199 Stoke Newington Church Street, N16 (7254 7497). Bus 73. **Open** 11.30am-11pm Mon-Sat; noon-10.30pm Sun. **Food served** noon-2.30pm Mon-Fri; noon-3.30pm Sat; noon-4pm Sun. **Credit** MC, V.

North

Successful restoration of the stone-flagged flooring; the preservation of the old Truman's wood panelling and listed deco windows; not just one, but two blazing fires in the colder months; and the unflagging good nature on both sides of the bar – all make the Rose & Crown something of a destination pub, pulling punters from far and wide. The beers are good too and usually include Adnams Best and Broadside and Marston's Pedigree, alongside an interesting choice of wines. Sunday roasts here have become legendary (and sometimes draw a packed crowd), as have the Tuesday quiz nights.
Babies and children admitted (until 7pm). Games (fruit machine, quiz machine). Quiz (8.30pm first Tue mth; £1). Tables outdoors (pavement). TV (satellite).

The Shakespeare

57 Allen Road, N16 (7254 4190). Bus 73. **Open** 5-11pm Mon-Fri; noon-11pm Sat; noon-10.30pm Sun. **Credit** MC, V.
After a bit of disruption a year or so ago while the rear wall and toilets were pushed back a few yards to make some more leg room, the Shakespeare remains on form. Thankfully, the longer walk to the loos is the only change; the pre-war French drinks posters still enliven an old wooden bar from which a fine selection of real ales (Timothy Taylor's Landlord among them) continues to be dispensed. The wine selection isn't bad either. Beaten-up church pews make up much of the seating, while a walled garden makes a convivial spot out of the wind (although sadly it tends to be out of the sun too). Best of all, the Shakey's justly famed jukebox continues to offer the choicest of selections – from Mingus to Madchester via Sinatra and the Clash.
Babies and children admitted. Jukebox. Quiz (8.45pm Mon; £1). Tables outdoors (garden). TV (satellite).

Also in the area...

Rochester Castle (JD Wetherspoon) 145 High Street, N16 (7249 6016).
Stoke Newington Tup 132 Church Street, N16 (7249 1318).

North

Swiss Cottage

Much like Lisson Grove and Hither Green, Swiss Cottage's name conjures up images of tranquillity and pastoral calm that make the grim urban reality even harder to take. Essentially a very busy A-road flanked by charity shops and discount furniture stores, this is not a destination to head to in a hurry.

Elbow Room

135 Finchley Road, NW3 (7586 9888/www.elbowroom.co.uk). Swiss Cottage tube. **Open** noon-midnight Mon-Thur; noon-1am Fri, Sat; noon-10.30pm Sun. **Food served** noon-10pm daily. **Happy hour** 5-8pm Mon-Fri. **Admission** £2 after 9pm Fri, Sat. **Credit** MC, V.
Remember the legend on the side of Del Boy's three-wheeler: 'Paris, New York, Peckham'? Well, there's something similar going on with the Elbow Room, the übercool pool bar chain whose other branches are in trend-central Islington, Westbourne Grove and Hoxton. How dismal old Swiss Cottage gatecrashed that hip trinity is anybody's guess. Enter through a fiercely solid metal door and head up the steps to a long corrider, one side filled by pairings of chair and table, the other hosting the pool tables. A larger corner space is given over to low chairs while at the end of the corrider looms the bar, serving standard cocktails and draught lager/stout. All credit Elbow Room for branching out to such an unfashionable area.
Function room. Games (pool tables). Music (DJs 9pm Fri, Sat). TVs (satellite).

Zuccato

Unit 8A, O_2 Centre, 255 Finchley Road, NW3 (7431 1799/www.etruscagroup.co.uk). Finchley Road tube.
Open/food served 10.30am-midnight Mon-Sat; 10.30am-11pm Sun. **Credit** AmEx, DC, MC, V.
The O_2 Centre is a huge hangar-like package of bleakest mall-life Americana. Theme restaurants, chain shops and a multi-screen cinema: it's the perfect setting for a shooting spree. Zuccato is at least a cut above its surroundings. It has a bit of that continental cafe look: stainless steel and dark brown furnishings, stiff black chairs, marble tables and curved bar. The drinks menu favours wine and bottled beers, as well as huge pitchers of cocktails (try the Pink Zuccato: peach schnapps, white wine, Grenadine and lemonade for £16) – although the idea of drinking cocktails in a shopping mall seems an odd one to us. Punters tend to be shoppers and cinema-goers – folk en route elsewhere, hence the huge station clock that hangs from the ceiling.
Babies and children admitted (restaurant, high chairs). Disabled: toilet. No-smoking area. Restaurant.

Also in the area...

JD Wetherspoon O_2 Centre, Level 2, 255 Finchley Road, NW3 (7433 0920).

Tufnell Park & Archway

A changing demographic seems to be breathing some much-needed life into the local beer economy. The area around Tufnell Park tube contains some old locals revived with young money (notably the **Progress Bar**), while other fleapits are being turned into gastropubs (this year we welcome the **Junction Tavern** and **Samphire**) faster than entrepreneurs can turn a buck on a council house.

Dartmouth Arms

35 York Rise, NW5 (7485 3267). Tufnell Park tube. **Open** 11am-11pm Mon-Fri; 10am-11pm Sat; 10am-10.30pm Sun. **Food served** 11am-10pm Mon-Fri; 10am-10pm Sat, Sun. **Credit** MC, V.
Despite its smart paint job (outside) and pared-down paint- and woodwork (inside), together with a long menu, the Dartmouth has managed to retain the feel of a real (but better than most) neighbourhood boozer. An early Tuesday evening visit unearthed more life than we'd bargained for. Groups of youth harangued anybody who'd listen on tabloid melodrama, Tony Blair and the contrasting fortunes of Spurs and Arsenal; older folk were settled back in the dingy snug slamming counters on the backgammon board. There's a well-kept beer selection, with Adnams beers and guest ales, plus a big choice of sandwiches, snacks like a half pint of prawns, and a full-blown gastro menu. On Sundays, the kitchen is overwhelmed by the demand for traditional roasts. Shelf-loads of books are there to buy or browse. It's an exceptional local.
Babies and children admitted (until 8pm; high chairs). Bookshop. Function room. Games (board games). Quiz (8pm every other Tue; £1). Tables outdoors (pavement). TV (satellite).

Junction Tavern

101 Fortess Road, NW5 (7485 9400). Tufnell Park tube. **Open** 5-11pm Mon-Fri; noon-11pm Sat; noon-10.30pm Sun. **Food served** 6.30-10.30pm Mon-Sat; noon-4pm, 6.30-9.30pm Sun. **Credit** MC, V.
The JT is yet another old boozer given the gastro-refurb treatment last summer. The restaurant is at the front, with open-plan kitchen and cookbooks lined up on the counter. The

food doesn't aim at fireworks but it's elevated by good taste, top ingredients, and nearly flawless skill in execution. The menu changes daily, but look for excellent vegetable soups and a killer chocolate cake that always seems to be on the menu. Tables are reasonably spaced, so you don't feel cramped even if the place is pretty busy; you can relax here. The laid-back quality is even more noticeable in the bar at the back, where there are sofas to lounge on while reading the papers. Beers include London Pride, Young's 'ordinary' and regular guests; the wine list, though nice and cheap (mostly £11-£16), could use a little more excitement. Staff are unbelievably friendly and, if the Junction Tavern could clone them, they would have other pub owners queuing to buy.
Tables outdoors (beer garden).

Lord Palmerston

33 Dartmouth Park Hill, NW5 (7485 1578). Tufnell Park tube. **Open** noon-11pm Mon-Sat; noon-10.30pm Sun. **Food served** 12.30-3pm, 7.30-10pm Mon; 12.30-3pm, 7-10pm Tue-Sat; 1-4pm, 7-9pm Sun. **Credit** MC, V.
Don't be fooled by the plain, unpretentious decor (duck-egg blue throughout, a couple of wine racks behind the large front bar and the odd flower arrangement), the Palmerston is a seriously class act. It's a place for culinary treats. The food is no-nonsense British but made with first-rate ingredients and prepared with flair, attention to detail and generosity. To drink, there are good beers, such as Courage Best or Marston's Pedigree, and a superior selection of wine, both by the glass and bottle. Sunseekers should make an early beeline for the benches at the front in summer. The only quibble with this place is that on busy nights and Sunday lunchtimes there never seem to be enough staff on hand to deal with the hungry crowds that flock here, so you might be in for a bit of a wait. But it's worth it.
Babies and children admitted. Function room. No piped music or jukebox. Tables outdoors (garden, pavement). TV.

Progress Bar

162 Tufnell Park Road, N7 (7272 2078/www.innprogress.com). Tufnell Park tube. **Open** noon-midnight Mon-Wed, Sun; noon-2am Thur-Sat. **Food served** 6-10.30pm Mon-Fri; 1-10.30pm Sat, Sun. **Happy hour** 6-9pm Tue, Thur. **Credit** MC, V.
Formerly the Tufnell Park Tavern, an ageing jazz venue, the new deep red flock wallpaper, charcoal tables and leather sofas evidence a stylish reincarnation as a DJ bar. In fact the concept is given a fun new spin, with regular residents jockeying from the bar counter itself. It's a large venue with plenty of standing room by the central bar, with quieter corners for more intimacy among close friends (or even friends of close friends). One corner is given over to a superb pool room with four tables backdropped by a London skyline in cool blue. Food involves a couple of specials along the Thai green curry line and the usual nachos and wedges, while drink is very much standard draughts and bottles. Regular fixtures include Saturday stand-up acts on loan from the Bound & Gagged comedy club at the **Fox** (*see p181*).
Babies and children admitted. Disabled: toilet. Function room (seats 120). Games (pool; £6-£10 per hour). Music (DJs 9pm, Thur-Sun; free. Bands 9pm Fri, Sat; £3). No-smoking tables. Tables outdoors (garden). TV (big screen, satellite).

St John's

91 Junction Road, N19 (7272 1587). Archway tube. **Open** 5pm-11pm Mon; 11am-11pm Tue-Sat; noon-10.30pm Sun. **Food served** 6.30-11pm Mon; noon-3.30pm, 6.30-11pm Tue-Sat; noon-4pm, 6.30-10.30pm Sun. **Credit** AmEx, MC, V.
Once a dingy old Irish boozer, this is now a less-dingy new gastropub: deep reds and greens, soft candlelight, leather sofas and appealing artwork creating a gloom conducive to the enjoyment of a fine menu. Clocking in at about £10-£15, main courses are not cheap, but a menu heavy on fish and game should appeal to the more adventurous diner. The wine list is extensive and beer drinkers are well served with Greene King Abbot, Marston's Pedigree plus a regularly changing guest ale on tap, as well as the standard range of imported bottled lagers. Indicative of the Junction Road area's gentrification is the fact that the place is rammed with diners most nights of the week. If you just want a quiet pint, you're best off leaving it until the post-prandial hour of 10pm.
Babies and children admitted. Tables outdoors (terrace).

Samphire

135 Fortess Road, NW5 (7482 4855/www.samphire_nw5.co.uk). Tufnell Park tube. **Open/food served** 6-10.30pm Mon-Sat; noon-9pm Sun. **Credit** MC, V.
Samphire occupies a space in a strip of Tufnell Park that seems to do for retail businesses what the Sargasso Sea does for mariners, but if there's any justice, this place will stay afloat where others have sunk. It is a seriously ambitious, seriously good local with reasonable prices and some cooking that would put many a West End trendy spot to shame. The decor is spare, with a small room on the ground floor and a larger one upstairs providing a good view – if you want one – of the unassuming shopping street where Samphire has pitched its tent. The beer range is standard, but the fact that this is a pub that sells itself on the quality of the food can be seen by the attention given to its interesting and sensibly priced wine list. The international food is exquisite, with charming service to go with it.
Babies and children admitted. No-smoking tables.

Settle Inn

17-19 Archway Road, N19 (7272 7872). **Open** noon-11pm Mon-Sat; noon-10.30pm Sun. **Food served** noon-3pm, 6-10pm Mon-Fri; noon-9.30pm Sat, Sun. **Credit** AmEx, DC, MC, V.
Scruffy Archway Road, just up from N19's notorious suicide bridge, and where one might expect to find the pub equivalent of Beachy Head, comes good with this positively life-affirming bar-restaurant. With gleaming windows, stripped floors and pine tables this pub, the offspring of a venture in more middle-class Battersea (*see p197*), skirts dangerously close to chain bar-ism chic. But in the short time that it's been open, the Inn's managed to pick up a dedicated local following, making for a very unchain-like buzzy atmosphere. Real ales include Courage Best and Bombardier, and a bustling open kitchen serves up sweet smelling dishes from a regularly changing menu: the Sunday roasts are recommended.
Babies and children admitted (Sun lunch only). Games (board games). Music (occasional jazz/acoustic). Quiz (music 8.30pm Sun; general 8.30pm Tue; free). TV (satellite).

West Hampstead

It's not as moneyed as neighbouring Hampstead proper or as scruffy as Kilburn, its neighbour on the other side; West Hampstead sits between the two poles of the pub spectrum. Quiet pints are to be had along West End Lane but nothing really stands out. One encouraging trend is the emergence of several bar-restaurants and DJ bars catering for the younger folk moving into the area.

Cane Bar

283-5 West End Lane, NW6 (7794 7817). West Hampstead tube/rail. **Open** 4-11.30pm Mon-Fri; noon-11pm Sat; noon-10.30pm Sun. **Happy hour** 5.30-8pm Mon-Fri. **Credit** MC, V.

Wander along otherwise peaceful West End Lane most nights of the week and the tranquillity's splintered by thumping bass. That's the Cane Bar. With its burgundy paintwork, ice blue lighting and black leather bed tucked in one corner, the place looks as if it is part chill-out room, part bondage parlour, and totally full-steam-on party box. Four nights a week, DJs let loose good time funk, hip hop and break beat to a massed fast-motion crowd – though you get the impression they could play Leonard Cohen and the punters would still be working up a lather. Preferred drinks match the night on the town ethos – bottled beers, cocktails and shots, served up by staff doing their best to maintain a studied cool amid the frenzy.

Function room. Music (DJs 7.30pm Tue, Thur-Sun; free). Tables outdoors (terrace).

Gallery

190 Broadhurst Gardens, NW6 (7625 9184). West Hampstead tube/rail. **Open** 4-11pm Mon; 4-11.30pm Tue-Thur; noon-midnight Fri, Sat; noon-11pm Sun. **Food served** *Bar* 5-8pm Mon-Fri; 12.30-4.30pm Sat, Sun. *Restaurant* 7-11pm Mon-Fri; 12.30-4.30pm Sat, Sun. **Happy hour** 5-7pm daily. **Credit** MC, V.

West Hampstead's movers and shakers were out in force the night we dropped by the Gallery, from art school fops to a well-spoken lass in a rugby shirt. The upstairs bar makes the most of an unpromising space, with the 'gallery' consisting of a small mezzanine adorned with dubious contemporary artwork. Drinks range from omnipresent lagers to rarer brands (Czech Kirin and Wells Banana Beer) and there's a bangers and mash-style bar menu until 8pm for comfort-seeking beer soaking. Downstairs, in a room that resembles a nuclear bunker furnished with antique auction leftovers, is a restaurant proper. We ate halibut with artichoke in a spinach bowl (£11.80) and left happy.

Babies and children admitted (until 6pm). Games (board games). Music (band 8pm occasional Mon). No-smoking tables. Tables outdoors (pavement).

No 77 Wine Bar

77 Mill Lane, NW6 (7435 7787). West Hampstead tube/rail/C11, 28, 139 bus. **Open** noon-11pm Mon, Tue; noon-midnight Wed-Sat; noon-10.30pm Sun. **Food served** noon-2.30pm, 7-10.30pm Mon, Tue; noon-2.30pm, 7-11.30pm Wed-Sat; noon-4pm Sun. **Credit** MC, V.

Forget the football and rugby shirts on the wall that suggest some kind of beer monster's delight, this chilled-out wine bar with friendly and unpretentious atmosphere is a firm and enduring neighbourhood fave with all-comers. Potted palms, woody furniture, candles and African-inspired artwork are a better indicator of tone. There's a bar area upfront, and an informal restaurant section at the back. The wine list is reasonable if a little static with some good value Old and New World selections, including reliable crowd-pleasers such as Chile's Santa Rita and California's Beringer. Definitely worth booking a table if you're intending to dine (it's good but it isn't cheap), and don't come if you're in a hurry, as service tends to be very leisurely.

Babies and children admitted (children's portions). Function room. Restaurant. Tables outdoors (pavement). TV (satellite).

Progress Bar. See p187

North

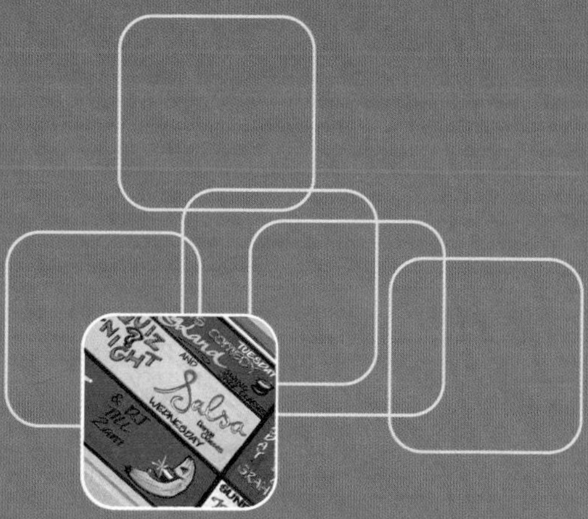

South

Balham

There's no doubt that Balham is on the up as far as eating, drinking and entertainment go. Old staples such as the **Bedford** have long garnered a loyal following, but it's the growing cafe/bar/restaurant culture that's finally turning the ugly duckling of SW12 into more than just a poor man's Clapham.

Bedford

77 Bedford Hill, SW12 (8682 8940). Balham tube/rail. **Open** 11am-11pm Mon-Wed; 11am-midnight Thur; 11am-2am Fri, Sat; noon-10.30pm Sun. **Food served** noon-2.45pm, 7-10pm Mon-Fri; noon-4pm, 7-10pm Sat; noon-4.30pm, 7-9.45pm Sun. **Credit** AmEx, MC, V.

This is Balham's best-known boozer, thanks in large part to a community-bonding programme of comedy shows, bands, magicians, quizzes, theatre, dance classes, fitness forums… You name it, it's happening. It's also a fine venue for simple boozing with a dog-leg bar (draught Miller, Kronenbourg, John Smith's plus 18 wines by the glass or the bottle) addressing the two main areas, each with their own cosy quarters, separated by arched alcoves or wooden railings. Beside is a modest but busy open kitchen serving up a full menu from soup of the day to lamb noisette. The weekday low-key vibe morphs into a free-for-all from Friday to Sunday but the atmosphere always remains the right side of convivial.

Babies and children admitted (until 6pm). Comedy (7.30pm Fri; £10. 6.30pm Sat; £13). Dance (line dancing 7.30pm Mon; £5. Swing classes 8pm Tue; £5. Salsa classes 7pm Wed; £5). Disabled: toilet. Function rooms (5). Games (board games, fruit machines). Magician (lunchtime Sun). Music (Jazz 8pm Sun; £5. Acoustic 9pm Wed; free. Bands 9pm Thur; admission vary). Nightclub (10.15pm-2am, last entry 11pm Fri, Sat; £5). Quiz (9pm Wed; £2). Theatre (8pm Mon-Thur; £10). TV (big screen, satellite).

Duke of Devonshire

39 Balham High Road, SW12 (8673 1363). Balham tube/rail. **Open** 11am-midnight Mon-Thur; 11am-2am Fri, Sat; noon-midnight Sun. **Food served** 11am-11pm Mon-Fri; noon-1am Sat, Sun. **Credit** MC, V.

A Young's pub, the Duke is stuck out between Balham and Clapham Common. From the outside it's a modestly fronted place, but indoors is as grand as it gets. A vast hangar of an interior is lidded by a maze-patterned ceiling, and dominated by a bar counter so vast that on Sunday mornings it serves local joggers as a running track. The home straight protrudes into the front of house, while behind is a dukedom all its own. The ornate back area has a weekend late-night music licence, and gives grand – that word again – entrance to a split-level terrace bar with kiddies' playground in summer. There are 15 wines served by the glass or bottle plus Young's fine ales.

Babies and children admitted (garden during daytime). Disabled: toilet. Games (darts, fruit machines, pinball, table football). Music (9.30pm-2am, last entry 11pm Fri, Sat; free). Tables outdoors (garden). TV (satellite).

Exhibit

Balham Station Road, SW12 (8772 6556). Balham tube/rail. **Open** 11.30am-11pm Mon-Thur; 11.30am-midnight Fri, Sat; 11.30am-10.30pm Sun. **Food served** noon-3pm, 7-11.30pm Mon-Sat; 12.30-4pm Sun. **Credit** MC, V.

Glass-fronted and eye-catching (despite having Balham tube opposite and Sainsbury's as a neighbour), Exhibit is a far cry from your usual depressing station tavern. Stylish and imaginative, it's a split-level bar of fab design and taste. Bauhaus-style seats are slung alongside long communal tables and low sofas separated by bamboo screens. At the far end, a sweep of bar counter operates as chat zone central against a backdrop photo mural of tomatoes, complemented by a postmodern fireplace and wall-length aquarium. Drinks include some intriguing house liqueurs and cocktails and an extensive wine list, but only Kirin, Stella, Guinness and Red Stripe for beer drinkers. Coffee mornings are popular, while weekend evenings see bouncers keeping eager visitors in good queuing order. Every tube stop should have one.

Babies and children admitted (until 7pm). Disabled: toilet. Restaurant. Tables outdoors (garden, pavement).

Grove

39 Oldridge Road, SW12 (8673 6531). Clapham South tube. **Open** 11am-11pm Mon-Sat; noon-10.30pm Sun. **Food served** noon-3pm, 6-10pm Mon-Sat; noon-6pm Sun. **Credit** MC, V.

Pity the Grove – all dressed up with nowhere to go. It's hidden (if a pub this big could ever be truly 'hidden') round the corner from Clapham South tube. The lack of custom on our recent visit seems to indicate that locals might be stepping further out to the brighter lights of the nearby High Road for their evening's entertainment. Bit of a shame, really, as the Grove is not unattractive (framed pictures, stucco ceiling and open fire) and a real effort has been made to maintain a comfortable trad feel while keeping things contemporary – for example, there's a surprisingly modish food menu and a selection of shooters to accompany the range of Young's ales.

Babies and children admitted (dining area only). Function area. Games (fruit machines). No-smoking area. TV (big screen, satellite).

Lounge

76 Bedford Hill, SW12 (8673 8787). Balham tube/rail. **Open** 5-11pm Mon, Tue; 5pm-midnight Wed-Fri; 11am-midnight Sat, Sun. **Food served** 6-10.30pm Mon-Fri; 11am-8pm Sat, Sun. **Credit** MC, V.

Really it's more of a cabin than a lounge, cowering beneath the roar of Balham railway bridge, blinds pulled down to shut out the headlights of passing traffic. It has a just-moved-in feel – a scant few raw pine tables and chairs, a couple of soft sofas and a plain wood bar counter. The drinks line-up is limited (Guinness, Carlsberg and Kronenbourg on draught) but backed up with bottles, plus cocktails, shots, half-a-dozen wines and a reasonable menu of Lounge burgers and similar. It's modest, but enterprising all the same and it attracts a crowd so laid-back they haven't seen upright for a while.

Babies and children admitted. Disabled: toilet. Function room. Tables outdoors (pavement). TV (satellite).

Point

16-18 Ritherdon Road, SW17 (8767 2660). Tooting Bec tube/Balham tube/rail. **Open** 10am-11pm Mon-Sat; 10am-10.30pm Sun. **Food served** 10am-10.30pm Mon-Sat; 10am-10pm Sun. **Credit** AmEx, DC, MC, V.

A rare find in the no man's land between Balham and Tooting Bec, the Point is plainly but nicely done out in pine and comfortable off-whites. The finer points of detail are reserved for the menu: cocktail and champagne mixes; jugs £15 for each. Red, white and rosé wine comes by the glass, with a broad bottled list including the £45 Château d'Angludet for any who wish to push out the boat. Hoegaarden and the little-tasted St Omer are on tap, and Castle, Leffe and London Pride in bottles; champagne mixes under £6, jugs £15 for each. Food is provided by the more than able restaurant out back.

Babies and children admitted (restaurant: children's menu, high chairs). Disabled: toilet. Restaurant. Music (bands 8pm Sun; free). Tables outdoors. TV

Bedford

Also in the area...

Moon Under Water (JD Wetherspoon) 194 Balham High Street, SW12 (8673 0535).

Battersea

Northcote Road is Battersea's Sunset Strip, a cruising joint full of sassy new style bars. Meanwhile, stripped-down gastropubs have erupted on every busy road, transforming previously seedy boozers faster than you can say 'gentrification'.

Artesian Well

693 Wandsworth Road, SW8 (7627 3353). Clapham Common tube/Wandsworth Town rail. **Open** 5-11pm Tue, Wed; 5pm-midnight Thur, Sun; 5pm-2am Fri, Sat. **Food served** 6-10pm daily **Admission** (club only) £3-£5 Fri, Sat. **Credit** AmEx, DC, MC, V.

The Marmite of all venues: people either love the Well or hate it. Opened in 2000 by Rudy Weller, sculptor of Piccadilly's *Horses in Helios*, its decor is childhood fantastical. This is where Harry Potter would want to drink when his voice breaks. Candle wax gloops from iron chandeliers, cracked glass pillars support the ceiling, intricately etched wooden chests punctuate the stone-tiled floor and foliage engulfs the wood panelled bar. The kitschy feel is married to quality food served in the large restaurant (also seriously OTT with vast mounted animal heads almost hidden amid the tack). Drinkers can nosh on bar food that reflects the Italian/English ownership (gnocchi, bangers and mash). Friday and Saturday nights slick-haired bouncers patrol the entrance to the club upstairs where DJs play funk rock to crowds on the pull.

Babies and children admitted (children's menu). Function room. Music (DJs 9.30pm Fri, Sat). Restaurant. Tables outdoors (pavement).

Babel

3-7 Northcote Road, SW11 (7801 0043/www.faucetinn.com). Clapham Junction rail. **Open** 11am-11pm Mon-Sat; noon-10.30pm Sun. **Food served** noon-10pm Mon-Fri; 11am-7pm Sat; noon-7pm Sun. **Credit** AmEx, MC, V.

Top spot for meeting en masse, less recommended for intimacy. By day, the leather sofas, scattered foliage and diffuse light filtered through swirly pink shades offer a welcome

alternative to the faceless chain bars occupying this stretch of Northcote Road (although the grey and brown decor could hardly be described as cheery). The place is cranked up for the weekend when aspiring sophisticates swoop in to fill the space between bar and lounge with liberating gyrations bolstered by a choice of more than 30 cocktails (plus a dull draught line-up) and DJs delivering acid jazz. Roasts and Bloody Marys cater for the morning-after crowd.
Babies and children admitted (until 6pm). Disabled: toilet. Music (DJs 7pm Thur-Sat, 4pm last Sun of month; free). Tables outdoors (patio). TV.

Boom

165-7 St John's Hill, SW11 (7924 3449). Clapham Junction rail. **Open/food served** 5-11pm Mon-Thur; noon-midnight Fri, Sat; noon-10.30pm Sun. **Happy hour** 7-8pm Mon-Fri; 6-7pm Sat; 7.30-9.30pm Sun. **Credit** MC, V.
Cheeky bars such as this – 'Trekky' futuristic with a dash of 1970s time warp – are scarce indeed. The curvy booths look made for table telephones with which to dial fellow drinkers. Unfortunately, Boom misses that particular trick but it's fun all the same: a long bar counter with pebble-dash panels fills the back wall; candlelit alcoves with deep-blue love seats offer intimacy; chunky white pillars break up the rest of the interior, especially the dining area, which has its own bar and fireplace. The crowd is young but moneyed. At happy hour, 16 Boom cocktails are at £3-£3.50 (a £2 reduction on normal prices). Beers are disappointing (draught Staropramen, Grolsch, Caffrey's; bottled Beck's, Peroni, Michelob), but overall, Boom is more than a cut above the local competition.
Babies and children admitted (until 6.30pm). Disabled: toilet. Games (board games). Function room. Music (DJs 8pm Thur-Sun; acoustic 6pm Sun; free). Tables outdoors (pavement). TV (big screen, digital).

Le Bouchon Bordelais

5-9 Battersea Rise, SW11 (7738 0307/www.lebouchon.co.uk). Clapham Junction rail/35, 37 bus. **Open** 10am-11pm Mon-Sat; 10am-10.30pm Sun. **Food served** 10am-10.30pm Mon-Sat; 10am-10pm Sun. **Credit** AmEx, MC, V.
A decade and a half has passed since Le Bouchon first popped its cork in Battersea. Though a touch fatigué, the croque, Kronenbourg and cafe noir combo still draws Francophiles through its sliding doors. The venue easily divides into the Bouchon Bordelais restaurant and the Bar des Magis, itself divided into stand-up zinc-countered bar and side cafe with plants, sofa and piano. The ambience of Parisian bar life is recreated by bartenders schooled in Gallic gruff, ceiling fans from Rick's Bar and copies of *Le Monde*. Waitresses deliver drinks and mini pots of pretzels between tables while flitting from French to English. In addition to croques monsieur et madame, there are baguettes and assiette de charcuterie to accompany a fine range of continental beers).
Babies and children admitted (children's menu, crèche 1-4pm Sat, Sun, high chairs). Function room. Tables outdoors (pavement). TV (satellite).

Castle

115 Battersea High Street, SW11 (7228 8181). Clapham Junction rail/19, 49, 319, 239, 344, 345 bus. **Open** noon-11pm Mon-Sat; noon-10.30pm Sun. **Food served** noon-3pm, 7-9.45pm Mon-Sat; noon-4.30pm, 6-9.30pm Sun. **Credit** MC, V.
The Castle is really a chalet, a Swiss hut built on the edge of a housing estate that blinks high into the distance. Uninspiring outside, inside it's as warm and welcoming as a St Bernard in the snow, with a fireplace and cosy sofas. Unshaven locals in sockless feet and loafers lounge behind the *Guardian*, while middle-aged couples in patterned sweaters dig in to the likes of wild boar sausages. A high-ceilinged conservatory, clad in rampant ivy, opens on to the spacious garden, a boon on fleeting warm days. Despite the trip hop trance and heavily pierced bartender, the bar is clean cut with spotlights picking out a cabinet of wine. The beers are Young's. There's also a lovely side bar with a piano and a fab mural of Chambéry.
Babies and children admitted (until 7.30pm). Function room. Games (board games). Tables outdoors (courtyard, garden). TV.

Circle

317 Battersea Park Road, SW11 (7627 1578). Battersea Park rail. **Open** noon-11pm daily. **Food served** noon-3pm, 6-9.30pm Tue-Thur; noon-3pm Fri, Sat; noon-7pm Sun. **Credit** AmEx, MC, V.
At the foot of a range of housing blocks sits this lime-green (yikes!) base camp, cousin to the well-established Circle of Stockwell. Huge windows flood light into a large, similarly lurid, interior dominated by a horseshoe bar counter surrounded by sci-fi stools. The tone abruptly changes toward the back where the room turns treacle red with a grand hearth and grand piano – the latter vying for attention with a widescreen TV tuned to the footie. No prizes for guessing which wins out. A table football skulks in a candlelit corner. Tall stalks of beer pumps (Löwenbräu, Stella and Tetley) line up under a blackboard of gastropub comfort cuisine. Get mini eggs, toffee and lollipops from the tuckshop sweet machines.
Function area. Games (board games, fruit machine, table football). TVs (big screen, satellite).

The Common Rooms

225 St John's Hill, SW11 (7207 1276). Clapham Junction rail/37, 39, 77A, 156, 170, 337, 670 bus. **Open** 11am-11pm Mon-Thur; 11am-1am Fri, Sat; 11am-10.30pm Sun. **Food served** 11am-10pm daily. **Happy hour** 6-8pm Mon-Fri. **Credit** MC, V.
This cocktail bar has already become one of Clapham's most stylish nightspots: Manhattan meets Kensington at the peak of St John's Hill. It's frequented by folk from surrounding 'hams' (Bal, Clap and Ful) who prefer Bellinis and Grey Goose Martinis to sucking down pineapple alcopops. The six-page drinks menu includes just shy of 30 cocktails, as well as seven brands of champagne and six draught beers. Enthusiastic bar staff are knowledgable and directed us expertly round the drinks list. The place looks good too, with a leather-panelled bar, soaked in a soft purple wash, flanked by fish tanks and made fragrant by vases of lilies. Must-order dishes include the roast, with meat by Harvey Nicks. The chef is from Bibendum.
Games (table football). Music (DJs 6-8pm Sun; free).

Corum

30-32 Queenstown Road, SW8 (7720 5445). Battersea Park or Clapham Junction rail. **Open** noon-3pm, 5pm-1am Mon-Fri; noon-1am Sat, Sun. **Food served** noon-3pm, 5pm-midnight Mon-Fri; noon-minight Sat, Sun. **Credit** MC, V.
Opened November 2001, this cutting-edge venue would look more at home among the glassy canyons of Docklands rather than down this shabby Battersea side-street. But owner Andy Jones seems to have hit the nail on the head when it comes to knowing what locals want – a metallic silver exterior, and beige cushion panelled walls, horizontal strips of mirror and brown sofas on the interior for that New York lounge-bar ambience. Clientele interact with Latino bartenders serving more than 32 varieties of cocktails in a fug of aftershave. Pics of Battersea power station add local colour. The restaurant is earning growing respect for its Mediterranean cuisine presided over by a chef formerly of the Ivy and the River Cafe.
Babies and children admitted. Disabled: toilet. Tables outdoors (terrace).

Drawing Room & Sofa Bar

103 Lavender Hill, SW11 (7350 2564). Clapham Junction rail/77, 77A, 345 bus. **Open** 5pm-midnight Mon-Fri; 11am-midnight Sat, Sun. **Food served** 6-10.30pm Mon-Thur; 6-11pm Fri; 11am-3pm, 6-11pm Sat; 11am-3pm, 6-10.30pm Sun. **Credit** MC, V.

With the exception of its laboured name, most everything about this bar is appealingly quirky. The drinks menu is a modified Ladybird book with 'duck in nappy' illustrations; there's an improbable display of starburst wall clocks (made from spoons), thick velvet drapes and threadbare armchairs; ornate teapots and tassel table lamps. In the toilets, tartan cotton substitutes for paper towels. A handpainted list in the Sofa Bar details a range of cocktails; alternatively, there's a decent range of bottled beers and quality wines by the glass, plus an eccentric range of teas in keeping with the hippie-chic image. A house special of vodka, infused with cucumber in the summer and vanilla in winter, serves as a light aperitif to a meal chosen from the monthly changing menu.

Babies and children admitted (toys). Function room. Tables outdoors (pavement).

Duke of Cambridge

228 Battersea Bridge Road, SW11 (7223 5662). Battersea Park or Clapham Junction rail/19, 49, 344, 345 bus. **Open** 11am-11pm Mon-Sat; noon-10.30pm Sun. **Food served** noon-2.30pm, 7-9.45pm Mon-Sat; noon-3pm, 7-9.45pm Sun. **Credit** MC, V.

While most locals rave about this multi-award-winning pub, there are dissenters who mourn the day Geronimo Inns ever stepped in and transformed it into what they say is a finely furnished 'stable for Sloanes'. How you feel about it depends on how at home you are among varnished wood, wicker chairs, French windows garnished by hops and the odd tweedy jacket. It's all unquestionably luxurious. However, the focus is still the bar where Young's pumps share space with a Hoegaarden tap. Food is consumed in the back area. Hanging there is a painting of the bar as gregariously busy as you'll see it today – unless it's summer, in which case you'd be wiser following the exodus out on to the pretty terrace.

Babies and children admitted. Disabled: toilet. Function room. Tables outdoors (garden). TV (satellite).

Eagle

104 Chatham Road, SW11 (7228 2328). Clapham Junction or Wandsworth Common rail. **Open** 11am-11pm Mon-Sat; noon-10.30pm Sun. **Credit** MC, V.

Serving the best pint of Pride in London (according to Fuller's, and it should know), this cosy pub proclaims itself 'the last true boozer in Battersea'. It might even be true. Manager Dave is passionate about his beer – best not to get him on the subject if you have other plans for the evening. He has a rotating array of ales that included Timothy Taylor's Landlord, Flowers Original and IPA on our visit. Otherwise, expect swirly carpets and worn leather sofas, bringing back memories of home pre-Habitat, and genial regulars: old timers, out-of-work thespians and antique/book/music sellers from Northcote Road (several of whom drop in on the dot of 5pm).

Babies and children admitted (until 7.30pm). Games (board games, quiz machine). Jukebox. Tables outdoors (garden, marquee). TVs (big screen, satellite).

Face Bar

2 Lombard Road, SW11 (7924 6090). Clapham Junction rail, then 239 bus. **Open/food served** noon-11pm. **Credit** AmEx, DC, MC, V.

Jakarta, Shanghai and now London, the Face is house bar to Lan Na Thai, an exotic Thai restaurant of Far Eastern origins that has mysteriously chosen to settle on a hazardous and forgotten bend linking Battersea Bridge with the known world. The brightly lit bar space – filled with artefacts and textiles all slow-boated in from the Orient, counter-flanked by the sculpted face of Buddha – boasts a menu of rare taste: 60-odd cocktails including 12 house creations (Phuket Beach, Jakarta Breeze, Dive in the Deepest Water). Top spot for sipping are the intricately designed Chinese wedding beds plumped with cushions. Views over the Thames and Chelsea Wharf are particularly fine when lit by night.

Babies and children admitted (high chairs). Disabled: toilet. No-smoking area. Tables outdoors (riverside).

Fox & Hounds

66 Latchmere Road, SW11 (7924 5483). Clapham Junction rail. **Open** 5-11pm Mon; noon-2.30pm, 5-11pm Tue-Thur; noon-11pm Fri, Sat; noon-10.30pm Sun. **Food served** 7-10.30pm Mon; 12.30-2.30pm, 7-10.30pm Tue-Thur; 12.30-3pm, 7-10.30pm Fri, Sat; 12.30-3pm, 7-10pm Sun. **Credit** MC, V.

Standard practice when transforming an old boozer into a stylish gastropub is to gut the place and refit with reclaimed, pseudo-rustic and pine throughout. Not at the Fox. Two years after renovation, many of the authentic trimmings remain, including Bass brewery mirrors, 1950s flowery pillars and dowdy wall prints. These sit comfortably with a bright, imaginative interior, complete with gastro-standard blackboards covered with scrawled listings of global fare with a Mediterranean slant. Greene King IPA and London Pride are on tap, and there's a good choice of wine by the glass. Just a shame about the location, surrounded by boarded-up shops and overshadowed by a leaky railway bridge.

Babies and children admitted (daytime). Disabled: toilet. Tables outdoors (garden). TV.

GII

339 Battersea Park Road, SW11 (7622 2112). Battersea Park rail. **Open** noon-11pm Mon-Sat; noon-10.30pm Sun. **Food served** noon-3pm, 6-10pm Mon-Fri; noon-10pm Sat; noon-9.30pm Sun. **Credit** MC, V.

Along bleak Battersea Park Road, GII appears like a Fabergé egg on a white elephant stall – invitingly sparkly and bright, and totally priceless. Enter to yellow walls, stripped-pine floors, full-moon ceiling lights, primary coloured sofas and waist-high palms. Old tiles on the wall bear drinking songs through the ages – these are allegedly a listed feature. On the bar counter sets of beer pumps in the shape of Scandinavian crosses dispense a standard selection of beers, supplemented by 14 cocktails and a selection of wines by the glass. There's an interesting and classy main menu, plus bar snacks (prawns in filo pastry). The back room, complete with fire and leather sofas, can be hired and there's a beer garden at the rear.

Babies and children admitted (lunch Sun). Function room. Music (DJs 7pm occasional Fri, Sat). Tables outdoors (garden). TV (digital).

Holy Drinker

59 Northcote Road, SW11 (7801 0544). Clapham Junction rail/35, 37 bus. **Open** 4.30-11pm Mon-Fri; noon-11pm Sat; 1-10.30pm Sun. **Credit** MC, V.

With its shadowy corners, pear-drop-patterned partitions and velvet furnishings, the Holy Drinker has burrowed a niche in the tête-à-tête market of Northcote Road. At twilight when the sun's gaze has steered eastwards from the voluminous windows, the lights are dimmed to a level advantageous only to moles, and music of Arabic descent engulfs the interior. It's divided into a trio of main spaces (mind the steps between): a street-level bar, a middle patch with its own fireplace, and a back brick alcove with another fireplace and a row of

velvet cinema seats. There's only one draught beer at the bar but a very fine array of bottles including Sam Smith's organic, Golden Promise and Fuller's Honey Dew. There's also an extensive wine list with a choice of seven by the glass. And the name? From a novel by Joseph Roth – 'a small masterpiece', says Amazon.com, and a bloomin' good bar, we add.
Babies and children admitted (until 7pm). Music (DJs 6pm occasional Sat, Sun). Tables outdoors (pavement). TV.

Inigo

642 Wandsworth Road, SW8 (7622 4884). Clapham Junction rail. **Open** 6pm-2am Mon-Fri; noon-2am Sat, Sun. **Food served** 6-10pm Mon-Thur; 6-9pm Fri; noon-9pm Sat, Sun. **Happy hour** 5-7pm daily. **Credit** MC, V.
Compressed between a snooker hall and a hydrotherapy surgery for dogs (we kid you not), Inigo's a dingily lit, grunge box where music comes well before style and decor – as advertised by the prominence of the Routemaster-sized speakers suspended from a yellowing ceiling. Chunky tables are placed at the front of the decorative oak panelled bar, a threadbare sofa chill-out zone towards the back. Before 9pm all shooters are £1 (served by a selection of shaven-headed or dreadlocked bartenders), which slightly compensates for the bland selection of beers. Ignition every Friday night attracts a hardcore crowd of weekend revellers up for late-night partying and prepared to queue for the privilege.
Disabled: toilet. Games (backgammon). Music (DJs 8pm daily). TV (video screen)

Latchmere

503 Battersea Park Road, SW11 (7223 3549). Battersea Park or Clapham Junction rail/44, 49, 344, 345 bus. **Open** noon-11pm Mon-Sat; noon-10.30pm Sun. **Food served** noon-9pm Mon-Sat; noon-6pm Sun. **Credit** AmEx, MC, V.
Although the place is seemingly forever changing hands, successive owners have so far been respectful enough not to tamper too much. This vast old corner pub still has bags of character, with studded leather seats, gorgeous lampshades high and low, fresh flowers on the bar counter and plants dotted around the fine woodwork. Upstairs, the wonderful 90-seat Latchmere Theatre is the cherry on the cake; little bigger than a train station waiting room, it's one of London's best fringe theatres. Theatre-goers can argue about performances over pints of Adnams Bitter or Greene King IPA. On a busy corner of Battersea, neither gastro nor retro, the Latchmere is easily but foolishly passed by.
Babies and children admitted (until 8pm). Function room. Games (fruit machine). Quiz (9pm Tue; £1). Tables outdoors (garden). Theatre (nightly; box office 7978 7040). TV (big screen, satellite).

Masons Arms

169 Battersea Park Road, SW8 (7622 2007). Battersea Park rail/44, 137, 344 bus. **Open** noon-11pm Mon-Sat; noon-10.30pm Sun. **Food served** noon-4pm, 6-10pm Mon-Sat; 12.30-4pm, 6-9.30pm Sun. **Credit** AmEx, MC, V.
Despite a location under a dripping railway bridge next to the Dogs' Home, the Masons always draws a decent crowd. Perhaps it's the steaming hob and the clatter of pots and pans (this was one of the area's first gastropubs), or the homely recycled wood and country kitchen ambience. In winter it could be the glowing fire, hemmed in by squishy leather sofas. Whatever, it's a comfortable place, a large L-shape with cosy alcoves, turning out food such as own-made steak and kidney pies. Adnams Bitter and Hoegaarden are the pick of the drinks on draught, while seven of 16 wines are served by the glass and there's an imaginative range of shooters.
Babies and children admitted. Disabled: toilet. Music (DJs 8pm every other Sat). Tables outdoors (pavement). TV.

Microbar

14 Lavender Hill, SW11 (7228 5300). Clapham Common tube/Clapham Junction or Wandsworth Road rail/77, 77A, 137 bus. **Open** 6-11pm daily. **Credit** AmEx, MC, V.
The quiet rebellion continues in Lavender Hill – a beer backlash where not only is 'Stella' a dirty word, but CAMRA comes in for some stick. Microbar is a simple, stylish bar (in beer-brown and burgundy) with a simple, admirable approach: drink less, drink better. Thus the beer connoisseur can mull over a long (and regularly updated) list of bottled brews painstakingly sourced from the world's best microbreweries, including the likes of Czech Herold Black lager and the Belgian Trappist Rochefort 8 (a whopping 9.2% abv). It's the antidote to a drinking culture dominated by bland pub chains. Draught beers include those from San Francisco's Anchor Steam Brewery. Our only criticism last year (apart from the awkward location) was the lack of food. That, management promises, will be remedied with the opening of a kitchen, all being well, in early summer 2003.
Games (backgammon).

S Bar

37 Battersea Bridge Road, SW11 (7223 3322). Clapham Junction rail/19, 49, 219, 345 bus. **Open** noon-11pm Mon-Thur; noon-midnight Fri, Sat; noon-10.30pm Sun. **Food served** noon-3pm, 6-9pm daily. **Credit** AmEx, MC, V.
The yellow awning of the S Bar is a last flash of colour before hitting the bridge over to Chelsea. Drivers hurtling by may not stop, but many pedestrians find it arresting. The beige walls, varnished wood and leather, ruby red sofas, tall ferns, high bar, plus the sheer size of the place, lend themselves to both intimacy and good-natured idiocy. Couples concealed by pillars are wined and dined at candlelit wooden tables. An unobtrusive TV catches the attention of rugby fans, not to mention the bar staff. Beers are disappointing (Caffrey's, John Smith's and Kronenbourg), lunches are simple and there's an upstairs conservatory handy for private parties.
Babies and children admitted (until 6pm). Disabled: toilet. Function room. Games (fruit machine). Music (DJs 8pm Fri; band Sat). Tables outdoors (pavement). TV (satellite).

Settle Inn

186 Battersea Bridge Road, SW11 (7228 0395). Clapham Junction rail. **Open** noon-11pm Mon-Sat; noon-10.30pm Sun. **Food served** noon-3pm, 6-10pm Mon-Fri; noon-10pm Sat, Sun. **Credit** AmEx, MC, V.
With doors opposite Battersea Park, this rectangular, airy pub is in pole position to catch at least some of the three million visitors reputed to walk in the leafy surrounds each year. It's a good place to relax after a healthy stroll, with high ceilings, deep leather sofas and lashings of modern art. Prime spot is in one of the high-backed Gothic armchairs set round the brick fireplace, but there are plenty of tables scattered throughout. A big screen draws in rugger types and footie fans, who hog the main bar swilling pints of Bombardier and London Pride; a more peaceful throng lounges near the vases of lilies at the far end, hidden from view by a chimney breast. In summer a garden comes into its own.
Babies and children admitted. Music (DJs 8pm Fri; free) Games (board games). Quiz (8pm Tue). Tables outdoors (garden). TV (big screen, satellite).

Tea Room des Artistes

697 Wandsworth Road, SW8 (7652 6526/www.sanctum.org). Wandsworth Town rail. **Open** 5.30pm-1am Fri, Sat; 5.30pm-12.30am Sun. **Food served** 6-10pm Fri-Sun. **Admission** £5 after 9.30pm Fri; £5 after 9pm Sat; £2 after 8pm Sun. **Credit** (restaurant only) MC, V.

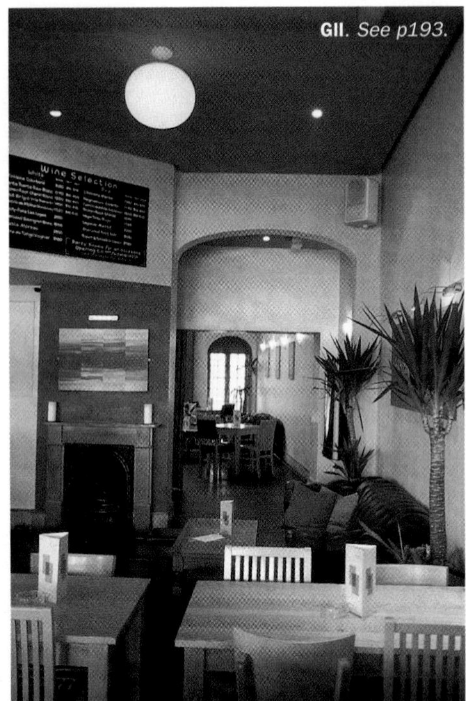

GII. *See p193.*

Despite local fears, the Tea Room appears to be suffering no ill effects from the arrival of the massive **Artesian Well** (*see p191*) next door. Every weekend, the pink neon sign ignites indicating permission to enter. It remains a wild squat-like hang out of eccentric charm: leopard-skin benches, multi-coloured fairy lights and *Star Wars* projected on the ceiling. Prices on bar snacks are deliciously reasonable although no prizes for the limited selection of wine and beers (Budvar, Hoegaarden, Leffe). Regularly filled with a loyal clientele happy to ignore any need to search for the next big thing, the Tea Room is sympathetic without having to labour the point.
Babies and children admitted (until 7.30pm). Function room. Games (table football). Music (DJs 9pm Fri, Sat; 5.30pm Sun). Restaurant. Tables outdoors (garden).

Woodman

60 Battersea High Street, SW11 (7228 2968). Clapham Junction rail. **Open** noon-11pm Mon-Fri; 11am-11pm Sat; noon-10.30pm Sun. **Food served** noon-2.30pm, 6-9pm Mon-Sat; noon-6pm Sun. **Credit** MC, V.
The unusual Woodman presents an intriguing taste of the past. With the pre-war paintings of hop-picking in Kent; the rows of half-pint mugs, jugs and tankards hung from the big bar counter; the mad scrapbook of sporting mementoes (Smokin' Joe Frazier, Palace stars of the '70s); and the Badger beers of Best and Tanglefoot beside authentic Bavarian taps of HB and Münchener Pilsner – it could be 1902 or 1972 in here. Somewhere along the line, a family feud or gentleman's agreement resulted in the renaming of a neighbouring hostelry, 'The Original Woodman'. This place feels like the public bar to its smarter brother. Bigger brother too, as a long cabin-like extension for TV sports, pool and darts adds half the space again to this strange, fine tavern.
Babies and children admitted (until 4pm). Games (board games, darts, fruit machine, Jenga, pool tables). Function room. Quiz (8.30pm Wed; £1 to play). Tables outdoors (garden). TV (big screen, satellite).

Also in the area...

All Bar One 32-8 Northcote Road, SW11 (7801 9951).
Asparagus (JD Wetherspoon) 1-13 Falcon Road, SW11 (7801 0046).
Fine Line 31-7 Northcote Road, SW11 (7924 7387).
O'Neill's 66A-C Battersea Rise, SW11 (7350 0349).
Pitcher & Piano 94 Northcote Road, SW11 (7738 9781).
Slug & Lettuce 4 St John's Hill, SW11 (7924 1322).

Bermondsey & Rotherhithe

All our recommended pubs are on the river, between King Stairs Gardens and the Hilton by Nelson Dock. The **Blacksmith's Arms** and **Ship** are locals' pubs frequented by the newly arrived loft dwellers because they are what they are: no-nonsense boozers selling decent food and good beer.

Blacksmith's Arms

257 Rotherhithe Street, SE16 (7237 1349). Canada Water or Rotherhithe tube. **Open** noon-11pm Mon-Sat; noon-10.30pm Sun. **Food served** 6.30-9.30pm Tue-Sat; noon-6pm Sun. **Credit** (restaurant only) AmEx, DC, MC, V.
A good, old-fashioned boozer, the Blacksmith's may sit next to the Rotherhithe Hilton (we're not kidding), but inside it's the same cosy two-bar boozer it ever was. The exterior is all

mock-Tudor frames, hanging baskets and bright spots, while inside it looks like a cross between Aunt Jane's front parlour of the 1960s and the Rover's Return, with a small games room to the back. Assorted blacksmith's tools are fixed to the wall and there's a piano for sing-songs and for keeping pictures on. We particularly like the library by the front door, offering magazines and books from all spectrums of the literary community. Being a Fuller's pub, the beers are faultless and the nosh is above average. A restaurant offers scallops with lime and ginger or pork wrapped in Parma ham. Well done.
Babies and children admitted. Games (darts, fruit machines, pool table). Tables outdoors (garden). TV.

Famous Angel

101 Bermondsey Wall East, SE16 (7237 3608). Bermondsey tube. **Open** 11.30am-11pm Mon-Sat; noon-10.30pm Sun. **Food served** noon-2.30pm, 6-9pm daily. **Credit** MC, V.

Famous? Certainly. Aside from being one of London's oldest boozers, this is where miserable genius Tony Hancock used to come to get away from things and learn his lines. An inn belonging to Bermondsey Abbey was established here in the 14th century to accommodate travellers taking boats from the adjacent Redriffe Stairs. Known as the Salutation until Charles II's day, Pepys wrote about it in his diaries and 'Hanging' Judge Jeffreys enjoyed watching pirates being drowned across the river at Executioner's Dock. The views, particularly of Tower Bridge, are still worth getting excited over, though the ground-floor bar is only exceptional for its three-dimensional Regency wallpaper and octagonal shape – it used to be five smaller rooms – around an island bar. Now under the wing of Tadcaster's Samuel Smith brewery, so expect beer at knockdown prices. A refurb has been threatened, so call to ensure it's open before you visit.
Function room. Games (fruit machine, quiz machine). Tables outdoors (riverside patio).

Mayflower

117 Rotherhithe Street, SE16 (7237 4088). Rotherhithe tube. **Open** noon-11pm Mon-Sat; noon-10.30pm Sun. **Food served** noon-3pm, 6.30-9pm Mon-Sat; noon-4pm Sun. **Credit** AmEx, DC, MC, V.

Arguably the best of the London seafaring inns, you can't fault the Mayflower for character or authenticity. The main bits date from 1550 and improvements have been made on a regular basis ever since. Its narrow settles, rackety wooden floors, bold stone fireplaces and small dark rooms are straight out of *Treasure Island*, and the rumour that it was partly reconstructed with timber from the Pilgrim Fathers' ship, the *Mayflower*, is not denied. It also makes a change to find a decent range of real ales: in this case IPA, Abbot and, if you're lucky, one other from the Greene King range. In hot weather the newly renewed outside decking is hotly contested. In winter, the motto above the giant has never rung truer: 'A warm hearth and fine wine soothes the soul and passes time.'
Babies and children admitted (restaurant). Games (fruit machine). Quiz (8.30pm Tue; £1). Restaurant. Tables outdoors (riverside terrace).

Ship

39-47 St Marychurch Street, SE16 (7237 4103). Rotherhithe tube. **Open** 11am-11pm Mon-Sat; noon-10.30pm Sun. **No credit cards.**

The combination of a proper Rotherhithe boozer and Young's beers at this almost riverside pub can prove irresistible. This red-carpeted, U-shaped, one-bar boozer attracts a good selection of old Rotherhithe locals and – as far as we could see – not too many of the loft-dwelling incomers. We found an atmosphere of quiet conversation and good-natured bonhomie. Unusually, every male in the place was drinking bitter while the gaggle of smartly dressed peroxide blondes at the bar were caning the Bacardis and Cokes. A shelf running around the beige walls holds a collection of decorative plates that wouldn't give the *Antiques Roadshow* much cause for concern, and a plethora of plants provides plenty of greenery into which shy drinkers in combat clothing can disappear.
Babies and children admitted. Games (fruit machine). Tables outdoors (garden). TV (satellite).

Spice Island

163 Rotherhithe Street, SE16 (7394 7108). Rotherhithe tube. **Open** 11am-11pm Mon-Thur; 11am-midnight Fri, Sat; noon-10.30pm Sun. **Food served** noon-9.30pm Mon-Sat; noon-8.30pm Sun. **Credit** AmEx, MC, V.

On our last visit, only Flowers IPA remained in what was once a strong real ale house. The food too has been toned down and the first-floor restaurant has been degraded to the status of what a sign describes as 'bar service and seating upstairs'. All change, then. This is a converted wooden riverside warehouse that was turned into a pub primarily for tourists and the incoming inhabitants of riverside lofts. From what we've seen, if the latter have arrived they're drinking elsewhere. Instead, Rotherhithe's young workers congregate here to drink lager and alcoholic pop. The music's loud and brash, and anyone stuck with nobody to chat up has more than enough fruit and video machines and pool tables to choose from. The ground-floor bar is a mass of wooden drinking areas around a central brick and wood bar. The heated terrace remains a popular feature and its views of Limehouse are as spectacular as only views of Limehouse can be.
Babies and children admitted (until 7pm; children's menu, high chairs). Disabled: lift, toilet. Games (fruit machine, pool, quiz machine). No-smoking area (restaurant). Restaurant. Tables outdoors (riverside terrace). TV (satellite).

Also in the area...

Surrey Docks (JD Wetherspoon) 185 Lower Road, SE16 (7394 2832).

Blackheath

Being on the coach road to Dover, Blackheath has old inns aplenty, now joined by a new breed of style bar. Henry V was welcomed home here after Agincourt, as was Charles II on the Restoration and Chris Evans 'courted' his bride-to-be in the Clarence Hotel.

Cave Austin

7-9 Montpelier Vale, SE3 (8852 0492). Blackheath rail. **Open** 11am-11.30pm Mon-Thur, Sun; 11am-1am Fri, Sat. **Food served** 11am-2.30pm, 6-10pm Mon-Sat; 11am-3pm Sun. **Credit** MC, V.

The small but comfortable downstairs bar has been closed the last couple of times we've been in, but we are big enough fans of the smart, modern ground-floor drinking area not to mind too much. Decked out in cream and light beige, with plenty of alcoves, there's a dining area to the left and a small chrome and glass serving area opposite. The restaurant offers Med standards, and the bar specialises in cocktails, wine and bottled beers (Stella, Beck's, Bud, yawn). There's also a lush little walled garden out back. The name refers to previous occupants – two grocers called Messers Cave and Austin.
Function rooms. Music (DJs basement bar, 9pm Fri, Sat; £5; musicians 8.30pm occasional Sun). Restaurant. Tables outdoors (garden). TV (big screen, satellite).

Crown

49 Tranquil Vale, SE3 (8852 0326). Blackheath rail. **Open/food served** 11am-11pm Mon-Sat; noon-10.30pm Sun. **Credit** AmEx, DC, MC, V.

Now proudly sporting the T&J Bernard badge that identifies it as part of the Scottish & Newcastle conglomerate , this 1740s boozer is one of SE3's more comfortable drinking holes. Old mirrors hang over delicious original Regency fireplaces, though the oak panelling, beige paintwork and thick carpet are from a more recent era. Outside is a squad of bench tables that, in warmer weather, are as sought after as gypsy gold. Expect five real ales (including standard Young's and Flowers IPA), ten wines by the glass and bottle, plus all the usual lagers and a (very) international menu. A former staging coach for horse-drawn buses to the City, these days it attracts the sort of mixed pubby crowd you'd expect to find in a colour supplement ad for real gas fires.

Games (fruit machine, video game). Tables outdoors (pavement). TV (digital and satellite).

Flame Bar

1 Lee Road, SE3 (8852 9111). Blackheath rail. **Open** 11am-11pm Mon-Sat; noon-10.30pm Sun. **Credit** MC,V.

The Flame Bar has sprung up in a cavernous former branch of NatWest. Where once cold efficiency and usury held reign, this high-ceilinged, split-level space is now where the bright young things of Blackheath come to imbibe cocktails and shooters (48 to choose from, all a fiver or less), plus Guinness, Staropramen and Gulpener Korenwolf draught Dutch wheat beer. Rebels opt for wine or bottled Beck's. The music was provided by the HitMix satellite channel, projected on to one wall, a pretty drab mix of Robbie, Eminem and Gareth. The place looks good, with vague beige and white paintwork augmented by fancy lighting effects and a huge shimmering carbon-rod chandelier. There's no food, but the twentysomething couples and groups of tie-askewed geezers we encountered seemed unconcerned. 'Are those real flames behind the bar or one of those wafty satin things?' asked one. Tricky.

TV (big screen, satellite).

Hare & Billet

1A Elliot Cottages, Hare & Billet Road, SE3 (8852 2352). Blackheath rail. **Open** 11am-11pm Mon-Sat; noon-10.30pm Sun. **Food served** noon-7.30pm daily. **Credit** MC, V.

Now that the Hogshead (sorry, hog's head) chain appears to have abandoned the concept of genuine real ale choice (just Flowers IPA and Adnams Bitter last time we toddled by), this unbranded outpost has removed much of the reason for trekking the extra way from the main drag. All right, so it's an old coaching inn dating back to 1700 – though the half-panelling and modern beige paintwork inside offer few clues to the history – and was once a haunt of highwayman Jerry Cruncher (great name for a WWF wrestler). But, aside from being a decent enough pub appealing to a general local crowd, it's not the pub it used to be. Food is the sort of corporate pub grub you'd expect and a blackboard points out that plenty of speciality beers (Belgians to the fore) are available in bottles.

Babies and children admitted. Games (quiz machine). No-smoking area (until 9pm). TV.

Princess of Wales

1A Montpelier Row, SE3 (8297 5911). Blackheath rail. **Open** noon-11pm Mon-Sat; noon-10.30pm Sun. **Food served** noon-9pm daily. **Credit** MC, V.

Not named after the late Lady Di, but after a much older royal called Caroline of Brunswick – George IV's old Dutch – this large and elegant L-shaped heathside pub is just shy of celebrating its 200th birthday. It's been elegantly kitted out, with panelled walls, cream paintwork and a carpet throughout. Comfortable sofas and armchairs are scattered around, walls are decked with historic prints and gilt mirrors and the overall effect is one of a low-rent gentlemen's club. Most regulars seem to come from Blackheath's underbelly of car dealers, City types and young local couples and – as Peter Cook used to say – you couldn't spit without hitting money. Real ales might include Timothy Taylor Landlord, London Pride and Draught Bass. The walled terrace garden is quite dinky, with flashing fairy lights. Coo.

Disabled: toilet. Games (fruit machine, quiz machine). No-smoking area. Tables outdoors (garden, patio).

Zero Degrees

29-31 Montpelier Vale, SE3 (8852 5619). Blackheath rail. **Open served** noon-midnight Mon-Sat; noon-11.30pm Sun. **Food served** noon-11pm Mon-Sat; noon-10.30pm Sun. **Credit** AmEx, MC, V.

Blackheath's own brewpub has established itself as a place to be seen in just a couple of years since opening. Customers are a diverse bunch, ranging from middle-aged geezers 'here for the beer' to young models and the odd media celebrity. Beers, emanating from the visible stainless steel brewery beside the bar, include pale ale, pilsner, black lager and seasonal brews. Though they're poured way too cold (zero degrees perhaps?), if you linger over your pint, it will eventually reveal its flavour. Food, served in a smarter dining area, revolves around good stone-baked pizzas, with 21 combos, ranging from cheese to salmon and mascarpone, roasted garlic chicken and Peking duck. Alternative main courses include bangers and mash and kilo mussel pots. Decor-wise, it's a cross between a TV space station and backstage at the Coliseum.

Babies and children admitted (high chairs). Music (jazz and blues 9pm Mon; free). Restaurant (available for hire). Specialities: own-brewed beers. TV (big screen, satellite).

Also in the area...

O'Neill's 52 Tranquil Vale, SE3 (8297 5901).

Borough & Southwark

Stretching along the Thames from Hays Galleria to where Borough High Street almost becomes Elephant & Castle, this is an area rich in history and thick with drinking dens. In fact, in our view, it's the single most rewarding area of London in which to booze. Just as Borough Market draws the foodies, so pubs like the **Market Porter**, **Lord Clyde** and **Royal Oak** cater to the connoisseur of beer, and **Wine Wharf** to the committed oenophile. For picturesque pints there's the **George Inn**, and for fine views, **Bridge House** and the **Founders Arms**.

Anchor Bankside

34 Park Street, SE1 (7407 1577). London Bridge tube/rail. **Open** 11am-11pm Mon-Sat; noon-10.30pm Sun. **Food served** noon-10pm daily. **Credit** AmEx, DC, MC, V.

This venerable old riverside pub – established 1775, though rebuilt after a fire in 1876 – has been closed for a while for a refit. Although the owners haven't changed the decor (old wood panelling, exposed stonework and historic oak beams), the beer range has taken a serious dive. Once, where you'd be able to find four or five real ales, you'll now only find kegs and the half-hearted offer of fetching a pint of Courage Best or Directors from the 'other bar'. In fact, the Anchor has myriad small bars as well as a restaurant where traditional pub grub can be had for prices that Dr Johnson would have

spent on a year's lodgings. The good Doctor is one of the pub's more illustrious patrons (Mr Thrale owned it), together with the likes of David Garrick, Oliver Goldsmith and Sam Wannamaker. Nowadays the clientele tends to be tourists laying claim to benches on the riverside terrace, besuited office wallahs and the odd escapee from nearby recording studios.
Disabled: toilet. Function rooms. Games (fruit machines). Tables outdoors (riverside patio).

Bridge House

218 Tower Bridge Road, SE1 (7407 5818). Tower Hill tube/Tower Gateway DLR. **Open** 11.30am-11pm Mon-Sat; noon-10.30pm Sun. **Food served** 11.30am-10pm Mon-Sat; noon-9.30pm Sun. **Credit** MC, V.
We found this modern-style Adnams bar on the southern end of Tower Bridge approach a bit smoky on our last visit – despite a state-of-the-art air filtration system – but the staff greeted us with friendly 'hellos', called 'thank you' as we left, and the beers (Broadside and Bitter) were their usual toothsome selves. Holding on to its title of best bar in the area – the nearby Wetherspoon's appears to specialise in very ordinary beers – this is a good place to sit and contemplate the pear-green and beige paintwork and IKEA furniture and wonder how you can get yourself a cushy job in pub design. The view from the front window is good-going-on-wonderful, though Ken's testicle does obscure the river vista beyond London Bridge. As this is a boozer that tries very hard to be a gastro-bar, you can expect many of the usual culinary suspects at prices slightly above what you'd want to pay. We were surprised to discover a Christian group holding an informal pub meeting over several tables.
Disabled: toilet. Function room. TV.

Founder's Arms

52 Hopton Street, SE1 (7928 1899). Blackfriars tube/rail. **Open** 11am-11pm Mon-Sat; noon-10.30pm Sun. **Food served** 9-11am, noon-8.30pm Mon-Sat; 9-11am, noon-7pm Sun. **Credit** AmEx, MC, V.
Built in 1979 and looking something like a German art museum annexe, this deceptively large Young's pub has great views across the river to St Paul's and of the Millennium Bridge. In balmy summer months the extensive concrete riverside terracing attracts tourists like flies to shitake, but when the weather is less kind, you have to make do with the view through expansive floor-to-ceiling plate glass windows. The beer comes from Wandsworth's Ram Brewery (thumbs up) and food that can be ranked somewhere between pub grub and gastro specials is offered up to the hungry office workers and refugees from the neighbouring Tate Modern who join the assorted backpackers and camera-toting Japanese munching fish and chips. Those in search of a quiet spot in which to sip bitter and munch curly sarnies will abhor this noisy pub.
Disabled: toilet. Games (fruit machines, quiz machine). No-smoking area. Tables outdoors (riverside patio).

George Inn

77 Borough High Street, SE1 (7407 2056). London Bridge tube/rail. **Open** 11am-11pm Mon-Sat; noon-10.30pm Sun. **Food served** noon-3pm, 5-10pm Mon-Fri; noon-4pm, 5-10pm Sat; noon-4pm Sun. **Credit** MC, V.
Rebuilt over medieval foundations following fire damage in 1676, this is London's last remaining galleried coaching inn. By the 1880s the inn – famous even then for its Shakespearean connections – had become a storehouse for the Great Northern Railway and could boast three sides of overhanging wooden galleries and mullioned windows surrounding the cobbled courtyard. In 1889 the railway decided that two were surplus to requirements and only the southern end was spared. Now owned by the National Trust and leased to the Laurel Pub Company, the decor is a mixture of corporate pub blackboards and olde worlde knick-knacks. There are four ground-floor rooms, offering plastered walls, old settles, bare wood floors and scrubbed dining tables. Drinkers are a mixture of office types and foreign visitors trying to work out whether 'deep fried fish, fries, peas and tartare sauce' is traditionally English. The beer range varies but between two and seven real ales can be had, over-chilled and at West End prices. .
Babies and children admitted. Function room. Games (darts, fruit machine). No-smoking area (daytime). Tables outdoors (courtyard).

Lord Clyde

27 Clennam Street, SE1 (7407 3397). Borough tube. **Open/food served** 11am-11pm Mon-Fri; noon-4pm, 8-11pm Sat; noon-7pm Sun. **Credit** AmEx, DC, MC, V.
Although an inn has stood here for 300 years, the name and current pile date from 1863, a memento of Scottish soldier and scourge of the sepoys Sir Colin Campbell, who kicked the balti that year. The elaborate, external, green and cream glazed earthenware tiles date from 1913 when landlord EJ Bayling took over and ensured his name appeared prominently beside that of the brewers, Trumans. Inside are two rooms: one long and L-shaped, the other square and small, dominated by a dartboard. The pub's been in the same family since 1956, with Michael and Lucy Fitzpatrick manning the pumps since 1975. The banquettes are red leather-like, the curtains rich vermilion velvet and walls are painted cream and dark red. Homely. Check out the photograph of EJ and a 1920s charabanc party, several delicious clocks and an enamelled sign proclaiming, 'Unrivalled mild ales and double stout'. No mild these days, just five cask ales: Young's 'ordinary', Courage Best, Greene King IPA, Shepherd Neame Spitfire and London Pride.
Games (darts, fruit machines). TV (satellite).

Market Porter

9 Stoney Street, SE1 (7407 2495). London Bridge tube/rail. **Open** 6-8.30am, 11am-11pm Mon-Fri; noon-11pm Sat; noon-10.30pm Sun. **Food served** noon-2.30pm daily. **Credit** AmEx, DC, MC, V.
With Borough Market now the world's trendiest place to buy chorizo, radiccio and ceps, the area is firmly on the upwardly mobile march. Bad news for old-style businesses like the Borough Cafe, but good for the Mints, Neal's Yard Creameries and Fishes that have sprung up around them. This traditional real ale pub has feet in both camps, but the combination of eight real ales and loyalty with the market traders and commuters who make up the bulk of the trade means it should go from strength to strength. Incoming trendies are starting to discover the joys of proper beer, making the Porter one of London's most perpetually busy boozers. Harveys Sussex Best is a constant and Courage Directors a regular, plus there are literally hundreds of guest ales coming in by the single barrel, many of which don't last the day. A recent makeover is now just a memory, and the wooden beam, stone and etched glass decor looks like it hasn't been touched for decades. Those brave and desperate enough will find the place in full swing from 6am to 8.30am for 'breakfast'.
Function room. Tables outdoors (pavement). TVs (satellite).

Old Thameside Inn

Pickfords Wharf, 1 Clink Street, SE1 (7403 4243). London Bridge tube/rail. **Open** noon-11pm Mon-Sat; noon-10.30pm Sun. **Food served** noon-3pm Mon-Fri; noon-4pm Sat, Sun. **Credit** AmEx, MC, V.
'Old Thameside Warehouse Conversion' might be a more apt title for this corporate boozer moored adjacent to the *Golden Hinde* replica. Although the outside looks more like the

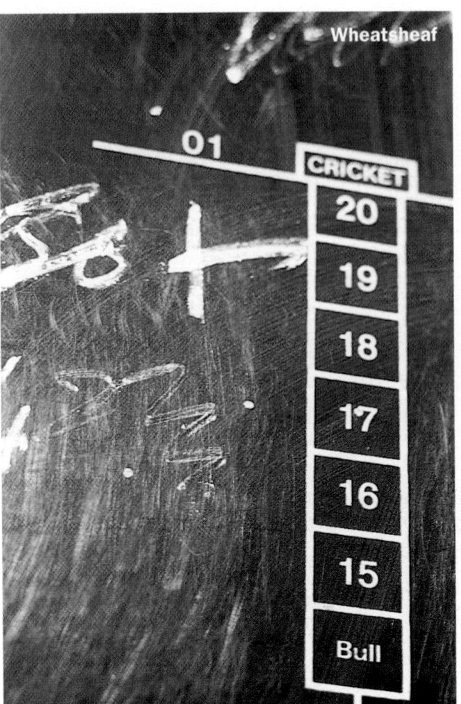

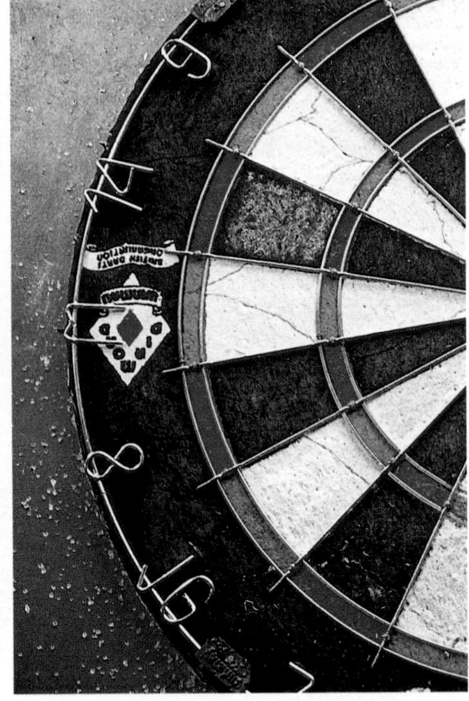

entrance to Soap PLC, inside there's slightly more of the olde worlde feel with the stereotypical bare brick walls, dark beams and flagstone flooring, enlivened by flashing fruit machine lights and jangling Capital Radio soundtrack. The smart dollar can be found in summer on the riverside terrace, where the pub's mix of office johnnies and media jills is augmented by armies of visitors in search of old Bankside. Beers include London Pride and Adnams Bitter, and food is standard pub grub. On Sunday afternoons, there used to be regular sea-shanty singing sessions (try saying that after six tequila slammers) on the terrace, but that particular avenue of enjoyment has disappeared.
Babies and children admitted. Disabled: toilet. Function room. Games (fruit machines, pool tables, quiz machine, video games). No-smoking tables (lunch). Tables outdoors (riverside terrace).

Royal Oak

44 Tabard Street, SE1 (7357 7173). Borough tube/London Bridge tube/rail. **Open** 11.30am-11pm Mon-Fri. **Food served** noon-2.30pm, 6-9.15pm Mon-Fri. **Credit** MC, V.
Tabard Street is named after the ancient inn where the pilgrims met in *The Canterbury Tales*. Modern-day pilgrims departing for Kent (via London Bridge) after a hard day's usury are spoilt for choice of boozers, but the more discerning among them zero in on this backstreet gem, joining the beer lovers and locals who keep it busy most of the day. Harveys of Lewes is one of the country's more dedicated regional brewers and this is its only London boozer. A full range of cask-conditioned ales is usually available, served in peak condition. Start with the XX Mild, then work your way through the canon with Sussex Pale, Best and the fruity Armada – not forgetting the regular seasonal brews. Good-to-average pub food is available from lunchtime until mid-evening. Nothing fancy, just good quality pies, own-made soups, grills and suchlike. The Oak's two bars are separated by a central serving area, all of it restored to neo-Victorian splendour in the 1990s, with plenty of carved mahogany and etched glasswork. This is *the* model traditional pub.
Babies and children admitted (until 5pm). Disabled: toilet. Function room. Quiz (8.30pm Tue).

Shipwrights Arms

88 Tooley Street, SE1 (7378 1486). London Bridge tube/rail. **Open** 11am-11pm Mon-Sat; noon-10.30pm Sun. **Food served** noon-2.30pm Mon-Fri; noon-4pm Sat, Sun. **Credit** AmEx, MC, V.
London was once full of these one-bar Victorian boozers with central serving areas, but now they're a rarity. Comfortably scruffy, the Shipwrights is a dark red and cream painted place with a nautical theme – framed seaman's knots, model ships and suchlike – topped off by a magnificent ceiling-high tile painting by Messrs Charles Evans & Co showing shipwrights righting shipping wrongs. The art nouveau exterior has been painted bright blue and white with a voluptuous figurehead above the main door. Although the signs suggest that this is a Courage pub, the two or three real ales on offer are more likely to come from smaller breweries and/or Young's.
Babies and children admitted. Function room. Games (fruit machines, quiz machines). Tables outdoors (pavement). TV (satellite).

Wheatsheaf

6 Stoney Street, SE1 (7407 7242). London Bridge tube/rail. **Open** 11am-11pm Mon-Fri; noon-8pm Sat. **Food served** noon-2.30pm Mon-Sat. **Credit cards** MC, V.

In the last couple of years the character of this small two-bar pub has changed beyond recognition. Once the scruffiest little boozer south of the river, in 2001 it was taken over by Young's of Wandsworth and now boasts a core clientele that would add value to any Clerkenwell style bar. The beers come up the river from Young's but, despite a hardcore of real ale aficionados, many of the newer customers seem intent on sucking alien bottled varieties and (God forbid!) Breezers. As in most Young's pubs, the wine list is comprehensive enough to stimulate large-scale cork-pulling. The two bar system was retained in the makeover, though the difference between the posh bit (carpet) and the public (lino) has eroded, with both now boasting superior floor coverings. Canned music tends towards the contemporary end of things and is largely why regulars have switched to the **Market Porter** (*see p199*).
Babies and children admitted. Games (darts). Tables outdoors (pavement). TV (satellite).

Wine Wharf

Stoney Street, SE1 (7940 8335/www.winewharf.co.uk). London Bridge tube/rail. **Open** 11am-11pm Mon-Sat. **Food served** noon-9.30pm Mon-Sat. **Credit** AmEx, DC, MC, V.
Tucked away on a quiet backstreet, Wine Wharf – the wine bar for Vinopolis (the wine museum) – offers a suitably extensive and global selection of interesting wines. If you like to experiment, this is the place to do it, where you can roam from an English gamay to a Uraguayan Tannat. The young wine-savvy staff are friendly and fun, plus they always let you try before you commit to buy. Options by the glass are strewn all over the menu, meaning choice is exceptional and quality is tip-top. Unfortunately, despite all the above – and the attractively modish wharf-style interior of bare bricks, beams and metal – the place doesn't seem to be pulling in the punters. Shame. London's wine lovers will lose a valuable resource if neglect forces the place out of business.
Babies and children admitted. Disabled: toilet. Function room.

Also in the area...

All Bar One 28-30 London Bridge Street, SE1 (7940 9981); 34 Shad Thames, Butlers Wharf, SE1 (7940 9771).
The Bermondsey (Davy's) 63 Bermondsey Street, SE1 (7407 1096).
Cooperage (Davy's) 48-50 Tooley Street, SE1 (7403 5775).
Hay's Galleria (Balls Brothers) Hay's Galleria, Tooley Street, SE1 (7407 4301).
Heeltap & Bumper (Davy's) Chaucer House, White Hart Yard, off Borough High Street, SE1 (7407 2829).
Hop Cellars (Balls Brothers) 24 Southwark Street, SE1 (7403 6851).
Mug House (Davy's) 1-3 Tooley Street, SE1 (7403 8343).
Pommeler's Rest (JD Wetherspoon) 196-198 Tower Bridge Road, SE1 (7378 1399).
Skinkers (Davy's) 42 Tooley Street, SE1 (7407 7720).
Slug & Lettuce 32 Borough High Street, SE1 (7378 9999).
Wetherspoon's Metro Central Heights, Newington Causeway, SE1 (7940 0890).

Brixton & Streatham

Local favourites from the 1990s – the **Dogstar** and **Fridge Bar** – now have a new contender in **Plan-B**, which looks set to kick-start a Hoxtonesque trend for cutting-edge DJ bars. Traditionalists can still stand their ground at such old-school drinking holes as the **Effra** and the **Trinity Arms**, but it's as a pre-clubbing destination that Brixton really shines.

Bar Lorca

261 Brixton Road, SW9 (7274 5537/www.barlorca.com). Brixton tube/rail. **Open** 5pm-2am Mon-Thur; noon-3am Fri, Sat; noon-midnight Sun. **Food served** 5-11pm Mon-Thur; noon-midnight Fri-Sun. **Admission** £3 after 9pm, £5 after 10pm Sat. **Credit** AmEx, DC, MC, V.
When the Brixton branch of Lorca opened a few years ago, some critics rated it a poor second to its Stoke Newington sibling. Yet this large and lively bar flourishes, due in no mean part to the multifarious weekly events it hosts. The Soca Professor dances in for Tropical Fever, a late-night session for Latin lovers, while Friday's regular Jazz Junction offers funk, soul and salsa to a tightly packed crowd. There are also regular dance classes and film screenings. A mosaic bar and Spanish chit-chat exchanged between bar staff lend a quintessentially continental flavour to proceedings, conducive to the downing of Havana Gold, San Miguel and Sol. Draught beers are fairly pedestrian – Stella, Carlsberg and Tetley's – while bottles are the familiar cluster of Beck's, Bud, Smirnoff Ices and Bacardi Breezers. Tapas helps soak it all up.
Babies and children admitted (children's menu, high chairs, nappy-changing facilities, toys). Dance classes 7.30-9.30pm Mon, Fri, Sat (salsa), Tue (samba); £5 one hour, £7 two hours. Disabled: toilet. Function room. Games (fruit machine, table football, quiz machine). Music (DJs 7pm Thur-Sun; world music 9pm every other Sun). Restaurant. Tables outdoors (terrace yard). TV (big screen, satellite).

Brixtonian Havana Club

11 Beehive Place, SW9 (7924 9262). Brixton tube/rail. **Open** noon-1am Tue, Wed; noon-2am Thur-Sat; 4pm-midnight Sun. **Food served** 7-11pm Tue-Sat; 4-11pm Sun. **Happy hour** 5.30-7.30pm Mon-Fri. **Admission** £3 after 10pm Thur; £5 after 10pm Fri, Sat. **Credit** MC, V.
Once with a branch in Covent Garden, this Caribbean bar decided to concentrate its energies south of the river in the late 1990s. Sporadic opening hours and an arbitrary kitchen timetable mean that succulent Caribbean-themed dishes sometimes appear to be on ration, but you've always been able to get a mean drink here (rum-based, natch). The sparkling bar, vibrant with splashes of pink and purple and dashes of red, is decked out with colourful bottles for cocktails; there's a menu of 32, including a stiff-backed Bahama Mama (with dark and white rum, ginger ale and lime juice) and the Grand Screwdriver (champagne, orange juice and Grand Marnier). Come weekend evenings, this is one of the liveliest dives in SW9.
Babies and children admitted. Dress: smart. Function room. Music (Cuban band 6pm Sun; jazz 10pm Thur; free). Tables outdoors (paved area).

Bug Bar

The Crypt, St Matthew's Church, Brixton Hill, SW2 (7738 3366). Brixton tube/rail. **Open** 7pm-1am Wed, Thur; 7pm-3am Fri, Sat; 7pm-2am Sun. **Credit** MC, V.
First opened in 1997, the cavernous stone crypt under St Matthew's Church still makes for a hugely impressive venue, still massively popular with south London stylists. Seating is a cluster of sofas in the centre and more velvet-topped chairs line the walls, but this is no spot for wallflowers – the focus is resolutely on the floor space, which gets packed with bump-and-grinders at weekends. Regular DJs and open-mic nights draw the punters, as do well-priced cocktails, bottled

beers and house wine served in generous-sized glasses. At the end of a curved hallway is the restaurant area where excellent fish and vegetarian options can be found among the meat on the eclectic menu. Massive toilets too.
Babies and children admitted (restaurant). Disabled: toilet. Music (DJs 7pm Wed-Sun; £4 9-11pm, £6 after 11pm). Tables outdoors (garden).

Dogstar

389 Coldharbour Lane, SW9 (7733 7515). Brixton tube/rail. **Open** noon-2am Mon-Wed, Sun; noon-2.30am Thur; noon-4am Fri, Sat. **Food served** 1-5pm Sun. **Admission** £4 10-11pm, £6 after 11pm Fri; £4 9-10pm, £5 10-11pm, £7 after 11pm Sat. **Credit** MC, V.
Back in the days of the riots (ah, nostalgia!), this was where the Atlantic Pub stood – a well-known domain for dominoes and trilby hats. The newer incarnation might have lost a bit of its former edge, but the Dogstar still draws in a loyal crowd, especially at weekends when bouncers are required to keep the queues of 'I Love Brixton' tourists in check. Come here during the day for a chilled vibe, as the expansive interior provides breathing space for chatterers and loungers. The well-worn DJ booth, overhead projectors and capacious floor space show that the venue is more geared towards its twilight role, but the Dogstar is still a good spot for brunchers.
Babies and children admitted (until 6pm). Disabled: toilet. Function room. Games (fruit machine, pinball machine, pool, video games). Music (DJs 9pm nightly). Tables outdoors (garden). TV (big screen).

Duke of Edinburgh

204 Ferndale Road, SW9 (7924 0509). Clapham North tube/Brixton tube/rail. **Open/food served** noon-11pm Mon-Sat; noon-10.30pm Sun. **Credit** MC, V.
Once upon a time, this off-the-beaten-track former Truman pub was a well-kept secret. Now, it's as over subscribed as an audition for *Big Brother*. There are low tables and sofas out front, and an ecclesiastical angle in the pub's back bar carried through carved wood, chunky church pews, stained glass, candles and raw brickwork. The DJ pulpit would be the most contemporary feature but for a huge overhead screen that has an unnerving habit of displaying images of Enrique Iglesias. Beers on tap are a poor line-up of Heineken, John Smith's and Stella. A huge garden makes the Duke even more of a crowd-puller come summer.
Games (fruit machine, pool, table football). Music (DJs, 8pm Thur-Sat; free). Tables outdoors (garden, heated marquee). TV (big screen, satellite).

Effra

38A Kellet Road, SW2 (7274 4180). Brixton tube/rail. **Open** noon-11pm Mon-Sat. **Food served** 1.15-8pm Mon-Sat. **No credit cards**.
What a splendid establishment. Cool without even being arsed. For its loyal locals it's home from home. The barman has even been known to walk home the odd overindulged customer. Drop by and you might feel you've entered the set of a 1970s British sitcom. Certainly, the curved dark-wood and gilt-edged trimmed bar seems to have changed little in the interim and there's even the odd ageing TV actor around to add to the mood. While the main bar is populated by Brixton's bright young things, the adjoining pool room is filled with Caribbean elders drawn here by the food and the Guinness on tap. All mix in the back, where regular jazz adds to the vibe. Warm baguettes are the main concession to pub fare, but there's also a fine line in jerk fish, chicken, pork or curried mutton – all come with rice at a reasonable £4.50.
Games (pool). Music (jazz 8.30pm Tue-Thur, Sat; reggae noon-11pm Fri; free). Tables outdoors (garden). TV.

Fridge Bar

1 Town Hall Parade, Brixton Hill, SW2 (7326 5100/ www.fridge.co.uk). Brixton tube/rail. **Open** *Main bar* 7pm-2am Mon-Thur; 7pm-4am Fri; 8pm-4am Sat; 8pm-3am Sun. *Chill-out bar* 5.30-11.30am Sat, Sun. **Admission** *Main bar* £5 before 11pm Fri, Sat, £8 after; occasional £5 Sun. *Chill-out bar* £5 Sat, Sun. **Credit** MC, V.
Absinthe, champagne and a late, late licence – that's the unholy trinity driving the booze-soaked punters who pack the Fridge Bar every weekend, seeking a good time and generally finding it, even if they can't remember its name the following morning. The grandaddy of Brixton club-bars, the Fridge is a legendary den of debauchery with erotic paintings on the wall setting a tone that the mixed-race, mixed-sex, mixed-sexuality punters are only too happy to buy into. Thumping beats provide the soundtrack and if the barmen aren't the most adept with a cocktail shaker – in the spirit of a 1980s revival we ordered a Sex on the Beach but it was more Limp Bizkit than *From Here to Eternity* – it really doesn't matter because nobody comes here looking for sophistication. Flowers and candles provide a chic balance to the mayhem. The crowd always looks as if it is having a whale of a time.
Dress: no trainers at weekends. Music (DJs 10pm nightly). Tables outdoors (pavement).

Hope & Anchor

123 Acre Lane, SW2 (7274 1787). Clapham North tube/ Brixton tube/rail. **Open** 11am-11pm Mon-Sat; noon-10.30pm Sun. **Food served** noon-2.30pm, 6-9pm Mon-Fri; noon-4pm Sat, Sun. **Credit** AmEx, DC, MC, V.
The sounds of the Sugarbabes give way to Abba – yep, you are entering MOR zone. Situated midway between Clapham and Brixton, this unassuming Young's pub, a uniformly beige hang out, caters to all: families, locals, and office workers. No gimmicks here, just a decent space to sup draught beer, wines and spirits. A large beer garden is conducive to the summer sprawl, which brings in the clans and broods of the local area. Things generally bubble along quite nicely due to friendly staff who are adept at emphasising last orders by maintaining benevolent smiles as they swoop on smoking ashtrays or freshly drained glasses.
Babies and children admitted (lunchtime only). Disabled: toilet. Function room. Games (fruit machines, golf machine). Tables outdoors (garden). TV (big screen, satellite).

Living

443 Coldharbour Lane, SW9 (7326 4040). Brixton tube/rail. **Open** noon-2am Mon-Thur, Sun; noon-4am Fri, Sat. **Happy hour** 6.30-8pm daily. **Admission** £5 after 10pm Fri, Sat. **Credit** AmEx, MC, V.
'You know the rules,' said the doorman pointing stoically at a customer's hat. The security-conscious but undeniably patronising 'no headwear' rule at Living has for some time been irking some Brixtonians – not least those using caps to store cascading dreadlocks. Still, this two-storey bar fills up on a regular basis with punters who have it logged as one of Brixton's funkier landmarks. Most activity takes place downstairs, where a mixed-up interior of '90s cool and '70s psychedelia forms the backdrop for a night on the cocktails: the likes of Woo Woos (a vodka, peach schnapps and lemon juice reviver) and Japanese Slippers (tequila, midori, lime and lemon juice). Shooters include lemon and peach and there are alcoholic milkshakes. Things get pretty snug, with standing room only most nights, but with double measures of spirits, punters are enjoying themselves too much to care.
Film screenings. Games (pool, table football, video games). Music (DJs 9pm nightly).

Plan-B

418 Brixton Road, SW9 (7733 0926). Brixton tube. **Open** noon-midnight Mon, Tue; noon-2am Wed, Thur; noon-4am Fri, Sat; noon-1am Sun. **Food served** noon-10pm daily. **Happy hour** 5-7pm daily. **Credit** AmEx, MC, V.

Most pub-goers in Brixton wouldn't know their *Wallpaper** from their cornice or their cornice from their Caipirinha, and think *Dazed & Confused* is a state of mind rather than a way of life. That, though, is set to change with the arrival of Brixton's first style bar, an attractively unobtrusive venue that squats nonchalantly on the site of a former Wimpy – a transformation that in itself offers evidence of the area's changing ways. Looking rather like a marketing meeting's idea of a Shoreditch bachelor pad, this low, sleek and spacious L-shaped venue offers overhead steel piping, brickwork and natural pine to provide textural variation. The back area is dominated by a long bar with a neon blue backdrop, mirrored by a large built-up DJ arena. Take your pick from low tables, high stools or the three-tiered bank of red cushioned seating. Young crowds, drifting down from Clapham where style bibles are all but compulsory, maximise their artful lounging while sipping well-made cocktails and picking at classy snacks. The beautiful people have arrived, and Brixton will never be the same again.

Babies and children admitted (until 6pm). Disabled: toilet. Music (DJs 9pm Wed-Sun; £3 after 10pm Thur or after 9pm Fri, Sat; £5 after 10pm Fri, Sat).

SW9

11 Dorrell Place, SW9 (7738 3116). Brixton tube/rail. **Open** 9am-11pm Mon-Thur; 9am-1am Fri; 10am-1am Sat; 10am-11pm Sun. **Food served** 10am-9pm Mon-Wed; 10am-10pm Thur-Sat; 10am-6pm Sun. **Happy hour** 4.30-7pm Mon-Fri, Sun. **Credit** MC, V.

The nearby **Brixtonian** (*see p201*) once occupied the site, but SW9 has now made this side alley its own, happy amid the breaker's yard and crumbling pavements of its surroundings. A compact space, it manages to squeeze in a decent amount of eating tables, a few bar stools and a comfy sofa at the back. Purple hues throughout are stylish, but scuffed and foot-marked pine floors make things seem a bit studenty. A winter canopy outside keeps a healthy amount of bums on seats in colder months. The bar boasts a good selection of rum and whisky, plus bottled beers and alcopops. Draughts include Guinness, Kirin and Erdinger, while Knob Creek Bourbon and Pusser's Rum are rudely displayed. Lunchtimes are popular for the £7-for-two-courses food offer. We rate the moist carrot cake and, of course, the big cups of hot melted and malted chocolate.

Babies and children admitted. Music (jazz 9pm Fri, Sat). Tables outdoors (heated patio).

Telegraph

228 Brixton Hill, SW2 (8678 0777). Brixton tube, then 49, 59, 118, 133, 159, 250 bus. **Open** noon-2am Mon-Thur; noon-4am Fri; noon-6am Sat; noon-midnight Sun. **Food served** 5.30-10.30pm Mon-Fri; 1-10.30pm Sat, Sun. **Credit** AmEx, MC, V.

Brixton Hill might be a hike too far, but it's worth the 15-minute stroll or eight-minute bus ride from Brixton tube to visit this enjoyable spot. Once a real old codgers' pub, the Telegraph has hoovered away the cobwebs and rebranded itself as a venue for live music and rave-style nights, much in the manner of neighbour the **White Horse** (*see right*). Locals Basement Jaxx once had a residency here in the cavernous back room. An open courtyard at the front is set slightly too close to the main road, but inside there's an intimate front bar and restaurant area serving Thai food at reasonable prices. Darkly lit in the daytime with red velvet curtains, a log fire in winter and scattered sofa-style seating, this likeable place deserves more custom and will surely soon get it.

Babies and children admitted (until 6pm). Function room (120). Games (pool table). Music (DJs 8pm Thur-Sat; bands 8pm Mon, Wed, Sun; £5 after 9pm). Tables outdoors. TV (big screen, satellite).

Tongue & Groove

50 Atlantic Road, SW9 (7274 8600). Brixton tube/rail. **Open** 8pm-2am Wed-Sat; 6pm-1am Sun. **Credit** AmEx, DC, MC, V.

Behind the blackened facade of T&G, you'll discover nights of swinging hips, spilt drinks and lizard lounging. This night-time bar resembles a '60s British bordello (er, apparently). Snakeskin, leopard skin, black leather, red velvet and erotic pictures all add to an 'anything goes behind closed doors' vibe, while DJs pull in music from all global angles; Cuban, kitsch and Afro-Beat hold sway for an open-minded crowd. Yet there's no denying a touristy element to the place, with wide-eyed or self-conscious drinkers looking like they've gate-crashed a slice of Brixton bedlam. Uniformed staff seem hand-picked to go with the sleek black-topped bar with overhead chrome. Double spirits and mixers, and fruit or champagne cocktails are dexterously served up.

Disabled: toilet. Music (DJs 9pm Tue-Sat; free).

Trinity Arms

45 Trinity Gardens, SW9 (7274 4544). Brixton tube/rail. **Open** 11am-11pm Mon-Sat; noon-10.30pm Sun. **Food served** noon-3pm Mon-Fri. **No credit cards**.

Situated on a quiet square, the aged Trinity Arms is a haven for *Racing Post* readers and flat-capped ale drinkers. But for all its stubborn olde worlde charm, this pub is a popular stomping ground for the area's cross-section of drinkers, who relish the relative calm. It's a Young's place, so all its standards and seasonal specials are served alongside Stella, Dry Blackthorn cider and Carling, and there's also a selection of malts including Laphroaig and 12-year-old Glenlivet. Wine is served by the glass (£2.55) or the bottle (£10.25). The obligatory garishly patterned carpet and polished dark wood fittings are pristine: untouched by unruly offspring who, according to a stern sign, are banished to the beer garden and away from the adult intimacy of the bar.

Games (fruit machine). Tables outdoors (garden). TV.

White Horse

94 Brixton Hill, SW2 (8678 6666). Brixton tube then 49, 59, 118, 133, 159, 250 bus. **Open** 5pm-1am Mon-Thur; 4pm-1am Fri, Sat; 2pm-1am Sun. **Food served** 5-10pm Mon-Sat; 2-6pm Sun. **Credit**. AmEx, MC. V.

The increasingly hip White Horse had a complete facelift a couple of years ago. It now presents a wide space with dark wooden flooring, nicely worn low leather seating and a DJ box. Things get quite tasty here at weekends, when Brixton's young lovelies come to make eyes at each other – a meeting of raging hormones and raging beats. Food and drink are as worthy of exploration as the clientele. Cocktails include a calorie-busting Toblerone with Baileys, Cointreau and honey blended with milk and Nuttella. Cuban Mojitos come with a very healthy dose of Havana Club rum, and there's also a fine selection of vodka shots. Olives, potato wedges and garlic mushrooms are all on the tapas menu, while main courses include the likes of marinated steak sarnies, broccoli and stilton soup with hunks of bread, and vegetarian chilli with coriander spiced rice.

Disabled: toilet. Games (pool). Music (9pm Thur-Sun; £3 after 10pm Fri, Sat). Tables outdoors (courtyard).

Windmill

122 Blenheim Gardens, SW2 (8671 0700). Brixton tube then 49, 59, 118, 133, 159, 250 bus. **Open** 11am-midnight daily. **Food served** 1-3pm Mon-Fri. **No credit cards.**

Very different to its Brixton Hill neighbours the **Telegraph** and **White Horse** (*see p203*), the Windmill caters to a slap-dash, boho, unfashionable, friendly and ridiculously open-minded clientele. Real people, then. From the outside, it's an unappealing venue – an ugly council estate concrete block of a pub – but inside is a darkened treasure of esoteric and hap-hazard decoration, ramshackle chairs and appalling toilets. At the longer end of the L-shaped bar (standard lagers and stouts) is a stage that faces a tucked-in lounging area of lazy sofas and candlelight. Every night something different takes place: comedy, acoustic folk, alt.country, punk, spoken word, fancy dress parties, even a socialist disco – on one occasion we watched kids mix drum and bass in one corner while a pair of elders studiously concentrated on their dominoes in the other. A great place. Trendies note: no attitude please.

Babies and children welcome (until 7pm). Function room. Music (8pm nightly). Tables outdoors (garden, pavement).

Also in the area...

Beehive (JD Wetherspoon) 407-9 Brixton Road, SW9 (7738 3643).

Crown & Sceptre (JD Wetherspoon) 2 Streatham Hill, SW2 (8671 0843).

Holland Tringham (JD Wetherspoon) 107-9 Streatham High Road, SW16 (8769 3062).

Camberwell

Camberwell has been on the up-and-up as a drinking destination for a while now, a result of thc overspill from neighbouring Brixton, attracted by (marginally) cheaper housing, and the presence of a student population from the art school. That has caused some friction between Camberwellians old and new, but also resulted in a vibrant scene and some of south London's better non-Brixton bars.

brb at the Grove

26 Camberwell Grove, SE5 (7703 4553). Bus 12, 36, 68, 68A, 171, 176, 185, 345. **Open** noon-11pm Mon-Sat; noon-10.30pm Sun. **Food served** noon-10.30pm Mon-Sat; noon-10pm Sun. **Happy hour** 5.30-7.30pm daily. **Credit** AmEx, MC, V.

The main space of the old Grove – a Camberwell landmark in the early '80s – is basically now a pizzeria, the only one of its size in the neighbourhood, with a long bar and stools so low you can rest your chin on the counter after the shock of discovering Hoegaarden is priced at £3.70 a pint. Settle for a Stella. Heavy, scrubbed wood tables of the rustic variety and chairs whipped from a place of worship, complete with little wooden slot on the back for a missal, can seat 80 diners – and it's always nearly full, especially on Fridays. The offers help: daily happy hours and two-for-one pizzas on Tuesday and two-for-one cocktails on Thursday. On the other side of this converted Victorian pub you'll find a spacious bar, predictably maroon in colour and exposing its bricks – the flooring's stripped and enormous screens drop down for football fans. Outside a small creeper-festooned yard is wall-to-wall in warm weather.

Babies and children admitted. Games (video games). Music (DJs 8pm Thur, Fri; free). Tables outdoors (garden, pavement). TV (big screen, satellite).

Funky Munky

25 Camberwell Church Street, SE5 (7277 1806). Oval tube/ Denmark Hill rail/12, 36, 171 bus. **Open** noon-midnight Mon-Wed; noon-2am Thur-Sat; noon-midnight Sun. **Food served** noon-3pm, 6-10pm Mon-Fri; noon-5pm Sat, Sun. **Happy hour** 5-7pm daily. **Credit** AmEx, MC, V.

In early evening the latest track from Massive Attack will wibble inoffensively in the background, but things can get a lot louder later on at this independently owned orangey-pink walled bar with its motley collection of tables and chairs (they are pushed outside in the summer when the pavement's heav-ing). Potted ferns and a vast red heart inscribed 'I Feel Love' hang above the door, perhaps particularly relevant at the weekends, when the decks are cleared and DJs appear from Kooba records. There are more DJs than variety of beers, in fact. Art students and local young couples collect here, drink-ing Beck's, Guinness and John Smith's; although some even sample from the small selection of interesting wines.

Babies and children admitted (daytime only). Function room. Games (board games). Music (DJs 9pm Thur-Sat; 7pm Sun). Tables outdoors (pavement).

Hermit's Cave

28 Camberwell Church Street, SE5 (7703 3188). Bus 12, 36, 171. **Open** 11am-11pm Mon-Sat; noon-10.30pm Sun. **Food served** 11am-4pm Mon-Sat; noon-5pm Sun. **No credit cards.**

'I feel sorry for people who don't drink. When they wake up in the morning, that's as good as they're gonna feel all day.' That's the message chalked up on the board along with the lunchtime specials – including a saliva-inducing garlic lamb – and all for under a fiver. Popular place, this. All the tables are usually taken in this gorgeously preserved pub, whose cut-glass frontage gracefully curves on a corner, the gleam reflect-ed inside by polished pumps, mirrors at the back of the bar and innumerable sparkly optics. A good collection of malts includes a ten-year-old Laphroaig – the bottle comes with the offer of becoming a lifelong leaseholder of one square foot of the island of Islay. Pewters hang overhead. Brendan, land-lord here for 15 years, points out that pewter will keep your ale much cooler than glass, and there's some good ales to be had in here. Expect suits at lunchtime, while profs from the art college hold court in the evening.

Babies and children admitted. Games (fruit machine). No piped music or jukebox. Tables outdoors (pavement). TV (big screen, satellite).

Red Star

319 Camberwell Road, SE5 (7703 7779). Denmark Hill rail/12, 36, 68, 68A, 171, 176, 185, 345 bus. **Open** 5pm-2am Tue-Thur; 5pm-4am Fri, Sat; 5pm-midnight Sun. **Happy hour** 5-8pm daily. **Admission** £2-£5 after 11pm Fri, Sat. **Credit** MC, V.

At the seedier end of Camberwell Green, just across the road from the Rock of Redemption prayer house and next door to the tattoo parlour and the Chinese acupuncturist, is the Red Star. And red it most certainly is, from the unmissable outside to the cavernous inside, where knackered and inviting sofas await beneath the ballroom mirror soon to spin and spin to Sonic Sabotage, breaks and grooves, Ballearic house, and the frighteningly popular and cheesy Jo Egg's bedroom '80s pop on Saturdays. The choice of draught beers is limited but there's a vast selection of optics to choose from and the cock-tails aren't too expensive. At weekends this becomes a pulling palace par excellence, or so rumour has it.

Disabled: toilet. Function room. Games (pool). Music (DJs 9pm nightly). Tables outdoors (garden). TV (big screen, projection).

Snug Bar

65 Camberwell Church Street, SE5 (7277 2601). Oval or Brixton tube/12, 36, 68, 68A, 171, 176, 185, 345 bus. **Open** 4pm-midnight Mon-Thur; 4pm-2am Fri; noon-2am Sat; noon-10.30pm Sun. **Food served** noon-6pm Sun. **Happy hour** 5-7pm daily. **Credit** AmEx, MC, V.

Everything's deeply upholstered – even the bar. And the Chesterfields – or are they Ottomans? – chaises longues stretch right to the back of this landscape of comfort. In the maroon back room hangs a huge golden moulded picture frame containing only a bare canvas. Not forgetting the bewildered bison transfixed above the blazing hearth, the potted palms and the cactus-filled windows. Where's the palm court orchestra hiding? You can almost feel a bossa nova coming on. At the weekends up-and-coming DJs from Brixton fill the dancefloors. On Sundays a roast is washed down with Kronenbourg, Strongbow or Foster's – and if you hang about there will be an acoustic jazz session later in the evening.

Function room. Music (DJs 8pm Mon-Sat; jazz 8pm Sun; free). TV.

Also in the area...

Fox on the Hill (JD Wetherspoon) 149-53 Denmark Hill, SE5 (7738 4756).

O'Neill's 15 Windsor Walk, Denmark Hill, SE5 (7701 8282).

Catford

Although Catford is the neglected end of Lewisham (especially when it comes to shopping facilities and transport links), it does house the borough's Town Hall and only big theatre. Pubs tend to be grim or great, with hardly any in between. Bars (what bars?), where they exist, tend to be half-hearted adjuncts to Caribbean or Italian restaurants.

Blythe Hill Tavern

319 Stanstead Road, SE23 (8690 5176). Catford or Catford Bridge rail. **Open/food served** 11am-11pm Mon-Sat; noon-10.30pm Sun. **No credit cards.**

This medium-sized Irish-run local exudes an air of friendly welcome, comfort and efficiency. Three joined bars form a U-shape around a central serving area. All are kitted out in faux dark beams, half-panelled, half-stippled walls and dotted with pub and brewery memorabilia. A couple of temperance signs point out that 'Abstinence brings Clearheadedness, Competency and Cash', while 'Alcohol injures Health, Home, Heart, Honour, Heads and Hands'. Who can argue with that? We were also impressed by a colourful wooden sign for 'Higgins – the beer that's clear'. We found the London Pride and Courage Best perfectly clear, as was the air, thanks to a state-of-the-art filtration system. There's a small garden and children's play area at the rear. One of London's best pubs: visit before it's turned into a gastropub.

Babies and children welcome (until 7pm). Function room. Games (darts, fruit machine). Music (8pm, 1st Thur of month). Tables outdoors (garden). TV (satellite).

Catford Ram

9 Winslade Way, SE6 (8690 6206). Catford or Catford Bridge rail. **Open** 11am-11pm Mon-Sat; noon-10.30pm Sun. **Food served** 11.30am-2.30pm, 7-9.30pm Mon-Sat. **No credit cards.**

It's not often you find a Young's pub in such an urban location, but this Tardis-like purpose-built boozer occupies a spot beneath a council housing block in the centre of Catford's grim shopping centre. Still, the nearness of Lewisham Town Hall, library and Broadway Theatre mean that the drinkers are a more urbane crowd than you might expect. The size of a giant Wetherspoon's, the long bar stretches from here to a big-screen TV, with paintwork that's a tasteful cream and beige concoction. Plenty of large mirrors and framed art deco prints make up for there only being one window. The real ales on offer are Young's Special, Ordinary and the seasonal brew. The Ram is renowned locally for well-cooked pub grub and you get plenty of it. Choose from mountainous portions of cottage pie, cauliflower cheese and steak and kidney pie.

Disabled: toilet. Games (darts, fruit machine, pinball machine). TV (big screen, satellite).

Rutland Arms

55 Perry Hill, SE6 (8291 9426). Catford Bridge rail/ 54, 185 bus. **Open** 11am-11pm Mon-Sat; noon-10.30pm Sun. **Food served** noon-2.30pm daily. **No credit cards.**

The current landlord was born here 60-odd years ago and between the time his family left and he took over in the early 1990s, it had been both a hang out for local villains and an '80s disco-pub. Under his renewed influence the emphasis is on jazz, real ale and home-cooking. For jazz read 'trad' and 'dixieland', although R&B of the old school is tolerated on Thursdays, when it packs in the thirty- and fortysomethings. Bands set up and play beside the baby grand. Decor is comfortably worn – green carpet, matching banquettes and framed beer posters. The Rutland's become something of a real ale shrine and regular cask ales include Bass, Young's, Adnams Best and Broadside, and Fuller's ESB and Pride.

Function room. Games (fruit machines). Music (trad jazz 8.30pm Mon, Sat; modern jazz 8.30pm Tue, 1pm Sun; pianist 8.30pm Wed, Fri, 8pm Sun; R&B 9pm Thur). Quiz (1st Sun of month; £1). Tables outdoors (pavement). TV (satellite).

Also in the area...

London & Rye (JD Wetherspoon) 109 Rushey Green, SE6 (8697 5028).

Tiger's Head (JD Wetherspoon) 350 Bromley Road, SE6 (8698 8645).

Clapham

Clapham probably has the widest variety of watering holes in south London. There are trad real ale boozers and noisy DJ bars, gay cruise joints and rugger-bugger meeting places, cocktail-sipping style bars plus, of course, the odd chain franchise, like the recently opened Revolution. But best of all, it boasts some of the most eccentric pubs in the capital, places like **Mistress P's** and the **Prince of Wales** where the imagination hasn't just run riot, it has tripped out into another dimension entirely.

Alexandra

14 Clapham Common Southside, SW4 (7627 5102). Clapham Common tube. **Open** 11am-11pm Mon-Sat; noon-10.30pm Sun. **Food served** noon-4pm Sun. **No credit cards.**

Right opposite Clapham Common tube station, the Alexandra is situated in an imposing, dome-topped building, but inside it's dark and dingy even in daylight, with beams hanging low, engendering a sense of claustrophobia that must be something like being below deck on an old sailing ship. The walls are covered in clutter, with vintage enamelled adverts Hall's Distemper Paint and Lux soapflakes struggling for space

Plan-B. See p203.

with contemporary booze promo posters and a baffling range of farming implements and equine paraphernalia. Up the stairs around the back is a grander space that shows big-screen sports and is often crowded. It's a good-natured place, with plenty of laughter above the shouty mainstream rock soundtrack, but this is essentially a utility pub rather than a venue you'd make a special journey for.
Function room. Games (fruit machine, pinball machine). Jukebox. Music (accoustic set 8pm Thur; £2) TV (big screen, satellite). **Map 11/K17**

Arch 635

15-16 Lendal Terrace, SW4 (7720 7343). Clapham North tube/Clapham High Street rail. **Open/food served** 5-11pm Mon-Thur; 4pm-midnight Fri, Sat; 4-10.30pm Sun. **Credit** MC, V.

It's hard to pull off the trick of being hip but relaxed at the same time, but Arch 635 – a converted railway arch, as its name suggests – just about manages it. The youngish clientele, a chatty mixture of media, marketing and advertising types, ease into the big red sofas or cluster around the industrial bar, looking sartorially sharp and unthreateningly laid-back. Friday and Saturday are the big nights here, but the soul, funk and house music never reaches headbanging velocity. You can also escape into the glass-roofed extension at the back, or attempt a game of table football as respite from the excitable pre-club guzzling.
Games (chess, pool, table football). Music (DJs 8.30pm Thur-Sun; free). TV (big screen, digital). **Map 11/L16**

Bar Local

4 Clapham Common Southside, SW4 (7622 9406). Clapham Common tube. **Open/food served** 5pm-midnight Mon-Thur; noon-midnight Fri-Sun. **Credit** AmEx, MC, V.

This narrow, corridor-like bar is dominated by a huge mural showing an aerial view of Clapham Common and adjacent parts. It's the most spacious thing about the place. Bar Local is loud, buzzy and packed of an evening, with funky beats blurting from the DJ decks and a crowd of dressed-down, clubby types knocking back the bottled beers and shouting to each other over the music. Staff wear T-shirts proclaiming 'Local Hero'. The bar is decorated in a kind of faux NYC, retro-futurist style, with big red sofas, high stools and some 'ironic' photos of street scenes on the walls. The space is so confined, however, that you'll find yourself endlessly spilling your drink and apologising as you attempt to hustle yourself some room.
Bar area available for hire. Music (DJs 8.30pm Thur-Sun; free). **Map 11/L17**

Bread & Roses

68 Clapham Manor Street, SW4 (7498 1779). Clapham Common or Clapham North tube. **Open** noon-11pm Mon-Sat; noon-10.30pm Sun. **Food served** noon-3pm, 7-9.30pm Mon-Fri; noon-4pm, 6-9.30pm Sat, Sun. **Credit** MC, V.

New Labour might have taken it down years ago, but the red flag is still flying here. The clean, modern feel wouldn't necessarily put the Blairites and organically minded liberals off, although this Clapham institution won't let them forget that good old socialist ideals haven't quite died out yet. Bread & Roses is home to the Workers' Beer Company, which provides all those beer tents you queue up in at festivals, and its name is taken from a song inspired by an American textile workers' strike in 1912. The booze too has a leftist theme, with Conspiracy Shooters and Revolutionary Cocktails (Moscow Mules, Mojitos and rum-based Che Guevaras). Draught beer includes Workers Ale and Adnams; there's hearty pub food (sausages and mash, etc); kids are particularly well provided for (with toys and high chairs in the conservatory); and a live African duo plays each Sunday just to remind you that the revolution must be globalised.
Babies and children admitted (until 9pm; high chairs, nappy-changing facilities). Comedy (£5, £3 concessions).

South

Disabled: toilet. Function room. Games (board games, Jenga). Music (call for details). No-smoking area (until 6pm). Quiz (8.30pm 3rd Mon of mth; £2). Tables outdoors (conservatory, heated garden, patio). **Map 11/L16**

The Calf

87 Rectory Grove, SW4 (7622 4019). Clapham Common tube. **Open** 5-11pm Mon-Fri; noon-11pm Sat; noon-10.30pm Sun. **Food served** 6-10pm Mon-Fri; noon-9pm Sat; noon-10pm Sun. **Credit** AmEx, MC, V.

The Calf, a bit out of the way down towards Wandsworth Road station, used to be a Firkin chain hostelry, but now it's a modish-looking gastropub with a little more character about it (and far less in the way of appalling puns adorning every available inch of wall space). It's a chilled-out sort of place, with staff to match, and the leather sofas and rickety furniture give it a certain lazy charm. Sunday afternoons are the most popular time to relax here, with a well-cooked roast on the table and a pint of Pride or a sample of the current guest beer (it was Old Speckled Hen on our visit), or perhaps a bottle from the small but entirely adequate wine list, and some funky beats in the background. A cheerful addition to the sometimes over-serious Clapham scene.

Games (Space Invaders, table football). **Map 11/K16**

Coach & Horses

173-5 Clapham Park Road, SW4 (7622 3815). Clapham Common tube. **Open** 11am-11pm Mon-Sat; noon-10.30pm Sun. **Food served** noon-2.30pm, 6-9.30pm Mon-Fri; noon-4pm, 6-9pm Sat; 12.30-6pm, 7-9pm Sun. **Happy hour** 6-7pm Tue, Fri, Sat. **Credit** MC, V.

This Georgian building was a bastion of Englishness, with its Marmite muffins and tea, and an English pub feel that survived modernisation. Of late, however, it has reached out towards the Antipodes, serving a range of Aussie bottled beers, and made its menu more eclectic (with Thai green curry and rainbow trout popping up alongside the fish cakes, bangers, mash, fat chips and lamb shank). There are also summer barbecues during rugby internationals. Nevertheless, the pub vibe endures, with well-priced Theakston's, London Pride and Adnams on draught. A worthwhile introduction is a 20-seater private dining room, meaning that parties wishing to avoid jostling among the drinkers and smokers can escape the fug and chatter.

Babies and children admitted (lunchtime only). Disabled: toilet. Function room. Tables outdoors (enclosed terrace). TV (big screen, satellite). **Map 11/L17**

Kazbar

50 Clapham High Street, SW4 (7622 0070). Clapham North tube/Clapham High Street rail. **Open/ food served** 4pm-midnight Mon-Sat; 4-11.30pm Sun. **Happy hour** 4-8pm Mon-Fri; noon-8pm Sat, Sun. **Credit** AmEx, DC, MC, V.

Searching for something loud, glitzy and ever so slightly tacky, with cheesy pop promos on constant rotation, mirror-balls, neon lights and helium balloons? This gay video bar should see you right. With chart poppets such as Kylie, Pink, Sugababes and Justin Timberlake on its screens and a DJ blasting out good-time house on a Saturday night, it may not be cool but that's not the point. Once a week the Crush Bar night offers two-for-one drinks each time a featured artist's record is played. For those who want to escape the constant caterwauling of *Heat* generation soap-pop, there's also a sofa den on the upper floor. And if you like the place that much, you can hire it for a private party.

Games (fruit machine). Music (video DJs 7pm nightly; free). Tables outdoors (pavement). TV (video screen). **Map 11/L16**

Landor

70 Landor Road, SW9 (7274 4386). Clapham North tube/ Clapham High Street rail. **Open** noon-11pm Mon-Sat; noon-10.30pm Sun. **Food served** noon-2.30pm, 6-9.30pm Mon-Fri; 1-9.30pm Sat; 1.30-6pm Sun. **Credit** DC, MC, V.

It looks like your average British boozer, full of dog-eared charm and regulars nursing halves in the corner, but there's more to the Landor than you might expect. Its upstairs room is also home to regular fringe shows, staging anything from Chekhov to Irvine Welsh. Which all sits oddly with the cabinet full of pool trophies, the giant canoes hanging from the ceiling and the inexplicable nautical decor that looks like it's come from some naval car boot sale (even the landlord can't explain it). But the ale's decent (Young's Special, Greene King IPA, London Pride) and, for those who care about such things, the bangers and burgers on the menu are organic.

Babies and children admitted (garden until 7pm). Games (fruit machine, pool, quiz machine). Quiz (8pm 1st Sun of mth; £2). Tables outdoors (garden). Theatre. TV (big screen, satellite). **Map 11/M16**

Mistress P's

29 North Street, SW4 (7622 5342). Clapham Common tube. **Open** 11am-11pm Mon-Sat; noon-10.30pm Sun. **Food served** noon-3pm Mon-Sat; noon-5pm Sun. **Credit** MC,V.

A bizarre and glorious fantasia of a public house, with a wonderfully dry-humoured landlady who's constantly adding new bits of tat to its eccentric decor. The latest additions to one of the most peculiar Clapham pubs are a piano – our host encourages punters to get up and bash out a tune or two – and a remote-control car-racing circuit on the end of the bar. This is on top of fairy lights and other glittering gewgaws. There's an idiosyncratic jukebox and south London's most cultish pub quiz, which is so popular it even draws participants from over the river (gasp!). Combine with a visit to the similarly eccentric and overloaded **Prince of Wales** (*see right*) down the road and a complete headfuck is guaranteed with no alcohol required. Oh, go on then, just a bit.

Games (fruit machine, remote-control racing car). Quiz (9.30pm Thur; free). Tables outdoors (pavement). TV (satellite). **Map 11/K16**

100 Pub

100 Clapham Park Road, SW4 (7720 8902). Clapham Common tube. **Open** 5-11pm Mon-Fri; noon-11pm Sat, Sun. **Food served** 6-10pm Mon-Sat; noon-7pm Sun. **Credit** MC, V.

Inviting tropical scenes are painted on the bright yellow exterior, but inside it's less exotic. This is a stripped-down, youth-orientated party pub – flavoured Wyborova vodkas and shooters are heavily promoted – with basic, utilitarian furniture and old-school hip hop mix tapes pumping out of the sound system. The bar staff are a little vague, but there's a rack of style mags to browse while you wait to be served. Entertainment includes stand-up comedy on Thursday. More enticing is the back courtyard. It boasts what the owners say is the biggest umbrella in England – all 49sq m of it. Food is basic; pizzas during the week, roast on the sabbath.

Babies and children admitted (until 7pm). Function room. Comedy (Thur). Games (table football). Tables outdoors (heated garden). TV (big screen, satellite). **Map 11/L17**

Polygon Bar & Grill

4 The Polygon, SW4 (7622 1199). Clapham Common tube. **Open/food served** noon-3.30pm, 6-11pm Mon-Fri; 11am-4.30pm, 6-11pm Sat; 11am-4.30pm, 6-10.30pm Sun. **Happy hour** 6-7.30pm daily. **Credit** AmEx, MC, V.

The style bar gone corporate. All the correct designer features are in place (pod-like stools that look like spacehoppers, spotlights, expansive glass window so passers-by can check how cool your new designer garms look), but it is strangely lacking in humanity or soul, as if assembled from a marketing department checklist. Although it's a relative newcomer to the Clapham scene, the blue chairs in the restaurant are already showing some signs of age, while the round tables look like they were appropriated from a college common room. The prices don't help either, with mains such as char-grilled swordfish and ribeye steak at around £14. Its most attractive features are the happy hour cocktails at £3 – then it's probably best to sup up and move on.
Babies and children admitted (restaurant; high chairs). Disabled: toilet. Restaurant (available for hire).
Map 11/K17

Prince of Wales

38 Old Town, SW4 (7622 3530). Clapham Common tube. **Open** 5-11pm Mon-Fri; 1-11pm Sat; 1-10.30pm Sun. **No credit cards.**

Stuffed birds and mongooses. Toy drums and aeroplanes. An antelope's head. A flag bearing the image of a young Bono. A plastic lobster. Paintings of military gents. Thai puppets. Traffic lights. The PoW looks as if a junk shop has exploded all over its walls and ceiling. To say it's cluttered is an understatement – kitschy curios cover every surface. Even some of the tables are old school desks. The beer's not bad either, with London Pride and Old Speckled Hen on tap, and Scrumpy Jack for the cider swillers. Great music too; we enjoyed late '70s new wave classics from the likes of Elvis Costello, the Jam, the Stranglers and Ian Dury. Vive la difference!
Babies and children admitted (until 7pm). Benches outdoors (pavement). Function room. TV. **Map 11/K16**

Rose & Crown

2 The Polygon, SW4 (7720 8265). Clapham Common tube. **Open** noon-11pm Mon-Sat; noon-10.30pm Sun. **Food served** noon-2.30pm Mon-Sat; noon-5pm Sun. **Credit** MC, V.

'Drunkenness is nothing but voluntary madness,' opines a slogan on the wall of this snug, wood-panelled, traditional pub opposite the bus terminus. But it's contented sipping rather than madly swilling that you'll be doing here, because the Rose & Crown is something of a temple to top-hole bevvy, with a constantly rotating selection of guest beers on offer (Abbot Ale, Dragon King and Wicked Hound on our visit) – at some of the most reasonable prices in the area. Further proving its dedication are the lovingly framed beermats from all over the country, including one for the rather heartlessly named Titantic Iceberg brew. Unlike many trad hostelries, it's remarkably neat and clean, and there's steak and kidney pud or sausage and mash if you need to soak up the beer.
Babies and children admitted (lunch only). Games (slot machine). No-smoking tables. Tables outdoors (garden, pavement). TV. **Map 11/K17**

Royal Oak

8-10 Clapham High Street, SW4 (7720 5678). **Open** noon-11pm Mon-Sat; noon-10.30pm Sun. **Food served** noon-10.30pm Mon-Sat; noon-10.00pm Sun. **Credit** AmEx, DC, MC, V.

The cutesy red and pink exterior suggests that the Royal Oak is just another unremarkable pub on the scruffier fringe of the Clapham manor. But behind the exterior, the place is a real find. Decorated in demure shades of brown and cream, with big comfy leather chairs and sofas to sink into, it has been converted in a way that's still publike but both inviting and individual. The food is a big plus too: solid breakfasts, a tasty variety of pies and sausages, doorstep sarnies and, if you fancy something a little different, a pint-pot of shell-on prawns or a plate of oysters with Guinness. Add subdued lighting, friendly and helpful bar staff, with cool chanson cooing on the sound system, and it's a real delight.
Babies and children admitted. Function room. Tables outside. **Map 11/K16**

Critics' choice
child friendly

Banner's (p164)
Part pub, part playgroup.

Bar Lorca (p185)
Clowns to entertain, high chairs to keep 'em captive.

Bread & Roses (p207)
Pub of choice for Clapham's junior socialist revolutionaries.

Crown & Greyhound (p211)
A sandpit and Wendy house in the garden, or just turn them lose in Dulwich Park.

Leather Bottle (p230)
Kids go Wombling free in a fine big Wimbledon garden.

Sand

156 Clapham Park Road, SW4 (7622 3022). Clapham Common tube/Brixton tube/rail, then 35, 37 bus. **Open/food served** 5pm-2am Mon-Sat; 5pm-1am Sun. **Admission** £5 after 9.30pm Fri, Sat. **Credit** MC, V.

Sand, a *TO* favourite situated close to the Brixton border, is beginning to age gracefully. Its olive-drab concrete and brick surfaces and chunky furniture are starting to look slightly worn and lived-in, and it rather suits the place, giving it a little more character than your average trendy bar. As the name suggests, it has a desert-chic look, and a rather deadly late licence, particularly if you've indulged in a couple too many of its rather fine whisky sours. Music on our last visit was funky soul classics provided by a female DJ. The menu is limited but contains plenty of good stuff, and you can order smaller portions if you're not keen on stuffing yourself. On Sunday there's a roast and the big papers to peruse.
Disabled: toilet. Function room. Games (board games). Music (DJs 10.30pm daily). **Map 11/L17**

SO.UK

165 Clapham High Street, SW4 (7622 4004). Clapham Common or Clapham North tube. **Open** 5pm-midnight Mon-Wed; 5pm-1am Thur; 5pm-2am Fri, Sat; noon-midnight Sun. **Food served** 5-10pm Mon-Sat; noon-10pm Sun. **Credit** AmEx, MC, V.

You can tell that this is intended to be one of Clapham's more fashionable (and pricier) drinking dens from the presence of Puff Daddy's fave, Cristal champagne, on the wine list. It even does its own CD too of hip electro-jazz. SO.UK, owned by actress Leslie Ash and former footballer Lee Chapman, affects a luxurious Arabic kasbah vibe (souk, geddit?), with hanging lamps, low sofas and sand-textured walls. The menu is a Morocco meets Japan meets Thai fusion, where tempura

Red Star. *See p205.*

prawns clash with couscous. The cocktail list is decent, and the vodka Martini certainly passed muster. The clientele? Bond Street designer shoes and Jennifer Aniston hair.
Disabled: toilet. Music (DJs 8pm Wed-Sat; free). Tables outside (pavement). **Map 11/L17**

2 Brewers

114 Clapham High Street, SW4 (7498 4971). Clapham Common or Clapham North tube. **Open** 5pm-2am Mon-Thur; 5pm-3am Fri, Sat; 2pm-12.30am Sun. **Admission** £2 after 11pm Tue-Thur; £3 9.30-11pm Fri, Sat; £5 after 11pm Fri, Sat. **Credit** AmEx, MC, V.

Boys, boys, boys, they're looking for a good time. This is a no-frills, no-nonsense gay pub (with a bit of a disco attached) whose entire raison d'être is hedonism. It's noisy, cruisy and ever so slightly sleazy (some call it the '2 Sewers'). There's throbbing handbag house and pop, with an '80s night on Tuesdays, plus cabaret turns – celebrity stewardess Pam Ann's Mile High Club show was a recent hit – and drag acts. But the main point is to check out other chaps' vital statistics before heading onwards for more serious investigations of the pleasure principle.
Cabaret (11.30pm Tue-Sat; 6.30pm Sun). Disabled: toilet. Games (fruit machines). Music (DJs 10pm nightly). TV (plasma screen). **Map 11/L16**

White House

65 Clapham Park Road, SW4 (7498 3388). Clapham Common tube. **Open** 5.30pm-2am Mon-Sat; noon-12am Sun. **Food served** 6-10.30pm Tue-Sun. **Happy hour** 5.30-7pm Mon-Fri. **Admission** £5 after 9pm Fri, Sat. **Credit** AmEx, DC, MC, V.

At weekends, burly bomber-jacketed bouncers stand sentinel outside this utterly un-publike white building, like bookends holding in place the snaking queue at the door. It's fashionably clad – 'painfully trendy', in the opinion of one local – and there's certainly a whiff of elitism about it. But those queues indicate that its combination of Tokyo-meets-NYC decor (tropical fish tank, intimate booths, swivelling barfly stools) and cool club tracks pumping through the speakers, plus a late licence, appeals to those who want a lounge club experience without actually going to a nightclub. It even has the *Sex and the City* cocktail, the Flirtini, on the menu. The gents, though, is the great leveller – a big steel trough just like you'd find in any housing-estate pub.
Disabled: toilet. Function room. Games (board games). Music (DJs Wed-Sun). **Map 11/L17**

Windmill on the Common

Clapham Common Southside, SW4 (8673 4578). Clapham Common tube. **Open** 11am-11pm Mon-Sat; noon-10.30pm Sun. **Food served** noon-2.30pm, 7-10pm Mon-Fri; noon-9pm Sat, Sun. **Credit** AmEx, MC, V.

This huge old Young's boozer has benefitted from a spring clean, with new carpets and chairs installed, so gone is the grime and stickiness of yesteryear. It remains rather soulless in a Beefeater kind of way (and the pictures on the walls are particularly artless), but who gives a toss when come summertime the Windmill has the common as its beer garden. Drinkers spill out over the grass, scattering plastic glasses everywhere as they bask in the rays. It was once a notorious meeting point for ravers during the acid house era, but now the intoxication is strictly liquid. There's standard pub grub

on the menu – shepherd's pie, chicken curry, ribeye steak. Some of the rooms have a hotel lobby vibe, which isn't surprising as this is also a three-star hotel.
Babies and children admitted (separate area; high chairs). Disabled: toilet. Function room. No-smoking area (restaurant). Restaurant. Tables outdoors (garden). TV (big screen, satellite). **Map 11/K18**

Also in the area...

Bierodrome 44-8 Clapham High Street, SW4 (7720 1118).
Boom Bar (Po Na Na) 165-7 St John's Hill, SW11 (7924 3449).
Fine Line 182-4 Clapham High Street, SW4 (7622 4436).
Pitcher & Piano 8 Balham Hill, SW12 (8673 1107).
Slug & Lettuce 4 St John's Hill, SW11 (7924 1322).

Deptford

A major centre of the navy in Pepys's day, the part of London bordered by Bermondsey, New Cross and Greenwich is currently undergoing a revival. The spectacular Laban Centre building (the focal point of modern dance in Britain) is down by the Creek and the arrival of the DLR has stirred up property prices. Still, change can't be rushed. Cool and groovy Farragos gave it a go but shut up shop this year.

Dog & Bell

116 Prince Street, SE8 (8692 5664). New Cross tube/rail/ Deptford rail. **Open** noon-11pm Mon-Sat; noon-3.30pm, 7-10.30pm Sun. **Food served** noon-2.30pm, 6-9pm Mon-Fri. **No credit cards.**
Regulars at this choice backstreet local include musicians – including one commercially partial to Bell's whisky – actors, writers, builders, market traders and lecturers and students from Goldsmiths and Greenwich Uni. Divided into three small and connected rooms, the walls are painted a pleasant shade of peach with plenty of rustic wood furniture scattered around. A small games area at the back hosts a bar billiards table, shove ha'penny board and dominoes. Winter evenings are enlivened no end by the annual pickle competition. The name comes from the method of duck hunting prevalent on the marshes around Deptford dockyards: the bell was used to scare the ducks into the air. You'll find up to five real ales (including London Pride and ESB) dispensed from a single serving area by affably knowledgeable barstaff. Not for nothing has this excellent Irish-run pub been a multiple winner of CAMRA's Pub of the Year Award.
Games (bar billiards, darts). Quiz (9pm Sun; 50p). Tables outdoors (garden). TV.

Royal George

85 Tanners Hill, SE8 (8692 2594). Deptford Bridge DLR/New Cross tube/rail. **Open** 11am-11pm Mon-Sat; noon-10.30pm Sun. **Food served** noon-8pm daily. **No credit cards.**
A Sam Smith's pub without real ale may seem a little like a sandwich shop bereft of bread, but the George is a community pub with enough life to satisfy most local drinkers. Although Tanners Road is perhaps the nearest New Cross comes to the Bronx, that can only serve to speed up your desire to arrive and, once inside this kitschy two-bar boozer, the welcome is genuine enough. Customers cross all divides and are as likely to include a drummer in a blues band as a chippie, a former glamour model as a resting actor and so on. A smallish room upstairs has variously seen service as a theatre (David 'Diddy' Hamilton brought his one-man show here a couple of years' ago) and as a minor music venue. Those looking for lagers served out of SS's curiously OTT pumps are well served and the Hefe Weisse and bottled stout and organic ales are worth a go.
Babies and children admitted. Function room. Games (fruit machine). Tables outdoors (garden, pavement). TV.

Dulwich

No, Dulwich is not the new Clapham, but walk down Lordship Lane of a Friday night and you could be forgiven for thinking so. **Franklin's** is typical of the genre of easy going gastrobars attracting young professionals, but there are half-a-dozen others. Historic taverns dot nearby Dulwich Village, with the **Crown & Greyhound** the grandaddy of them all.

Crown & Greyhound

73 Dulwich Village, SE21 (8299 4976). North Dulwich rail. **Open** 11am-11pm Mon-Sat; noon-10.30pm Sun. **Food served** noon-10pm Mon-Sat; noon-3pm, 4.30-9pm Sun. **Credit** MC, V.
Affectionately known as 'the Dog', the Crown & Greyhound's Victorian grandeur imposes itself on the heart of Dulwich Village. A recent makeover has not damaged its traditional feel nor historic roots as a staging post between London and Sevenoaks, and has enhanced its drink and food selections while allowing more light into the previously dowdy atmosphere. The curved central bar now serves Staropramen, Leffe, Young's, Fuller's Pride and Bass on draught with Pilsner Urquell a welcome addition in bottles. A regenerated kitchen offers an updated snack/meal menu with smarter wines. From the old days, there's no change to the no-smoking area, split-level garden, three bar areas or conservatory. It remains the perfect stop off after a stroll in Dulwich Park.
Babies and children admitted (high chairs, nappy-changing facilities). Disabled: toilet. Function rooms. No-smoking area (restaurant). Restaurant. Tables outdoors (garden). TV (big screen).

East Dulwich Tavern

1 Lordship Lane, SE22 (8693 1817). East Dulwich rail. **Open** 11am-11pm Mon-Wed; 11am-midnight Thur-Sat; noon-10.30pm Sun. **Food served** 6-10.30pm Tue-Sat; 11am-4pm Sun. **Credit** MC, V.
The EDT is at the gateway to the heart of the area, its imposing Victorian edifice towering over Goose Green roundabout. Several facelifts in recent times have eroded a murky past and now the EDT can mix it with the best, offering all the benefits of a well-run community pub: friendly service, good music, excellent screen area and lots of space. Watch out for the changing backlit photo staring at you as you order draught Grolsch, Staropramen, Young's Special or bottled Tiger, Budvar or Leffe from the bar. Since the passing of East Dulwich Cabaret comedy to the nearby Magdala, the upstairs area has been converted into a quality pizzeria with additional roasts on Sunday. In what was a barn of a space, an impressive and tidy job has been achieved to create a relaxed and intimate vibe.
Function room. Games (quiz machine, table football). Restaurant. Tables outdoors (pavement). TV (big screen).

Franklin's

157 Lordship Lane, SE22 (8299 9598). East Dulwich rail. **Open** 5-11pm Mon; noon-11pm Tue-Thur; noon-midnight Fri, Sat; noon-10.30pm Sun. **Food served** 6-10.30pm Mon; 1-5pm, 6-10.30pm Tue-Sun. **Credit** AmEx, MC, V.

Despite a growing number of bars and cafes to have sprung up along this lively stretch of Lordship Lane, Franklin's has deservedly retained its mantle as the influential leader of the burgeoning East Dulwich scene. Much of its reputation is based on a superbly distinctive Modern British menu using carefully chosen ingredients and changed daily, but it also wins plaudits for the bringing together of gastro and bar camaraderie while managing to be kiddie-friendly at the same time (important in an area that is very popular with young families). Conviviality is ensured with a haphazard seating arrangement; endearing quirks come courtesy of a fantastic back-bar mirror feature and charmingly creaky door. The regular throng enjoys draught Beck's, Young's, Weston's Organic Cider or a wicked Bloody Mary with their Saturday brunch. A grouchy manager fuels the banter.
Babies and children admitted (high chairs). Disabled: toilet. Function room. Restaurant. Tables outdoors (pavement).

The Green

58-60 East Dulwich Road, SE22 (7732 7575). East Dulwich rail. **Open** 10am-11pm daily. **Food served** noon-3.30pm, 6-10.30pm daily. **Credit** AmEx, MC, V.
On the corner of Ady's and East Dulwich Road, this recent arrival has enhanced a previous blind spot in the area. The large frontage opens on to a wide pedestrian thoroughfare, great for sunnier days. Two nights a week, the front becomes a live jazz bar, leading into two designated restaurant areas surrounded by offerings from local artists: the Green Art Gallery. Poetry readings are another attraction, but there's plenty of space to hide in when necessary. The seafood bar menu is a plus, as is the premium spirit portfolio of a range of Havana Clubs, vodkas and single malts. An excellent pint of Bitburger is the solitary draught lager option.
Babies and children admitted. Disabled: toilet. Function room. Music (jazz 8-11pm Tue, Thur; free). No-smoking tables. Tables outdoors (terrace).

Also in the area...

Postal Order (JD Wetherspoon) 33 Westow Street, SE19 (8771 3003).

South

Forest Hill

Centred around a railway station that spent much of its life called Dartmouth Road, Forest Hill is part dormitory suburb for central London workers and part inner-city Lewisham. Neither aspect is appealing for the drinker, something proved by us giving a Wetherspoon pub a rare commendation.

Capitol

11-21 London Road, SE23 (8291 8920). Forest Hill rail. **Open** 10am-11pm Mon-Sat; noon-10.30pm Sun. **Food served** 10am-10pm Mon-Sat; noon-9.30pm Sun. **Credit** AmEx, MC, V.
This giant cinema conversion represents the best and the worst of the JD Wetherspoon chain. The best is the work and detail that have gone into the renovation. The building's a Grade II-listed former cinema, first opened for business in 1929, closed in 1973. In the 30 years since it suffered 18 years of bingo and two stints of neglect. The new pub begins in the foyer, where the former ticket booth and sweet counter have been converted into colourful little alcoves. Up the stairs there's a combined no-smoking/dining area, leading to the splendour of what were the stalls. The walls and tall ceiling are restored to the original cinematic colours – several shades of blue and purple – with amber, gold and ivory highlights. Then there's the worst: at 10pm on a Friday night there were only two servers on duty and just two real ales (Spitfire and Courage Best) on offer. Hardly worth waiting for, so after five minutes lingering while large groups of confident late-teens bought up piles of cut-price alcopops, we left.
Disabled: lift, toilet. No piped music or jukebox. No-smoking area. Tables outdoors (garden).

Railway Telegraph

112 Stanstead Road, SE23 (8699 6644). Forest Hill rail/122, 185 bus. **Open** 11am-11pm Mon-Sat; noon-10.30pm Sun. **Food served** noon-2.30pm Mon-Fri. **Credit** MC, V.
This fairly large outpost of Faversham's Shepherd Neame brewery was recently knocked through to make a single bar. The result is a cross between a designer's idea of a Parisian cafe-bar and an inner-city boozer. The walls are yellow, cream and gold, a long serving area takes up almost one wall, the others are hidden under a mixture of railway memorabilia, framed art deco posters and Hogarthian prints. A couple of real ales are usually available (usually Spitfire and Master Brew), plus Hurliman and Orangeboom lager and the usual gaggle of nitrokegs. Customers are a lively mix of locals, from young couples out to party to older groups moaning about the price of petrol, pies and Proust. Food is a mishmash of Cafe Uno-style faux Mediterranean nosh and pub grub staples. Darts are still played down one end, while the giant TV dominates events opposite.
Babies and children admitted (until 7pm). Games (darts, fruit machines, pool, quiz machines). Jukebox. Tables outdoors (garden, pavement). TV (big screen, satellite).

Greenwich

Greenwich has an easily defined geography but a tricky identity when it comes to bars. Tourists are delighted that it makes full use of its maritime location and history – the **Cutty Sark Tavern**, **Trafalgar Tavern** and so on – but locals are more attracted to boozers around the weekend market, ones with a little style (**North Pole**) and ones with superb ales (the **Ashburnham** and **Union**). Everything's an easy walk from the mainline or DLR station. Superb for lazy weekend boozing.

Ashburnham Arms

25 Ashburnham Grove, SE10 (8692 2007). Greenwich rail/DLR. **Open** noon-3pm, 6-11pm Mon-Fri; 11am-11pm Sat; noon-10.30pm Sun. **Food served** noon-2.30pm, 6-10pm Mon-Sat; noon-10pm Sat. **Credit** (food only) AmEx, MC, V.
Just off the well-trod tourist track but only a couple of lurches away from the rail/DLR station, the Ashburnham's long been a favourite boozing oasis for the local grognoscenti. Real ales from the Kent-based Shepherd Neame brewery (including a delicious bottled organic Whitstable Bay ale) continue to pull in the beer hunters, and food availability has been extended since a recent management changeover. There's nary a whiff of 'new-broom paranoia' either, since the distinctive features of the place – compact and friendly front bar, bordered by an area with an original bar billiards table, comfy side space leading to the blue vaulted ceiling of the back dining conservatory, beyond which a tranquil garden beckons – have been gratefully retained.
Babies and children admitted (conservatory only; children's menu, high chairs). Games (bar billiards). Quiz (9pm Tue; free). Tables outdoors (garden, patio).

Coach

13 Greenwich Market, SE10 (8293 0880). Greenwich rail/DLR. **Open** 11am-11pm Mon-Fri; 9am-11pm Sat; 9am-10.30pm Sun. **Food served** noon-3.30pm, 5-10pm Mon-Fri; 9am-10pm Sat, Sun. **Credit** AmEx, MC, V.
An exercise in the utilisation of space, the Coach somehow manages to avoid clutter within the confines of its restricted L-shaped environment, and yet still offer a bijou two-settee chill-out zone. Broad windows give the place a light and airy feel, and allow for oggling the tourists gazing upon the wares for sale in the covered market outside. Real ales on offer are Bombardier, London Pride, Old Speckled Hen and Tetley's, and there's also the increasingly common (but very welcome) Wieckse Witte Dutch beer. Overcast skies can be counteracted with a Blue Heaven cocktail. The lunch menu entices with wild mushroom ravioli at £6.50 and roasted salmon with baby veg and vanilla sauce for £10.50.
Babies and children admitted (until 9pm). Tables outdoors (patio).

Cutty Sark Tavern

Ballast Quay, off Lassell Street, SE10 (8858 3146). Greenwich rail/DLR/Maze Hill rail. **Open** 11am-11pm Mon-Sat; noon-10.30pm Sun. **Food served** noon-9pm Mon-Fri; noon-6pm Sat, Sun. **Credit** MC, V.
Well, shiver me timbers, there's some serious wood in here: low beams, chunky staircases, robust gallery and what looks like cannon ball-proof panelling. And barrels galore, some of which are converted into tables on which you can tuck into lamb chops in red wine and rosemary gravy or filo-wrapped shredded duck with port and damson sauce. The wine list is adequate if not ground-breaking, while London Pride, Cambridge Bitter and IPA counterbalance the grim, Carling-dominated lager range. Still, it's not the beer but the view from the upper storey that's the Cutty Sark's principal attraction and indeed a flashpoint for the oft-repeated Battle of the Bow Window, when punters regularly jostle for the optimum vantage point from which to take in the wide sweep of the river or to sneer at the continuing folly that is the Dome.
Babies and children admitted (children's menu). Games (fruit machine). Jukebox. Tables outdoors (riverside terrace).

Greenwich Union

56 Royal Hill, SE10 (8692 6258). Greenwich DLR/rail. **Open** 11am-11pm Mon-Sat; noon-10.30pm Sun. **Food served** 12.30-3pm, 5-8pm Mon-Fri; 1-4pm Sun. **Credit** MC, V.
About 18 months ago Alastair Hook came across a suitable venue from which to purvey the fruits of his passion-led brewing labours. A mere half-hour's stroll – in his case, probably along the surface of the Thames – from his Charlton-based Meantime Brewing Company, the pub formerly known as the Observatory was transmogrified in double-quick time into the Greenwich Union. Flagstone floor was retained, along with sections of wood panelling; vibrant yellow and orange paint dutifully applied; customer-friendly staff enlisted and then…Tally ho! The beers are simply one revelation after another, a carnival of palate-ticklers from the Vienna-style Amba lager, through the pleasantly tart raspberry-flavoured Red, to the surprisingly uncloying Chocolate beer, via a distinctive White brew, and the pokey Golden Pilsner. The label on the Union ale – a chap with foam-bedecked top lip and brain-checking eyes rolled heavenwards – adds wryness to this unique and innovative establishment. Hats off.
Babies and children admitted. Games (board games). Music (jazz 7pm Sun; piano 8pm Mon). Tables outdoors (garden, patio). TV (satellite).

North Pole

131 Greenwich High Road, SE10 (8853 3020). Greenwich rail/DLR. **Open** noon-11pm Mon-Sat; 9.30am-10.30pm Sun. **Food served** noon-3pm Mon-Sat; 9.30am-4pm, 6.30-10pm Sun. **Happy hour** 6-8pm Thur-Sun. **Credit** AmEx, MC, V.
Faux zebra pelt adorns the bar stools and cheat's cheetah covers the roomy settees that grace the sectioned-off lounge room next to the welcome-to-Europe chrome bar, which boasts its own 'I can't believe it's not leather' quotient of comfy sofas. But no actual animals were harmed in the making of this bar. Whew! The first floor of the triple-decked North Pole is a spacious mecca for the palate-conscious, where warm crab cake with chillies, coriander and herb sauce (£5) can precede the likes of lamb chump and sweet parsnip tatin (£13). All very scrumptious. At ground level, the main bar amply caters to the cocktail-exploring predilections of its twenty-to-thirtysomething clientele. Bar food of the garlic risotto/goat's cheese, grape and walnut salad ilk is available, along with a beer choice that includes Hoegaarden and Staropramen. The South Pole DJ bar, a pet project of deck-loving bar custodians Nick and Ollie, opens Thursday to Sunday in the basement.
Babies and children admitted (children's menu, high chairs). Function room. Music (DJs 7.30pm Thur-Sun; jazz 7.30pm occasional Thur). Restaurant. Tables outdoors (pavement). TV (big screen, digital).

Richard I

52-4 Royal Hill, SE10 (8692 2996). Greenwich rail/DLR. **Open** 11am-11pm Mon-Sat; noon-10.30pm Sun. **Food served** noon-2pm, 6-9pm Mon-Sat; noon-3pm, 6-9pm Sun. **Credit** MC, V.
Greeted by a belligerent then reluctantly apologetic barman, we eventually warmed to the honesty of this well-established and popular drinking hole that, apart from the virtually compulsory booth-removal, is the same, 'all local life is here' boozer it's always been. Young's ales and an adequate range of wines and champagne are steadily consumed in wood-to-the-fore, hint-of-nicotine coloured surroundings by a mixed-sex crowd. Standard pub food along the lines of garlic and herb chicken, Cumberland sausages and lamb shank is available for those seeking more sustenance than the delightful, and strikingly red, home-pickled eggs can provide. Outside to the front of the pub, a couple of tables permit the enjoyment of watching life stroll by on the picturesque Royal Hill, while at the back a garden heaves with sun-loving loungers when the weather deigns to behave itself. Shame about the attitude-problem of some of the staff, though.
Babies and children admitted (garden only). No piped music. Tables outdoors (garden, pavement). TV.

Trafalgar Tavern

Park Row, SE10 (8858 2437). Cutty Sark Gardens DLR/Maze Hill rail. **Open** 11.30am-11pm Mon-Sat; noon-10.30pm Sun. **Food served** noon-3pm Mon-Wed; noon-10pm Thur-Sat; noon-5pm Sun. **Credit** MC, V.
The Trafalgar Tavern has certainly had a few incarnations since its 1837 inception: skint by 1908, after which it became a seaman's hostel, then a working men's club, followed by a period of relative dereliction, before being restored in the 1960s. Rooms are stately, ceilings lofty and the panelling in the Collingwood restaurant fittingly grand. The fish-centric menu attracts a steady stream of venerable lunchtime diners. Face-furnitured representatives of the 19th century and more recent celebs peer down from photographs mounted high on the walls. Real ales include the Porter-like Monkey's Magic, Morning Glory and the nigh-on ubiquitous Old Speckled Hen. Weekday evenings tend toward the quiet but the place comes

into its own on Mondays and at the weekend when live jazz ensures a varied and enthusiastic clientele. And we should also mention the splendid river views.
Babies and children admitted (children's menu, high chairs). Function rooms. Music (jazz 9pm Sat; free). Restaurant.

Also in the area...

Davy's Wine Vaults 161 Greenwich High Road, SE10 (8858 7204).
The Gate Clock (JD Wetherspoon) Cutty Sark Station, Creek Road, SE10 (8629 2000).

Herne Hill

Perched midway between Brixton and Dulwich, Herne Hill exhibits some of the edge of the former and much of the gentility of the latter. Trendification was inevitable at some point, and it's just starting to bite, particularly with the opening of **Escape**. All the drinking options are concentrated within a minute's walk of each other, around what is essentially a six-road interchange. The choice isn't huge at present but things are changing fast. Watch this space.

Cafe Provençal

4-6 Half Moon Lane, SE24 (7978 9228). Herne Hill rail. **Open** noon-11pm Mon-Fri; 10am-11pm Sat; 10am-10.30pm Sun. **Food served** noon-10.30pm Mon-Fri; 10am-10.30pm Sat; 10am-10pm Sun. **Credit** MC, V.
Cafe Prov is a winning neighbourhood restaurant – a hippie-chic ambience, amiable staff and good, filling grub (steak and chips, red onion and goat's cheese tart, et al) – with, at one end of its rambling premises, a small bar with a handful of tables. It's not a place to spend an entire evening drinking, but it provides an admirable, funkily laid-back pit stop for a bottle or two of Mort Subite (£3) or Brugs white beer (£3.30). (Only Guinness and Beck's are available on draught.) There's also a reasonable selection of wines (eight or so reds and a similar number of whites, starting at £9.95). You can eat from the main menu at the bar, or just munch on a big bowl of chunky chips, while perusing the slung together decor, complete with framed classic LP covers and (compulsory in Herne Hill, frustrated artists all) artworks for sale.
Art exhibitions. Babies and children admitted (restaurant until 7pm). Tables outdoors (pavement).

Escape Bar & Art

214-16 Railton Road, SE24 (7737 0333). Herne Hill rail. **Open** 7am-midnight Mon-Fri; 10am-midnight Sat, Sun. **Food served** 7am-10pm Mon-Fri; 10am-10pm Sat, Sun. **Credit** MC, V.
The opening of Escape in February 2003 next to the solidly trad Commercial pub illustrates new and old Herne Hill in microcosm. While the latter has framed rugby shirts filling the walls, Escape aims at something rather more ambitious with monthly changing art exhibitions. It's a big, white-painted space, with a long bar to one side, sofas at the far end and really rather groovy underlit tables with pebbles-in-resin tops. The drinks list is unremarkable (Red Stripe, Hoegaarden and Guinness on draught), but the food is pretty good – pizzas (around £4.20), salads (£3.80-£4.20) and filled ciabattas (£3). Although it would benefit from more sympathetic lighting (having a drink in an art gallery isn't everyone's idea of relaxation), Escape's a laudable attempt to try something different. And signs are that Herne Hillers are impressed.
Art exhibitions. Games (board). Music (DJs 8pm Fri, Sat; occasional jazz). Tables outdoors (pavement).

Half Moon

10 Half Moon Lane, SE24 (7274 2733). **Open** noon-11pm Mon-Sat; noon-10.30pm Sun. **Credit** MC, V.
With dizzyingly high ceilings, lashings of dark wood and etched glass a-go-go, this is a classic Victorian London alehouse – the division of public bar (with pool table and jukebox), saloon bar and snug has been maintained (there are some rather lovely bird paintings on the mirrors in the latter). The beers are entirely unremarkable (on draught: Courage, Kronenbourg, Beck's, Guinness), and there is, in truth, an air of decay about the place. But the staff and regulars are cheery, and the Tuesday night quiz (8.30pm start) is always fun and friendly. For many years the Half Moon was a famous music venue (the Police and U2 both let rip here in its heyday), and it's recently been revived as such, with rock and pop gigs on Thursdays and Saturdays, followed by an indie DJ until 1am.
Function room. Games (pool). Jukebox. Music (bands 7pm Thur-Sat). Quiz (8.30pm Tue).

Pullens

293-5 Railton Road, SE24 (7274 9163). **Open/food served** 11am-11pm Mon-Sat; 11am-10.30pm Sun. **Happy hour** 5-7pm. **Credit** MC, V.
The bar at Pullens is essentially an adjunct to a restaurant, yet it's also an immensely congenial (if spatially challenged) spot for a chinwag and a schooner of vino (the list is short but not obvious; it's good to see a viognier as house white – £10.75, or £6 during happy hour). The vibe is 100% bistro, with bare floorboards, candlelight and a constant bubbling of chat from the youngish, hippish clientele, who nibble on classic snacks like oysters (£1.35 each) devilled whitebait (£4.25) or fish cakes (£4.50). There are no draught beers, but you won't be complaining when you spy the heavenly, honeyed St Peter's Organic Ale among the bottles. A scattering of tables are set out on the pavement in summer, though you'll have a scrap on your hands to secure one.
Babies and children admitted. No-smoking area. Tables outdoors (pavement).

Kennington, Lambeth & Oval

The area between Waterloo in the north, Stockwell in the west and the Elephant in the east is another example of divergent cultures and income groups living practically cheek-by-jowl. The **Greyhound** by the Oval has long been a haunt of interesting locals, while a couple of hundred metres away, the drinkers you'll find in the **Prince of Wales**, Cleaver Square, are much more likely to be rugger-playing ex-public schoolboys. **South London Pacific** is a new arrival that could easily put Kennington on the tourist map.

Beehive

60 Carter Street, SE17 (7703 4992). Kennington tube/ 12, 68, 68A, 171, 176, P5 bus. **Open** 11am-11pm Mon-Sat; noon-10.30pm Sun. **Food served** noon-3pm, 5.30-10pm Mon-Fri; noon-10pm Sat, Sun. **Credit** MC, V.
An old lag coming back to sunny Walworth after a ten-stretch would be shocked to find his old local treated in such a cavalier fashion. Gone are the chipped lino, threadbare furnishings and smoke-drenched air, in their place are smart beige and light primrose paintwork, book-lined walls and enough bare board to make any timber merchant beam with pride. And the air is as clean as local traffic will allow, with maybe a vague hint of balsamic vinegar. Food is a major part of what the Beehive does and those large tables in the candlelit back

South

bar aren't just for resting Stella on. We came across specials of a seafood platter, marinated lamb chops and potato and leek soup at prices that wouldn't upset anyone, even old lags. Beers of choice include Directors, London Pride, 6X and Old Speckled Hen, with a wide selection of malts and a wine list offering vino for practically every occasion and pocket.
Babies and children admitted (until 7pm; children's menu). Tables outdoors (patio). TV (satellite).

Dog House

293 Kennington Road, SE11 (7820 9310). Kennington or Oval tube. **Open** noon-11pm Mon-Fri; 6-11pm Sat; noon-10.30pm Sun. **Food served** noon-3pm Mon, Tue; noon-3pm, 7-10pm Wed, Thur; noon-3pm Sun. **Credit** MC, V.
Being sent to the Dog House would be a welcome punishment, provided this is the establishment in question. Formerly an Irish music pub of some notoriety, it has made a name for itself over the last few years as a boho bar, appealing to SE11's trendy young drinkers. The decor is of the old furniture, potted plant and mystical imagery type with a quasi-gastropub type emphasis on blackboard art. Sunday roasts (and their vegetarian equivalents) are worth seeking out, while during the rest of the week the emphasis is on posh sandwiches – ciabatta with roast vegetables – and suchlike. There are signs of a mellowing, with a tasty Nina Simone soundtrack playing the last Friday we visited and more thirtysomethings sipping wine (a blackboard of just over a dozen to choose from) and real ale (Flowers IPA) than pre-clubbers guzzling bottled lagers and Breezers.
Babies and children admitted (Sun lunch only). Games (board games). Tables outdoors (pavement).

Greyhound

336 Kennington Park Road, SE11 (7735 2594). Oval tube. **Open** 11am-11pm Mon-Sat; noon-10.30pm Sun. **Food served** noon-3pm daily. **Credit** MC, V.
This long, thin, old-school boozer is one of the area's cosiest and most popular locals. Although featured in many of Ken Bruen's novels of London noir as the venue for gangland confrontations and 'coming-out parties' – we don't mean for Rodene gals, either – it's real-life role is as a friendly community pub where anyone sensible is welcomed. The beer range is good – including Marston's Pedigree, Courage Best and London Pride – although the Guinness is rated by many of the Irish expat regulars as the best east of the Liffey. Lunchtime pub grub is lasagne meets bangers and mash. It's deceptively long, with the main front bar giving way to two smaller rooms through doorways framed by patterned china plates. Being so close to the Oval cricket ground it's natural that the pub should enjoy a sporting theme, and here it extends to an appreciation of TV football and darts.
Babies and children admitted (Sun lunch only). Games (fruit machine). Jukebox. Tables outdoors (pavement). TV (big screen, satellite).

Prince of Wales

48 Cleaver Square, SE11 (7735 9916). Kennington tube. **Open** noon-11pm Mon-Sat; noon-10.30pm Sun. **Food served** noon-2.30pm, 6-8.30pm Mon-Thur; noon-2.30pm Fri-Sun. **Credit** MC, V.
You'd never guess that this used to be a gangland boozer and a haunt of the notorious Richardson family in the 1960s, nor that it became a posh, red-velvet kind of place after that, where leading politicians took their mistresses. It's all true, even if this secluded pub – now under the wing of Faversham's Shepherd Neame brewery – is more of a sofa, blackboard and bare board kind of upmarket boozer. The small back room may feature framed pictures of famous criminals, and the larger front bar is festooned with politician's mug shots but the tone now is designed to appeal to the area's upmarket young homeowners. If there are typical customer types, they're twentysomething, she something in the media, he a banker. Food is chosen from a huge blackboard over the bar and is likely to involve sausages or pasta. Beers include real ales such as Master Brew and Spitfire and Orangeboom Dutch lager (brewed in Kent).
Tables outdoors (pavement).

South London Pacific

340 Kennington Road, SE11 (7820 9189). Oval tube. **Open** 6pm-midnight Tue, Wed; 6pm-1am Thur; 6pm-2am Fri, Sat; 6pm-midnight Sun. **Happy hour** 6pm-1am Thur. **Food served** 6-9pm Fri, Sat. **Credit** MC, V.
If it's a one-off, then this cod but very kitsch South Seas bar deserves to become a tourist attraction; if it's the first of a chain of clones, then gawd help us. From the blue-painted Easter Island totems outside to the colourful carvings of grotesquely distorted faces and hula-hula girls within, it's a colourful, tongue-in-cheek, psychedelic homage to the most romantic of destinations. Imagine *South Pacific* in a set designed by an absinthe-fuelled Lawrence Llewellyn-Bowen and you'll be halfway there. Inside it's big, with a stage at one end and more potted yuccas than should be found in one spot. Beers are the standard Scunthorpe variety (Beck's, Stella, etc) but the array of cocktails with names like Pago Pago, Royal Hawaiian and Bahama Mama are what anybody should be drinking. We found a young crowd – many of the women with flowers in their hair – getting in to the vibe. Regular events include DJs, cabaret, Elvis-worshipping and live bands. The themed table football table must be seen to be believed.
Disabled: toilet. Games (table football, pinball machine). Music (Brazilian dance 7pm Tue; free. swing dance 7pm Wed; free. bands 7pm Thur; £3-£5. DJs and/or bands 7pm Fri; £3-£5 after 10pm).

Three Stags

67-9 Kennington Road, SE1 (7928 5974). Lambeth North tube. **Open** 11am-11pm Mon-Sat; noon-10.30pm Sun. **Food served** noon-8pm Mon-Fri; noon-6pm Sat, Sun. **Credit** AmEx, MC, V.
This impressively grand Victorian corner pub's Charlie Chaplin connection is understandably milked for all it's worth – his father drank himself to death within these very walls, so the story goes – as is the proximity to the Imperial War Museum, so pictures of cinema's first star and various military memorabilia battle for supremacy on the tastefully papered walls. We arrived just as a group of young Swedes invaded and so had to wait a little before we were let loose on the Greene King ales (Abbot and IPA) the pub specialises in. The staff are keen, friendly and well versed in dealing with groups of 12 who order and pay for identical half-pints individually and so we were soon ensconced in our wood and glass alcoved corner, watching the world go by. Hard to imagine that only a couple of years ago this was an Oirish music pub called Brendan O'Grady's.
Babies and children admitted. Disabled: toilet. Function room. Games (fruit machine). Karaoke (8pm Sat; free). Music (jazz 8pm Mon; singer Tue; free). No-smoking area. Tables outdoors (pavement). TVs.

White Bear

138 Kennington Park Road, SE11 (7735 8664). Kennington or Oval tube. **Open** 11am-midnight Mon-Sat; noon-10.30pm Sun. **Food served** 11am-3pm Mon-Fri. **Credit** AmEx, MC, V.
The White Bear Theatre Club – entrance through the doors at the rear of this large one-bar boozer – is forever winning awards, but it's got to be said that the pub that bears its name

isn't likely to follow suit. Expect to find solitary men sitting on stools around the oval island bar, drinking lager and Guinness (real ale is off the menu) and tapping along to the 'Spirit in the Sky'/Wham '80s soundtrack. Similar couples sit at tables around the edge, staring glumly into space and totting up the cost of another round of Caffrey's and melon Breezer. The walls are orange and blue ragged and show the signs of multiple posters. No luvvies here on any occasion we've visited, just geezers and their geezerettes. The bar staff once locked us in after hours and wouldn't let us out again.
Babies and children admitted (until 7pm). Games (fruit machines). Jukebox. Tables outdoors (courtyard, garden). Theatre (8pm Tue-Sat; 4pm Sun; £7-£8). TV (big screen, satellite).

Lee

The area triangled by Catford, Hither Green and Grove Park is centred around the railway station and not usually known for its fantastic pubs. Bars tend to be illegal affairs on the tenth floor of council blocks, where cans of Red Stripe and spliffs change hands for a couple of coins.

Crown

117 Burnt Ash Hill, SE12 (8857 6607). Lee rail. **Open** 11am-11pm Mon-Sat; noon-10.30pm Sun. **Food served** noon-2.30pm, 7-9pm Mon-Sat; noon-4pm, 7-9pm Sun. **Credit** MC, V.
This large Young's pub is perpetually busy, but as it's a fair way off the beaten track, this must have more to do with doing things right than with attracting passing trade. Most customers are known by name and have been coming here for a while. We tend to find twentysomething couples, older groups of men and the odd gaggle of late-teen girls whenever we stop by. Want a plumber, an electrician or a drama coach? Look no further. The large main bar is scattered with chunky wooden dining tables, grandad chairs and the odd armchair. There's a cosy snug by the front door and a sporty little spot at the rear. The full range of Young's bitters are available and are kept in fine condition and food is very serious: upmarket fry-ups, fish and chips, cottage pie, that sort of thing. Bench tables on the flowery terrace attract summer drinkers like flies to a fishing convention.
Function room. Games (fruit machine, quiz machine). Quiz (8.30pm Sun; £1). Tables outdoors (garden). TV.

Also in the area...

Edmund Halley (JD Wetherspoon) 25-7 Leegate, SE12 (8318 7475).

Lewisham

Most boozers in the centre of Lewisham are OK, if unremarkable, but when the admittedly well-run local Wetherspoon (the Watch House) becomes the centre of market life you know there's something lacking elsewhere. On Friday and Saturday nights hordes of local yoof descend on the supposedly pedestrianised High Street and the Yates' Wine Lodge, Broadway Bar and others take on the atmosphere of Wild West saloons.

Sand. *See p209.*

South

Dacre Arms

11 Kingswood Place, SE13 (8244 2404). Lewisham DLR/rail then 321 bus/Blackheath rail. **Open** 11am-11pm Mon-Sat; noon-10.30pm Sun. **Credit** MC, V.

Proving that management can make or break a boozer, the Dacre is an oasis among a desert of dodgy pubs north of the Lee High Road. Home for a complete cross-section of locals, this is a pub at the heart of the community. A noticeboard keeps regulars informed of local affairs (not the sexual kind, that would be rude) as well as proposed beer price hike notices from the brewery. The decor is trad and cosy, with rust banquettes, matching stools and armchairs, and enough bric-a-brac to keep Camden Passage or Church Street in business for a week. An enclosed beer garden proves a popular sun trap in clement weather. Cask-conditioned beer is something of a feature, with Courage Best joined by three guests – we found Greene King IPA, Shepherd Neame Spitfire and something tasty from Scotland.

Games (fruit machine). No-smoking area. Tables outdoors (16, garden). TV.

The Jordan

354 Lewisham High Street, SE13 (8690 2054). Ladywell rail. **Open** 11am-11pm Mon-Sat; noon-10.30pm Sun. **Food served** noon-2pm Mon-Fri, Sun. **Credit** AmEx, MC, V.

When Jordan (not that one, we mean Mr Jordan) took over the tenancy of this small and traditionally decorated former Hogshead, it seemed only natural to change the name. The only other apparent differences are a rather fetching external makeover in brown and black and an improved beer selection. You'll normally find three or four real ales available on pump plus a couple dispensed straight from the barrel. Add a healthy selection of British, Belgian and other continental bottles plus a range of country wines and the traditionalist and drinks connoisseur will be happy as a hog in hooch. The decor of bare stone, distressed oak beams and fake rustic style will remain. As will the enclosed back beer patio. Being sited slap-bang next to Lewisham University Hospital, many drinkers are off-duty doctors, nurses and students, with a regular contingent of porters propping up the bar.

Babies and children admitted (summer only; beer garden). Games (fruit machine, quiz machine). Tables outdoors (garden). TV (satellite).

Also in the area...

Watch House (JD Wetherspoon) 198-204 Lewisham High Street, SE13 (8318 3136).

New Cross

Barlife in New Cross is concentrated around Goldsmith's College, surrounded by six focal pubs (the Marquis of Granby, New Cross Inn, Goldsmith's Tavern, Rosemary Branch and the **Hobgoblin**, which is the only one we review here – draw your own conclusions). The area is crying out for a cool, late-opening haven for the area's musicians, artists and comedians – any takers?

Hobgoblin

272 New Cross Road, SE14 (8692 3193). New Cross Gate tube/rail/36, 89, 136, 171, 177 bus. **Open** 11am-11pm Mon-Sat; noon-10.30pm Sun. **Happy hour** (students with ID only) 2-8pm Mon-Fri. **Food served** noon-8.30pm Mon-Fri; noon-4.30pm Sat; noon-4pm Sun. **No credit cards.**

The Hobgoblin gives the lie to the general rule of thumb that makes 'refurbishment' synonymous with 'ruination' because the place actually seems to have been improved. The space, both inside and out, has been well utilised: the interior has been opened up, a conservatory added, and the former boxing ring out the back has been bench-tabled and shrubbed-up to take advantage of those balmy afternoons and evenings when winter has the decency to depart. The ever increasing student presence of the area has been successfully targeted and the mainly youthful customers seem more than willing to invest their loans in the fairly standard booze – Stella, Fosters, a couple of real ales, and perfectly acceptable wines – and the hearty grub on offer. It gets lively and chocker at the weekends, with sports-loving punters sobbing quietly into their pints over the Sky-screened ineptitude before them.

Babies and children admitted (conservatory, garden). Disabled: toilet. Games (fruit machines, quiz machines). Jukebox. Music (DJs 8pm Fri; free). Tables outdoors (conservatory, garden). TV (satellite).

Walpole Arms

New Cross Road, SE14 (8692 2080). New Cross tube/rail. **Open** 11am-11pm Mon-Sat; noon-10.30pm Sun. **Food served** 12.30-10pm daily. **Credit** MC, V.

If anything points to a possible change in fortunes for the area, then it's the Walpole Arms, right by New Cross station and well within the catchment area for Goldsmiths College's new halls of residence the other side of the busy A2. Gentrification would be an overstatement but it does have Thai food, fan heaters, picture windows, scrubbed wood furniture and a hip-level bar counter. The clientele, however, remain unreconstructed young locals, drawn by cheap shooters, a party atmosphere, events nights and easy mixing. If you can't pull here, you can't pull anywhere. Continental terrace furniture – outside the last building in a long line of chip shops, taxi firms and giro-dispensing post offices – completes the incongruity.

Babies and children admitted (lunchtimes only). Games (board games, fruit machine). Music (DJs 8pm Wed, Fri-Sun; jazz 8pm Mon; vocalists 8pm Thur; free). Tables outdoors (pavement).

Peckham

Peckham itself has little to recommend it. Visitors need only concern themselves with the better pubs around Peckham Rye, a 15-minute walk away. The **Clock House** would fit nicely in Dulwich or Camberwell – here, it's the only real alternative.

Clock House

196A Peckham Rye, SE22 (8693 2901). East Dulwich or Peckham Rye rail/12, 37, 63, 176, 185, 312 bus. **Open** 11am-11pm Mon-Sat; noon-10.30pm Sun. **Food served** noon-2.30pm, 6-9pm Mon-Fri; noon-9pm Sat, Sun. **Credit** MC, V.

The timepiece-heavy Clock House revels in tradition. Dark green walls serve as a backdrop for classic images and framed certificates that acknowledge the esteemed green-fingered horticultural talents of the owner; a 100-year-old unblinking 20lb pike hovers in its glass case above the fireplace in a cosy, elevated little side room. Via two substantial skylights, spring sunshine bathes the customers in the airy and spacious lounge at the back. Outside, a panoply of benches await that time when the good weather and bloomnificence combine to attract a constant stream of drinkers and diners. Young's real ales and the usual humdrum, lager suspects link up with a wine list that features a Vacqueyras red at £13.50 a bottle and the reliable Torres Via Sol for £11

South

to tempt imbibers. Good-quality food is on offer at lunchtimes and throughout the weekend. OK, we give up: what exactly is the time?
Disabled: toilet. Quiz (9pm Tue; £1). Tables outdoors (patio).

Also in the area...

Kentish Drovers (JD Wetherspoon) 71-9 High Street, SE15 (7277 4283).

Putney

Putney's young swingers congregate at its high street bars, noisily supping on bottled beers and pheromones. Deeper into the hinterland you'll find Young's pubs of a more individualistic stamp: the **Half Moon** for music, the **Green Man** for country living. But it's down by the river that the area's at its best, where half a dozen venues offer soul-soothing views to the background slap and ooze of the Thames. Just leave your chin at home if you're visiting on Boat Race Day.

Bar M

The Star & Garter, 4 Lower Richmond Road, SW15 (8788 0345). Putney Bridge tube/Putney rail. **Open** 11am-11pm Mon-Sat; noon-10.30pm Sun. **Food served** 11am-10pm Mon-Thur; 11am-9pm Fri, Sat; noon-9pm Sun. **Credit** AmEx, DC, MC, V.
Being situated on the Embankment next to Putney Pier means this civilised haunt makes a fine venue to watch the start of the University Boat Race. You'll find Bar M underneath the Star & Garter hotel. The 'M' stands for 'minimalistic' (a decor of very light pastel greens and unfussy furniture), 'modern' (a spacious, airy interior with one of the longest bars in Putney) and 'Mediterranean' (the menu contains a somewhat limited array of mostly shellfish and chicken dishes). There's a nice choice of white wines, hailing from Chile, Italy, New Zealand, Spain and France. A small deep-red cellar bar is a cosier alternative to upstairs, but sofas and chairs pointing towards the big screen and brick bar, not the river. Castle lager at six for £5 suggests a South African following – and a get-pissed-quick mentality – and there's no real ale.
Babies and children admitted (until 7pm, high chairs). Function rooms. Games (fruit machine, quiz machine). TV (big screen, digital).

Coat & Badge

8 Lacy Road, SW15 (8788 4900). Putney Bridge tube/ Putney rail/14 bus. **Open** 11am-11pm Mon-Sat; noon-10.30pm Sun. **Food served** noon-3pm, 7-9.30pm Mon-Fri; noon-7pm Sat, Sun. **Credit** MC, V.
Named after the notorious four-mile boat race (the oldest continuous sporting event in the country), the Coat & Badge has, not surprisingly, the usual Putney punt-art lining the wall. But it also has its eccentricities, like the toilets that are entered through a wall-mounted bookcase (actually a door). The front bar offers low-slung traditional comfort – rouge, cream and oak, candles and fake real fire. In contrast, the more modern, striped seated rear room seems to have been built to cater for the overspill, and a tiny alcove with a bench seat serves no other purpose than for those in hiding. Food is reassuringly down to earth: a mixture of hearty English staples sprinkled with lighter Mediterranean offerings.
Babies and children admitted (until 7pm). Function room. Games (board games). Tables outdoors (terrace). TV (digital).

Duke's Head

8 Lower Richmond Road, SW15 (8788 2552). Putney Bridge tube/265 bus. **Open** 11am-11pm Mon-Sat; noon-10.30pm Sun. **Food served** noon-2.30pm, 6-10pm Mon-Fri; 11am-10pm Sat; noon-9pm Sun. **Credit** MC, V.
A Young's house, the Duke's Head was rebuilt in its current form in 1864 and thankfully, its grand Victorian features remain. There are three bars in total: the saloon, the public bar and dining room. Head to the public and you'll realise why Putney's wealthy business folk and couples continue to flock to this grand, mahogany-adorned pub. The armchairs are large and comfortable, the fire is a cosy touch, and the huge bay windows offer a fabulous view of the river – this is a great spot to watch Oxford and Cambridge slog it out on the river during the annual boat race. For the rest of the year, get the common touch in the road side saloon bar where you can join the Chelsea fans shouting at the telly or challenge the locals at a spot of table football.
Games (table football). No piped music or jukebox. Tables outdoors (riverside patio). TV (satellite).

Green Man

Wildcroft Road, Putney Heath, SW15 (8788 8096). East Putney tube/Putney rail/14, 39, 85, 93, 170 bus. **Open** 11am-11pm Mon-Sat; noon-10.30pm Sun. **Food served** noon-2.30pm daily. **Credit** MC, V.
The Green Man dates back to the 1700s when Putney Heath was a popular duelling spot. The decor in its two bars looks as if it hasn't changed much since the days when highwayman Jerry Abershaw was a regular (he was caught here and ended up on the gibbet outside). Nowadays this canine-friendly haunt is a relaxed hangout for a mature crowd of dog walkers in need of a lubricating stop off. It's a little cramped inside, but the presence of Putney Heath opposite means that the outside seating area comes into its own in summer (as does the outside gents' toilet). It's a Young's pub, so the beer's good, and prices are also very reasonable.
Games (darts, fruit machine). No piped music or jukebox. Quiz (8.30pm Thur; £1). Tables outdoors (garden, patio).

Half Moon

93 Lower Richmond Road, SW15 (8780 9383). Putney Bridge tube/Putney rail. **Open** noon-11pm Mon-Sat; noon-10.30pm Sun. **Credit** MC, V.
Synonymous with live music and holder of the area's only seven-day-a-week music licence – names large and small, well known and home grown, have cut their teeth here, including kd lang, Elvis Costello and the Rolling Stones. Big names still feature on the poster-clad walls – Bunsen burning madman John Otway and Fairport Convention were there in spring 2003 – alongside up-and-coming talent and cheesy covers bands. Even if you don't part with the few quid for entrance to the well-trodden and well-danced rear music room, the vast front bar is open and inviting of all. Friendly pierced staff, oak-panelled walls, a rockin' jukebox and windows concealed with plants give the Half Moon genuine character that you'd be hard put to find anywhere else local.
Games (fruit machines, pool). Jukebox. Music (bands 8.30pm Mon-Sat; from £2. Jazz 2-5pm occasional Sun). Tables outdoors (garden). TV (big screen).

Putney Bridge

Embankment, 2 Lower Richmond Road, SW15 (8780 1811). Putney Bridge tube. **Open** noon-midnight Mon-Thur; noon-1am Fri, Sat; noon-10.30pm Sun. **Food served** noon-2pm, 7-10.30pm Mon-Sat; noon-3pm Sun. **Credit** AmEx, DC, MC, V.

Drink a drink a drink, beneath an Elisabeth Frink a Frink a Frink. Classic Frink bronze nudes add classy cred to this ultra stylish, architecturally proud, riverside bar-restaurant (sporting a Michelin star). The ground-floor bar was designed by David Collins: polished wood-panelled walls, leather sofas you can get lost in, lights that are low-key enough to make the place a fine venue for a romantic date, and a signature touch of an engraved glass partition that separates the long cocktail bar from the cigar lounge at the rear. To drink, the swanky, money-soaked white-collar crowd enjoys an admirable range of flamboyantly prepared cocktails (£5.25 each, which isn't bad at all) complemented by an adventurous array of bar snacks: Spanish almonds, marinated olives, spring rolls, samosas and the like. These are just teasers for the main Anthony Demetre run restaurant upstairs.
Babies and children admitted (lunch; restaurant only). Disabled: toilet. Function room. Restaurant. Tables outdoors (riverside terrace).

Whistle & Flute

46-8 Putney High Street, SW15 (8780 5437). Putney Bridge tube/Putney rail. **Open** noon-11pm Mon; 11am-11pm Tue-Sat; noon-10.30pm Sun. **Food served** noon-10pm Mon; 11am-10pm Tue-Thur; 11am-9pm Fri, Sat; noon-4pm, 6-9pm Sun. **Credit** AmEx, DC, MC, V.
Never mind the windows overlooking Blockbuster and Pizza Hut and another bloody Starbucks, this place proves that it is possible for a high street pub to maintain character and serve good booze. Well-kept Fuller's (Cask Marque approved), a decent '60s soundtrack, and a pub menu that's heavy on the seafood (£6.95-£10.50) that you'd be proud to foist upon your parents are part of the appeal. Terracotta and cream with wood floors, the main bar area has a couple of mute TVs largely ignored by the pretty young crowd – too busy munching on boar sausages (£6.95). Rugby days, however, are a very different story. A limed oak-panelled room to the rear echoes to middle-aged laughter emanating from deep red sofas; a crass fake bookcase is a poorly concealed fire exit. *Big Brother*'s Nasty Nick and some of *The Office* cast have been spotted here, making this more high street comic-reality TV than Hollywood blockbuster.
Disabled toilet. Games (fruit machine, quiz machine). TV (satellite).

Also in the area...

Fez (Po Na Na) 200B Upper Richmond Road, SW15 (8780 0123).
O'Neill's 90-90A High Street, SW6 (7384 3573).
Railway (JD Wetherspoon) 202 Upper Richmond Road, SW15 (8788 8190).
Slug & Lettuce 146-8 Putney High Street, SW15 (8785 3131).

South Norwood

South Norwood isn't exactly a beacon for chic drinkers. Its pubs, clustered in and around the High Street, are functional and, unless you're a local, the only reason to visit them is if you're heading for Selhurst Park and looking for a pre-match livener. Anyone wanting something slightly above the bog-standard should look to sup elsewhere.

Alliance

91 High Street, SE25 (8653 3604). Norwood Junction rail. **Open** 11am-11pm Mon-Sat; noon-10.30pm Sun. **Food served** noon-2pm Mon-Fri. **No credit cards.**
A tad more welcoming than most of the nondescript drinkeries that line South Norwood's convenience-store strip, the Alliance, next to the clocktower, was built in 1860 and has so far resisted the drive to modernisation. It remains an unashamedly old-fashioned tavern. Which means chaps straight out of work discussing the latest football transfers and racing results, elderly gents nursing pints of Best; dark wood, beams, yellowing paint and prints of old Norwood and Crystal Palace decorating all spare wall space. And brass. Lots of it. Coal scuttles, pans, kettles and jugs dangle from walls and ceilings, while battalions of brass figurines mass above the bar. The beer's decent (Courage, Greene King) and there are some satisfyingly obscure guest ales (Jennings Sneck Lifter on our visit). Visitors to Crystal Palace FC's nearby Selhurst Park ground will find it a more than acceptable pre-match warm-up.
Games (fruit machines). Jukebox. TV.

Goat House

2 Penge Road, SE25 (8778 5752). Norwood Junction rail. **Open** noon-11pm Mon-Sat; noon-10.30pm Sun. **Food served** noon-4pm daily. **Credit** DC, MC, V.
Drinkers who've crossed the railway bridge to the wrong side of the South Norwood tracks will be cheered up when they're greeted by the manager's excitable (and rather frisky) little bijou poodle skittering across the tiled floor. This cavernous, wood-panelled Fuller's establishment, with its leather bench seats and armchairs, makes much of its 'sports pub' credentials: there are games areas for pool, darts, computer games and pinball. But it's not just a lads' playground, there's also a lovely little alcove to hide away in and while away an hour or so with a book and a pint of Pride, as many locals do – although the peace is shattered on Friday by karaoke and at other times by big-screen Premiership footie. In summer, during the daytime kids are allowed into the bar and there's a big sunny (well, sometimes) beer terrace.
Babies and children admitted (until 7pm). Disabled: toilet. Games (darts, fruit machines, pinball, pool table). Tables outdoors (patio). TV (big screen, satellite).

Also in the area...

William Stanley (JD Wetherspoon) 7-8 High Street, SE25 (8653 0678).

Stockwell

In a hard and neglected neighbourhood, Stockwell's redeeming feature is undeniably the spicy character provided by a long-standing and thriving Portuguese element at the north end of South Lambeth Road and the south end of Stockwell Road. That aside, a few whitewashed hidden squares show that SW8 has potential that is waiting to be fulfilled.

Bar Estrela

111-15 South Lambeth Road, SW8 (7793 1051). Stockwell tube/Vauxhall tube/rail. **Open/food served** 8am-midnight Mon-Sat; 9am-11pm Sun. **Credit** AmEx, MC, V.
At the Little Portugal end of South Lambeth Road, Bar Estrela is the loudest and largest of this area's myriad small but buoyant contingent of Latin bars, restaurants and delis. Under a star-flecked ceiling, busy waiters clad in black slacks, waistcoats and crisp white shirts slip effortlessly between the bar and the cafe area, avoiding the children that run amok while their parents sip on espresso, booze on Sagrès or dine on arroz de mariso, the Iberian answer to paella. Often a male-dominated enclave, football and politics are discussed here

London drinking: sports bars

Where's the style in London's sports bars?

The revolution shared by all last summer – early opening hours across the nation to watch World Cup 2002 – has not left a new generation of sports bars in its wake. While DJ bars, cocktail bars and specialist spirit bars have improved dramatically in the capital, the sports bar appeals to the lowest common denominator in terms of drink, decor and ambience.

What we're stuck with are either sports bars aping the American model – glass frames protecting tacky sports shirts steaming up with the unimaginative grilled offerings emerging from the kitchen – or traditional gems dotted around town, more meeting places for those in the know than considered commercial operations.

Of the bog-standard sports bars of the type found from Warsaw to Wicklow, the main one in London is the **Sports Cafe** in the Haymarket, but there are any number of similar operations, **JD Young Sports Bar** in Camden and **F3K** by West Ken tube to name but two. In addition, every other pub boasts a poster in its window promoting upcoming offerings by Sky Sports, Setanta Sports or terrestrial competitors. Maxiscreens dominate proceedings; for the uninitiated, walking into one on a Premiership Sunday, rugby Saturday or Champions League Tuesday is a cross between walking into a tiny cinema halfway through the crucial piece of the film, and recreation time at the local remand school. Expect ugliness if England are involved.

Alongside, there is a handful of chains specifically not of the US or moronic Anglo type – in particular the **Tups** and **Shoeless Joe's** (*see p16*) – which attract rugger types to engage in friendly banter with antipodeans in between overs or during a long-winded line out.

In the main, there's nothing wrong with any of these bars – they provide alcohol, a screen, food, furniture, a toilet – but few go any further than that. The Sports Cafe is looking to broaden its agenda, with longer opening hours and participatory (rather than gulp-and-gawp) events such as pool nights, communal games, etc. The Tup chain deserves particular praise for involving (and funding) regulars in the local community who play in teams at the local park, before (ideally) gathering at the bar afterwards.

Football, however, is not on the agenda. Of those in the gem category, it's a case of pick your sport. For boxing, head to **The Ring** (*see p103*) in Waterloo. For cricket, the **Australian** (*see p53*) in Knightsbridge. For rugby, the **White Swan** (*see p245*) in Twickenham. Each have a footnote in sporting history and through geography or the whim of a landlord, engender a sporting passion in the best sense.

Six of the Best

Bar Kick (*see p121*) 127 Shoreditch High Street, E1 (7739 8700).
Cafe Kick (*see p108*) 43 Exmouth Market, EC1 (7837 8077).
F3K (*no review*) 171 North End Road, W14 (7603 6071).
Sports Cafe (*see p59*) 80 Haymarket, SW1 (7839 8300).
Tup chain (*see p16*) Branches in Balham, Camden, the City, Fulham, Islington, Kingston, Marylebone, Stoke Newington, Twickenham, Wandsworth and off the Strand. See **Also in the area...** for addresses.
JD Young Sports Bar (*see p162*) 2 Lidlington Place (7387 1495).

And what of the rest? What about somewhere that's cool, convivial, knowing but not bragging about the game at hand? Where sport comes first, but not at the expense of communal enjoyment? Step forward, **Cafe Kick**. Started as a wacky gimmick in 1996, with its three table football tables and continental touches, this bar loves its football and has enough flair to put pleasure back into watching a game here. No American Football helmets, no bland dumbing down in terms of drink, food or decor. Apart from a second branch in Shoreditch, **Bar Kick**, where else gives the modern sports bar its best shot? *Peterjon Cresswell*

with vigour, much aided by a TV screen that works as a magnet during the football season. Don't be intimidated, though, all are made to feel welcome in this comfortable environment.
Babies and children admitted (high chairs). Games (pool table). Restaurant. Tables outdoors (pavement). TV (satellite).

Circle

348 Clapham Road, SW9 (7622 3683). Clapham North or Stockwell tube. **Open** noon-11pm Mon-Sat; noon-10.30pm Sun. **Food served** noon-3pm, 7-10pm Mon-Thur; noon-3pm Fri, Sat; noon-4pm, 5-9pm Sun. **Credit** MC, V.
Midway between SW4 and SW9, this spacious venue is much more Clapham than Stockwell. The product of two inexperienced design graduates taking over a run-down boozer on a desolate stretch of busy road between Stockwell and Clapham North, the Circle has become a buzzingly successful location. Twentysomethings meet and greet each other as if on *Friends*, particularly on Sundays when brunches and lunches feature sizzling roasts of lamb, beef, chicken or veg with Yorkshire puds and rosemary. A square bar counter is flanked by the kitchen to one side, and to the other, a table football game and TV projections of the real thing on an overhead screen. Drinks include draught Löwenbräu, Tetley's and the usual range of cocktails. For a venue that's stuck in a bit of a south London wasteland, the Circle has made quite a name for itself.
Function room. Games (board games, fruit machine, table football). Music (DJs 8pm Sat; free). Tables outdoors (garden). TV (big screen, satellite). **Map 11/M15**

Priory Arms

83 Lansdowne Way, SW8 (7622 1884). Stockwell tube. **Open** 11am-11pm Mon-Sat; noon-10.30pm Sun. **Food served** noon-3pm Mon-Sat; 12.30-3.30pm Sun. **Credit** MC, V.
This compact spot round the back of Stockwell is intimate, friendly and tranquil and particularly beloved for its fine selection of beverages and brews, indicated by the endless display of beer mats that stretch along the walls and into a good part of the bar area. The beer list stretches to rare Belgians and Germans (Schneiderweisse? Schumacher?), plus plenty of cask ales (five are always available) and country fruit wines including apricot, birch and dandelion. It's all a bit cheek-by-jowl, especially on the slightly raised level seating where tables, stools and cushioned perches are jumbled together, and a jovial buzz of conversation flows. Around the main bar area regulars confidently stake out their territory and chew the fat with the bar staff. The food never aims above pie and mash, and doesn't really need to – everyone is perfectly happy with their lot here. Quiz nights and cricket club meetings enhance the social glue.
Babies and children admitted (until 8pm; no pushchairs). Function room. Games (fruit machine). Quiz (9pm Sun; free). Tables outdoors (garden). TV (satellite).

Royal Albert

43 St Stephen's Terrace, SW8 (7735 8095). Stockwell tube. **Open** noon-11pm Mon-Sat; noon-10.30pm Sun. **Food served** noon-3pm, 6-9.30pm Mon-Sat; 1-6pm Sun. **Credit** MC, V.
Nestling comfortably in a quiet pocket of Stockwell, the Royal Albert binds the whitewashed St Stephen's Square and the adjacent brownstoned estates together. Two bar areas represent separate factions. The bawdier, testosterone-fuelled front bar caters to drinkers who cluster around the pool table, or bellow at the large overhead screen that is typically tuned to Sky Sports. The quieter back area is a dark wood haven, complete with bookshelves, a plump Chesterfield, and a modest bank of dining tables, where socialist workers gather around the log fire to compare notes on bygone peace marches and the general state of the nation. Occasional two-fer deals on burgers and chips excite food sales, while other options include steak and ale pie, sausage and mash, nachos and Cajun chicken. London Pride is a popular addition to the bar, while weekly quiz nights and an upstairs pool room add to the entertainment.
Babies and children admitted. Function room. Games (darts, pool table, quiz machine). Tables outdoors (garden, pavement). TV (big screen, satellite).

Surprise

16 Southville, SW8 (7622 4623). Stockwell tube/Vauxhall tube/rail. **Open** 11am-11pm Mon-Sat; noon-10.30pm Sun. **Food served** noon-3pm daily. **Credit** MC, V.
A trad boozer, complete with a resident Labrador to fetch your beer mat and drool on your toes. It's a tiny place, found at the end of one of Stockwell's myriad slightly dodgy-looking side streets, although this one sits on the edge of Larkhill Park, which means ample sociable summertime drinking that extends beyond the adjoining beer garden. The park encourages barbecues, boules competitions and other pub activities that raise this a cut above most locals. Expect to be slightly blinded by the garish carpet and harsh lighting, particularly in the back bar where hangs a collection of framed caricatures of what could either be regular visitors or very badly drawn celebrities. On tap are Young's beers, supplemented by a modest menu of daily food specials.
Games (board games, boules pitch, fruit machine). Music (occasional band Fri; free). Tables outdoors (patio). TV (satellite).

Swan

215 Clapham Road, SW9 (7978 9778/www.theswanstockwell.com). Stockwell tube. **Open** 5pm-2am Thur; 5pm-3am Fri; 7pm-3am Sat; 7pm-2am Sun. **Admission** £2 after 10pm Thur; £3 after 7pm, £5 after 9pm Fri; £3 after 7pm, £6 after 9pm Sat; £3 after 10pm Sun. **Credit** AmEx, DC, MC, V.
Home for at least one night to every terrible tribute covers band that has ever played in London, the Swan sits bang opposite Stockwell tube station and is almost impossible to miss. Massive crowds of weekenders regularly cause road-blocks as they queue for the easy entertainment, cheap, fizzy beer and mammoth pulling potential that the Swan offers. Straddling both Stockwell and Clapham Roads, the expansive dark green venue with blacked-out windows also attracts a regular stream of Celts and Aussies. Inside is divided into a small Gothic bar with rusted metal chandeliers, gargoyles and numerous nitrokegs on tap. From there, step into a larger cavern with low wooden beams, faded red velvet curtains, upholstered stone walls and a humble stage. The Swan's upper deck, a huge bar area and whopping great stage, is where the hardcore action takes place. Not a place for the discerning or faint hearted.
Babies and children admitted (until 7pm weekdays). Dress code (weekends). Games (fruit machine). Music (DJs 8.30pm nightly; bands 9.30pm nightly). TVs.

Sydenham

Although close to Dulwich Common, much of Sydenham has an air of defeat about it. On Sydenham Hill, the **Dulwich Wood House**, the **Bricklayers Arms** and the **Woodman** reflect taste and tradition, but in the squalid crush around the train station, boozers are stacked back-to-back, one for every takeaway and dingy shop.

Bricklayers Arms

189 Dartmouth Road, SE26 (8699 1260). Forest Hill or Sydenham rail/122, 176, 202, 312 bus. **Open** 11am-11pm Mon-Sat; noon-10.30pm Sun. **Food served** noon-3pm, 5-8pm Mon-Fri; noon-7pm Sat, Sun. **No credit cards**.

A corner pub on the busy road between Sydenham and Forest Hill appealing to sporty types, families and ale aficionados. The only Young's pub in the immediate vicinity, the Bricklayers also boasts a reasonable wine list, chalked up in the smaller front bar area; in the bare floorboarded back room, home of the Wig and Pen FC, a dartboard, sports TV and pool tables. In a side room there's a fireplace and a children's room, which leads through to a modest garden. The food (burgers and curries) is genuine pub grub, and new management is looking to attract locals by putting on regular jazz and free weekends in Paris on the strength of talent at karaoke. It's an easy walk from either Sydenham or Forest Hill train stations.

Babies and children admitted. Games (darts, fruit machine, pool). Music (occasional bands; free). Tables outdoors (garden). TV (satellite).

Dulwich Wood House

39 Sydenham Hill, SE26 (8693 5666). Sydenham Hill rail/63, 202 bus. **Open** 11am-11pm Mon-Sat; noon-10.30pm Sun. **Food served** noon-9pm Mon-Sat; noon-6pm Sun. **Credit** MC, V.

Prominent public house set between Sydenham and Dulwich Common, with a panoramic view over south London at the 202 bus stop nearby. It's a beautiful building, designed by Sir Joseph Paxton, whose Crystal Palace is pictured all ablaze inside, alongside eminent snuff-guzzling Georgians in portrait and Grand Prix legend Graham Hill. The interior is neatly divided into fireplaced alcoves, a main bar offering the full range of Young's brews, and a lower-level no-smoking spacious restaurant area giving on to a large, pretty garden dotted with beer tables and a children's playground. Oh yes, and there's a small room for serious darts players, electronic scoreboard and all. Excellent food too.

Babies and children admitted (playground). Games (fruit machines, quiz machine). Quiz (7.30pm last Wed of mnth; £1). Tables outdoors (garden). TV.

Two Half's

42 Sydenham Road, SE26 (8778 4629). Sydenham rail. **Open** 11am-11pm Mon-Sat; noon-10.30pm Sun. **Food served** noon-3pm, 6-9pm daily. **Credit** AmEx, DC, MC, V.

A strange place this, separated from the High Street mass of takeaways and tacky shops by a small fence and terrace. Once inside, a cavernous sports bar appears, with a food hatch at the back, and main counter in the shadow of a maxiscreen the size of Canada. In the afternoon, locals gather to curse the racing from oversized armchairs placed around the front pool table; it's only a couple of steps to the bar (Hofmeister, Foster's) where there's a box of betting slips. Pay outs are at the bookies the other side of Budgen's next door. In the evenings, £3.50 cocktails and £2.50 shooters attract a younger crowd, who congregate around a second pool table at the back. The recent addition of a chef allows for a Caribbean-influenced menu, although on Sunday roasts take the place of curried goat. Elsewhere, this place would clear up.

Babies and children admitted (until 8pm). Disabled: toilet. Karaoke (7.30pm Sun; free). Music (band 7.30pm Sat; free). Tables outdoors (pavement). TV (big screen, digital and satellite).

Also in the area...

Windmill (JD Wetherspoon) 125-31 Kirkdale, SE26 (8291 8670).

Tooting

Now that property developers are shoehorning young professionals into SW17, entrepreneurs are catching on to the idea that maybe not everybody wants to schlep over to Clapham or Balham for a drink. For a long time **Spirit** was the only alternative to ropey old boozers. Now the renovation at the **King's Head** and the appearance of designer bar **smoke bar diner** suggest things are finally on the turn.

King's Head

84 Upper Tooting Road, SW17 (8767 6708). Tooting Bec tube. **Open** 11am-11pm Mon-Sat; noon-10.30pm Sun. **Food served** noon-9pm daily. **Credit** AmEx, MC, V.

The ornate Victorian decor of this honest Tooting boozer, built in 1896, has survived a recent takeover and makeover by Scottish & Newcastle. Sensibly, the new owners have raised the tone of the place without stripping it of character – nor alienating the lucrative throng of football fans who crowd the back room on match nights. There's promise of a new garden hosting summer events and regular pub promotions. No longer is the side bar a secretive den of iniquity and pool-sharking; the green baize has been relegated to the back room and in its place is an altogether smarter dining area. The food has improved and in among the taps (Bombardier, Pride and guest ales such as Rosy Nosey) on the tarted-up island bar are vases of exotic blooms and a display of champagne bottles. We haven't noticed anyone ordering the Bolly yet, but you have to admire the optimism.

Disabled: toilet. Games (pool, quiz machine). Tables outdoors (patio). TV (big screen, satellite).

smoke bar diner

14 Trinity Road, SW17 (8767 3902/www.smokebardiner.com). Tooting Bec tube. **Open** 5.30pm-midnight Mon-Fri; noon-midnight Sat; noon-11pm Sun. **Food served** 6.30-10.30pm Mon-Fri; noon-5.30pm, 6.30-10.30pm Sat; noon-5pm, 6.30-10pm Sun. **Credit** MC, V.

A few doors down from the tube station is Tooting Bec's first proper designer bar (you can tell it's designer by the lower-casing). The owner's credentials – he used to manage Montana in Fulham – are apparent from the slick contemporary neutrals-and-leather decor and retro touches. The biker in the monochrome print dominating the bar is his uncle, no less. Beers include Leffe on tap, and Staropramen, Modelo and Bombardier in bottles. Wines are mostly Old World and cocktails (£4.75-£6) are mostly classics with the odd modern take but nothing leery or inelegant. Food enters gastropub territory. Dare we say it but the Sunday roast rivals mum's. Beef (£8.95) is organic, the veggies firm and the roasties crunchy. So far so good. The downside, however, is that at peak times the place is rammed – a tell-tale sign of an up-and-coming area crying out for decent venues. So take our advice: avoid the crowds and try Sunday lunch. Just don't tell mum.

Disabled: toilet. Function room. Music (DJs 5pm Sun). Tables outdoors (pavement). TV (satellite).

Spirit Cafe Bar

94 Tooting High Street, SW17 (8767 3311). Tooting Broadway tube. **Open** 4pm-midnight Mon, Tue; 11am-midnight Wed-Sat; 11am-10.30pm Sun. **Food served** 4-10pm Mon-Thur; 3-8pm Fri; noon-6pm Sat, Sun. **Credit** AmEx, MC, V.

An early front runner in the Tooting nightlife stakes, Spirit still draws the local hipsters. Space is at a premium, so interior fripperies are limited to a fairy-lit twig atop the bar that pulsates to pumping dance tracks. The windowless back

room is saved from dinginess by the splash of designer red on the wall and some trance-enducing light projections. Drinks of choice tend to be shots, alcopops, cheeky cocktails such as Sex on the Grass, and wine, although Leffe, Stella and Staropramen are on tap. The small, flickering TV screens add little to the clubby vibe, although they do come into their own when the Sunday lunchers settle down for an afternoon of football and fodder. Last orders, usefully, are at midnight and weekend breakfast is served, sportingly, until 4pm.
Babies and children admitted. Function room. Tables outdoors (pavement). TV (satellite).

South

Trafalgar Arms

148 Tooting High Street, SW17 (8767 6059). Tooting Broadway tube. **Open** noon-11pm Mon-Sat; noon-10.30pm Sun. **Food served** noon-9pm daily. **Credit** MC, V.
Formerly the shabby William IV pub, the revamped and renamed Trafalgar has become a reliable favourite with local twenty- and thirtysomethings. It's a welcoming place with a big open fire, candlelit tables and cutesy canvasses (available for purchase at remarkably low prices). TVs are forbidden and the jolly disco tracks are kept low enough to create a vibe without spoiling conversation. Food's a tad steep at more than seven quid for the cheapest main, a risotto, but beers are good and guest ales have included Old Speckled Hen. The owner seems keen to inject a little fun into the place, hence the recent Kylie Night, complete with drag queen act. No shrinking violet himself, he's threatened a monthly talent competition. Hope it does better than the Friday fancy dress night we attended – just a lone cardboard-gun-toting cowgirl.
Babies and children admitted (until 9pm). Games (board games, fruit machines). Tables outdoors (pavement).

Also in the area...

JJ Moons (JD Wetherspoon) 56A Tooting High Street, SW17 (8672 4726).

Vauxhall

Away from the patch of Little Portugal that edges down from Stockwell and the vibrant gay scene that centres round the (in)famous and ever lively **Vauxhall Tavern**, there's little here for the mainstream crowd. That is possibly because Vauxhall has never been a mainstream crowd sort of place – though things may soon change with the completion of the multi-million-pound Vauxhall Cross development. After all, even spies need somewhere to drink.

Canton Arms

177 South Lambeth Road, SW8 (7820 7921). Stockwell tube/Vauxhall tube/rail. **Open** 11am-11pm Mon-Sat; noon-10.30pm Sun. **Food served** noon-2.30pm, 6-9.30pm Mon-Fri; 12.30-3pm, 6.30-9pm Sat; 12.30-4pm, 7-9pm Sun. **Happy hour** 6-7pm Fri, Sat. **Credit** DC, MC, V.
Describing itself as an 'ale and food house', this revamped boozer has relaunched in a parade midway between Vauxhall and Stockwell among the many Portuguese bakeries and tapas bars that inhabit this surprisingly cosmopolitan manor. The two public areas, wrapped horseshoe-like around a central serving area, are bright, with huge semi-mullioned windows spilling light over cheerfully mismatched furniture and low-slung sofas. The colour scheme is an unlikely but winning pairing of navy and lime (yum!). Real ales are tasty Greene King IPA, Old Speckled Hen and Theakston Coolcask. Nosh largely features gastropub standbys such as fish cakes, fish and chips and lamb shank, generally competitively priced between £3.95 and £7.50. Service is friendly and keen, with a diverse bunch of drinkers, ranging from new media types puffing on roll-ups, to old-style locals drawing on, er, roll-ups.
Games (table football). Tables outdoors (patio). TV (big screen, satellite).

Greenwich Union. *See p213.*

Fentiman Arms

64 Fentiman Road, SW8 (7793 9796). Vauxhall or Oval rail/tube. **Open** 11am-11pm Mon-Fri; noon-10.30pm Sun. **Food served** noon-3.45pm, 7-9.45pm Mon-Sat; noon-4pm, 7-9.45pm Sun. **Credit** MC, V.

Until quite recently the Fentiman Arms was a dingy boozer, frequented by crusty old men with hacking coughs. But gentrification comes to all that wait, and since being acquired by Geronimo Inns the place has been buffed and polished to serve as an extended sitting room for the up-and-coming residents of Fentiman Road. Crustiness is now confined to the pastry nestled on top of wholesome chicken pies and the like. On the rainy Monday evening of our visit, it was comfortably busy, welcoming mainly middle-aged couples and portly types in grey suits. There's Greene King IPA drawn from gleaming pumps, a reasonable selection of wines by the glass (four red, four white), plus the aforementioned food – hearty fare like bangers and mash, steak and chips, with prices starting around the £8 mark. In summer patrons get to enjoy a fully decked walled garden out back. The 'How to create a perfect gastropub' manual has been followed a bit too closely, and a few eccentricities would perk the place up no end.

Babies and children admitted. Function room. Tables outdoors (garden). TV (satellite).

Vauxhall Tavern

372 Kennington Lane, SE11 (7582 0833). Vauxhall tube/rail. **Open** weekends only but hours vary – phone for details. **No credit cards**.

History oozes from the Vauxhall's sweaty walls: the Krays are rumoured to have hung out here (the gay one, anyway), Lily Savage got her start tending bar here – can you imagine the banter? More recently, the Real IRA launched a mortar bomb attack on MI6 from behind the park. Never a dull moment, then. Well, except during the week, when the place is boarded up. Friday club nights are sporadic, but Saturday nights are home to the legendary Duckie, a post-gay extravaganza where the London Readers Wifes (*sic*) spin a mix of punk and trash to a mixed crowd of indie kids and old queens, with a bit of avant-garde cabaret thrown in. Sunday afternoons host Slags Chillout, a comedown session for hardcore clubbers who need to recharge their batteries for Sunday evening, when the hi-NRG kicks in, the poppers come out and the tops come off. So much for Monday morning.

Wandsworth

With the exception of **Tír Na Nóg** (which, frankly, would be an exception in any locality), most drinking venues in this district stick to a well-thought-out, smart formula: premium beer, classy wine, decent food, rugby in preference to football. They target the more demanding clientele: often couples who decamped here from town when children came along (more house for your money), giving rise to the area's nickname of Nappy Valley.

Alma Tavern

499 Old York Road, SW18 (8870 2537). Wandsworth Town rail. **Open** 11am-11pm Mon-Sat; noon-10.30pm Sun. **Food served** noon-4pm, 6-10pm Mon-Sat; noon-4pm, 6-9.30pm Sun. **Credit** AmEx, DC, MC, V.

On a corner opposite the station, this imposing pub with original green-tiled exterior, grand mahogany staircase and ornate mirrored panels, is smart and traditional, like its punters who come to witness England's battles on the rugby pitch. The pub takes its name from a real battle – the opening salvo of the Crimean War – as commemorated in the gilded tablets on the walls. The drinking area skirts around a huge island bar behind serving Young's ales (they haven't travelled far; it's a mere 400 yards to the brewery) and some equally

well-kept wines. The back-room restaurant (with elegant wall frieze) offers gastropub fare, most notably organic meat from the farm of the owners: Charles and Linda Gotto, whose empire includes the neighbouring **Ship** (*see right*), and the **Cooper's Arms** (*see p31*) in Chelsea.
Babies and children admitted (high chairs). Function room. No piped music or jukebox. Restaurant. TV (big screen, satellite).

ditto

55-7 East Hill, SW18 (8877 0110). Wandsworth Town rail. **Open** noon-11pm Mon-Sat; noon-10.30pm Sun. **Food served** noon-3pm, 7-11pm Mon-Sat; noon-4pm, 6-9pm Sun. **Credit** MC, V.
When faced with a sliver of a bar-restaurant with scant natural light what do you do to avoid dinginess? You make it dark and interesting. Try boxy bar stools, sofas you could get lost in (under an avalanche of earthy scatter cushions), and stacks of backgammon boards and newspapers to massage the intellect. The art-for-sale wall hangings are pricey (upwards of £240), but small beer to the affluent locals and Putney overspill that congregate here. Owners Christian Duffell and Giles Cooper (ex of Scotts of Mayfair and the Ritz Carlton bar) have compiled a sophisticated wine list and there's a monthly line-up of cocktails (£4-£7). Beers on tap include Hoegaarden and Boddingtons. The more formal restaurant, running parallel to the bar, has a classy Modern European menu (two courses for £15.50, three for £19.50). Want to know how to make the cocktail of the month in your own home? Get on the mailing list.
Babies and children admitted (restaurant only). Function room. Games (backgammon). Restaurant. TV (satellite).

East Hill

21 Alma Road, SW12 (8874 1833). Wandsworth Town rail. **Open** 11am-11pm Mon-Sat; noon-10.30pm Sun. **Food served** noon-3pm, 7-10pm Mon-Fri; noon-8pm Sat, Sun. **Credit** MC, V.
The caramel and black exterior of the East Hill screams 'smart modern pub'. So too does the TV-garden makeover decking – an odd adornment in a residential street. You wouldn't stumble across this place from Wandsworth Town station, so it's safe to assume it relies on local trade: the locals in question being affluent thirtysomethings. The interior is one big room with butcher's block tables, Conranesque stripy soft furnishings and rug-strewn wooden floors. The space is broken up by open bookshelves providing little sofa-ed alcoves. A semicircular bar stocks quality wines by the glass or bottle, and numbers Bitburger, Affligem and Wieckse Witte among its more interesting draught beers. A menu of decent pub food changes monthly.
Babies and children admitted. Games (bar billiards, board games). Tables outdoors (paved area). TVs (satellite).

Hope

1 Bellevue Road, SW17 (8672 8717). Wandsworth Common rail. **Open** noon-11pm Mon-Sat; noon-10.30pm Sun. **Food served** noon-9.45pm Mon-Sat; noon-9pm Sun. **Credit** AmEx, MC, V.
First a dreary boozer then a Firkin, the Hope was, for many years, largely left untroubled by the gentlefolk of Wandsworth. Recently, however, all has changed. The Hope's benefitted from a kitchen makeover, new à la mode decor and art-for-sale wall furniture. The sexy sunken seating isn't as comfy as it looks, but the sofas are. There's even talk of a roof terrace – cash allowing. Otherwise, the outside chairs and tables provide the perfect vantage point from which to spot rare patches of grass between hordes of summer drinkers on the common. Staropramen, Leffe, cloudy cider Addlestone's and Adnams lead the draught offerings (along with occasional guest ales), and there's an eclectic mix of easy drinking wines (£10.75-£25). In a retro touch, a vintage games machine features Pacman and Space Invaders.
Disabled: toilet. Games (arcade table). Tables outdoors (patio).

Nightingale

97 Nightingale Lane, SW12 (8673 1637). Clapham South tube/Wandsworth Common rail. **Open** 11am-11pm Mon-Sat; noon-10.30pm Sun. **Food served** noon-2.15pm, 7-9.30pm Mon-Fri; 1-3pm Sat, Sun. **Credit** MC, V.
On the slope of Nightingale Lane sits this commendable, communal and charitable institution. It's just passed the 150-year mark and has about it a kind of rites of passage air: sons, grandsons and great-grandsons can sup from the same spot where their previous kin once stood. The tavern and its patrons also have a prodigious history of philanthropy as evidenced by the charity-issued photos of sponsored labradors: all pictured tongue happy before a lifetime of servitude in blind reins. Regulars squeeze around a D-shaped bar counter, built for socialising, and sup Young's beers, plus bottles of Beck's. There's a modest evening menu. Three thumps can occasionally be heard from the dartboard in one corner, while diagonally opposite, a patio decked in hops and the sacks once filled with them leads to an intimate walled beer garden.
Babies and children admitted (separate area). Games (darts, fruit machine, golf machine). No-smoking area. Quiz (7.30pm first Mon of mth; £1). Tables outdoors (garden). TV (satellite).

Ship

41 Jew's Row, SW18 (8870 9667). Wandsworth Town rail. **Open** 11am-11pm Mon-Sat; noon-10.30pm Sun. **Food served** noon-10.30pm Mon-Fri; noon-4pm, 7-10.30pm Sat; noon-4pm, 7-10pm Sun. **Credit** AmEx, DC, MC, V.
The walk up to the Ship doesn't bode well, but persist past McDonald's and London Transport's huge Wandsworth garage and there, nestled between the overflowing skips and the rusting hulk of an old sailing barge on the river, believe it or not, is a very pleasant pub. The front is made up of two traditional, dark and small snugs serving fine Young's ales. As this is the Gottos' flagship boozer – the others being the **Alma** (*see p225*) and the **Cooper's Arms** (*see p31*) in Chelsea, there's a knowing wine list. At the back, a sizeable conservatory and adjoining restaurant overlook a split-level riverside beer garden with some serious barbecue equipment and beach-hut bar. If you strain your ears, over the not-so-distant roar of the traffic from Wandsworth roundabout, you can even make out the sound of seagulls.
Babies and children admitted. Function room. Restaurant. Tables outdoors (riverside garden).

Tír Na Nóg

107 Garratt Lane, SW18 (8877 3622). Earlsfield rail. **Open** 11am-11pm Mon-Sat; noon-10.30pm Sun. **Credit** MC, V.
Imagine if Albert Steptoe a) existed b) was Irish and c) decided to give up his rag and bone cart to open a public house. The end result would look something like Tír Na Nóg. On an innocuous bend of Garratt Lane, among housing estates and warehouses, this quirky, fairy-lit Irish pub reveals its junkyard-chic interior as you peer through the glowing windows crowded with bric-a-brac. Every conceivable space (even the ceiling) is littered with vaguely Irish odds and sods – a cartwheel here, a drinking jar there. Wax-laden bottles serve as candelabras on rickety mismatched tables. The bar offers little of note, but is kept by Irish staff and standard

Irish labels are well represented. Irish music on Saturday nights comes courtesy of Foxy & Friends. Is Foxy, we wonder, the stuffed one suspended over the piano?
Babies and children admitted. Games (darts, fruit machine, pool). Music (Irish bands 9pm Sat; DJs 8pm Sun; free). Tables outdoors (garden). TV (big screen, satellite).

Also in the area...

Grid Inn (JD Wetherspoon) 22 Replingham Road, SW18 (8874 8460).
Pitcher & Piano 11 Bellevue Road, SW17 (8767 6982).
Rose & Crown (JD Wetherspoon) 134 Wandsworth High Street, SW18 (8871 4497).
Tonsley Tup 1 Ballantine Street, SW18 (8877 3766).

Wimbledon

South Londoners will grimace but for Wimbledon read also Earlsfield, Colliers Wood and Southfields. Drinking options vary wildly in this vast area, from charismatic old pubs around the common to designer bars in the more salubrious Wimbledon village and Earlsfield. Wimbledon's main drag is blighted by the predictable bog-standard chains, but improved by quirky newcomer **Bar Sia**.

Alexandra

33 Wimbledon Hill Road, SW19 (8947 7691). Wimbledon tube/rail. **Open** *Pub* 11am-11pm Mon-Sat; noon-10.30pm Sun. *Wine bar* noon-11pm Mon-Thur; noon-1am Fri, Sat; noon-10.30pm Sun. **Food served** noon-2.30pm, 6-9.30pm daily. **Admission** £5 (wine bar only) after 9.30pm Fri, Sat. **Credit** AmEx, DC, MC, V.
A grand old (built 1874) Young's pub, resplendent with wood panelling and low ceilings. Ignore the main bar and slip into the sports bar – featuring spit roasts over an open fire in winter – or ditch the fags and try the smoke-free saloon bar as both score highly in the cosy drinking stakes. The pub's adjoining 'Smart Alex' wine bar is elegant, in a Parisian cafe kind of way, with a lengthy wine list and a zippy seasonal menu of Modern British dishes for around £6.50-£10.50. The pretty roof terrace is the place in summer (although not for its views, which are of busy A-roads), when hordes of sun worshippers threaten to bow the ancient beams under their feet as they assemble up top to toast the last rays of the day.
Disabled: toilet (wine bar). Dress: smart casual (wine bar). Games (fruit machine, quiz machine, golf machine). Music (band 9.30pm Fri, Sat). No-smoking area. Tables outdoors (garden, pavement). TV (big screen, satellite).

The Bar Cafe

153-63 The Broadway, SW19 (8543 5083). South Wimbledon tube/Wimbledon tube/rail. **Open/food served** 11am-11.30pm daily. **Happy hour** noon-8pm daily. **Credit** AmEx, MC, V.
This sleekly cavernous yearling preaches an appealing philosophy: 'Eat, drink, dance'. The first imperative is catered for with snacks and food-to-share (sandwiches, salads, pasta and a rather incongruous afternoon tea, £5.95) and a range of seating options from chairs and tables to leather-clad TV booths. The second is catered to by a simplistic wine list from £9.95 a bottle, and an up-for-it menu of dirt-cheap cocktails complete with taunting come-ons – the Flatliner: 'Can you handle a fiery mouthful of tequila, sambuca and tabasco?' Further encouragement comes with noon to 8pm happy hours. Dance is accommodated by a smallish floor (enhanced by a wall of mirrors), a midnight licence and a DJ. Casual crews should take note that when the DJ is in the house, jeans and trainers are out. Nice to see that some turntable jocks still have sartorial sensibilities.
Disabled: toilet. Dress: weekend evenings, no jeans or trainers. Music (DJs 8pm Fri, Sat). Tables outdoors (patio). TV (satellite).

Bar Sia

105-9 The Broadway, SW19 (8540 8339). South Wimbledon tube/Wimbledon tube/rail. **Open/food served** noon-11pm Mon-Thur; noon-midnight Fri, Sat; noon-10.30pm Sun. **Credit** AmEx, DC, MC, V.
The sign on the door reads 'Lounge, cocktails, music, baths'. Yes, 'baths'. The premises (a listed building dating from 1910) used to house a Turkish-style hamam. The current owners discovered the downstairs plunge pool when renovating and incorporated it into a bar/DJ area. The mezzanine ground floor is more conventional; two aluminium light-boxes depicting a woman bathing – created by the bar's architect – greet all-comers entering the green and aubergine front area where, on Wednesday or Thursday, a jazz duo takes up residence in the window. Upstairs, one of the heaviest bars in SW19 (made of solid terrazzo) offers a predictable beer list, lolly drinks, a short wine list (£9.50-£16.50), another of champagnes, and a raft of cocktails from the classic to the cheeky (G-spot, strawberries and champagne, £6.90).
Dress: smart casual. Function room. Music (jazz 8pm alternate Wed and Thur; DJs 8pm Fri, Sat). TV (satellite).

Common Room

18 High Street, SW19 (8944 1909). Wimbledon tube/rail. **Open** 11am-11pm Mon-Sat; 11am-10.30pm Sun. **Food served** 11am-10pm Mon-Sat; 11am-9.30pm Sun. **Credit** AmEx, MC, V.
Heralding the end of the neutrals and dark wood decor that has been all the rage recently, the not awfully common Common Room has gone pink: pastel in the front bar, racier in the back. The refurb has also extended to the bar – quite literally, as it now stands a good metre further forward into the room for swifter service. Not that anyone is encouraged to rush. An elegant, relaxed vibe is enhanced by architectural blooms and mellow music, so local ladies who lunch can chat demurely, or watch and be watched through the acres of glass frontage. The wine list offers an interesting round-the-world selection (£12-£30) with most available by the glass (£3.25-£7.25). A food menu leans toward casual comfort dishes such as smoked haddock cakes (£9). Evenings, when the place fills with after-workers, are the testing time for the 'bigger bar, swifter service' theory. Anyone got a stopwatch?
Babies and children admitted (children's menu, high chairs). Games (board games). No-smoking area (until 6pm). Tables outdoors (garden).

Earl Spencer

260-262 Merton Road, SW18 (8870 9244). Southfields tube. **Open** 11am-11pm Mon-Sat; noon-10.30pm Sun. **Food served** 12.30-2.30pm, 7-10pm Mon-Sat; 12.30-3pm, 7-9.30pm Sun. **Credit** MC, V.
Beneficiary of the full gastropub makeover, this grand Edwardian drinking palace has been cleared out, stripped down, and cleaned up. A bookshelf by the open kitchen door is lined with well-thumbed classic cookery books, while just-baked loaves of bread rest on the bar counter (prior to being cut into soldiers for diners). All of which is fine and dandy, but what about the booze? Well, thankfully, the old Earl still operates as a proper pub. It's got a real log fire and three cask-conditioned ales: Hook Norton, Courage Directors and Fuller's London Pride. There is no separate dining area,

Vauxhall Tavern. *See p225.*

and everyone has to muck in together, drinkers grudgingly conceding space to diners. The daily-changing menu is chalked on blackboards, in the usual way, and although service can be slow, dishes are well worth the wait.
Babies and children welcome (until 7pm). Function room. Games (board games). Tables outdoors (patio).

Eclipse Wimbledon

57 High Street, SW19 (8944 7722/www.bareclipse.com). Wimbledon tube/rail/93 bus. **Open/food served** 5.30pm-midnight Tue, Wed; noon-1am Thur-Sat; noon-10.30pm Sun. **Admission** £5 (after 11pm Thur; 10.30pm Fri, Sat). **Credit** AmEx, MC, V.
Formerly just Eclipse, now Eclipse Wimbledon. Perhaps, as this diminutive bar is still the area's premier cocktail spot, the name has been modified as a pointer for any who lose their bearings after a night of heady excess, lulled into a stupor by the mesmeric rhythm of the bongo drums (10pm-1am Thur-Sat). Even the addled should steer clear of the stools at the tiny tables where there are angled mirrors above that serve to draw attention to the merest hint of a receding hairline or balding spot. Not the look the trendy young things are hoping for. Dab-hand staff serve up the usual wanton hedonism of Martinis, champagne cocktails, shorts, talls and shots, and there are brief wine and champagne lists. During Wimbledon fortnight the bar also does a successful sideline in fruit smoothies. Food includes bite-sized sushi at £6-£12 per half-dozen set. Ensure you arrive before 11pm or you'll cop a £5 door charge.
Babies and children admitted (until 5pm). Dress: no trainers. Tables outdoors (pavement). TV (big screen, tennis only).

Fire Stables

27-9 Church Road, SW19 (8946 3197). Wimbledon tube/rail, then 93, 200, 493 bus. **Open** 11am-11pm Mon-Sat; 11.30am-10.30pm Sun. **Food served** noon-3pm, 6-10.30pm Mon-Fri; 11.30am-4.30pm, 6-10.30pm Sat; 11.30am-4.30pm, 6-10pm Sun. **Credit** AmEx, MC, V.
Also known as the 'Wimbledon Glue Pot'; you fancy a quick half of something tasty, maybe Belgian brew Affligen or the Dutch Wieckse Witte, or a glass of quality wine, so you nip into the Fire Stables. But the classy contemporary interior, low-slung tables and even lower-slung sofas are just so wrap-around comfortable, so enticing, that before you realise it you've downed a third drink and are pawing over the bar menu. Order a lamb burger and chips (£8.50) or some other beautifully executed fare from the Modern European menu and kiss goodbye to the rest of the day. You're stuck. Canny punters know the pitfalls. They avoid sitting and remain standing instead. For the less experienced just keep repeating this mantra: 'Only a quick half. Only a quick half.'
Babies and children admitted (high chairs). Disabled: toilet. No-smoking area.

Fog

2 Groton Road, SW18 (8874 2715). Earlsfield rail. **Open** 11am-11pm Mon-Sat; noon-10.30pm Sun. **Food served** noon-2.30pm daily. **Credit** MC, V.
In a bold statement of isolationism (or is it blissful ignorance?), the Fog has resisted all temptation to sell out and its decor remains resolvedly 'old boozer'. It has eschewed the glass frontage, shunned the leather sofa and, in fact, you're more likely to see HM the Queen snowboarding than Fog bar staff twirling cocktail shakers. A poster warns that anyone caught selling drugs will be barred for life, but it's hard to imagine a less likely set of dealers than these punters. They'd rather prop up the bar discussing the burning issues of the day (such as who won the 2.50 at Aintree) over pints of ale or a few frames of pool. The menu of typical pub grub makes exciting reading for the tight of wallet and specials are chalked up on the blackboards. One day there will be pub theme-pubs and the Fog will be the model.
Games (darts, fruit machine, pool). TV (satellite).

Fox & Grapes

9 Camp Road, SW19 (8946 5599). Wimbledon tube/rail. **Open/food served** 11am-11pm Mon-Sat; noon-10.30pm Sun. **Food served** noon-9.45pm Mon-Sat; noon-9.30pm Sun. **Credit** AmEx, DC, MC, V.
The owner's a Kiwi, but this is far from being your average antipodean pub. In fact, the Fox & Grapes blends the best of the Old and the New Worlds: a traditional 18th-century building, wood-panelled with wingback armchairs by a roaring fire and Bombardier, Adnams and Directors on tap, plus an up-to-the-minute wine list. At the top end is a Montrachet at £56.50 and there's lots from Down Under, particularly some cracking New Zealand producers, such as Saint Clair, Goldwater and Cloudy Bay (sauvignon blanc £29.50). Throw into the mix a lovely spot on the common next to a riding school (the gentle clip-clopping transports you far from city stresses) and an interesting – if not particularly cheap – bar menu including the likes of Steinlager-battered fish and chips with green-lipped mussels served in newspaper (£9.50). Is it, as the pub claims, the best boozer in Wimbledon? With, as it also claims, the best wine list in London? Debatable on both counts. But who cares? It's good enough.
Babies and children admitted. Function room. No-smoking area. TV (big screen, satellite).

Garage

20 Replingham Road, SW18 (8874 9370). Southfields tube. **Open** noon-11pm Mon-Sat; noon-10.30pm Sun. **Food served** noon-9pm daily. **Credit** AmEx, MC, V.
Last year this was the 'Old' Garage but presumably the aged prefix didn't sit well with the bar's youthful aspirations, evident to all in the photos of shiny-faced big kids displayed at the entrance. Encouragement – in the form of free drinks – is offered to anyone exhibiting true 'party spirit', by which management presumably means turning up in saucy (ladies) or ridiculous (lads) school uniform, and that sort of thing. Other frequent opportunities for personal exhibitionism/humiliation (including Wednesday night karaoke) are listed on a blackboard. Staff behind the snaking bar counter dispense the usual bottled and draught lagers, plus alcopops and so-so wines by the glass. Pitcher and doubles promotions speed the descent into blurry misbehaviour – rewarded no doubt with yet more free booze. Smile for the camera.
Disabled: toilet. Games (fruit machines). TV.

Hand in Hand

6 Crooked Billet, SW19 (8946 5720). Wimbledon tube/rail. **Open** 11am-11pm Mon-Sat; noon-10.30pm Sun. **Food served** noon-2.30pm, 7-9.30pm Mon-Sat; noon-4pm, 7-9pm Sun. **Credit** MC, V.
This ancient Young's pub on Wimbledon Common, a bakehouse of old, is rumoured to have its own ghost, but don't let that scare you off what is one of the more charismatic drinking options in the vicinity of the village. Tipplers here must have a little decorum. Signs request 'quiet' when leaving so as not to wake up the privileged offspring of the privileged neighbours, and only plastic glasses can be carried outside on to the large and lovely grass expanse outside the front doors of the pub. May we suggest that into one of those plastic glasses you ask to have poured something from the house selection of fruit wines; choose from the likes of apricot, damson and a very delicious elderberry (£2.15 a glass). Alternatively, when was the last time that you were

in a pub serving 'mead'? Otherwise, staff behind the attractive island bar dispense more standard offerings including fine Young's ales, wines and reasonable pub grub.
Babies and children admitted (separate area; children's menu). Games (darts, quiz machine). No-smoking area. Tables outdoors (courtyard).

Hartfield's Wine Bar

27 Hartfield Road, SW19 (8543 9788/www.hartfields.com). Wimbledon tube/rail. **Open** noon-11pm Mon-Fri; 6pm-midnight Sat. **Food served** noon-2.30pm, 6-10pm Mon-Fri; 6-10pm Sat. **Happy hour** 5-11pm Mon; £5 bottle of house wine. **Credit** AmEx, DC, MC, V.

An unpretentious neighbourhood wine bar with a list that, while harbouring no great surprises, offers around 40 unstuffy bottles, many of which can be sampled by the glass (£2.50-£5.30). Apart from a bias towards French whites, there's an almost pedantic symmetry with one rosé, a solitary sticky and two organics (a red and a white), plus three sparklers. Beer drinkers must settle for one of a trio of bottled lagers (Beck's, San Miguel, Foster's Ice, all £2.50). To soak up the alcohol, bar snacks such as calamari are £3 a pop, or £25 for all ten. The menu proper offers simple dishes such as steak with stilton sauce (£10.50) or the more niche sea bass with pernod and fennel sauce (£10.75). Incredibly, this narrow space plays host to musicians (duos or soloists, clearly) on Saturdays. A regular newsletter encourages further fostering of the community spirit.
Babies and children admitted. Disabled: toilet. Music (acoustic guitarist or jazz 8pm Sat; free). No-smoking area. Quiz (7.30pm last Mon of mth; free).

Leather Bottle

538 Garratt Lane, SW17 (8946 2309). Earlsfield rail. **Open** 11am-11pm Mon-Sat; noon-10.30pm Sun. **Food served** noon-3pm, 6-8.30pm daily. **Credit** MC, V.

The Leather Bottle has witnessed some changes since its 18th-century beginnings. Then it served the rural hamlet of Garrett and overlooked the village green, on which mock elections took place for the 'Mayor of Garrett' to lead residents against local land closures. Ultimately, you'd have to say their protests failed as the Grade II-listed Young's pub is flanked by shops, houses and busy Garratt Lane, a blight and eyesore to anyone hoping to enjoy a quiet pint sat out on the front-of-pub seating. Better to face inwards and admire the building's incongruous exterior (noting the iron hoops to which horses were once tethered). The rural theme is taken up inside with farming ephemera, stuffed animals and historical photographs. Top spot in winter is by one of the fireplaces nursing a pint of the fine and seasonal Winter Warmer. And in summer? Enjoy a barbecue (and the not-so-country air) in the rear beer garden.
Babies and children admitted (garden play area only). Disabled: toilet. Tables outdoors (garden). TV (satellite).

Rose & Crown

55 High Street, SW19 (8947 4713). Wimbledon tube/rail/93 bus. **Open** 11am-11pm Mon-Sat; noon-10.30pm Sun. **Food served** noon-2.30pm, 6-9.30pm Mon-Sat; noon-3pm Sun. **Credit** MC, V.

One of London's oldest surviving pubs, the Rose was established here in 1659, gaining its 'Crown' a century later. It became a literary watering hole, most famously frequented by the poet Swinburne during its time as a Victorian fop-house. Horrified when his custom was remarked upon in the *Pall Mall Gazette*, Swinburne would then sneak in by a side door in desperate stab for anonymity. It's doubtful he'd recognise the place now it's become a Young's hotel: the recent refurbishment has knocked the bar through into the conservatory and pleasant rays of light seep in from the beer garden. To get a feel of the pub of old, grab a seat under the front windows, either facing inwards (admiring the rare 18th-century prints of London) or looking out over the High Street. Settle down to standard lunch specials or the new express business lunch (£5-£14), supplemented with something tasty from the range of fine Young's ales.
Babies and children admitted. Disabled: toilet. Games (fruit machine). No-smoking area. Quiz (7.30pm Sun, £1). Tables outdoors (garden). TV (satellite).

Sultan

78 Norman Road, SW19 (8542 4532). Colliers Wood or South Wimbledon tube/Wimbledon tube/rail. **Open** noon-11pm Mon-Sat; noon-10.30pm Sun. **No credit cards**.

Not named in tribute to the only halfway decent song that Dire Straits ever knocked out but in honour of a champion racehorse from the 1830s. This stately boozer may be hidden on a residential backstreet but that's never stopped the CAMRA folk heaping awards on the place, the sole London outpost of Salisbury brewer Hop Back. Summer Lightning, Thunderstorm, Entire Stout, GFB and a Hop Back beer of the month are on tap, and available to take home. Most cost under two quid and even less during the Wednesday Beer Club (£1.50 a pint 6-9pm). Decor-wise, it's a two-roomed vision in beige (only one is open at night), with aged Turkish carpets, dartboard and trophy case, fires in winter and a little garden that comes into its own in September when the pub holds weekend barbecues and a beer festival. Dylan the Old English sheepdog dozes oblivious through it all, Miggy the cat miaows at anyone who'll listen. Remember: pubs with pets are good pubs indeed.
Disabled: toilet. Games (fruit machine). Quiz (8.30pm Tue; £1). Tables outdoors (patio).

Willie Gunn Restaurant & Wine Bar

422 Garratt Lane, SW18 (8946 7773). Earlsfield rail. **Open/food served** 11am-11pm Mon-Sat; 11am-10.30pm Sun. **Credit** AmEx, MC, V.

Willie Gunn remains Earlsfield's smartest venue for a fashionably oversized glass of wine (or a premium lager if you must). Strangely, the attempt to warm up the decor by replacing duck egg blue with 'misty lilac' has rendered it, if anything, more frigid than before. Carefully chosen pictures and candlelit tables in the front bar and grander rear dining room complete the demure look. The sizeable wine list hedges its bets, starting at £11 for house wine but rising considerably for the vintage stuff. For beer drinkers there's Stella Artois on tap and a few premium bottled lagers. A regularly changing menu offers upmarket takes on old favourites, such as Angus beef burger with fries (£8.50) or there's the provocative selection of unpasteurised cheeses (£5.75), and bar snacks. A restorative full English breakfast is served from 11am until 1pm daily.
Babies and children admitted (high chairs, children's menu on request). TV (big screen, satellite).

Also in the area...

All Bar One 37-9 Wimbledon Hill Road, SW19 (8971 9871).
O'Neill's 66 The Broadway, SW19 (8545 9931).
Pitcher & Piano 4-5 High Street, SW19 (8879 7020).
Po Na Na 82 The Broadway, SW19 (8540 1616).
Slug and Lettuce 21 Worple Road, SW19 (8971 6790).
Wibbas Down Inn (JD Wetherspoon) 6-12 Gladstone Road, SW18 (8540 6788).

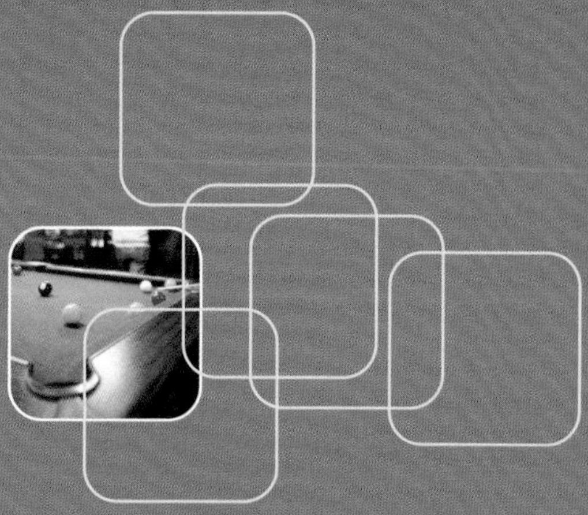

West

Acton

The area's most celebrated pub, the **Grand Junction Arms**, lies at Acton's northernmost tip, on the Grand Union Canal. Most others are found near the junction of Uxbridge Road, the high street and Steyne Road. High Street, in particular, offers a slew of big, newish bars aimed at the under-25 market.

Grand Junction Arms

Acton Lane, NW10 (8965 5670). Harlesden tube. **Open** *Front bar* 11am-11pm Mon-Sat; noon-10.30pm Sun. *Back bar* noon-11pm Mon-Thur; noon-1am Fri; noon-midnight Sat; noon-10.30pm Sun. **Food served** noon-3pm, 6-9pm Mon-Thur; 9pm-12.30am Fri; 9-11.30pm Sat. **Credit** MC,V.

One of four canalside pubs, all with the same name, opened in the early 19th century by the Grand Junction Canal Company (forerunner of the Grand Union Canal) and originally catering specifically for bargees and lock-keepers. These days, customers can still arrive by boat – the pub has its own moorings and waterside terrace. Inside is a spacious public bar offering pool tables and satellite sport. A middle saloon bar caters to less sporty tastes and barside chats have a habit of turning to mooring fees, lock issues and rollicks. There's an excellent range of wines and Young's beers, and a good food menu, including a daily roast. Shouts of 'Ahoy!' to passing barges will probably be met with icy stares.

Babies and children admitted (garden play area). Disabled: toilet. Function room. Games (darts, fruit machine, golf machine, pool table, quiz machine). Music (band or karaoke 9pm Fri). No-smoking tables. Tables outdoors (garden). TV (big screen, satellite).

Also in the area...

Red Lion & Pineapple (JD Wetherspoon) 281 High Street, W3 (8896 2248).

Barnes & Mortlake

For much of its history, Barnes and neighbouring Mortlake were relatively remote villages, set apart from London and linked only by the river and marshy Barnes Common. Even now, Barnes has the air of a self-contained village, with one of its best-known pubs, the **Sun Inn**, facing Barnes Green. The other pubs listed are all either on the river or, in the case of the **Coach & Horses**, a very short distance away.

Bull's Head

373 Londsdale Road, SW13 (8876 5241). Hammersmith tube, then 209 or 283 bus/Barnes or Barnes Bridge rail. **Open** 11am-11pm Mon-Sat; noon-10.30pm Sun. **Food served** noon-2.30pm, 6-10.30pm daily. **Credit** AmEx, MC, V.

Since 1959 the Bull's Head has been renowned as one of London's most respected jazz venues. The pub consists of a main room, with a lot of brick and yellow paintwork and a huge central bar that specialises in malt whiskies (80 of them) and Young's beers. A smaller side room has its own fire and window tables, which would overlook the river across the road if it weren't for a concrete parapet that blocks the view. On our visit the clientele was, as ever, largely middle aged, with just the odd youthful face. It's not the cosiest pub you've ever seen (too much empty space for that) but the benches along the walls are comfortable enough. A recent addition is a self-contained restaurant, Nuay's Thai Bistro, with its entrance round the corner in Barnes High Street.

Babies and children admitted (family area). Function room. Games (board games). Music (jazz 8.30-11pm Mon-Sat; 8-10.30pm Sun; £5-£10). No-smoking tables. Tables outdoors (terrace). TV (big screen, satellite).

Coach & Horses

27 Barnes High Street, SW13 (8876 2695). Hammersmith tube, then 209 or 283 bus/Barnes or Barnes Bridge rail. **Open** *Winter* 11am-3pm Mon-Thur; 11am-11pm Fri, Sat; noon-10.30pm Sun. *Summer* 11am-11pm Mon-Sat; noon-10.30pm Sun. **Food served** *Winter* noon-2.30pm Mon-Fri; noon-4pm Sat, Sun. *Summer* noon-3pm, 6-8.30pm Mon-Sat; noon-4pm Sun. **Credit** MC, V.

A former 19th-century coaching inn, the C&H has managed to retain much of its original layout – you still have to go out the bar and across the old stable block to use the toilets, though these days the stable yard itself serves as a very popular summer garden. The pub's single room is primarily a den for drinkers, with Young's beers on draught and a reasonable wine list available to be ordered from the unusual iron-latticed serving area. Frosted glass keeps the outside world at bay, and the air of tranquillity is enhanced by the absence of a jukebox or piped music.

Babies and children admitted (garden, children's play area). Function room. Tables outdoors (garden). TV.

Ship

10 Thames Bank, SW14 (8876 1439). Mortlake rail. **Open** 11am-11pm Mon-Sat; noon-10.30pm Sun. **Food served** noon-3pm, 6.30-9.30pm daily. **Credit** AmEx, DC, MC, V.

The Ship is a riverside pub, a short stagger from the Budweiser brewery whose yeasty fragrance pervades the air seven days a week. It's a sprawling place with several linked seating areas including a conservatory and a huge outside terrace for those who wish to sit by the bleak stretch of river that acts as the finishing line for the annual Varsity boat race. For decoration, the owners have made a vague stab at Victoriana, in the form of striped wallpaper and brownish walls, but the place has yet to acquire a strong identity other than as a once-a-year destination for rowing enthusiasts and associated pissheads. Busy and cheerful, with dogs much in evidence and two ales – Directors and London Pride – on tap.

Babies and children admitted (until 8pm). Function room. Games (bar billiards, board games, fruit machines, quiz machine). Tables outdoors (garden). TV (satellite).

Sun Inn

7 Church Road, SW13 (8876 5256). Hammersmith tube, then 209 or 283 bus/Barnes or Barnes Bridge rail. **Open** noon-11pm Mon-Sat; noon-10.30pm Sun. **Food served** noon-9.30pm daily. **Credit** MC, V.

Dating from 1750, this classic Barnes pub was until recently the haunt of the more mature drinker and Sunday luncher. It's now remodelled itself as a venue for the moneyed young (a giveaway is that the telly only comes on when there's a rugby match to whinny over). It remains a deep, dark, rambling place but with a modernist veneer such as blood red walls, stripped floors, a huge free-standing carved elephant and butcher's blocks as tables. We found the place sparsely populated; whether the current incarnation will still exist in a year's time is anyone's guess. But we were impressed by the fine range of beers: Hoegaarden, Leffe, Adnams Broadside and a rarity, Jeffrey Hudson Bitter, were all on tap. The fine seating area at the front, with its timeless view of the village green and pond, remains happily unchanged.

Babies and children admitted (until 7pm). Games (table football, video game). No-smoking tables. Tables outdoors (terrace). TV (rugby only).

Duke of York. See p235.

Ye White Hart

The Terrace, Riverside, SW19 (8876 5177). Barnes Bridge rail/209 bus. **Open** 11am-11pm Mon-Sat; noon-10.30pm Sun. **Food served** 11am-2.30pm daily; 11am-2.30pm, 6.45-9.30pm Tue-Sat. **Credit** AmEx, MC, V.
One of the best of the many west London riverside watering holes, the, sorry, Ye White Hart is a big, raucous Victorian pub, occupying a palatial four-storey building. Inside you'll find a vast single room with central bar, and countless nooks and crannies around the circumference. Lavish decoration comes in the form of chintzy curtains, bubble glass, mirrors and brass – not to mention the large skiff suspended from the ceiling – but the place is so big that none of this seems at all over bearing. There's the full range of Young's beers on draught. Outside is a large terrace overlooking the river, which includes a charming pagoda with seating for two. If you fancy Sunday lunch, best come early.
Function room. Games (fruit machine). Tables outdoors (balcony, riverside terrace). TV (big screen, satellite).

Chiswick & Kew

Filling a thick peninsula formed by a dramatic loop of the Thames, until the 1850s Chiswick consisted of a series of riverside hamlets, one of which, Strand-on-the-Green, is now the site of west London's best riverside pubs. Cross at Kew Bridge and you'll find yourself in Kew Green, site of one of London's best-preserved coaching inns, the **Coach & Horses**.

Bell & Crown

11-13 Thames Road, Strand-on-the-Green, W4 (8994 4164). Gunnersbury tube/rail. **Open/food served** 11am-11pm Mon-Sat; noon-10.30pm Sun. **Credit** AmEx, DC, MC, V.
A first-rate riverside pub with a colourful history to boot: it was used by Oliver Cromwell to flee his Royalist pursuers (he is said to have taken a tunnel running from the cellar to Oliver's Island in midstream) and also by 18th-century smugglers to stash their booty. Today, the exceptionally deep bar ends in a conservatory overlooking the river, from which you can step out and down to a little south-facing garden, with hanging flower baskets and wrought-iron tables and chairs. Beyond that again is the Thames towpath. Beers come courtesy of Chiswick's own Fuller's brewery. The place is deservedly popular – on our visit, the clientele ranged from office crowds to singletons enjoying a pint and a book.
Babies and children admitted (until 7pm). Dress: smart. Function room. No-smoking tables. Tables outdoors (heated riverside patio).

City Barge

27 Strand-on-the-Green, W4 (8994 2148). Gunnersbury tube/rail/Kew Bridge rail. **Open** 11am-11pm Mon-Sat; noon-10.30pm Sun. **Food served** noon-9.30pm daily. **Credit** AmEx, DC, MC, V.
Despite the modern-looking exterior, the river-facing City Barge positively brims with history. Dating from 1484, when it was known as the Navigator's Arms, it acquired its present name in 1788 in homage to the Lord Mayor of London's state barge *Marie Celeste*, which was moored nearby. Much of the pub was destroyed during a World War II air raid, then carefully rebuilt; the Beatles shot a scene for the film *Help!* here in 1965. These days, the place falls into two distinct halves: the modern, woody ground-floor bar, and the more secluded subterranean basement, which protects itself from frequent inundations with a watertight flood door. Food is limited but attractive (Thai chicken curry and warm salmon salad).
Babies and children admitted (until 9.30pm). Games (darts). Music (live jazz 8.30-11pm Thur). No-smoking tables. Tables outdoors (riverside terrace).

Coach & Horses

8 Kew Green, Surrey (8940 1208). Kew Gardens tube/rail. **Open** 11am-11pm Mon-Sat; noon-10.30pm Sun. **Food served** noon-2.30pm, 7-9.30pm Mon-Sat; noon-3.30pm, 7-9pm Sun. **Credit** AmEx, MC, V.

A sympathetic refit has improved the already excellent Coach & Horses in the form of lemon shading, solid panelling and tasteful Victorian prints. One of the few former coaching inns in the metropolis still offering board and lodging, the owners have recently beefed up the accommodation, making the place a pub-cum-hotel rather than the pub-with-a-couple-of-rooms that it was for many years. Fresh fish (obviously not from the Thames, then) has long been a feature of the menu and there's a full selection of Young's beers with which to wash it all down. The extensive outdoor seating area offers a lovely view of Kew Green – but also of the rather less lovely South Circular Road that lies between.

Babies and children admitted (food area). Disabled: toilet. Function room. Games (board games, fruit machines, quiz machine). No-smoking tables. Tables outdoors (patio, garden). TV (satellite).

Duke of York

107 Devonshire Road, W4 (8994 2118). Turnham Green tube. **Open** 11am-11pm Mon-Sat; noon-10.30pm Sun. **Food served** noon-3pm Mon-Sat; noon-6pm Sun. **No credit cards**.

The Duke's a basic two-bar boozer within easy jogging distance of the Hogarth Roundabout. Built around 75 years ago, it leerily occupies a backstreet corner. Inside the public bar are bare boards, eye-catching stained glass and dark wood screens, unchanged since Adolf and Neville's day, with contrasting red carpet adding to the rich old feel. In a small games room down one end, locals argue over pool and chuck darts. Aside from the beer (ambrosial London Pride, only £2.15 a pint), it's worth visiting for unfussy lunchtime food (liver and bacon, £4.50) and a photograph in the gents of two men shaking hands through their flies.

Babies and children admitted (dining area). Function room. Games (darts, pool table). Tables outdoors (garden). TV (big screen, satellite).

George & Devonshire

8 Burlington Lane, W4 (8994 1859). Turnham Green tube. **Open** 11am-11pm Mon-Sat; noon-10.30pm Sun. **Food served** noon-8pm daily. **Credit** AmEx, MC, V.

Just yards from the ferociously busy Hogarth roundabout, where traffic fumes mingle with the thick, sweet-and-sour fragrance of the nearby Fuller's brewery, the George & Devonshire offers two large, separate drinking areas. The public bar is traditional, functional and – on our visit – 100% male, with a pool table dominating the room and further entertainment provided by an ageing but boisterous Jack Russell. The saloon bar, reached by a separate door, is much bigger, carpeted and altogether more salubrious, resembling the lobby of a small country hotel. Fuller's beers dominate and many of the customers are off-duty brewery workers.

Function room. Games (darts, fruit machines, pool table). Jukebox. Tables outdoors (patio, pavement). TV (big screen, satellite).

Mawson Arms

110 Chiswick Lane South, W4 (8994 2936). Turnham Green tube. **Open** 11am-8pm Mon-Fri. **Food served** noon-3pm Mon-Fri. **Credit** AmEx, MC, V.

Together with its neighbour, the **George & Devonshire** (*see above*), this is one of the two house pubs of the Fuller's brewery. The Mawson takes its name from the family that took it over in 1685 and the place passed through several hands before the Fuller clan arrived on the scene in the 1820s. Tours of the brewery start in the bar and, not surprisingly, there's a huge range of Fuller's products on sale. The pub consists of a single dog-leg bar in relaxed, minimalist decor – wood floor, cream walls. Fine if you're prepared to create your own atmosphere. Note the unusual opening hours – though, with the official brewery shop situated just next door, there's always the option of taking some merchandise home with you for a more prolonged sample.

Babies and children admitted. Function room. TV.

Old Pack Horse

434 Chiswick High Road, W4 (8994 2872). Chiswick Park tube. **Open/food served** 11am-11pm Mon-Sat; noon-10.30pm Sun. **Credit** MC, V.

A large red-brick pub on the busy corner of Acton Lane and Chiswick High Road, the Old Pack Horse boasts a main bar that's all dark wood, leaded glass and log fires. The Thai restaurant area (all dishes are under a fiver) at the rear is more modern, chillier-looking and rather unimaginatively furnished. The modest selection of wines, available by the glass or bottle, has been specifically chosen to complement Thai food. But the place does well as a drinker's pub too. A Fuller's establishment, it has most of the usual suspects on tap – plus extras, such as Adnams Bitter and Hoegaarden. Try to grab the tiny alcove with its own fire, at the very end of the main bar on the left –by far the best seats in the house.

Babies and children admitted. Function room. Games (quiz machine). Tables outdoors (pavement, garden).

Pilot

56 Wellesley Road, W4 (8994 0828). Gunnersbury tube/rail. **Open** noon-11pm Mon-Sat; noon-10.30pm Sun. **Food served** 12.30-4pm, 6.30-10pm Mon-Sat; 12.30-4pm, 6.30-9.30pm Sun. **Credit** AmEx, MC, V.

A newcomer to the constantly expanding west London gastropub scene, the Pilot is already a firm local favourite judging by the phalanx of young office staff we found ensconced there on a weekday evening visit. Most were drinking rather than eating – the emphasis is on wine (bottles range from £13 to £39) and draught lagers. The menu, though modest in length, changes twice a day, and includes intriguing international fare such as Chinese duck and smoked haddock with crème fraîche and pecorino. Given all that, you'd expect the decor to be bare wood with plain cream walls interspersed with arty photographic prints – and you'd be right. The young staff are notably smart, efficient and approachable. Music is strictly of the foreground variety, so unless you're a talented lip reader this is not the place for a cosy head-to-head.

Babies and children admitted (noon-4pm daily). Disabled: toilet. Function room. Tables outdoors (garden).

Ealing

Several of the area's oldest, most attractive pubs can be found in the vicinity of St Mary's Road, where the original Ealing village developed. However, recent arrivals such as **Baroque** have been concentrated along the area's hitherto unglamorous east-west thoroughfare, Uxbridge Road.

Baroque

94 Uxbridge Road, W13 (8567 7346). West Ealing rail. **Open** noon-11pm Mon-Sat; noon-10.30pm Sun. **Food served** noon-3pm, 6-10pm daily. **Happy hour** 5-7pm Mon-Fri. **Credit** AmEx, MC, V.

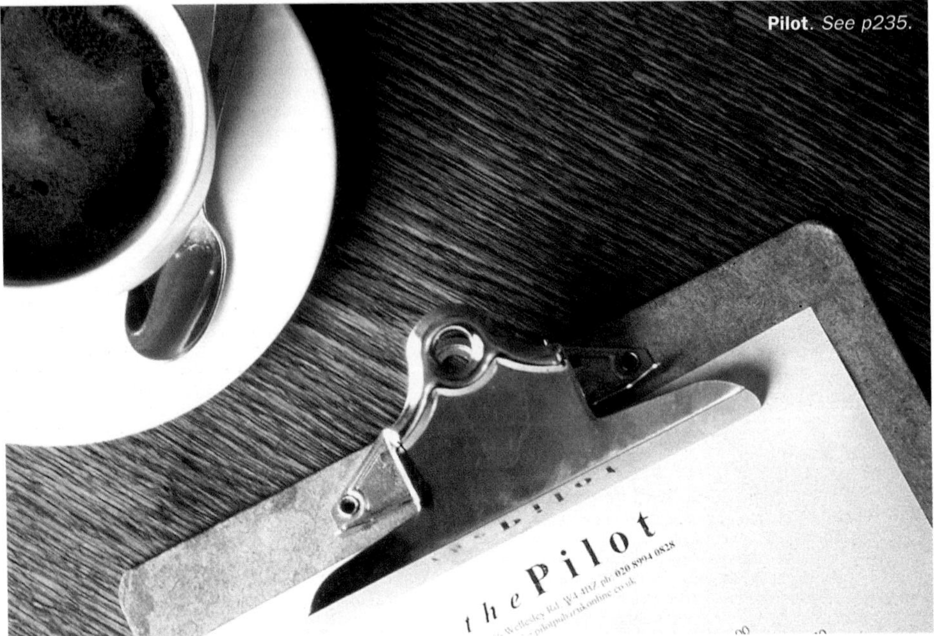

Pilot. *See p235.*

The OED defines baroque as 'certain stylistic tendencies in 17th- and 18th-century arts, characterised by exuberance and extravagance' – none of which seems applicable to this bar's candy-coloured furniture, walls in varying shades of mauve and tasteful black and white photographs of power stations and Manhattan skyscrapers. Baroque stakes its reputation on its cocktails, champagne and otherwise (prices around £6 a pop); we were also impressed by the non-alcoholic varieties (all £2.50), such as La Brisa Nida (orange juice shaken with coconut and cream). The chill cabinet features VB, the beer that's as bog-standard as Foster's in its native Oz but considered a bit of a novelty over here. Staff are pleasingly informal while remaining quietly efficient. From April the smart terrace garden comes into play.
Dress: smart. Function room. Games (board games). Music (DJ 1st Sat of mth 7-11pm; free) Tables outdoors (garden).

Drayton Court

2 The Avenue, W13 (8997 1019). West Ealing rail. **Open** 11am-11pm Mon-Sat; noon-10.30pm Sun. **Food served** noon-10pm Mon-Sat; noon-9pm Sun. **Credit** MC, V.
A popular, grey-brick Victorian pub (complete with turrets), just north of Ealing Broadway, the Drayton's main claim to fame is a basement theatre that on our visit was presenting Chekhov. Less cerebral pleasures come in the form of Fuller's beers (plus Hoegaarden and Caffrey's on tap), a pool room and table football. The decor might benefit from some attention – it currently features yellow walls, dubious woodcuts and a reproduction of the Bayeux Tapestry – but we do like the small balcony, with metal flooring and tables, that overlooks the pub's wonderful landscaped garden.
Babies and children admitted (until 9pm). Disabled: toilet. Function room. Games (board games, darts, fruit machine, pool table, quiz machine). Music (jazz 8pm Wed). Tables outdoors (garden). TV (big screen, satellite).

Ealing Park Tavern

222 South Ealing Road, W5 (8758 1879). South Ealing tube. **Open** 11am-11pm Mon-Sat; noon-10.30pm Sun. **Food served** noon-3pm, 6-10.30pm Mon-Sat; noon-4pm, 6-9pm Sun. **Credit** AmEx, MC, V.
A bulging mock-Tudor pub on the corner of Ealing Road and Carlyle Road, the EPT comes with fashionably muted look of dark wood and plain white walls relieved by large, abstract paintings. Distant ceilings and mirrors expand the available space. Though a member of the Courage chain, the long bar also serves draught Brakspear, Old Speckled Hen and Adnams Broadside, in addition to a good wine list. Upmarket bar snacks of goat's cheese and cold meats are speciality. The clientele is diverse and on our visit, most of them had gravitated to the main restaurant, divided from the bar by an arch; it serves substantial dishes such as Roquefort and red pepper tart or slow-roast pork. An excellent all-rounder.
Babies and children admitted. Games (board games). Tables outdoors (garden).

Grange Tavern

Warwick Road, W5 (8567 7617). Ealing Broadway tube/rail/Ealing Common tube. **Open** 11am-11pm Mon-Sat; noon-10.30pm Sun. **Food served** noon-2.30pm, 6-10pm Mon-Sat; noon-9.30pm Sun. **Credit** AmEx, MC, V.
A big, popular local overlooking a corner of Ealing Common, the Grange has two main bar areas. The one facing as you enter, with bottles of claret neatly arranged behind the counter, is for wine only. On our visit there were about 25 varieties on offer, including champagne, but from a wide range of countries including New World hotspots such as Chile and Argentina. Decoration is funereal, with Victorian-style wallpaper and an imposing stone fireplace, the effect of which is ruined by the ugly virtual-football machine installed a few inches away. The main bar is brighter, with a standard range of beers, and windows overlooking the pub garden.

Babies and children admitted (family area). Function room. Games (arcade machines, board games, darts, fruit machines, giant Jenga, pool table, table football). Tables outdoors (garden).

Parade

18-19 The Mall, W5 (8810 0202). Ealing Broadway tube/ rail/Ealing Common tube. **Open** 12.30-2.30pm, 6-11pm Mon-Sat; 12.30-3pm Sun. **Food served** 12.30-3pm, 7-10pm Mon-Sat; 12.30-3pm Sun. **Happy hour** 6-8pm Mon-Thur. **Credit** AmEx, MC, V.

It can be rather intimidating to visit a bar where the staff meet you at the door, show you to a seat and go away to fetch your drinks; fortunately, at Parade they turn out to be as amiable as they are efficient. The place comes with the bright lighting and modern art obligatory to the modern urban bar, though we wonder if there might be an element of self-parody in the picture of a goldfish in a bowl. The place specialises in pre-dinner cocktails – about 20 of them to choose from at around £5.50 each. On our Saturday night visit, most of the middle-class clientele – many of them families – were moving on to the restaurant area at the back. But if you're not planning on eating, the extraordinarily fat, round little leather seats in the bar area turn out to be very comfortable indeed.

Babies and children admitted. Disabled: toilet. Function room. TV (children's TV room Sun).

Red Lion

13 St Mary's Road, W5 (8567 2541). South Ealing tube. **Open** 11am-11pm Mon-Sat; noon-10.30pm Sun. **Food served** noon-2.30pm, 7-9.30pm Mon-Sat; noon-5pm Sun. **Credit** AmEx, MC, V.

A recent refurbishment, which had inspired some trepidation in the regulars, seems to have left this Ealing institution more or less unscathed. The dark wood, thick upholstery and brass fittings of the main bar area remain; as you walk through you'll find a modestly proportioned conservatory area with a garden behind. The Red Lion's alternative name is Stage 6, in homage to the actors and film crews who called in for a snifter after a day's work on stages 1 to 5 of nearby Ealing Studios. Inevitably, stars of the big and small screen – ranging from Jack Hawkins to Basil Brush – adorn the walls. There were plenty of customers during our Saturday afternoon visit, but the atmosphere was hushed, and although piped music has now been introduced, the volume was kept pleasantly low.

Disabled: toilet. Tables outdoors (garden).

Fulham & Parsons Green

Our Fulham boundary stretches far and wide, taking in everything from the riverside to the busy lower stretches of the King's and Fulham Roads. Pastoral pleasures are to be found by Parsons Green – the **White Horse** is one of London's finest boozers – but generally this is a lively playground for SW6's young carousers and football supporters along to watch Fulham and Chelsea at the nearby grounds.

Atlas

16 Seagrave Road, SW6 (7385 9129). West Brompton tube. **Open** noon-11pm Mon-Sat; noon-10.30pm Sun. **Food served** 12.30-3pm, 7-10.30pm Mon-Sat; noon-3pm, 7-10pm Sun. **Credit** DC, MC, V.

Although the praise-worthy food is a big draw (choose from a regularly changing Mediterranean menu scratched up on a blackboard, mains £7.50-£11.50), the Atlas works equally well as a decent down-to-earth boozer. In contrast to the modish cuisine, the look of the place is strictly and attractively trad (scuffed wood floor, brick-surround open fires, darkwood panelling). Real ales are limited to Brakspear, but there's a long and good wine list, with a fair choice by the glass, priced £2.50-£4.90. Noise levels were high on our last visit, but then it was early evening Saturday and Chelsea had just won at home. With no designated eating section, diners compete for table space with drinkers; less of a problem in summer when a beer garden soaks up the overflow.

Babies and children admitted (until 7pm). Function room. Tables outdoors (heated courtyard). TV.

Black Bull

358 Fulham Road, SW10 (7376 7370). Fulham Broadway or Earls Court tube. **Open** noon-11pm Mon-Fri; noon-11pm Sat; noon-10.30pm Sun. **Happy hour** noon-9pm Mon-Thur, Sun; noon-8pm Fri, Sat. **Credit** MC, V.

The exterior suggests nothing more than a bog-standard Queen Vic-era public house with little hint of the £250,000 spent inside to create one of the sexiest boozers in town. The result: an ultra-chic lounge bar with a blood red ceiling and matching drapes, flock wallpaper and fake fireplace, candles, candles, candles, tom-tom stools and sumptuous arse-swallowing sofas – how much must management make from harvesting the loose change that slips between the crevices of those cushions? A respectable roster of DJs (Wed-Sun) adds glam and good time sounds. The dull drinks may be the least appealing part of the package – although the cocktails are at least cheap (£4.50). The lack of a late licence is a downer, but for weeknight slouching or as a weekend pre-club venue (or even, fingers cross, a venue in its own right should we get the promised licencing review), then it's a Bull's-eye.

Function room. Games (cards, Jenga). Music (DJs funky house 8pm Thur-Sat; open decks noon Sun; free). Tables outdoors (pavement).

The Bridge

451 Fulham Road, SW8 (7352 8636). Fulham Broadway tube. **Open/food served** noon-11pm Mon-Wed; noon-midnight Thur-Sat; noon-10.30pm Sun. **Happy hour** 5.30-7.30pm daily. **Credit** AmEx, DC, MC, V.

Edging towards the Sloane Square end of the area, the brash and busy Bridge has an air of naughtiness. Behind the matt-black frontage Chelsea boys in best shirts and Chelsea blondes in glitter halter tops strive to suggest shaggability with casually artful poses and self-consciously sensually hip-swaying to whatever the DJ is offerings (chart, house and funk over the weekend). Industrial metal piping, a long metal bar, low tables and beanbags are the props, with a chandelier made of glass tea cups and art on the walls as last ditch conversation starters – the art's for sale but mention Hockney here and they'll probably think you're talking about an East End Hooch. Drinks prices are provocatively low (two-for-one cocktails on Thursdays) while mini-vibrators excite the easily excitable when their pizza orders are ready. Upstairs is quieter with more formal seating and a great corner window overlooking the Fulham Road.

Disabled: toilet. Function room. Music (DJs 8.30pm Fri-Sat; free). Tables outdoors (garden). TV (big screen, satellite).

Crabtree Tavern

Rainville Road, SW6 (7385 3929). Hammersmith tube. **Open** noon-11pm Mon-Sat; noon-10.30pm Sun. **Food served** noon-9pm daily. **Credit** MC, V.

Once a bawdy boozer of the old school, the Crabtree has paid heed to prevailing trends and converted itself into the full terracotta walled, dark green windowed, bookcased and

West

squeaky chaired den for the middle classes as beloved by gastropub owners all over London. It also makes full use of its riverside location, with a plum courtyard by the Thames that comes into its own during the summer, when a wrought-iron Victorian awning provides cover for barbecues and alfresco diners alike. The long bar inside pulls a pint of Fuller's or guest ale, though most punters are more interested in the extensive wine list and international menu. A large oil painting by the bar is a pointer of how things used to be, but those days are long gone and judging by the contended looks on the faces of the regular clientele, they're not being mourned.
Disabled toilet. Games (fruit machines). Quiz (8pm Tue; free). Tables outdoors (beer garden). TV.

Duke of Cumberland

235 New Kings Road, SW6 (7736 2777). Parsons Green tube. **Open** 11am-11.30pm Mon-Sat; noon-11am Sun. **Food served** noon-2.30pm Mon-Sat; 1pm-3.30pm Sun. **Credit** AmEx, MC, V.

Across the green from the **White Horse** (*see p240*), this dark and imposing green-tiled Victorian boozer was built in 1894 on the site of a 17th-century tavern and is named after a cretinous murderer. The eponymous Duke (1771-1851) was a busy chap, guilty of murder, incest, adultery and indecent assault – a plaque above the door tells his sordid tale. Regulars don't seem that put off by the association. The only thing this lot could murder is a pint. A local breed, Fulham born and bred, they scatter themselves about a scuffed wooden-floored front bar that is large enough to happily accommodate sofas, table football, TVs and chairs without feeling cramped. The treacle-lacquered bar churns out Young's ales. The rear bar is warmed by a red carpet, wood panelling, a hearth and kitchen serving standard pub grub.
Babies and children admitted (before 8pm). Disabled toilet. Function room. Games (fruit machines, table football). Tables outdoors (pavement). TV (big screen, satellite).

The Durell

704 Fulham Road, SW6 (7736 3014). Parsons Green or Putney Bridge tube. **Open** noon-11pm Mon-Thur; noon-midnight Fri; 11am-midnight Sat; 11am-10.30pm Sun. **Food served** noon-10pm Mon-Thur; noon-10.30pm Fri, Sat; 11am-9pm Sun. **Credit** AmEx, DC, MC, V.

This is the pub as modern bachelor pad: spacious and uncluttered, brightened by stylish ocean blue throughout, leather sofas, big TV, a couple of pool tables with plenty of elbow room, arcade games, table football and pizzas freshly oven-baked to order. Not forgetting the large bar with its attention grabbing offers of cut-price shooters – Brain Haemorrhage! £2.50!! – and cheapo cheapo cocktails at £3.75 (although of course, if this was the ideal bachelor pad, the drinks would all be free and administered by Winona Ryder). Unsurprisingly, the place is usually thronged with young male professionals becoming progressively more shouty as the night wears on and Britney's chased by Christina chased by the Ketchup Girls, chased by tATu, and damn, where's the bed? You mean we can't actually crash here?
Babies and children admitted (until 7pm). Disabled: toilet. Games (fruit machine, pool table, quiz machine, table football). Music (DJs 8pm Fri; free). Tables outdoors (patio). TV (big screen, satellite).

Eclipse Lounge

108-110 New King's Road, SW6 (7731 2142/ www.bareclipse.com). Parsons Green tube. **Open/ food served** 5-11pm Tue-Sat. **Credit** AmEx, MC, V.

At the wrong end of New King's Road (though you could well argue that there isn't a right end), Eclipse boasts that 'the price you pay for the life you choose' in a notice that greets all visitors. Very Fulham, but also particularly apt in this case, because Eclipse was recently forced to slash prices – a cunning ploy that's brought powerful cocktails, long and short, down to £3.50 a pop and enticed a batch of Fulham's standard-issue leggy blondes and slack-tied trend-setters into its worn leather sofas. Red drapes mask sedate drinkers from the outside world as they move amid the flicker of candles and Japanese art and staff conjure up fruity drinks behind the marble bar. At these prices, the mandatory 'optional' 12.5% surcharge, though annoying, seems almost insignificant.
Bar available for hire. Tables outdoors (pavement).

Eight Bells

89 Fulham High Street, SW6 (7736 6307). Putney Bridge tube. **Open** 11am-11pm Mon-Sat; noon-10.30pm Sun. **Food served** 11am-10.30pm daily. **Credit** MC, V.

It's a lovely old boozer, the Eight Bells, though it often gets mistaken for just another commuters' pub, stuck as it is between the tube and bus station. Faded, warm and cosy, it dates back to 1690 and has made few concessions to modern Fulham. 'It's cleaner,' claims the new landlady, but deep down, this is a pub you're lucky to find and unwilling to leave. Putney Bridge locals remain true, enjoying Young's and Fuller's ales amid the film posters and assorted curios (a sombrero collection) and local historical prints. To the left of the small, horseshoe bar, a grandfather clock sits shoulder to shoulder with a fruit machine. To the right, beyond the open fire, stuffed fish and wooden benches, the kitchen belts out typical tucker to the dozing clientele.
Babies and children admitted (until 3pm). Games (fruit machine). Music (jazz 7-10.30pm Sun; free). Tables outdoors (pavement). TV (satellite).

Fiesta Havana

490 Fulham Road, SW6 (7381 5005). Fulham Broadway tube. **Open/food served** 5pm-2am Mon-Sat; 5pm-1am Sun. **Admission** £3 after 10.30pm Mon-Wed; £5 after 10.30pm Thur; £5 after 9pm; £8 after 11pm Fri-Sat; £3 after 10pm Sun. **Happy hour** 5pm-7.30pm Mon-Fri, Sun. **Credit** AmEx, DC, MC, V.

A leading light on the Castro-pub scene, Havana's beautiful brown-tiled exterior is the packaging for seven nights a week of heavy duty hip swivelling. On any given evening dozens of sweaty bodies get up close and personal on (and off) the dance floor. Professionalism is not a requisite – although being extrovert is a help – and amateurs are more than welcome (regular dance classes offer the chance to brush up on moves). Animal-print couches provide for diners; most folk opt for giant tapas platters to share. Drinks are mid-priced Latino cocktails like Mojitos and Caipinrinho (£5.25 each). For those whose who want something fat and Cuban in their mouths, there's a serious cigar list that starts at a Don Ramos No 3 (£5.20) and ends at the Romeo y Julieta No 1 (£9).
Disabled: toilets. Dress: smart casual. Music (DJs nightly; samba classes 7.30pm Mon; salsa classes 7.30pm Tue-Thur; £6 Tue; Latin bands 9pm occasional Thur, Fri). TV.

Fox & Pheasant

1 Billing Road, SW10 (7352 2943). Fulham Broadway tube. **Open** 11am-11pm Mon-Sat; noon-10.30pm Sun. **Food served** noon-2.30pm Mon-Fri. **Credit** MC, V.

Stained glass and hanging tankards aren't unusual in tucked-away boozers, nor is the gentle whiff of real fire and real dog, but this cosy pub deserves recognition for its character. The pub dog, Nelson, can even open doors with his paws! An unlikely find tucked away down the barricaded private Billing Road, this ale-mine is a poorly aimed goal-kick away from Stamford Bridge. This timeless boozer is home to the

West

more senior Chelsea fans – the kind who shudder when they recall Mickey Droy – supping Greene King IPA and Abbot Ale. Tar-yellowed walls, treacle-brown glossed woodwork and hunting pictures span both little bars. The lack of music is a joy, allowing gentle conversation punctuated only by the thwack of arrows in the dartboard and the odd yelp from Nelson – the two noises are only rarely connected.
Games (darts). Tables outdoors (heated garden, pavement). TV (satellite).

Harwood Arms

Walham Grove, SW6 (7386 1847). Fulham Broadway tube. **Open** 11am-11pm Mon-Sat; noon-10.30pm Sun. **Food served** noon-2.45pm, 7-9.45pm Mon-Sat; noon-4pm, 7-9.30pm Sun. **Credit** MC, V.
Colonial outpost meets Fulham gastro. This spacious light yellow pub will have you reaching for a G&T – a picture of a Panama hat, scattered bookshelves and an ancient typewriter complete the Graham Greene look. Smart suits chew cigars and discuss property while quaffing London Pride and Hoegaarden; other cash-flush customers sprawl across the fireside sofas stretching legs and lunch hours to the max. Former England spinner Phil Tufnell drinks here, and a local recording studio feeds the pub a constant diet of popstars: Stereophonics and Dido, to name a couple. A small TV plays mute sport, while the dining area to the rear is marked by images of a knife and fork and a framed poor review. The Harwood fish cakes (£5.95 to £8.50) were fantastic and the olives (£2.45) fresh, fat and tasty.
Babies and children admitted (until 7.30pm). Games (board games). TV (satellite).

Ifield

59 Ifield Road, SW10 (7351 4900). Earl's Court, Fulham Broadway or West Brompton tube. **Open/food served** 5-11pm Mon-Thur; noon-11pm Fri, Sat; noon-10pm Sun. **Credit** AmEx, MC, V.
Flanking the cemetery that sits in the shadows of Chelsea FC's imposing East Stand, the Ifield is a vibrant spot on a sleepy road that serves as little more than a cut through to the Earl's Court exhibition centre. A massive and decidedly unsubtle turquoise sign bellows its presence from its corner premises, attracting all to its brash and bawdy interior of pop art and vivid blue seating. Madonna, once of these parts, has been known to be tempted as have that dashing pair of princes William and Harry. Drinks can be selected from the global wine list or pulled from the pump marked Adnams Broadside, depending upon taste. Round the back of the pub you will find a restaurant that is run by owner and TV chef Ed Baines. His Modern British menu goes at anything between £8.75 and £13.95 for main courses.
Babies and children admitted (daytime only). Function room. TV.

Lunasa

575 King's Road, SW6 (7371 7664). Parsons Green tube. **Open** 11am-11pm daily. **Food served** noon-4pm, 6-9pm daily. **Credit** AmEx, DC, MC, V.
Lunasa's not your average pub. It's a place out to impress and, we have to say, it succeeds. It's a star-flocked haven of chic, chicks and class, a place where informality means casually strewn fur coats. Front of house is dominated by a stylish, woody bar and parlour palms, while the back is occupied by a big-screen TV, small dance floor, DJ decks, comfortable chairs and low tables. Upstairs is a spacious function room adorned with a large nude on canvas who looks plain ugly compared to the ravishingly perfect customers. Jay Kay and Kylie have been spotted here, as have WestLife (best not to ask about the champagne bucket incident). Should you find yourself sharing air with a genuine celeb, the bar sells disposable cameras. Gorgeous as a spot for a quiet drink, come the end of the week the whole place can get pretty manic. Armchair and newspaper or party with the beautiful people, either way Lunasa has it nailed.
Disabled: toilet. Function room. Music (DJs 9pm Thur-Sat; free). Restaurant. Tables outdoors (pavement). TVs (big screen, satellite).

La Perla

803 Fulham Road, SW6 (7471 4895). Parsons Green tube. **Open** 5-11pm Mon-Fri; noon-11pm Sat; noon-10.30pm Sun. **Food served** 5-10.15pm Mon-Fri; noon-10.30pm Sat; noon-9.45pm Sun. **Happy hour** 5-7pm daily. **Credit** AmEx, MC, V.
Le Perla's a very friendly place. Friendly like a randy chihuaua with designs on your leg. This joint is like Jack Nicholson's idea of a singles bar. Must be something to do with all the margaritas downed by the patrons of this Mexican/surf-styled gaff. Or perhaps fellow drinkers are hoping somebody will succumb to temptation and buy them a £100 shot of Cuevo 1800 Coleccion Tequila, which comes with the promise of having the big spender's name added to a list on a plaque behind the wall. Corona is a more affordable £2.85 and at happy hour you can get two for the one to share with your new friends. Food is of the Mexican tapas variety. Cheesy latin and soulful jazz play in the background, never loud enough to interrupt your conversation with the stranger on the next bar stool. Like we said, it's friendly.
Babies and children admitted (restaurant only).

Po Na Na Fez

222 Fulham Road, SW10 (7352 5978). Fulham Broadway tube. **Open** 9.30pm-2am Mon-Sat. **Credit** AmEx, DC, MC, V.
This late-night basement grotto of a club has taken the Fez theme to bizarre levels – a leopard skin cigarette machine seems too camp for Cubs to us. But at least the scattered jewels and mosaic mirrors are thoughtfully placed to warn taller punters about the low ceilings. Cavelike, and riddled with private alcoves, this corporate club with a sparkle of originality attracts a mix of young revellers, post-pub stragglers, fat-walleted blokes on the pull and the odd celeb – Lawrence Dallaglio and Jay Kay (again!) have been sighted. Chunky cocktails, Grolsch and bottles of champagne at £45 are speedily served from the busy bar, and the mood progresses throughout the night from relaxed pool playing, to steamy dancing. The music is varied, but always loud.
Games (board games). Music (DJs 11pm nightly; £4 after 11pm Mon-Wed; £5 Thur; £6 Fri; £7 Sat).

Salisbury Tavern

21 Sherbrooke Road, SW6 (7381 4005). Fulham Broadway tube. **Open** 11.30am-11pm Mon-Sat; noon-10.30pm Sun. **Food served** noon-2.30pm, 7-11pm Mon-Sat; noon-3.30pm, 7-10.30pm Sun. **Credit** AmEx, MC, V.
Bright pink backlighting shines behind the bar and images of sports stars stare down from every wall (Botham grabbing a bunny girl is a particular highlight). The attached restaurant (international cuisine from £8 to £15) is also Liberace-led pink, but those put off by such bold colours will be soothed by the cream scheme in the main bar. Fulham idlers, advertising scruffs and sporting toughs lounge in high-backed benches, ogling built-in TVs. Drinks are a choice of three changing real ales, San Miguel and Hoegaarden. Mobile phones are asked to stay on vibrate, a policy that doesn't seem to deter the punters. Perhaps other places could give it a try.
Babies and children admitted (until 7pm). Disabled: toilet. Games (board games). TV (big screen, satellite).

White Horse

1-3 Parsons Green, SW6 (7736 2115). Parsons Green tube. **Open** 11am-11pm Mon-Sat; 11am-10.30pm Sun. **Food served** noon-3pm, 6-10pm Mon-Fri; 11am-10pm Sat, Sun. **Credit** AmEx, MC, V.

Smug on the cusp of Parson Green the White Horse is the boozer of choice for the posh young locals that have earned it the nickname the Sloaney Pony. It's a grand place, with hand-painted tiles of Shakespeare's Doll & Pistol at the entrance and a big statue of a white horse up on the roof. The original saloon bar stained glass was taken by a departing landlord in 1979. Drink and food are treated lovingly here, both served by slow, capable staff. Ale is a speciality with plenty on tap (Bass, Gales and Harveys and regular guests) and a festival that sees the sprawling front garden extend out on to the green itself, as the whole area becomes awash with merry drinkers. There are also plenty of continental brews and a handsome 120-strong wine list. It's a pleasure to see beer taken so seriously. The interior bar is dark wood, broad and sweeping; a horseshoe that's right arm leads to the newly installed conservatory/restaurant out back. Food is Modern European (salmon fish cakes; tarragon everywhere) and good.

Babies and children admitted. Function room. No-smoking area (restaurant). Tables outdoors (garden).

Also in the area...

All Bar One 587-591 Fulham Road, SW6 (7471 0611).
Fine Line 236 Fulham Road, SW10 (7376 5827).
Fulham Tup 268 Fulham Road, SW10 (7352 1859).
Legless Tup 1 Harwood Terrace, SW6 (7610 6131).
Pitcher & Piano 871-3 Fulham Road, SW6 (7736 3910).
Slug & Lettuce 474-6 Fulham Road, SW6 (7385 3209).

Hammersmith, Ravenscourt Park & Stamford Brook

Hammersmith offers two distinct types of pub. The first is likely to be encountered in the network of streets that converge near the tube station: big, noisy, youth-oriented and packed to the gunnels on a Saturday night. The second can be found on the river, has changed little since the 18th century and is personified by the **Dove**.

Autumn House

133-5 King Street, W6 (8600 0941). Hammersmith tube. **Open** 11am-11pm Mon-Thur; 11am-midnight Fri, Sat; noon-10.30pm Sun. **Food served** noon-10pm Mon-Thur; noon-10.30pm Fri, Sat; noon-9.30pm Sun. **Credit** MC, V.

A £500,000 refit has transformed Autumn House from a standard boozer to – guess what? – yep, a gastropub aimed squarely at the wealthier end of the market (the toilets are the most pristine we have ever seen on licensed premises). The place is split between a pubbish area, with low-slung leather couches and tables, and a restaurant for serious grazing. The bar itself is resplendent in Pompidou Centre-inspired shiny metal plumbing. Other innovations include the speed lunch (simple dishes such as moules marinieres and chilli con carne, ordered, cooked and scoffed within 20 minutes), and a variety of two-for-one offers on wines, beers and spirits.

Disabled: toilet. Games (board games, fruit machine). Music (DJs 8pm Fri, Sat; blues and jazz 8pm two Sun per mth).

Blue Anchor

13 Lower Mall, W6 (8748 5774). Hammersmith tube. **Open** 11am-11pm Mon-Sat; noon-10.30pm Sun. **Food served** noon-2.30pm, 6-8.30pm Mon-Sat; noon-3.30pm, 6-8pm Sun. **Credit** MC, V.

Gustav Holst, who was once director of music at St Paul's Girls' School in nearby Brook Green, is said to have been inspired to write *Hammersmith* while sitting by the window of this superb little riverside pub. Visiting it on a dark winter's afternoon, we found it tantalisingly close to perfection: mist rising off the river, candles on the tables and Michael Holliday crooning dreamily over the speakers. We were also taken by the two full-sized racing canoes hanging from the ceiling – just the things for a good drunken dare – the venerable pewter-topped bar and nicely contrasting dark panels and cream paintwork. The useful £4.95 breakfast, riverside breeziness and general air of quiet introspection could also be just the ticket for recovery from a hangover.

Babies and children admitted (daytime only). Function room. Tables outdoors (riverside). TV.

Brook Green Hotel

170 Shepherd's Bush Road, W6 (7603 2516). Hammersmith tube. **Open** 11am-11pm Mon-Sat; noon-10.30pm Sun. **Food served** noon-3pm, 6-10pm Mon-Sat; noon-9.30pm Sun. **Credit** AmEx, DC, MC, V.

Prominently sited on the main Hammersmith-Shepherd's Bush road, a short walk from the area's most popular and almost pornographically tacky nightspot School Disco, the Brook Green Hotel is an amply proportioned Victorian pub, with a cavernous interior and huge orb-like hanging lamps over the bar. Decor is similarly bold and bright: scarlet and gold walls, yellow ceiling, check upholstery. Young's is responsible for the draught beers and on busy nights it opens up the Brooks wine bar in the basement. A hotel in more than just name, the Brook Green also provides accommodation, with no fewer than 14 air-con bedrooms for those who think heading back to their own cot after a night's imbibing might be a bit beyond their capabilities.

Comedy (8pm Fri; £6). Disabled: toilet. Games (fruit machines, games machine). No-smoking area. Tables outdoors (garden). TV (satellite).

Dove

19 Upper Mall, W6 (8748 5405). Hammersmith or Ravenscourt Park tube. **Open** 11am-11pm Mon-Sat; noon-10.30pm Sun. **Food served** noon-2.30pm, 6.30-8.45pm Mon-Sat; noon-4pm, 6.30-8.45pm Sun. **Credit** AmEx, DC, MC, V.

One of a row of small 18th-century houses built along a small alley, the immortal and adorable Dove features the smallest snug bar in the country according to that venerable and utterly reliable guide *Guinness World Records*. A conservatory, complete with snaking vines, overlooks the riverside terrace and is one of the most popular vantage points to watch the Oxford and Cambridge Boat Race. Indeed, views of the river here are exceptional whatever the time of year. Former regulars include the poet James Thomson who lived in a room upstairs and wrote 'Rule, Britannia!' in the bar; AP Herbert, who included the Dove, thinly disguised as the Pigeons, in his novel *The Water Gypsies*; and the designer William Morris, who would pop in here from his house over the road. The names of hundreds more visitors – from Alma Cogan to Zachary Scott – have been faithfully transcribed in a list over the fireplace in the snug bar. The selection of beers and wines is average, but you're here for atmosphere and history.

No piped music or jukebox. Tables outdoors (riverside terrace).

Old Ship

25 Upper Mall, W6 (8748 2593). Hammersmith, Ravenscourt Park or Stamford Brook tube. **Open** 9am-11pm daily. **Food served** 9am-10.30pm daily. **Credit** AmEx, MC, V.

Like a modernist version of the **Blue Anchor** *(see p240)*, the Old Ship also boasts canoes hanging from the ceiling, but here the setting is bright, modern and lightly woody. A vast bar at the back hosts fairly bog-standard beers but a lengthy wine list, lots of flavoured vodka and hot toddies. Hospitable, relaxed staff dispense a mixture of standard pub food and more up-to-date fare such as paninis and there are also several breakfast options to choose from. The multiple state-of-the art TV sets are neither here nor there – major sporting occasions apart, does anyone really want to watch TV in a pub? – making the best feature the waterfront veranda, which is where everybody heads given half-decent weather.

Babies and children admitted (children's menu, high chairs, nappy-changing facilities). Disabled: toilet. Function rooms. Games (fruit machine). Tables outdoors (riverside balcony, terrace). TV (big screen, satellite).

Raven

375 Goldhawk Road, W12 (8748 6977). Stamford Brook tube. **Open** noon-3pm, 5-11pm Mon-Sat; noon-3pm, 5-10.30pm Sun. **Food served** noon-3pm, 6-10.30pm daily. **Credit** AmEx, DC, MC, V.

True, the tables and paintwork are worn and chipped, but a makeover would surely kill the Raven. Built almost directly under the arch of Stamford Brook tube station, this former stable inn continues to offer solace to travellers along a particularly bleak section of Goldhawk Road. Furnishings are a medley of squashy armchairs, sofas and back-to-back settles, the cosiness only slightly marred by over insistent piped music. The neon-lit bar offers a good selection of cocktails and shots, and food is a cut above your average pub nosh (pan-fried corn-fed chicken and feta cheese salad were on offer when we dropped by). You'll also find a restaurant and garden at the back.

Babies and children admitted. Function room. Tables outdoors (garden)

Stonemason's Arms

54 Cambridge Grove, W6 (8748 1397). Hammersmith tube. **Open** noon-11pm Mon-Sat; noon-10.30pm Sun. **Food served** noon-3pm, 6.30-10pm Mon-Fri; 12.30-3.30pm, 6.30-10pm Sat, Sun. **Credit** AmEx, MC, V.

Despite its workaday name, the Stonemason's Arms is the sort of place where they give you a straw to drink your orange juice. Situated on the corner of Cambridge Grove and Glenthorne Road, the place has much to commend it. Despite its barnlike dimensions, the well-chosen forest green and cream decor has a genuinely relaxing quality, and the spectacular arched windows let in plenty of natural light. The bar is also superbly stocked – there are some 30 wines to choose from, including dessert wines, plus a dazzling variety of cocktails and shots. One part of the pub is given over to dining, and much entertainment is to be had watching the chefs perform in their open kitchen up behind the bar. Be warned: the varying floor levels can be hazardous to the unwary and/or alcoholically challenged.

Babies and children admitted. Function room. Tables outdoors (pavement).

Also in the area...

Bar 38 1 Blacks Road, W6 (8748 3951).
William Morris (JD Wetherspoon) 2-4 King Street, Swan Island, W6 (8741 7175).

Kensal Green

A compact area bounded to the west by Wormwood Scrubs and to the south by the Grand Union Canal, Kensal Green is generally synonomous with its celebrated cemetery. Socially, it's a very mixed area, and this diversity is reflected in its pubs, which range from the faintly intellectual **Paradise** and **William IV** to the unpretentious **North Pole** on the fringe of the infamous nick.

Astons

2 Regent Street, NW10 (8969 2184). Kensal Green tube/Kensal Rise rail. **Open** noon-11pm Mon-Wed; noon-midnight Thur-Sat; noon-10.30pm Sun. **Food served** noon-3.30pm, 6.30-10pm daily. **Credit** MC, V.

Not, as the name would suggest, a crummy Brummie wine lodge circa 1982, but a striking, bright, all-purpose bar with a big island serving area, chandeliers and long windows letting in plenty of light. Its location is probably a mixed blessing – being in the same side street as **Paradise** *(see below)* has no doubt helped attract attention from those entering that venerable institution but also limits any chance of enticing random passers-by. The owners seem to be pushing hard for an upmarket clientele: ads for champagne are much in evidence, and what at first glance appears to be a posh jukebox turns out to be a humidor dispensing fat cigars. Food is top drawer and includes the likes of mussels in rosé wine, thyme and garlic (£5.50) and smoked haddock fish cakes (£8.75). Check out the rear of the bar, where you'll find comfy armchairs and settees and, in winter, a roaring fire.

Babies and children admitted (high chairs). Music (DJs 7pm Sun). Tables outdoors (patio).

North Pole

13-15 North Pole Road, W10 (8964 9384). Latimer Road or White City tube. **Open** noon-11pm Mon-Sat; noon-10.30pm Sun. **Food served** noon-4pm, 6-10pm daily. **Credit** AmEx, MC, V.

This modish gastropub has a big open-plan bar area, windows the size of cinema screens and a scattering of leather sofas, armchairs and calf-high tables. You've seen it countless times before, but it's feet-up comfortable and it works. The bar dispenses a reasonable range of draught beers including Beck's, Kronenbourg, Bombardier and London Pride, and an adjacent kitchen turns out variants on pub nosh such as lamb and coriander burger, and crab and papaya salad. A welcome feature, particularly if you've come in search of the hair of the dog, is the range of breakfasts – including a vegetarian option and eggs benedict – served between noon and 4pm every weekend (though be warned, the thumping music may not be the best thing if you're nursing a headache).

Babies and children admitted (until 6pm). Tables outdoors (pavement).

Paradise by Way of Kensal Green

19 Kilburn Lane, W10 (8969 0098). Kensal Green tube/Kensal Rise rail/52, 302 bus. **Open** 12.30-11pm Mon-Sat; noon-10.30pm Sun. **Food served** 12.30-4pm, 7.30-11pm Mon-Sat; noon-9pm Sun. **Credit** MC, V.

The unwieldy name comes from a GK Chesterton poem, the text of which is inscribed on the front of the pleasantly shabby, indeterminately coloured bar. The place resembles a run-down Gothic mansion. The main bar has a mix of spindly wrought-iron furniture and battered antique velvet armchairs and sofas, placed under the sightless gaze of a massive cemetery angel. A room to the side is divided by two impressive wood and glass doors. Inside is a fireplace with a

lion sculpture, plus random second-hand books (an unfortunate cliché). Helpful bar staff serve under another large grounded angel fixed to the wall; expect lagers, ales and stouts, a good selection of wines (roughly £15 a bottle) and shooters at £3.50 a go. The restaurant at the back serves pricey gastro fare.
Babies and children admitted (high chairs, menus, nappy-changing facilities). Dance classes (7.30pm Mon; £7.50). Disabled: toilet. Function room. Tables outdoors (garden).

William IV
786 Harrow Road, NW10 (8969 5944). Kensal Green tube. **Open** noon-11pm Mon-Wed; noon-midnight Thur-Sat; noon-10.30pm Sun. **Food served** noon-3pm, 6-10.30pm Mon-Wed; noon-3pm, 6-11pm Thur, Fri; noon-4pm, 7-11pm Sat; noon-4.30pm, 7-10pm Sun. **Credit** MC, V.
Prominently sited on the corner of Harrow Road and Warfield Road, the William IV is a smart gastropub with a big open-plan interior roughly divided into three areas, one of which is the restaurant. There's a slight 1930s feel to the place, created by lots of pale-green oak panelling. Modern features include two fireplaces covered with mirrored mosaics. Seating is well spaced out, with leather sofas and armchairs among wooden tables. One end of the long, gently curving bar serves as a DJ station. Visiting on a Saturday lunchtime, we found the place frequented by west London intelligentsia, sporting designer spectacles and brandishing serious novels. An accomplished Med-influenced menu is served throughout the bar, with mains in the £8-£14 price range. There's also an attractive rear garden for those who favour drinking in the sunshine.
Babies and children admitted (until 6pm). Function room. Music (DJs 8.30pm Thur-Sat; free). Tables outdoors (garden).

Kingston-upon-Thames

A chunk of suburbia focused on a busy but unlovely shopping area, Kingston lacks the cachet of neighbouring Richmond. Two of its best pubs lie well away from the town centre – the **Park Tavern**, on the edge of massive Richmond Park, and the **Boaters Inn**, down by the riverside.

Boaters Inn
Canbury Gardens, Lower Ham Road, Kingston-upon-Thames, Surrey (8541 4672). Kingston rail. **Open** 11am-11pm Mon-Sat; noon-10.30pm Sun. **Food served** noon-10pm Mon-Sat; noon-9pm Sun. **Credit** AmEx, MC, V.
Well screened behind the foliage of Canbury Gardens, this former cafe looks unprepossessing as you approach but turns out to offer a fine panoramic view of the river. Bright, open and woody, the Boaters backs straight on to the towpath (you can take your drink outside should the weather prove acceptable). After a brief and scorned hiatus, the real ales for which the pub is renowned are back with a vengeance: we found Greene King IPA, Abbot Ale and Shepherd Neame's Spitfire on draught, plus a good range of cocktails and shooters. The place hosts occasional beer festivals that feature some 40 real ales and it also puts on Sunday evening jazz. Boat crews qualify for a 10% discount, if you want to put your oar in.
Babies and children admitted (children's menu, nappy-changing facilities). Games (board games, fruit machines). Music (jazz 8.30pm Sun; free). No-smoking area. Restaurant. Tables outdoors (riverside patio, front balcony). TV.

Canbury Arms
49 Canbury Park Road, Kingston-upon-Thames, Surrey (8288 1882). Kingston rail. **Open** 11am-11pm Mon-Sat; noon-10.30pm Sun. **Credit** MC, V.
A scruffy but friendly boozer, the Canbury Arms doesn't appear to have been refurbished since they introduced vinyl roofs on the Cortina. What passes as interior decoration comes in the form of an elaborate display of beer mats and Artexed walls. But who cares: the pub's selling point is its range of real ales, numbering six when we dropped by, including HSB, Wychwood Hobgoblin and Red Lion Rebellion. Excellent.
Babies and children admitted (separate room). Games (board games, fruit machines, pool table). Music (bands 9pm Fri, Sat; free). Quiz (8.30pm Sun; £1). Tables outdoors (forecourt, garden). TV (big screen, satellite).

Park Tavern
19 New Road, Kingston-upon-Thames, Surrey (no phone). Norbiton rail. **Open** 11am-11pm Mon-Sat; noon-10.30pm Sun. **No credit cards**.
An old-fashioned freehouse, the Tavern features French-style shutters and a useful little patio by the front door that benefits from the lack of passing traffic. Inside there's London Pride and Young's 'ordinary' on draught, while eclectic design features include a wall with holes bored in it, like an early recording studio, and a mirror with chintz curtains on either side – do they ceremoniously fling them apart at opening time? Thanks to a mysterious marble shelf at navel level, users of the gentlemen's lavatories are well advised to check their shoes before returning to public gaze.
Games (fruit machine). Jukebox. Tables outdoors (garden, patio). TV (big screen, satellite).

Wych Elm
93 Elm Road, Kingston-upon-Thames, Surrey (8546 3271). Kingston rail. **Open** 11am-3pm, 5-11pm Mon-Fri; 11am-11pm Sat; noon-10.30pm Sun. **Food served** noon-2.30pm Mon-Sat. **No credit cards**.
The Wych Elm takes a traditional approach to pub layout, offering a separate saloon and public bar – the former in Fuller's trademark unmatching upholstery, the latter sporting a lino floor and incongruous gilt mirror and chandelier. The saloon bar also features wood panelling, an ornate fireplace and terracotta-coloured walls. In summer, the Wych Elm's best feature is its exterior floral display, there's a garden at the back and a full range of Fuller's beers on draught.
Babies and children admitted (dining area only). Games (darts, fruit machine). Tables outdoors (garden). TV.

Also in the area...
Kingston Tup 88 London Road, Kingston-upon-Thames, Surrey (8546 6471).
King's Tun (JD Wetherspoon) 153-7 Clarence Street, Kingston-upon-Thames, Surrey (8547 3827).
O'Neill's 3 Eden Street, Kingston-upon-Thames, Surrey (8481 0131).
Slug & Lettuce Turks Boatyard, Thames Side, Kingston-upon-Thames, Surrey (8547 2323).

Richmond, Isleworth & Twickenham

Richmond and Twickenham both started life as riverside fishing villages, and most of their finest pubs can be found on the river. Richmond, which has a bigger town centre, also has several

London drinking: gastropubs

How the ploughman's was put out to grass.

Not too long ago, London pub lunches were appalling affairs: scotch eggs – lower case 's' due to them having Anglo-Indian not Hibernian origins – curly-edged sandwiches and pork pies as hard as crabshells. Occasionally you could find a boozer where the landlady would cook up liver and bacon at the drop of Fanny Craddock's hat, but usually the best you'd hope for was a hot cabinet, where leathery sausages would irradiate for days on end.

Then along came the ploughman's. Not the rustic labourer's standby as we'd always assumed, but a 1950s invention of the English Country Cheese Council. Pubs were issued with free colour posters showing a generous wedge of sweating cheddar plonked next to a molehill of pickle and a chunk of oh-so-chic french bread. The idea proved so successful, it was adapted to other foods and for a brief halcyon period London's boozers were swamped with the likes of the huntsman's (cold roast beef), the fisherman's (scampi) and (gawd help us) the highlander (scotch egg).

In 1975, fewer than 10 per cent of London's pubs sold hot food. Now, thanks to a renewed interest in food and cooking, the figure is more than 90 per cent, even if much of it is pre-cooked and reheated in the infernal microwave ('The devil's tumble-drier,' as Peter Cook called them).

Now, it seems that the birth of the gastropub was inevitable, with the **Eagle** in Farringdon widely recognised as London's first. Opened in 1991 by David Eyre, it was located suitably close to the offices of the *Guardian* and was a catalyst for a new approach to pub cuisine. Who knows when the queasy coupling of 'gastro' and 'pub' was coined (it first appeared in *Time Out*'s annual *Eating & Drinking* guide in 1997) but, by God, it's caught on.

Ubiquitous almost to the point of nausea, there are standard ingredients: stripped pine flooring; chunky wooden furniture; big windows; open kitchen; serving staff with that just got out of bed look. Similarly, expect a menu (lettered on a blackboard) of a Mediterranean slant with something seared, something char-grilled, and enough accents to make the average punter regret having left the complete set of Collins European dictionaries at home.

It's an easily copied formula and one that has already been applied to chains of pastel-fronted pubs. A slew of former Firkins have been turned into gastropubs by the massive Spirit Group. Given that these are the people behind Wacky Warehouses, you'd expect the worst, but in fact Spirit's **Fire Stables** in Wimbledon won Best Gastropub category in the 2001 *Time Out* Eating & Drinking awards, with sibling **Lots Road Pub & Dining Rooms** picking up the same accolade in 2002.

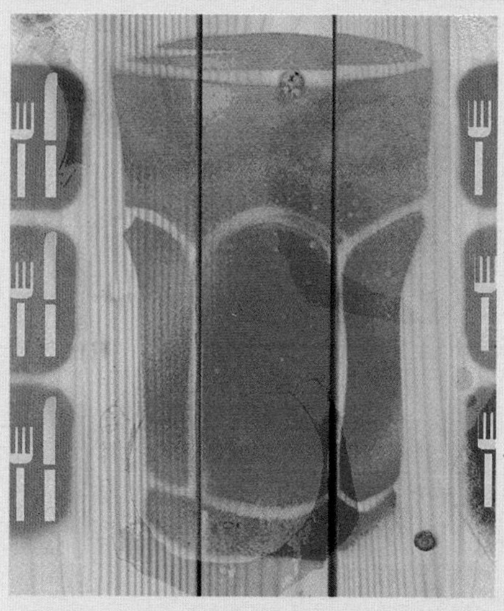

Fine dining times ten

Anglesea Arms (*see p246*) 35 Wingate Road, W6 (8749 1291).
Cow (*see p68*) 89 Westbourne Park Road, W2 (7221 5400).
Crown (*see p143*) 223 Grove Road, E3 (8981 9998).
Eagle (*see p111*) 159 Farringdon Road, EC1 (7837 1353).
Fire Stables (*see p229*) 27-9 Church Road, SW19 (8946 3197).
Golborne House (*see p69*) 36 Golborne Road, W10 (8960 6260).
Junction Tavern (*see p186*) 101 Fortess Road, NW5 (7485 9400).
Lansdowne (*see p183*) 90 Gloucester Avenue, NW1 (7483 0409).
Lots Road Pub & Dining Rooms (*see p33*) 114 Lots Road, SW10 (7352 6645).
Perseverance (*see p50*) 63 Lamb's Conduit Street, WC1 (7405 8278).

For the most part, though, gastropubs remain in the domain of the independent, which is where you find the most interesting developments. Twin operations the rough-edged **Endurance** (*see p81*) and the kitschy **Perseverance** are notable for being two of the few West End gastropubs (Islington and Notting Hill are the more usual environs), while the **Crown** and **Duke of Cambridge** offer a purely organic menu (drinks included). *Andrew Driver*

long-established places in the vicinity of Henry VII's one-time jousting venue, Richmond Green. Isleworth, the least glamorous neigbourhood of the trio, boasts another venerable waterfront pub, the **London Apprentice**, but most other places of note are hidden away in drab, anonymous streets well away from the Thames.

Barmy Arms

The Embankment, Twickenham, Middx (8892 0863). Twickenham rail. **Open** *Apr-Nov* noon-11pm Mon-Sat; noon-10.30pm Sun. *May-Oct* 11am-11pm daily; noon-10.30pm Sun. **Food served** noon-3pm, 6-9pm Mon-Sat; noon-3pm Sun. **Credit** AmEx, DC, MC, V.

A raffish riverside hostelry, next door to the Mary Wallace theatre and near the junction of Riverside and Church Lanes, the BA has a nautical rather than an inland waterway theme. Maritime prints and photographs of deck life in the days of rum, sodomy and the lash adorn the walls, and hot navy rum is a house special. Other characteristics include big blue shutters without, and low ceiling, worn carpet and studied distressed paintwork within – though the latter is now genuinely distressed through the passage of time and tide. Draught ales include Abbot, IPA and Courage Directors, and there's a huge seating area overlooking the river.

Function room. Games (fruit machines, board games). Tables outdoors (patio). TV.

Bridge Inn

457 London Road, Isleworth, Middx (8568 80088). Isleworth rail. **Open** 11am-11pm Mon-Sat; noon-10.30pm Sun. **Food served** 11am-10.30pm Mon-Sat. **Happy hour** 7-11pm Thur. **Credit** MC, V.

It looks like a dive from the outside but appearances can be very deceptive. Despite its bashed about and scruffy appearance and seriously unpromising location (near a railway arch on the corner of London and Linkfield Roads), the Bridge Inn turns out to be a neatly laid-out establishment lit by art deco wall lamps and incorporating a full-sized Thai restaurant (dating back a decade to 1993 and therefore surely one of the first such establishments to have been attached to a pub). Seating in the bar is arranged on three sides of the main serving area. Design-wise it's standard stuff: framed Guinness posters and sepia photos of London scenes. Abbot Ale is on draught, and four-pint pitchers of Kronenbourg are £9.50. It also offers accommodation.

Babies and children admitted (restaurant). Games (cards, fruit machines, pool table). TV (big screen, satellite).

Coach & Horses

183 London Road, Isleworth, Middx (8560 1447). Syon Lane rail. **Open** 11am-11pm Mon-Sat; noon-10.30pm Sun. **Food served** noon-3pm, 6-10pm Mon-Sat; noon-4pm Sun. **Credit** MC, V.

One of countless roadhouse pubs to be found on the main arterial roads into London, the Coach & Horses started life as a coaching inn and has been a Young's pub since 1831. For a tied house, the range of beers could hardly be better – we found Young's ordinary, Special, Winter Warmer and pilsner on tap, plus Bristol IPA. Sport's a big feature – on a Saturday afternoon you're likely to find competing events on the two TVs; if that puts you in the mood for a run around, Syon Park's next door. Other features include real coal fires and the inevitable Thai restaurant, although Sundays there's the option of a traditional roast.

Babies and children admitted (until 8pm). Games (fruit machines). Music (bands 9.30pm Mon-Sat; 2.30pm Sun; free). Quiz (Wed 9pm). Tables outdoors (courtyard). TV (satellite).

Cricketers

The Green, Richmond, Surrey (8940 4372). Richmond tube/rail. **Open** 11am-11pm Mon-Sat; noon-10.30pm Sun. **Food served** noon-3pm, 6-9pm Mon-Fri; noon-6pm Sat, Sun. **Credit** MC, V.

The location's the thing – the Cricketers stands on the outside edge of Richmond Green and its first-floor balcony offers a perfect view of the village cricket played there during the summer months. The leather-willow theme continues in the downstairs bar where the walls are decorated with famous quotes about this most pastoral of pastimes. The pub also fields its own team. Cricket apart, it's rather a spartan place, with a curiously empty area in front of the bar. Draught options include estimable Abbot Ale, Old Speckled Hen and Greene King IPA.

Babies and children admitted (restaurant). Comedy (8.30pm Tue; £3). Function room. Games (fruit machines). Music (jazz 8pm 1st Sun of mth; free). Restaurant. Tables outdoors (pavement). TV (big screen, satellite).

Eel Pie

9 Church Street, Twickenham, Middx (8891 1717). Twickenham rail. **Open** 11am-11pm Mon-Sat; noon-10.30pm Sun. **Food served** noon-3pm daily. **Credit** MC, V.

Eel Pie island – the nearby islet from which this hostelry takes it name – was once the most rock 'n' roll island in England (yes, even more so than Lindesfarne). This wonderfully obscure slab of land featured a club that in the '60s played host to the Animals, the Yardbirds, the Rolling Stones, Rod Stewart and the Who. The club burnt down in 1970, condemned as a 'beatnik-infested vice den'. No such complaint could be made of the boozer that now faces it from the riverbank. The Eel Pie does a convincing imitation of a country pub in a quiet village street. Spacious but intimate, it features the obligatory rugby photos – in this case Twickers in the '30s – with low reddish lighting and hop bines suspended from the ceiling. Featured beers are Badger ales and Hoffbrau.

Babies and children admitted (until 7pm). Games (bar billiards). Quiz (9pm Thur; £1). TV (satellite).

London Apprentice

62 Church Street, Isleworth, Middx (8560 1915). Isleworth rail. **Open** 11am-11pm Mon-Sat; noon-10.30pm Sun. **Food served** 11am-2.30pm, 6-9.30pm Mon-Thur; 11am-9.30pm Fri, Sat; noon-9pm Sun. **Credit** AmEx, DC, MC, V.

Located in a part of Isleworth undergoing Docklands-style gentrification, the Apprentice belongs to the area's past. It dates back to Tudor times; until 1739 it was open all night for the benefit of river travellers. It's said to have been a popular haunt for highwaymen, including Dick Turpin, and a tunnel for quick getaways once ran between the cellars and the vaults of nearby All Saints church. Henry VIII, Charles I, Charles II, Nell Gwynne and Oliver Cromwell are all rumoured to have called in, which must have been one hell of a party. The bar's done out in orange and features miniature glasses in cabinets – both of which seem to be a feature of Isleworth pubs.

Babies and children admitted (until 9.30pm, dining area only; children's menus). Function room. Games (bar billiards, darts, fruit machine, video games). No-smoking area. Tables outdoors (riverside terrace). TV.

Marlborough

46 Friars Stile Road, Richmond, Surrey (8940 0572). Richmond tube/rail. **Open** noon-11pm Mon-Sat; noon-10.30pm Sun. **Food served** noon-10pm daily. **Credit** MC, V.

Once a very forgettable local, the Marlborough has recently acquired a big glassy lobby area at the front and another seating area with ox-blood walls and diamond paned

windows at the back. Outside there's a garden and patio. Ironically, the place started life as a 19th-century temperance hotel. These days it stocks numerous brands of the devil's buttermilk, including Fuller's London pride, beers from Adnams and lovely Leffe. The view from nearby Terrace Gardens is one of the best in London.
Babies and children admitted (until 7.30pm; garden, play area). Function room. Music (band 1pm Sun; free). Tables outdoors (garden, patio).

Old Ship

3 King Street, Richmond, Surrey (8940 3461). Richmond tube/rail. **Open** 11am-11pm Mon-Sat; noon-10.30pm Sun. **Food served** noon-8pm daily. **Credit** MC, V.
A long, dark pub on a busy shopping street, the Old Ship is a long-established fixture of Richmond town centre. In its early days, mail coaches used to stop here six times a day on route to Hampton Court, and the place would probably still be recognisable to the river rats and stagecoach passengers who originally frequented it. The clientele is noticeably more down-to-earth than the cricket-sweater-and-*Daily Telegraph* types who form the base clientele of so many other Richmond pubs. Beers are from Young's and there's a hot plate warming traditional pub grub; it also does Thai.
Function room. Restaurant. TV (satellite).

Red Lion

92 Linkfield Road, Isleworth, Middx (8560 1457). Isleworth rail. **Open** 11am-11pm Mon-Sat; noon-10.30pm Sun. **Food served** noon-4pm Sun. **Happy hour** 4-7pm Mon-Thur. **No credit cards**.
Perhaps the ultimate example of a particular type of west London pub – an unsung haven in a quiet residential street, where the core customers have become an extended family. We found a haze of communal cigarette smoke in the saloon bar, swathing a pride of middle-aged lions who looked up lazily as we came in before returning to an intricate saga of extra-marital affairs in neighbouring streets over the past 20 years. Gripping stuff. The second bar offers a pool table, TV tuned to sport and a younger, more vocal clientele. Well respected by CAMRA, the Red Lion (founded 1846) takes its real ales seriously – we found three on draught, including a wonderful rarity, Woodforde's Wherry, from Norfolk.
Babies and children admitted. Disabled: toilet. Games (board games, darts, fruit machines, pool tables, quiz machine, table football). Tables outdoors (garden). TV (satellite).

White Cross

Riverside, Richmond, Surrey (8940 6844). Richmond tube/rail. **Open** 11am-11pm Mon-Sat; noon-10.30pm Sun. **Food served** noon-3.30pm Mon-Sat; noon-4pm Sun. **Credit** MC, V.
Biggest and arguably the best of the Richmond riverside pubs, the Cross attracts huge crowds at the weekend, particularly on summery and/or bright winter days. The pub dates from 1835, and the site was previously occupied by the Monastery of the Observant Friars, from whose symbol derives the name. There's the full range of Young's beers, and the separate food bar dishes up appetising fare; on our visit there was a big run on nursery puddings and custard. A first-floor sitting room and huge outdoor area (the latter with its own servery during the summer) have excellent views of the river. The cobbled dockside is prone to flooding, which causes considerable and very public amusement on the frequent occasions when a punter's car is overtaken by the rising tide. Signs unashamedly proclaim the absence of facilities for kids, but dogs were much in evidence in the bar – a classically British sense of priorities for a classically British boozer.
No piped music or jukebox. Tables outdoors (garden).

White Swan

26 Old Palace Lane, Richmond, Surrey (8940 0959). Richmond tube/rail. **Open** 11am-11pm Mon-Sat; 11am-10.30pm Sun. **Food served** noon-3pm, 6.30-10pm Mon-Sat; noon-3pm Sun. **Credit** MC, V.
Near the river, but not on it, the White Swan is a popular weekend watering hole for Richmond's well-heeled mums, dads, Jacks and Chloes. The main bar is appealingly decked out in yellow and green, and in winter you'll usually fine a good fire going. There's an extensive wine list (worth saving for), but the range of beers is routine. There's also a smallish food menu. Arrive early so you don't have to eat in the spartan dining area with its corrugated plastic ceiling. Yuk! Thankfully the garden beyond is much more attractive.
Babies and children admitted. No-smoking area (restaurant). Restaurant (available for hire). Tables outdoors (garden, pavement).

White Swan

Riverside, Twickenham, Middx (8892 2166). Twickenham rail. **Open** *Winter* 11am-3pm, 5.30-11pm Mon-Thur; 11am-11pm Fri, Sat; noon-10.30pm Sun. *Summer* 11am-11pm Mon-Sat; noon-10.30pm Sun. **Food served** noon-2.30pm, 7-9pm Mon-Thur; noon-3pm Fri-Sun. **Credit** MC, V.
This White Swan overlooks a quiet stretch of the Thames and includes both a raised terrace and a beer garden on the riverbank. This stretch of the river is liable to be flooded at little notice, and the dank stairs and passageway leading to the toilets have seen so much excess Thames they resemble a dungeon during the French Revolution. However, the place dates back more than 300 years so it shouldn't fall into the river any time soon. The back bar is, like so many pubs in the area, is a shrine to the oval ball; the modest serving area offers Charles Wells Bombardier and Shepherd Neame Spitfire.
Babies and children admitted. Bar area available for hire. Music (band Wed, Sat). Tables outdoors (balcony, riverside garden). TV (satellite).

Also in the area...

All Bar One 9-11 Hill Street, Richmond, Surrey (8332 7141); 26-8 York Street, Twickenham, Surrey (8843 7281).
Moon Under Water (JD Wetherspoon) 53-7 London Road, Twickenham, Middx (8744 0080).
Pitcher & Piano 11 Bridge Street, Richmond, Surrey (8332 2524).
Slug & Lettuce Riverside House, Water Lane, Richmond, Surrey (8948 7733).
Twickenham Tup 13 Richmond Road, Twickenham, Middx (8891 1863).

Shepherd's Bush

Benefitting from the Notting Hill overspill and the constant presence of the BBC, Shepherd's Bush has developed quite a drinking culture of its own. The split is a straightforward: bright young bars for bright young things or serious gastropubs for TV execs whose expense budgets don't stretch to the Ivy.

Albertine

1 Wood Lane, W12 (8743 9593). Shepherd's Bush tube. **Open** 11am-11pm Mon-Fri; 6.30-11pm Sat. **Food served** noon-10.45pm Mon-Fri; 6.30-10.45pm Sat. **Credit** MC, V.
The Albertine is the archetypal neighbourhood wine bar, with small wooden tables, candle lighting, wreaths of drifting cigarette smoke and muted jazz. Other than a few Parisian

prints on the walls, there's almost no decoration – unless you count the functional but beautiful display of racks and racks of wine above the tiny bar. Staff are relaxed and low key, and food, such as grilled goat's cheese and cod and leek gratin, is seemingly intended to complement the wine rather than the other way round. There are more than 100 wines to choose from, ranging from £10.50 to £29. A single bottled beer (Budvar) is available. Order it if you dare.
Function room.

Anglesea Arms

35 Wingate Road, W6 (8749 1291). Goldhawk Road or Ravenscourt Park tube. **Open** 11am-11pm Mon-Sat; noon-10.30pm Sun. **Food served** 12.30-2.45pm, 7-10.45pm Mon-Sat; 1-3.30pm, 7-10.15pm Sun. **Credit** MC, V.
It looks like a local, but those lucky enough to live near the AA are the well-heeled inhabitants of Brackenbury Village, an enclave of extremely desirable Victorian terraces and villas just east of Ravenscourt Park. It's a wonderful pub for a winter afternoon with friends (not that it's a wash-out in the summer). The panelled main bar is exceptionally dark: on our visit it was lit only by the flames of the fire – for once, a real one, with logs and kindling piled nearby to prove it. Beyond the bar there is a more brightly lit, brick-walled food area, decorated with a large mural. Food is outstanding. There's a longish wine list, and home-made lemonade is a speciality.
Babies and children admitted. No piped music or jukebox. Restaurant. Tables outdoors (patio).

Bush Bar & Grill

45A Goldhawk Road, W12 (8746 2111/www.bushbar.co.uk). Goldhawk Road tube. **Open** noon-11pm Mon-Sat; noon-10.30pm Sun. **Food served** noon-3pm, 6.30-11.30pm Mon-Sat; noon-4pm, 6.30-10.30pm Sun. **Happy hour** 5-7pm daily. **Credit** AmEx, MC, V.
This trendy bar-restaurant, well hidden behind a row of shops near Shepherd's Bush Green, is popular at evenings and weekends with a trendy young crowd who appreciate its minimalist industrial decor and warm, flattering lighting. The smallish bar area is separated from the dining section by a platform of small circular tables with banquette seating; alternatively, you can sit at the long stone bar and ogle attractive bar staff preparing delicious cocktails from an impressive list (£6-£7, although a selection is available for just £3 during happy hour). Bottled beers include Stella, Hoegaarden and Staropramen and there's a good selection of wines. If you're feeling flush, consider eating as well, because the food is often excellent. Hard to believe it is just 100 yards away from the grot magnet that is Shepherd's Bush Green.
Babies and children admitted (restaurant only; high chairs). Disabled: toilet. Function room. Restaurant.

Crown & Sceptre

57 Melina Road, W12 (8746 0060). Goldhawk Road or Shepherd's Bush tube. **Open** noon-11pm Mon-Sat; noon-10.30pm Sun. **Food served** noon-4pm, 6-10pm Mon-Sat; noon-4pm, 6-9.30pm Sun. **Credit** MC, V.
Well concealed amid a warren of side streets near tiny Cathnor Park, the Crown & Sceptre is a newish gastropub. The wide seating area consists of two distinct sections. One is a dead-traditional public bar, with red padded benches resembling the upholstery of an old Morris 1100; the other consists of a pizzeria-like food bar, served from the ubiquitous open kitchen and offering dishes such as smoked salmon and lamb couscous. On our early evening visit it was quiet, but past visits suggest this may have been the calm before the storm.
Babies and children admitted (high chairs). Disabled: toilet. Games (games machines). No-smoking area. Tables outdoors (garden, pavement). TV.

Havelock Tavern

57 Masbro Road, W14 (7603 5374). Hammersmith or Shepherd's Bush tube/Kensington (Olympia) tube/rail. **Open** 11am-11pm Mon-Sat; noon-10.30pm Sun. **Food served** 12.30-2.30pm, 7-10pm Mon-Sat; 12.30-3pm, 7-9.30pm Sun. **No credit cards**.
Another of the quietly excellent pubs to be found in the upmarket residential streets of Shepherd's Bush, the Havelock offers a decent range of beers (Brakspear Bitter, Marston's Pedigree and Stella on tap), together with more than a dozen each of red and white wines, plus rosés and dessert wines, starting at £9.50 a bottle. It's an L-shaped pub, with an especially cosy little seating area right at the back, and just the right blend of interior decoration – cream walls, chocolate-painted wood and discreet lighting. The young, laid-back staff are a definite bonus. The food is also highly recommended (char-grilled tuna, Thai red chicken curry and similar). An unpretentious, quality place – like Arnie and the two old guys we saw playing dominoes in the corner, we'll be back.
Babies and children admitted (high chairs). Games (board games). No piped music or jukebox. Tables outdoors (garden, pavement).

Seven Stars Bar & Dining Room

243 Goldhawk Road, W12. (8748 0229/www.sevenstarsdining.co.uk). Goldhawk road tube. **Open** noon-11pm Mon-Wed; noon-midnight Thur-Sat; noon-10pm Sun. **Food served** noon-3pm; 6-10.30pm Mon-Sat; noon-10pm Sun. **Credit** MC, V.
World of Leather meets Cape Canaveral at this spectacularly refurbished Victorian pub on the busy Goldhawk Road roundabout, featuring squashy brown sofas, lots of wood and gigantic light fittings apparently modelled on the engines of Saturn V. Friendly staff serve a good range of beers, wines, cocktails and shots. Beyond the bar, a coy half-hitched curtain reveals the dining room, decorated in even more wood and leather and ending in a spectacular metal food bar dispensing reasonably priced, predominantly meaty and fishy dishes with an all-day roast on Sundays. Yummy! Booze on!
Disabled: toilet. Tables outdoors (garden). TV.

Vesbar

15-19 Goldhawk Road, W12 (8762 0215). Goldhawk Road or Shepherd's Bush tube. **Open/food served** 11am-11pm Mon-Fri; 10am-11pm Sat; 10am-10.30pm Sun. **Credit** AmEx, DC, MC, V.
With its big central eating area, neon bar and steady clientele of almost interchangable BBC researchers and yoof TV presenters, Vesbar looks at first glance like one of them new fangled sushi bars with weirdy robotic drinks dispensers. In fact, the menu is restricted to pasta, burgers and upmarket pizzas, with an adequate but unexciting bar list (Kirin and Hoegaarden are on draught) to soothe the throat. Service is gratifyingly friendly and slick. The best position is next to the floor-to-ceiling windows, where leather settees give you a panoramic view of the busy Shepherd's Bush Green traffic. If you've got time to kill before going to a play or gig nearby, there are far worse places to sit and watch the world go by.
Bar area available for hire. Disabled: toilet.

West 12

74 Askew Road, W12 (8746 7799). Shepherd's Bush tube, then 207 bus/266 bus. **Open** 4pm-midnight Mon-Sat; 11am-10.30pm Sun. **Food served** 5-10.30pm Mon-Sat; 11am-10pm Sun. **Credit** MC, V.
Homely like a womb, the West 12 is a cove of lush red and purple that transports you back to the comfort of your mummy's tummy. Not that your mummy's tummy would

have featured the amount of alcohol available here (unless she was a particularly bad, Jerry Springer-style screaming white trash mummy, that is). Bottled lagers (Tiger and Sapporo) and Guinness and Stella on tap are supped early evening, but later drinkers tend to favour one of two dozen cocktails priced at £6 a throw. There are dozens of wines too, often taken with the international menu, which boasts of a reliance on seasonal produce.
Babies and children admitted (until 7pm). Disabled: toilet. Function room. Music (singer 7pm Wed). No-smoking tables. TV (digital).

Also in the area...

O'Neill's 2 Goldhawk Road, W12 (8746 1288).
Slug & Lettuce 96-8 Uxbridge Road, W12 (8749 1987).
Walkabout Inn 58 Shepherd's Bush Green, W12 (8740 4339).

Southall

Way out west on the M4 corridor and renowned for its superb range of Indian restaurants and markets, Southall has so far made only a modest contribution to London pub life. It is, however, home to the unique **Glassy Junction**, as well as a smattering of more traditional hostelries.

Beaconsfield Arms

63-7 West End Road, Southall, Middx (8574 8135). Southall tube. **Open** 11am-11pm Mon-Sat; noon-10.30pm Sun. **No credit cards**.
Locals don't come much more local than this. Next to a muddy car park halfway down an anonymous residential street, the roomy Beaconsfield makes little attempt to attract passing trade but, having won several CAMRA awards, it probably doesn't need to. The real ale buffs rate it especially highly for its commitment to dark milds, one of which, Rebellion, we found on draught. Surroundings are pleasantly low key – dark wood, green and cream striped wallpaper – and conversation around the bar as lively and parochial as you would expect at a neighbourhood boozer. There's a beer garden at the back.
Games (darts, fruit machines, pool table, table football). Tables outdoors (garden). TV (satellite).

Glassy Junction

97 South Road, Southall, Middx (8574 1626). Southall rail. **Open** 11am-11.30pm Mon-Wed; 11am-2am Thur-Sat; noon-11pm Sun. **Food served** noon-10.30pm Mon-Wed; noon-midnight Thur-Sat; 12.30-10pm Sun. **No credit cards**.
There's no mistaking the Glassy Junction. This Sikh-run Southall institution – the first pub in Britain to accept payment in rupees – proclaims its existence with a row of 20ft statues of bhangra musicians along its outside wall. Inside you'll find Indian beers such as Kingfisher and Lal Toofan on draught, alongside John Smith's and Foster's, and an extensive Indian menu offering a range of dishes you would expect to find in a high street tandoori. The echoing main bar is a bit too big for its own good – there are acres of empty space between the glitzy bar and the tables and stools fringing the edges – but the clientele on our visit was a harmonious mix of youngish Asians and late middle-aged white men.
Babies and children admitted. Function room. Games (pool table). TV (satellite).

Seven Stars Bar & Dining Room

West

Where to go for...

Critics' choice index

COMEDY

DISABLED TOILETS

Index

DJ BARS

EARLY LICENSES

FOOD

Breakfasts

GASTROPUBS

GAMES

GAY & LESBIAN

HAPPY HOURS

HISTORIC PUBS

NO-SMOKING TABLES/AREAS

OUTDOOR DRINKING

Advertisers' Index

Please refer to relevant sections for addresses/telephone numbers

Index

A-Z Index

CVO Firevault p41
36 Great Titchfield Street, W1 (7580 5333).

d

Dacre Arms p218
11 Kingswood Place, SE13 (8244 2404).
Daniel Defoe p185
102 Stoke Newington Church Street, N16 (7254 2906).
Dartmouth Arms p186
35 York Rise, NW5 (7485 3267).
De Hems p56
11 Macclesfield Street, W1 (7437 2494).
Denim p56
4A Upper St Martin's Lane, WC2 (7497 0376).
Detroit p36
35 Earlham Street, WC2 (7240 2662).
Dickens Inn p138
St Katharine's Way, E1 (7488 2208).
Dirty Dick's p131
202 Bishopsgate, EC2 (7283 5888).
District p148
19 Amhurst Rd, E8 (8985 8986).
ditto p226
55-7 East Hill, SW18 (8877 0110).
Dive Bar p56
48 Gerrard Street, W1 (no phone).
Dog & Bell p211
116 Prince Street, SE8 (8692 5664).
Dog & Duck p79
18 Bateman Street, W1 (7494 0697).
Dog House p216
293 Kennington Rd, SE11 (7820 9310).
Dog House p79
187 Wardour Street, W1 (7434 2116).
Dogstar p202
389 Coldharbour Lane, SW9 (7733 7515).
Dorchester Bar p64
Dorchester Hotel, 53 Park Lane, W1 (7629 8888).
Dove p240
19 Upper Mall, W6 (8748 5405).
Dove Freehouse p148
24-28 Broadway Market, E8 (7275 7617).
Dover Castle p60
43 Weymouth Mews, W1 (7580 4412).
Dovetail p109
9 Jerusalem Passage, EC1 (7490 7321).
Down Mexico Way p57
25 Swallow Street, W1 (7437 9895).
Dragon p125
5 Leonard Street, EC2 (7490 7110).
Drapers Arms p172
44 Barnsbury Street, N1 (7619 0348).
Drawing Room & Sofa Bar p193
103 Lavender Hill, SW11 (7350 2564).
Drayton Arms p88
153 Old Brompton Rd, SW5 (7835 2301).
Drayton Court p236
2 The Avenue, W13 (8997 1019).
dreambagsjaguarshoes p125
34-6 Kingsland Rd, E2 (7739 9550).
Dublin Castle p160
94 Parkway, NW1 (7485 1773).
Duke of Cambridge p193
228 Battersea Bridge Rd, SW11 (7223 5662).
Duke of Cambridge p172
30 St Peter's Street, N1 (7359 3066).
Duke of Cumberland p238
235 New Kings Rd, SW6 (7736 2777).
Duke of Devonshire p190
39 Balham High Rd, SW12 (8673 1363).
Duke of Edinburgh p202
204 Ferndale Rd, SW9 (7924 0509).
Duke of Wellington p61
94A Crawford Street, W1 (7224 9435).
Duke of York p235
107 Devonshire Rd, W4 (8994 2118).
Duke (of York) p49
7 Roger Street, WC1 (7242 7230).
Duke of York p184
2A St Anne's Terrace, NW8 (7722 1933).
Duke of York p111
156 Clerkenwell Rd, EC1 (7837 8548).
Duke's Head p219
8 Lower Richmond Rd, SW15 (8788 2552).
Duke's Hotel Bar p90
Duke's Hotel, 35 St James's Place, SW1 (7491 4840).
Dulwich Wood House p223
39 Sydenham Hill, SE26 (8693 5666).
The Durell p238
704 Fulham Rd, SW6 (7736 3014).
Dusk p61
79 Marylebone High Street, W1 (7486 5746).
Dust p111
27 Clerkenwell Rd, EC1 (7490 5120).

e

Eagle p193
104 Chatham Rd, SW11 (7228 2328).
Eagle p111
159 Farringdon Rd, EC1 (7837 1353).
Eagle Bar Diner p41
3-5 Rathbone Place, W1 (7637 1418).
Ealing Park Tavern p236
222 South Ealing Rd, W5 (8758 1879).
Earl Spencer p227
260-2 Merton Rd, SW18 (8870 9244).
East Dulwich Tavern p211
1 Lordship Lane, SE22 (8693 1817).
Easton p111
22 Easton Street, WC1 (7278 7608).
East Hill p226
21 Alma Rd, SW12 (8874 1833).
Eclipse p69
186 Kensington Park Rd, W11 (7792 2063).
Eclipse Wimbledon p229
57 High Street, SW19 (8944 7722).
Eclipse Lounge p238
108-110 New King's Rd, SW6 (7731 2142).
Edgar Wallace p93
40 Essex Street, WC2 (7353 3120).
The Edge p81
11 Soho Square, W1 (7439 1313).
Eel Pie p244
9 Church Street, Twickenham, Middx (8891 1717).
Effra p202
38A Kellet Rd, SW2 (7274 4180).
Eight Bells p238
89 Fulham High Street, SW6 (7736 6307).
Elbow Room p186
135 Finchley Rd, NW3 (7586 9888).
Elbow Room p173
89-91 Chapel Market, N1 (7278 3244).
Elbow Room p125
97-113 Curtain Rd, EC2 (7613 1316).
Elbow Room p69
103 Westbourne Grove, W2 (7221 5211).
El Vino p118
47 Fleet Street, EC4 (7353 6786).
Electric Brasserie p69
191 Portobello Rd, W11 (7908 9696).
Elusive Camel p101
121 Lower Marsh, SE1 (7633 0270).
Embassy Bar p173
119 Essex Rd, N1 (7359 7882).
The Endurance p81
90 Berwick Street, W1 (7437 2944).
Engineer p183
65 Gloucester Avenue, NW1 (7722 0950).
Enterprise p160
2 Haverstock Hill, NW3 (7485 2659).
Escape Bar & Art p215
214-16 Railton Rd, SE24 (7737 0333).
Evangelist p118
33 Blackfriars Lane, EC4 (7213 0740).
Exhibit p190
Balham Station Rd, SW12 (8772 6556).

f

Face Bar p193
2 Lombard Rd, SW11 (7924 6090).
Famous Angel p197
101 Bermondsey Wall East, SE16 (7237 3608).
Fentiman Arms p225
64 Fentiman Rd, SW8 (7793 9796).
Ferry House p144
26 Ferry Street, E14 (7537 9587).
Fiesta Havana p238
490 Fulham Rd, SW6 (7381 5005).
Fifteen p125
15 Westland Place, N1 (7251 1515).
Film Cafe p103
NFT, South Bank, SE1 (7928 3535).
Filthy McNasty's p173
68 Amwell Street, EC1 (7837 6067).
Finch's p33
190 Fulham Rd, SW10 (7351 5043).
Fire Stables p229
27-9 Church Rd, SW19 (8946 3197).
Fire Station p103
150 Waterloo Rd, SE1 (7620 2226).
FireHouse p90
3 Cromwell Rd, SW7 (7584 7258).
Fitzroy Tavern p42
16 Charlotte Street, W1 (7580 3714).
Flame Bar p198
1 Lee Rd, SE3 (8852 9111).
Flask p168
77 Highgate West Hill, N6 (8348 7346).
Flask p166
14 Flask Walk, NW3 (7435 4580).
Fleetwood Bar p131
36 Wilson Street, EC2 (7247 2242).
The Florist p141
255 Globe Rd, E2 (8981 1100).
Fluid p111
40 Charterhouse Street, EC1 (7253 3444).
Fog p229
2 Groton Rd, SW18 (8874 2715).
Founder's Arms p199
52 Hopton Street, SE1 (7928 1899).
Fox p181
413 Green Lanes, N13 (8886 9674).
Fox & Anchor p112
115 Charterhouse Street, EC1 (7253 5075).
Fox & Grapes p229
9 Camp Rd, SW19 (8946 5599).
Fox & Hounds p193
66 Latchmere Rd, SW11 (7924 5483).
Fox & Hounds p33
29 Passmore Street, SW1 (7730 6367).
Fox & Pheasant p238
1 Billing Rd, SW10 (7352 2943).
Fox Dining Room p125
28 Paul Street, EC2 (7729 5708).
Fox Reformed p185
176 Stoke Newington Church Street, N16 (7254 5975).
Franklin's p211
157 Lordship Lane, SE22 (8299 9598).
Freedom p81
60-6 Wardour Street, W1 (7734 0071).
Freedom Brewing Company p37
41 Earlham Street, WC2 (7240 0606).
Freemasons Arms p166
32 Downshire Hill, NW3 (7433 6811).
French House p81
49 Dean Street, W1 (7437 2799).
Freud p37
198 Shaftesbury Avenue, WC2 (7240 9933).
Fridge Bar p202
1 Town Hall Parade, Brixton Hill, SW2 (7326 5100).
Funky Munky p205
25 Camberwell Church Street, SE5 (7277 1806).

g

Gallery p188
190 Broadhurst Gardens, NW6 (7625 9184).
Gallery p74
1 Lupus Street, SW1 (7821 7573).
Garage p229
20 Replingham Rd, SW18 (8874 9370).
The George p132
40 Liverpool Street, EC2 (7618 7400).
George & Devonshire p235
8 Burlington Lane, W4 (8994 1859).
George & Dragon p126
2 Hackney Rd, E2 (7012 1100).
George Inn p199
77 Borough High Street, SE1 (7407 2056).
George IV p93
28 Portugal Street, WC2 (7831 3221).
Gil p193
339 Battersea Park Rd, SW11 (7622 2112).
Glassy Junction p247
97 South Rd, Southall, Middx (8574 1626).
Goat House p220
2 Penge Rd, SE25 (8778 5752).
Golborne House p71
36 Golborne Rd, W10 (8960 6260).

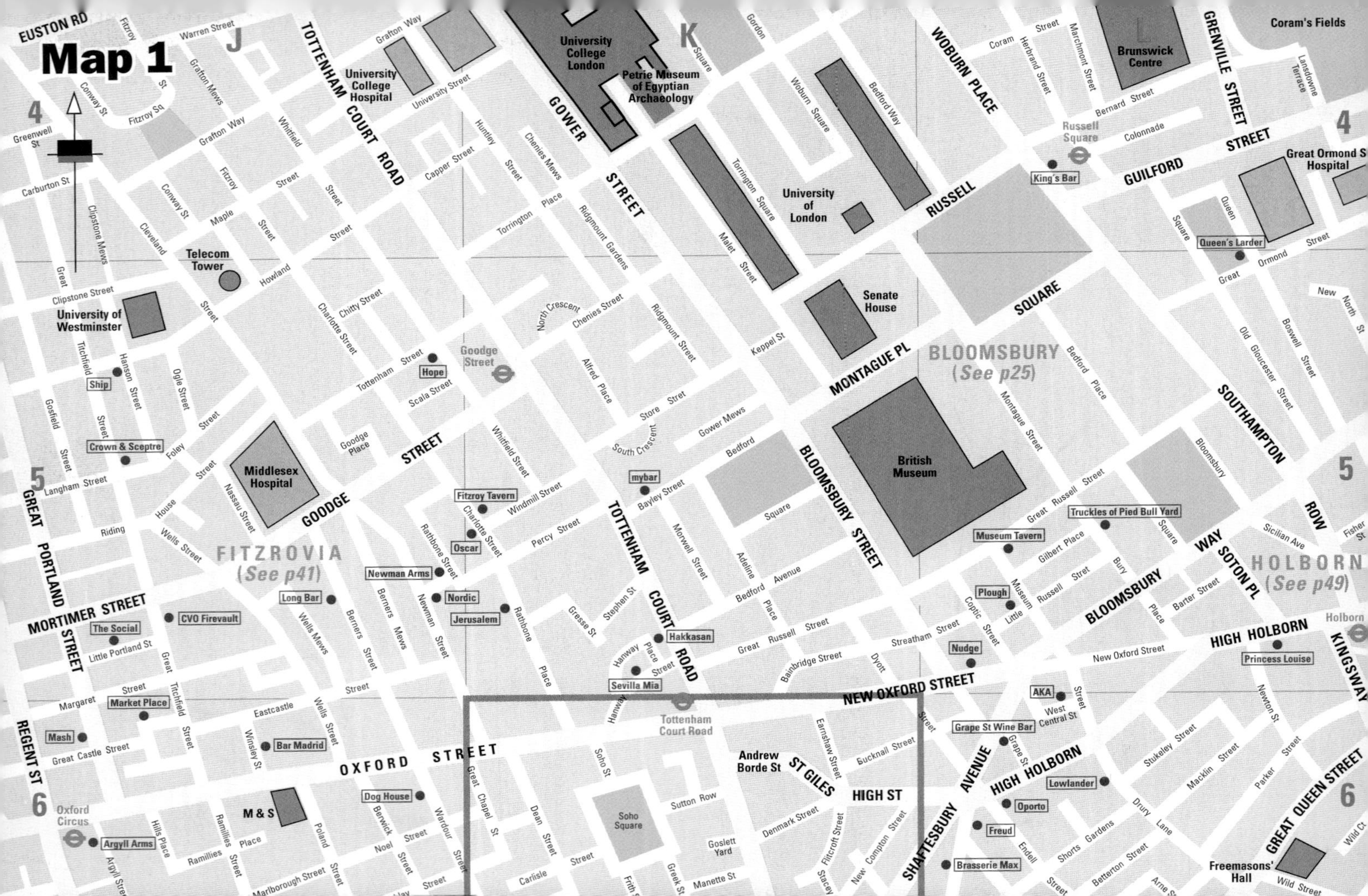
Map 1
EUSTON RD
TOTTENHAM COURT ROAD
GOWER STREET
WOBURN PLACE
GRENVILLE STREET
GUILFORD STREET
RUSSELL SQUARE
MONTAGUE PL
BLOOMSBURY STREET
SOUTHAMPTON ROW
BLOOMSBURY WAY
SOTON PL
HIGH HOLBORN
KINGSWAY
NEW OXFORD STREET
GREAT QUEEN STREET
SHAFTESBURY AVENUE
ST GILES HIGH ST
OXFORD STREET
REGENT ST
GREAT PORTLAND STREET
MORTIMER STREET
GOODGE STREET
BLOOMSBURY
(See p25)
FITZROVIA
(See p41)
HOLBORN
(See p49)
University College London
Petrie Museum of Egyptian Archaeology
University College Hospital
University of London
Senate House
British Museum
Brunswick Centre
Great Ormond St Hospital
Coram's Fields
Telecom Tower
University of Westminster
Middlesex Hospital
Soho Square
M & S
Freemasons' Hall
Russell Square
Goodge Street
Tottenham Court Road
Oxford Circus
Holborn
King's Bar
Queen's Larder
Truckles of Pied Bull Yard
Museum Tavern
Plough
Nudge
AKA
Princess Louise
Grape St Wine Bar
Lowlander
Oporto
Freud
Brasserie Max
mybar
Hakkasan
Sevilla Mia
Hope
Fitzroy Tavern
Oscar
Newman Arms
Nordic
Jerusalem
Long Bar
CVO Firevault
The Social
Ship
Crown & Sceptre
Market Place
Mash
Argyll Arms
Bar Madrid
Dog House

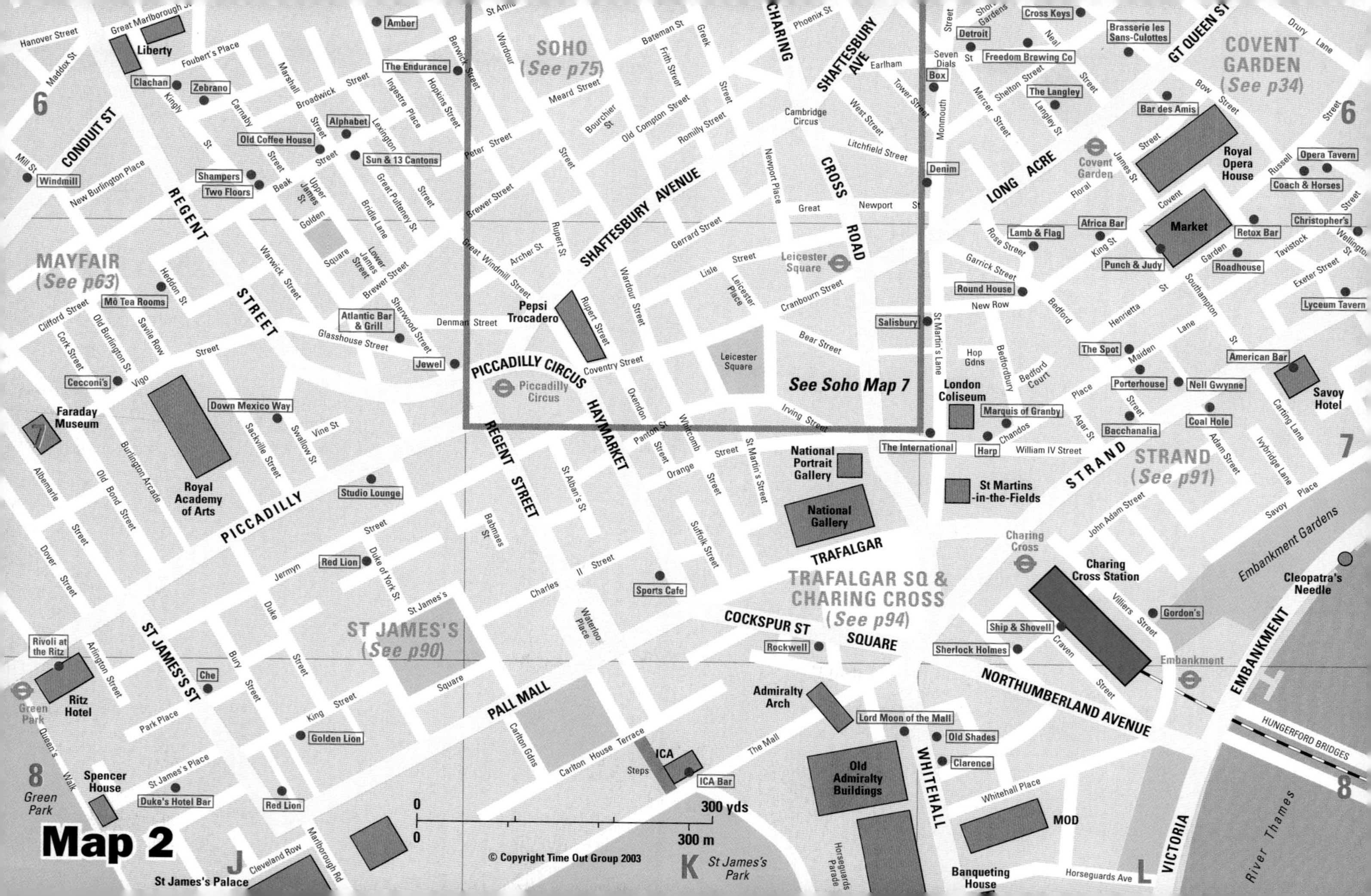
Map 2
SOHO (See p75)
COVENT GARDEN (See p34)
MAYFAIR (See p63)
STRAND (See p91)
ST JAMES'S (See p90)
TRAFALGAR SQ & CHARING CROSS (See p94)
See Soho Map 7
Liberty
Clachan
Zebrano
Windmill
Amber
The Endurance
Alphabet
Old Coffee House
Sun & 13 Cantons
Shampers
Two Floors
Mô Tea Rooms
Atlantic Bar & Grill
Jewel
Cecconi's
Down Mexico Way
Studio Lounge
Red Lion
Sports Cafe
Rockwell
Che
Rivoli at the Ritz
Golden Lion
Duke's Hotel Bar
Red Lion
ICA Bar
Lord Moon of the Mall
Old Shades
Clarence
Sherlock Holmes
Ship & Shovell
Gordon's
The International
Harp
Marquis of Granby
Bacchanalia
Coal Hole
Porterhouse
Nell Gwynne
The Spot
American Bar
Salisbury
Round House
Lamb & Flag
Africa Bar
Punch & Judy
Roadhouse
Retox Bar
Christopher's
Coach & Horses
Opera Tavern
Lyceum Tavern
Bar des Amis
Brasserie les Sans-Culottes
Cross Keys
Detroit
Freedom Brewing Co
The Langley
Box
Denim
Pepsi Trocadero
Faraday Museum
Royal Academy of Arts
Ritz Hotel
Spencer House
St James's Palace
ICA
Admiralty Arch
Old Admiralty Buildings
MOD
Banqueting House
National Portrait Gallery
National Gallery
St Martins -in-the-Fields
London Coliseum
Charing Cross Station
Cleopatra's Needle
Savoy Hotel
Royal Opera House
Market
Leicester Square
Piccadilly Circus
Covent Garden
Charing Cross
Embankment
Green Park
St James's Park
Horseguards Parade
River Thames
HUNGERFORD BRIDGES
EMBANKMENT
VICTORIA
NORTHUMBERLAND AVENUE
WHITEHALL
PALL MALL
COCKSPUR ST
TRAFALGAR SQUARE
STRAND
PICCADILLY
PICCADILLY CIRCUS
HAYMARKET
REGENT STREET
SHAFTESBURY AVENUE
SHAFTESBURY AVE
CHARING CROSS ROAD
LONG ACRE
GT QUEEN ST
CONDUIT ST
ST JAMES'S ST
Hanover Street
Maddox St
Mill St
Great Marlborough St
Foubert's Place
Kingly St
Carnaby Street
Marshall Street
Broadwick Street
Berwick Street
Wardour Street
Ingestre Place
Hopkins Street
Lexington Street
Beak Street
Upper James St
Golden Square
Lower James Street
Bridle Lane
Great Pulteney St
Brewer Street
Peter Street
Great Windmill Street
Archer St
Rupert St
Rupert Street
Denman Street
Glasshouse Street
Sherwood Street
Warwick Street
Heddon St
New Burlington Place
Clifford Street
Cork Street
Old Burlington St
Savile Row
Vigo Street
Sackville Street
Swallow St
Vine St
Burlington Arcade
Old Bond Street
Albemarle Street
Dover Street
Arlington Street
Bury Street
Duke Street
King Street
Park Place
St James's Place
Queen's Walk
Cleveland Row
Marlborough Rd
Jermyn Street
Duke of York St
St James's Square
Charles II Street
Babmaes St
St Alban's St
Waterloo Place
Carlton Gdns
Carlton House Terrace
Steps
The Mall
Suffolk Street
Orange Street
Whitcomb Street
Panton St
Oxendon Street
Coventry Street
St Martin's Street
Irving Street
Bear Street
Leicester Place
Lisle Street
Gerrard Street
Cranbourn Street
Newport Place
Great Newport St
Litchfield Street
West Street
Tower Street
Earlham Street
Monmouth Street
Seven Dials
Shorts Gardens
Neal Street
Shelton Street
Mercer Street
Langley St
Cambridge Circus
Phoenix St
Greek Street
Frith Street
Bateman St
Romilly Street
Old Compton Street
Bourchier St
Meard Street
St Anne's
St Martin's Lane
New Row
Garrick Street
Rose Street
Floral Street
King St
James St
Covent Garden
Bow Street
Drury Lane
Russell Street
Wellington St
Tavistock Street
Exeter Street
Southampton St
Henrietta Street
Maiden Lane
Bedford Street
Bedfordbury
Bedford Court
Hop Gdns
Chandos Place
Agar St
William IV Street
Adam Street
Ivybridge Lane
Carting Lane
Savoy Place
John Adam Street
Villiers Street
Craven Street
Embankment Gardens
Whitehall Place
Horseguards Ave
0
300 yds
0
300 m
6
7
8
J
K
L
© Copyright Time Out Group 2003

Map 3
See Map 9
CLERKENWELL & FARRINGDON (See p106)
HOLBORN (See p49)
GRAY'S INN ROAD
KING'S CROSS RD
ROSEBERY AVENUE
SKINNER STREET
PERCIVAL STREET
GOSWELL ROAD
ST JOHN STREET
CALTHORPE STREET
GUILFORD STREET
THEOBALD'S ROAD
CLERKENWELL ROAD
CLERKENWELL RD
FARRINGDON ROAD
HATTON GARDEN
CHARTERHOUSE STREET
LONG LANE
SMITHFIELD
Mount Pleasant Sorting Office
Eastman Dental Hospital
Coram's Fields
Dicken's House
Great Ormond St Hospital
Gray's Inn Gardens
Gray's Inn
House of Detention
Museum of the Order of St John
Charterhouse
Charterhouse Square
St Barts Medical College
Smithfield Market
Northampton Square
Farringdon
Chancery Lane
Barbican
O'Hanlon's
Easton
Cafe Kick
Pakenham Arms
Al's Bar Cafe
Calthorpe Arms
Eagle
Lamb
Duke (of York)
Perseverance
Rugby Tavern
King's Arms
Vats Wine Bar & Restaurant
Duke of York
Potemkin
Clerkenwell House
Three Kings of Clerkenwell
Crown Tavern
Sekforde Arms
Peasant
Mint
The Well
Cicada
19:20
Sutton Arms
Dovetail
Match
Bear
Dust
Jerusalem Tavern
St John
Fox & Anchor
Fluid
Charterhouse
Hope
Smiths of Smithfield
Abbaye
Cock Tavern
Bishops Finger
Rising Sun
Hand & Shears
Cellar Gascon
Bleeding Heart Tavern & Bistro
Ye Old Mitre
Cittie of Yorke

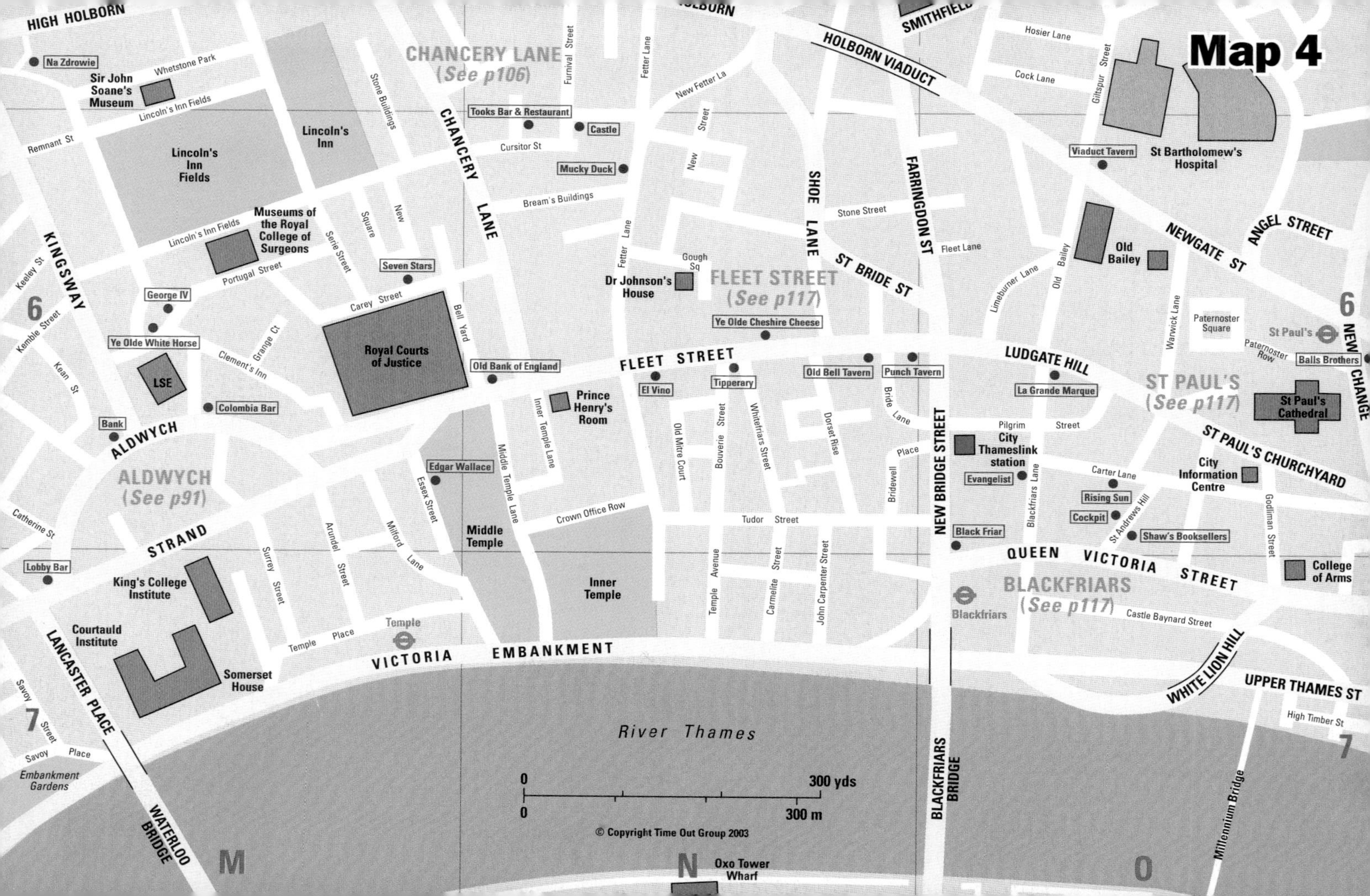
Map 4
HIGH HOLBORN
Na Zdrowie
Sir John Soane's Museum
Whetstone Park
Lincoln's Inn Fields
Remnant St
Lincoln's Inn Fields
Lincoln's Inn
CHANCERY LANE
(See p106)
Stone Buildings
Furnival Street
Tooks Bar & Restaurant
Castle
Cursitor St
Mucky Duck
Bream's Buildings
Fetter Lane
New Fetter La
New Street
SHOE LANE
FARRINGDON ST
HOLBORN VIADUCT
SMITHFIELD
Hosier Lane
Cock Lane
Giltspur Street
Viaduct Tavern
St Bartholomew's Hospital
Stone Street
Fleet Lane
ST BRIDE ST
Limeburner Lane
Old Bailey
NEWGATE ST
ANGEL STREET
Warwick Lane
Paternoster Square
St Paul's
NEW CHANGE
Paternoster Row
Balls Brothers
ST PAUL'S
(See p117)
St Paul's Cathedral
ST PAUL'S CHURCHYARD
City Information Centre
Godliman Street
College of Arms
KINGSWAY
Keeley St
Kemble Street
Kean St
Museums of the Royal College of Surgeons
Portugal Street
Serle Street
Square
Seven Stars
George IV
Ye Olde White Horse
Carey Street
Grange Ct
Clement's Inn
Royal Courts of Justice
Bell Yard
LSE
Colombia Bar
Bank
ALDWYCH
ALDWYCH
(See p91)
Old Bank of England
FLEET STREET
Dr Johnson's House
Gough Sq
FLEET STREET
(See p117)
Ye Olde Cheshire Cheese
El Vino
Tipperary
Old Bell Tavern
Punch Tavern
LUDGATE HILL
La Grande Marque
Prince Henry's Room
Inner Temple Lane
Middle Temple Lane
Old Mitre Court
Bouverie Street
Whitefriars Street
Dorset Rise
Bride Lane
Bridewell Place
NEW BRIDGE STREET
Pilgrim Street
City Thameslink station
Evangelist
Blackfriars Lane
Carter Lane
Rising Sun
Cockpit
St Andrews Hill
Shaw's Booksellers
Black Friar
Catherine St
Edgar Wallace
Essex Street
Middle Temple
Crown Office Row
Tudor Street
STRAND
Lobby Bar
King's College Institute
Surrey Street
Arundel Street
Milford Lane
Inner Temple
Temple Avenue
Carmelite Street
John Carpenter Street
QUEEN VICTORIA STREET
BLACKFRIARS
(See p117)
Blackfriars
Castle Baynard Street
Courtauld Institute
Somerset House
Temple Place
Temple
VICTORIA EMBANKMENT
WHITE LION HILL
UPPER THAMES ST
High Timber St
LANCASTER PLACE
Savoy Street
Savoy Place
Embankment Gardens
River Thames
300 yds
300 m
BLACKFRIARS BRIDGE
Millennium Bridge
WATERLOO BRIDGE
© Copyright Time Out Group 2003
Oxo Tower Wharf
6
7
M
N
O

Map 5

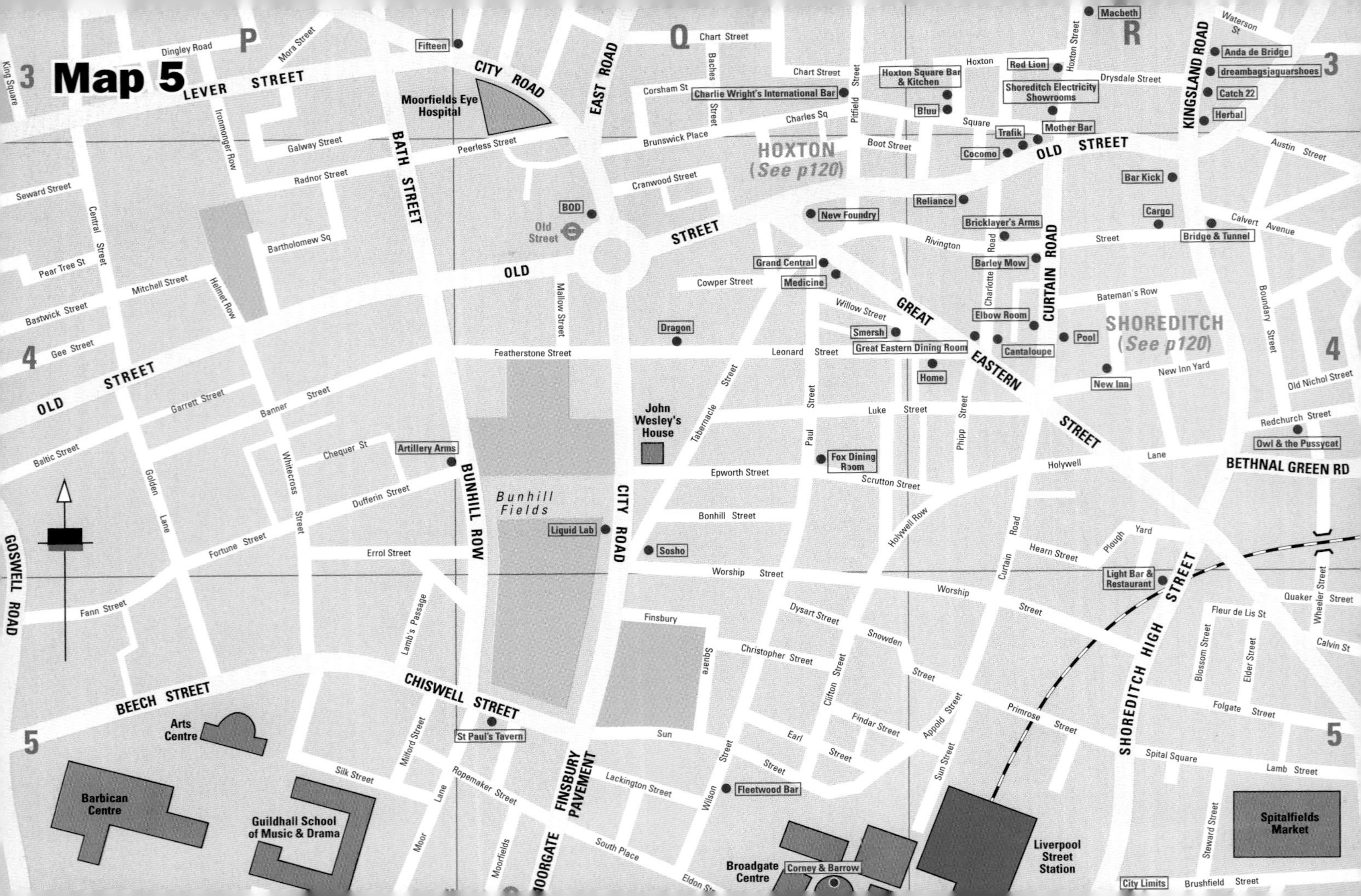

Map 5
Moorfields Eye Hospital
Old Street
HOXTON
(See p120)
SHOREDITCH
(See p120)
John Wesley's House
Bunhill Fields
Arts Centre
Barbican Centre
Guildhall School of Music & Drama
Broadgate Centre
Liverpool Street Station
Spitalfields Market
Fifteen
Macbeth
Anda de Bridge
dreambagsjaguarshoes
Catch 22
Herbal
Red Lion
Hoxton Square Bar & Kitchen
Bluu
Shoreditch Electricity Showrooms
Mother Bar
Trafik
Cocomo
Charlie Wright's International Bar
Bar Kick
Cargo
Bridge & Tunnel
Reliance
Bricklayer's Arms
New Foundry
Barley Mow
Grand Central
Medicine
Elbow Room
Pool
Smersh
Great Eastern Dining Room
Cantaloupe
New Inn
Home
Owl & the Pussycat
BOD
Dragon
Fox Dining Room
Liquid Lab
Sosho
Artillery Arms
Light Bar & Restaurant
St Paul's Tavern
Fleetwood Bar
Corney & Barrow
City Limits
LEVER STREET
CITY ROAD
EAST ROAD
BATH STREET
OLD STREET
BUNHILL ROW
CITY ROAD
GREAT EASTERN STREET
CURTAIN ROAD
KINGSLAND ROAD
BETHNAL GREEN RD
SHOREDITCH HIGH STREET
CHISWELL STREET
BEECH STREET
GOSWELL ROAD
FINSBURY PAVEMENT
MOORGATE
King Square
Dingley Road
Mora Street
Chart Street
Baches Street
Corsham St
Charles Sq
Pitfield Street
Hoxton Street
Hoxton Square
Drysdale Street
Waterson St
Austin Street
Boot Street
Brunswick Place
Peerless Street
Galway Street
Ironmonger Row
Radnor Street
Cranwood Street
Seward Street
Central Street
Bartholomew Sq
Pear Tree St
Mitchell Street
Helmet Row
Bastwick Street
Gee Street
Garrett Street
Banner Street
Baltic Street
Golden Lane
Whitecross Street
Chequer St
Dufferin Street
Fortune Street
Errol Street
Fann Street
Lamb's Passage
Milford Street
Silk Street
Moor Lane
Ropemaker Street
Moorfields
South Place
Eldon St
Mallow Street
Featherstone Street
Cowper Street
Willow Street
Leonard Street
Tabernacle Street
Paul Street
Luke Street
Epworth Street
Bonhill Street
Worship Street
Finsbury Square
Christopher Street
Dysart Street
Snowden Street
Clifton Street
Earl Street
Findar Street
Appold Street
Sun Street
Wilson Street
Lackington Street
Sun Street
Primrose Street
Scrutton Street
Holywell Row
Phipp Street
Charlotte Road
Rivington Street
Calvert Avenue
Bateman's Row
Boundary Street
New Inn Yard
Old Nichol Street
Redchurch Street
Holywell Lane
Curtain Road
Hearn Street
Plough Yard
Fleur de Lis St
Blossom Street
Elder Street
Folgate Street
Spital Square
Lamb Street
Steward Street
Brushfield Street
Quaker Street
Wheeler Street
Calvin St
P
Q
R
3
4
5

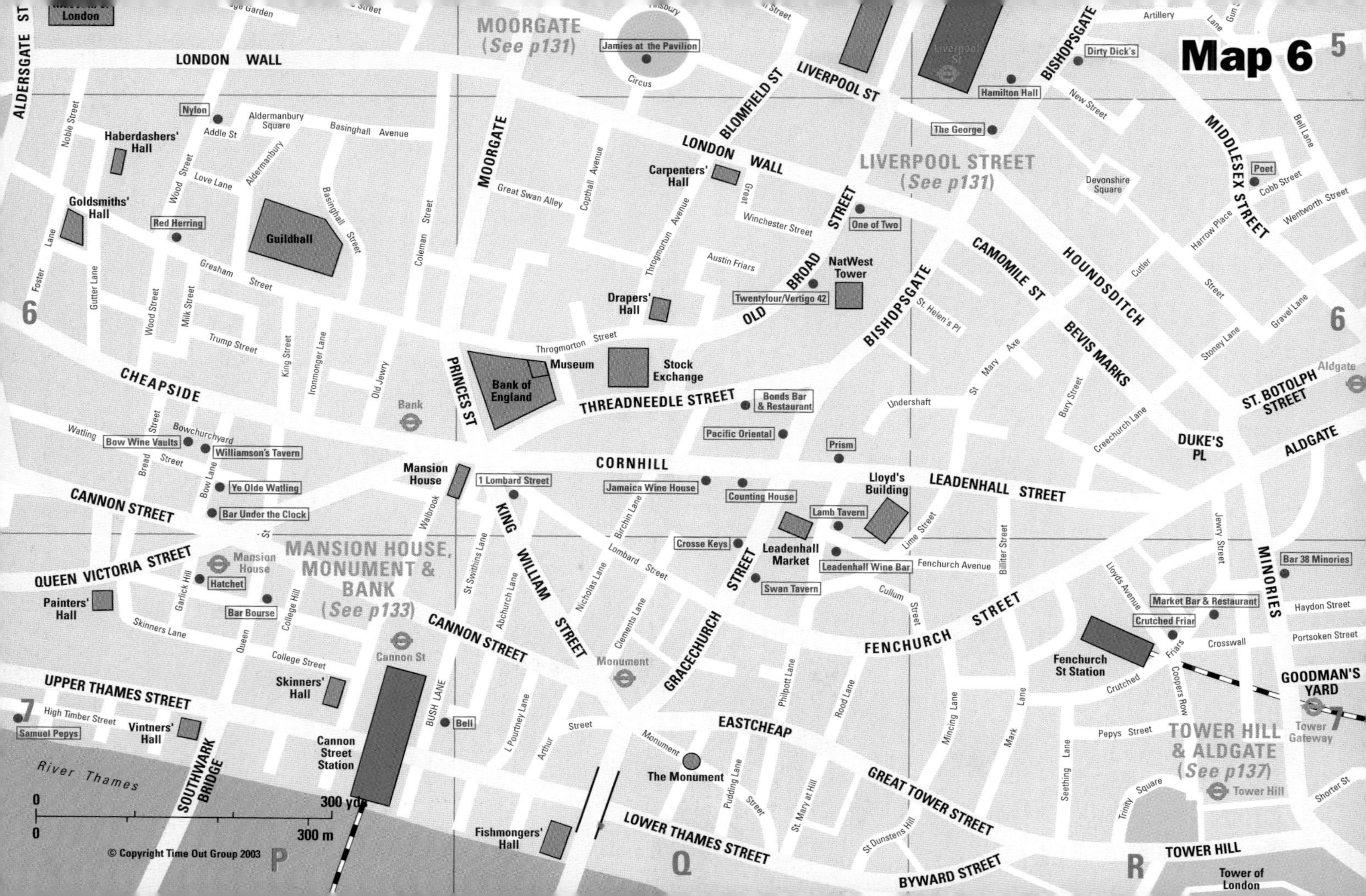

© Copyright Time Out Group 2003

Map 7 - Soho
FITZROVIA
(See p41)
Bradley's Spanish Bar
Rathbone Pl
Eagle Bar Diner
Hanway Street
Tottenham Court Road
NEW OXFORD STREET
Point 101
Dyott
ST GILES
(See p25)
OXFORD
STREET
K
Pop
Soho Street
The Edge
Earnshaw Street
Bucknall Street
ANDREW BORDE ST
ST GILES
HIGH STREET
Angel
Great Chapel Street
Couch
Opium
Dean Street
Sutton Row
Soho Square
CHARING
CROSS
ROAD
Denmark Street
Goslett Yard
Crobar
Flitcroft Street
New Compton Street
Toucan
Carlisle Street
Candy Bar
Manette Street
Frith Street
Greek Street
Pillars of Hercules
Wardour Street
6
St Anne's Court
Revolution
Player
Akbar
Thirst
The Soho
Dog & Duck
Phoenix Artist Club
Phoenix Street
Stacey Street
SHAFTESBURY
AVENUE
Bateman Street
Crown & Two Chairmen
Lab
SOHO
(See p75)
Wardour
Earlham
Café Boheme
Spice of Life
Tower S
Meard Street
Berwick Street
Bar Sol Ona
Coach & Horses
Bar Soho
Romilly St
Cambridge Circus
Intrepid Fox
Old Compton Street
Kettner's
West Street
Two Thirty Club
Waikiki
Street
Freedom
Admiral Duncan
French House
Ku Bar
Peter Street
Litchfield Street
Newport Pl
Comptons of Soho
De Hems
Village Soho
Brewer Street
AVENUE
Saint
Yard
Rupert Street
Great
Newport St
SHAFTESBURY
Dive Bar
CHARING
CROSS
ROAD
Rupert St
Gerrard Street
West Central
brb
Archer St
Bar Code
LONG ACRE
Great Windmill Street
Lisle Street
Leicester Square
Leicester Place
Wardour Street
Blue Posts
Cranbourn Street
Cork & Bottle
Rupert Street
LEICESTER SQ &
PICCADILLY CIRCUS
(See p55)
7
Denman St
Trocadero
Waxy O'Connor's
On Anon
Bear Street
PICCADILLY CIRCUS
Coventry St
Leicester Square
Oxendon Street
0
150 yds
0
150 m
Piccadilly Circus
REGENT ST
HAYMARKET
© Copyright Time Out Group 2003
The Interval
Irving Street

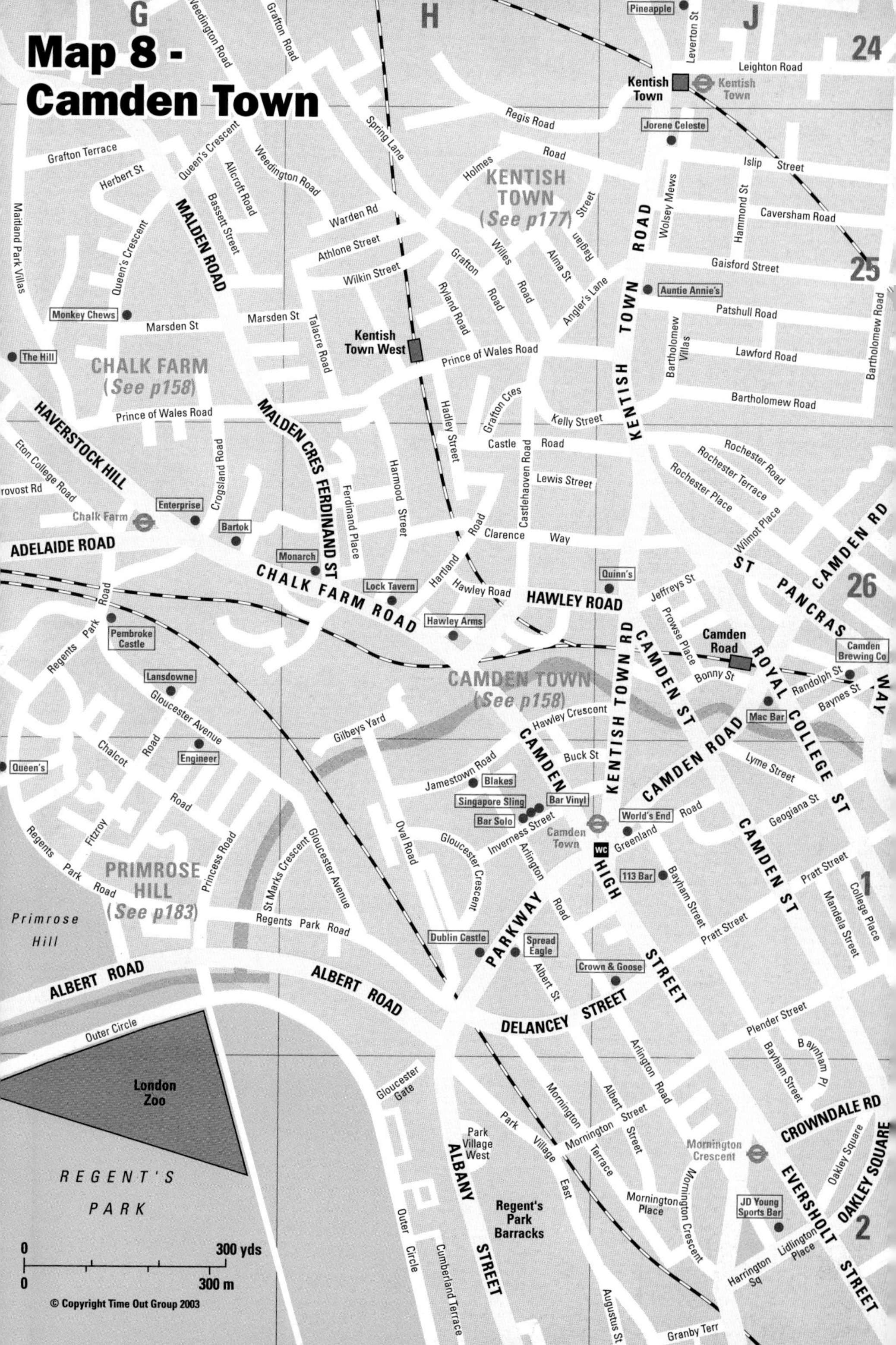

Map 8 - Camden Town
G
H
J
24
25
26
1
2
Kentish Town
Kentish Town West
Camden Road
Chalk Farm
Camden Town
Mornington Crescent
KENTISH TOWN (See p177)
CHALK FARM (See p158)
CAMDEN TOWN (See p158)
PRIMROSE HILL (See p183)
Primrose Hill
REGENT'S PARK
London Zoo
Regent's Park Barracks
Pineapple
Jorene Celeste
Auntie Annie's
Monkey Chews
The Hill
Enterprise
Bartok
Monarch
Lock Tavern
Hawley Arms
Quinn's
Pembroke Castle
Lansdowne
Engineer
Queen's
Camden Brewing Co
Mac Bar
Blakes
Bar Vinyl
Singapore Sling
Bar Solo
World's End
113 Bar
Dublin Castle
Spread Eagle
Crown & Goose
JD Young Sports Bar
MALDEN ROAD
MALDEN CRES
FERDINAND ST
HAVERSTOCK HILL
ADELAIDE ROAD
CHALK FARM ROAD
HAWLEY ROAD
KENTISH TOWN ROAD
KENTISH TOWN RD
CAMDEN ST
CAMDEN ROAD
ST PANCRAS WAY
ROYAL COLLEGE ST
CAMDEN RD
CAMDEN HIGH STREET
PARKWAY
ALBERT ROAD
DELANCEY STREET
CROWNDALE RD
EVERSHOLT STREET
OAKLEY SQUARE
ALBANY STREET
0
300 yds
300 m
© Copyright Time Out Group 2003

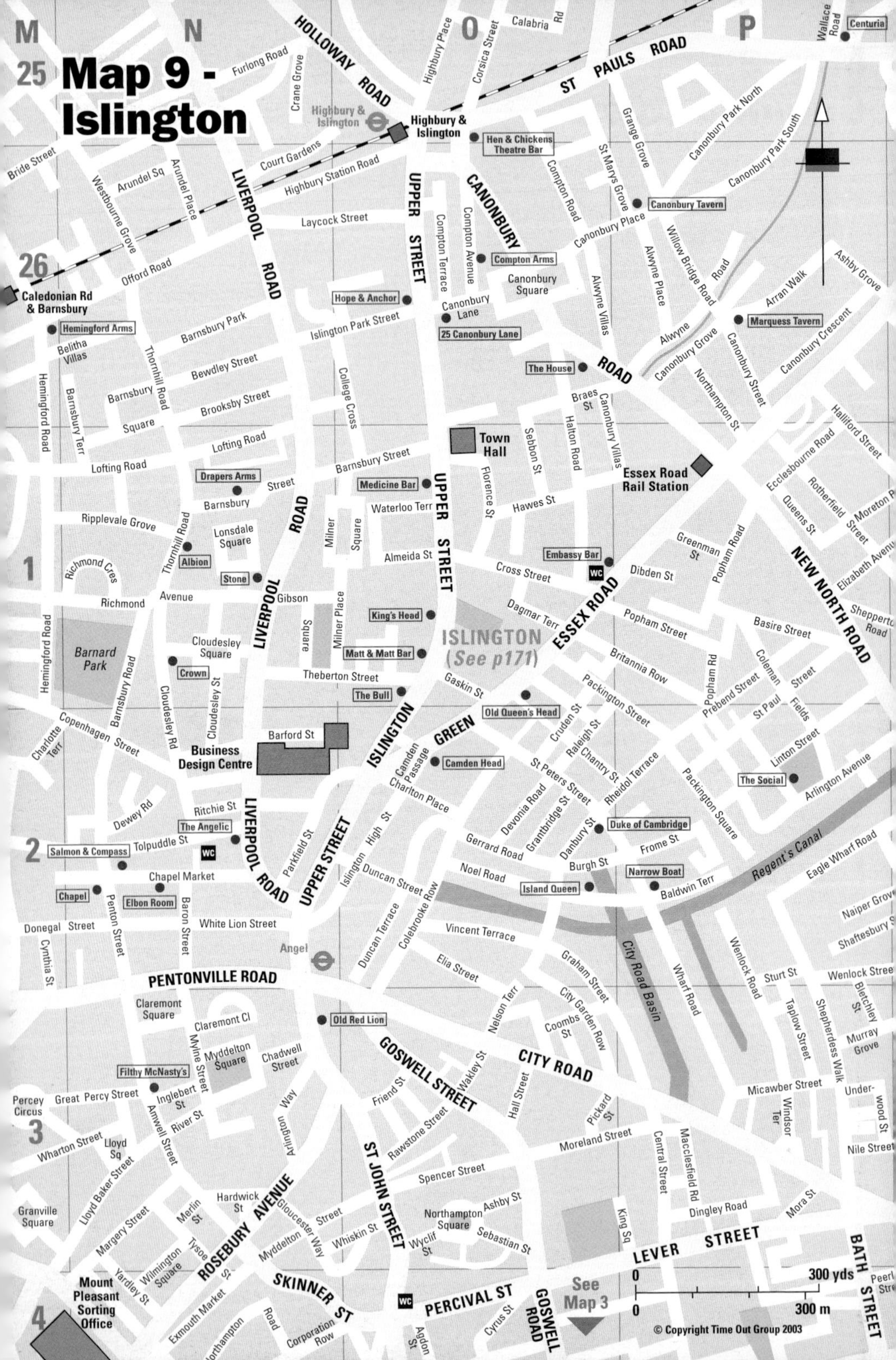

Map 9 -
Islington
M
N
O
P
25
26
1
2
3
4
HOLLOWAY ROAD
Highbury Place
Corsica Street
Calabria Rd
Wallace Road
Centuria
ST PAULS ROAD
Furlong Road
Crane Grove
Highbury & Islington
Highbury & Islington
Hen & Chickens Theatre Bar
Bride Street
Court Gardens
Arundel Sq
Arundel Place
Westbourne Grove
Highbury Station Road
LIVERPOOL ROAD
UPPER STREET
CANONBURY
Compton Road
St Marys Grove
Grange Grove
Canonbury Park North
Canonbury Park South
Canonbury Tavern
Laycock Street
Compton Terrace
Compton Avenue
Compton Arms
Canonbury Place
Willow Bridge Road
Alwyne Place
Alwyne Villas
Canonbury Square
Offord Road
Caledonian Rd & Barnsbury
Hope & Anchor
Canonbury Lane
25 Canonbury Lane
Islington Park Street
Marquess Tavern
Arran Walk
Ashby Grove
Hemingford Arms
Belitha Villas
Barnsbury Park
Thornhill Road
Bewdley Street
College Cross
The House
ROAD
Alwyne
Canonbury Grove
Canonbury Street
Canonbury Crescent
Northampton St
Hemingford Road
Barnsbury Terr
Barnsbury Square
Brooksby Street
Braes St
Canonbury Villas
Halton Road
Sebbon St
Town Hall
Essex Road Rail Station
Halliford Street
Ecclesbourne Road
Lofting Road
Lofting Road
Barnsbury Street
Medicine Bar
Drapers Arms
Barnsbury Street
Waterloo Terr
Florence St
Hawes St
Rotherfield Street
Queens St
Moreton Rd
Ripplevale Grove
Thornhill Road
Lonsdale Square
Milner Square
Greenman St
Popham Road
NEW NORTH ROAD
Elizabeth Avenue
Albion
Almeida St
Embassy Bar
WC
Cross Street
Dibden St
Richmond Cres
Stone
ESSEX ROAD
Shepperton Road
Richmond
Avenue
Gibson Square
Milner Place
King's Head
Dagmar Terr
Popham Street
Basire Street
Hemingford Road
Barnard Park
Cloudesley Square
Matt & Matt Bar
ISLINGTON (See p171)
Britannia Row
Coleman Fields
Barnsbury Road
Crown
Cloudesley Rd
Cloudesley St
Theberton Street
The Bull
Gaskin St
Packington Street
Popham Rd
Prebend Street
St Paul Street
Old Queen's Head
ISLINGTON
GREEN
Cruden St
Raleigh St
Copenhagen Street
Charlotte Terr
Barford St
Business Design Centre
Camden Passage
Camden Head
Chantry St
Rheidol Terrace
Linton Street
The Social
St Peters Street
Packington Square
Arlington Avenue
Charlton Place
Devonia Road
Grantbridge St
Dewey Rd
Ritchie St
The Angelic
LIVERPOOL ROAD
Parkfield St
UPPER STREET
Islington High St
Duke of Cambridge
Danbury St
Regent's Canal
Eagle Wharf Road
Salmon & Compass
Tolpuddle St
WC
Gerrard Road
Frome St
Burgh St
Chapel Market
Noel Road
Narrow Boat
Chapel
Elbon Room
Duncan Street
Colebrooke Row
Island Queen
Baldwin Terr
Naiper Grove
Penton Street
Baron Street
Donegal Street
White Lion Street
Duncan Terrace
Vincent Terrace
Shaftesbury St
Cynthia St
Angel
Elia Street
Graham Street
City Road Basin
Wharf Road
Wenlock Road
Sturt St
Wenlock Street
PENTONVILLE ROAD
Claremont Square
Claremont Cl
Old Red Lion
Nelson Terr
City Garden Row
Taplow Street
Shepherdess Walk
Bletchley St
Myddelton Square
Chadwell Street
Mylne Street
GOSWELL STREET
Wakley St
CITY ROAD
Coombs St
Murray Grove
Filthy McNasty's
Percey Circus
Great Percy Street
Inglebert St
Friend St
Hall Street
Pickard St
Micawber Street
Windsor Terr
Under-wood St
River St
Amwell Street
Arlington Way
Rawstone Street
Wharton Street
Lloyd Sq
ST JOHN STREET
Moreland Street
Central Street
Macclesfield Rd
Nile Street
Lloyd Baker Street
Spencer Street
Granville Square
Hardwick St
ROSEBURY AVENUE
Gloucester Way
Street
Northampton Square
Ashby St
Dingley Road
Mora St
Margery Street
Merlin St
Myddelton
Whiskin St
Wyclif St
Sebastian St
King Sq
LEVER STREET
BATH STREET
Wilmington Square
Tysoe St
Mount Pleasant Sorting Office
Yardley St
SKINNER ST
WC
PERCIVAL ST
GOSWELL ROAD
See Map 3
0
300 yds
0
300 m
Peerless Street
Exmouth Market
Northampton Road
Corporation Row
Agdon St
Cyrus St
© Copyright Time Out Group 2003

Map 10
Notting Hill
Az
A
B
4
5
6
7
WESTWAY A40 (M)
GREAT WESTERN ROAD
Regent's Canal
HARROW RD
WESTBOURNE GROVE
(See p68)
NOTTING HILL
(See p68)
BAYSWATER
(See p18)
HOLLAND PARK
(See p50)
HIGH STREET KENSINGTON
(See p47)
WESTBOURNE PARK ROAD
LADBROKE GROVE
CHEPSTOW ROAD
PEMBRIDGE VILLAS
PEMBRIDGE RD
NOTTING HILL GATE
KENSINGTON CHURCH STREET
PALACE GARDENS TERRACE
HOLLAND PARK AVE
Golborne House
Grand Union
Bed
Under the Westway
Westbourne
Cow
Prince Bonaparte
Harrys Social Club
Eclipse
Electric Brasserie
192
Market Bar
Lonsdale
Elbow Room
Portobello Star
Beach Blanket Babylon
Portobello Gold
Leinster
Pharmacy
Mall Tavern
Ladbroke Arms
Academy
Castle
Churchill Arms
Windsor Castle
Westbourne Park
Ladbroke Grove
Notting Hill Gate
Holland Park
0
200m
0
200 yds

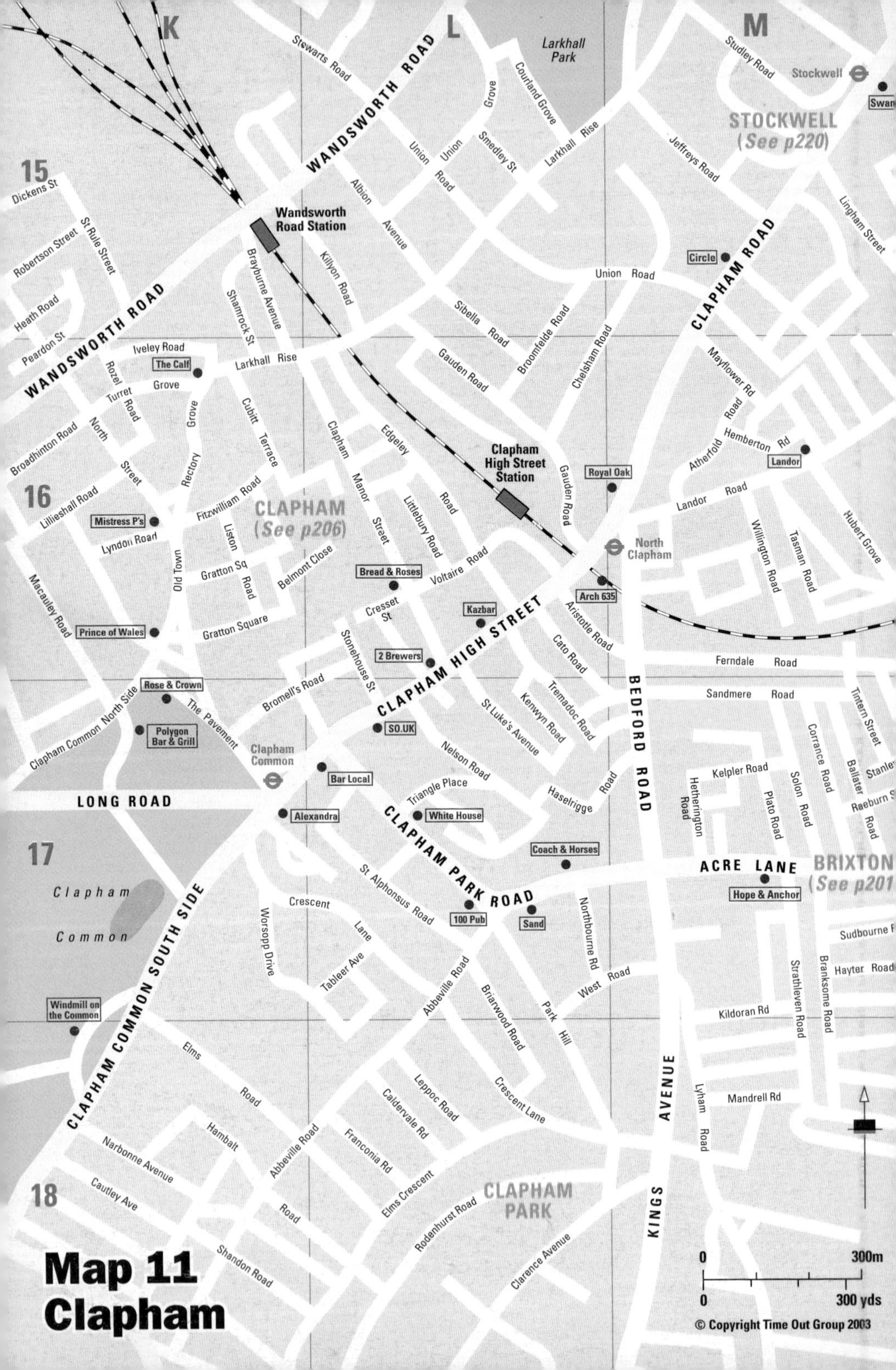
K
L
M
15
16
17
18
Larkhall Park
Stockwell
Swan
STOCKWELL
(See p220)
Wandsworth Road Station
Clapham High Street Station
North Clapham
Clapham Common
CLAPHAM
(See p206)
BRIXTON
(See p201)
CLAPHAM PARK
WANDSWORTH ROAD
CLAPHAM ROAD
CLAPHAM HIGH STREET
CLAPHAM PARK ROAD
BEDFORD ROAD
ACRE LANE
KINGS AVENUE
LONG ROAD
CLAPHAM COMMON SOUTH SIDE
Clapham Common
The Calf
Mistress P's
Prince of Wales
Rose & Crown
Polygon Bar & Grill
Bread & Roses
Kazbar
2 Brewers
SO.UK
Bar Local
Alexandra
White House
Coach & Horses
100 Pub
Sand
Royal Oak
Arch 635
Circle
Landor
Hope & Anchor
Windmill on the Common
Map 11
Clapham
0
300m
0
300 yds